C0-AOX-886

Mid Tem
Nov 19.
2, 3, 4, 5, 6
10, 11, 12, 13, 22

SOME FREQUENTLY USED SYMBOLS

BUSINESS FINANCE: THEORY AND MANAGEMENT

BUSINESS FINANCE:

by

STEPHEN H. ARCHER

and

CHARLES A. D'AMBROSIO

with the collaboration of
WILLIAM F. SHARPE

DEPARTMENT OF FINANCE AND STATISTICS
UNIVERSITY OF WASHINGTON

HG
173
.A8

THEORY

AND MANAGEMENT

THE MACMILLAN COMPANY, NEW YORK

COLLIER-MACMILLAN LIMITED, LONDON

HIEBERT LIBRARY
Fresno Pacific College - M. B. Seminary
Fresno, Calif. 93702
WITHDRAWN

106055

© Copyright, The Macmillan Company, 1966

All rights reserved. No part of this book may be reproduced or utilized in any form or by any means, electronic or mechanical, including photocopying, recording or by any information storage and retrieval system, without permission in writing from the Publisher.

Third Printing, 1969

Library of Congress catalog card number: 66-12639

The Macmillan Company
Collier-Macmillan Canada, Ltd., Toronto, Ontario

Printed in the United States of America
Design: Natasha Sylvester

PREFACE

To a large extent a textbook represents a philosophy about the topic it proposes to cover. At the elementary level the selection of topics and their organization reveal in an explicit way part of the general philosophy of the author or authors, and the actual exposition systematically reveals this philosophy in an implicit manner. Although these comments are applicable to this book, a partial statement of philosophy and orientation may also be useful at this point.

It is the authors' belief that the operational aspects of the relevant theory of financing business enterprises are the central concern of the study of business finance. But we also feel that if meaningful operational decisions are to be made, a frame of reference is necessary. The frame of reference in this text takes the form of aggregate considerations as well as microeconomic and noneconomic considerations that seem to bear most importantly on the firm's financial decision-making processes. The structure resulting from this frame of reference may be briefly summarized as follows.

Part I presents the basic theoretical and environmental frame of reference for financial decision making. Because financial decision making is part of a larger frame of reference than that of the firm itself, in Part I are set forth aggregate topics such as supply of capital and saving, demand for capital and investment, determination of "interest" rates, and the creation and flow of capital in the economy. A theoretical model established in Part I is utilized in subsequent chapters to describe and perhaps explain certain aspects of macro- and microphenomena. This part also deals extensively with the concepts of the capital market in both a theoretical and real-world fashion. To a much greater extent than heretofore has been the case in a book of this sort and at this level, the topic of risk is explicitly developed and incorporated into analysis. This is done in both an intuitive and quantitative, though not rigorous, fashion.

Part II deals with those aspects of the behavior of the firm that are for the most part financial in character. The material of this part is both descriptive and theoretical. All of it focuses on those characteristics of financing business enterprises that are absolutely essential to the student's understanding. In general, there is no attempt to make these financial aspects operational; implementation is left to Part III. Although some of our colleagues object to so-called institutional and descriptive material and view those topics as externals rather than essentials, we believe that a beginning course in business finance is incomplete without a modicum of such material. To summarize, this part of the text begins with a discussion of the nature of business enterprise and continues with discussions of profits; which are the presumed objective of an enterprise, and the firm's demand for, the supply of, and the price of capital.

Part III is devoted to financial management—the implementation of the conceptual, theoretical, and descriptive materials in Parts I and II. At the outset the nature of the finance function is briefly delineated in order to place the financing of business firms in operational perspective. We then turn to the discussion of short-run and long-run liquidity, investment management, expansion and contraction of the enterprise, financing decisions, adjustments of the sources of capital, and financial analysis. Presentation of the last topic does not follow the usual ratio analysis approach. Rather, we have set forth traditional financial analysis from the point of view of the suppliers of capital—a point of view of which financial management must be cognizant. Hence, this discussion centers on the implications the ratios have for the cost of capital to the firm and consequently for the profits of the owners.

For the student who may feel that review is necessary, Appendix A summarizes some of the major characteristics of the chief forms of business organizations. Appendix B contains a description of the major forms of securities used by firms as well as the provisions typically contained in them. No attempt has been made to be exhaustive in either of these appendixes. Appendix C contains present value tables and a table of standard normal curve deviates.

This book is intended for use in either a one-quarter or one-semester introductory course in business finance at the junior, senior, or graduate level. If a shorter treatment is required, selected chapters may be eliminated. However, certain chapters appearing in the later part of the text rely quite heavily on chapters in the first and second parts. For example, the risk and capital budgeting aspects of financial management should be handled by preparing the student with Chapters 4, 5, and 6 of Part I and Chapters 11, 12, and 13 of Part II. Some chapters are intended as a review for students who have had exposure to economic theory either through a principles course or a course in money and banking. These—

specifically Chapters 2, 3, 6, 7, and 9—can be given lighter treatment than others, although they are necessary to develop complete perspective. As a final structural note, not all the questions at the end of each chapter can be answered precisely, with or without the aid of the text material of the chapter. Some are designed to extend the student's thought processes and hence are "open-end" in that sense.

In order to maintain internal consistency and preciseness of usage, we have defined rather specifically such terms as *income, profits,* and *capital,* which are so frequently used in a book of finance. At the risk of causing some confusion based upon our readers' previous knowledge or use of these terms, we have attempted to pin down the meanings of at least some of the terminology used in the financial field. Consequently, we do not intend to present the student with a complete array of historical definitions and historical uses of various terms. We have committed ourselves in some cases to use only one meaning of such terms as *income, profit, wealth, working capital,* and *funds.* It has been our experience in using the original manuscript that such a treatment is pedagogically sound and efficient.

It is expected that students using the book will have taken basic courses in accounting and economic theory. A previous course in statistics will facilitate the use of the text but is not necessary; all of the statistical presentations are reasonably self-contained. No mathematics is required; a modest memory of elementary algebra is sufficient.

This book, like all others, has somewhat obscure origins and bears the imprint of many events in the development of the authors. The pioneers of the subject matter, the teachers we worked with during our formal education and retain even today by virtue of their scholarly works, and last, but significantly, other textbook writers—all of these have been a source of stimulation and at times consternation to the authors. Our debt to them is great and so is our gratitude. We are especially indebted to Professor William F. Sharpe of the University of Washington for his major contributions to Chapters 4, 5, and 10 and for his review of several other early chapters. Finally, but most important of all, our gratitude extends to our students, both graduate and undergraduate, who served so well as educational guinea pigs during the time the original manuscript was used in a formal way from the fall of 1962 to the spring of 1965, in the daytime program, evening program, and summer sessions. Naturally, all sins of omission or commission are the exclusive property of the authors.

S. H. A.
C. A. D.
Seattle, Washington

CONTENTS

BUSINESS FINANCE: THEORY AND MANAGEMENT

PART I THE CONCEPTUAL FRAMEWORK: CAPITAL AND THE ECONOMY

Chapters 2–8 constitute the basic structure and conceptual framework that will be used throughout the text. The concepts and ideas introduced in this part provide the basis for building Parts II and III, wherein are contained analyses which are dependent to a very large extent on the material in these chapters. Thus it will be to the framework of Part I that persistent reference should be made; it will serve as our analytical setting within which to cast problems concerning the financing of business enterprises. Perforce, then, much of this part is theoretical in nature; some of it is analytical; some of it is descriptive. All of it is necessary for a thorough understanding of Parts II and III, for in Part I are contained the beginning notions concerning the forces at work in the financial environment of business firms. Such topics as the capital market and the expected rate of return and risk—among many others—will be developed in this section and persistently refined in Parts II and III.

CHAPTER 1 INTRODUCTION

Too often students fail to read the introduction of a textbook. At times this omission is justified. Usually, however, the introduction sets forth the setting of the text and thus becomes an integral part of the book. Even though much of what follows in this chapter might otherwise be placed in a preface, because of its significance to the student's perspecuity it is included as a separate chapter. Indeed, it is hoped that this chapter will be the first and last one assigned so that the rest of the chapters may have greater meaning.

A LOOK AT THE PAST, THE PRESENT, AND THE FUTURE

In the development of any academic discipline, several persons always stand out. Their work within that discipline leaves indelible marks on their field. Business finance recognizes several men of importance to the field, even though this art, as we understand it today, is very young. And it is to these that we look to trace the development of the study of business finance. It is the intent of this brief chapter to review the development of the study of business finance as evidenced by the appearance of textbooks in the field. Two basic, identifiable approaches to the study of business finance—the "traditional" and the "managerial"—will be explored. A third approach will be recommended, itself a fusion of the two approaches currently popular.

The Traditional Approach

The first formal book dealing exclusively with what might broadly be termed business finance was that by Greene.[1] Although it was scarcely a scholarly treatment of the subject in any modern-day sense of the word, in that book is nevertheless to be found the embryo of the subsequent academic development of the field. It, as well as its immediate successors, mirrored the nature of business organizations and their financial problems within their contemporary environment as perceived by the author. Emphasis was given to the major events in the financial life of a firm as

[1] Thomas L. Greene, *Corporation Finance* (New York: Putnam, 1897).

3

opposed to the day-to-day managerial problems. Indeed, the external affairs of large business enterprises, which were widely publicized, received considerable attention from the writers of books on private finance. For example, trusts and trust financing, which were centers of national controversy because of their allegedly monopolistic practices, gave birth to Edward Sherwood Meade's *Trust Finance*.[2] Meade analyzed the financial characteristics of trusts, techniques of periodic or external financial management, and the basis and justification of trust capitalization. Throughout the discussion of the book, Professor Meade constantly wove in environmental factors influencing the financial aspects of the firm, including the economics of competition, the nature of trust law, and various types of regulation. But trusts did not receive exclusive attention in the study of business finance; railroads and other public utilities, perhaps because their securities were the only ones of private enterprises held in significant magnitudes by the public, also received considerable study by textbook authors of that time.

In 1910, Professor Meade published a second book entitled *Corporation Finance*.[3] This book, as distinguished from his *Trust Finance*, dealt not only with trusts but with corporations as well. Notably, at this time he covered such topics as the determination of profits, promotion, sale of securities, dividend policy, holding companies, consolidation, lease, readjustments and reorganizations.

A further significant development occurred when Arthur Stone Dewing published his well-known *Corporate Promotions and Reorganizations*.[4] This book primarily used a case approach to deal with the issues of promotion and reorganization of corporations and with some financial aspects of corporate consolidations.

During this same time (early 1900's) William Z. Ripley published four books, although only one was a finance book in any genuine sense of the word. It was devoted to railroad finance and reorganization—a near classic work and a major step in the development of the finance field and study of business.[5] Ripley followed in the tradition established by Green, Meade, and Dewing, dealing with major episodes of external financial management of railroads and the influence of the security markets thereon. He discussed capitalization, types of securities, market prices, speculation,

---

[2] Edward Sherwood Meade, *Trust Finance* (New York: Appleton, 1903).

[3] Edward Sherwood Meade, *Corporation Finance* (New York: Appleton, 1910).

[4] Arthur Stone Dewing, *Corporate Promotions and Reorganizations* (Cambridge, Mass.: Harvard U.P., 1914).

[5] This volume was entitled *Railroads: Finance and Organization* (New York: Longmans, 1915). The other three books were: *Trusts, Pools and Corporations* (New York: Ginn, 1905); *Railway Problems* (New York: Ginn, 1907); and *Railroads: Rates and Regulations* (New York: Longman, 1912).

stock watering, state regulation of security issues, valuation problems, organization of railroads, and combinations.

In 1919, Dewing published his first general text in corporation finance: *The Financial Policy of Corporations.*[6] Unlike his previous work, it contained few case descriptions. This book, along with its subsequent revisions, was to become a classic in the field and established the pattern of finance books for the next thirty years. It, as well as its revisions,[7] focused attention on the major episodes in the life cycle of a business and the implications these episodes held for the financing of the firm.

Since Dewing's first edition, several other excellent books have been cut out of the same essential mold, although they vary in emphasis and organization. One which is of particular significance is Lyon's *Corporations and Their Financing.*[8] Although the emphasis continued to be on episodic financing of business enterprises, the major force of the book lay at what Lyon felt was the heart of financing business: the so-called incidents of ownership. By this was meant that a concomitant aspect of financing business enterprises was the apportionment of three basic factors "incidental" to all business firms: risk, income, and control. This meant that the financing of corporations was primarily a matter of apportioning the risk associated with the business firm, as well as its income and control, among the various suppliers of capital. At one extreme, for example, were the bondholders who assumed, presumably, the least amount of risk, received the least amount of income (or at least were entitled to the least amount), and had the minimum degree of control, if any. At the other extreme were the residual claimants of the enterprise—common stockholders, partners, or proprietors (depending on the legal form of organization)—who assumed the maximum amount of risk, were entitled to the maximum return on their investment, and possessed exclusive legal control. With the demise of effective public control over large, publicly held corporations, the significance of Lyon's work today lies in his emphasis on risk and income.

A number of other books have emphasized major financial episodes in the life cycle of firms as well as institutional factors that bear on them.[9]

[6] Arthur Stone Dewing, *The Financial Policy of Corporations* (New York: Ronald, 1919).

[7] The last edition of this scholarly, well-documented book was published in 1953. See: Arthur Stone Dewing, *The Financial Policy of Corporations,* 5th ed., *Vols. I and II* (New York: Ronald, 1953).

[8] Walter Hastings Lyon, *Corporations and Their Financing* (Boston: Heath, 1938). This book was preceded by three other finance books by the author, two of them predating Dewing's *Financial Policy.*

[9] Among the more pertinent ones are: Chelcie C. Bosland, *Corporate Finance and Regulation* (New York: Ronald, 1949); Floyd F. Burchett, *Corporation Finance* (New York: Harper, 1934); Charles W. Gerstenberg, *Financial Organization and Manage-*

Several of them are still extremely popular today. All of them tended to follow, in one way or another, the Greene-Meade-Dewing-Lyon tradition. All of them, including their sires, typically use what may be referred to today as the "traditional" approach to the study of business finance, emphasizing as they do major episodic financial events in the life cycle of a firm and institutional factors that bear on them.

The Managerial Approach

A second direction taken by the development of the study of business finance emphasizes the so-called "managerial" approach, in which day-to-day operations of financial management receive the focus of attention, with periodic or episodic financial events being relegated to a position of lesser importance. The precursors to this approach are to be found in the works of Gerstenberg [10] and Lincoln [11] in a rather rudimentary form, and in that of W. Mackenzie Stevens [12] in a more detailed and analytical form. The latter also combined the episodic approach of Dewing and Meade with the routine, managerial or internal, administrative approach. It dealt with such managerial topics as budgetary control, sales forecasting, financial control of production, control of expenses and assets, and coordination of financial administration. This approach to instruction was not popular, however, until the post-World War II period, when Hunt and Williams' *Case Problems in Finance* [13] was published. The text employed cases in which to analyze the internal financial problems of firms and is the contemporary landmark of this approach. A few years later *An Introduction to Business Finance*,[14] by Howard and Upton, was published. This represented a further step in the transition from the traditional corporate finance emphasis upon episodes to an emphasis on the day-to-day management of financial problems of all businesses. It contains an extended, intuitive discussion of Lyon's incidents of ownership with special emphasis on risk as well as a lengthy treatment of cash budgeting.

---

ment of Business, 4th ed. (Englewood Cliffs, N. J.: Prentice-Hall, 1959); and Harry G. Guthmann and Herbert E. Dougall, *Corporate Financial Policy*, 4th ed. (Englewood Cliffs, N. J.: Prentice-Hall, 1962). The latter two books were originally published in 1924 and 1940 respectively.

[10] Charles W. Gerstenberg, *Materials of Corporation Finance* (Englewood Cliffs, N. J.: Prentice-Hall, 1915).

[11] Edmonds Earle Lincoln, *Problems in Business Finance* (Chicago: Shaw, 1921).

[12] W. Mackenzie Stevens, *Financial Organization and Administration* (New York: Am. Bk. Co., 1934).

[13] Pearson Hunt and Charles M. Williams, *Case Problems in Finance* (Chicago: Irwin, 1949).

[14] Bion B. Howard and Miller Upton, *An Introduction to Business Finance* (New York: McGraw, 1953).

Since 1953 several other excellent texts emphasizing the internal financial management of the business enterprise have been published. So popular has this approach become during the past fifteen years that it rivals those which emphasize corporate episodes, although there is no conclusive evidence as to which is more popular.

A Third Approach

Thus it is that two distinct approaches characterized the development of business finance. One focused attention on those aspects of financial operations of business which occur only periodically and the influence of institutional arrangements that impinged upon these essentially discontinuous decisions. The other stressed internal financial management with special emphasis on day-to-day financial activities, viewing them as essentially continuous propositions.

In this process of organic, yet seemingly dichotomous evolution to the present well-written texts in the field of business finance, the dependence of the art of private business finance on the science of economics is a persistent, although sporadic, characteristic. At times the discipline and principles of economic theory have been misused, abused, and confused when applied to the context of business finance. At times this science has been relegated to a position of seeming unimportance. At times the principles of economics are only inferentially present. The economics of business finance, however, has never been more prominent than it is today.

Perhaps the major impetus to the vigorous, although scarcely complete, application of economic theory to business finance was given by Keynes' *General Theory*.[15] The core of that epoch work as applied to business finance is to be found in the macroeconomic concept that the level of aggregate economic investment depends on two factors: the additional expected rate of return on that investment, and the additional cost of capital. This concept was distilled over the years down to the micro level of business finance and is currently referred to as *capital budgeting*—the process of comparing the expected rates of return of individual investment projects against the cost of capital. Although the theoretical concepts and processes employed were not new, they were not widely known in any operational sense until the 1950's. Early in that decade Joel Dean's book, *Capital Budgeting*,[16] led to a resurgence of interest in the economics of business finance. The result has been a vast profusion of literature emanat-

[15] John Maynard Keynes, *The General Theory of Employment, Interest and Money* (New York: Harcourt, 1936).
[16] Joel Dean, *Capital Budgeting* (New York: Columbia U.P., 1951).

ing from scholars of both economics and finance.[17] As the principles of these two fields tended to be fused more and more, the Ford Foundation underwrote the research and publication of a high-level, scholarly book [18] that would encourage even greater fusion. This book is an excellent distillation of prevailing economic theory applied to the context of business finance. Its design is to diffuse the prevailing knowledge in the field as approached by the "new" school of thought which places expected returns of investments and the cost of capital to firms in the forefront of financial decision making.

Thus a third dimension is given to the study of business finance, one which gives greater emphasis to the economics of business financing. But the precursor to this "new" approach may be found in Buchanan's *The Economics of Corporate Enterprise*,[19] a work which has received inadequate attention in the recent development of the study of business finance. This work was unique in its approach because it integrated the prevailing economic theory of the firm with the dominant financial and legal aspects of corporate enterprise. Probably no work since Dewing's has been referred to more frequently as fundamental background for advanced students of private finance. Yet, as noted above, until just recently very little had been developed along these lines on advanced levels, and nothing at all on the undergraduate level. The authors maintain that some of the Buchanan-Solomon emphasis ought not to escape even the first student of business finance.

Moreover, because the subject of business finance is influenced by institutional forces at work in the economy and by the economic behavior of business enterprises, attempted integration of that which is useful in the traditional approach, the managerial approach, and the newer "economic" approach should be made. Both aggregative as well as micro data and analysis bear on business operations and the making of financial decisions and hence need to be included in a thoroughgoing text. Thus a frame of reference is established which will provide adequate understanding of the operations of the business firm within which the art of finance is practiced. Consequently, we have attempted to integrate what we deemed the intuitively appropriate but not rigorous economic theory into the study of business finance.

Moreover, we have attempted to present some of the underlying con-

[17] A valuable collection of many of the leading scholarly articles pertaining to the capital budgeting topic is to be found in: Ezra Solomon (ed.), *The Management of Corporate Capital* (New York: Free Press, 1959).

[18] Ezra Solomon, *The Theory of Financial Management* (New York: Columbia U.P., 1963).

[19] Norman S. Buchanan, *The Economics of Corporate Enterprise* (New York: Holt, 1940).

cepts and logic appropriate to financial behavior and management of private business enterprise in a market economy. Economic theory has frequently dealt with such important concepts of finance as income, profit, capital, and—in a rather careful way—analysis of firm optimizing behavior in an effort to achieve its goals. Traditional economic theory of the firm tends to deal with these topics only conceptually, however, with the objective of lending meaning or understanding to them rather than making them operational or measurable. It concerns itself with the problem of allocating scarce resources among competing ends and with seeking out equilibrium solutions. Although equilibrium situations never may be attained, the gravitational tendencies toward equilibrium are the valuable attributes of economic conceptualization. But the dynamic aspects of shifting equilibria and adjustment to change are also worthy subjects of study by the student of business finance. An important contribution of economic theory to the study of the enterprise is its ability to trace neatly the impacts of changing economic variables upon the behavior of the economy and the firm while other, less relevant, factors are of necessity relegated to that limbo of inactivity designated as *ceteris paribus*. These processes of continuous adjustment to changing costs, shifting interest rates, new products, and the like in the market economy are invaluable to an understanding of the financial behavior of the firm and need to be translated into meaningful operational procedures.

Moreover, although we do not maintain that the economic behavior of the business is the only aspect of its behavior worth review, it is the most highly developed behavioral system available for the study of business enterprise. Other disciplines, although they have latent potential contributions, cannot bring to bear upon the analysis of business the one outstanding virtue that economic theory possesses: namely, nearly complete, traceable behavior under assumptions which are sufficiently realistic for a significant portion of the economic system.

To a much greater extent than heretofore, we have also attempted to emphasize the concept of risk in the theory and analysis of financial problems. Business decisions are not made under conditions of certainty. On the contrary, the world in which we live is one of change and uncertainty. The study of business enterprise in general and business finance has too long been an unrealistic preserve of rational decision-making in the face of rigid certainty assumptions which yield specific outcomes depending on the strategy selected by financial management. This oversimplification, although perhaps necessary as a theoretical mechanism, distorts the understanding of firm behavior. Decisions that commit the resources of the firm are subject to uncertainty conditions, as are decisions regarding the proper mix of sources of capital. As a consequence, an adequate treatment of business finance needs to tackle this difficult area.

Conclusions

Obviously, the study of business finance at the introductory level assumes that students have previously studied elementary economic theory, business law, accounting, and elementary statistics. We do not, however, presume a complete command of these subjects even at an elementary level. Instead, we have tried to present an intuitive and less than rigorous review of some of these concepts as they are introduced. We recognize that this is done at the risk of some redundancy and overgeneralization, but we are hopeful that the additional pedagogical gains to be realized far outweigh any incremental losses that might arise.

Also, it is our belief that the episodic aspects of the study of business finance, although significant in its impacts upon financial management and replete with valuable lessons to be gained from experience, are materials more profitably studied in a second course in finance or as supplementary reading in the first course. Moreover, the managerial approach, which some texts treat exclusively, should be presented as a part of a greater theoretical framework, the foundations of which lie primarily in microeconomic analysis with an emphasis on capital theory.

A central issue of business financing, whether it be long-run or short-run in nature, is the matching of expected gains and expected costs of sources of capital (with due consideration given to uncertainty) in light of the goals of the firm and available investment projects. The term *investment projects* is used in an extended sense to include everything to which a financial commitment is or can be made. A firm, for example, makes "investments" in its cash position, its level of receivables, its inventories, its bonds when it redeems them before maturity, and its stock when it buys it in the open market. In these, as well as in other investments, the central issue is whether the commitment is profitable—a judgment which can be made only when expected benefits are matched against expected costs, both economic and noneconomic. Hopefully some optimal solution of each commitment can be approached as well as an equilibrium solution of the total mix of commitments.

But these financing decisions have to be set in a greater context, for the influence of a larger sphere of activity on firm behavior can be significant. The broader context necessary to the understanding and operation of financing on the firm level deals with certain aspects of aggregative economic activity, capital theory, risk analysis combined with indifference analysis (where the trade-off is between magnitudes of risk and magnitudes of expected returns), and institutional factors. The most important of the latter are the securities markets, and the forces at play there, and appropriate legal factors that bear on financing business firms.

ORGANIZATION OF THE BOOK

So conceived, such aggregative economic activities as saving, investing, the price of capital, and the creation and flow of capital as it operates in the total economic organization of a national economy are necessary to the study of business finance. It is this framework and environment which leads to the understanding of the economic progress of a nation, of the factors involved in determining the cost of capital in the economy, and the processes by which capital is allocated and transferred from suppliers to users. This is the major financial environment within which the business firm operates; a clear understanding of this environment is necessary for a fuller understanding of the role of financial management in the complex of macroeconomic activity. Part I deals with these aggregative, environmental factors.

But the study of business finance should also be concerned with the normative and descriptive behavior of the business enterprise, the economic organization in which the activities of private financing operate. The firm's ability to generate profits, its decisions to save or to invest, its activities related to its demand for capital, the sources of capital available to it, and the manner by which it allocates its supply of capital among various competing alternative ends are central to this frame of reference. These aspects of financing business enterprises are taken up in Part II.

Finally, all of this would be of little value unless it were related to the operational activities and functions of financing and financial management. Business finance is concerned with the provision and administration of resources to generate profits. Customarily, the ultimate responsibility for these resources or command over resources resides with the financial manager. He is concerned with providing sufficient dollars to achieve the goals of the firm and with securing the proper mix of supplies of these dollars in the money and capital markets. The operational implications of the aggregate, normative, and descriptive material is the goal of the study of business finance and is the subject matter of Part III.

Because the corporation dominates business enterprise today, much of the discussion which follows presumes this legal form of organization, even though proprietorships and partnerships are larger in terms of numbers of units. But our preoccupation with large-scale corporations in no way detracts from the body of the conceptual framework and tools of management presented, for they apply to all forms of enterprise.

If he is not already familiar with them, the reader may be interested in reviewing the nature of the form of organization of different types of firms. This information is found in Appendix A, which deals with the nature of proprietorships, partnerships, and corporations. Appendix B describes the general nature of corporate securities and other business contracts commonly used to raise capital.

SUGGESTED READINGS

In the chapters to follow as well as in this one, the suggested readings are intended either to substantiate the material presented in the chapter or to lead the student to new and relevant subject matter. These references, however, are to be supplemented by those given in the footnotes for almost no duplication of cited material is made in the chapter-ending bibliographies.

Moreover, only on occasion will the works of other texts be noted in the selected readings. There are a number of fine texts available to the student, and we encourage him to peruse their tables of contents for supplementary reading. Some of these texts are cited below. In some cases, chapters which may prove to be particularly valuable adjuncts to the content of this text's chapters have been noted.

SUGGESTED READINGS—GENERAL

BERANEK, WILLIAM. *Analysis for Financial Decisions.* Homewood, Ill.: Richard D. Irwin, Inc., 1963.

BRADLEY, JOSEPH F. *Administrative Financial Management.* New York: Holt, Rinehart & Winston, Inc., 1964.

DEWING, ARTHUR STONE. *Financial Policy of Corporations,* 5th ed. New York: Ronald Press Co., 1953.

FISHER, IRVING. *The Nature of Capital and Income.* London: Macmillan & Co., 1912.

———. *The Rate of Interest.* New York: The Macmillan Company, 1907.

GORDON, MYRON J. *The Investment, Financing and Valuation of the Corporation.* Homewood, Ill.: Richard D. Irwin, Inc., 1962.

GUTHMANN, HARRY G., and HERBERT E. DOUGALL. *Corporate Financial Policy,* 4th ed. Englewood Cliffs, N.J.: Prentice-Hall, Inc., 1962.

HUNT, PEARSON, CHARLES M. WILLIAMS, and GORDON DONALDSON. *Basic Business Finance,* rev. ed. Homewood, Ill.: Richard D. Irwin, Inc., 1961.

JOHNSON, ROBERT W. *Financial Management,* 2nd ed. Boston: Allyn & Bacon, Inc., 1962.

SOLOMON, EZRA (ed.). *The Management of Corporate Capital.* New York: The Free Press of Glencoe, Inc., 1959.

———. *The Theory of Financial Management.* New York: Columbia University Press, 1963.

WESTON, J. FRED. *Managerial Finance.* New York: Holt, Rinehart & Winston, Inc., 1962.

WILLIAMS, J. B. *The Theory of Investment Value.* Cambridge, Mass.: Harvard University Press, 1938.

SUGGESTED READINGS FOR CHAPTER 1

BUCHANAN, NORMAN S. *The Economics of Corporate Enterprise,* Chap. 1. New York: Holt, Rinehart & Winston, Inc., 1940.

CALKINS, FRANCIS J. "University Courses in Finance," *The Journal of Finance, 4* (September 1949), 244–65.

DAUTEN, CARL A., JOHN SAGAN, *et al.* "Toward a Theory of Business Finance," *The Journal of Finance, 10* (May 1955), 107–51.

HAGEMANN, H. F., JR. "Recent Developments at Home and Abroad in Business Finance: Discussion," *The Journal of Finance, 7* (May 1952), 371.

HALLEY, DONALD M., FRANCIS J. CALKINS, PEARSON HUNT, CHELCIE C. BOSLAND, and R. MILLER UPTON. "Materials and Methods of Teaching Business Finance," *The Journal of Finance, 5* (September 1950), 270–92.

SOLOMON, EZRA (ed.) *The Management of Corporate Capital.* New York: The Free Press of Glencoe, Inc., 1950. Pp. 13–17.

———. *The Theory of Financial Management.* New York: Columbia University Press, 1963. Chap. 1.

UPTON, R. MILLER. "Conference on the Teaching of Business Finance," *The Journal of Finance, 4* (September 1949), 243.

CHAPTER 2   THE INDIVIDUAL,
THE FIRM,
AND THE ECONOMY

The purpose of the book is to introduce the reader to an understanding of the function and activity of financing a business enterprise. Very generally, the activity of financing in a business enterprise is that of obtaining the tools (or the ability—i.e., dollars—to command tools) which can be used in the productive process to achieve the aim of the business. A thorough understanding of the field is impossible, however, without an understanding of the environment within which a business operates and in which financial decisions are made, and an understanding of the purposes for which man utilizes the business firm. To understand the pertinent environmental factors that bear on financial decision-making, at least a cursory study of the individual and his behavior regarding capital and finance is important.

In this regard Figure 2-1 is a useful diagram for an over-all conceptualization of the problems and processes of financial decision-making. At the very core of these concentric circles are the financial decisions themselves. Each of the factors contained in the outer circles bear on this core and any or all of them will have influence on any given decision. As a generalization the more distant from the core one gets, the less important each of the outer circles tends to become to most financial decisions of most firms. Also, the farther one moves from the core, the less the importance of financial decisions for each of the areas bounded by the outer circles. Obviously, this is not universally the case. The point here is that financial decisions are not made in a vacuum; rather, financial management will need to consider a host of relevant factors, the most important being those depicted by the circles emanating from the core. The extent to which each of the outer circles needs to be considered in making financial decisions depends on the importance of the decision and the influence of the outer circles on the decision itself. At this point, one might be inclined to say that everything and anything has a bearing on financial decision-making— and, in a sense, this is true. It is equally true, in a restricted sense, that financial decisions influence almost everything and anything. But the significance of the decision-maker's environment and the impact his decision has on this environment varies from case to case. A small business

14

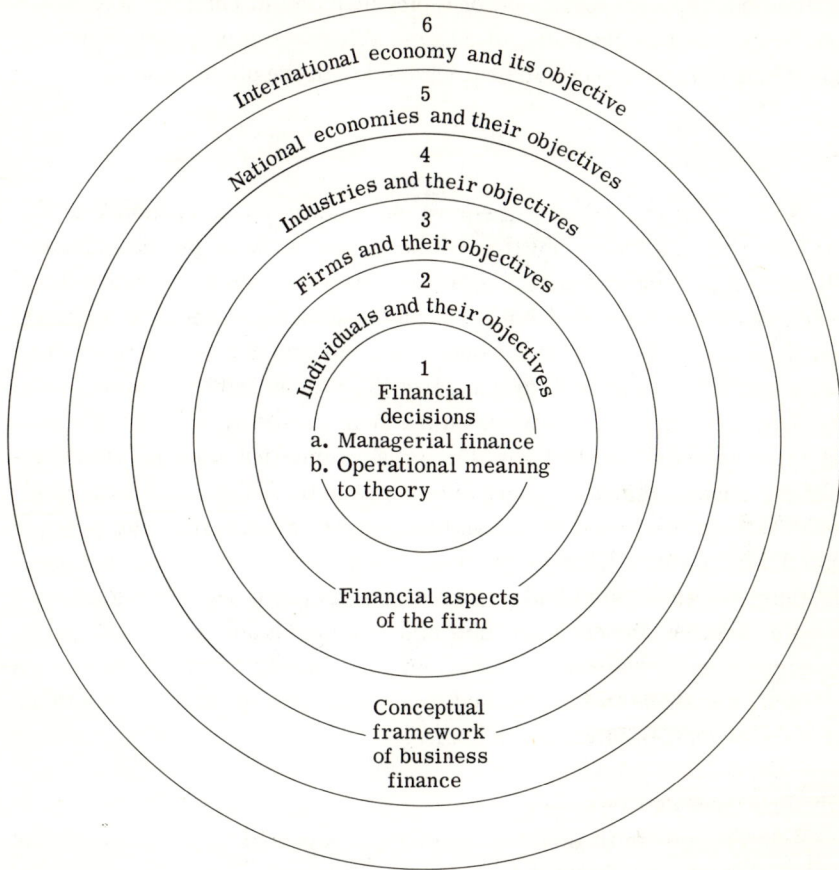

6
International economy and its objective

5
National economies and their objectives

4
Industries and their objectives

3
Firms and their objectives

2
Individuals and their objectives

1
Financial
decisions
a. Managerial finance
b. Operational meaning
to theory

Financial aspects
of the firm

Conceptual
framework
of business
finance

Figure 2-1 Financial Decision Making and the Environment of Business Finance

firm's decision to prepay a $16,000 note to its bank will have fewer repercussions than a decision by American Telephone and Telegraph Company to raise $1 billion through the sale of common stock. Also, a decision to establish a trade area such as the European Common Market, with its concomitant tariff charges on imported goods, has considerably greater influence on those firms outside the trade area that export goods to countries in it than on firms outside the trade area that do not. Even though the ramifications of each of the environmental factors set forth will vary from case to case, the diagram remains a useful tool which helps one to envision this over-all environment. For the present, we will deal primarily with the topics included in Circles 2, 3, and 5. Circle 1 represents what is termed *managerial finance* and the discussion of that topic is reserved for Part III of the book. Specific discussion of topics included in Circles 4 and 6 will not be included in this initial discussion. Wherever appropriate, however, discussion of these topics will be integrated with the other material.

THE INDIVIDUAL

Because the individual is the most elementary unit of economic analysis, it is with the individual that we begin our study of business finance. Because it is the individual who makes financial decisions, we are interested in certain aspects of human behavior that have special significance for the study of finance. At the outset, we can probably say without criticism that individuals seek to maximize the present value of future satisfactions. That is, they seek to maximize their well-being, which is the sum of their expected satisfactions. But satisfactions that one individual receives from a certain activity are different from those that other individuals receive. Thus, we would expect and do observe different behavior patterns for different individuals in pursuing what each envisions as his satisfactions. But each individual regards each action he takes as being, in some way or another, beneficial to him and he regards all his actions, when combined, as yielding some maximum total benefit or satisfaction. As a general rule, then, we can say that individuals attempt to achieve a maximum of benefits from various actions.

The Time Dimension

Interestingly, most of these benefits are expected to occur over some future period, thereby introducing a time dimension to our general rule. The most significant aspect of the time dimension is the time alloted to achieve a specific benefit. This we will call the *planning horizon*. There are several important facets to the time dimension. First, it will vary from person to person and according to the specific benefits sought. That planning horizons vary among individuals is apparent when a moment's reflection is given to the matter. For example, a young man has a planning horizon which may be considerably longer than that of an older man.

Another facet of the time dimension is that individuals plan with reference to the level of satisfactions to be derived tomorrow as well as today, although the more distant the flow of benefits is from the present the less valuable they are likely to seem. Hence, one might further generalize behavior by stating that individuals attempt to maximize their satisfactions for some expected time period. As a result, most present activities of individuals are related to the *flow of satisfactions* in the future, recognizing that the maximizing of satisfactions today may result in a loss of satisfactions in later periods. For example, individuals, concerned about the existence as well as the degree of future consumption, sacrifice some current pleasures of consumption in order to increase the level of satisfaction in future periods. This is the familiar concept of *saving*, formally defined in economics as nonconsumption of current income. Thus, individuals are usually well aware that it is possible through various means to adjust their flow of satisfactions through the activity of saving, the act of giving up present satisfactions. In this regard saving usually accomplishes two things. First, it redistributes the flow of income and, therefore, the command of certain satisfactions over time. But individuals are not interested only in *redistributing the flow* of income, as evidenced by retirement payments and other such *accumulations;* they are also desirous of *enhancing the flow* of satisfactions, which is the second major aspect of saving. This enhancement may be accomplished by *investing*, which—from an individual's standpoint—will be defined as the placement of savings into some productive use such that the sacrifice made today will hopefully give greater satisfaction in the future and increase his total satisfactions, his well-being. Investment, based on the anticipations of an increased flow of satisfaction, may take the form of either financial assets, such as common stock and savings accounts, or real assets, such as education (designed to increase the level of future earnings) and a power lawn mower, all of which are expected to alter the net level of satisfaction for some time in the future, where "net satisfactions" may be described as the difference between gross satisfactions and dissatisfactions—the difference between positive benefits and negative ones.

Individual Capital

The accumulated amount of net investment may be termed *capital*. But it is capital in a very special sense: it applies to individuals and tends to augment their expected future satisfaction. The *return to capital* is the incremental (additional) flow in satisfaction—monetary or nonmonetary, material or nonmaterial—that results from its use. The amount of capital accumulated can be viewed as either the total value of the incremental flow of the income arising from the investment, valuing flows in later years successively less as they are further from the present, or it can also be approximated in another sense by the cost of the sacrifice necessary to generate this capital (accumulated saving). These concepts, presented as skeletons here, will take on greater form subsequently. But for now the general rule will be: *Individuals in society are interested in maximizing their present and future satisfactions, most of which take the form of future benefits over an expected time period; they accomplish this by acts of consuming, saving, and investing.*

THE ECONOMY

The individual does not act alone in the process of personal saving and investing. These personal economic activities are affected by similar actions of numerous other individuals with whom he must interact. The individuals and their economic activities, when aggregated, can be loosely termed *the economy.* But once aggregated, both personal and impersonal forces interact which partially transcend individual action, performing functions for them that they cannot perform themselves or can perform only imperfectly and at greater costs. From a financial point of view, the economy as a whole is concerned with the well-being of all individuals. Inasmuch as most of the activities of individuals in society are directed at future flows of satisfactions, the economy too is preoccupied with these flows. These flows are described as national income—although, in the measurement of national income, nonmonetary aspects of income (because they cannot be quantified) must necessarily be excluded.

In the economy saving is roughly the sum of the savings of individuals and firms. As some individuals may be dissaving and some saving, the sum is an aggregate of negative and positive amounts. In the same manner, aggregate investing is the sum of the individual investments. *Investments,* in this sense, refers only to net additions to the physical and/or human capital of society which result in increasing present and/or future income. As some capital is continuously being used up to generate this income, it must be replaced. Thus, the problem of maintaining the aggregate flow of income to society is one of maintaining the proper aggregate amount of capital. Generally, it is only when investment exceeds the amount of capital consumed that the economy will be able to increase further the aggregate income.

Divergence of Behavior Patterns of the Economy and of Individuals

Behavior patterns of the economy, however, differ in several significant respects from those of individuals. For instance, the economy—at least theoretically—does not have as limited a planning horizon; its life may be infinite. Thus, although the economy may be viewed as the simple sum of the activities of its individual components, each of which has finite planning horizons, it may also be viewed as a group of people acting jointly to achieve somewhat common aims, among which is the survival and per-petuation of society. This latter consideration gives rise to a theoretically infinite planning horizon for the economy. But the interplay among indi-viduals relying on each other to achieve these long-run goals might evolve behavior patterns at any given moment in time that represent short-run interests or compromises of the planning horizons of individual citizens. What influence will this have on the long-run continuity of the economy? In part, individual decisions made at various points in time tend to reflect the desire for long-run satisfactions. In so doing individuals seek out those benefits which will promote this well-being. In a general way, through the market-allocation system, resources will tend to flow to their most de-sirable uses, provided there are not too many constraints to this flow. Be-cause individuals comprise society and because the "economy" refers to that facet of society which is concerned with the economic well-being of individuals in it, these individual decisions should tend to promote the long-run survival and welfare of the economy as a whole. But there are many effective constraints on the allocation mechanism, and governmental action is often required. This is a key ingredient to ensure survival and the long-run welfare of the economy. All this may seem a bit precarious at first glance, but inasmuch as the economy consists of the total activities of individuals, the risks facing the economy (owing to the pooling of risks, a process to be explained at a later point) may well be less than the sum of the risks facing each individual. It is because these risks are reduced on an aggregate basis and because of the productive advantages arising from interdependency that the economy can act in a fashion other than that of the members who constitute it.

The tools which the economy uses to produce national income are the productive resources available to it. Traditionally, economists grouped these resources into the categories of land, labor, and capital. Land and labor were viewed as natural resources; capital, as a resource created by man. A characteristic of capital is that it allows for specialization of pro-duction functions which, in turn, provide for roundabout methods of gen-erating income so that its flow can be increased. As simple as the break-down of the various resources may appear, in actual circumstances it should be evident that little land today is successfully worked by labor without substantial investments in soil fertility, conservation, and other activities that tend to enhance its long-run production. Labor too involves considerable training and development—an investment which is referred to as *human capital*. Consequently, land and labor are ordinarily insepara-ble from capital.

Income of the Economy

The sum of the efforts of all the factors of production is referred to as *national income*. National income consists of rent, wages, and interest and profits, as payment for land, labor, and capital. It may also be expressed as the sum of the income returns which flow to households in payment for the resources used by firms. The circular flow of funds in the economy is roughly represented in Figure 2-2. Firms (F) produce a flow of goods and services paid for by households (H) with the money income they receive from the employment of their factor services.

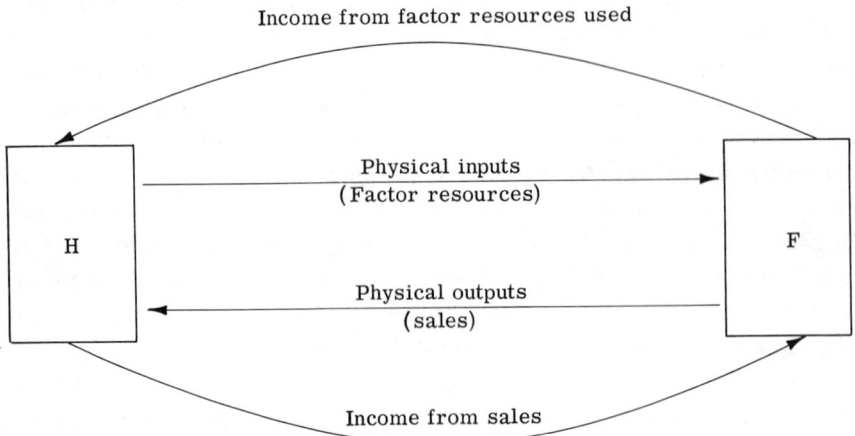

Figure 2-2   Circular Flow of Income

THE FIRM

The firm is an organization employing factors of production and producing economic goods and services to achieve the objectives of the enterprise. These goods and services are economic in that they are scarce and useful. They are of such a nature that they can be possessed by and used for the welfare of each individual, which usually distinguishes them from most government services, the benefits of which do not customarily or intentionally accrue to the benefit of any one individual, but to many concurrently. Because these goods and services are desired by households, a firm produces them with the view to satisfying this demand while generating income for itself. As noted in Figure 2-2, a firm employs factor resources in this production mechanism and makes payment for their use, thereby providing income to the household.

A firm, as compared with an individual, may have longer planning horizons—particularly if it is relatively large. But it is generally presumed that firms have an existence shorter than that of the economy. On the other hand, the life of a firm is generally long enough to be viewed as an intermediary to the extent that it aids individuals to pursue their long-run goal: the maximization of the present value of their satisfactions. In this context, the firm's activity is used to achieve these objectives of the individual. The firm may consist of one individual employing no factors other than household labor, land, and/or capital, or it may be a vast organization involving the joint venture of many individuals who hire many factors of production. These firms may be proprietorships, partnerships, or corporations. This point is further exemplified by Figure 2-3, which is a variant of Figure 2-2. The firm is pictured as an intermediary in that it is a basic mechanism for satisfying the basic material and non-material, short-run and long-run needs of society. Although we do not intend to treat this topic exhaustively, it should be evident that in any general conceptual context, the firm is essential to the maximization of individual satisfactions. By providing physical output, it satisfies the material needs of society. Some goods or services are consumed immediately or in a very short period of time. Other goods, as we know, are not consumed in the short run but give up their utilities over a more extended period. These are usually referred to as *consumer durable goods.* Some goods, usually referred to as *capital goods,* are typically used to produce other goods and services. Net additions to goods that will produce other goods and/or services are called *economic investment.* Thus the firm is an intermediary in still another sense—that is, to the extent that it facilitates net additions to the capital stock of society. This is *capital formation* and tends to satisfy the future basic material needs of individuals.

To the extent that it provides a stage for the creativity of individuals, especially in problem-solving, and to the extent that nonmaterial needs of individuals (such as the desire for power and prestige and other psychological and esthetic needs) are satisfied within its setting, the firm can be viewed as an intermediary through which the nonmaterial needs of individuals are also satisfied, at least in part. The firm, by hiring the various factors of production, provides monetary income for individuals with which they can also satisfy their basic material needs. In this regard, they perform another very important intermediate role.

Customarily, firms involving more than one individual or at least more than one owner are formed to pool the risks to which their economic activity is exposed. This is done with the hope of reducing each participant's risk below that which it would be were he to undertake the activity himself. When a firm is a joint operation of several owners, however, there are likely to be some intragroup conflicts which must be re-

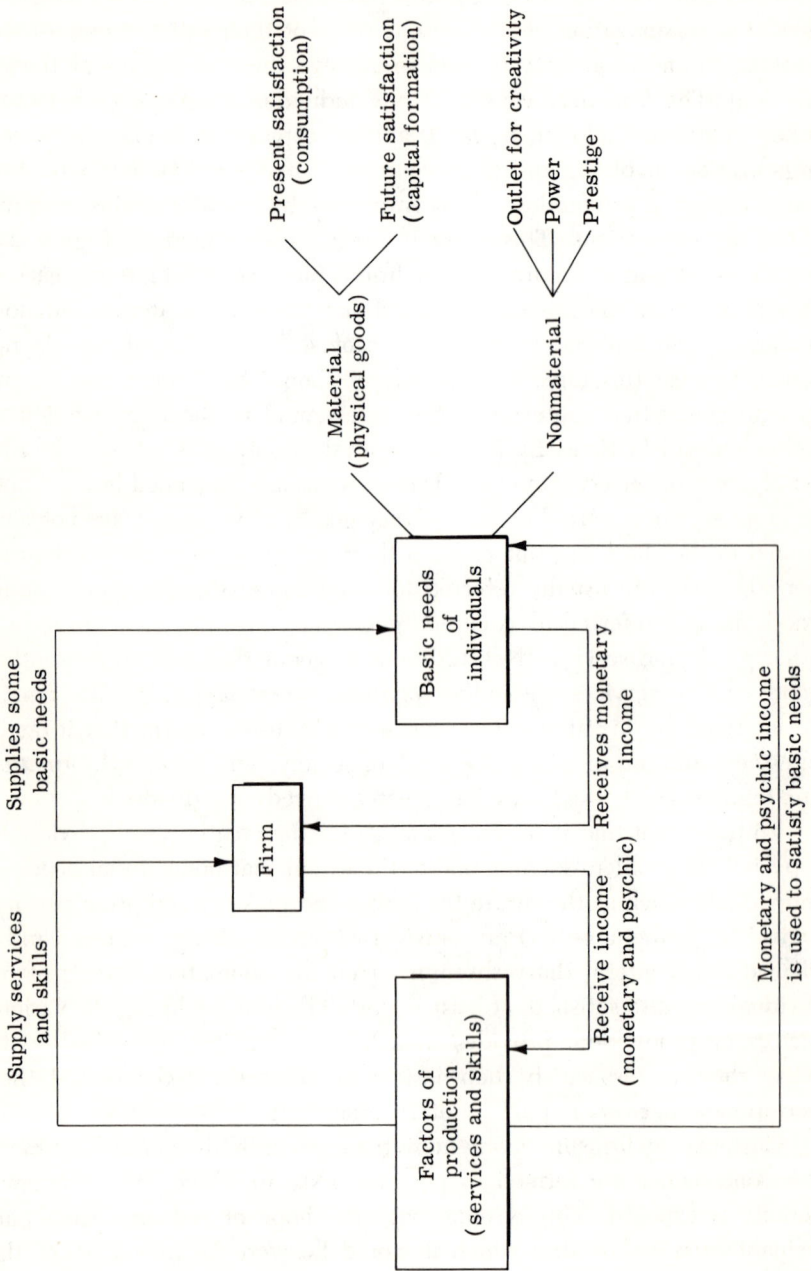

Present satisfaction (consumption)

Future satisfaction (capital formation)

Material (physical goods)

Outlet for creativity

Power

Prestige

Nonmaterial

Basic needs of individuals

Supplies some basic needs

Firm

Receives monetary income

Supply services and skills

Factors of production (services and skills)

Receive income (monetary and psychic)

Monetary and psychic income is used to satisfy basic needs

Figure 2-3   The Firm as an Intermediary

solved through some political, economic, and/or social process. A compromise of views or a degree of domination by one or several persons over the others will result. This will be viewed by outsiders as firm behavior. Under such circumstances, the problem of determining the objective of the firm is a difficult one. In any given firm, it is likely to be some mix of rather complex and diffuse individual objectives. As we shall discuss in Chapter 9, however, there are a number of reasons for restricting our attention in this text to one predominant objective upon which to base our behavioral analysis. Hopefully, this objective is sufficiently representative of the bulk of firms' objectives.

SUMMARY

The individual, the most elementary unit in our economy, is a person seeking to maximize his satisfactions both in the present and in the future. To secure the capital needed to accomplish the objective, savings—his own or those of others—must be employed. The economy, viewed as the totality of individuals pursuing their economic goals, also seeks to maximize the total satisfactions—present and future—of its members. This is accomplished by saving part of the current output of society and investing it in goods that will enhance the flow of satisfactions in future years. The firm, as the fundamental production unit in society, is essentially an intermediary, providing both material and nonmaterial satisfactions to members of society. In doing this it also attempts to satisfy the present and future satisfactions of its owners and/or managers. As a result, it too must employ capital to enhance future flows of satisfactions. To acquire this capital, it can employ its own savings or those of others.

SUGGESTED READINGS

ANDREWS, P. W. S., and E. BRUNNER. "Productivity and the Business Man," *Oxford Economic Papers, 2* (June 1950), 197–225.

BUCHANAN, NORMAN S. *The Economics of Corporate Enterprise.* New York: Holt, Rinehart & Winston, Inc., 1940. Chap. 2.

DUE, JOHN F., and ROBERT W. CLOWER. *Intermediate Economic Analysis,* 4th ed. Homewood, Ill.: Richard D. Irwin, Inc., 1961. Chap. 1.

FERBER, ROBERT. "Research on Household Behavior," *American Economic Review, 52* (March 1962), 19–63.

GOLDBERGER, ARTHUR S., and MAW TIN LEE. "Toward a Microanalytic Model of Household Sector," *American Economic Review, 52* (May 1962), 241–51.

MARSHALL, ALFRED. *Principles of Economics,* 8th ed. New York: The Macmillan Company, 1920.

ORCUTT, GUY H. "Microanalytic Models of the United States Economy: Need and Development," *American Economic Review,* 52 (May 1962), 229–40.

TOBIN, JAMES. "Money, Capital, and Other Stores of Value," *American Economic Review,* 51 (May 1961), 26–37.

VON MISES, LUDWIG. *Human Action.* New Haven, Conn.: Yale University Press, 1949.

QUESTIONS

2.1 Examine your activities today and classify them according to whether they involve current satisfaction to you or they are expected to affect future satisfaction.

2.2 What activities do you undertake that you do not expect to yield satisfactions to you in some form or another?

2.3 Estimate the proportion of time you devote to saving. How would you expect this to differ from a person aged seventy-five?

2.4 What are the forms of investment you are making?

2.5 Does the success of your saving and investing depend upon others? If so, do you anticipate any conflicts with these others in the achievement of your goal? How should these be reconciled?

2.6 What is the role of the firm in your efforts to achieve your goal?

2.7 What satisfactions do not involve the firm in some manner?

2.8 In examining your career objective, how do you anticipate the firm's contribution to your goal?

2.9 What do you believe is the role of governments in contributing to the satisfactions of individuals?

2.10 How long is your planning horizon? How would your flows of satisfaction be altered if your planning horizon were shortened? Lengthened?

2.11 "All courses of action are designed to enhance satisfactions." Comment on the reality or lack of reality in this statement. Would your answer be any different if you assumed the point of view of the firm? That of the economy? That of the individual?

CHAPTER 3   THE CAPITAL RESOURCE

Because capital is so very important to the creation of goods and services —and thus to the creation of income—it is to a discussion of this concept that we now turn. We will limit ourselves, however, to general observations regarding capital. Because the other traditional factors of production —land and labor—are not created by man, most economies are rather powerless to exert control over them except over very long periods of time.[1] As a result, the role of capital takes on great significance because man attempts to lift himself to a higher level of consumption and satisfaction. He does this essentially with the use of capital in its various forms. Not only will we concentrate upon gaining an understanding of capital, but we will also examine the relation of capital to money and credit and try to elicit a rather intuitive "feel" for the processes by which capital is created.

THE NATURE OF CAPITAL

The term *capital* has been used in many ways by many people. It is difficult to define the term in a manner broad enough to include all shades of its meaning. Despite such hazards, however, we shall at this point give a rather general meaning to the term. This definition is one of convenience; it is most appropriate to the immediately ensuing discussion. In subsequent parts of the book the definition will be refined wherever necessary.

Definition

In a broad, general sense, *capital* consists of resources *to be used in the creation of income.* This relatively simple statement requires considerable elaboration if it is to be understood. *Resource* refers to something over which the economy, organization, or individual has control. The term *resource* is used to include the traditional economic factors of production, such as land, labor, and capital, as well as such monetary factors as cash and receivables. The term *resource* is also used to differentiate it from the

---

[1] The "quantity" of labor may be affected by programs which affect either the birth rate or the death rate or both.

25

term *asset,* which connotes that something is owned. In the broad context of business finance, all items contributing to the generation of income fall under the heading of capital resources. Ownership of resources is not a necessary element; at least partial control is the primary requisite. For example, businesses often lease equipment or contract for skilled management or labor. In both cases, the firm has made an investment, a commitment, for the purpose of making profits. Although these resources are not owned, a modest degree of control is maintained over them while they are employed in productive uses. In this highly important sense they are considered part of the total resources devoted to profit generation—as capital.

Closely allied to the definition of capital is the definition of *profit.* Although the term *profits* will be discussed thoroughly in later portions of the book, we should state the general lines along which this complex word will be used. For our purposes *profits are changes in the value of ownership during some time period plus any nonwage distributions to owners during the period minus any cash contributions made to the firm by owners.*[2] Although this definition may seem simple enough, there exist many problems in the measurement of profits. We shall find that the data available in an objective and verifiable form dictate that a method of approximating these profits be found. Accountants have developed some rather elaborate rules and procedures in their attempts to measure profits. Their measurement, however, does not conform to our definition. Hence, we differentiate "our" profits from those of the accountant by designating the former as profits and the latter as *accounting profits.* To confuse the issue even more, neither *profit,* as we use it, nor *accounting profit* is identical to the economist's use of the term. The economist views profit as a type of surplus or windfall, a return beyond that which is considered normal.

To go a step further, *income is the return to a factor of production during some time period.* Income is measured in monetary terms ordinarily and takes the name of *wages* as *returns to labor, rents* as *returns to land,* and *profits* and *interest* as *returns to capital.* Profits and interest, then, are the returns to one factor: capital. Interest is the return to that capital which is not supplied by the owners of the firm. Nonmonetary returns or incomes also exist but are difficult to identify and measure and, to a large extent, they are beyond the scope of this book.

Various economic activities have as their objective an increase in the flow of income to some factors of production in preference to others. The

[2] For the time being, suffice it to say that for a corporation changes in the value of ownership may be measured by changes in the market value of the firm under review; nonwage distributions are dividends; and cash contributions may take the form of purchases of new stock issues.

firm's objective may be to increase its profits relative to the shares of other factors of production. In the economy, society may seek to limit or eliminate profits as sources of income in order to increase returns to some other factor, such as labor (ignore human capital for the moment). This problem of the distribution of income among the various factors engaged in the production process is paramount for all economics, for excessive payments to selected resources customarily result in disproportionate increases or decreases in the supply of the factors, which may result in inefficient utilization and combination of these resources. For example, insufficient returns to capital relative to the other resources may prevent those increases in capital which are necessary to the maintenance and growth in the total income of the economy.

As far as a firm in the United States economy is concerned, capital is customarily used for the purpose of securing profits, although losses may actually result. That is to say, although losses may result in an *ex post* sense, in an *ex ante* sense the expectations are that profits will be realized whenever capital investments are made and combined with the other income-producing factors. Although it might be argued that in some cases capital has been employed for the purpose of creating losses, at least on the surface, such behavior usually has other, unexposed ramifications which, if recognized, would indicate that the objective was still the creation of profit. For example, intentional use of capital to create a loss may have as its ultimate objective a higher total after-tax profit when combined with other profits.

From the individual's standpoint, we may consider another type of income in addition to dollar income. We might state that an individual has psychic income, satisfaction, or utility—derived from some good or act. This form of income can be only subjectively measured and then only by the individual himself as he compares different levels of satisfaction derived from different types of behavior. Dollars elicit psychic income primarily through their command over food, clothing, amusement, and other pleasures of various sorts. They also contribute to psychic income by the security or mental assurance that they provide. When income is used in this broader sense, other items the individual controls then become capital items—as, for example, his home (perhaps even his wife, if he controls her).

As a final point, some experts have argued that a resource, to be classed as capital, must also be exchangeable. That is, the resource must be capable of having a market value. This position customarily requires that the resource be physically separable from the user and that (unlike a resource, which is used profitably in the generation of *one* firm's profit) it also have value to another firm. From the point of view of the firm, however, some equipment may be so installed as to render its transfer impossible. In the same sense a firm may have invested considerable sums in its employees, orienting them to its particular methods of operations. This investment, called *human capital,* is irrevocable, being invested in the form of knowledge about the operations of their particular firm. This value can not be sold or even recovered for use by the departing employee's replacement. Yet this human resource is used in the generation of profits and can be treated as capital. Exchangeability is not a requirement for our definition of capital.

Types of Capital

Viewed from the context of the nation, the firm and the household, all of which employ it to seek some sort of income, capital assumes different —at times very specific—meanings. Capital for individuals includes items usually different from those of the firm. Likewise capital items of the firm often differ from those of the national economy. For example, a purchase of equipment from one firm by another results in a change in the mix of their respective assets. From the standpoint of the entire economy, however, there has been no change in the real capital stock of the nation, although the income-producing capabilities of two constituent firms has changed, presumably for the better. That is, from an aggregate point of view, there has been a transfer of capital items but no change in the total amount. Also, the exchange of a stock certificate by a firm for cash from an individual changes their respective forms of capital; but on the national scene, this transfer, taken by itself, does not affect the total amount of capital. Because of these and other similar examples the student could think of, it is necessary to differentiate among the various elements of capital as they pertain to the household, the firm, and the nation. Common to all three, however, is the fact that capital is owned and/or controlled and is capable of and intended to generate some sort of monetary and/or psychic income.

In the national economy capital consists of all the tools which are or will be capable of generating goods and services. This capital—consisting of plant, equipment, and inventories—is capital in the "economics" sense and usually is referred to as *real capital.* That is, these are the physical productive resources themselves as opposed to any monetary claims on them, such as bonds and stocks. The transfer of these tools, either their ownership or their control, among firms or governmental units involves no capital additions to the economy, although greater income may be generated as a result of more efficient capital allocation. In the economy, real capital is created or formed only when a new plant is constructed, new equipment is manufactured, or greater inventories are accumulated. Furthermore, land may be so altered through investment that it is capable of generating more income than before. Consequently, efforts to enrich the soil and the investment in flood control and irrigation systems create capital.

To such capital items as inventories, plant and equipment and improved land, we may also add *human capital*.[3] When an economy invests in its labor resources the knowledge and abilities necessary to enhance their productivity, these resources become capable of generating greater income. Thus society's aggregate capital has been enhanced in the form of human capital. In an indirect sense, the advance of knowledge or the dissemination of new or existing knowledge becomes a sort of "supercapital," for it eventually makes possible an increased flow of income. It is obvious that knowledge must be disseminated to become embodied in either human or physical capital where it can operate to enhance income. Advances in knowledge are viewed by many as a mixed blessing. Specifically, there seems to be some question whether such advances in knowledge will make capital relatively more important among the factors of production and thereby render existing real capital goods obsolete because of changes in technology. Although the issue is by no means resolved, the advances are customarily viewed as causing the use of greater capital relative to other factors. For example, data-processing equipment replaces a considerable amount of labor. However, if the technological change is of the capital-saving type (making for more efficient production, perhaps by more roundabout techniques), the amount of capital required to produce a unit of given output may be reduced, thereby reducing the demand for capital. On the other hand, technological change may also increase the risk of obsolescence and thus act to deter the incorporation of new techniques into the production process.

From the firm's point of view, its assets in the form of plant, equipment, fixtures, inventories, accounts receivable—and even its cash—are tools that are employed to increase profits. Because these resources may be either owned or controlled, some of the firm's capital items are not usually displayed on the conventional accounting balance sheet. Among these are goodwill and other intangible items, as well as human capital items. The

---

[3] For a fine treatment of this intriguing and important concept, the student is referred to: Theodoore W. Schultz, "Investment in Human Capital," *The American Economic Review*, 51 (March 1961), 1–17.

investments made in orientation programs, on-the-job training, management seminars, and other forms of employee education are all items which are expected to contribute to profits and possess all the other characteristics of capital. Because they are not owned, they are not assets in the same sense that other balance-sheet items are. But they are controlled in the sense that they are hired and are used in the generation of profits; hence they constitute a part of a firm's capital just as much as any recorded balance-sheet item.

From the individual's viewpoint, capital consists of those resources he owns or controls which are used to generate income. As a student, his goal may be to enhance his skills, increase his knowledge, or develop further his reasoning capacity. This increase in capital, human capital, is a resource which at some time will probably be committed to some form of economic activity. In the case of some students, part or all of the expenditures might be directed toward such courses as music appreciation, art, and literature. These investments (consumptive investments) are made for consumption by the individual alone and usually would not be thought of as contributing to the productive processes of the national economy (except in a very indirect manner). They are capital in the individual sense, however, for they enable him to achieve, presumably, a higher level of consumption; consumption in this case is the satisfaction derived from listening to Bach or reading Dante's *Inferno*. His investment in a law degree is more indirect; presumably this investment will later yield dollar income which, in turn, may be used to obtain a multitude of material satisfactions. Other forms of individual capital would consist of stocks, bonds, investments in real estate, savings accounts, and other items used or to be used to create income.

The use of capital is a roundabout method of generating income—greater income (fish) can be had by Robinson Crusoe were he to employ the roundabout method of using a net to catch fish as opposed to the direct method of catching fish by hand. It can also be said that capital is not a homogeneous factor of production. The only characteristics common to all forms of capital are: (1) they are owned or controlled, and (2) they generate either monetary or nonmonetary income. But because no two items of capital are alike in all respects, we can say that capital items as a class are heterogeneous. For example, it is difficult to conceive of one individual's human capital as being identical to another's. Moreover, the fact that one plant has a location different from another may make it more or less valuable. Or one plant may be older than another and as a consequence they are not identical because different costs, taxes, and the like will have prevailed in each case.

MONEY AND CAPITAL

As you may recall from your studies of elementary economics or money and banking, an economy such as ours relies very heavily on money. Money, of course, performs many important functions. It serves as a medium of exchange and thus becomes the lifeblood of our economic system, which is renowned for its heavy reliance upon specialization, division of labor, and roundabout methods of production. Money also performs the important function of being a measuring unit of economic values; with money we tend to establish a hierarchy of values among a vast array of goods and services. Such goods and services are exchanged for one another in proportion to their relative values in ratios stated in terms of prices. Prices are therefore the dollars-and-cents measurements of the exchangeable value of goods and services.

Money and capital resources are related through the functioning of our financial system. The financial system of our economy—banks, investment firms, and other financial institutions—facilitates the transference of money into capital items and vice versa. It measures the value of the resources expended to create an item of capital and the exchangeable value of capital items; usually it also measures the cost of creating capital. And finally, to create capital both savings and investment are necessary and to a large extent the financial system (the money and capital markets) provides the link between the saving and investment activities of the economy.

THE STOCK OF CAPITAL

Our next consideration concerns accounting for the amount of capital. We have talked very generally about the nature of capital but have not as yet discussed the problem of measuring any quantity of capital. In a theoretical sense two approaches to determining the amount of capital can be taken: the first values capital as the cost incurred in the creation of the capital item; the second associates the value of capital with its capacity to generate income.

Measurement by Costs

In its simplest form, the first approach suggests that the value of a capital item should be the sum of cash outlays necessary to create it or purchase it. This approach appears operationally simple and is the one which conventional accounting systems attempt to follow. In fact, however, it is simple only to the extent that original cash outlays are identifiable and can be easily assigned when an asset is initially committed. It will soon become apparent that this is a somewhat difficult approach to adhere to after the capital has been put to use or when existing capital is purchased. This is so because of the changing character of value. Yet it remains more operationally feasible than the measurement-by-income approach, especially on the firm level. Capital, under the present approach, is recorded at the cost expended to secure it. In terms of real capital, costs are expressed as the sacrifices made by foregoing present consumption opportunities (the resources devoted to the formation of real capital must be taken away from the production of consumer goods). In a practical sense, the accountant would not record the dollar value of the sacrifices directly in terms of consumption given up, but in terms of the dollar cost to the firm purchasing the capital (the purchase price). These dollar values are objective, and thus quantifiable, for they result from the purchase and sale of resources in the market economy which is based upon the money system. In this sense, dollars—through money exchanges—measure the cost of most of the resources going into the creation of capital.

Generally speaking, acquired assets would be recorded by accountants as having a value equal to the purchase price. Over time, the original cost of the asset would be reduced on the books to recognize the estimated pro-rated amount of original value that has been "used up." Obviously, this procedure can give an inaccurate idea of the value of an asset. Changes in the supply of and demand for a recently acquired asset could change its value considerably. Also, and in recent years this has been even more important, general price increases may change the value of assets recorded on the basis of original-cost-less-depreciation. Despite these difficulties, there appears no adequate substitute that is as operationally meaningful (although there are many schemes which are conceptually more significant), and the measurement is generally accepted in business practice. Consequently, we continue to use that which we have available, while recognizing its shortcomings and making efforts to compensate for them.

But the concept of cost can and should be expanded to include all dollar outlays needed to purchase and place in operation a capital item so that it will contribute to income. This concept of cost includes more than the direct dollar outlay required to purchase a capital item. It also includes all installation and transportation costs, although, admittedly, both of these may be included in the purchase price.

Measurement by Income

Although the more operational cost approach is easily quantifiable, it is also unsatisfactorily rigid. Part of the difficulty with it is that capital items, once created, often do not contribute to income either the exact amounts originally anticipated or at the planned times. Consequently, after the decision to create or purchase a capital item (recorded at original cost) is used, its actual and/or expected contribution to income varies continuously. Because the true value of capital items is dependent on income, if income is ever-changing, it follows that the true value of capital is ever-changing also; rarely does it equal the cost of the resources expended to purchase it. Thus a more flexible approach measures the value of any capital item according to its contribution to income.[4] This capital item can be construed to be either physical or nonphysical; therefore, we might state, for example, that the present economic value of a person would to some extent reflect his future income flows. In the valuation of human capital, however, we must be careful to include in future income flows only those items of his personal income which result from the human capital contribution. For most measurement purposes we should not include, for example, future transfer payments which he might receive, but only those items of income which result from contributions of human capital. The same is true of an item of physical capital, such as a machine, the value of which at any moment depends upon its expected income over the future. In this sense not only is value constantly changing, but it is also obviously difficult to maintain an up-to-date recording of its quantity. However, periodic income estimates may be made and the value of capital approximated by the use of such data. Inasmuch as the estimates of future incomes are predictions, the value is based upon estimates of income that are likely to bear a certain degree of variability depending upon many environmental conditions.

Measuring the Capital Stock in the United States

Since both approaches to the measurement of individual capital items are at best difficult, to take inventory of just the stock of physical capital of an economy is an even more ominous task. Notwithstanding, it is logical to ask: What is the magnitude of capital stock that is generating our flow of national income and what magnitude will be needed in future years to accommodate expected levels of national income? Although quantification itself is fraught with innumerable difficulties, any measurement of physical output should be sensitive to quality differences in the capital; it should be comparable to stocks of capital in different time periods. For this reason, measurement by original cost is inadequate. It's like adding apples and oranges: the result is meaningless.

Measurement by income is more satisfactory theoretically but more difficult to apply. In practice, however, capital would be valued at less

---

[4] This measure will be developed extensively in Chapter 10.

than its full potential value. This is so because (1) it is not always and everywhere fully employed and (2) it is not fully mobile and therefore may not be employed in its best alternative use in the economy. Given these considerations, any plan to improve the reallocation of capital not employed in its best alternative use would increase our capital evaluation without a concomitant increase in investment and/or savings (aside from reallocation costs). In practice, difficulties also arise when this measure is used to separate the returns to capital from returns to other factors of production. The problems of obtaining an agreed-upon, unbiased estimate of future earnings of each item of capital are so great as to render such individual accounting impossible.

The value of the stock of capital for any economy is incapable of precise measurement because of the overwhelming statistical task. Yet the rapid capital formation in the United States appears to have been the dominant characteristic in the growth of the economy. A very rough approximation of the United States' physical capital stock may be made on the assumption that it must be about three times annual output; this ratio has been estimated by economists to be proper for the United States.[5] Thus if output were $700 billion, a crude estimate of capital would be $2,100 billion.

Additions to economic capital consist of the sum of net private domestic investment, net foreign investment, and net social investment. By *social investment* we mean the additions to the tools provided by society through government and used to generate monetary or psychic income. The contribution of public capital—such as highways, airports, and development of natural resources—is an important part of the ability of firms to generate profits. Although the importance of these contributions to monetary incomes is beyond question, they are so diffuse and interwoven with other returns as to make their quantification virtually impossible.[6]

Our federal government does, however, estimate net foreign investment and net private domestic investment. Very roughly *net foreign investment* occurs when we sell more goods and services abroad than we buy. Disinvestment occurs when we buy or give away more goods and factor services than we sell. In 1964, for example, we disinvested in this manner about $5 billion.

Net private domestic investment is measured as the sum of new construction, new producer's durable equipment, and changes in business in-

---

[5] Simon Kuznets, *Capital in the American Economy: Its Formation and Financing* (Princeton, N. J.: Princeton U.P., 1961), p. 80.

[6] National income statistics include all government expenditures. Not all of this is economic investment, however, thus precluding use of these data even as a rough approximation of total social investment.

ventories. As some of these capital items were consumed during the period —they were used up—the gross amount would be reduced by an estimated capital consumption allowance in order to produce a net figure. As set forth in Table 3-1, in 1964, gross private domestic investment was $87.3 billion, capital consumption allowances were $53.7 billion, and net investment was $33.6 billion.

Table 3-1
1964 U.S. Private Capital Additions
(Billions of Dollars)

Gross private domestic investment	$87.3
Less capital consumption allowances	53.7
Net private domestic investment	33.6
Net foreign investment	7.0
Total U.S. capital additions*	$40.6

* Other than by U.S. federal, state, and local governments.
Source: Federal Reserve Bulletin (January 1965), 174, 175.

RETURNS TO FACTORS

Profits

In order to place our discussion of returns to the various factors of production in proper perspective, it is necessary to describe two important concepts. The first deals with *time*. Because profit and income are being generated continuously, in order to estimate returns to factors of production a time period must be chosen which is relevant for the study of the economy as a whole as well as of its components. Most frequently, this period is one year, although income or profit is often estimated for shorter periods. Moreover, measurement of the profit or income flow requires rather careful allocation to the periods in which they actually are earned. This problem of allocation among time periods is a difficult one; it has plagued accountants for many years.

The second point to be delineated concerns adjustment of recorded data that are often used in the computation of returns. For example, much of what is often referred to loosely as "profits" in the firm may be nothing but wages, rent, and interest under another title. Implicit interest, implicit rent, and implicit wages are names given to this part of "reported profits." These *implicit returns* are necessary to keep the various factors employed over the long run, but failure to recognize them for what they are can lead to highly erroneous analyses. For example, a store proprietor whose salary is lower than what he could receive if he hired out his services will have included in his "profit" the implicit factor cost of wages. Only after a fair deduction of this implicit income in the form of wages can he determine profits. The same general observation can be made of the whole economy. Only after implicit payments to various factors of production are made can we determine profits.

The Sum of Returns to Factors of Production: National Income

For the accounts of the economy, government statisticians have devised a measure of the national income. It is one measure of the total economic effort of the economy for a period of one year and is defined as the sum of the income payments to each of the factors of production. The national income in the United States in 1964, for example, consisted of the items set forth in Table 3-2. The wages and salaries paid to individuals are measured before the deductions made by the federal government for income taxes. Income taxes, corporate profits tax, and property taxes are deductions from the returns to factors, but are part of the common revenue of society. These income payments in turn are spent or saved by society either individually or collectively. It is the saving (nonconsumption of current income) which permits diversion of some currently produced resources to additions to capital stock.

Table 3-2
1964 National Income
(Billions of Dollars)

Compensation of employees	$364.8
Proprietor's income	52.1
Rental income	12.4
Corporate profits	58.1
Net interest	27.1
	$514.5

Source: *Federal Reserve Bulletin* (January 1965), 174.

In measurements of national income, the returns to capital are net of the amount of capital used up during the designated period. Capital has been used to generate this "income" and is customarily replaced before dividing the total product among the factors producing it. Also, factors of production do not work alone; they work jointly to produce goods and services. They interact with each other, usually complementing one another's effectiveness. Sometimes, however, these factors will compete with rather than complement one another. For example, labor and capital may be substituted for each other to a certain point—as when a data-processing system supplants a number of clerical workers. Thus the demand for a factor—and hence its return—depends, among other things, upon the prices of all the factors.

The Return to Capital

Let us re-emphasize that capital is a factor of production created by man involving an indirect method of production which is intended to increase the total income available to him. Increased human capital increases one form of return to man, usually embodied in the national statistical accounts in the return to the labor factor called wages. Increased physical capital also increases the income flow. Its contribution to productivity is expressed in standard terms as a return to capital generally called profits or interest. The return to capital, usually expressed as an annual percentage, includes profit as the return to ownership capital and interest as a return to borrowed capital. The analysis of these capital returns, although commonly associated only with physical capital, may be applied to all forms of capital in the context of the economy, the firm, or the household (which consists of one or many individuals).[7]

Depending upon the viewpoint adopted toward the factors of production, a large part of national income could be called a return to capital. This is especially so when we introduce the concept of human capital. How much of the "compensation to employees" would then be a return to human capital and how much is a return to labor? This is a difficult question, but it would seem that most of labor's productivity, at least that part which consists of special talents and skills, would arise from human capital. Moreover, investments required in land today make it difficult, if not impossible, to separate the return to land from the return to capital. Even though rents are commonly referred to as the return to land, a great deal of that return probably arises from the capital improvements made to land.

In an economy, the productivity of capital is affected by many elements, such as the political and institutional environment in which it is employed and the complementary aspects of other factors of production. At various times, this productivity may be subject to considerable fluctuation. During the depression of the 1930's, the aggregate demand for goods was such that the net productivity of capital decreased to such a low level

[7] At least a portion of the activity of the household frequently is similar to that of a firm. The line between much of household activity and that of a proprietorship, partnership, or even a small corporation is often very difficult to draw. Purchases of stocks, bonds, and pieces of land are activities engaged in by both firms and households and usually for the same reason—profit.

that no stimulus for increasing the supply of physical capital existed. For a period, capital was not being replaced, and the economy thus was apparently regressing. Such a depletion of capital does the economy considerable future damage in terms of the levels of expected income.

CAPITAL FORMATION

As mentioned earlier, capital items result in so increasing the productivity of labor that we attribute to this factor a net productivity or contribution viewed as profit and interest. This net productivity may be expressed in the form of a rate per annum. The demand for capital depends upon the expectation of this productivity. In other words, the demand for capital is a derived demand, derived ultimately from the demand or value of consumption goods which are produced directly or indirectly by the use of capital items. Its net productivity would be the gross contribution of capital after all costs of capital replacement and other maintenance expenses.

In situations in which capital is very scarce relative to other elements in the productive process—such as labor, human capital, and, in some cases, land—physical capital will tend to have a high net productivity. Because of this, funds for the creation of physical capital will command relatively high prices for their use for there will exist a strong demand in the economy for resources to devote to physical capital formation. For example, if the net productivity of physical capital were as high as 20 or 30 per cent, it would be profitable to divert factor resources in the economy to capital creation if returns to other factors were relatively low. The money necessary for capital creation would be generated for the most part indirectly by the giving up of consumption out of current income—that is, by saving. Savings in a high-income economy may come from a large number of widely scattered economic units and frequently are directly placed in capital creating activities, indirectly invested in documents representing capital investments (for example, stocks and bonds), or invested indirectly in capital through the financial system. These savings, representative of foregone present consumption, can be used for the production of consumer goods to increase inventories, or for the production or creation of real capital. This process is referred to as *capital formation*.

In more advanced nations, 10–20 per cent of the national income may be used in capital formation. In the less advanced countries, the rate of saving and investment may be less than 5 per cent. The population of many of these countries is growing so rapidly that even reproducing the primitive tools they now use leaves little savings available for progress.

Moreover, much of the saving of some of these countries goes into the hoarding of gold and jewelry. Owing to inflation and—perhaps more important—the risks of alternative investments, the attraction of hoarding may be much greater than an investment in internal, more productive schemes. Wealthy members of these societies, in the absence of effective exchange controls, frequently invest their savings in more secure ventures abroad, leaving little for internal national development.

In the economically underdeveloped areas of the world, per capita income is very low and the pressure for rapid economic growth is very strong. Although no one has yet developed a formula guaranteed to bring about growth, it is agreed that among other necessary ingredients capital is of primary importance. The importation of physical capital paid for with great sacrifices of consumption or through loans or gifts from outside sources is perhaps not as much of a problem to these countries that wish to achieve rapid growth as is the problem of finding the proper proportion of human capital to use with physical capital. Human capital may also be imported, but this is frequently politically undesirable—at least to any significant extent—even though development of their own human capital takes time. Aside from these needs, a proper level of consumption must be maintained so as to absorb the increasing productive capacity; consequently, saving must not increase too rapidly. Political stability and the moral attitudes of the people are also customarily viewed as important variables in growth; they affect the risk of investment and thus its desirability. So it can be seen that the act of investment and the provision of capital play an important role in the economic growth of all nations.

SUMMARY

This chapter has been devoted to a discussion of the nature of capital. Capital is one factor of production; its use results in increased productivity and income. Capital, like other factors of production, is not homogeneous and may exist in either physical or human form. It may be measured as the cost of the resources required to create it or (preferably) by the value of its contribution to total income. Profit and interest are the returns to capital: profit, the return to that part of capital supplied by the owners of the business; interest, the return to capital supplied by lenders. National income is the return to all factors of production in an economy. Increases in capital are encouraged by high net productivity rates; the higher these rates relative to other factors, the more rapid the growth and formation of capital. Capital in all its forms plays a vital role in economic development.

SUGGESTED READINGS

ACKLEY, GARDNER. *Macroeconomic Theory*. New York: The Macmillan Company, 1961. Chaps. 2 and 3.

FRIEDMAN, MILTON. *Price Theory*. Chicago: Aldine Publishing Company, 1962. Chap. 13.

HAAVELMO, TRYGVE. *A Study in the Theory of Investment*. Chicago: The University of Chicago Press, 1960.

HOOVER, E. M. "Capital Accumulation and Progress," *American Economic Review, 40* (May 1950), 124–35.

KENDRICK, JOHN W. "Some Theoretical Aspects of Capital Measurement," *American Economic Review, 51* (May 1961), 102–11.

KEYNES, JOHN MAYNARD. *The General Theory of Employment, Interest and Money*. New York: Harcourt, Brace & World, Inc., 1936. Chap. 16.

MACHLUP, FRITZ. *The Production and Distribution of Knowledge in the United States*. Princeton, N.J.: Princeton University Press, 1963.

SAMUELSON, P. A. and R .M. SOLOW. "A Complete Capital Model Involving Heterogeneous Capital Goods," *Quarterly Journal of Economics, 70* (November 1956), 537–62.

SMITH, DAN THROOP. "Capital Formation and the Use of Capital," *American Economic Review, 53* (May 1963), 314–22.

SOLOW, ROBERT M. "Technical Progress, Capital Formation and Economic Growth," *American Economic Review, 52* (May 1962), 76–86.

WESTON, J. FRED. "Some Perspectives on Capital Theory," *American Economic Review, 41* (May 1951), 129–44.

QUESTIONS

3.1 Discuss whether a highway toll road is capital to the economy, to the firm, and/or to the individual.

3.2 Consider the demolition of an old warehouse to make way for a new apartment building. Does this involve a gain or loss to the economy?

3.3 If an oil rig were transferred from the Southwest to Alaska, would there be a gain or loss to the Southwest regional economy? To Alaska?

3.4 Is there such a thing as a unit of labor or human with zero human capital? (Begin your discussion by setting forth your understanding of human capital.)

3.5 A firm makes expenditures for stock bonuses, pension funds, and free insurance to employees. Are these expenditures for capital items?

3.6 If an egg-producing chicken is considered capital, how would you view the concepts of saving, investment, and consumption?

3.7 Are the expenditures in the location of labor in the economy through such mobility-stimulating outlays as employment information services considered capital? If so, what kind of captial? If not, why not?

3.8 Determine your personal stock of capital by estimating the costs of (1) all the items used to generate your monetary income, and (2) all the items used to generate psychic income.

3.9 Consider the operation of a one-man shoe-repair shop. After deducting costs for materials, rent, and utilities from his receipts, discuss the nature of the remainder as a return to the productive factors.

3.10 Discuss the factors influencing economic development of an economy, including any not mentioned in this chapter that come to mind.

CHAPTER 4   THE CAPITAL MARKET

We have dealt with many aspects of the capital resource: its nature, its measurement, and the manner in which it comes into being and is rewarded. On the other hand, we have not as yet discussed the answer to an extremely important question: What determines the magnitude of the reward to capital? This task occupies not only this chapter, but also the two following. There are two reasons for devoting so much space to it. First, it is without doubt the most important single aspect of the financial environment within which the firm operates. Furthermore, the techniques which are needed to explain the determination of the reward to capital constitute some of the most important basic tools of the financial manager. For this reason, a clear understanding is necessary if some of the essential concepts to be presented later are to be grasped.

In general, an *investment* involves an *exchange*. There are two quite different aspects to such a transaction. The first is the time element—one gives up something today in order to receive something in the future. Such action is contrary to a general (but not universal) tendency to prefer something today to an equivalent thing in the future, a characteristic called *time preference*. The second element of the capital decision involves risk—one gives up something certain today for something less than certain in the future. This too is contrary to a widely observed human characteristic, the desire to avoid risk, usually called *risk aversion*. Obviously, transactions will take place if, and only if, the terms are such as to compensate the investor for bearing risk and for waiting; he expects to get more in the future than he gives up in the present. But how much more? This will depend on the length of time he must wait and on the risk involved. Although such a statement goes a long way towards describing the problem, there is, unfortunately, much more to it than that. In order to approach the problem we shall break it down into its several aspects. First we will consider only the time aspect of the capital decisions, leaving out risk entirely. This task will occupy the remainder of this chapter. Chapter 5 will add to the discussion by considering risk. Finally, Chapter 6 will introduce some of the effects of governmental actions, changes in tastes, and other factors that impinge on this problem.

THE INVESTMENT PROCESS

We have defined investment as the act of devoting some resource to a use which will not yield satisfaction in the present, in the anticipation that it will yield satisfaction in the future. In any particular year an economy such as that of the United States has a tremendous amount of capital in a multitude of forms—goods, human beings, knowledge and skill, and natural resources. Ordinarily, we would expect an economy to invest some of its current income, although in most economies the new investment in any given year is far short of that year's income. The economy must decide how much to invest, what particular goods to devote to the investment process, and the manner in which they are to be combined to produce future goods. Our task in this chapter is to begin to analyze such decisions, concentrating for the moment on the time aspect of the decision.

To make the discussion somewhat more simple, we will assume (1) that time comes in two convenient doses—the present and the future—and, (2) that the future is exactly one year away from the present. We will move into a more realistic world in Chapter 6, but for the present our simplified picture will prove difficult enough.

The second simplification concerns risk. We will assume that everyone knows with certainty just what the result of a particular investment will be. In other words, we assume, for example, that every farmer knows exactly what his crop will be if he plants a certain amount of seeds in a certain manner with a certain type of fertilizer; every businessman knows exactly what his sales will be if he makes a particular type of car; and so on. In brief, we assume a world which is extremely unrealistic. We will bring realism back into the world in Chapter 5.

We characterize the investment process as one in which members of an economy forego present satisfaction from goods in order to obtain satisfaction in the future; in other words, investment is really an exchange of present goods and services (hopefully) for (greater) future goods and services. Although this is true, the usual method by which the process is carried out involves intermediate exchanges using money, the medium of exchange in any highly developed economy. Thus to the individual the investment process is likely to take the following form: *exchange present money for future money* foregoing the present goods and services which the present money could have bought in order to get some future goods and services with the future money. It is in this sense that it is reasonable to view the investment process as one involving investment of money by individuals in return for future money. Remember, however, that money is primarily a "veil" in this context (we will want to qualify this notion in Chapter 6); the real trade is present goods for future goods.

With the above distinction clearly in mind, we may talk about the supply of *investment funds,* that is, the amount of present money and/or credit which people in the economy wish to invest instead of the supply of *present goods.* This will greatly simplify our discussion and conform more to the viewpoint of the individual investor.

THE RATE OF RETURN

The first concept necessary for an understanding of the investment process is the rate of return. We shall see later that this can be a rather tricky notion, but for the conditions to which we are limiting ourselves here, it is, fortunately, quite straightforward. The rate of return is *a measure of the relationship between the amount an investor gets back from his investment and the amount invested.* Thus, if we were to invest $1.00 this year and obtain $1.15 next year, we have earned a rate of return of 15 per cent for the year.[1]

If one invests $1.00 this month and receives $1.15 in return next month, he has earned 15 per cent *per month.* Note that the rate of return is a rate per month, year, day, or whatever time period one might specify. A rate of interest of 12 per cent certainly sounds different from a rate of 1 per cent, but they may be quite similar (e.g., if the former is 12 per cent per year and the latter is 1 per cent per month). In the absence of any period quoted, the rate is assumed to be annual. In general, when an investor foregoes $X now and receives in return $Y after some time period, his rate of return (R) is

$$R = \frac{\$Y - \$X}{\$X}$$

per time period. The table below gives several examples of such calculations:

Amount Invested Now ($X)	Amount Received Later ($Y)	Time Period Between Investment and Receipt	Rate of Return
$100	$120	1 year	20%/year
200	210	1 month	5%/month
500	700	2 years	40%/2 years

[1] We are ignoring taxes at present.

In general, we find rates of return expressed in terms of time periods other than a year rather difficult to compare so we often convert such rates as 5 per cent per month and 40 per cent per two years into comparable annual rates. To illustrate, when the time period is a fraction of a year, an estimate of the comparable annual rate of return can be found by dividing the rate of return by the fraction the time period is of a full year as, for example,

$$5\% \text{ per month} = 5\% - 1/12 = 60\% \text{ per year}$$

When the time period is more than a year, the comparable annual rate can be found by dividing the rate of return by the number of years in the time period:

$$40\% \text{ per 2 years} = 40\% \div 2 = 20\% \text{ per year}$$

We will see later that, because of "compounding," these rules tend to understate the comparable annual rate when the time period is less than a year and to overstate it when the period exceeds a year. For many purposes, however, the estimates are close enough to the true rates.

In the examples in this and the next chapter, we will be concerned always with the same time period (between the present and the future). For convenience we assumed that this period is one year; thus all rates of return will automatically be on an annual basis.

THE SUPPLY OF INVESTMENT FUNDS

One of the difficulties in understanding the investment process concerns the relationship between capital and income. Before proceeding, it might be well to review this relationship and indicate its importance in the present discussion. In viewing the workings of an economy, we often focus our attention on discrete time periods—frequently a year. Thus we speak of the annual income of an economy as the total value of goods and services produced by that economy during a particular year. There are many goods, services, and resources available to an economy at any time besides those produced during the current year. These we called *capital*, the results of investment during past years. When investigating the investment process, we usually retain the distinction between time periods, concentrating on the amount invested during a particular time period. Thus we speak of the annual net investment of an economy as being the total change in its stock of capital during the year. In most cases the net change will be positive; capital will increase. But it may be negative, as in the case of a country at war.

The danger with concentrating on the total amount of investment is that it tends to obscure the actual process. Consider an economy which on net adds to its total stock of capital during a year. Although the total value of capital will increase, this does not imply that every capital item in existence at the beginning of the year is in existence at the end; quite to the contrary, many will have been consumed during the year. Similarly, the fact that investment on net is, say, 10 per cent of current income does not mean that 10 per cent of currently produced goods and services will be devoted to investment. The actual amount will be larger, to offset the items of previous capital which were actually consumed. To understand the decision process underlying investment, it is essential to realize that both items of capital and currently produced goods and services are available for either consumption or investment during the year. To emphasize this point, we will use the term *wealth* to indicate the sum of both capital stock and current income and speak in terms of the decision to invest all or part of wealth. In most cases we would expect to find that an economy chooses to invest an amount of its wealth so that its capital will increase, but this need not necessarily be the case. In any case, our analysis should lead us to the correct answers.

To begin our analysis of the investment process, we must examine the individual, for in a capitalistic economy the majority of decisions are made by private parties (exceptions will be considered in Chapter 5). With the exception of governmental activities, the majority of the economy's wealth is under the direct or indirect control of individuals. Some of this is direct and identifiable, such as an individual's house, or personal business, while some is highly indirect, such as the property right of a share of stock. Nevertheless, individual owners, to a greater or lesser extent, make decisions concerning the disposition of their resources. For our present discussion the important decision concerns the allocation of their wealth between present satisfactions and future satisfactions.

What determines the amount of personal capital that an individual will want to devote to the future? The answer obviously depends on many things. Certainly the size of his *present total wealth* will have some effect. Although we cannot say that wealthier people devote a higher proportion of their wealth to the future, it seems quite likely that they devote a higher absolute amount than poorer people. An individual's *time preference* also plays a major role. The impatient will eat, drink, and be merry today, devoting little thought to the future; those who are willing to wait will be more inclined to devote wealth to the future. Obviously the individual's *expectations* concerning the future will play a role in his decision. Thus in economies threatened by war, revolution, inflation, or some other equally consequential occurrence, people are extremely reluctant to invest (save) much of their wealth. Connected with this is the factor of *risk;* we shall disregard it here, reserving its discussion in Chapter 5.

All the factors described above are important in determining an individual's willingness to devote resources to the future—that is, to supply investment funds to the market. But one crucial factor has not yet been indicated; to put it bluntly, the person will not be able to make up his mind on this point until he knows "what's in it for him." What does he get in the future for giving up something now?

We have described a measure which relates future amounts of wealth to present amounts. This we called the rate of return (R). In theory, there is some standard rate of return available on *riskless investments.* Economists define this as the pure rate of interest ("pure" because it includes no compensation for risk).

What is the pure rate of interest? Formally, it is a relationship between future goods and services and present goods and services, indicating the rate at which one can be traded for the other. Ordinarily, it is characterized as the *price of money.* But this is not strictly accurate, for money—to return to our earlier discussion—is only the medium of exchange. The *real exchange* is that of present goods for future goods. To the extent that money serves as a standard of value also, however, we can and do express any and all exchanges in terms of it. The result is a price, the ratio of various goods and/or services to other goods and/or services expressed in money terms. To repeat, however, the real exchange is that of goods and/or services, with money acting only to facilitate the exchange. Thus the pure rate of interest indicates the terms on which one can trade present wine for future wine, present gin for future tonic, or present milkshakes for future Cadillacs. In short, it is the *price of time,* indicating the reward for *waiting,* or the rate of exchange between present and future goods.

But what determines the magnitude of this reward? It is not surprising to learn that the answer an economist would readily give to such a question is: demand and supply. In other words, the pure interest rate in an economy will depend on people's desires to invest and the availability of investment projects; but both of these are, in turn, dependent on the pure interest rate. The standard way out of this "circle" is to isolate the effects of the pure interest rate on the supply-and-demand sides of the market and then bring the resultant analyses together to determine the rate which clears the market. We follow that procedure here.

Figure 4-1 indicates graphically the typical relationship between an individual's desire and ability to invest and the pure rate of interest (a supply curve of capital). Its major characteristics are fairly straightforward.

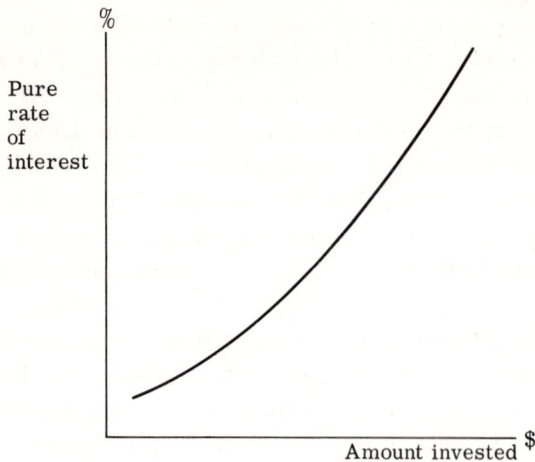

'Figure 4-1   An Individual's Supply of Capital

The higher the pure rate, the more an individual supplies to the invest-ment market (if all other influences on him remain the same), because at a high pure rate he will receive much more in the way of future goods for a given amount of present goods given up. Or, to put it another way, for a given amount of future goods, he will have to forego fewer present goods.

In a hypothetical economy in which all wealth is controlled by individ-ual owners, the total supply of the "economy" is merely the sum of the supply curves of the individual members. To characterize the investment desires of such an economy, we need only sum up the desires of its indi-viduals. Figure 4-2 illustrates the process graphically for an economy com-posed of two individuals, A and B. The left-hand curves are the supply schedules of A and B, respectively, while the right-hand curve, labeled A + B, is the supply of investment funds by the entire (two-man) riskless economy. This is obtained simply as follows. For any possible rate of in-terest (e.g., r) determine the amount A wishes to invest (here it is QZ). Then determine the amount B wishes to invest (QW). The total amount which the economy wishes to invest (at r) is merely the sum of these (QX). Repeating the process for every possible rate of interest, we obtain the full schedule. Note that this schedule, like its components, slopes upward (higher rates of interest induce desires to invest more). As higher rates of interest are reached, some individuals choose to invest more and more in-dividuals who previously had not wished to invest at all will enter the market.

We have discussed individual investment desires by characterizing

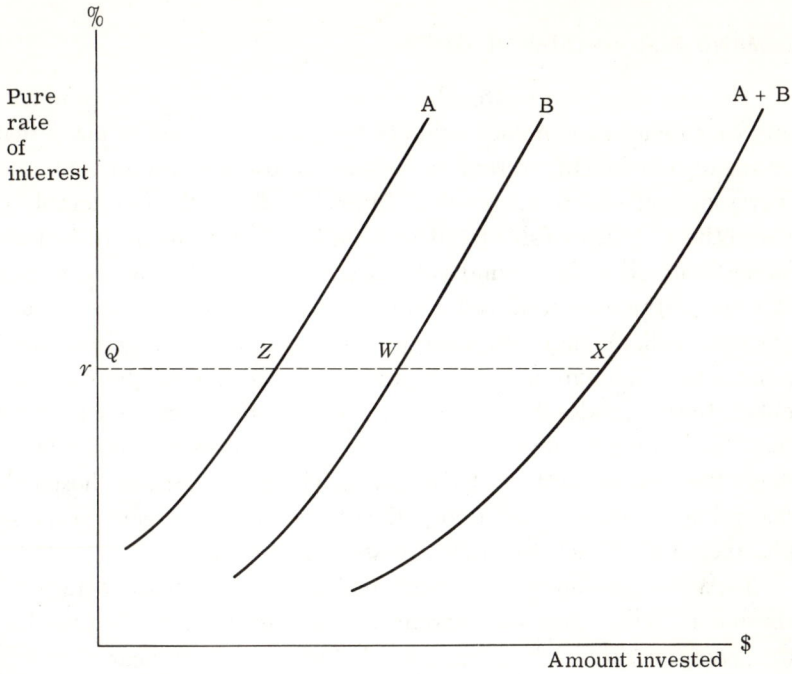

Figure 4-2 The Economy's Supply of Capital

them in terms of a supply curve of investment funds and indicating their response to various levels of the pure interest rate. In any perfectly free-enterprise economy, it is thus possible to represent the desires of the economy in the same manner: namely, by merely summing up the individual desires into a total investment funds supply curve and indicating the amount which would be forthcoming at each of various interest rates. The nature of such a curve depends on the positions of its component curves, which in turn depend upon such things as individuals' time preferences, expectations concerning the future, and present level of wealth. Although greater emphasis will be placed on these variables in later discussions, it should be apparent at this juncture that we can expect the total supply curve to change as these underlying influences change. If wealth should somehow be transferred from a patient man to an impatient one, the total supply of investment funds will shift; the new curve will lie to the left of the old one since at any given rate of interest a smaller supply would be forthcoming on net. If people suddenly decide an atomic war is imminent, the curve will shift violently to the left. On the other hand, a relaxation of international tension would probably lead to a shift to the right.

DEMAND FOR INVESTMENT FUNDS

The rate of return relates the money value of the goods produced by an investment to the money value of the goods required to make that investment. Obviously, present goods may be used in any of a number of ways, some of which will produce future goods worth considerably more than others. A dead fish placed in a vault is hardly likely to increase in value; if placed in the ground as fertilizer, it may contribute to an increase in value of the crop fertilized. On the other hand, wine placed in a vault (or wine cellar) might increase in value by a rather large amount. The point is that there are many alternative methods of using present goods to obtain future goods. If a decision has been made to invest a good rather than to consume it, efforts would be made to use it in a fashion which produces the greatest future value of goods. The particular use chosen would depend upon, among other things, the physical characteristics of the goods plus the relative prices of various goods in the future.

There are any number of goods which could be invested rather than consumed. Which ones are chosen? The answer is extremely complex but the general nature of the process is relatively simple. We can start best by considering the single commodity and then moving to several commodities.

The Return from Investing in One Good

Assume that in a particular year a rather small crop of unique grape is produced. This grape can be consumed as grape juice or put aside to make wine. The physical relationship is quite simple; one quart of grape juice placed in a cask will yield one quart of wine in one year. The casks are available for the entire crop if desired, and the physical relationship is the same regardless of the amount of the crop placed in the wine cellar. Will the rate of return on the investment (making wine instead of drinking grape juice) be the same regardless of the amount invested (the amount of grape juice placed in the cellar)? Perhaps not. The price of the wine produced will probably depend on the quantity produced. If only one cup of grape juice were invested, the wine might be quite rare and command a fairly high price,[2] yielding a handsome rate of return on the investment. On the other hand, if the entire crop were placed in the wine cellar, the wine might be quite commonplace and command a relatively low price, resulting in a mediocre or perhaps even negative rate of return.

This situation is not necessarily typical. In many cases there are certain

[2] Needless to say, this magnitude of the price would depend on many factors, such as the availability of relatively similar wines, the extent to which the qualities of this wine are generally known and appreciated, and so on.

economics of scale [3] associated with a production process. Even though a larger quantity of wine may lead to lower prices per bottle, the efficiency gained through large-scale production might more than offset the price effect, causing total income per dollar invested to be larger for some medium-scale investment than a small-scale operation. On the other hand, such economies of scale cannot be obtained continually as the scale of production is increased. Eventually the advantages of large-scale production are not sufficient to offset the disadvantages in terms of price reduction, for to sell larger and larger quantities the manufacturer must eventually resort to lower prices. The net effect is thus typically similar to that shown in Figure 4-3. In the range from *O* to *M*, additional investment results in economies of scale sufficient to more than offset price reductions. But from *M* on, the required price reductions more than offset any additional gains from economies of scale.

The possibility of economies of scale appears to make it impossible to assume that the rate of return from investing in a particular operation will fall as more is invested; actually this is not the case. It should fall, and unless an investor is severely constrained in the amount available to him for investment, he will never choose to cease investing in a process as long as there remain economies of scale more than sufficient to offset any required price reductions from increased production. He will cease to invest only when the marginal rate of return equals the marginal cost of capital (under certainty). In general, if any investment in this process is to take place, it will equal or exceed *OM*. And in the range above *OM*, the curve

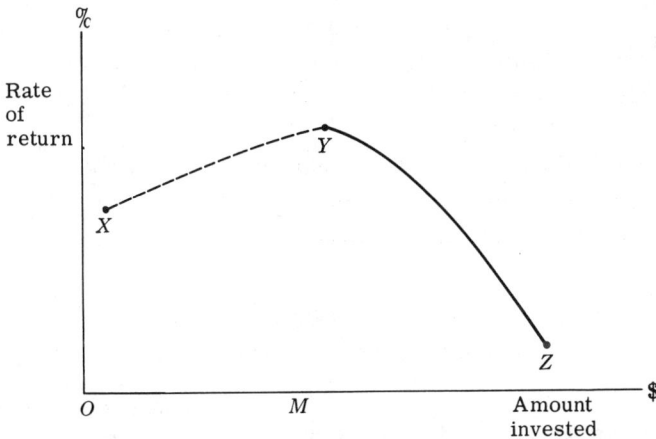

Figure 4-3   Rate of Return and Economies of Scale

[3] Economies of scale prevail where, through some range, the average cost per unit falls as the total output is increased.

does fall. Thus it is reasonable to assume that, over a relevant range of operations (or investments), the return from investment in a single good will fall as more is invested—at least within the range of investment to be considered.

The Return from Investing in More Than One Good

We now turn from a single investment to the possibility of investing in diverse ways. Assume that a firm employs two workers, each performing the same task and receiving the same salary. The managers are considering investing in them by foregoing for some time the work they can perform while they go to a special trade school to increase their skill. One of the workers has an IQ of 100 while the other has an IQ of 150. If the firm decides to send (invest in) only one worker, it would undoubtedly send the brighter one, as he presumably offers a potentially better return on the investment (he will either learn more in a given time or learn the same amount in a shorter time). On the other hand, if the firm wishes to invest more (let us assume it can send both workers), the result would be a lower rate of return on its additional investment. The simple principle of taking the best first leads to the inevitable conclusion that the more invested, the smaller the rate of return.

THE MARGINAL EFFICIENCY OF CAPITAL

In the previous section we obtained a curve indicating the amount of investment funds provided by individuals; we now need a comparable schedule to indicate what can be done with such funds. For such a schedule to be rational, it must reflect the obvious rule that the best is done first. A curve that performs this task is known as the Marginal Efficiency of Capital (*MEC*) curve; in the context of our discussion, it constitutes the demand for investment.

The marginal efficiency of the capital curve can best be understood by examining a simple case. Table 4-1 shows the characteristics of four investments available in a simple mythical economy.

Table 4-1
Investment Opportunities

Investment	Rate of Return	Amount of Investment Required
A	10%	$100
B	20	100
C	5	400
D	15	200

If the manager of a socialist economy were presented with this list, he would undoubtedly rearrange it with the best investment first (the "best" being the one giving the highest rate of return). We can be certain that the profit motive in a free-enterprise economy would also result in better investments being taken first, so we can rearrange it in the same manner. This is done in Table 4-2.

Table 4-2
Investment Opportunities (Arranged)

Investment	Rate of Return	Amount of Investment Required	Cumulative Amount of Investment Required
B	20%	$100	$100
D	15	200	300
A	10	100	400
C	5	400	800

Notice that we have added a final column to the table, the cumulative amount, indicating the total amount of investment funds required to support all the investments equal to or better than each investment. The meaning of this colunm should become clearer after the following discussion.

How might we graph the information concerning the investments open to an economy? Each investment has two important aspects: its rate of return and the amount required. A two-dimensional figure can be used to represent an investment; we can represent each investment by a rectangle with width equal to the amount of investment funds required and height equal to the rate of return, lining such boxes up in order, with the best to the left, as shown in Figure 4-4. Notice that this technique allows us to read the total amount of investment required to undertake a project and all better projects directly from the horizontal scale. Thus to undertake B, D, and A (B and D are better than A) will required a $400 ($100 + $200 + $100) investment.

Figure 4-5 repeats the information of Figure 4-4 without the internal vertical lines of the original boxes; Line ZZ is drawn as a hypothetical fit of the relation between rate of return and investment. We shall call the data of Table 4-2 the Marginal Efficiency of Capital schedule and Line ZZ in Figure 4-5 the *MEC* curve. Let us see how it can be used.

If the members of the economy choose to invest in all projects with a rate of return greater than 9 per cent, how much would they invest? Start-

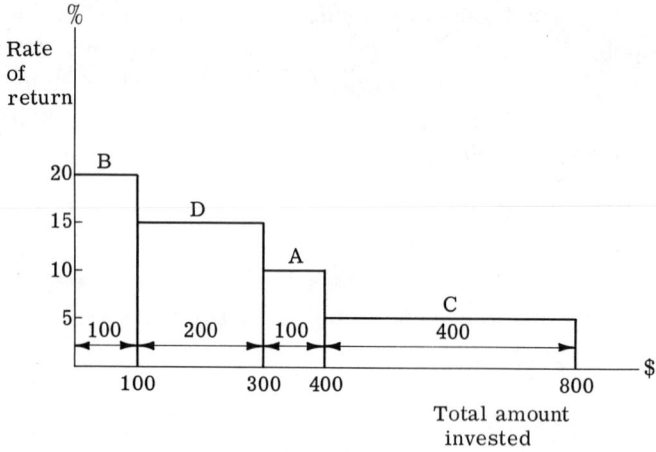

Figure 4-4   Array of Investment Opportunities, Cumulative

ing at 10 per cent on the vertical axis and reading over to the *MEC* curve, we find that the answer is $400. Which projects would be undertaken? All those with greater rates of return. Such projects must lie to the left of the point at which we contacted the *MEC* curve; in this case they are Projects B, D, and A. Similarly, if the economy wished to invest in all projects with rates of return greater than 14 per cent, it would invest $300. It is in this way that the riskless *MEC* curve can be used to indicate the amount required to support investments with rates of return greater than or equal to any particular amount.

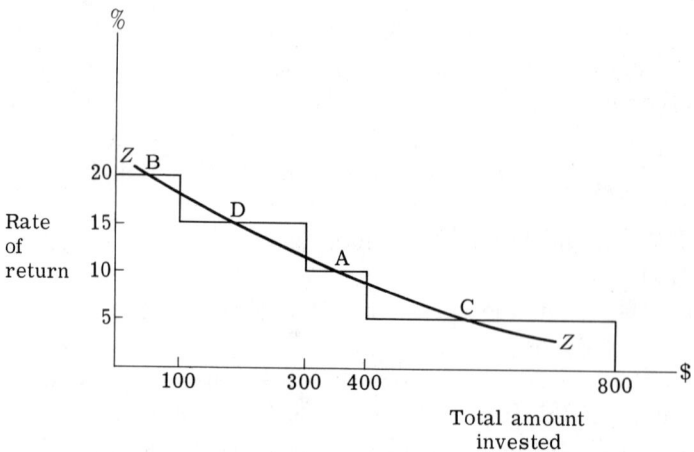

Figure 4-5   Cumulative Array of Investment Opportunities

The *MEC* curve can be used in the opposite manner too. If the members of this economy wished to invest $400 in the best possible fashion, what investments would be undertaken? Starting at $400 on the horizontal axis, we read up to the *MEC* curve. We find that for $400 they can undertake investments that yield at least 10 per cent. Thus all investments with a rate of return in excess of 10 per cent would be undertaken. Again, such investments lie to the left of the intersection; in this case they are B, D, and A. The *MEC* curve can be used, then, to indicate the minimum rate of return available if a given total amount of funds is to be invested. Put another way, it indicates the rate of return given by the least attractive investment plan; this latter is a *marginal* investment. The rate of return can be considered a measure of *efficiency*, and *capital* is required to support the investment—hence the name, Marginal Efficiency of Capital.

In our mythical example we assumed that the economy in question had available only four separate investment projects, each of which was virtually on a take-it-or-leave-it basis. In real economies, the picture is considerably more complex. There are hundreds of thousands of possible types of investments, most of which can be taken in either greater or lesser amounts. Thus the *MEC* curve for a real economy would include the possibility of investing in many projects and also the possibility of investing more in projects already considered. Nevertheless, the principle is the same. The better alternatives would be taken first, so the curve will slope downward, as we have drawn it. But the multiplicity of possibilities will make it appear almost perfectly continuous as in Line ZZ, rather than a series of horizontal and vertical lines.

We wish to construct a graph that will indicate the amount which would be invested at various pure rates of interest. What projects should be undertaken given a rate of interest? Obviously those with greater rates of return. Because the *MEC* curve shows the total amount which can be invested at rates of return greater or equal to any given rate of interest, it thus performs the desired function exactly. It *is* the demand for investment in an economy. The only task remaining in this chapter is that of putting our two curves together to see how they mutually determine the pure rate of interest in the economy.

THE PURE RATE OF INTEREST

Figure 4-6 combines the results of our earlier discussion to indicate the manner in which the pure rate of interest is determined in an economy. Both the *MEC* curve (indicating what can be done with investment funds) and the supply curve (indicating the terms on which such funds

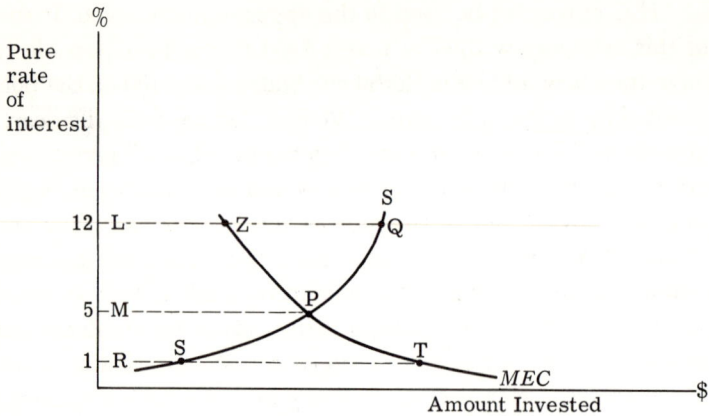

Figure 4-6 Determination of Equilibrium Pure Rate of Interest

will be forthcoming) are shown. In this example they intersect at a rate of 5 per cent. We will now see why this must be the prevailing pure rate of interest in the riskless economy pictured.

Assume for the sake of argument that the interest rate were higher than 5 per cent—for example, 12 per cent. People would like to invest an amount shown by the length *LQ* at such a rate of interest. What projects would they invest in? The *MEC* curve indicates that only *LZ* of projects with rates of return in excess of 12 per cent are available. In their attempt to invest in these attractive projects, people will bid up their prices. But because the rate of return measures the relative magnitude of future dollars to present dollars, at a higher price an investment will give a lower rate of return. Thus the effect of people's attempts to bid away the relatively scarce projects from one another will cause a drop in the rate of interest.

Assume next that the rate of interest were below 5 per cent—say, 1 per cent. At this rate of interest people would be interested in relatively little investment; in this graph it amounts to *RS*. But if only *RS* were invested, a great many projects with rates of return in excess of 1 per cent would remain untaken, a situation which could not long prevail. The conclusion is that only at the rate of interest where the two curves cross—where the quantity of funds people wish to invest at or above the prevailing interest rate is equal to the opportunities for them to invest on these terms—will there be no pressure for a change in the rate. Thus the pure rate of interest will tend to settle at the rate indicated by the intersection of the *MEC* curve and the Supply of Investment curve.

We have shown that the pure rate of interest will be determined by factors of demand and supply. Obviously, as the underlying factors influencing the demand and supply curves change, the curves will shift, yielding a new intersection and a new pure rate of interest. The process by which that new rate of interest is reached has only been alluded to here because it is extremely complex, involving financial intermediaries, various types of contracts, and numerous other factors. The analysis presented here represents a simple model which focuses on the basic determinants of the pure interest rate in a purely free-enterprise system. The effects of governmental activities, banks, and other financial intermediaries will command our attention in later chapters.

An indication of the simplicity with which the analysis provides answers can be gained from some simple examples. Assume that a new technique for producing some good is discovered. This will add a new investment opportunity to the set described in the MEC curve, causing it to shift to the right. What will happen to the pure interest rate and the amount invested? Figure 4-7 indicates the answer. The MEC curve shifts from MEC_1 to MEC_2, causing the rate of interest to rise from r_1 to r_2 and the amount of investment in the economy to increase from Q_1 to Q_2. Will the change in the MEC manifest itself more in a rise in the pure rate or in the amount invested? This will depend on the nature of the supply of the investment funds. If the supply curve is relatively flat, indicating that people will wish to invest considerably more at slightly higher interest rates, the major effect will be felt in the amount of investment; the pure rate of interest will respond relatively little. On the other hand, if the supply curve is quite steep, indicating that people require major increases in the interest rate to induce them to increase investment appreciably, the opposite effect will obtain; most of the impact will be on the pure rate.

Figure 4-8 provides another example of the use of the analysis. Suppose

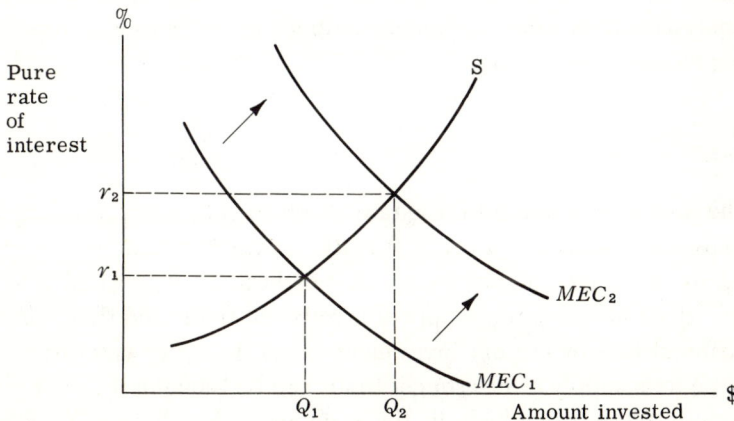

Figure 4-7 Changes in the Pure Rate of Interest Given a Shift in Demand

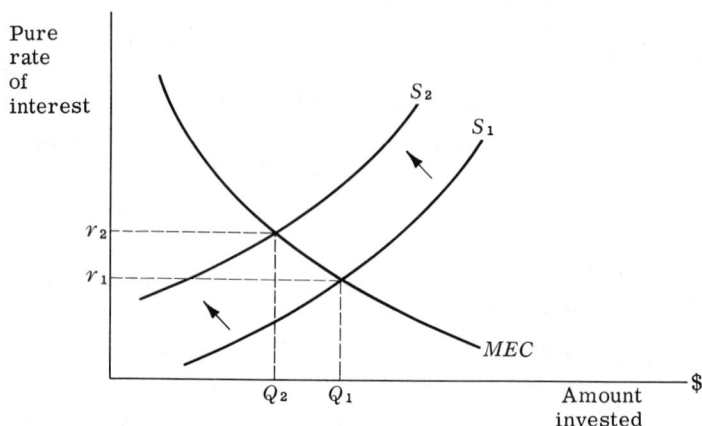

Figure 4-8   Changes in the Pure Rate of Interest Given a Shift in Supply

that a new progressive income tax were instituted in an economy, trans-ferring income from the rich to the poor. Furthermore, assume that the poor were inclined to spend more of their income than the rich. The net effect would be a fall in the supply of investment funds, indicated in Figure 4-8 by the shift from curve S_1 to curve S_2. The effect would be felt in two ways: the pure rate of interest would rise and the amount invested would fall. What would determine the relative magnitudes of the two effects? Obviously the slope of the MEC. If the MEC is flat, the major effect would be on the amount invested. If it were steep, however, the pure interest rate would absorb most of the impact.

The student is encouraged to test his understanding of the demand-and-supply analysis described in this chapter with some other possible examples (several are given as problems at the end of this chapter); this will also serve to provide an insight into the wide range of applicability of the analysis and its value for understanding the underlying factors deter-mining the pure interest rate.

SUMMARY

The pure rate of interest is the rate of return generally prevailing in an economy for riskless investments; it is the reward for waiting. It is deter-mined by a number of factors which can best be segregated into two groups: those affecting the supply of investment funds and those affecting the demand for (or use of) investment funds. In a free-enterprise econ-omy, the total supply of investment funds can be thought of as the sum of the amounts the individuals in the economy are willing to supply. In general, this will be a function of an individual's wealth, his time preference, and the pure rate of interest. For purposes of understanding the determination of the last factor, we usually concentrate on the relationship between the pure rate of interest and the amount of funds which individuals are willing to supply. A curve which indicates this relationship will generally slope upward, indicating that people are willing to invest more at higher rates of interest.

The demand for funds is best viewed as a schedule indicating the highest rate of return which can be earned on the projects that would be undertaken at various levels of total investment. A curve indicating this is called the Marginal Efficiency of Capital (*MEC*) curve. It is constructed on the premise that in a free-enterprise economy there are strong forces which will cause better investment projects to be preferred to poorer ones.

The pure rate of interest in a free-enterprise economy is determined by the forces of demand and supply. The only rate consistent both with people's preferences and with the opportunities available is that rate at which the amount of funds supplied equals the amount demanded. Graphically this is simply the intersection of the Suppy of Investment Funds curve and the *MEC* curve. If one of these curves shifts, the pure rate of interest will shift. The magnitudes of the two effects will depend on the underlying nature of the curves.

SUGGESTED READINGS

DUE, JOHN F., and ROBERT W. CLOWER. *Intermediate Economic Analysis.* 4th ed. Homewood, Ill.: Richard D. Irwin, Inc., 1961. Chaps. 13, 16, and 17.

EARLY, JAMES S. "Capital and Interest: Discussion," *American Economic Review, 41* (May 1951), 177–80.

HAMMER, FREDERICK S. *The Demand for Physical Capital: Application of a Wealth Model.* Englewood Cliffs, N. J.: Prentice-Hall, Inc., 1964.

KEYNES, JOHN MAYNARD. *The General Theory of Employment, Interest and Money.* New York: Harcourt, Brace & World, Inc., 1936. Chaps. 11–13.

LEIGH, ARTHUR H. "An Equilibrium Rate of Interest," *American Economic Review, 41* (May 1951), 166–74.

WESTON, J. FRED. "Some Perspectives on Capital Theory," *American Economic Review, 41* (May 1951), 129–44.

QUESTIONS

4.1 What is the rate of return if $50 invested now returns (a) $60 two years from now, (b) $57 six months from now, and (c) $49 one month from now? Convert these to approximate annual rates.

4.2 In Y Land the total capital at the beginning of the year 1916 was $500,000. The economy's total gross production for that year was $325,000 and $25,000 of capital was used during the year to produce the income. (a) What percentage of gross production must be reinvested to maintain the capital stock? (b) If the same ratio of income (gross production less capital consumption) to capital stock were expected to continue, how much capital would be required to produce an income of $450,000? (c) If 10 per cent of gross production was invested during 1916, what would the net addition to capital be in 1916?

4.3 How is your time allocated between consumption and investment? What factors determine this rate?

4.4 Why should individuals be willing to save more at higher interest rates?

4.5 Explain the meaning of the words "marginal efficiency" as they apply to the *MEC* curve.

4.6 Would the closure of the Panama Canal have any tendencies to affect the demand for capital? The supply of capital? Explain.

4.7 How does a desire on the part of individuals to invest more at the prevailing interest rate affect the prevailing rate itself?

4.8 Would the knowledge of the pure rate of interest determinants be of any value to a large cattle rancher who sells steers to a packer each year?

4.9 A new and cheaper technique for producing a good is developed. What would be the impact on the *MEC* curve? The pure rate of interest?

4.10 Analyze the effect of the following on the rate of interest: (a) an increase of $300 in the federal personal income tax; (b) a nuclear war scare; (c) an increase in demand for solar batteries; and (d) a decline in national and therefore personal income.

4.11 Why should the pure interest rate tend to move toward the intersection of the *MEC* curve and the Supply of Investment Funds curve?

4.12 What characteristics would you expect a riskless investment to have?

RISK AND THE CAPITAL MARKET

THE PROBLEM OF RISK

In Chapter 3 we made an extremely limiting assumption: namely, that every investment was made under conditions of certainty. There are no investments which have this characteristic and any realistic appraisal of the world in which financial decisions are made would have to conclude that the usual case is far different. The investor does not know before he makes the investment just what he will obtain in return; he is not certain about the outcome; there is *risk* attached to the investment. Any analysis of the workings of our financial system which hopes to provide insights into the essential operation of the system must acknowledge this fact explicitly. Inclusion of risk in the analysis is the task of this chapter.

The nature of risk can be indicated by the simplest of examples. Assume your firm is considering the following "investment." You give $1.00 to someone who promises to flip a coin at the end of one year. If the coin comes up heads he will pay you back your original dollar; if it comes up tails, he will give you $1.20. What is the rate of return on such an investment? *After* it is over, you will be able to determine readily what the rate of return *was;* it was either 0 per cent ($1.00 - 1.00/1.00$) or 20 per cent ($1.20 - 1.00/1.00$). But you must decide whether or not to invest before the outcome is known. What rate of return do you assume in making your decision—20 per cent, 0 per cent, or something else? We will see that investment decisions most commonly encountered can be approached in a manner similar to that which is appropriate for this extremely uncommon investment and, thus, that the answer to this question is of considerable practical importance. Before attempting to answer it, however, let us examine the relationship between such a relatively clear-cut case and the typical business investment.

The coin-flipping investment has one very satisfying property. Assuming that the coin to be used is fair (perhaps it has been subjected to laboratory tests), you can be certain about the *chances* of each possible outcome (in this case they are fifty-fifty); it is possible to assign numbers indicating such chances with precision for there is a considerable body of evidence concerning the manner in which coins behave, and there is a procedure by which one can determine whether the coin in question is similar to all those on which evidence is available. A careful examination of the circumstances determining the two events in this case provides the basis for concluding precisely what the chances are in this and similar cases.[1] Unfortunately, such a situation is rarely found in the usual investment situation.

One rarely even finds an investment whose outcome is determined by known factors that are readily measurable and subject to known patterns of behavior and on which a large body of past experience has been collected and evaluated. In cases in which these conditions are met—the obvious example exists in most (but not all) types of insurance—actuarial calculations can be used to predict the chances of various outcomes with a very satisfactory degree of accuracy. In the more usual case, a basis for such objective calculations is either nonexistent or insufficient, and the manager must resort to some alternative method of predicting the chances of various outcomes. Scientific sampling procedures may be applied in some situations. However, even statistical estimating devices may not be suitably used in a large number of situations. This is true for most investment situations where prediction of outcomes depends upon a large number of interrelated and sometimes unknown variables. Where predictions must be based partly or wholly on judgment rather than on results from some manipulation of data from the past, they are called *subjective predictions* or *subjective probability estimates*. When predictions take the form of a set of numbers indicating the chance or probability of each possible outcome, the total set is referred to as a *subjective probability distribution*, a concept fundamental to the investment process.

CERTAINTY, RISK, AND UNCERTAINTY

Before proceeding with the discussion, however, it might be well to devote some attention to three commonly used terms which, like many words, often mean quite different things to different people. This examination will also indicate the nature of the use of the terms in business investments to be used in this book.

If a manager feels he knows exactly what the outcome of an investment will be and is willing to act as if no alternative were possible, we say that

---

[1] The chances in this example are known and referred to as the probabilities of the outcomes or events. A probability can be defined as the *relative frequency* of the outcome over an *infinite* number of *repeated trials* of the same experiment. Needless to say, almost all probabilities must be estimated from a quantity of evidence varying from case to case in the quantity of observations and in the quality (in the scientific sense) of observations. The use of the term *probability*, however, in this text shall mean implicitly estimated probability.

he is acting under conditions of *certainty;* there is no risk (in his mind, at least) attached to such an investment. If, however, he is not willing to act in this manner and if he is to use any consistent set of decision rules, he must adopt some method that will enable him to recognize and measure risk. Risk would involve assigning the true theoretical probabilities to various outcomes as in the coin-flipping example. For business situations, however, these probabilities can only be estimated. If the manager feels that they are correct, such conditions are formally defined as conditions of risk. On the other hand, usually he is unsure about the probabilities themselves. These cases are normally defined as conditions of uncertainty. Practically, however, the distinction between risk and uncertainty becomes academic because there exists no generally accepted technique for dealing explicitly with uncertainty. For better or worse, the manager estimates the possibilities of various outcomes using either objective or subjective techniques (remember that the latter can include some objective calculations), and *acts as if they were correct*. For this reason we will generally use the terms *risk* and *uncertainty* interchangeably, maintaining only the distinction between certainty and the lack thereof.

MEASURES OF ESTIMATED FUTURE PERFORMANCE

Having defined our terms fairly carefully, we are now ready to indicate a manner in which risk can be quantified for our purposes. It will be useful to do this with the aid of an example which is more like the standard business investment than was the coin-flipping case. Assume a construction company is considering investing $25,000 in a restaurant that is to be sold shortly after construction is completed. Upon completion, the restaurant will have some unique decorations on the front, a strange overall shape, unusual interiors, and be located in a part of the city largely used for warehouses. Extensive analysis by the firm has indicated that there is considerable uncertainty concerning the public's reception of such a restaurant. The analysis can best be summarized as follows:

(1) There is one chance in ten that the restaurant as built will be a tremendous success. If so, it can be sold for $50,000.
(2) There are two chances in ten that it will be well received and require only minor alterations by the purchaser, who will pay $40,000.
(3) There are four chances in ten that the restaurant will not be very well received. But with some remodeling by the purchaser of some of the more unusual features it can still be operated as a restaurant. If this turns out to be the case, the sale price will be about $30,000.
(4) There are two chances in ten that the situation will be a little worse

than that described above, requiring even more extensive remodeling by the purchaser. If so, the sale price would be about $20,000.

(5) There is one chance in ten that the whole idea of a restaurant in the location chosen will prove in error. If this happens, the building will have value only as a (unique) warehouse. Total sales price would be about $10,000.

The Expected Value

In order to translate these estimates into subjective probabilities we need only state them in terms of "so many chances in 100," or, better yet, as a relative frequency of occurrences. To do this, we merely add the possible outcomes to find the total, then divide each one by that total, as shown in Table 5-1.

Table 5-1
Subjective Probability Distribution of
Outcomes for a Restaurant Investment

Sales Price	Chance(s)	Probability
$50,000	1	1/10 = .10
40,000	2	2/10 = .20
30,000	4	4/10 = .40
20,000	2	2/10 = .20
10,000	1	1/10 = .10
	10	1.00

Figure 5-1 displays the situation graphically. The possible outcomes from the investment are shown along the horizontal axis while the height of each bar indicates the likelihood of each outcome. Such a *subjective probability distribution* is now a formal and complete description of the manager's feelings about the results from the investment. We will not concern ourselves here with the manner in which the manager attempts to fill in such a graph (we will see that he need not be this complete in most cases); for the present we will concentrate on the question of what he would do once he had filled in the graph.

In the analysis of the last chapter, we talked about "*the* rate of return" for investment. In other words, we related some outcome to the initial cost in order to determine a single performance figure. Now we have a case in which there are several possible outcomes. If we wished to represent this situation by one single rate of return, we would need to use a single possible outcome. What procedure might we follow?

Probability

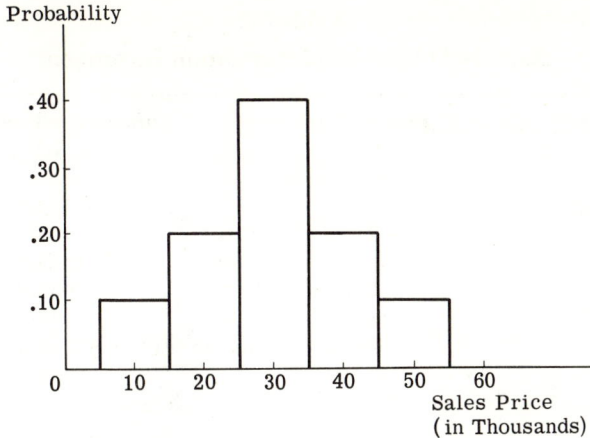

Figure 5-1   Subjective Probability Distribution of Outcomes for a Restaurant Investment

Statisticians face similar problems in describing data in a summary fashion concerning past performance (e.g., life expectancy among a particular class of people). Most of the measures which they use for this purpose have the convenient mnemonic device of beginning with *M:*

(1) The maximum.
(2) The minimum.
(3) The mode.
(4) The median.
(5) The mean.

For our example, the magnitude of each of these measures is as follows. The Maximum is the highest possible outcome; in our example it is $50,000. The Minimum is the lowest possible; here it is $10,000. The Mode is the outcome most likely to occur; in our case it is $30,000. The Median is the "middle" outcome; it is $30,000. The Mean is the familiar *average*. In this context it is better named the *expected outcome* (*EO*) or *expected value* of the outcome instead of mean or average. It is found, like a weighted average, by multiplying each possible outcome, X_i, by its likelihood, P_i, and adding, as shown in Table 5-2.

Which of these five values is the most useful for a rate of return calculation? An extremely pessimistic manager might use the Minimum on the grounds that it would indicate the worst possible outcome. But this completely ignores other possible outcomes and hence would scarcely be the sort of measure used in normal business practice. Because there is

Table 5-2
Expected Outcome of Restaurant Investment

Outcome (X_i)		Probability (P_i)		Outcome × Probability (X_iP_i)
$10,000	×	.1	=	1,000
20,000	×	.2	=	4,000
30,000	×	.4	=	12,000
40,000	×	.2	=	8,000
50,000	×	.1	=	5,000
			Expected outcome (EO) =	$30,000

or

$$EO = \sum_{i=1}^{n} X_iP_i$$

typically a relatively small chance that most investments will result in financial disaster, the manager who looked only at the worst possible outcome fails to consider the possible gains.

The Maximum is an equally unattractive measure, but for opposite reasons. The financial officer who uses it is oblivious to all but the rosiest prospect. Because there is usually only a slight chance of an unusually large gain from an investment, this criterion would lead one to an extremely high rate of return, for it fails to take into consideration the smaller or less satisfactory outcomes. Obviously, this is not a very satisfactory measure.

The Mode suffers from the same criticism directed at the Maximum and Minimum; it takes into account too little of the information available concerning the situation described. In our example, the most likely single outcome hapens to be the Mode—$30,000. Frequently, however, the Mode may be one of the extreme outcomes; this is true in skewed distributions. If one were to use the Mode, our measure of return would fail to account for the magnitude of the other possibilities. It depends entirely on the most likely value and takes no consideration of other outcomes, either their position or likelihood of occurrence.

The Median is the middle-position outcome. It ignores the relative likelihoods of the various outcomes and ignores the differences in value. It is concerned only with being central in a rank order by value of the outcomes. Obviously, like the Mode, the Median is an unacceptable measure.

By process of elimination, we are left with the Mean, or expected outcome, as the best of the five discussed. Unlike the others, it takes into account both the magnitudes (in this case, sale value) of the possible outcomes and their likelihood (probability) of occurrence. Any change in the manager's outlook will affect the value of this measure. If a given prospect looks rosier (its payoff is better), the expected outcome will increase; if it looks bleaker, it will decrease. If the financial manager decides that the more attractive outcomes are relatively more likely than he had previously thought, the expected outcome will rise. Hence, of these measures, which can be calculated by simple mathematical techniques, the expected outcome is the best.

It is important that the true meaning of the expected outcome be felt intuitively, rather than merely being able to define it formally. In almost no actual business situation does a manager draw up a subjective probability distribution and then calculate its expected outcome. Instead, he thinks about the possibilities for a while and then writes down some number. The number corresponds to an expected outcome and he does the calculation in an extremely rough and generally implicit manner. To put it simply, he writes down a number which reflects the various outcomes he considers possible, according each an importance relative to its likelihood.

From our example in Table 5-2 we can derive an expected rate of return (*ER*). With an expected outcome of $30,000 and an initial cost of $25,000, the *expected rate of return (ER)* is 20 per cent—(30,000 − 25,000/ 25,000).

Let us summarize the expected-rate-of-return approach. If there is uncertainty about the outcome of an investment, the manager can write down the expected outcome of all possible outcomes and calculate the rate of return of the investment using that amount. If he does this, he has found what we will call the expected rate of return. Note that *ex post*, the firm will undoubtedly have earned a rate of return other than the expected. There is .6 probability that the return will not be $30,000 (the expected outcome) or 20 per cent (the expected rate of return) and only .4 probability that it will be 20 per cent.

The expected rate of return (*ER*) could also be computed by figuring the rate of return for each outcome and then finding the weighted average (the mean) of these as we did with the outcome. Table 5-3 computes it in this fashion. What both the expected outcome and expected rate of return suggest is that an average outcome of $30,000 and an average rate of return of 20 per cent could be secured from an investment of $25,000 were we able to *repeat* this identical investment situation for an infinite number of times, assuming our estimates of outcomes and probabilities were correct.

Table 5-3

Expected Rate of Return on Restaurant Investment

Outcome	Rate of Return	Probability	Probability Rate
$10,000	− .60	.1	− .06
20,000	− .20	.2	− .04
30,000	+ .20	.4	.08
40,000	+ .60	.2	.12
50,000	+ 1.00	.1	.10

Expected rate of return (ER) = $\overline{.20}$ or 20%

Unfortunately, the investor cannot secure the same identical investment for a large number of successive investments. It is likely that there is only one chance to play the game. He may get $10,000, $50,000, $20,000, $30,000, or $40,000, but his best estimate of the value of the investment is 20 per cent. Obviously, the expected rate of return needs some additional measure that accounts for risk. The need for such an additional measure can be readily seen by returning to our first "investment" in which the manager was to pay $1.00 one year hence if a coin came up heads and $1.20 if it came up tails. The expected outcome from this investment is obviously $1.10 (.50 × $1.00 + .50 × $1.20), giving an expected rate of return of 10 per cent. A manager using only the expected rate of return would be led to the conclusion that such an investment is as desirable as any other with the same expected return. Assume that he had an alternative investment available with a second individual who would use the coin but with the following payoffs: heads, $1.05; tails, $1.15. This other investment also has an expected return of 10 per cent (.5 × $1.05 + .5 × $1.15 = $1.10). Are the two investments equally desirable to the manager? They are not equally desirable, and to understand decision-making we must include some measure of risk in our analysis.

Measuring Risk

The expected outcome of an investment's performance is a measure which, in general terms, indicates the center (or central tendency) of the range of possibilities (taking into account, of course, their likelihood). It does not, however, tell us anything about the range of the outcomes or, to put it another way, about the dispersion of the outcomes from that which can be expected on the average. The coin example illustrates this point well. The graphs of the outcomes of the two investments are shown in Figure 5-2. They have the same expected outcome, $1.10, but Case A is more "spread out" than Case B. The actual outcome will diverge further

Case A

Probability

Case B

Probability

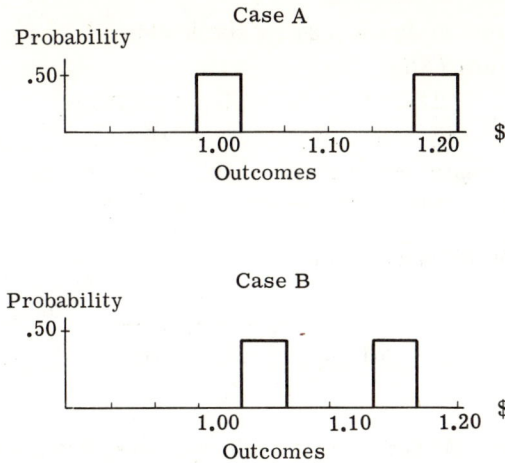

Figure 5-2   Range of Expected Outcome as a Measure of Risk

from the expected outcome (either above or below it) than Case B. In common parlance, we would typically say that the first investment involved more *risk* than the second. This is what we wish to measure as risk: the *extent* to which an investment may turn out *better or worse* than expected. We measured the expected outcome by using a weighted average, although in actual practice it is frequently determined in a rather crude and implicit fashion. In order to provide an appropriate measure of risk, we can again turn to the statisticians, who have been facing the problem of measuring the *dispersion* of distributions for some time.

As one might imagine, there are many measures of dispersion just as there are many measures of central tendency. The *range* of outcomes is one such measure of dispersion. Fortunately, we need not repeat the kind of discussion which we gave the measures of central tendency for the principles we used in that selection apply here equally well. The range uses only two outcomes and we wish to use a measure which will take into account both the magnitude of each possibility and its likelihood. For a number of reasons, which are complex and need not be treated here, the most generally accepted measure is the standard deviation,[2] which, as you may recall, can be calculated as follows.

(1) Measure the extent to which a possible rate of return (R_i) diverges from the expected rate of return (ER).

(2) Multiply the amount in (1) by itself (i.e., square it).

[2] Harry M. Markowitz, *Portfolio Selection* (New York: John Wiley & Sons, Inc., 1959), pp. 294–97.

(3) Multiply the answer in (2) by the likelihood (P_i) of the particular rate of return (SR).

(4) Perform (1), (2), and (3) for each possible rate.

(5) Add all these figures in (4).

(6) Take the square root of the sum; this is the *standard deviation* of the rate of return (SR).

The formula for this calculation is

$$SR = \sqrt{\sum_{i=1}^{n} (R_i - ER)^2 P_i}$$

The *standard deviation of the rate of return* is a measure of risk. It does not measure the prospects that expected returns will not be realized, nor does it reflect only chances of loss. It *is* a measure of the dispersion of possible outcomes. The *standard deviation of the rate of return* conforms to the usual notion of risk.

Calculation of the standard deviation of return for the restaurant example is shown in Table 5-4.

Table 5-4

Measurement of Risk for Restaurant Investment

Outcome (Rate of Return)	Deviation from *ER* of 20%	(Deviation)²	Proba- bility	Probability × (Deviation)²
− .60	.80	.64	.1	.064
− .20	.40	.16	.2	.032
.20	.0	.0	.4	.0
.60	.40	.16	.2	.032
1.00	.80	.64	.1	.064
				.192

Standard deviation of the rate of return = $\sqrt{.192}$

SR = .438

= 43.8%

Thus far we have presented our measure of risk as the standard deviation of the rate of return. Let us consider two investment alternatives with the same standard deviation. Investment A has an expected rate of return of 10 per cent and a standard deviation of the rate of return of 5 per cent; Investment B has an expected rate of return of 100 per cent and a standard deviation of 5 per cent. Is the risk the same in both cases? If they were, one would also have to agree that an investment of one cent with a return of one cent and a standard deviation of one cent reflects no greater risk than an investment of one cent with a return of a million dollars and a standard deviation of one cent. As can be seen, the problem with the standard deviation of the rate of return as a measure of risk is that it does not reflect the magnitude of the expected outcome. To allow for this, we should be more properly concerned with relative dispersion. Only by such a relative measure are we able to make meaningful comparisons of risks existent in differing investments. To make the standard deviations comparable, we may express them in relation to the respective means. The ratio of SR/ER is referred to as the *coefficient of variation*. This ratio of the standard deviation of the rate of return to expected rate of return will hereafter be our measure of risk.[3] Investment A has a coefficient of variation of .05/.10, or .5; Investment B has a risk of .05/1.00, or .05. According to this measure, the risk in B is definitely less than that of A.[4]

As we shall develop more fully later, for a given wealth level of an individual or firm, the desirability of an investment may be affected not only by ER and SR/ER, but also by the size of the investment relative to the wealth position. For the general market case, however, large numbers of investors of differing wealth will be entering the market and the individual circumstances of each may be bypassed for the present.

In order to understand more fully our measure of risk, we should examine its behavior while altering some of the values in its computation. Taking our restaurant example, let's change one outcome. Assume, for example, that the most favorable outcome was $100,000, not $50,000. The reader may verify the computations on his own, but the expected return would now be 40 per cent, and the standard deviation of the rate of return would be 95.4 per cent. As a result of making just one outcome more

---

[3] Alexander Barges, *The Effect of Capital Structure on the Cost of Capital* (Englewood Cliffs, N.J.: Prentice-Hall, 1963), Chap. 2. See also: L. Fisher, "Determinants of Risk Premiums on Corporate Bonds," *Journal of Political Economy*, 67 (June 1959) pp. 217–37; Stephen H. Archer, "Diversification and Risk Reduction," *University of Washington Business Review*, 23 (April-June 1964) pp. 19–25; and Neil R. Paine, "Uncertainty and Capital Budgeting," *The Accounting Review*, 39 (April 1964) pp. 330–32.

[4] It should be noted that in relying on this measure of risk, we are ignoring any differences that might exist in the confidence placed in the estimates of possible outcomes and their expected relative frequency of occurrence. We have no satisfactory method for dealing with such differences in uncertainty. Consequently, these differences are ignored in this treatment of decision problems.

Perhaps the chief difficulty encountered in using the coefficient of variation lies in the fact that it is a relative measure, a ratio. As such, if the denominator should be near 0, the value of the coefficient becomes very large. Realistically, however, *ex ante* investments with expected returns near 0 would be discarded so that the qualification here is not great.

favorable, the *SR* has increased considerably over the 43.8 per cent in the original example. The coefficient of variation in the rate of return, however, has remained approximately unchanged at 2.2. One might be inclined to suggest that the alteration of the example to make one outcome more favorable ought to produce lower risk. This would be an error in reasoning, for although the expected return is further removed from a negative return, the risk is in a sense a measure of confidence in the mean and not a measure of risk of loss. If we are willing to accept the larger value as a measure of return, we must also accept the increased absolute dispersion about this estimate. It happens in this case that we have caused an increase in expected return without a significant alteration in risk. Other changes in the original restaurant problem, such as a change in the probabilities, will also cause changes in the risk and expected return values. In practice, managers do not normally form specific ideas about the future in probabilistic terms and then perform mathematical manipulations of them to determine the expected rate of return; this is undoubtedly also the case with the coefficient of variation of the rate of return. Nevertheless, managers do make investment decisions. Typically they do this by writing down an estimate of future performance and then deciding whether this estimate promises a rate of return sufficient to compensate them for the risk involved.

CHOOSING AN INVESTMENT

The previous section developed two important concepts for understanding the process by which firms choose investments. The first was a measure of expected rate of return; the second, a measure of risk. How can these measures be used by firms to choose among the hundreds of thousands of investment opportunities available to them? We shall approach the answer to this question in two stages. At first we will assume that the firm has no alternative financing schemes available to it other than the one postulated and that it must choose *one, and only one,* investment from the given array of opportunities. Then we will introduce situations in which there are alternative investment combinations.

Investment Preference (No Alternatives)

Assume that a firm's total capital is $1,000, (contributed entirely by owners) and that the firm's manager is attempting to choose one of five investment opportunities, each of which requires the full $1,000. They are as follows:

Investment	Expected Rate of Return	Risk
A	6%	1/2
B	10	.1
C	6	6/5
D	10	2
E	13	2

The possibilities are plotted in Figure 5-3.

A careful inspection of the opportunities will reveal certain investments which the firm would not make, as long as its owners had the usual preferences and acted according to the *dominance principle* which states that

(1) Among investments with the same risk (SR/ER), they prefer the one offering the greatest expected return (ER), and
(2) Among investments with the same expected return (ER), they prefer the one with the smallest risk (SR/ER).

Examining the investments in the light of these virtually universal characteristics, we can conclude that Investments C and D should not be chosen. These investments are dominated by at least one alternative; that is, there is at least one investment which is better in at least one respect and no worse in any respect. Investment C is dominated by Investment A, which offers the same expected rate of return (6 per cent) with much less risk (1/2 instead of 6/5). Investment D is dominated by two investments. E offers the same risk (2) but a higher expected return (13 per cent instead of 10 per cent), while B offers the same expected return (10 per cent) but less risk (1 instead of 2). Obviously, the firm need concentrate

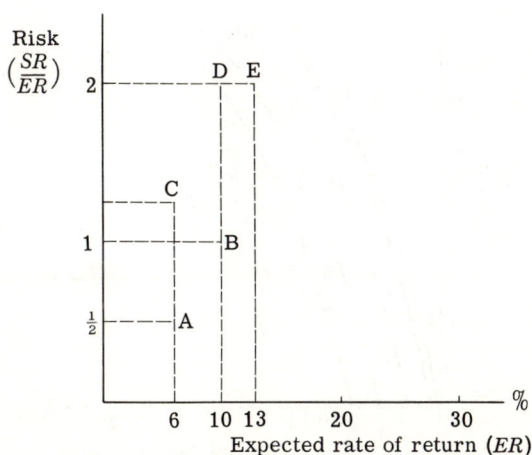

Figure 5-3   Investment Opportunities and the Dominance Principle

only on the choice among Investments A, B, and E. Investments C and D are relatively inferior investments when compared (according to their respective risks and expected rates of return) to the other investment opportunities (A, B, and E).

But which of these remaining investments should be selected? The answer is not at all obvious. Investment B offers a higher expected return than does A, but at the cost of a higher risk. Similarly, E is better than either A or B with regard to expected return but worse with regard to risk. The proper choice for an individual or firm must depend on the owner's attitudes toward risk relative to expected return: How much of the former are they willing to bear in order to get more of the latter? A convenient device for summarizing any single individual's attitude on this point is a graph which uses a family of indifference curves such as that shown in Figure 5-4.

These curves are constructed in the following manner. Starting with some possible investment, say, D (which has an expected return of 10 per cent and a risk of 2), we ask the investor to tell us about all possible invest-ments which he considers equally as attractive as D. Obviously, such in-vestments will have either a higher expected return (which makes them better) and a higher risk (which makes them worse) or a lower expected return (which makes them worse) and a lower risk (which makes them better). By combining all the points representing such investments, to form one indifference curve (II), the individual indicates alternatives along which he is indifferent. If we had begun our questioning of this individual by selecting a different investment, say, E, we would have

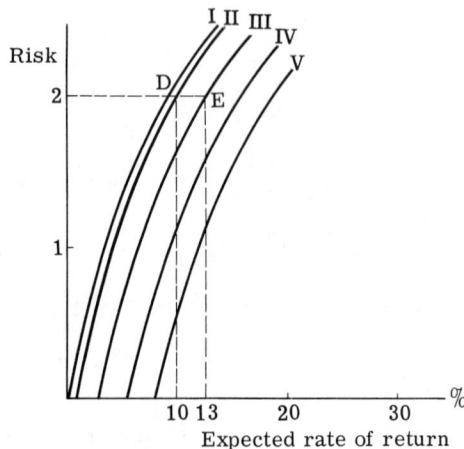

Figure 5-4   Selection of Investments D and E by use of Indifference Curves

elicited a different curve. In this case, it would have been III. That is, he considers as equal any two investments represented by two points on the same curve. Curves I, II, III, IV, and V are such curves, each one representing a combination of points to which the investor is indifferent. He does have preferences as to curves, however; he prefers II to I, III to II, IV to III, and so on. Actually he would prefer that curve that lies as far right as possible (however, investments may not be available on such curves). There are virtually an infinite number of such curves which could be drawn for any given individual. They usually appear similar to those indicated in the figure and have the following characteristics.

(1) They slope upward.[5] That is, to make the individual equally happy, he must be given a greater expected return to compensate for increased risk. This reflects the fact that *people like expected return and dislike risk.*

(2) The curves become more horizontal as they go up. That is, to induce someone to take on more and more risk, he must be compensated with an increasing amount of expected return.

(3) Moving to the right along any horizontal line, one reaches curves which represent higher over-all levels of satisfaction (the same degree of risk prevails but the expected return increases). This is a reflection of the individual's desire for greater expected return.

(4) Moving downward along any vertical line, one reaches curves which represent greater over-all levels of satisfaction; the same expected return is achieved but there is less risk. This is a reflection of the individual's dislike for risk.

Figures 5-5(a) and 5-5 (b) repeat the information about the three investments under consideration in addition to the indifference curves of two different individuals. Individual 1 is represented in 5-5 (a) and Individual 2 is represented in 5-5 (b). If the firm in question were owned by Individual 1, the best investment would be E, for it falls on a higher indifference curve than either A or B. The reason this individual prefers E is clear. His indifference curves are quite steep, indicating that his degree of risk aversion is relatively low; he is willing to accept large amounts of additional risk with relatively little increase in expected return. It is not surprising that such an individual would prefer the riskiest investment.

[5] The slope is, of course, changing as one moves along the curve, but in a rather intuitive sense we say that the curve in general is steep, meaning the slope at most points is fairly large or the first derivative of the function at various points takes on values greater than 1. Values less than 1 would suggest a more horizontal curve.

It should be recalled that the slope gives the ratio of the rate of change in SR/ER to the rate of change in ER. A perfectly horizontal line has a zero slope and a vertical line a slope of infinity.

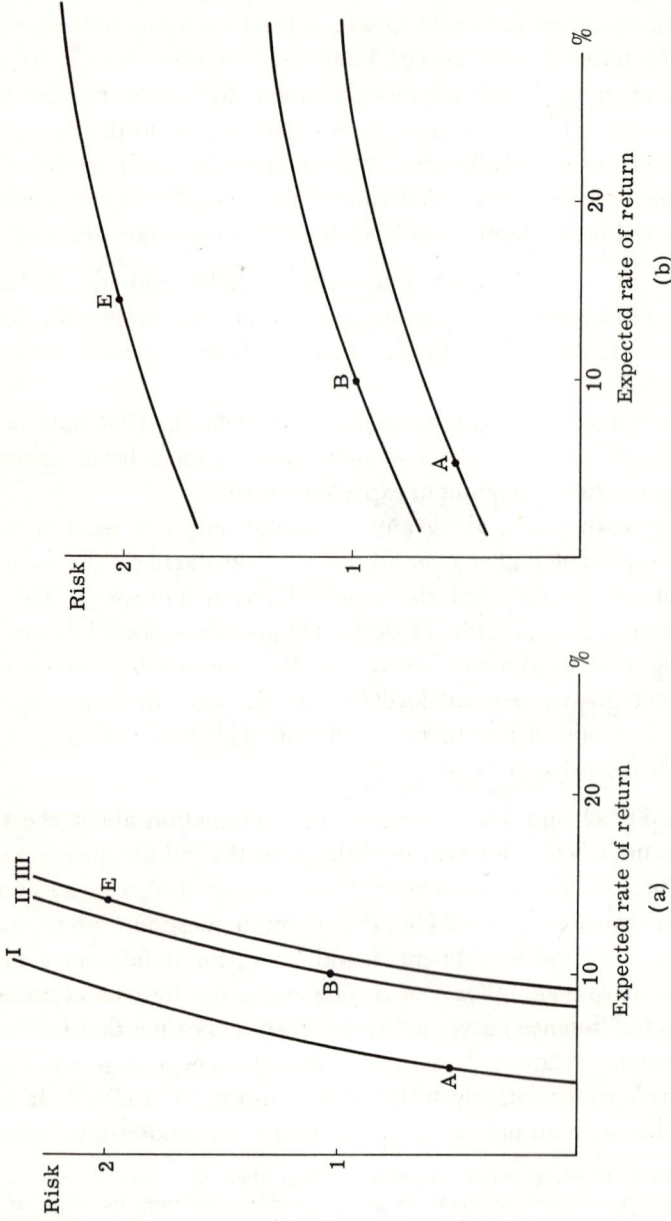

Figure 5-5   Indifference Curves of Two Individuals

The situation would be completely different, however, if the firm were owned by Individual 2, whose indifference curves are quite horizontal indicating a high degree of risk aversion (he requires large increases in expected return to compensate him for additional risk). In this case the best investment is A, the most conservative of the three.

If a firm were in a position similar to that presented in either one of these two cases, the only answer to the question of choice among alternative investment opportunities would be to choose the one that was best in the light of the preferences of the owners (having first removed from consideration those which are dominated by other investments). Needless to say, such an answer leaves something to be desired, especially when there are many owners (imagine the dilemma of the manager if *both* Individuals 1 and 2 owned the firm!). Fortunately, we will see that when a more realistic case is considered, the answer becomes more straightforward.

The nature of the indifference curves can be expected to change if the amount of the investment being made on this "play" were altered. If the investment were one dollar instead of one thousand (the total capital of the firm), the firm's indifference curve would be expected to reflect less aversion to risk such as depicted by the curves of Individual 1. Later we shall discuss further this sort of impact upon investment decisions of the firm.

Investment Preferences (With Alternatives)

We are now in a position to add some realism to our example and, in so doing, to solve some (but not all) of the problems encountered thus far. We wish now to add two alternative actions to those allowed our mythical firm. First, there is the possibility of additional financing through borrowing. Second, there is the opposite possibility of placing some of the owner's funds in risk-free assets (negative borrowing or lending).

To keep the discussion simple, we will assume that firms can in both cases make contracts at the pure rate of interest; obviously this is less likely when a firm seeks to borrow money than when it wishes to invest it. Nevertheless, the principles derived from this assumption will require only slight modification when the full complexity of the conditions under which a firm can borrow are taken into account. (We will postpone introducing this complexity until Parts II and III.)

Borrowing—The Use of Debt

We have shown Investment B with an expected rate of return of 10 per cent and a risk of 1. Let us assume that this investment is one which costs $1,000 and has a fifty-fifty chance of an outcome of either $1,000 or $1,200. The calculations below show that such a prospect does in fact have an expected rate of return of 10 per cent and a risk of 1.

Outcome (%)	Probability	Outcome × Probability
.00	.5	.0
.20	.5	.10

Expected outcome = $\overline{10\%}$

Outcome (%)	Divergence from Expected Outcome	(Divergence)²	Probability	Probability × (Divergence)²
.00	.10	.01	.5	.005
.20	.10	.01	.5	.005
				$\overline{.01}$

Standard deviation of outcome = $\sqrt{.01} = .10$

Coefficient of variation in rate of return = $\dfrac{.10}{.10} = 1$

Now assume that another project, just like Investment B in all respects, is available to the firm. What would be the owners' position if an additional $1,000 to finance the second project were borrowed at the pure rate of interest (which, in this case, we shall assume to be 5 per cent)? The answer is relatively simple. If the projects turn out badly, each will return $1,000 for a total of $2,000. Of this total, $1,050 (the $1,000 loan plus 5 per cent interest) must be repaid to the firm's creditors, leaving $950 for the owners. On the other hand, if they turn out well, the total amount will be $2,400, leaving $1,350 for the owners.[6] Such an arrangement thus converts the owners' position from one in which they have a fifty-fifty chance of earning $1,000 or $1,200 to one in which they have a fifty-fifty chance of earning $950 or $1,350. As shown below, such a situation gives them an expected return of 15 per cent and a risk of 1.33—both elements being greater than before.

Outcomes	Probability	Outcome × Probability
− .05	.5	− .025
.35	.5	.175

Expected outcome = .15

[6] We assume that the two projects are identical in all respects and therefore if one fails, both fail; if one succeeds, both succeed.

Outcome	Divergence from Expected Outcome	(Divergence)²	Probability	Probability × (Divergence)²
− .05	.20	.04	.5	.02
.35	.20	.04	.5	.02
				.04

$$\text{Standard deviation of outcome} = \sqrt{.04} = .20$$

$$\text{Coefficient of variation in rate of return} = \frac{.20}{.15} = 1.33$$

For present purposes, we shall view the commitment of owners' capital and borrowed capital ($2,000) to two B-type projects as one investment. Designating this investment B′ and plotting it on Figure 5-3, we find that it dominates Investment E. For convenience, Figure 5-3 with Investment B′ is reproduced in Figure 5-6. Remember, Investments C and D were already eliminated from consideration by applying the dominance principle. Now, by the same process, Investment E can be eliminated for B′ has a greater return and less risk than E.

Negative Borrowing—Purchase of Risk-Free Assets

What if the firm wished to offer its owners *less* risk rather than more; what might it do? An answer is to use no debt financing *and* invest in conservative projects. One way of doing this would be to choose an investment of a more conservative nature than B (such as A). An alternative to this choice would be to invest only part of the firm's capital in B, placing the rest in an extremely safe investment. For our illustration we will as-

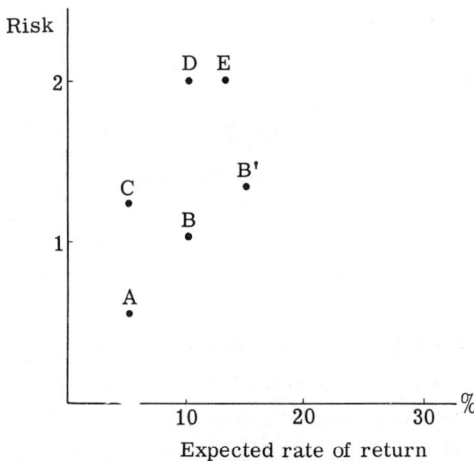

Figure 5-6 Investment Opportunities with the Addition of Investment B′

sume that it is possible for the firm to invest just $500 in the project, taking a proportionate cut in the outcome (assume some other firm will split the cost of $1,000 and the outcome with our firm). We wish to determine the owners' position if their $1,000 is used to finance $500 of Project B and the remaining $500 invested in a risk-free investment at the pure interest rate (5 per cent) with no outside debt financing to be used. This combination of commitments we shall designate as investment B".

Again the answer is relatively straightforward. The possible returns from the $500 invested in Project B are $500 (½ of $1,000) or 0 per cent and $600 (½ of $1,200) or 20 per cent. The return from the other $500 will be $525 (the principal plus 5 per cent interest). Thus the firm has a fifty-fifty chance of a total income of $1,025, the sum of $500 and $525, or $1,125, the sum of $600 and $525. Such a prospect gives the owners an expected rate of return of 7.5 per cent and a risk of 2/3—both lower than before, as shown below.

Outcome	Probability	Outcome × Probability
.025	.5	.0125
.125	.5	.0625
		.0750

Expected outcome = 7.5%

Outcome (%)	Divergence from Expected Outcome	(Divergence)²	Probability	Probability × (Divergence)²
.025	.05	.0025	.5	.00125
.125	.05	.0025	.5	.00125
				.0025

Standard deviation of outcome $= \sqrt{.0025} = .05$

Coefficient of variation in rate of return $= \dfrac{.05}{.075} = 2/3$

Investment B" can be added to the previous plot of Figure 5-6. Other combinations may also be added. For example, Investment B''', a combination investing $300 in B and $700 in the risk-free assets, would produce an expected return of 6.5 per cent and a risk of approximately .46. The reader may wish to verify these computations. By observing the plot with the addition of B" and B'''. Figure 5-7 exhibits the dominance of B''' over A. In fact, as it turns out, Investments A, C, D, and E of our original example

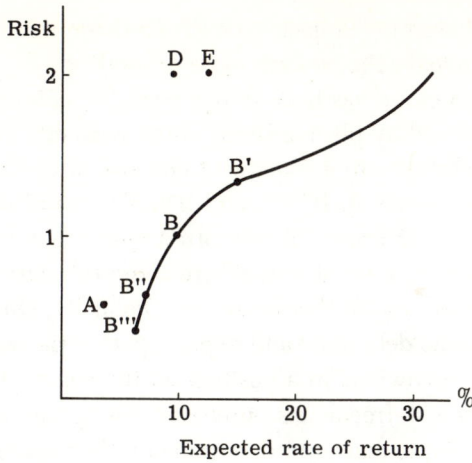

Figure 5-7 Investment Opportunities D and E with a Series of B–Type Investments

are dominated by Investment B in some combination of negative or positive borrowing at the pure interest rate.

Figure 5-8 shows the original Investment B, the new alternatives—B′ (debt financing), B″, and B‴ (purchase of risk-free assets)—and Investments A and E. It should be recalled that we show the prospects for the *owners* of the firm only.

Up to this point, we have shown that neither Investment A nor E *as originally described* or any others are worth considering when the possibilities of alternative schemes based on B are examined. But what about

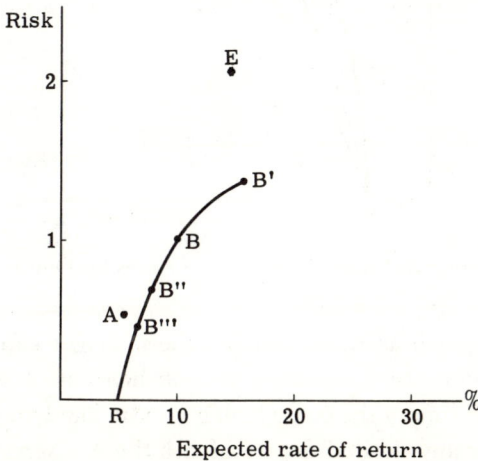

Figure 5-8 Investment Opportunities A and E with a Series of B–Type Investments

similar schemes based on Project A or E? To determine the best over-all policy, we need to make the analysis more general.

In Figure 5-8 a curve has been drawn from the point representing the performance achieved by placing funds at the pure rate of interest (Point R, with an expected return of 5 per cent and risk of 0) through the point representing Investments B, B', B", and B'''. The use of debt financing to increase the amount of Project B supported must place the firm's owners in a position shown by a point somewhere along this curve above Point B (the more debt used, the farther away from Point B). On the other hand, the decision to use no debt at all and to place part of the capital in risk-free assets will place the owners in a position on the curve somewhere below Point B (the more risk-free assets purchased, the farther away from Point B). Thus, it is a simple matter to determine all the possibilities which the firm can provide its owners with financial policy built around Project B; they all lie on such a curve drawn from Point R through B.

Figure 5-9 shows the general method by which a firm can determine which of a group of alternative investment projects is best. By drawing the curves from the point representing the pure interest rate through each

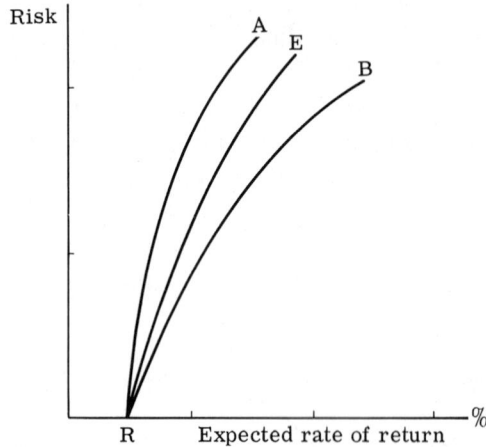

Figure 5-9   Various Investment Opportunity Curves for One Firm

possible project (such as A, E, and B), the manager can determine the alternatives available to the owners if each investment is selected. The best investment is simply the one which gives the line lying farthest to the right, because for any desired degree of risk there is *some* financing plan which in conjunction with this investment will give a higher expected return than any financing plan in conjunction with any other investment.[7] Even at that, however, the manager has not escaped the problem of satisfying his owners' preferences, for he must still choose a financing plan. If only one owner were involved, this would be relatively simple, for no possibility of conflicting attitudes toward risk would arise. The solution is shown in Figure 5-10 at Point B*, where an indifference curve just touches (is tangent to) the curve representing the alternative financing schemes from the best investment (B). This must be the best point, for the curve which cuts the line (I) represents smaller levels of satisfaction and the curves which lie below the line cannot be attained.

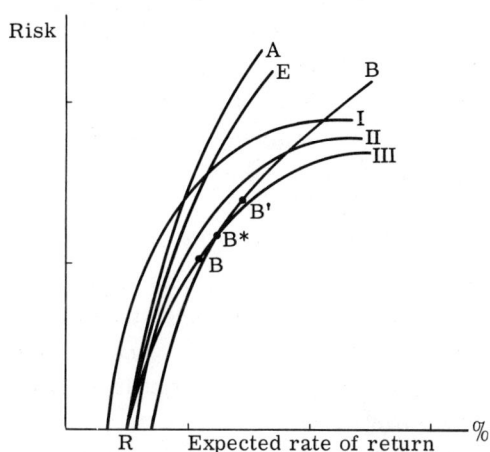

Figure 5-10 Selection of a B–Type Investment by use of Indifference Curves

In the case shown in Figure 5-10, the best financing scheme involves some borrowing, since Point B* lies above Point B. Note, however, that the amount required is less than in our previous example represented by Point B'. On the other hand, if Point B* had fallen below Point B, the best financial plan would, of course, have involved negative borrowing—an investment in risk-free assets.[8]

---

[7] We have intentionally excluded many alternatives open to the firm (primarily the possibility of combining two or more investments) and assumed away one important aspect of most real cases—the fact that projects cannot usually be divided into convenient common sizes nor can they be undertaken at virtually any desired level. We shall suggest methods of handling these aspects in Parts II and III but for the purposes of understanding the general relationships in the capital market the presentation given here will prove satisfactory.

[8] One might conjecture what the situation would be like if the indifference curves were more vertical; that is, the manager were not so averse to risk. In that case, the optimal point would lie farther to the right. We would continue to move to the right

Although the choice of a financial plan is thus relatively straight-forward when only one owner is involved, the more usual case—many owners—continues to present some difficulties; we will see later that an alternative argument suggests that the choice of a financial plan need not be made with reference to the owners' attitudes toward risk at all. In any event, we shall postpone our discussion of this problem until Part II.

THE CAPITAL MARKET

We now have the tools required to explain the over-all operation of the capital market (provisionally defined as the market for investment funds) in a free-enterprise system. To begin with, consider the situation shown in Figure 5-8. As indicated in the previous section, *any* one firm examining the investment projects shown there would be led to choose Investment B, regardless of its owners' attitudes. Obviously, if every firm in the economy agreed on the prospects surrounding each of the investments pictured, they would all be led to the same conclusion. The result would be a strong demand for the resources required by Project B and, conversely, a lack of demand for investment purposes for the resources required by the other projects, Investments A and E. Needless to say, it is unlikely that there will be complete unanimity of opinion concerning the prospects of various investments among *all* firms, nor will all firms be aware of all projects. Nevertheless, agreement among enough firms is likely to obtain and hence yield results similar to those described.

What would be the result of these shifts in demand for resources? The prices of the resources in question would change. Owners of the resources required for Projects A and E would be forced to accept lower prices for their resources. The result would be a change in the relative attractiveness of these projects. In time, Project B would also become less attractive as the increase in demand for resources necessary for Project B caused the resource prices to rise and profits to fall. Adjustments will also take place in the prices commanded by the goods produced by the various invest-ments as their relative quantities are affected. For equilibrium to be at-tained, these various prices and costs must continually adjust until all investment projects whose nature is generally known are equally attrac-tive, for the existence of exceptionally attractive or exceptionally un-

---

on successive indifference curves until we can no longer find one further to the right that has a point in common with an investment curve. In this unusual example, risk does not increase very much as borrowing is increased. It is these exceptional invest-ment situations that allow small increases in risk for large increases in return. In this example there is no loss possible except interest costs; as a result an investor with great wealth relative to this investment (tending in a near vertical indifference curve) should be willing to borrow the maximum available.

attractive alternatives will lead to further adjustments. Under what conditions would all investments be considered equally attractive?

We have shown that one investment is better than another if the curve drawn from the point representing the pure rate of interest through the point representing that investment lies to the right of a similar curve drawn through the other investment. Obviously, if two investments are to be equally attractive, this cannot be the case. The conclusion is simple: two investment projects are equally attractive if, *and only if,* they both lie along the same curve drawn from the point representing the pure interest rate. This is the equilibrium condition for the capital market. The majority of investments will offer combinations of expected return and risk lying along such a curve running through the point representing the pure rate of interest. (If the market were perfect, they would all lie on such a curve.) Some investments, however, will offer combinations lying above (and to the left) of the line, but these will be avoided by knowledgeable firms. Investments placed at a point lying below and to the right of the line would command such attention that their costs would be bid up and they would move up to the line if their qualities were widely known and there were no other effective barriers to attaining them. Because in an equilibrium condition no pressures on prices exist, such a situation would not prevail.

The firm or individual using a reasonable amount of common sense in the selection of investments can generally expect to obtain a combination of expected rate of return and risk lying along a single curve such as RQ in Figure 5-11. Such a curve summarizes the generally prevailing terms in the capital market at any one point of time. We shall call it the Capital Market Curve (CMC).

There are a number of reasons why the relationship between risk and expected return in the capital market is likely to be only approximately a curve such as CMC. Imperfections in the various markets (factor, goods, and capital), lack of information about some investments, and the inability of firms to borrow at the pure rate of interest or very extensively at some bank prime rate are among the more important reasons. These problems will lead us to suggest that in some cases a firm may need to ascertain more precisely the exact conditions it faces in the capital market. This approach belongs, however, to the topics of Parts II and III of this text. For a description of the general conditions prevailing in the economy, the CMC provides a thoroughly adequate analytical tool.

What will determine the position of the CMC? In a sense, everything. It is influenced on the supply side by all the factors that determine people's willingness to supply capital, such as their time preference and their risk

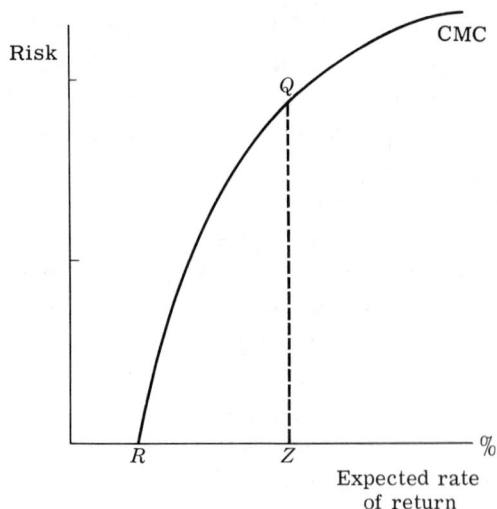

Figure 5-11   The Capital Market Curve as a Summary of Risks and Expected Rates of Return

aversion. On the demand side, it is influenced by all the elements which determine the probable outcome of capital investments, such as the physical relationships between resources and the products which they can produce, the risk of future price changes, and changes in demand and policy. All these many factors converge in the capital market and react on one another. The result is a set of combinations of risk and expected return best described by the *CMC*. Naturally, as the underlying factors change, so will the market conditions.

For some purposes it is easiest to think of the *CMC* simply as a line. We have already said that the pure rate of interest is one of the results of the forces at work in the capital market. It is, of course, the point at which a line approximating the curve touches the horizontal axis. Because the pure rate locates one point of the line, we need only indicate its steepness to describe it entirely. Fortunately, the steepness of the line has an extremely simple meaning. In Figure 5-11, for example, it could be measured by the ratio of the distance *RZ* to the distance *QZ*. Just what would this ratio mean? Simply that the market rewards the investor with *RZ* additional expected return if he is willing to accept *QZ* additional risk. In other words, this indicates the additional expected return received per unit of additional risk; it is the slope of the function.[9] We can thus think of the

---

[9] Since the approximation of the *CMC* is a straight line, the ratio or slope will be the same for any part of the line; that is, the slope is constant. In the curve, however, the slope is constantly changing from point to point and therefore the "trade-off" be-

Capital Market as determining two elements of the reward to capital: the pure rate of interest, and the premium per unit of risk. The expected return from any given investment will thus be made up of the pure rate of interest plus an additional amount, the *risk premium,* equal to its risk times the generally prevailing premium per unit of risk.

Before summarizing the chapter, we need to emphasize exactly what the *CMC* does represent and what it does not represent. It is intended to show the opportunities available in the general market from investments whose qualities are generally agreed upon. Because these opportunities are widely known, it is unlikely that people will provide a firm with funds on any poorer terms. Thus the *CMC* also indicates the combinations of terms on which money is generally available. But note, and this is of crucial importance, that we have not said that *all* investment projects will lead the firm to combinations lying on this curve, nor have we said that *all* sources of funds will be offered on terms lying on this curve. Quite the contrary, the entire *raison d'être* of the firm in a free-enterprise economy is to marshal special knowledge and talent to find the investment project which is better than generally available projects and/or to find sources of funds which are better than those generally available. This task is so crucial that we will define the term *profit* to measure the firm's success in doing just this. The *CMC,* then, is simply an indication of the generally available, run-of-the-mill opportunities for investment and sources of funds. It provides a standard of comparison for the firm in its search for something better and provides a useful indication of the general conditions in the capital market. But it is by no means indicative of terms available from *all* investments nor of the costs of *all* sources of funds.

SUMMARY

A complete understanding of the workings of the capital market is impossible without taking adequate account of risk—the chance that an investment project may turn out better or worse than expected. In order to evaluate an investment whose outcome is not certain, a manager must take some position, explicit or implicit, about the chances of various possibilities. If he spells these out in detail but bases his estimates at least partly on judgment, he has described the project with a subjective probability distribution. This can, in turn, be described in terms of the expected rate of return (a measure which takes into account not only the magnitude

---

tween risk and return changes as we move along the curve. The function giving the ratio or slope for any point on the curve would, of course, be the derivative of the original function.

of all possible outcomes but also their likelihood) and the risk (measured by the coefficient of variation in the rate of return, another measure taking into account both the magnitude and probability of each possible outcome). In practice, these items are usually estimated by using some short-cut process rather than by explicitly thinking in terms of an actual subjective probability distribution.

The choice of an investment by a firm depends on both the financing alternatives available and the attitudes of its owners toward risk. If little is available in the way of debt financing, the manager of a firm must select investments primarily on the basis of his assessment of the owner's attitudes, particularly their degree of risk aversion. But if rather wide latitude is available with regard to financing and if purchase of near-risk-free assets by the firm is an additional possibility, the manager may be able to select an investment project without considering explicitly the attitudes of the owners toward risk, although he may have to consider this when selecting a financing scheme.

The ability of firms (and, for that matter, individual investors) to borrow or lend at near the pure rate of interest gives rise to the requirement that for the capital market to be in equilibrium, all generally available and widely known investments must offer terms lying along a single CMC. The position of this curve is determined by all the forces at work in the capital market and changes whenever those forces change. It can best be described by its two components: the pure rate of interest, which indicates the reward for riskless investments; and the premium per unit of risk, which indicates the additional reward expected for each additional unit of risk associated with an investment. The CMC summarizes the conditions prevailing in the general capital market and also provides a standard against which the firm can evaluate investment projects and potential sources of funds.

SUGGESTED READINGS

ARCHER, STEPHEN H. "The Structure of Management Decision Theory," *Academy of Management Journal,* 7 (December 1964), 269–87.

ARROW, KENNETH J. "Alternative Approaches to the Theory of Choice in Risk-Taking Situations," *Econometrica, 19* (October 1951), 404–37.

———. "Functions of a Theory of Behavior under Uncertainty," *Metroeconomica, 11* (April–August 1959), 12–20.

BERANEK, WILLIAM. *Analysis for Financial Decisions.* Homewood, Ill.: Richard D. Irwin, Inc., 1963. Chaps. 1 and 2.

BERNOULLI, DANIEL. "Exposition of a New Theory on the Measurement of Risk," *Econometrica, 22* (January 1954), 23–36.

BIERMAN, HAROLD, JR., LAWRENCE E. FOURAKER, and ROBERT K. JAEDICKS. *Quantitative Analysis for Business Decisions.* Homewood, Ill.: Richard D. Irwin, Inc., 1961. Chaps. 2 and 3.

HICKS, J. R. *Value and Capital.* 2nd ed. Oxford, England: Oxford University Press, 1946. Chaps. 1–3.

HILLIER, FREDERICK S. "The Derivation of Probabilistic Information for the Evaluation of Risky Investments," *Management Science, 9* (April 1963), 443–57.

HIRSHLEIFER, JACK. "Risk, the Discount Rate, and Investment Decisions," *American Economic Review, 51* (May 1961), 112–20.

KNIGHT, FRANK. *Risk, Uncertainty and Profit.* Boston: Houghton Mifflin Company, 1921.

KRELLE, W. "A Theory on Rational Behavior under Uncertainty," *Metroeconomica, 11* (April–August 1959), 51–63.

LATANÉ, H. A. "Criteria for Choice among Risky Ventures," *Journal of Political Economy, 67* (April 1959), 144–55.

LINTNER, JOHN. "The Valuation of Risk Assets and the Selection of Risky Investments in Stock Portfolios and Capital Budgets," *The Review of Economics and Statistics, 47* (February 1965), 13–37.

SCHLAIFER, ROBERT. *Statistics for Business Decisions.* New York: McGraw-Hill Book Company, Inc., 1961. Chaps. 1–3 and 14.

SHARPE, WILLIAM F. "Capital Asset Prices: A Theory of Market Equilibrium," *The Journal of Finance, 19* (September 1964), 425–42.

STREETEN, P. "The Effect of Taxation on Risk-Taking," *Oxford Economic Papers, 5* (October 1953), 271–87.

WILLET, ALLAN H. *The Economic Theory of Risk and Insurance.* Philadelphia: University of Pennsylvania Press, 1951. Chaps. 1, 3, 5, 6, and 8.

QUESTIONS

5.1 Classify the following according to whether they are situations of certainty, risk, or uncertainty: (a) sales estimates of a furniture manufacturer for next year; (b) a turn of a roulette wheel; (c) the proportion of bad debts in the existing accounts receivable of a firm; and (d) the mixture of two parts hydrogen with one part oxygen.

5.2 How likely is it that complete uncertainty would be encountered in business situations? What probability should be attached to, say, eight possible outcomes in the case of complete uncertainty?

5.3 If a contemplated investment has an expected return of 10 per cent and a risk of 1/2, is it possible to earn more than 15 per cent on the investment? Explain.

5.4 Explain what is meant by *negative borrowing*. Why would it be likely that negative and positive borrowing rates would differ?

5.5 Given the following investments, which of them dominate others?

Investment	Return	Risk
A	15%	1/2
B	20	1
C	12	1
D	10	1/2
E	15	5/8

A 7B

A > D   Higher Return Same Risk   A > E Same return and

B > C

5.6 Would an indifference curve of investments change for a firm if the size of the average investment were $500,000 instead of $500? Explain.

5.7 What are the advantages of the *CMC* over the pure interest determination of the last chapter in describing the investment alternatives of the market?

5.8 In Figure 5-7 the right tail of the slope of the *B* investment curve changes after Investment B'. Comment on the reality or lack thereof of that portion of the investment curve extending beyond B'.

5.9 Why is it that as more and more of a homogeneous investment is taken on through the use of borrowed funds that the risk and the expected rates of return of a firm increase? Explain fully.

PROBLEMS

5.10 During a meeting of your class, the number of questions asked may vary from 0 to ___. (a) Construct a subjective probability distribution for the possible outcomes. (b) Compute the expected outcome.

5.11 For the restaurant example in this chapter, determine the risk for both of the following conditions: (a) A recent warehouse fire created a demand for space so that there are now 2 chances in 10 of selling the building for $50,000 and 1 chance in 10 of selling it for $40,000. (b) The top sales price was $100,000 instead of $50,000 (1 chance in 10).

5.12 The subjective probability distribution of outcomes for an investment of $10,000 for one year is given below:

Outcome		Estimated Probability	
$20,000	×	.10	2000
15,000	×	.15	2250
12,000	×	.20	2400
10,000	×	.25	2500
8,000	×	.20	1600
7,000	×	.10	700

[handwritten: ER = 11,450 - 10,000 / 10,000 ; 1450 / 10,000 = .145]

[handwritten: 11,450 EO]

Calculate the expected return, standard deviation of the rate of return, and risk. *[handwritten: for SD find ER for each of above. Then take ER -]*

[handwritten: ① 20,000 - 10,000 / 10,000 ② 15,000 - 9000 / -9000]

5.13 Given the following rates of return and subjective probability distribution find the mean and standard deviation of the distribution. What is the expectation that the return will exceed 7 per cent? *[handwritten: 45%]*

[handwritten left margin: Rate]

Return	Estimated Probability
5%	.10
6	.20
7	.25
8	.20
9	.10
10	.15

[handwritten: add over 7 = ×5% ; Mode 7% ; Median 7.5]

5.14 The following are the investments available in the market:

	Risk	Expected Return
A	1/2	10%
B	1/2	12
C	5/8	15
D	3/5	15

(a) Plot the four investments. (b) If the pure rate of interest is 5 per cent, construct a hypothetical *CMC* on your original diagram. (c) Now draw a curve representing your approximate indifference to combinations of risk and expected return (your risk aversion). (d) Which investment did you choose? Would the situation have changed if you had to borrow half the money necessary to undertake the project?

5.15 (a) What do you estimate the nature of your risk aversion to be: high, low, or somewhere in between? (b) What factors did you consider in arriving at this determination? List them. (c) Plot your indifference curve to combinations of risk and expected rate of return. Remember, this should demonstrate your risk-aversion feelings. (d) Would your plot in (c) be any different if you had the following data? If so, plot your new indifference curve given these data. (e) Which of these investments do you choose?

Investment	Risk	Expected Return
A	1/2	5%
B	1/4	9
C	3/8	16
D	3/4	18
E	1	16
F	1/8	25

CHAPTER 6 THE RATE OF EXCHANGE
OF MONEY CAPITAL

Heretofore we referred to saving and investment as the exchange of present goods and services for future goods and services. To the participants in the process, however, the exchange is likely to be one of present money for future money, although the real trade is present goods for future goods. The pure rate of interest in an economy was shown to be determined by the marginal efficiency of capital schedule and the supply of funds schedule; this analysis was based upon the assumption of a riskless economy and supplies little of the realism of the components or forces behind the determination of the pure rate of interest—the return to riskless investments.

It is of considerable importance to examine more closely such a riskless rate, for the base of our CMC is the pure rate. As should be obvious from the discussion which developed the concept of the CMC, changes in the pure rate will tend to cause entire shifts of the CMC, which reflects the whole structure of rates of return to capital. Changes in inclination of suppliers of money capital toward risk causes changes in the shape, however, without a change in the pure rate. Changes in attitudes toward the assumption of risk arise more from psychological factors; these are too complex to be easily and completely identified and only a few of the more superficial forces will be referred to here.

At this stage we recognize that there is no such theoretical pure rate in the real world. Our discussion of the pure rate in Chapter 4 represents a theoretical ideal which can at best be only approximated in the real world—such as, for example, by the return to short-term United States government obligations. In this chapter, the determination of the *rate of interest* will, in theory, refer to the interest rate in general and, in reality, represent a whole structure of rates. The discussion of this chapter is directed to the determination of the interest rate, a money rate of exchange, and later to the structure of rates the analysis represents.

It is important to realize in a money economy that money is a lubricant in the financial process of directing saving into real capital formation. Non-consumption, or saving, enables resources to be diverted to the creation of capital. Saving of individuals and businesses may be accumulated in the form of money and offered in the funds market as money to be used to buy the resources to create the capital. If the money is in the form of a bank demand deposit, the bank, in turn, may offer the funds. If, however, the money is held in the form of hoarded currency, it may not reach the funds market. Resources freed by saving in such a case can only be directed to users through money expansion by banks or by government spending with the aid of banks.

Real saving results when an economy does not use up all of its currently produced physical output. If, for example, in a Robinson Crusoe economy, five fish are caught in one day, the total current physical output of that economy consists of the five fish. This is also the total income for that period. Now the stranded sailor is faced with a decision concerning the disposal of his total output (or income). He can consume all the fish, none of the fish, or part of the fish. Were he to consume all the fish, there would be none left for the next day's use and he would once more have to attempt to catch fish. If he were to consume none of the fish, although his hunger pains may be severe, he would have saved the total amount for future use—either for consumption, for use in the form of fertilizer, or for some combination of both. His choice may be to consume part of his income (total output) and not consume (i.e., save) the rest in order to provide for future consumption and/or some other use. Capital is formed in this case just by saving, because our definition of *capital formation* includes not only the creation of goods used in the production of other goods but also the accumulation of inventories.

In more advanced economies, where money is used as a medium of exchange, society's saving needs to be translated into real capital formation. The mechanism by which this is accomplished is the subject of Chapter 8. In a society in which money is used, interest rates then may be, in part, a monetary phenomenon. This phenomenon was first reflected in the more traditional theory of interest, which was introduced in Chapter 4 and secondly in the *CMC* discussion of Chapter 5. In this chapter we will expand upon the forces influencing such a market.

The interest rate is also a monetary phenomenon in a later theory of interest—that of J. M. Keynes. His theory of the rate determination depended upon the stock of money and people's preferences for liquidity. Behind all the monetary façade, however, lies the more fundamental determinants of the interest rate: the real productivity of capital. Realizing that this factor lies behind the monetary structure, we shall concentrate our efforts on the determination of the rate of interest in a general or average sense in the monetary world and follow with an examination of the whole structure of interest rates as theoretically introduced in Chapter 5 by the *CMC*.

DETERMINATION OF THE RATE OF INTEREST

The rate of interest, or the price for the use of money, may be determined by the demand for and the supply of loanable funds—according, at least, to the traditional theorists. If we ignore risk for the moment, one way in which to anticipate better interest-rate changes is to disaggregate the total demand and the total supply of loanable funds.

Aggregate Demand for Loanable Funds

The demand for loanable funds comes from three segments of the economy: the consumer sector, the business sector, and the government sector. When aggregated, all three constitute the total demand for loanable funds. Let us now turn our attention to these three sectors of our economy.

In the post-World War II years, the consumer sector has become an increasingly important segment of the total demand for loanable funds. Bank investments in consumer installment paper, and the rapid and substantial growth of financial institutions which lend to consumers, attest to this phenomenon. The underlying motive for consumer credit is to be found in the desire of consumers to possess present goods, many of which are durables yielding up services over time, while intending to pay for them out of future income. So characteristic of our society have consumer loans become in the past two decades that it has been stated that people no longer buy, say, a consumer durable as such; rather they buy a service and a payment and will shop for the most of a given consumer durable service that a particular payment can secure.

The business demand for loanable funds is usually regarded as the most important from the standpoint of the entire economy, for private investment, unpredictable as it is, is the most economically destabilizing factor in our society. The need for investment funds by business firms in recent years has been substantial and has been satisfied to a very large extent through retained earnings and depreciation accruals. The source of demand for loanable funds for business firms can be, as we saw in the preceding two chapters, reflected in a marginal efficiency of capital schedule and is based on expectations concerning future conditions, however much such expectations may be based on historical fact. Thus they are *ex ante* investment opportunities and are subject to all the vicissitudes associated with any decision-making process.

Government demand for loanable funds in recent times has been substantial. The federal government has been a consistent borrower of funds for the last several decades. Most significantly, efforts to shore up the economy during the depression of the 1930's led to deficit financing (borrowing the difference between income and outgo). Efforts to win World War II caused the greatest expansion in federal debt and since then periods of economic decline have witnessed further deficit financing in order to prevent a worsening in economic activity.

State and local governments have also been substantial sources of demand for loanable funds in the past few decades. The demand for more and better roads, schools, and welfare plans, for example, have made many of our states heavy demanders of loanable funds.

When the three sectors are aggregated, the total demand for loanable funds is derived. A demand curve for loanable funds will slope down to the right, indicating that as the interest rate declines the demand for loanable funds in the aggregate will probably increase. What the precise response to changes in the interest rate in loanable funds will be cannot be determined. As a general statement, we can say that there is a tendency for the quantity demanded to increase as the interest rate decreases, and vice versa. It is frequently suggested, however, that changes in interest rates produce less than proportionate changes in the quantity of loanable funds demanded by consumers. This may be so because consumers are relatively invariate in their demand for goods and because interest rates have proportionately less impact on the total amount paid by consumers on most of their purchases. With respect to changes in interest rates on home mortgages, however, the case may have a different impact for the time period involved is much longer, making for a more meaningful magnitude of change in the total cost of the object purchased. Nevertheless, aggregate consumer demand for loanable funds is presumed to be as depicted in Figure 6-1. That is, it is presumed to be, for the most part, highly inelastic; consumers' demand for loanable funds are thought to be relatively insensitive to changes in the interest rates.

The federal government demand for loanable funds is presumed to be extremely inelastic, for any changes in interest rates probably will not deter government borrowing plans. This is true with respect both to upward as well as to downward changes. Local or state governments may be constitutionally constrained from borrowing, however, by upward changes in interest rates. The demand schedule for loanable funds of state and local governments probably is elastic only at higher rates; in all other segments it is probably as highly inelastic as it is for the federal government. When combined with federal government demand for loanable funds, the demand schedule of the entire government sector is presumed to be inelastic —that is, virtually nonresponsive to changes in the interest rate. Figure 6-2 illustrates this inelasticity.

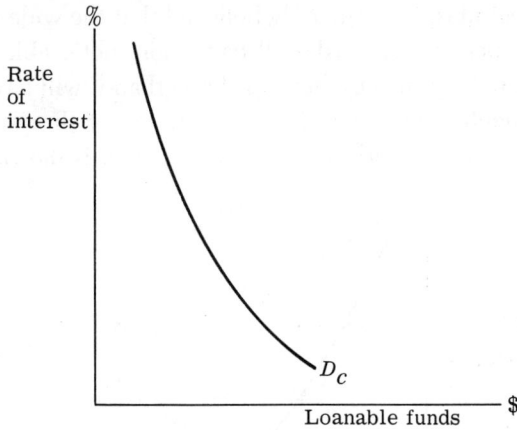

Figure 6-1 Consumer Demand for Loanable Funds

The demand schedule for loanable funds by business firms is probably the most elastic of all, but even in this instance it is frequently argued that there is a high degree of inelasticity. In some investment decisions the interest expense associated with the acquisition of funds is so small relative to the profit prospects of the outlay that at least small variations in the level of interest rates will have little or no effect on the quantity of loanable funds demanded. It is generally presumed that the demand schedule for loanable funds by business firms is more elastic than those for either the consumer or government sectors of the economy. That is to say, although empirical studies are readily available attesting to the fact that business-men do not generally regard the interest rate as an important consideration

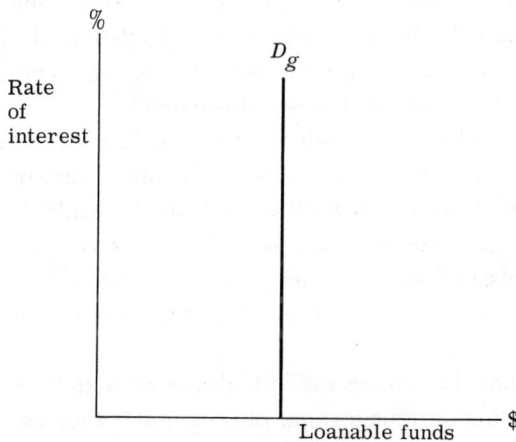

Figure 6-2 Government Demand for Loanable Funds

in financing decisions, it is generally believed that the wide changes in the
interest rate, especially upward, will have more noticeable affects on the
demand for loanable funds by business firms than it will have for consumers or governmental units. A graphic illustration of the presumed nature
of demand for loanable funds by the business sector is shown in Figure 6-3.

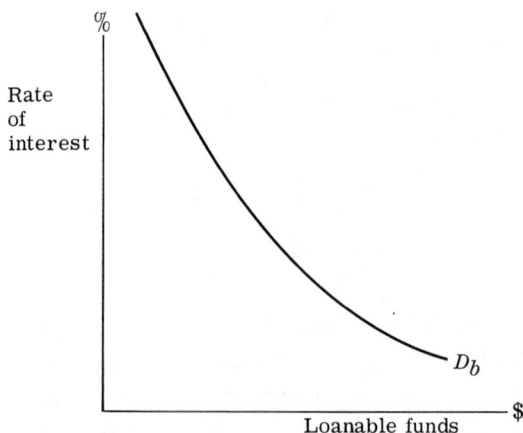

Figure 6-3   Business Demand for Loanable Funds

Figure 6-4 represents the aggregation of all three sectors of demand for
loanable funds.

Aggregate Supply of Loanable Funds

Although it is assumed that the supply of and demand for loanable
funds determine the interest rate, a disaggregation of the demand for
loanable funds and the supply of loanable funds is necessary for a more
thorough understanding of interest-rate changes.

The supply of loanable funds is determined by a complex of forces all
acting on and reacting to one another. In broad outline, the supply of
loanable funds is derived from the funds made available by individuals,
business units, and governments as well as by changes in the supply of
money. The reasons for a changing supply of loanable funds lies in the
factors to be discussed below. We will first focus our attention on individual savers.

There are only two things individuals can do with their income or their
wealth (including current income plus capital): they can use it for consumption expenditures, or they can save it. The reason the individual saves
part of his income is attributable essentially to desires to redistribute in-

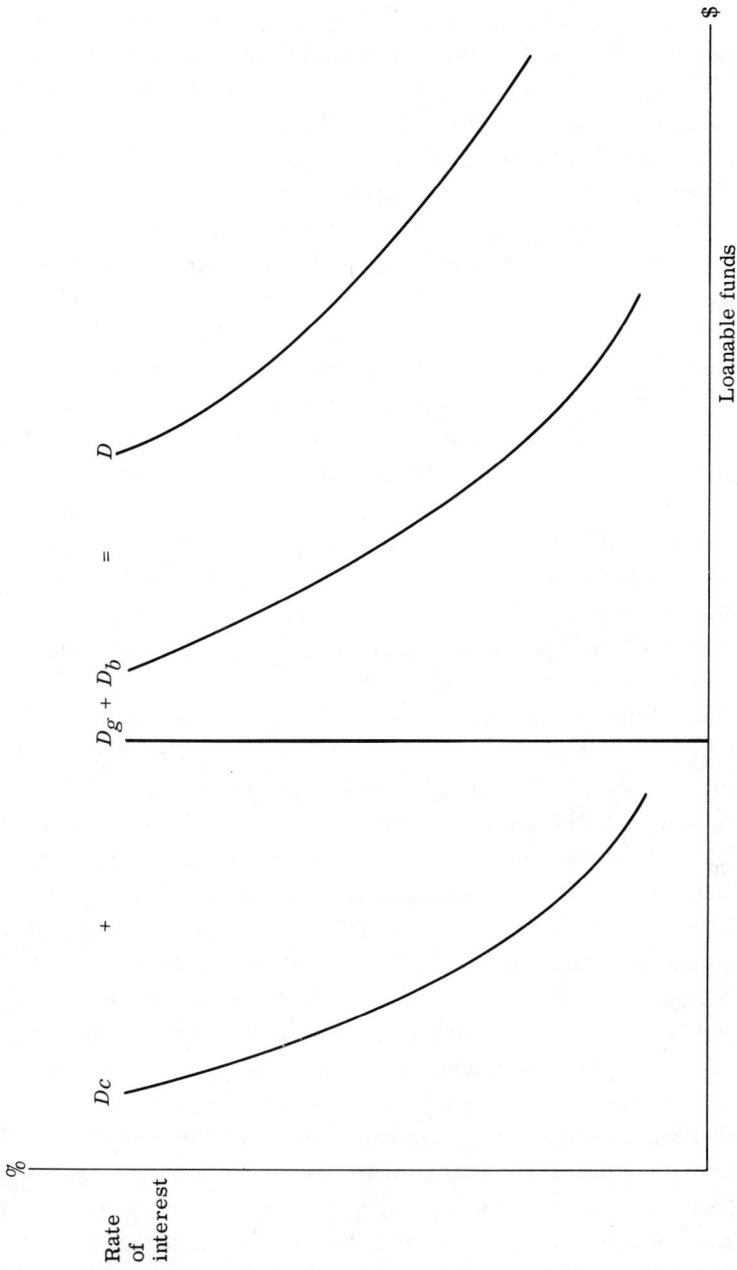

Figure 6-4   Aggregated Demand for Loanable Funds

come over the life of the saver and to increase his income in the future. Although a great deal of one's income is devoted to satisfying present consumption needs, some of it may be diverted to future needs by way of saving (not consuming all of one's current income). Increased present satisfactions may be desired over future satisfactions by many, and individuals may even borrow against future income.

The inclination to future satisfactions arises from the desire to redistribute income and to augment it. Some of these desires are reflected in the creation of contingency funds to provide needs in case of loss of income, to provide for the education of children, to provide for the marriage of daughters, or to provide for the years of retirement. Also, as we saw in Chapter 4, the level of the interest rate itself may be a factor. Theoretically, as interest rates tend to rise, the level of saving should tend to increase, for the saver can augment his income more in the future with the higher rates available. How important this factor is in practice is subject to question. The saving habits of individuals, in fact, seem to be relatively unresponsive to (at least small) changes in the interest rate. Finally, the amount of wealth a person already has, his level of income and such noneconomic factors as "keeping up with the Joneses" all have a significant bearing on the level of saving expected from individuals.

Even beyond these considerations, however, there are other important factors to be recognized. One is the fact that saving does not mean that loanable funds are directly enhanced. Indeed, they may not be. Individual expectations, saving habits, and even apathy may prevent savers from making their funds available. For example, persons expecting a nuclear war might tend to withhold their funds from the loanable-funds market; Civil Defense authorities recommend that a sum of cash be kept on hand in one's fallout shelter for just such an eventuality. Moreover, persons may feel that their money is safer at home than in the bank or some other medium of saving. Funds hoarded, however, are not spent and the goods and resources not demanded are available for capital formation. To maintain stability, the monetary authorities would be expected to create enough funds to replace those hoarded.

The reverse side of this proposition is also true, however. More loanable funds may be forthcoming from this sector of the market than is indicated by the amount of current saving—as, for example, when previously hoarded currency is put on the market. Thus an easing of Cold War tensions may persuade people to reduce the number of dollars stored in their fallout shelters. Also, habits in general may change so that less cash is kept at home than was the case before. Monetary authorities tend to adjust to these conditions by reducing the money supply.

The business sector of the economy also can provide loanable funds through the retention of earnings and depreciation accruals. The sum of these two is referred to as *internally generated funds;* these constitute a segment of the total supply of loanable funds as much as those of individuals because they "compete" with other sources of funds. Admittedly, however, the need of these funds within the firm is also part of the total demand for loanable funds. This aspect of funds is discussed more completely in Chapter 8. For the present it is sufficient to recognize that business "saving" in the form of retained earnings and depreciation accruals, covered in part or in whole by net revenues collected, constitute a source of loanable funds. This supply may or may not appear on the market. If these funds are used internally, the supply provides funds which otherwise would have had to have been secured from the market.

In addition to the supply of loanable funds provided by households and business units, the capacity of the banking system to add to this supply is significant. Banks may offer an increment to the supply either on their own volition or under the stimulus of federal agencies (the Treasury Department and the Federal Reserve System). Because it is presumed that the student has been exposed to this notion in other courses, only the basic outlines of the money-creating aspects of the system will be presented below.

The money-creating capacity of a commercial banking system is based on the maintenance of fractional reserves to back up deposits. That is to say, any deposits brought to a bank need not be supported completely with cash or deposits. On the contrary, only a fraction need be kept in a cash or deposit form. The remainder may be lent. The banker knows from experience that only a small part of the total deposits committed to his bank can be expected to be withdrawn over a period of normal operations. The funds not needed to meet legal reserve requirements, day-to-day currency withdrawals (which are usually relatively small), or operating expenses (also usually small in magnitude) would just lie idle if the bank did not put them to use. Because the bank is in business for a profit, it actively seeks out those investments which are most consistent with its policies and with the regulations surrounding the banking industry. But if a businessman seeks and is granted, say, an $800 loan from a bank, the bank ordinarily does not give him $800 in currency. It extends him credit by giving him a checking account in that amount. Because checking accounts (demand deposits) are defined as part of the money supply, by extending credit to the businessman the bank has taken the first step in expanding the money supply. For example, assume that someone deposits $1,000 in currency in The First Liberal National Bank. Assume further that the bank is required to keep on deposit with a Federal Reserve Bank or in currency 20 per cent of all its demand deposits. To simplify matters we will assume that the bank needs to make no other appropriations of cash (to meet day-to-day expenses, for example) other than those required by the Federal Reserve. Under these assumptions, the bank's balance sheet would look like that below:

The First Liberal National Bank

Assets		Liabilities	
Required reserves	$ 200	Demand deposits	$1,000
Excess reserves	800		
	$1,000		$1,000

The bank would have $800 in excess of the amount required by the Federal Reserve. If a businessman comes in for a loan of $800, the bank is in a position to lend him that amount. If the businessman wanted a loan of, say, $1,000, he would be unable to get all of it from this bank. The bank itself can lend only the amount it has in excess of reserves, for as the borrower spends his loan it is likely that checks will be deposited in other banks, thus reducing the lending bank's reserves. For example, assume a loan for $800 has been made and the bank gives the businessman a checking account in that amount. The balance sheet will look as follows:

The First Liberal National Bank

Assets		Liabilities	
Required reserves	$ 360	Demand deposits	$1,800
Excess reserves	640		
Loans and investments	800		
	$1,800		$1,800

This is a very temporary situation for the bank. Because it is one bank within a system of banks, the likelihood of checks written on the bank returning to it might be very small. Let us assume that none of the checks written on the bank by the businessman will be redeposited in the lending bank. Assume they are deposited in another bank. When all the checks written on the bank by the businessman are cleared, the bank must have $800 on hand to make payment on them. Thus once the loan is made, the bank has no excess reserves because of the expected $800 fall in deposits and reserves. After the checks have been made and are cleared, the balance sheet of the bank will look like this:

The First Liberal National Bank

Assets		Liabilities	
Required reserves	$ 200	Demand deposits	$1,000
Loans	800		
	$1,000		$1,000

The bank will still have $1,000 in resources: $200 in required reserves, $1,000 in demand deposits, and $800 in the loan made to the businessman, which is now an earning asset for the bank. The entire amount of excess reserves has been lent out. But what happens to the checks cleared through this bank? For simplicity's sake, let us assume they are all deposited in The Second Conservative National Bank, whose balance sheet will then look like this:

The Second Conservative National Bank

Assets		Liabilities	
Required reserves	$160	Demand deposits	$800
Excess reserves	640		
	$800		$800

This bank in turn can make loans to the extent of its excess reserves, in this case $640. If we were again to assume that the total loans made by The Second Conservative National Bank were withdrawn and deposited in The Third Compromise National Bank, their respective balance sheets would look like this:

The Second Conservative National Bank

Assets		Liabilities	
Required reserves	$160	Demand deposits	$800
Loans	640		
	$800		$800

The Third Compromise National Bank

Assets		Liabilities	
Required reserves	$128	Demand deposits	$640
Excess reserves	512		
	$640		$640

The Third Compromise then could make loans to the extent of its excess reserves, in this case $512.

This illustration could be carried on and on, and, under the given assumptions that all checks made on a bank are placed in another bank, the system as a whole could generate a total of about five times the amount of the original deposit; that is, it could generate demand deposits of $5,000, unless limiting factors such as increased currency needs held the figure below this level. By this process the banking system has clearly expanded the money supply of the economy by the difference between the original deposit of currency and the final aggregate amount of demand deposits. In this case the difference amounts to $4,000.

Contraction of the money supply would take place in a reverse manner. Withdrawal in cash of the $1,000 demand deposit in The First Liberal would require it to come up with $1,000. But it only has $200 in required cash reserves on which to draw. Where does it get the rest? It calls in the loan it made or it borrows from the Federal Reserve Bank, if possible. If the loan is called (assuming it can be retired upon call of the bank), The Second Conservative will be faced with precisely the same problem that faced The First Liberal; its demand deposits will have been withdrawn to pay the loan and it will be short of cash to meet the withdrawal. In order to make good on the withdrawal, it has the same alternatives as The First Liberal, but again we will assume that it calls in its loan. This will put pressure on The Third Compromise to generate cash to meet the withdrawal to pay the loan caused by The Second Conservative's action because, under the given conditions, the only source of funds for meeting withdrawals is to call in loans. This action forces the individuals to whom the loans have been made to withdraw their deposits—which, in turn, sets in motion another process of loan-calling and demand-deposit contraction. Thus the expansion model set forth earlier is perfectly reversible.

The process of creating and destroying money, demonstrated here in abbreviated fashion, is the result of fractional reserve banking and depends on the excess reserve position of banks and their willingness to make loans. The most important influences on the excess reserve positions of commercial banks, aside from loan demand, are the actions of the

Federal Reserve Bank and the Treasury. It is now in order for us to discuss briefly the impact of monetary policy on the loanable-funds market.

The economic objectives of our nation are to provide high levels of employment and income, to promote growth, and to maintain a reasonably stable price level. To achieve these objectives, fiscal and monetary policies have been extensively resorted to in recent years. Fundamental to an understanding of the supply of and demand for loanable funds is a comprehension of monetary policy.

Monetary policy is concerned primarily with conscious manipulation of the excess reserve position of commercial banks in order to control the money supply so as to influence the level of interest rates, the availability of funds, and national economic activity. As noted above, individual banks can make loans (or investments) only to the extent that they have excess reserves and that a demand exists. The system, moreover, can expand the total money supply only to the extent that banks have excess reserves and do, in fact, make loans or investments. It is important to remember, however, that the money provided by commercial banks is not the only constituent of total loanable funds. Savings out of current income by individuals and business firms, and dishoarding, also must be included. Monetary authorities have no direct control over these latter elements.

The monetary policies of our country are administered, for the most part, by the Federal Reserve Board and executed by the various Federal Reserve Banks in order to promote the economic objectives of our society. There are several tools or instruments at the Board's disposal for execution of its responsibilities; among these are open-market operations, changes in required reserve ratios, and discounting paper (making loans to commercial banks). The most notable of these is the open-market operation of the Open Market Committee of the Federal Reserve Board. This entails buying and selling government securities in the open market in order to influence the reserves of commercial banks and, in turn perhaps, the interest rates on securities.

The fact that the Federal Reserve may buy substantial amounts of bonds in itself tends to increase the demand for bonds. Now, other things being equal, this "extra demand" will cause bond prices to rise. As seen above, if bond prices rise, yields must go down. Thus the level of interest rates is directly affected by the Federal Reserve's buying and selling United States government securities. Changes in the yields on these securities affect the prices and yields of other securities.

But the level of interest rates is further affected by open-market operations insofar as the reserve positions of commercial banks are affected. If the reserve positions of commercial banks are affected, the money supply and therefore the total loanable funds will also be affected. Suppose, for example, the Federal Reserve were to sell bonds to the public. We know that this action will tend to increase yields. Suppose further that you bought one of these bonds for, say, $1,000. It is conceivable that you might have that much cash at home or in a safety deposit vault and can draw on these idle cash balances to pay for the bond. More likely you, as well as all the other purchasers, would write a check in the amount of $1,000. In other words, you will make out a check to the Federal Reserve (we assume) for that amount. What happens when demand deposits are drawn down? A withdrawal of deposits has the tendency to contract the money supply. The specific impact of a withdrawal will depend on the extent to which the banks have excess reserves and on their magnitudes. Without getting into the various ramifications of these notions, we will say that sales of bonds by the Federal Reserve have the tendency to reduce the money supply. For precisely the opposite reasons, purchases of bonds have the tendency to increase the money supply. What would a bank do that sees its deposits going down and its excess reserve position either eliminated or reduced considerably? It probably will reduce its rate of making loans. It will either take the most preferred of risks (thereby precluding other borrowers who would then in turn have to go elsewhere for funds, usually at a higher cost), charge more for the loans it does make to reduce demand, or engage in a combination of these two procedures. Both actions will have the tendency to increase interest rates. The obverse of the proposition is true also; increasing deposits tends to swell excess reserve positions, and there is a tendency to employ them. When interest rates are reduced and less credit-worthy risks are taken on, this tends to reduce interest rates.

The other instruments employed by the Federal Reserve to control the rate of interest are also designed to affect the excess reserve position of commercial banks. Discounting paper brought to the Federal Reserve bank is a mild panacea for a commercial bank which is short on excess reserves, although it is temporary in nature. Most commercial banks use this device but may prefer to sell some of their "secondary" reserves (Treasury Bills, for example) if conditions warrant it. Changing the required proportion of reserves to deposits is unquestionably the bluntest of all the instruments available to the Federal Reserve; as a consequence, it is resorted to only rarely.

The federal government, through its efforts to refinance a portion of the debt almost on a continuous basis, may have an impact on the rate of interest. Changes in debt-management policies may induce changes in the structure of interest rates. On the other hand, the operations of the

Treasury Department are not executed without reference to the operations of the Federal Reserve. When a large "roll-over" of government debt is impending, the Federal Reserve may take action to provide the banking system with sufficient reserves to facilitate the Treasury's operations.

Financial managers may anticipate the actions of the monetary authorities to an extent by keeping an eye on economic conditions. As economic conditions tend to the "full" employment level, it is not unreasonable to expect the Federal Reserve to restrain the expansion of the money supply (in order to raise the level of interest rates to prevent inflation).

During periods of economic decline the opposite might be expected to take place. In order to promote investment expenditures, efforts by the monetary authorities will be directed at lowering interest rates. If the interest rate declines and if the marginal efficiency of the capital schedule remains the same, the level of investment should increase, thereby tending to promote economic recovery. By buying securities in the open market the Federal Reserve tends to bid up prices and, concomitantly, the interest rate declines. The impact on the money supply depends on from whom the bonds are bought. Presumably they will be bought from sellers who would be expected to deposit the dollars in commercial banks or from the banks themselves. This would then tend to increase the banks' excess reserves and, thereby, the supply of loanable funds.

Thus the total supply of loanable funds is derived from the savings both of individuals and of business firms as well as from the money created by both the monetary authorities. Figure 6-5 indicates the presumed nature of the supply curve of loanable funds. The supply curve slopes up

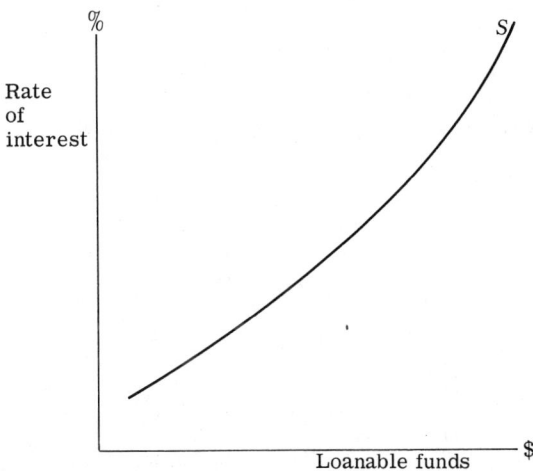

Figure 6-5 Aggregate Supply of Loanable Funds

to the right, indicating that as interest rates go up more loanable funds will be forthcoming. At low levels of interest rates few loanable funds may be forthcoming.

As in the determination of the pure rate of interest in Chapter 4, the equilibrium in the loanable funds market is demonstrated in Figure 6-6. The quantity demanded for loanable funds is imposed on the curve of the quantity supplied. Any efforts to move away from this position either by supplying more funds than are demanded or by demanding more funds than are supplied will induce reactions in the market for funds. Thus, given the equilibrium conditions set forth in Figure 6-6 (equilibrium is at Point E), any effort on the part of those attempting to supply additional loanable funds while the demand for them remains the same would tend to lower interest rates; the supply of loanable funds would shift to the right (perhaps because of open-market purchases by the Federal Reserve). There the level of interest rates is reduced because of an increase in the quantity supplied of loanable funds, and a new equilibrium would exist.

LIQUIDITY PREFERENCE

Another approach to examining changes in the interest rate is through the controversial liquidity-preference analysis. People and business firms may desire to hold money instead of earning assets for a number of reasons, and the extent to which they do so can affect interest rates. We will first discuss the reasons for holding money; later we will examine their impact on interest rates.

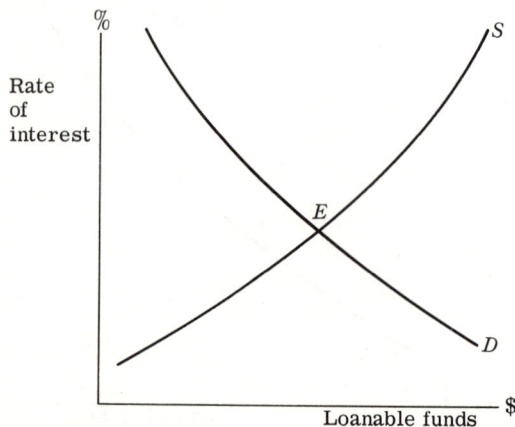

Figure 6-6 Equilibrium in Loanable Funds Market

Motives for Holding Money

The liquidity-preference theory is in part concerned with the reasons for holding money.[1] It attempts to establish the general concepts regarding preferences for liquidity and their impact on the rate of interest. There are three basic reasons to hold money. The first of these is the need to bridge the gap between income and outgo. Because receipts and expenditures are not coincidental, some sort of budgeting is required. As a matter of course, most economic units hold back a portion of their periodic money inflow from immediate use in order to take care of the day-to-day routine expenditures of the budgeted period. This preference for maintaining liquidity is called the *transactions motive*. The aggregate amount of money required to satisfy this motive in the economy is primarily a function of the level of national income; for the individual it is a function of individual income and frequency of payment. As the level of economic activity declines, less income is received and the amount of transactions, both for persons and for firms, declines so that fewer dollars are used to take care of day-to-day activities. The reverse is also true.

The second motive for maintaining liquidity is to establish contingency reserves. These are in the nature of a "rainy-day fund." Individuals, as well as firms, are aware that certain infrequent events may arise unexpectedly in the future—events over which they have no control but which will require cash outlays beyond those capable of being met by current money income. Such a desire for liquidity arises from the so-called *precautionary motive*. Serious illness on the part of the breadwinner would be a case in point. A fire in a factory is another. To meet such eventualities, it is usually suggested that funds be set aside in liquid form.

Another reason why people prefer liquidity is to be found in the so-called *speculative motive*. This refers to the desire of persons to hold sums beyond those needed to satisfy the transaction and precautionary motives. People may prefer to hold money, for example, because they expect a change in profit potentials as a result of a change in the level of interest rates. Thus this motive depends to a large extent on the changes in factors affecting prices of earning assets or other purchases (even consumptive purchases). It is speculative in the sense that the individual anticipates lower prices of earning assets or consumptive goods.

These motives can be combined into an aggregate preference for liquidity. Keynes suggested that the rate of interest is determined by the nature of liquidity preference of individuals and the stock of money. The

[1] John M. Keynes, *General Theory of Employment, Interest and Money* (New York: Harcourt, Brace & World, Inc., 1936), pp. 194–209.

nature of such a determination is illustrated in Figure 6-7. The liquidity-preference function (*LP*) slopes down to the right; when the stock of money (*M*) increases, given such liquidity preferences, the rate of interest tends to fall. Over time, as individuals and businesses change their attitudes toward holding money, the liquidity-preference function will shift, causing changes in the rate of interest. If people as a whole expected a depression, they would attempt to hold more money based upon speculative and precautionary motives and, unless *M* increased, the interest rate would rise.

THE STRUCTURE OF INTEREST RATES

In the earlier discussions concerning the determination of the rate of interest, it was generally assumed that there existed perfect mobility of funds, perfect knowledge of opportunities, no risk differences in securities, and no other market imperfections. This theory thereby gave the illusion that there is but one, and only one, interest rate. Moreover, it oversimplified other aspects of the market for funds. Yet the theory does indicate the tendencies one would expect in the market. But the market for loanable funds in the real world is not a perfect one and its shortcomings, plus other factors, result in a whole array of interest rates (a structure of interest rates) rather than just one.

In determining the rate of interest, we made the implicit assumption that there was perfect mobility of loanable funds in the sense that there was only one national market and funds moved freely to that market,

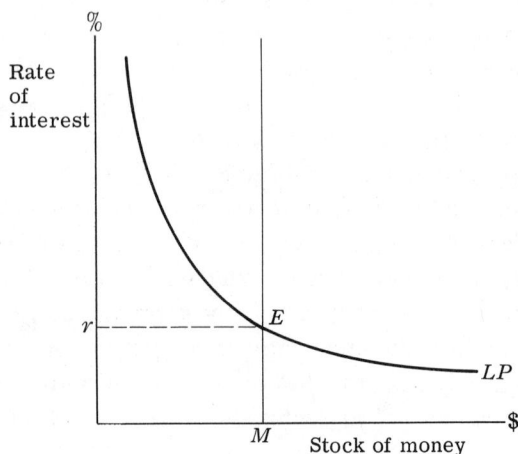

Figure 6-7   Liquidity Preference Determination of the Interest Rate

making the funds available to any user who can pay the price. This obviously is not true. Some funds are restricted to certain geographical areas, such as those of savings and loan associations. Other funds are restricted as to the nature of the investments into which they can be placed, such as the funds of life insurance companies and commercial banks. Still others are circumscribed by personal limitations or lack of knowledge in their management. Finally, the forms of contract under which loanable funds flow is, in practice, a heterogeneous group, although there are only two general classes of legal form—creditorship and ownership. This heterogeneity makes for specialization among potential lenders of loanable funds and thus tends to limit even further the mobility of funds. Thus, for example, savings and loan associations and mutual savings banks restrict most of their investments to mortgages; life insurance companies place a substantial amount of their funds in corporate securities (especially bonds); and commercial banks are assuming ever-greater proportions of consumer credits.

Another flaw in the market is the lack of perfect knowledge both on the part of the supplier and on the part of the demander. If the supplier of loanable funds is an institution,[2] it will likely be better informed as to its alternative opportunities than an individual would be. This, in fact, is one of the vital services provided by financial institutions; they provide special skill and knowledge to investment decisions that individuals in and of themselves often are unable to provide. Similarly, if the demander of loanable funds is a large business corporation or a governmental unit, chances are they have more knowledge of alternative sources of funds than do individuals.[3]

Another imperfection, administrative in nature, suggests the reasonableness of more than one interest rate. The administrative cost as a percentage of the loan is greater on smaller loans than it is on large loans. The data presented in Table 6-1 indicate this fact in part.[4] Notice that as the size of short-term commercial loans increases from the smallest category ($1,000–$10,000), the interest rate per annum declines significantly. The differentials cannot be accounted for exclusively by administrative per unit costs, as we shall see, but the point to be made is that

[2] Financial institutions to a great extent supply loanable funds as intermediaries (except commercial banks). A further discussion of this point is to be found in Chapter 8.
[3] This is not necessarily so in all cases. The emphasis is on the likelihood that they are better informed than individuals. Individual cases have illustrated a certain ineptness in seeking out alternative sources of funds.
[4] In part, lower rates on larger loans is no doubt due to the generally, but not universally, better credit standing of large borrowers as opposed to small ones.

Table 6-1
Bank Rates on Short-Term Business Loans
(Percentage per Annum)

Year	Size of Loan (Thousands of Dollars)			
	1–10	10–100	100–200	200 and Over
1955	5.0	4.4	4.0	3.5
1956	5.2	4.8	4.4	4.0
1957	5.5	5.1	4.8	4.5
1958	5.5	5.0	4.6	4.1
1959	5.8	5.5	5.2	4.9
1960	6.0	5.7	5.4	5.0
1961	5.9	5.5	5.2	4.8
1962	5.9	5.5	5.2	4.8
1963	5.9	5.5	5.2	4.8
1964	5.9	5.6	5.3	4.8

Source: Federal Reserve Bulletin (January 1965), 141.

just about the same amount of paper work, overhead cost, and supervision is required of small loans as is required of larger ones. The larger ones are potentially more profitable on a per unit basis (per $1,000 unit) than the smaller ones. Consequently, lower rates may be charged them as opposed to the smaller loans.

Another element making for a structure of interest rates is that nemesis of all creditors: risk. An investor is concerned primarily with being paid back his principal commitment with interest and under the conditions specified in the contract between him and the debtor. His major task is to estimate the probability of not realizing various possible returns. Not all borrowers are of the same grade or quality. Some are naturally better than others. The United States government is unquestionably a "preferred risk" because there is little question that it will meet its obligations. In fact, although there is no riskless investment, United States government securities are the nearest to it; they command less of a risk premium than any other securities. At the other extreme may be the newly formed firm in a new industry, with a differentiated product but with no known sales appeal. The chance of not being repaid in full by this firm may be great. Between these extremes lie many other securities. Table 6-2 indicates the differences that arise from differing degrees of risk associated with one form of security contract: bonds. Notice that government bonds are the least costly, because they carry the least risk. At the other end of the spectrum are securities with a substantially greater likelihood of failing to come close to the expected return.

Table 6-2
Yields on Long-Term Bonds
(December 1964)

Securities	Yields
U.S. Governments	4.16
Corporates:	
Aaa	4.44
Aa	4.50
A	4.58
Baa	4.81

Source: Survey of Current Business (January 1965), 5–20.

As one would expect, variations occur even within a group of rather homogeneous securities. For example, differentials in yields occur in different United States government securities. This is illustrated in Table 6-3.

Table 6-3
Market Yields on Government Securities
(January 1965)

Securities	Yields
Three-month bills	3.87
Six-month certificates	3.96
Nine-to-twelve-month issues	3.93
Three-to-five year issues	4.07
Long-term bonds	4.16

Source: Federal Reserve Bulletin (January 1965), 142.

All these obligations are essentially the same in every respect except one: time. Some come due in a very short period of time—three months or less, for example, in the case of Treasury Bills. Others came due in ten to twenty years. The differential in yields is accounted for almost exclusively by the fact that the further the repayment of principal is from the present, the more uncertain do future events become and there is a natural inclination to prefer a higher interest return on securities having a longer maturity than on those having a shorter one. This is the so-called interest-rate risk associated with long-term securities. Long-term bonds fluctuate more widely in market price when interest rates change than do short-term bonds. Consequently, the uncertainty surrounding the potential price of a ten-year bond is greater than that associated with an obligation having a maturity of only three months. The former will usually command a higher yield than the latter in order to compensate for the additional risk (there are exceptions, however).

From the foregoing it is clear that a whole structure of rates of return to investors exists for securities. This structure is determined primarily by certain risk characteristics and by the nature of the security itself. Among the risk characteristics, three stand out. The first is the uncertainty that the issuing agent will be able to meet all the terms of the bond contract— usually the expected payment of interest and principal. The second risk factor is the interest-rate risk (sometimes called the money risk) and is primarily a function of maturity and the volatility of interest rates. The third is the risk associated with changes in real rates of return caused by changes in the price level. If uncertainty exists as to future general price levels, confidence in the estimates of the real rates of return is reduced. Generally securities with fixed dollar commitments involve more uncertainty as to real rates of return.

Another risk, normally of lesser consideration, is that of market risk. An investment which may be expected to require some time to sell increases uncertainty of the "immediate" liquidation price.

The security contract may also carry a variety of provisions. These provisions vary considerably and every security offered for sale usually will contain a "package" of provisions that vary from most other securities already on the market.[5] These variations in many cases cause some small yield differentials; however, they will warrant further consideration later in the text.

These factors combine to require investors to demand a risk premium. Risk aversion, characteristic of most of our institutions, influences the market to such an extent that premium must be paid to induce the assumption of greater risk. The indifference curve for the market as a whole is the CMC. It indicates the market consensus of indifference. Wealth positions, incomes and attitudes toward risk tend to make individuals prefer a particular point on such a curve.

The fact that some investments may be smaller than average may require that the gross return before administrative costs be large enough so that the net return after costs represents the appropriate "risk point" on the CMC. An investment requiring an unusually large commitment is unavailable for all practical purposes to investors with small wealth positions and, if taken by other investors, prevents them from diversifying into several

---

[5] United States government bonds are probably as close to an exception to this statement that one could find. Even in this case, however, there is considerable lack of "standardization."

investments. Consequently it may have to yield a larger yield than if it were available in smaller amounts.

It has been suggested before that lack of knowledge and the lack of full market mobility leads one to expect that points representing combinations of risk and return not on the *CMC* will exist.

It would be an overwhelming task even to attempt to compute all the risks of many securities in order to offer an empirical *CMC*. But our thesis, based upon our deductive and inductive reasoning, suggests that such a curve should appear as that in Figure 6-8.

The supply of funds, the demand for funds, the attitude of suppliers toward risk—all contribute to the basic form of such a structure. It is to be expected that it will be constantly changing to reflect current conditions. It is in the sense of Figure 6-8 that we refer to a structure of interest rates or, in other words, to a structure of rates of return.

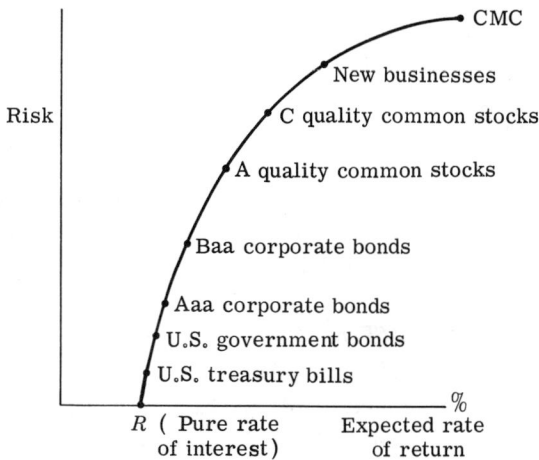

Figure 6-8 Hypothetical Structure of Returns to Investors

SUMMARY

The importance of the interest rate is to be found in the allocation of resources to capital formation. The interest rate is determined by many factors. The aggregate demand for loanable funds represents one group of influences on the rate. It can be broken down into three basic sectors: the consumer, the business, and the government. The aggregate supply of loanable funds is another influence on the interest rate. Essential to the determination of this supply are the commercial banking system, with its ability to create and/or destroy money, and the saving inclinations of individuals, firms, and governments. The Federal Reserve System, through its impact on the reserve position of banks, and the Treasury, especially in its role of manager of the nation's debt, also affect the interest rates. Because of several imperfections in the market for loanable funds, a whole structure of interest rates exists in reality. From this structure of rates we can derive our *CMC*, which represents the indifference curve of the nation toward risk and returns.

SUGGESTED READINGS

CULBERTSON, J. M. "The Term Structure of Interest Rates," *Quarterly Journal of Economics, 71* (November 1957), 485–517.

FISHER, L. "Determinants of Risk Premiums on Corporate Bonds," *Journal of Political Economy, 67* (June 1959), 217–37.

HART, P. E. "The Business Propensity to Save," *The Review of Economic Studies, 29* (February 1962), 147–50.

JACOBY, NEIL H. "The Demand for Funds by American Business Enterprise, Retrospect and Prospect," Parts 1 and 2. *The Journal of Finance, 3* (October 1948), 27–38, and 4 (March 1949), 47–59.

LUCKETT, D. G. "Professor Lutz and the Structure of Interest Rates," *Quarterly Journal of Economics, 73* (February 1959), 131–44.

MALKIEL, B. A. "Expectations, Bond Prices, and the Term Structure of Interest Rates," *Quarterly Journal of Economics, 76* (May 1962), 197–218.

MEISELMAN, DAVID. *The Term Structure of Interest Rates.* Englewood Cliffs, N.J.: Prentice-Hall, Inc., 1962.

MORTON, W. A. "The Structure of the Capital Market and the Price of Money," *American Economic Review, 44* (May 1954), 440–54.

O'LEARY, J. J. "The Institutional Savings-Investment Process and Current Economic Theory," *American Economic Review, 44* (May 1959), 455–70.

QUESTIONS

6.1 (a) Suppose $30 was all that was available to you for spending during the coming month. If a savings bank offered you 5 per cent for the month on whatever dollars you placed with them this month, how much would you invest? If they offered 10 per cent? 20 per cent? 35 per cent? 50 per cent? 100 per cent? (b) In view of your response, comment on the upward-sloping nature of the curve of the supply of loanable funds.

6.2 Can the amount of loanable funds exchanged be different from savings? Explain.

6.3 Discuss the impact of social security and medicare upon the level of saving.

6.4 (a) How does the action by the Federal Reserve to sell bonds on the open market affect the amount of consumer spending? (b) What impact would this have on business investment?

6.5 If the Federal Reserve during full employment of resources permits expansion in bank reserves which is followed by credit creation which is used by banks to make loans and investments, does real saving expand in the economy? Comment.

6.6 If a banker receives new reserves, can he expand his deposits? Can he always find outlets for his funds? Discuss.

6.7 If you expect inflation, how will this affect your liquidity preference? Your inclination and ability to save? Discuss.

6.8 If war were an imminent threat, what would be the forces operating on the liquidity-preference function? Analyze the impact in terms of transactions, precautionary, and speculative motives for holding cash.

6.9 What are the monetary tools used by the Federal Reserve to control the money supply? Discuss the effectiveness of these tools from the view of their effects on the interest-rate structure.

6.10 What factors might a banker consider in determining what rate to charge you, as an individual, for a loan of $100? A loan of $10,000?

6.11 How are monetary policies related to the shape of the *CMC*?

6.12 (a) Using the sources indicated, update Tables 6-1, 6-2, and 6-3. (b) What particular changes do you see?

6.13 Using United States Treasury Bills as a first approximation to the pure interest rate, construct a *CMC* similar to that shown in Figure 6-8.

CHAPTER **7** THE ALLOCATION
OF CAPITAL

One of the earliest lessons learned in the study of economics is that the subject is based upon the principle of scarcity. If all goods and services were in unlimited supply (like the air we breathe), then they would be what economists call *free goods;* there would be no price on them. But almost all goods and services are in limited supply and have a price attached to them. These are called *economic goods.* Most economic goods require some sort of processing by man or other factors of production before they are usable. Because the resources required for such processing are also limited, infinite quantities of various goods and services are technologically impossible to produce and man's desires for goods and services cannot be totally satisfied. If an infinite amount of all goods and services could be produced (fully satisfying man's material wants), it would not matter whether resources were improperly allocated, an excess of any particular good were produced, or factors of production were poorly combined. But because factor resources are scarce, they should be so allocated as to produce that combination of goods and services which results in the greatest total level of satisfaction to society. If the factors are poorly combined, output could be increased by a shift to a more efficient mixture of resources. This would tend to increase society's total satisfaction. In most cases, however, the essential method of allocating resources and goods and services in any economy is through the price mechanism.

Moreover, in general, greater output can be achieved with the use of greater capital. Increasing the amount of capital employed in an economy requires giving up some presently produced consumption goods so that the resources may be diverted to the production of additional capital. Thus capital is created only at a cost—the nonconsumption out of current income or wealth. Cost, in this sense, cannot be precisely measured. What, for example, is the cost of consumption given up by a poor man as opposed to that given up by a wealthy individual? In terms of total satisfaction foregone, the cost to wealthier individuals is likely to be less than it is to poorer ones. And the more advanced and wealthy an economy, the easier it is to save and to increase the absolute quantity of capital.

To the extent that capital is a limited resource, care must be taken to insure that it is efficiently combined with other productive factors and allocated in such a way as to maximize the flow of goods and services to society. But proper allocation of capital is a subject of concern for the economy as a whole, as well as for the individual firm. Society is interested in maximizing the total flow of satisfactions, expressed from our economic standpoint in terms of maximizing the present worth of future income. The firm, or more properly the owners of the firm, are interested in maximizing profits, the return on their investment. The allocation of capital within the firm, among competing or alternative uses, will be discussed in Parts II and III of the book. The allocation of capital in the economy is the brief subject of this chapter.

ALLOCATION IN A PRIVATE FREE-PRICE SYSTEM

Let us direct our attention first to the purely competitive economy, even though the economy of the United States—or any economy, for that matter—is far from being a purely competitive, private, free-price system. The behavior of this theoretical economy presents an interesting illustration of the structure of an abstract economic system. It is instructive to discuss this model because a portion of our existing mixed economy tends to behave in this fashion. It is also a useful comparison for other economic models. Notably, the capital market is a close approximation to the purely competitive model, despite some of its shortcomings.

The Purely Competitive Model

One of the very attractive aspects of the competitive system is the manner in which the system selects the goods and services to be produced. If enough consumers seek certain goods and services, the economy will devote the necessary resources to their production. If enough demand exists for the products, the prices of these products will be high enough, relative to the cost of production, that substantial economic profits can be made by existing producers of these goods. Entrepreneurs in control of capital will be attracted to this investment opportunity in the expectation of participating in the profits being generated in this industry because businessmen are inclined to invest in those areas of production where potential profits are the greatest. Thus, any shifts in consumer demand for or costs of producing different commodities will lead eventually to shifts in the volume of production of the various goods demanded. Freely moving prices are the characteristic mechanism by which such an economy indirectly (and impersonally) makes decisions about which goods shall be produced (based on the profit motive), and therefore how the resources shall be allocated among industries and firms in the economy. They are the core of the competitive system's functioning.

If, for example, the demand for television sets were increasing, prices, at a low-volume level of production, would rise and profits would tend to increase. Because entrepreneurs outside the television industry are interested in employing capital in activities which are expected to yield the highest profits and the largest rate of return on investment, those capable of doing so will enter the production of television sets. The entrance of more firms in response to the potential profits that are available thus draws more resources into the production of television sets. As production is increased and supply increases relative to demand, prices will tend to fall and profits will tend to disappear, choking off further additions of resources to this investment alternative.

This example briefly illustrates the behavior of a perfectly competitive economy (in this case assumed to be purely competitive) and the forces which stimulate the allocation of the limited supply of capital in the economy among competing industries. This is illustrated by Figure 7-1. In State I, at time $t = 0$, the industry produces 100 sets, operates at less than full capacity, sells them for $100 each and receives an annual rate of return on investment of 1 per cent. This return is not likely to stimulate entrepreneurs to seek additional capital for investment in this industry as it would not be sufficient to pay them for the cost of capital and the risks they assume when they make the investment.

In State II, time $t = 1$, consumers have increased their demand for television sets while the capacity to produce remains constant. Firms in the industry find it worthwhile to produce at full capacity, for at this level profits are greatest; it is assumed that entrepreneurs still do not find additional returns on additional investments sufficient to warrant an increase in capacity.

In State III, time $t = 2$, consumers again have increased their demand for the industry's product. Relative to State II, price increased and supply remained constant at full capacity. Average returns now amount to about 23 per cent on existing investment. At this point, entrepreneurs decide returns from additional investment will more than compensate them for the additional cost of capital and the additional risks involved. Consequently, existing firms will increase aggregate investment or new firms will enter the industry, or some combination of both might result. As capacity cannot be expanded instantaneously, they must wait until time $t = 3$ to provide the greater volume of sets which consumers have been seeking.

By State IV, time $t = 3$, capacity has increased and although demand remained at the same level as in State III, prices are lower, the volume is

State I, $t = 0$	State II, $t = 1$	State III, $t = 2$	State IV, $t = 3$

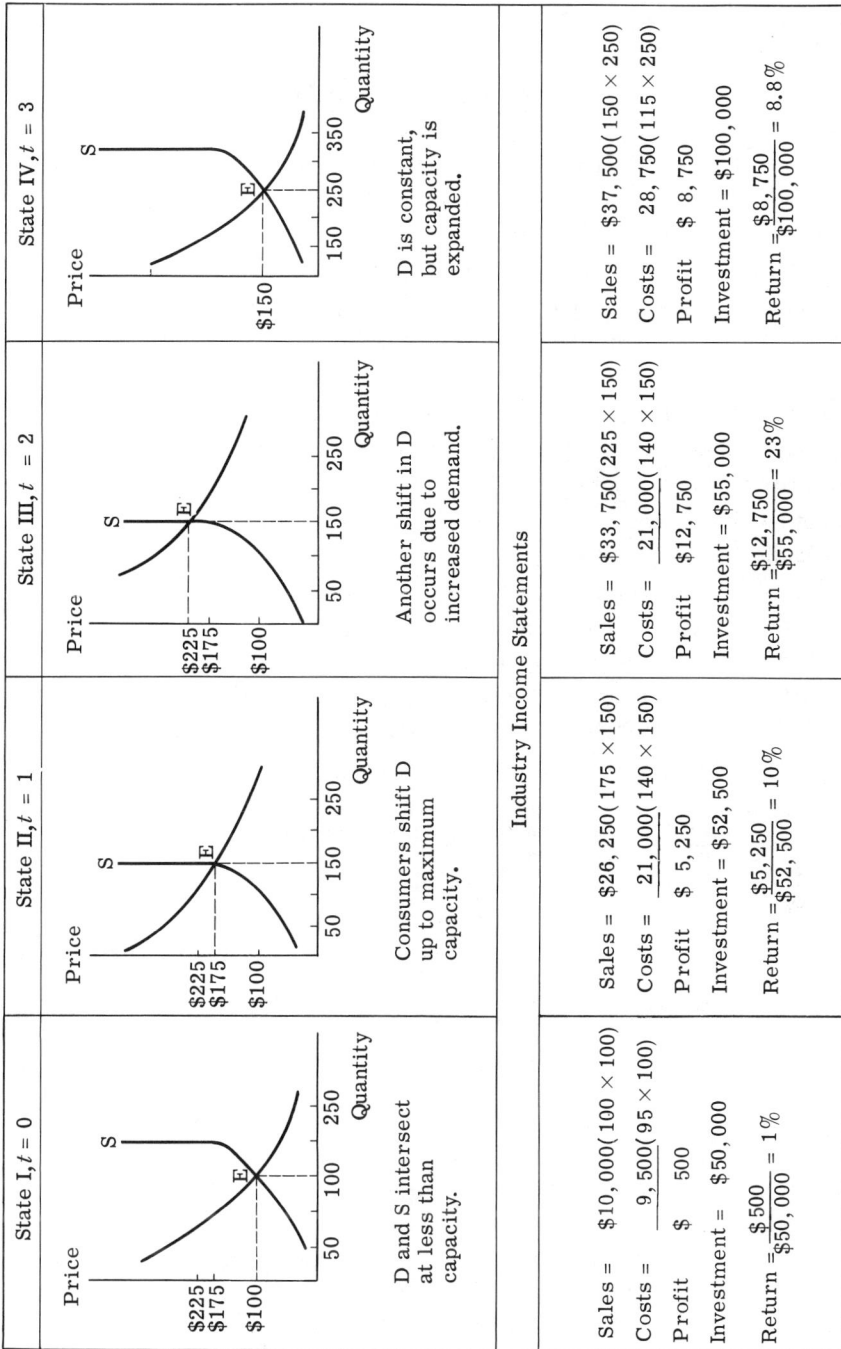

State I, $t = 0$

D and S intersect at less than capacity.

State II, $t = 1$

Consumers shift D up to maximum capacity.

State III, $t = 2$

Another shift in D occurs due to increased demand.

State IV, $t = 3$

D is constant, but capacity is expanded.

Industry Income Statements

State I:

Sales = $10,000(100 \times 100)$

Costs = $9,500(95 \times 100)$

Profit $ 500

Investment = $50,000

Return = $\dfrac{\$500}{\$50,000} = 1\%$

State II:

Sales = $26,250(175 \times 150)$

Costs = $21,000(140 \times 150)$

Profit $ 5,250

Investment = $52,500

Return = $\dfrac{\$5,250}{\$52,500} = 10\%$

State III:

Sales = $33,750(225 \times 150)$

Costs = $21,000(140 \times 150)$

Profit $12,750

Investment = $55,000

Return = $\dfrac{\$12,750}{\$55,000} = 23\%$

State IV:

Sales = $37,500(150 \times 250)$

Costs = $28,750(115 \times 250)$

Profit $ 8,750

Investment = $100,000

Return = $\dfrac{\$8,750}{\$100,000} = 8.8\%$

Figure 7-1 Development of Industry T

greater, and the rate of return on the aggregate investment is now lower. Investment would continue to expand as time passed, as long as entrepreneurs believed sufficient returns could be received that would at least pay for the capital employed and compensate them for the anticipated risks that are associated with the investment.

In the whole economy, similar dynamic changes in response to changes in consumer demand are occurring in many industries. In some industries, demand may be falling and investment will gradually be reduced, whereas in others, investment will be increasing because of increasing demand. Thus investment in the whole economy during a time period is the sum of investment in all industries (some negative investment and some positive).[1] To secure the resources needed to expand facilities, the entrepreneur(s) will seek funds (money and credit) in the capital market. The aggregate demand for funds by entrepreneurs is roughly represented in the current curve of marginal efficiency of capital for the economy. If the model of the capital market were represented as in Chapter 6 (ignoring risk), the demand for funds might be represented by MEC in Figure 7-2.

In this riskless economy, entrepreneurs interested in building factories to produce television sets would constitute part of the total funds supplied (at 5 per cent) of $30 billion, part of which would be allocated to expanding the capacity to produce television sets. The $30 billion would be allocated to those projects for which the anticipated return equals at least 5 per cent and no funds would be allocated to those expected to yield less.

[1] Real investment is measured in economics, however, as the sum of negative and positive investments in plant, equipment, and inventories, excluding other types of assets of the firm.

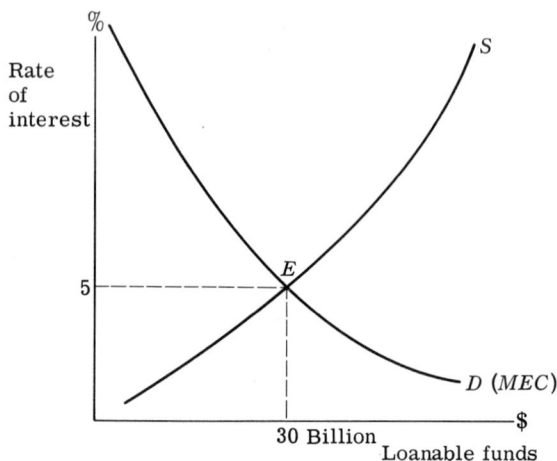

Figure 7-2   Demand for and Supply of Funds

On the marginal efficiency of capital schedule, as illustrated by Figure 7-3, $30 billion would be allocated to all the projects to the left of the $30 billion mark. If we assume the capacity of the television industry to double and anticipated a return of 12 per cent (requiring $450 million), it could be represented by Block T in Figure 7-3. That is, $450 million of the $30 billion total would be allocated to entrepreneurs expanding television-set production. This demand is derived from the increased demand for television sets by consumers. It is in this way that the economy provides the mechanism which enables capital to be allocated according to consumer wishes.

As established in Chapters 5 and 6, however, this allocation model is excessively simple. It ignores the differential risks of various projects requiring capital. To illustrate, the television industry expansion project mentioned above may be represented as a point, T, in a two-dimensional graph such as that in Figure 7-4. This point reflects its particular combination of expected rate of return and risk. For the whole economy during the same time period, the state of alternative projects seeking capital is represented by numerous points in this two-dimensional illustration. There exists, we assume, a *CMC* in the economy representing the terms of risk and expected return of run-of-the-mill investments well-known in the

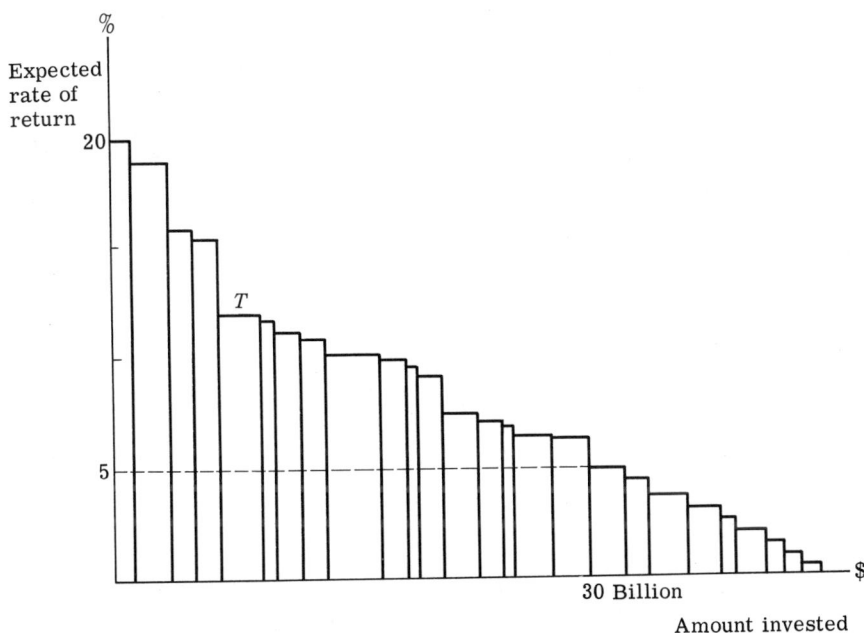

Figure 7-3   Marginal Efficiency of Capital Schedule

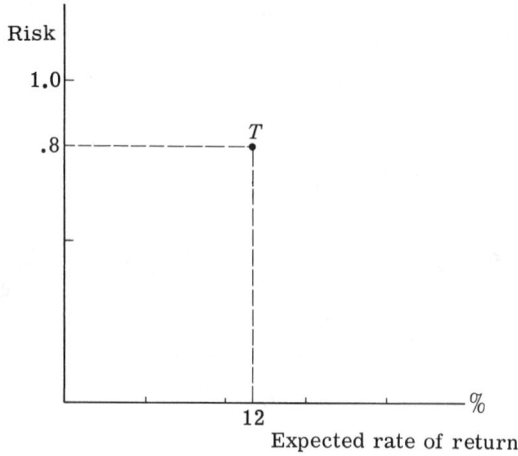

Figure 7-4   Risk, Expected Rate of Return, and Industry T

economy (such as shown in Figure 7-5). Recall that the *CMC* may be viewed as a curve of best fit toward which the majority of well-known investment opportunities in the economy tend to gravitate. All investments lying on the *CMC* represent average rates of return, given their risks. By *average rate of return* we mean one that is necessary to compensate the investor for the sum of pure interest—5 per cent in this case—and a premium for risk. Anything to the left of *CMC* would represent an investment overvalued by investors. Anything to the right of *CMC* is an "undervalued" case; that is, there are profits accruing to their investments in excess of what are needed to induce persons or firms to undertake them.

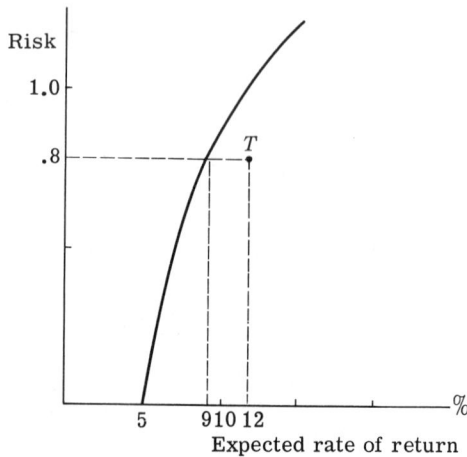

Figure 7-5   The Capital Market Curve and Industry T

Thus, in Figure 7-5 the project indicated by Point T represents an investment alternative obviously more attractive than the average investments available. If competing suppliers of capital were well-informed as to risk and return, the television industry ought to be able to secure their $450 million of capital at a rate of about 9 per cent, paying a risk premium of 4 per cent above the pure rate of interest of 5 per cent. Investment would tend to continue to go into the industry and over time the expected rate of return would decline to 9 per cent (and/or risk may increase) at which time further investment would not be forthcoming. Although the firms of the television industry should secure capital at 9 per cent, knowledge of sources of funds may be inadequate and they may pay more; they could also pay less than 9 per cent if suppliers were unaware of the *CMC* or made errors in evaluating the risk or the expected rate of return.

Several interesting observations can be made regarding the *CMC*. If there were a perfectly competitive economy, including the funds market, all investments would lie along the *CMC* in equilibrium. Both suppliers and demanders of funds have *knowledge* of all investments and are of such equal size that no one supplier or one demander may influence price; demanders compete for funds and suppliers compete for outlets. Individual suppliers will not, therefore, be able to secure outlets for their funds to the right of the *CMC* for their knowledge of all outlets and competition will force the price of such outlets up to the point where it rests on the *CMC*. Individual demanders competing for funds will likewise, being informed of supply, be unable to secure funds at more favorable rates than those offered on the *CMC*. This would hold true not only for securities but also for real investments such as an investment in the production of television sets. The *CMC* model represents equilibrium conditions of the whole capital market. The *CMC*, on the one hand, represents the feelings of all demanders of funds regarding risk and their expected returns (ER), and, on the other, those of suppliers of funds regarding risk and their expected returns, even though demanders and suppliers are often separate and distinct elements of the capital market.[2]

Any deviations from the *CMC* would tend to put in motion a whole series of actions and reactions which would return the system to equilibrium. Our television industry example (Point T in Figure 7-5) is helpful in illustrating this point. As depicted, the risk magnitude of this investment is assumed to be .8. For average, run-of-the-mill investments of equal risk, a rate of return of 9 per cent is the most that can be expected. For the tele-

---

[2] Retention of earnings can be viewed as part of the supply of capital in the market in the sense that this source of funds competes with all other sources. It also satisfies demands for funds.

vision industry, however, ER is 12 per cent—at this point in time, better than average. For any number of reasons—such as lack of adequate information, lack of mobility of resources, or different appraisals of risk and ER—suppliers of capital are willing to provide funds at 9 per cent. The difference between the 9 per cent average cost of capital and the 12 per cent ER represents excess profits to the television industry. Knowledge of this fact is presumed to be generally available and there are assumed no effective barriers to entry, so that new firms will be formed to produce television sets or existing firms will expand output. The shares of the market of previous producers will be reduced if new firms enter. In either event, the cost of factor resources will probably be increased and prices of television sets may be reduced, all causing either a reduction in expected returns, an increase in risk, or some combination of both. If the market is perfectly competitive, T must settle somewhere on the CMC.

This brief exercise is useful for explaining general tendencies in the capital market. It demonstrates that, in the absence of any barrier, an investment outlet should not long stay to the right of the capital market line. This is not to say that in the real world investments do not exist to the right of the CMC. On the contrary, they do. Trademarks, patents, imperfect knowledge on the part of investors, and other considerations all are effective restraints to the rapid entry of firms into an industry experiencing a high expected return or the expansion of existing ones. Nevertheless the general tendencies exist and capital will tend to be allocated to projects to the right of the CMC. As illustrated in Figure 7-6(a), investment projects to the right of the CMC will receive allocations of funds in the economy and projects to the left will tend to be ignored. Assume for the moment that the points to the right of the CMC in Figure 7-6(a) require an amount of capital exceeding that available on these terms. These conditions would not last long. Projects competing for a limited supply of funds would bid up the price, screening out those projects with less attractive combinations of risk and expected return than others. The rise in rates would tend to call forth some increased supply. The new CMC might be represented as in Figure 7-6(b), with a pure rate of interest of 6 per cent. The new pure rate of interest results from changes in the relationship between the quantity demanded of loanable funds and the quantity supplied. An increase would indicate that the former exceeded the latter and vice versa. In this model, as in the loanable-funds model, the allocation of capital is in part a response to shifts in consumer demand for goods and services. The upward shift in the structure of interest rates could be attributed to an increase in demand while the supply of funds remained the same.

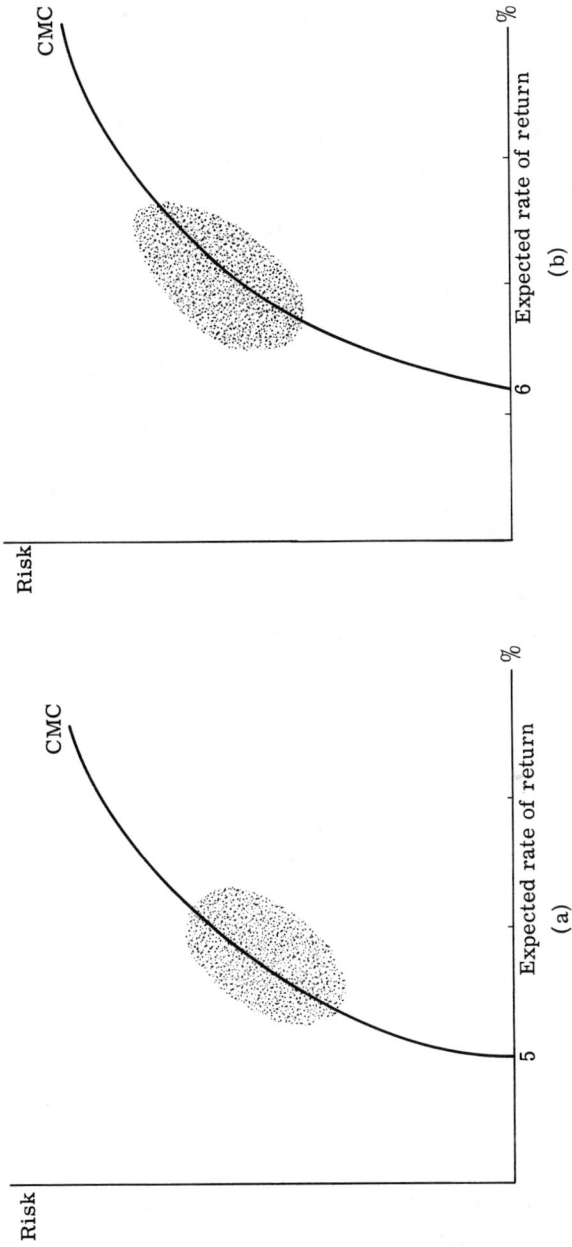

Figure 7-6   A Shift in the CMC

Businessmen hire factors of production and owners of productive resources will seek the employer who offers them the highest price—whether the price be wages, interest, or rent. Consequently, owners of productive resources are encouraged to shift their employment to those activities that receive the greatest rewards.

Entrepreneurs presumably always tend toward the most profitable mix of resources to be used in production. Traditional marginal analysis of the firm indicates that the firm under price competition will seek to operate at the most profitable output level—that is, where its marginal cost equals its marginal revenue. The firm will expand output so long as the additional costs are less than the sales value of its marginal product. Analogously, expansion of inputs used will continue so long as additional revenues derived are greater than the prices of the additional productive factors. Thus the businessman hires additional workers and buys additional raw materials and equipment as long as the wages and capital costs he pays are less than the amount each new unit of input will add to his revenues. Through his desire to maximize profits, he acts in a manner consistent with consumer preferences by bidding factors into his firm and away from less valuable uses. He therefore adds resources as long as the worth to consumers of the addition of these resources exceeds that which entrepreneurs of other businesses will bid for their services. In this way, the firm, seeking to maximize profits, provides an effective service in helping to allocate resources according to consumer preferences and the interests of resource owners. In other words, factors will be employed in a most efficient manner and in such quantities that the marginal unit of each resource will be contributing an equal value to the product (per unit cost of the resource).

At an abstract level of analysis, the optimum allocation of the factors of production in the economy would exist when the present value of the sum of future satisfactions of individuals is maximized. This would mean that the allocation of capital among alternative uses is such that no increase in total consumer satisfaction could be obtained by any reallocation of capital among the firms producing the existing goods and services, including the production of capital, which is, in effect, the allocation between current goods and future goods. At the optimum, the last unit of any resource added to a particular use would yield the same economic value in all possible uses for this resource. The only objective way by which we can measure consumer satisfaction is by the prices consumers are willing to pay for goods. In a purely competitive economy, where buyers are indifferent to the source of supply, prices may reflect that satisfaction. Also, in the purely competitive system, no restriction would be placed upon the entry of firms or resources into an industry or their exit from it. If there were perfect mobility of resources, equilibrium would exist when there were no firms or resources entering or leaving an industry; marginal revenues would be equilibrated to marginal costs for all firms; and all factor payments would be equal to the marginal value product of resources supplied. In this event, no alternative uses would exist in which any resources could receive any greater amount of economic value. Capital, then, would be allocated to those uses consistent with consumer preferences and used in combination with other factors in an efficient manner. Theoretically, capital would be employed by a firm (allocated to a firm) up to the point where the cost of the last unit of capital employed was just equal to the return from investing the last unit of capital. In a realistic economy, the whole stock of capital is not perfectly mobile and firms therefore may not be able to secure the capital desired even though it could be employed at a rate of return greater than some existing uses.

The Government in the Competitive Economy

So far we have discussed only the private aspects of the allocation of factor services under the purely competitive system. The government in this system theoretically would expand the production of social goods and services to the point where the marginal social benefit of these goods is just equal to the marginal social cost. *Marginal social benefit* is the additional benefit that society derives from the production of additional units of a social good or service. *Marginal social cost* is the additional sacrifice resulting from having a marginal unit of resource used to produce the social good in question rather than an alternative private good.

The collective nature of most social goods, however, makes it quite impossible to use such a mechanism based upon individual exchange. Indeed, an important characteristic of social goods and services is that government output is not divisable—no individual can have exclusive possession of the goods. These goods and services are customarily allocated to all members of the community by a political process rather than through a market mechanism. In a democratic nation, the individual citizens voice decisions involving the diversion of economic resources from private to public use by means of the ballot box. And although the benefits of social goods theoretically accrue to all individuals, the distribution of the tax burden determines who pays for the costs of public goods and services. Taxation legally takes power over resources and indirectly these taxes are voted upon by society. Thus the costs of social goods normally are covered by the process of taxation (although occasionally by inflation).

Some Inadequacies of the Competitive Model

The competitive model of the economy appears to be theoretically sound, but the workings of the system are not without their difficulties. The reliance of the system upon the consumers' dollar-voting as a way of choosing the goods and services to be produced ignores the fact that not all citizens have equal voting power, nor is it necessarily clear that they should. Different capabilities, in themselves, will generate unequal incomes. But the price system registers only actual money demands; it can give very little consideration to desires not backed up by the ability to pay. Consequently, the desires of the poor regarding what should be produced have less influence than the desires of citizens with more income. A wealthy man's basic satisfactions may be easily taken care of with his income. He may be more interested in allocating more of society's productive effort toward the expansion of output in the future and therefore may save a considerable portion of his income, stimulating the production of real capital goods.

As a result of free, individual consumer choices, the system also tends to create a degree of instability and insecurity. Unpredictable shifts in consumer demand create risks for the entrepreneur—the risk of not being able to recover all of the capital committed to the provision of certain goods or services. Whether or not this is a necessary prerequisite of the system, there has been increasing emphasis toward security and stability in the United States economy (which is only partially based on the competitive model) at the expense of maximizing the private consumer's influence over resource use. Society, through its government, hesitates to allow complete freedom of movement of resources as consumer demands tend to shift. On the other hand, there is also an unwillingness to infringe upon the freedom of the individual.

During periods of prosperity, there usually tends to be a relatively heavy allocation of factor resources to the production of capital goods and consumer durables. On the other hand, in recessions there tends to be a lower level of investment of resources into these items and proportionately more factors are devoted to the production of consumer nondurable goods and services. In these periods of economic prosperity and decline, there is little reason to expect that the plans for the allocation of resources between consumer goods production and capital formation will exactly match the plans for allocation of income between current spending and the saving of individuals and businesses, especially in a perfectly competitive system. Consequently, the allocation of resources between future consumption (investment) and present (consumption) does not always "jibe" with the desires of people to save. As long as this is so, there will be destabilizing forces in the economy. Moreover, those investing in real capital goods cannot turn the process on and off as if it were a continuous flow so that investment may continue to go on. Thus the level of investment of capital goods may not shift with the desires for savings and a disequilibrium condition results, setting off the dynamic forces of the economy which tend to restore equilibrium.

Even in a very competitive economy there would realistically exist certain short-run restrictions on mobility of resources—a certain inertia toward the shift of resources to uses in which they would receive maximum payment. In reality, resources may be highly immobile for extended periods of time. Because of these mobility imperfections, economic profits will not in fact be completely eliminated and the proper resource allocation will perhaps never obtain the theoretically desirable state of equilibrium. Only the more mobile productive resources will be allocated in a way such that the anticipated value of marginal products will tend toward the average expenditures on them, reflecting the opportunity cost [3] of not using such resources in other uses.

In each firm and each industry, the resources were assumed to be employed to the point where the marginal (and average) expenditures equaled the sale value of the marginal product. The value of the marginal product is the measure of the factors' worth in this use. But in a condition of less than full employment resulting from the instability of the system, problems may be encountered in moving resources from one use to another. Theoretically, a resource moves to an employment in which it makes the maximum contribution to the production of the goods desired. Some employed resources, however, hesitate to accept employment and remain idle because their expectations are for future, better opportunities. Therefore, they withhold their services in order to take advantage of future openings. These idle resources remain unemployed and limit national income. Unemployment compensation for labor and land (not capital), as it is used in the United States, results in making even less likely the employment of marginal resources, because for some resources their marginal revenue products may be too near the payment they receive under unemployment compensation to bring about mobility. Although the allocation of employable resources may follow consumer preferences, the allocation between employment and unemployment may not.

Consequently, the monetary and fiscal activities of the government attempt to bring about a degree of stabilization in the aggregate level of

[3] An opportunity cost is the amount that could be received by a factor in its best alternative use.

economic activity and to promote full employment. In fact, many governmental activities are designed to do just that. We also saw that the economic system distributes incomes according to the economic contribution of productive resources in their most remunerative employments and that therefore unequal incomes must exist. The government may—and does, through its taxing and spending process—attempt to redistribute incomes. The redistribution of income unfavorably affects factor incentives as well as the allocation of resources between the public and private sectors. The employment of these tools to achieve the desired stabilization and redistribution of income produces sufficient additional impacts on the economy so that it no longer behaves as the purely competitive model.

ALLOCATION IN A PARTIALLY COMPETITIVE ECONOMY

The Private Economy

The economy of the United States does not and has not behaved like the model of the purely competitive system. In some industries the competitive model may seem appropriate, but for a large portion of the economy this model does not explain the behavior of our system. In most industries competition takes a considerably different form. Indeed, we customarily describe our economy as a *mixed economy* because it possesses some of the characteristics of the competitive system and some of the characteristics of a monopolistic system. A great deal of the competition that does exist in a mixed economy is of a nonprice nature, and resources tend to be allocated in a manner unlike that of the purely competitive system. Advertising, for example, plays a significant role in the allocation mechanism. It attempts to attract customers to a particular product and, in some cases, creates an illusion of product differentiation which may not in reality exist, but which permits charging higher prices. Advertising certainly affects consumers' ideas of what satisfactions are important and how they should vote their consumer dollars, and it may also be informative, leading consumers to select purchases more nearly in accord with underlying preferences.

In the mixed economy, if too few resources are allocated to industries characterized by monopoly conditions—which implies that entry is at best difficult—then a disproportionate amount of resources will be forced into the more competitive areas where entry and exit are more easily effected. Consequently, too many resources may be devoted to the production of goods in competitive industries and too few factors may be used in monopolistic industries. In industries characterized by monopoly or monopolistic competition, the consumer may pay a relatively high price for an unduly limited product, for the monopolist maximizes profits at a volume of output which is less than the optimum that would prevail under perfectly competitive conditions.

In some circumstances near-monopoly conditions may exist as a result of inherent natural economies of large-scale production; in other cases monopolistic conditions are contrived. Trademarks, patents, and advertising are often responsible for restricting competitive influences. The patent system of the United States provides an incentive to innovation and supports new investment, but it also grants a temporary monopoly. This restrictive form of economic activity reduces the incentive to lower costs which otherwise would exist in a competitive situation. Yet such restrictions upon the entry of others tends to propagate existing profits and distort resource allocations. Not only does profit by contrived scarcity limit incentives to lower cost, but the inflexibility of prices reduces the sensitivity of the supply of goods in response to shifts in consumer dollar voting.

Furthermore, because it is unlikely that such firms would be fully aware of changes in consumers' tastes and therefore may overproduce in one industry and underproduce in another, businessmen in our economy must operate with less than perfect information. They simply do not know completely the methods of other producers and, consequently, costs cannot fall as rapidly as desired.

The problem of a mixed economy is that of achieving reasonably effective workable competition. On the whole, the United States economic system remains a price-oriented private-enterprise system. The price system is not perfect, but neither are any known alternatives.

The allocation of private capital by business firms in the United States during 1961 is shown in Table 7-1. The figures given are only for plant and

Table 7-1
Allocation of Funds for Plant and Equipment Expenditures, 1965
(First Quarter Annual Rates)

Industry	Billions of Dollars Expended
Manufacturers (durable goods)	8.76
Manufacturers (nondurable goods)	8.96
Mining	1.16
Railroads	1.52
Other transportation	2.12
Public utilities	5.08
Communications, commercial and other	14.72
Total	42.32

Source: U.S. Department of Commerce, Office of Business Economics, *Survey of Current Business* (June 1964), S-2.

equipment expenditures. Firms also allocate funds to inventories and financial assets which include cash, highly marketable securities, and receivables.

The Public Domain

In the production of some goods there may arise certain hidden costs of production which may not be paid by the producer but may be borne involuntarily by society. These costs are frequently difficult to measure and to associate with any one given producer. For example, in the process of refining oil a considerable amount of soot may result which may contribute to smog conditions and other problems for society resulting in what is referred to as a *social cost*. Social cost is not included in the cost calculations of producers; therefore, the prices charged will be lower than the true private and social costs justify, although in the long run society may be charged to cover the total cost by means of taxation, the proceeds of which will be used to control, for example, smog or water pollution.

In certain other cases, activity may result in social benefits, which are not reflected in the prices as determined by consumer voting. The social benefits of educating members of the populace will not be entirely measured in the revenues received by the members from the educational process. Nevertheless, as long as society feels it is desirable to provide such education, it simultaneously decides to support and subsidize the educational process for individuals.

In a mixed economy, a political process of sorts decides upon the allocation of resources between the public and private sectors. The assumption underlying the proper allocation of resources is that the individuals in the economy make considered decisions and exert their influence in equal weight upon their political representatives. The argument continues that these representatives achieve an approximation to proper allocation which, under a competitive system, would exist when the marginal social cost equals the marginal social benefit. Other arguments suggest that a bias exists in the system so that too few resources are devoted to public purposes. Others would argue that "government does too much." In any event, when the number and amount of social costs that must be met by society and the collective benefits that accrue to many public expenditures are fully considered, it is evident that government participation in and influence on economic activity is considerable.

Society is requiring an increasing proportion of our resources to be expended by the government for collective consumption, although these resources are not expended entirely for consumption items (goods and services which satisfy wants directly); governments also make capital additions (goods and services that give satisfactions indirectly and over an extended time period) through highway improvement, and the construction of bridges, school facilities, dams, and so forth. These expenditures generally enable private business to operate at lower costs than would be the case had the public real capital not been created. In this regard as well as others, public capital is a necessary element in any economic advancement.

Capital allocation among firms in our economy can be analyzed with the same models discussed in earlier sections. There we saw that all resources, capital included, tend to be allocated to firms which can afford to pay the highest price. Firms capable of paying relatively higher prices are those with the greatest profit expectations. Thus we would expect them to be most eager to secure capital and most capable of getting it. But, given the realities of our mixed economy, the allocation of capital is affected by the shortcomings of the competitive system, by the impacts of restrictions upon competition, by the immobility of resources, and by the influence of the government in restricting resource mobility and directing some resources into less productive areas. Nevertheless, there is a general tendency to allocate capital to those areas which are most able to pay even though their ability to pay may be influenced by governmental activities or monopolistic practices.

ALLOCATION IN A SOCIALISTIC SYSTEM

Our economy is frequently described by the adjective, *capitalistic*, because it is characterized by extensive use of privately owned capital. In our mixed economy, the legal property rights of individuals are only relative; they are limited by society. Society determines how much of its property a man may pass on to his heirs. Society determines how much the owners of public utility companies can earn and how, in some degree, they must run their business. Thus ownership of capital in our economy is not unrestricted. In fact, most of society's economic income—human earning power—cannot be capitalized at all into private property; human earning power is forbidden by law to be considered property, for man is not free to sell himself.

Under socialistic economic systems, as theoretically described, productive property is collectively owned by society and the returns from real capital goods accrue to the government rather than directly to individuals. The factor resource payment to land and capital is paid to the government, which then decides how this income is to be distributed among them as social dividends. Even in this type of system, the final cost of consumer goods must include the sum total of all factor costs necessary to produce the good. The demand for a factor in this case, as in the private competitive economy, is an indirect or derived demand, dependent upon the demand for consumer goods. If the full factor cost of each of the factors of production were not included in consumer good costs, the resource would not be allocated according to its optimum use and the market pricing of finished goods would not lead to maximum consumer satisfaction.

In cases in which "socialism" has been tried, the economy has in fact been only a mixed economy, not fully socialistic, and the balance between public and private ownership of productive resources has varied. The differences between our economy and the semisocialistic economies are not too significant. In Sweden and Denmark, for example, the role of private property is somewhat limited in the sense that some industries have been nationalized and the unearned profits from increases in land value are also frequently limited; but even in our free-enterprise economy the rights of private property are somewhat restricted. The socialistic economies rely more heavily upon coordinated planning than on the profit motive to guide the economy. Advertising is customarily restricted; workers and professional people are encouraged to develop skills of craftsmanship rather than motives of profit maximization. The government, through its taxing and spending power, attempts to reduce wealth and redistribute individual incomes.

These so-called semisocialistic economies might be considered just an extension of the trend to the welfare state in the United States. To date the operations of socialistic economies have not significantly interfered with the detailed allocation of capital among the various industries of the economy; most of these nations are content to blend the market mechanism with government planning. The government attempts to set the aggregative level of capital creation and, through planning boards and by other means, to influence the economy to attain the goals set. They remain largely responsive to consumer dollar votes for the types of services they choose to produce and permit relatively free flow of factor resources among employments. For example, using the loanable-funds allocation model, the government might consider setting the pure rate of interest at an artificially low rate such as the 4 per cent shown in Figure 7-7, where market equilibrium occurs at the intersection of D and S_1.

In this case, however, the gap between supply of funds as indicated by S_1 and the amount demanded requires the government to supply the additional amount from their coffers (which might contribute to inflation), to force increased saving through rationing to restrict consumption (in which

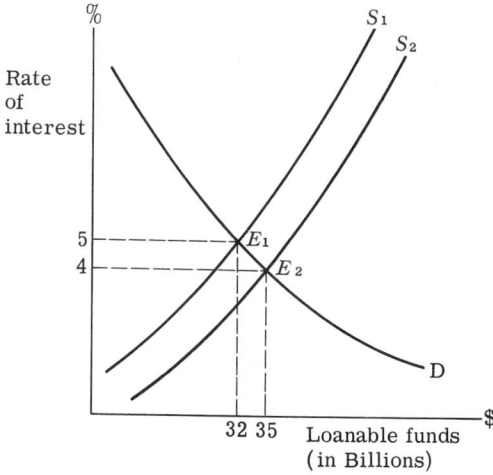

Figure 7-7   Contrived Equilibrium in a Socialist State

case the supply, S_2, would shift to equilibrium at 4 per cent), or to ration $32 billion in capital to priority uses. For example, building permits might not be granted for construction of recreational facilities.

Although it is chiefly the aggregative level of capital formation with which these economic systems are basically concerned, there are some industries in which capital allocation may come under close scrutiny and management. These industries are usually key ones in the economy, with the economic well-being and growth of society heavily dependent on them. Moreover, those industries typically are efficient, large-scale producers and tend to behave as monopolies.

The operations of these economic systems are little different from those of many underdeveloped countries of the world that seek their real capital by importation. In both, the foreign exchange control system is frequently used to determine what types of capital and which industries shall receive the limited supply of foreign currencies necessary to secure the equipment for their industry. Consequently, it is difficult to distinguish clearly the socialist societies from many of the capitalistic societies. In the United States the aggregate levels of investment and capital formation are strongly influenced by our government, and the government agencies involved are primarily of an advisory or "staff" relationship to the operating or line segments of our federal government. In the socialistic economies, this function of influence upon the aggregate levels of investment is performed by control or planning agencies which are more closely tied to the executive branch of the government.

In the socialistic economy, capital goods are recognized to have a net productivity. Consequently, a price must be attached to capital, and the price is generally referred to as an interest rate. This is used to allocate savings of the economy to their best use. Whatever the amount of national income society has decided to invest in capital goods, the actual allocation to various productive uses cannot be made well without an interest rate to screen out uses with low productive potentials. (The interest rate, among other things, is a rationing device of capital in capitalistic systems as well.) In most of the socialistic systems, however, it would be argued that the rate of interest should not also determine the allocation between current consumption and the production of capital goods, as it does in the competitive model. In the socialist system, the decision of how much should be saved and invested in capital is determined by the state in light of national and social needs, not by individuals. In other words, the government attempts to set the interest rate for the economy. The level of saving and capital accumulation having been determined, the interest rate is used to allocate the supply of capital to its most efficient uses in order of the priority of alternative projects. The allocation of capital in today's socialistic economy does not tend to interfere directly with the allocation of capital resources to the production of goods; it interferes only with the allocation of effort between present and future consumption. Only in the communist economies, such as the U.S.S.R., does the government attempt to exert complete control over capital allocation among productive activities; in other economies, this type of allocation is left in large degree to the influence of consumers through their purchases of goods and services.

SUMMARY

The limited supply of productive resources—land, labor, and capital—and the unfulfilled nature of consumer wants dictates the scarcity of goods and services. In all forms of economic systems in use—capitalistic, socialistic, and communistic—scarce factors must be efficiently allocated for society to approach any maximum satisfaction from the limited productive availability. Consequently, an interest rate—the price of capital—is used by all systems to allocate capital to its various alternative uses. The interest rate, however, may not be freely used in any economy to allocate the production between current and future consumption. In capitalistic economies, allocation between current consumption and the production of capital goods is influenced by the state in an indirect manner; in socialistic economies, this allocation becomes a more direct responsibility of the government.

SUGGESTED READINGS

BORNSTEIN, MORRIS. "The Soviet Price System," *American Economic Review,* 52 (March 1962), 64–103.

FOLDES, LUCIEN. "Imperfect Capital Markets and the Theory of Investment," *The Review of Economic Studies,* 28 (June 1961), 182–95.

GOPAL, M. H. "Allocation of Capital Resources in a Planned Economy," *Indian Economic Journal,* 3 (October 1955), 127–53.

GRANICK, DAVID. "On Patterns of Technological Choice in Soviet Industry," *American Economic Review,* 52 (May 1962), 149–57.

HAAVELMO, TRYGVE. *A Study in the Theory of Investment,* Parts II and III. Chicago: University of Chicago Press, 1960.

HIRSHLEIFER, JACK. "Efficient Allocation of Capital in an Uncertain World," *American Economic Review,* 54 (May 1964), 77–85.

KEIRSTEAD, B. S. *Capital, Interest and Profits.* New York: John Wiley & Sons, Inc., 1959.

LESTER, R. D. "Advertising, Resource Allocation, and Employment," *Journal of Marketing,* 15 (October 1950), 158–66.

LINTNER, J. "Effect of Corporate Taxation on Real Investments," *American Economic Review,* 44 (May 1954), 520–34.

MALINVAUD, E. "Capital Accumulation and Efficient Allocation of Resources," *Econometrica,* 21 (April 1953), 233–68.

NEVIN, E. "Social Priorities and the Flow of Capital," *Three Banks Review,* 19 (September 1953), 27–43.

SAMUELSON, PAUL A. "Parable and Realism in Capital Theory: The Surrogate Production Function," *The Review of Economic Studies,* 29 (June 1962), 207–18.

SOLOW, ROBERT M. *Capital Theory and the Rate of Return.* Amsterdam: North-Holland Publishing Company, 1963.

―――. "Substitution and Fixed Proportions in the Theory of Capital," *The Review of Economic Studies,* 29 (June 1962), 207–18.

QUESTIONS

7.1 Under what conditions of the purely competitive model will the best factor mix be obtained?

7.2 What factors determine the price of capital? Compare these factors with those determining the price of a good, such as a gallon of milk.

7.3 How would you expect the impact of a 100 per cent inheritance tax upon all estates to affect the allocation of capital in the United States between current and future goods?

7.4 What are some examples in our economy that illustrate less than complete mobility in the factors of production?

7.5 How has the federal government's policy toward the agricultural industry tended to affect the distribution of the limited supply of resources in the United States?

7.6 What contribution do government capital expenditures make to society's total income?

7.7 Compare the allocation of capital in a mixed capitalistic system with that of a socialistic system.

7.8 Should the interest rate determine the allocation of effort between current consumption and capital goods? Why?

7.9 What is the result when an economy attempts to exclude costs of capital from the pricing of goods and services?

7.10 What would be the impact on a socialistic economy which set an artificially low price on capital?

7.11 What would be the impact on the *CMC* of (a) increasing uncertainty of economic conditions, (b) an increase in liquidity preference (c) increasing aversions to risk by suppliers of capital and (d) an increase in profitable innovations available?

7.12 In your household, can you determine what proportion of your total resources are devoted to current consumption and what proportion to capital creation? How is this created capital allocated among members of your household?

7.13 If you were an economic planner of an underdeveloped country and were given aid amounting to $100 million, how would you decide to allocate these funds to (1) the creation of industry to produce capital, (2) the creation of industry to produce consumer goods, and (3) the direct purchase of consumer goods? Which allocation would tend to give the greatest increases in incomes in the distant future? Which the least?

7.14 How realistic is it in the study of business finance, as you understand it at this point, and to the study of capital markets, to analyze the allocation of resources in a free-price market economy?

7.15 What differences in the shape of the *CMC* would you expect in a planned economy, such as Sweden, for example, as opposed to that of a mixed economy, such as the United States?

7.16 How can the *CMC* (1) shift, (2) tilt, or (3) stay the same when new investment opportunities to the right of a given *CMC* present themselves? Discuss fully.

7.17 Given the information below, answer the following questions:

Investment	Risk	Expected Rate of Return
Pure Rate of Interest	0	5%
A	3/16	7
B	5/16	9
C	5/8	14
D	5/8	11
E	5/8	24
F	11/16	16
G	14/16	23
H	1	20

(*a*) How can the differential in expected rate of return between Investments C and E be accounted for? (*Hint:* It might be helpful to plot these data before attempting to answer the question.) (*b*) If, of all these investments, an investor (a firm) chose D, what would be the maximum price of capital this firm would be willing to pay?

CHAPTER **8** THE STRUCTURE OF
THE FINANCIAL SYSTEM

From the standpoint of the entire economy, the discussion has so far proceeded in terms of capital definitions, the formation of capital, the manner in which the demand for capital is formulated, the supply of capital, the cost of capital, and the allocation of capital in our society. We have not discussed how capital is obtained. This is accomplished through a market mechanism and with the use of money as the medium or exchange; command over capital resources is secured (and each economic unit seeking the services of various resources does so) in competition with all other units seeking these resources. Important to an understanding of capital and capital formation are the institutions which comprise the financial system of society, for it is primarily by these vehicles that saving is channeled into investment.

These institutions are indigenous to a capitalistic society in which the majority of savers and investors are ordinarily distinctly different groups and in which capital formation takes place in substantial magnitude. The economy is characterized to a large degree by financial institutions which *accumulate the savings* of a large number of persons and purchase either the ownership or creditorship instruments of business firms. Yet, a significant part of the demand for funds is satisfied directly by the savers themselves, who have no direct need for the financial system here described. In general, the financial system is designed to provide money for those economic units which need more than they have available and at the time they need it. It is the task of the present chapter to discuss this financial system. We shall discuss both the flow of funds in our system and the institutions that facilitate the flow. Moreover, we will be concerned almost exclusively with those institutions which affect the supply of funds to business firms—recognizing, however, that the institutions which supply money to individuals as well as to governmental units, either on a long- or short-term basis, are competitive with the intermediaries supplying funds to businesses and thereby affect the price that business firms will pay for their funds. We shall also emphasize institutions providing long-term funds. Finally, because the demand for funds by business firms can be satisfied either internally, through retained earnings and capital consumption allowances, or externally, through the issuance of securities,[1] we will incorporate these distinctions into the discussion to follow wherever appropriate. For the most part, however, we will be concerned primarily with the external markets for long-term funds and the institutions which bear most importantly on them. Because financial institutions as such are generally not yet directly involved with its formation, human capital, important as it is, will not be included in the present discussion.

CAPITAL FORMATION AND FINANCIAL INSTITUTIONS

It was previously noted that at any moment in time there are economic units in society that have an excess of funds (money and credit) over their need for them. At the same time there are economic units which have a need for more funds than they possess. The demand for these funds by all business firms is represented by a schedule of investments, referred to as the *marginal efficiency of capital schedule*. The total demand for loanable funds includes demands by individuals and governments as well. The supply of loanable funds is, to a large extent, directed to users through a system of financial institutions—complex and dynamic in nature—which pools the savings of millions of economic units (whose desires for individual investment outlets are many and varied but rarely coincidental with the demand for funds) and which channel these funds to investors (whose needs are varied but rarely coincidental with the supply of funds). One of the important functions of financial institutions, then, is to bridge the acts of saving and investing.

Moreover, much of the money needed by business firms to command resources is supplied by individuals. Much is provided by business firms themselves. Finally, the commercial banking system as a whole may increase the money supply because of the nature of fractional reserve banking. But the intriguing thing about our savings-investment process is that the majority of savers supply money for the use of other economic units; less often are these funds directly channeled to the users. In turn, financial institutions—possessing, as they do, expert investment staffs—seek to allocate their investable funds among the best opportunities consistent with the objectives (and regulations) of their institution. That is, they allocate funds to those economic units which seek them and are capable of paying for their use. To the extent that the real stock of capital is increased by the units using these funds, capital is formed and these financial institu-

---

[1] For present purposes, *securities* may be viewed as consisting of any obligation of the firm which has a right to (or claim on) the assets, earnings, and/or control of the firm.

tions can be viewed as performing yet another important function: namely, they are "capital-facilitating" in nature.

But funds saved by individuals may not always be in the amount or form necessary for investors. Indeed, the funds saved by individuals are frequently very small in any given period while the needs of business firms seeking funds are relatively large. Furthermore, the form in which the funds may be let to investors may not be suitable for either party. (By *form* we mean primarily the degree of risk involved and the rate charged for the use of the funds; we do not mean the legal forms of debt and ownership.) Financial institutions, by gathering funds together, convert the individuals' saving into the amounts desired by businesses and, in most cases, into the forms they need. For example, from the firm's point of view the form is materially different when using the accumulated funds of a financial institution from what it might be, had it to resort to individual savers. The problem of securing funds is appreciably reduced because the firm receives the amount of funds it needs at the time it needs them.

And, to the extent that a firm usually needs to deal with only one financial institution (as opposed to a multitude of small savers), the cost of securing funds is also reduced. This pooling arrangement also benefits the individual savers in that they have a ready outlet for their savings; institutions will accept small amounts of funds whereas investors today generally require large sums which the vast majority of individuals are incapable of providing. In addition, in many savings institutions the savings of individuals are insured, thereby reducing the risk to individuals. Also, because financial institutions tend to diversify commitments, the risk-reducing advantages of this policy accrues to the benefit of the savers who committed their funds to the institutions.

To business firms, however, as we have already seen, money is a form of capital, because by our definition *capital* is something over which they have control and which can be directed toward the achievement of the goals of the firm. These economic units enter the market place and hire the various factors of production with the view to selling the products or services produced by them at prices which tend to exceed the costs of the factors. The result, hopefully, will be a residue or profit. To the extent that these firms, in the aggregate, increase the total productive capacity (real stock of capital, including inventories) of society, capital formation has taken place. These current savings in the form of money are then channeled to economic units desiring them and able to pay for them by purchasing firms' debt or ownership securities. This can be done either directly or indirectly, through financial institutions. The economic units then use the funds to command resources which may be used to form capital. But the claims issued for money by business units are distinct from the physical capital which may be formed. As we shall see later, the issuance of so-many-millions-of-dollars of bonds by a business corporation may or may not result in capital formation. The bonds themselves are merely financial claims (credit) on the firm. Credit is often used in advanced economies as an equivalent for cash.[2] Thus the intangible claims issued for money or credit by business firms and intermediaries that pool savings need to be differentiated from the actual formation of tangible goods.

Lastly, to the extent that financial institutions make the formation of capital easier and cheaper, they tend to promote the economic welfare of society; that is, they tend to promote a higher standard of material well-being for the members of society. To achieve the maximum economic well-being, goods and services need to be provided in sufficient quantities and with proper regard for quality so as to satisfy the material needs and desires, both today and in the future, of its citizens. The search for this goal requires an ever-increasing stock of capital goods in order to increase total productivity. In a complex society, in which direct investment by many individuals is difficult and inefficient, a method of directing the savings of millions of economic units—individual, business, and government—is all-important. In our society, financial institutions provide just such a service. We sometimes call them *financial intermediaries,* implying that they are the link between the ultimate saver of funds and the ultimate user. Their intermediate position is such as to pool the current savings of the various economic units of society in exchange for various claims on them. In turn, they direct the use of the amalgamated funds into those investment opportunities that appear most satisfactory in exchange for other types of claims. Their major function, however, is to facilitate capital formation. But because capital formation is designed to increase productivity, it can be said that financial intermediaries perform the vital role of increasing productivity, thereby contributing to the economic well-being of society.

THE FINANCIAL SYSTEM

In our society, in which the free marketplace is predominant, an over-all mechanism for extending the use of funds to those desiring it has developed. This mechanism is the *securities market,* which may be defined as the institutional arrangement for effecting exchanges of claims on consumers, governments, and businesses for cash or credit. We will concentrate on that aspect of the securities markets that applies most appropri-

---

[2] *Credit* is a claim on the future money savings (usually with interest) of those using it.

ately to business firms, primarily corporations. The summary view of securities markets set forth in Table 8-1 is not intended to be all-inclusive; rather, it is concerned only with those institutions which bear most directly on financing business enterprise. Hence the table is just a convenient grouping of securities markets and is intended to illustrate the basic interrelationships that are pertinent to business financial decisions.

Thus, for example, securities markets can be differentiated according to types. There are those which involve new isues of securities by business firms and there are those which result in purchases and sales of securities already outstanding but which do not directly affect business firms. The former is called the *primary market,* for it is here that funds are secured by business. The latter is called the *secondary market,* where the transactions have to do with buying and selling of "second-hand" or existing securities. In the primary market new securities are exchanged for new cash, credit, or other securities. In the secondary market existing securities are exchanged for cash or credit.

Both the primary market and the secondary market can be further subdivided according to time. Thus, for example, transactions in securities having a duration of a year or more (i.e., long-term in nature) are consummated in the *capital markets.* Those having a duration of a year or less (i.e., short-term in nature) are consummated in the *money markets.* Thus the claims (for example, bonds) of business firms issued for new funds and for a long duration will be sold in the primary capital markets. The claims (for example, commercial paper) of business firms seeking new cash for a short period will take place in the primary money markets. Further, the existing claims (for example, bonds) of business firms that are exchanged among individuals (no new funds going to the firm) will take place in the secondary capital markets. Finally, excess accumulations of funds by business firms seeking a temporary outlet may be channeled into existing short-term United States government securities (for example, Treasury Bills) and this transaction will take place in the secondary money market.

Securities markets can also be differentiated according to place. In general, it needs to be mentioned, however, that a market for securities exists wherever a transaction can be consummated. There is no specific, physical location in which most securities transactions are consummated, although New York City and its financial district constitute the hub of our economy's financial activities. This is as close as one can come to locating *the* securities markets. Nevertheless, there are two general classes of securities markets, differentiated partially according to place. The first of these entails transactions consummated by a negotiated agreement for an exchange of securities for funds but in no specific, formal location.

Table 8-1
Differentiation of Securities Markets

Securities Markets

Differentiation	Primary (New Securities)		Secondary (Existing Securities)	
Type				
Duration of issue	Capital markets (long-term securities)	Money markets (short-term securities)	Capital markets (long-term securities)	Money markets (short-term securities)
Location of transaction	Over-the-counter markets		Securities exchanges and over-the-counter markets	Over-the-counter markets
Institutions involved*	Investment bankers Insurance companies Private pension funds	Federal Reserve Banks Commercial banks U.S. Government and its agencies Finance companies	Investment firms Investment companies Insurance companies Private pension funds Other institutions Individuals	Commercial banks Business firms Federal Reserve Banks
Impact on capital formation	Funds exchanged may or may not result directly in capital formation. If capital formation is to take place at all, however, it will be through the mechanism of the primary markets.		No capital formation directly takes place. These markets are "capital facilitating," however.	

* Although not part of the securities markets *per se*, internal cash flows, consisting of retained earnings and depreciation accruals, do provide a substantial degree of competition for other types of funds, and hence in a sense ought to be regarded as part of the market for "securities."

These are referred to as *over-the-counter transactions.* The second encompasses those transactions which take place on an auction basis at a specifically defined location designed for that purpose and under highly formalized conditions. These are referred to as transactions consummated on *securities exchanges.*

Not all transactions are so neatly differentiated as those mentioned above. Indeed, a firm may purchase long-term government bonds in secondary over-the-counter capital markets even though it intends to hold them for a short period. Furthermore, there is a definite interrelationship between the capital markets and money markets, the primary and secondary markets, and the over-the-counter market and securities exchanges, for buyers of securities are active in all and can move with some—although not perfect—dexterity among them. Borrowers of funds also can move from the primary capital market to the primary money market and vice versa with some facility. For our purposes, however, it is useful to differentiate securities markets according to (1) types of transactions (those for new securities and those for existing securities), (2) time (long-term or capital markets and short-term or money markets), and (3) the nature and location (over-the-counter and securities exchanges).

As Table 8-1 indicates, however, securities markets can be *further differentiated according to the major intermediaries* active in each of the various segments. Particular notice should be made of the fact that sales of all new securities issues take place in the over-the-counter markets. Brokers and dealers, acting in the over-the-counter market, can purchase or sell new securities or existing ones. By contrast, transactions on securities exchanges are exclusively associated with secondary securities—that is, existing ones.

Money Markets

Money markets are defined as the market for short-term funds. From the financial manager's point of view, the major "securities" offered in the money market are short-term government securities, commercial paper, short-term commercial bank loans, and bankers' acceptances. Of these, the market for short-term government securities is by far the most dominant. A thorough discussion of short-term governments with respect to money markets, however, is not within the direct purview of the present chapter. Nevertheless, a brief comment on this segment of the money market, as well as other forms of "securities" frequently encountered, will be presented in order to lend perspective to the present discussion.

Perhaps the single most important characteristic of short-term government securities is their impact on interest rates of all short-term securities.

The rate of interest charged for other types of short-term securities is dominated by changes in the rate charged on short-term governments. As we have seen previously, the pure rate of interest was the result of the supply of and demand for loanable funds where no risk existed. We suggested at that time that the closest our society comes in practice to meeting this requirement is to be found in United States government securities of short duration. Beyond these, however, every other security offered, as it were, has a greater degree of risk associated with it than found in governments. Because of this [3] the rate of interest in these securities will be greater than those found on governments. Because the United States government is so predominant an influence in the money markets and because the vast majority of its securities are of a short-term nature usually requiring refunding, their impact on money market rates is quite pervasive.

In addition, because United States governments constitute so large a proportion of total transactions, the Federal Reserve is another factor which has an important bearing on the money markets. Through its use of various tools of monetary control, it may provide excess reserves for commercial banks from which loans can be made. The chief tool used in recent years to affect the excess reserve positions of commercial banks has been the buying and selling of United States government securities which, in turn, also affects the level of interest rates. The Federal Reserve Banks have been highly important in this segment of the securities market.

The commercial banks are also important to the money markets for the obvious reason that they provide short-term loans directly to businesses that need them to finance seasonal upswings in business or for other purposes. Commercial banks are also important to the extent that they are the main purchasers of United States government securities of a short-term duration. Furthermore, they deal in bankers' acceptances. Bankers' acceptances are drafts drawn on a bank ordering it to pay another party, either at the present or at some future date, the amount stipulated on the draft. They usually run for periods of one to three months. Once accepted by the bank, receipt of the funds by the third party will be realized. The bank, in turn, will expect the funds to be forthcoming shortly from the drawer of the draft. The major use of these securities is in international trade, and commercial banks are of critical importance to their use.

A less obvious but equally important aspect of the money markets for our purposes is the amount of funds supplied by commercial banks to investment bankers in their efforts to sell new issues of securities. Although investment banking is treated more fully later, it should be pointed

[3] The increased degree of risk on some securities of short duration may be quite small, however.

out here that the distribution of securities to the public by investment dealers is greatly facilitated by loans made by commercial banks on a short-term basis (usually less than thirty days). In this respect the commercial banks indirectly aid the financing of business enterprises.

Loans derived from the use of commercial paper have increased significantly in the post-World War II era after having experienced a rather precipitous decline since the 1920's. Commercial paper may be defined as promissory notes which are issued by prime credit risks in large denominations and traded in open markets. They are usually sold through a dealer in commercial paper who in turn sells them to banks throughout the country. Thus, in another indirect way, commercial banks provide a substantial sum of money for business firms that use this medium. It is important to recognize that, in order to take advantage of the usually low cost of commercial paper, a firm has to have an excellent and well-known credit standing. For this reason, only very large, well-established firms with good earnings records can expect to use this method of financing. These notes are issued for varying lengths of time, although the majority of them have a duration of three to six months.

Capital Markets

Investment Banking

With respect to the primary capital markets generally, several institutions are important to the financial manager. One of these is the investment banker, although he is not a banker in the generally accepted sense of the word. Investment banking firms do not participate in the activities normally associated with commercial banks. Like commercial banks, however, they operate in both the primary and secondary markets for securities and facilitate the channeling of funds to business firms. They do not accept deposits of any sort, nor do they have the ability to create money which are the two chief characteristics of commercial banks. The activities of investment bankers in the primary market, to which we will now direct our attention, will reveal other dissimilarities which may suggest the appropriateness of referring to them as merchants of securities.

A firm desiring to raise new cash through the issuance of ownership or debt securities may or may not engage the services of an investment banker. But because firms seek new cash in the primary capital markets only infrequently, they ordinarily do not possess the skill, knowledge, or insights necessary for a successful flotation of securities and hence reliance upon the services of an investment banker is often required. Most important, the banker has the ability to gather or pool large amounts of funds from his network of clients. Consequently, the professional services of an investment banker are usually desirable. As an investment banker, he may perform any or all (and in varying degrees of each) of three functions: buying, selling, and underwriting securities issues.

The buying function requires many activities before the investment banking firm makes a final commitment to purchase an issue. These activities take the form of a thorough investigation of the firm wishing to sell an issue. This study has to do primarily with its economic and financial condition; it entails securing audited statements of income and condition and engineering reports, estimating the prospects of the company with respect to new products and competition, and a host of other factors that any prudent buyer might want to examine before purchasing. The buying function also involves the creation of a "package" of covenants which are suitable both to the issuer and to potential buyers. The factors that influence this "package" vary, but the conditions of the securities markets, the size and nature of the issue, the size and nature of the firm, and last—but by no means least—the prevailing whims of investors, all come to bear on the construction of the "package."

The selling function focuses primarily on forming a marketing organization which will distribute the securities efficiently once offered for public sale. The size of the marketing group will vary according to the size and the nature of the issue to be sold. For small, high-grade debt issues the marketing organization will likely be small, consisting of no more than a handful of firms that have previously shown competence in distributing this type of issue. Similarly, the major portions of these issues are likely to be bought by a few investors. For large issues of common stock of some of the more prominent companies, the selling organization may consist of hundreds of firms because each of the persons from whom the funds are raised takes a relatively small proportion of the total amount. Thus more contact and effort is needed to raise the necessary amount. Additionally, any one investment banking firm, regardless of how large it might be, has access only to a relatively limited number of buyers of securities. To tap the vast sources of funds needed for a successful flotation of relatively large issues and to spread the risk of not being able to sell the entire issue or of selling it at a loss, usually a syndicate is formed to purchase and sell the issue. The syndicate is a partnership which usually lasts for a short period (a few days). Its major goal is to raise the capital by selling an issue as rapidly as possible after it is initially offered for public sale. Moreover, because the profit margin on the sale of any given issue is relatively small, it could be eliminated by small fluctuations in market price. The low margin gained on the sale of securities is customarily offset by a rapid turnover of the financial resources of the selling firm. This gives added incentive for investment bankers to sell the issue rapidly. The investment banking house may have a substantial portion of its own funds tied up in the offering, which may preclude it from participating in further flotations.

Underwriting an issue of securities means guaranteeing the business firm that it will receive the funds previously agreed upon under the purchase agreement, whether or not the investment banking group sells the entire issue. As long as they promise to deliver the previously committed dollars to the business (usually seven to ten days after the first day of the sale), the underwriters must come up with that amount. If the security is not completely sold out by then, the investment banking group will have to borrow the difference between the amount sold and the amount that must be delivered. Thus the function of the investment banker in this respect is to insure the firm against potentially adverse risks such as delay in receiving the desired funds or even failure to sell part or all of the issue. He does this by relieving the issuing firm of the risks of selling the issue. In this sense, the price paid to the investment banker may be viewed in part as a risk or insurance premium. In part, it is a cost for the other services which the investment banker may perform, such as selling the issue and advising the company or helping in the preparation of a registration statement (if it is required by the Securities and Exchange Commission).

Because of the risks that are obviously involved, the compensation to the investment bankers, although seemingly high in some cases, needs to be commensurate with their efforts. The size and quality of the issue will determine, along with the conditions of the capital markets, the extent of compensation required by bankers. For very large issues of high-grade bonds issued in strong markets, the total cost to the firm could be as little as $0.25 on $100. For common stock issues of small, relatively unknown firms or of firms of relatively inferior quality and for small issues in a relatively weak market, the cost to the firm may run as high as $15–$20 on $100, if it is underwritten at all. Between these extremes there are, of course, imperceptible gradations among security flotations.[4] Interestingly, the cost of flotation declined considerably from the middle 1930's to the early 1950's. Since then it has remained fairly stable.[5] Nevertheless, it cannot be stressed too much that the underwriting function is crucial for

[4] United States Securities and Exchange Commission, *Cost of Flotation of Corporate Securities, 1951–1955*, 1957.

[5] Avery B. Cohan, *Cost of Flotation of Long-term Corporate Debt Since 1935*. Research Paper No. 6. (Chapel Hill, North Carolina: University of North Carolina, School of Business Administration, 1961), p. 7.

business firms and for the economy as a whole for it assures firms, presumably with profitable investment opportunities, that they will receive the needed funds and presumably at prices considerably lower than might otherwise have been the case. This in turn tends to aid in the efficient allocation of funds to what appear to be the most profitable uses. Firms with unprofitable outlooks would be unable to pay the costs of capital; these costs are estimated by the investment banker who "measures" the market and advises the firm on the pricing of an issue.

Aside from these general considerations, there are numerous modifications of the functions described, such as stand-by underwriting, best-efforts selling agreements, market support for the sale of existing securities, and the role of investment bankers as "finders" for direct placements. (These and other related topics will be discussed later in the text.)

The investment banker is one of many financial institutions and because of changes in the pattern of corporate financing his contributions to business financing in dollar terms has varied significantly over the years although the absolute magnitude of his activity has increased. More and more in the last several decades, corporate bonds have been sold directly to large financial intermediaries, especially life insurance companies which have taken up about 90 per cent of total private placements of corporations.[6] In these cases investment bankers have acted as "finders" for almost 50 percent of total private placements.[7] Their services in this respect, however, are less important than those provided when issues are sold to the public.

The change in the nature of investment banking functions also reflects the deleterious effects of the increasing importance of internally generated funds and the sale of additional common stock to existing stockholders. To see this more clearly and to add perspective to the present chapter, a discussion of the sources and uses of funds is in order.

Sources and Uses of Funds

Since World War II significant changes have occurred in the pattern of corporate financing. Table 8-2 and Figures 8-1 and 8-2 illustrate some of these changes. Table 8-2 indicates the relative importance of the various sources of funds (internal, long-term external and short-term external) and the uses to which these funds were put (increases in physical assets and increases in financial assets). It is interesting to note that an average of almost 63 per cent of total funds was acquired by internal sources during

---

[6] Richards C. Osborn, *Corporation Finance* (New York: Harper and Brothers, 1959), p. 248.
[7] *Ibid.*

Table 8-2

Percentage Composition of Total Sources and Total Uses of Corporate Funds, 1946–1963*

Sources and Uses	1946	1947	1948	1949	1950	1951	195
Internal sources, total	52.4	51.2	64.6	96.1	47.0	48.0	57.8
Retained profits†	32.2	35.2	43.3	50.3	29.4	25.3	24.0
Depreciation	19.2	16.0	21.3	45.8	17.6	22.7	33.8
External long-term sources, total	19.2	19.4	24.7	27.7	9.2	19.7	30.5
Stocks	5.9	4.3	4.1	10.3	3.8	6.8	9.7
Bonds	5.0	9.3	16.1	21.3	4.5	9.1	15.9
Other debt	8.2	5.9	4.5	− 3.9	1.1	3.8	4.9
Total long-term debt	13.2	15.2	20.6	17.4	5.6	12.9	20.8
Short-term sources, total	28.8	29.3	10.7	−23.9	43.4	32.3	11.7
Bank loans	16.9	13.9	4.5	− 1.9	19.9	6.8	8.8
Trade payables	− 7.3	6.5	3.1	−14.2	16.5	10.9	−10.1
Federal income tax liabilities	9.6	4.3	1.7	−11.0	4.8	9.8	5.2
Other	9.6	4.6	1.4	3.2	2.3	4.8	7.8
Increase in physical assets, total	102.1	73.7	8.13	77.0	58.9	79.5	79.0
Plant and equipment	53.9	52.0	66.4	98.8	37.3	54.7	74.7
Inventories (book value)	48.3	21.7	14.8	−21.8	21.6	24.8	44.3
Increase in financial assets, total	− 2.1	26.3	18.7	23.0	41.1	20.5	21.0
Receivables	20.7	23.2	14.5	3.6	30.4	11.9	19.3
Consumer	4.7	4.3	4.6	9.1	4.0	2.0	7.3
Other	15.9	19.0	9.9	− 5.5	26.5	9.9	12.0
Cash and U.S. government securities	−20.3	3.1	3.5	19.4	9.9	7.1	0.3
Cash (including deposits)	4.7	6.7	1.1	7.3	3.5	4.8	2.7
U.S. government securities	−25.0	− 3.7	2.5	12.1	6.4	2.3	− 2.3
Other assets	− 2.6	0.0	0.7	0.0	0.7	1.5	1.3

* Excludes banks and insurance companies.

† Includes depletion.

Source: 1946-1957, U.S. Department of Commerce, Office of Business Economics, *U.S. Income a Output; A Supplement to the Survey of Current Business* (1958) 195, Table V-10; 195 1961, U.S. Department of Commerce, Office of Business Economics, *Survey of Curre Business* (May 1964) 11.

the period 1946–63. Short-term sources constituted an average of about 15 per cent, and total external long-term sources, interestingly, constituted slightly less than 23 per cent of the total.

Within each of these categories, of course, notable relationships are present. For example, at the beginning of the period, of total internal sources roughly two thirds were derived from retained earnings (as illustrated in Figure 8-1). At the end of the period this source of internal funds constituted slightly more than 23 per cent of internal funds, thereby evidencing the substantial rise in importance of depreciation accruals as a source of internal funds. In this period, the average ratio of retained earn-

Table 8-2

Percentage Composition of Total Sources and Total Uses of Corporate Funds, 1946–1963*

1953	1954	1955	1956	1957	1958	1959	1960	1961	1962	1963	Average
64.8	89.2	52.9	63.1	71.1	66.0	54.5	68.9	61.8	65.1	63.3	62.7
26.0	28.4	21.7	23.1	21.9	14.5	16.6	16.5	14.1	13.1	13.2	24.9
38.8	60.8	31.2	40.0	49.1	51.5	37.8	52.4	47.9	52.0	50.0	38.2
25.0	28.8	17.1	25.1	30.2	27.7	16.6	22.2	21.4	22.0	18.6	22.5
7.6	9.5	5.4	6.8	8.5	9.1	6.5	6.8	8.7	3.9	1.0	6.6
15.8	17.1	8.3	10.9	18.7	15.0	7.2	11.3	9.8	9.3	9.0	11.9
1.6	2.3	3.4	7.5	3.0	3.6	3.2	3.9	2.7	7.8	8.5	4.0
17.4	19.4	11.7	18.4	21.7	18.6	10.4	15.2	12.5	17.1	17.5	15.9
10.2	−18.0	30.0	11.8	− 1.2	6.6	28.9	8.8	16.8	23.5	24.9	15.2
1.3	− 0.9	7.4	4.3	1.5	− 1.0	9.5	2.9	0.8	5.6	7.3	4.2
2.0	−14.0	10.9	6.1	− 2.7	9.6	9.3	5.9	11.6	10.3	11.2	7.9
0.3	− 5.0	7.6	− 3.2	− 4.7	− 6.3	3.7	− 3.4	1.2	1.7	2.0	− 0.4
7.2	1.8	4.2	4.5	4.7	4.3	6.5	3.6	3.3	6.0	4.2	4.7
39.8	87.4	61.1	89.9	90.0	68.0	65.6	81.3	64.8	66.8	64.9	76.6
33.6	94.1	47.8	70.2	85.6	74.8	53.2	74.9	61.3	49.7	57.6	66.7
6.3	− 6.7	13.2	19.7	4.4	6.8	12.7	6.3	3.7	7.1	7.3	10.9
10.1	12.6	38.9	10.1	9.9	32.0	34.4	18.7	35.2	33.2	35.1	23.3
3.8	9.2	23.5	18.1	8.6	19.0	20.9	18.5	19.9	21.1	22.0	17.2
6.3	2.9	6.5	2.8	2.4	0.8	4.6	3.9	0.2	4.3	3.9	4.2
2.4	6.3	17.0	15.3	6.3	19.5	16.1	14.6	19.7	16.7	18.1	13.0
6.3	0.0	9.9	−10.1	− 4.7	7.6	5.6	− 7.5	5.2	2.2	1.5	2.2
0.7	9.7	2.4	1.2	− 0.3	7.1	− 2.1	− 0.5	6.0	1.3	0.7	3.2
5.6	− 9.7	7.5	−11.3	− 4.4	0.6	7.7	− 7.1	− 0.8	0.7	1.0	− 1.0
0.0	3.7	5.5	2.1	6.0	5.4	7.9	7.5	10.1	9.9	11.5	3.9

ings to total internal sources amounted to 43 per cent; the remainder was derived from depreciation accruals.

The reasons for this change within the internally generated funds category are complex and multidimensional in character. Nevertheless, it is worthwhile to pursue some of them.

At the end of World War II, the nation's usable stock of peacetime production facilities was extremely low. The problem of converting plant and equipment from the production of "war" goods to "peace" goods was enormous. Moreover, facilities then in existence were built during a period of relatively low prices. Also, many of the facilities used during the war had been amortized under government-issued certificates of necessity which allowed firms to depreciate their facilities at rates higher than usual. Thus, because of the relatively small stock of real capital, the low prices at which the facilities had been purchased and the relatively small

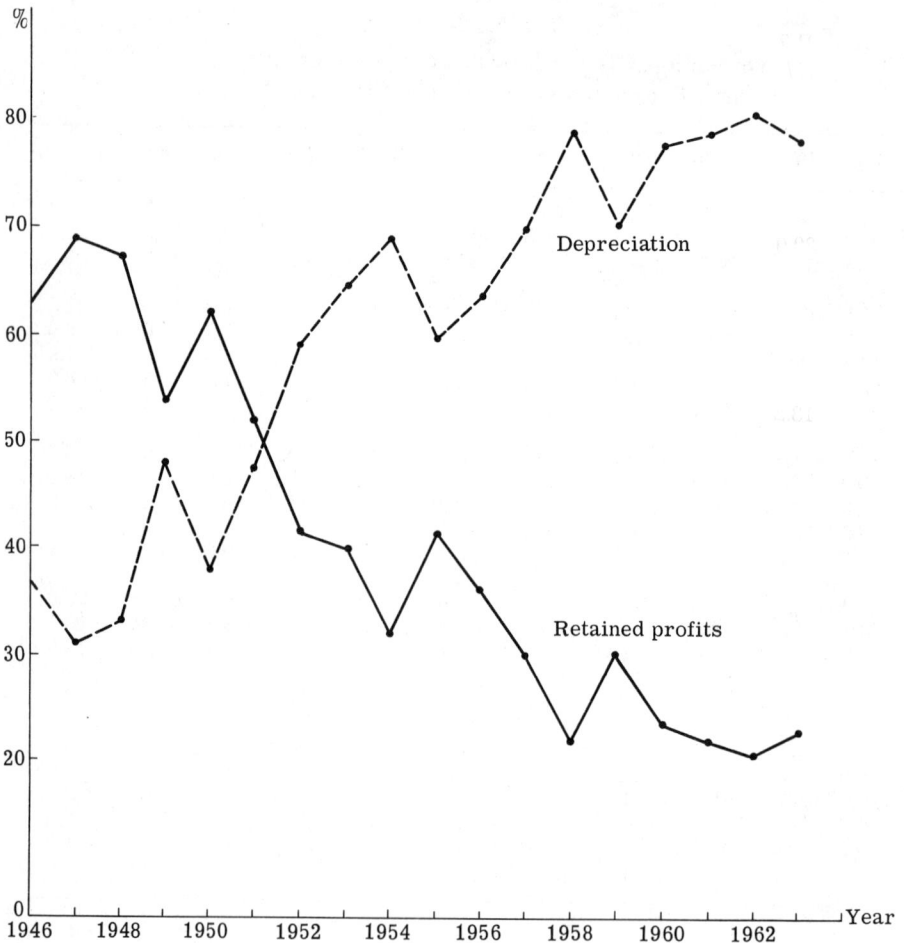

Figure 8-1   Percentage Composition of Internal Sources of Funds 1946–63.
Source: Compiled from various issues of the *Federal Reserve Bulletin.*

base on which to take depreciation, depreciation was not a major source
of internal funds for current capital outlays. The generally low dividend
disbursements of most corporations immediately after the war made it
possible for larger amounts to be retained in the business.

A few years later the picture began to change. New capital expenditures rose substantially after the war, thus adding greatly to the stock of
depreciable assets. More liberal methods of depreciation also enhanced
this segment of internally generated funds. In addition, there was a
gradual increase in the amount of funds paid to stockholders, thus leaving
fewer dollars to be retained. These are the paramount reasons why depreciation is now the chief source of internal funds.

Also of importance has been the development of long-term external sources of funds. Figure 8-2 illustrates the variations of total external long-term and permanent sources of funds secured by business firms in this period. An average of almost 32 per cent was in the form of stocks, although there is no really discernible trend in the stock financing of firms. On the other hand, there has been a significant rise in the use of bonds as a medium of securing external long-term funds. In this period bonds amounted to an average of 52 per cent of total long-term external funds. This rise was at the expense of other long-term debt, which took the form primarily of term loans and directly negotiated debts (such as mortgages). The average for this type of debt was slightly more than 16 per cent. For the aggregate of debt, however, there has been no significant trend, this category having averaged slightly more than 68 per cent of total long-term external funds.

Among the many reasons for extensive reliance on debt during this period, two stand out. One reason is traceable directly to the successful efforts of the Federal Reserve to peg interest rates at relatively low levels in order to accommodate Treasury financing (at first) and to promote (subsequently) relatively high levels of aggregate investment and employment. Both efforts, especially in the years 1946–51, made debt financing by business firms extremely cheap and, therefore, attractive. Moreover, because interest was (and is) deductible for tax purposes, high levels of federal taxation provided added encouragement to use debt. These inducements tend to explain why corporations depended upon debt financing so extensively. But another reason may be found in the fact that many corporations came out of the war years with substantial equity and considerable debt-paying capacity. Funds accumulated during the war, either through profits or through depreciation, were used to scale down their then-existent debts. Moreover, much of the debt corporations had was refinanced at substantially lower interest rates. Even during the later years of this period interest costs, although rising, remained substantially below those of the prewar years. In addition, profits rose substantially during this period. All these factors enhanced the debt-paying capacity of corporations considerably and established the basis upon which debt securities could be sold.

Short-term sources of funds displayed rather erratic movements during the period. This is to be expected for the major items of this category—bank loans, trade payables, and federal income tax liabilities—all move together to some degree with the relative level of actual or anticipated economic activity. But although they fluctuated erratically throughout the period, there were no significant trends in any of the categories. The only

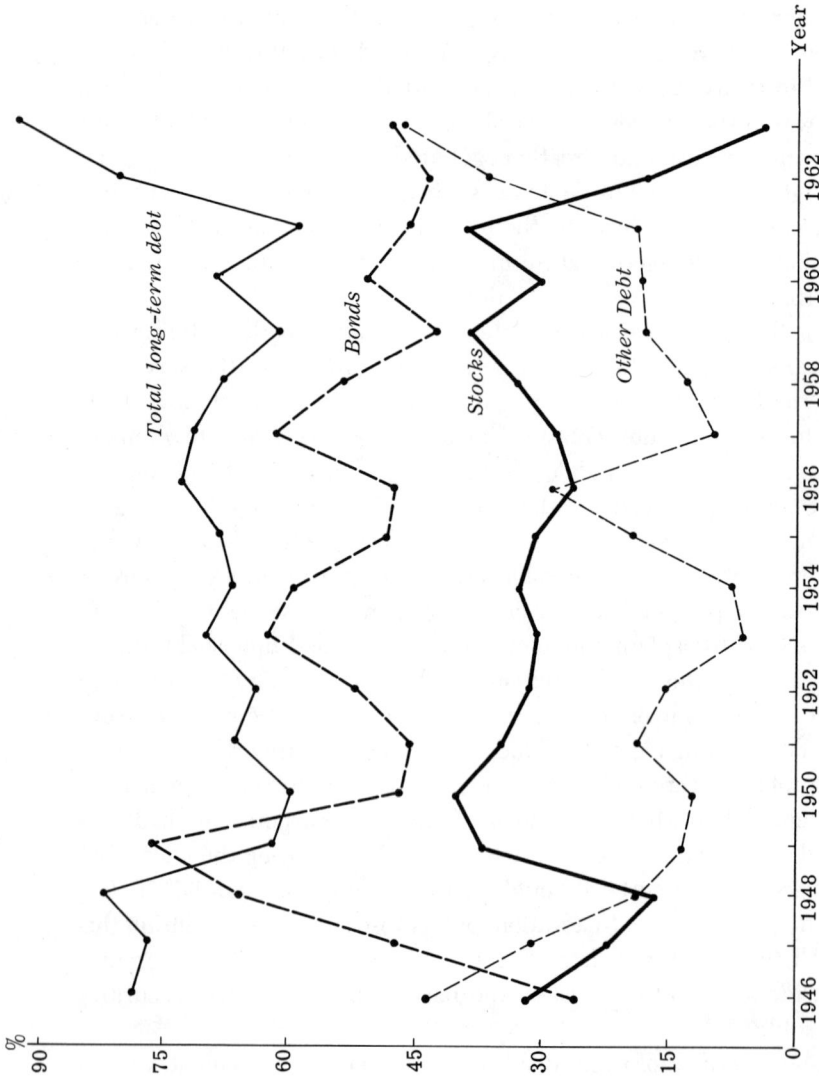

Figure 8-2 Percentage Composition of External Long-Term Sources of Corporate Funds, 1946–1963. *Source:* Compiled from various issues of the *Federal Reserve Bulletin,* and the *Survey of Current Business.*

significant fact seems to be that very little increase in the absolute magnitudes of short-term debt was in evidence, so that the relative importance of the group as a whole declined.

Finally, the vast majority of all funds was used to replace or expand physical assets, primarily plant and equipment, and this was usually accomplished during periods of relative prosperity. Indeed, much of the fluctuation in the pattern of external financing can be explained by general movements in over-all economic activity.

Private Placements

Although the precise magnitude of the shifts in importance of investment banking is not known, some inferences can be made from information available. It has been shown that the major sources of funds to business firms in the post-World War II era were internally generated. Long-term and permanent external sources—the ones in which investment bankers are most interested—constituted, on the average, only 22.8 per cent of total sources. Of the external sources, 31.7 per cent was in the form of stocks; the rest was in the form of debt.

From Table 8-3 it can be seen that of all issues publicly offered—not only during this period but since 1934—a substantial proportion was privately placed (securities sold to one or a handful of institutions). By 1963, more securities were privately placed than publicly sold. When debt issues alone are considered, the proportion of private placements to total debt issues is even higher. If we combine this information with the fact that many of the stock issues are sold to the firm's existing stockholders, we can reasonably infer that serious incursions into the investment banking business from the standpoint of financing large business enterprises have taken place in recent decades. This is so because all the situations described above—the extensive use of internal funds, the great proportion of debt to total external funds, the increase in importance of private placements (especially in debt securities), and the sale of stocks (most of which are common stock) to existing stockholders—do not require the services of an investment banker, or if so, to a minor extent only.[8]

When the types of firms using the private placement technique are divided into categories, the data are even more revealing. Figure 8-3 shows that ever since 1935 private placement of debt securities of industrial, financial, and service firms, taken as a whole, averaged in excess of 45 per cent of the total debt offerings of these firms, although it has been

---

[8] Often, investment bankers will act as "finders" for private placements. Also, where stocks are sold to existing stockholders, a "standby" agreement or "underwriting only" agreement is often made with the investment banker. Neither of these activities, however, is completely consonant with the three primary functions discussed above.

Table 8-3 A Summary of Corporate Securities Publicly Offered and Privately Placed in Each Year From 1934 Through 1963 (Millions)

Calendar Year	Total			Public Offerings			Private Placements			Private Placements as Per Cent of Total	
	All Issues	Debt Issues	Equity Issues	All Issues	Debt Issues	Equity Issues	All Issues	Debt Issues	Equity Issues	All Issues	Debt Issues
1934	397	372	25	305	280	25	92	92	0	23.2	24.7
1935	2,332	2,225	108	1,945	1,840	106	387	385	2	16.6	17.3
1936	4,572	4,029	543	4,199	3,660	539	373	369	4	8.2	9.2
1937	2,309	1,618	691	1,979	1,291	688	330	327	3	14.3	20.2
1938	2,155	2,044	111	1,463	1,353	110	692	691	1	32.1	33.8
1939	2,164	1,979	185	1,458	1,276	181	706	703	4	32.6	35.5
1940	2,677	2,386	291	1,912	1,628	284	765	758	7	28.6	31.8
1941	2,667	2,389	277	1,854	1,578	276	813	811	2	30.5	33.9
1942	1,062	917	146	642	506	136	420	411	9	39.5	44.8
1943	1,170	990	180	798	621	178	372	369	3	31.8	37.3
1944	3,202	2,670	532	2,415	1,892	524	787	778	9	24.6	29.1
1945	6,011	4,855	1,155	4,989	3,851	1,138	1,022	1,004	18	17.0	20.7
1946	6,900	4,882	2,018	4,983	3,019	1,963	1,917	1,863	54	27.8	38.2
1947	6,577	5,036	1,541	4,342	2,889	1,452	2,255	2,147	88	34.0	42.6
1948	7,078	5,973	1,106	3,991	2,965	1,028	3,087	3,008	79	43.6	50.4
1949	6,052	4,890	1,161	3,550	2,437	1,112	2,502	2,453	49	41.3	50.2
1950	6,362	4,920	1,442	3,681	2,360	1,321	2,680	2,560	120	42.1	52.0
1951	7,741	5,691	2,050	4,326	2,364	1,962	3,415	3,326	88	44.1	58.4
1952	9,534	7,601	1,933	5,533	3,645	1,888	4,002	3,957	45	42.0	52.1
1953	8,898	7,083	1,815	5,580	3,856	1,725	3,318	3,228	90	37.3	45.6
1954	9,516	7,488	2,029	5,848	4,003	1,844	3,668	3,484	184	38.5	46.5
1955	10,240	7,420	2,820	6,763	4,119	2,644	3,477	3,301	176	34.0	44.5
1956	10,939	8,002	2,937	7,053	4,225	2,827	3,886	3,777	109	35.5	47.2
1957	12,884	9,957	2,927	8,959	6,118	2,841	3,925	3,839	86	30.5	38.6
1958	11,558	9,653	1,906	8,068	6,332	1,736	3,490	3,320	170	30.2	34.4
1959	9,748	7,190	2,558	5,993	3,557	2,436	3,755	3,632	122	38.5	50.5
1960	10,154	8,081	2,073	6,657	4,806	1,851	3,497	3,275	221	34.4	40.5
1961	13,147	9,435	3,713	8,149	4,706	3,443	4,999	4,729	270	38.0	50.1
1962	10,770	9,016	1,754	6,127	4,487	1,640	4,643	4,529	113	43.1	50.2
1963	12,237	10,872	1,364	5,965	4,714	1,251	6,271	6,158	113	51.2	56.6

Source: U.S. Securities and Exchange Commission, *Twenty-ninth Annual Report*, 171; 1963 data are from the *Federal Reserve Bulletin* (June, 1964), 757.

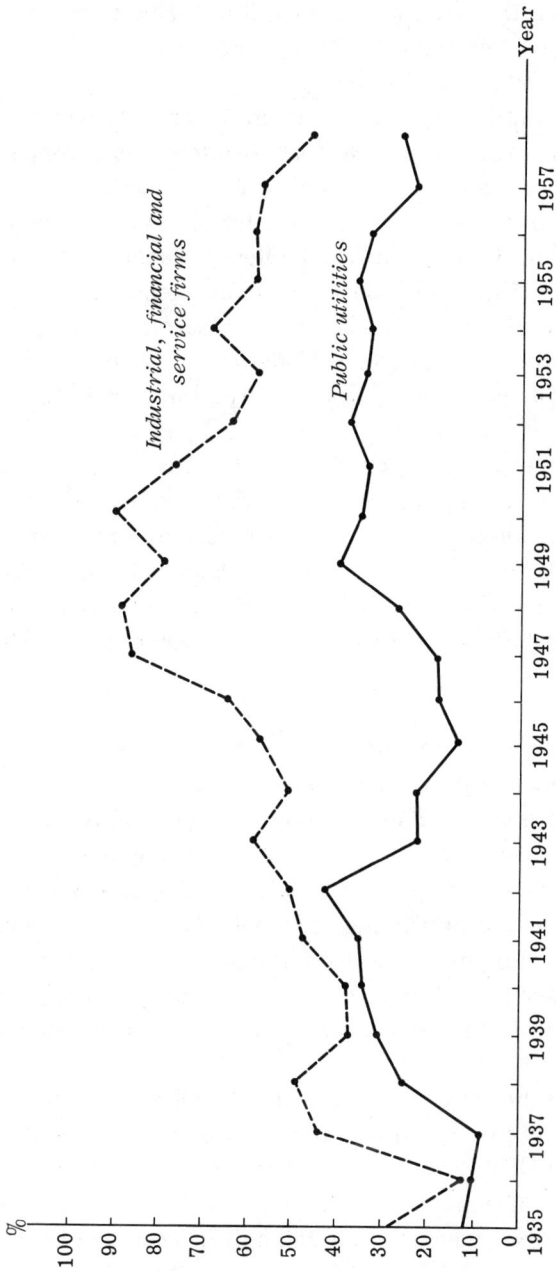

Figure 8-3   Private Placements of Cash Debt to New Cash Debt Issues for Industrial, Financial, Service and Public Utility Firms.

declining since 1950. On the other hand, private placement of debt securities has not been used as extensively in the public utility field as it has in the industrial, financial, and service firms. This is because most public utility commissions require firms within their jurisdiction to sell their securities by competitive bidding.[9]

The rise of privately placed securities, particularly debt issues, can be traced to several factors. First, the cost of flotation is materially less for such securities than it is for public offerings. Second, the time involved before the firm gets its money is considerably shorter than it is in the case of public sales. Third, securities so offered usually need not be registered with the Securities and Exchange Commission. A firm may thus avoid disclosing information it wishes to keep secret. Finally, changes in the contract between borrower and lender can be made more easily because there is usually only one or, at best, a handful of creditors with which to negotiate.

Despite these factors, to the extent that investment bankers provide a highly specialized service for business firms and can sell securities to the public much more easily, they tend to reduce the cost of funds to the firm. They must be more efficient in raising capital to be useful, and—other things being equal—if the demand for investment remains constant, the lower the cost of funds to the firm, the greater the investment (capital formation) will be.

Other Financial Institutions

Similar to investment banking activities in the primary market are other financial intermediaries that make substantial sums available to business enterprises and thereby tend to facilitate capital formation. The most relevant of these for our purposes are life insurance companies, commercial banks, and private pension funds. The rest of the financial institutions participating in the market for long-term funds, such as savings and loan associations and mutual savings banks, although important and competitive with those mentioned above, provide few funds for business enterprises.

The securities of business firms held by life insurance companies constitute over 40 per cent of the insurance companies' total resources. The vast majority of these are bonds. Because of the regulation and apparent inclination of insurance companies, few of their funds have been channeled into stocks, which constituted only 4.7 per cent of their total assets

---

[9] Avery B. Cohan, *Private Placements and Public Offerings: Market Shares Since 1935*, Technical Paper 1, (Chapel Hill, N. C.,: School of Business Administration, University of North Carolina, 1961), p. 8.

in 1962. Of the stocks they do hold, however, about 60 per cent are common stocks and the vast majority are in the industrial (mining, manufacturing, and merchandising) category.

The asset growth of life insurance companies since 1940 has been enormous. In the period 1940–62, the total assets of life insurance companies increased from $30.8 billion to $133.3 billion, as can be seen from Table 8-4. Figure 8-4 demonstrates this fact even more emphatically. In that same period the composition of these assets changed significantly, particularly as they apply to the financing of business firms. This period witnessed (as shown in Table 8-5) a considerable shift away from railroad bond holdings and a significant increase in public utility and industrial and miscellaneous bond holdings. Not all these increases in securities represent new issues of business firms. On the contrary, a great many were the result of purchases in the secondary markets—that is, of securities already outstanding. Although the precise amounts of new issues acquired by life insurance companies may never be determined, we do know that they are the single most important category of institutions in the direct placement of corporate bonds. One study indicates that life insurance companies consistently took up more than 80 per cent of all privately placed corporate securities in the postwar years.[10] In another study it was found that 72 per cent of the total bond purchases in 1949 resulted from direct placement. By type of industry, in turn, 22 per cent of railroad bonds, 50 per cent of public utilities bonds, and 87 per cent of industrial and miscellaneous firms bonds were directly placed.[11] For example, in the period ending 1961 it was estimated that of the total life insurance holdings of $28.7 billion of industrial and other nonutility type bonds, $24 billion was the result of private placements. This was almost 84 per cent of the total holdings of these securities by life insurance companies.[12] It is further suggested that, had there been no required competitive bidding, the amounts directly placed would be even greater.[13]

In addition, life insurance companies extend mortgage funds to numerous businesses, especially small ones, and hence the extent to which they aid in the financing of business firms is understated if only their bond

[10] U. S. Securities and Exchange Commission, *Privately Placed Securities—Cost of Flotation* (1952), p. 6.

[11] Merwin H. Waterman, *Investment Banking Functions* ("Michigan Business Studies," Vol. XIV, No. 1; Ann Arbor, Mich.: Bureau of Business Research, School of Business Administration, University of Michigan, 1958), pp. 120, 121; citing: Frazer B. Wilde, *The Pros and Cons of Direct Placement* (Chicago, 1950).

[12] *Life Insurance Fact Book,* Institute of Life Insurance (1961), p. 82.

[13] Merwin H. Waterman, *Investment Banking Functions,* p. 121. Railroad securities and all securities of public utilities coming under the jurisdiction of the Securities and Exchange Commission and the Federal Power Commission must be bid for on a competitive basis.

Table 8-4 Distribution of Assets of U.S. Life Insurance Companies (Millions)

Year	U.S. Government Securities	Foreign Government Bonds	State Provincial and Local Bonds	Railroad Bonds	Public Utility Bonds	Industrial and Miscellaneous Bonds	Stocks	Mortgages	Real Estate	Policy Loans	Miscellaneous Assets	Total
1917	$ 70	$ 163	$ 329	$1,813	$ 113	$ 49	$ 83	$ 2,021	$ 179	$ 810	$ 311	$ 941
1920	830	169	350	1,775	125	49	75	2,442	172	859	474	7,320
1925	637	154	530	2,238	687	97	81	4,808	266	1,446	604	11,538
1930	319	160	1,023	2,931	1,631	367	519	7,598	584	2,807	977	18,880
1935	2,853	189	1,685	2,625	2,114	575	583	5,357	1,990	3,540	1,705	23,216
1940	5,767	288	2,392	2,830	4,273	1,542	605	5,972	2,065	3,091	1,977	30,802
1941	6,796	396	2,286	2,858	4,873	1,842	601	6,442	1,878	2,919	1,840	32,731
1942	9,295	511	2,045	2,712	5,165	1,830	608	6,726	1,663	2,683	1,693	34,931
1943	12,537	684	1,773	2,734	5,220	1,888	652	6,714	1,352	2,373	1,839	37,766
1944	16,531	792	1,429	2,777	5,299	1,883	756	6,686	1,063	2,134	1,704	41,054
1945	20,583	915	1,047	2,948	5,212	1,900	999	6,636	857	1,962	1,738	44,797
1946	21,629	1,010	936	2,872	5,587	3,316	1,249	7,155	735	1,894	1,808	48,191
1947	20,021	1,037	945	2,844	6,941	4,969	1,390	8,675	860	1,937	2,124	51,743
1948	16,746	1,140	1,199	3,002	8,741	7,151	1,428	10,833	1,055	2,057	2,160	55,512
1949	15,290	1,130	1,393	3,017	9,764	8,680	1,718	12,906	1,247	2,240	2,245	59,630
1950	13,459	1,060	1,547	3,187	10,587	9,526	2,103	16,102	1,445	2,413	2,591	64,020
1951	11,009	922	1,736	3,307	11,235	11,441	2,221	19,314	1,631	2,590	2,872	68,278
1952	10,252	755	1,767	3,545	11,953	13,702	2,446	21,251	1,903	2,713	3,088	73,375
1953	9,829	586	1,990	3,643	12,827	15,527	2,573	23,322	2,020	2,914	3,302	78,533
1954	9,070	481	2,549	3,757	13,511	16,926	3,268	25,976	2,298	3,127	3,523	84,486
1955	8,576	410	2,696	3,912	13,968	18,179	3,633	29,445	2,581	3,290	3,742	90,432
1956	7,555	357	3,011	3,877	14,520	19,787	3,503	32,989	2,817	3,519	4,076	96,011
1957	7,029	332	3,163	3,863	15,252	21,717	3,391	35,236	3,119	3,869	4,338	101,309
1958	7,183	320	3,510	3,843	15,938	23,439	4,109	37,062	3,364	4,188	4,624	107,580
1959	6,868	349	4,135	3,774	16,455	25,105	4,561	39,197	3,651	4,618	4,937	113,650
1960	6,427	437	4,576	3,668	16,999	26,728	4,981	41,771	3,765	5,231	5,273	119,576
1961	6,134	476	5,039	3,594	16,999	28,690	6,258	44,203	4,007	5,733	5,683	126,816
1962	6,170	659	5,349	3,496	17,330	30,718	6,302	46,902	4,107	6,234	6,024	133,291

Source: Life Insurance Fact Book, Institute of Life Insurance (1963), 64.

Table 8-5 Percentage Distribution of Assets of U. S. Life Insurance Companies

Year	U.S. Government Securities	Foreign Government Bonds	State Provincial and Local Bonds	Railroad Bonds	Public Utility Bonds	Industrial and Miscellaneous Bonds	Stocks	Mortgages	Real Estate	Policy Loans	Miscellaneous Assets	Total
1917	1.2%	2.8%	5.6%	30.5%	1.9%	0.8%	1.4%	34.0%	3.0%	13.6%	5.2%	100.0%
1920	11.3	2.3	4.8	24.3	1.7	0.7	1.0	33.4	2.3	11.7	6.5	100.0
1925	5.4	1.3	4.6	19.4	6.0	0.8	0.7	41.7	2.3	12.5	5.3	100.0
1930	1.7	0.9	5.4	15.5	8.6	1.9	2.8	40.2	2.9	14.9	5.2	100.0
1935	12.3	0.8	7.3	11.3	9.1	2.5	2.5	23.1	8.6	15.2	7.3	100.0
1940	18.7	1.0	7.8	9.2	13.9	5.0	2.0	19.4	6.7	10.0	6.3	100.0
1941	20.8	1.2	7.0	8.7	14.9	5.6	1.8	19.7	5.7	8.9	5.7	100.0
1942	26.6	1.5	5.8	7.8	14.8	5.2	1.7	19.2	4.8	7.7	4.9	100.0
1943	33.2	1.8	4.7	7.3	13.8	5.0	1.7	17.8	3.6	6.3	4.8	100.0
1944	40.3	1.9	3.5	6.7	12.9	4.6	1.9	16.3	2.6	5.2	4.1	100.0
1945	45.9	2.1	2.3	6.6	11.6	4.3	2.2	14.8	1.9	4.4	3.9	100.0
1946	44.9	2.1	1.9	6.0	11.6	6.9	2.6	14.8	1.5	3.9	3.8	100.0
1947	38.7	2.0	1.8	5.5	13.4	9.6	2.7	16.8	1.7	3.7	4.1	100.0
1948	30.2	2.0	2.2	5.4	15.7	12.9	2.6	19.5	1.9	3.7	3.9	100.0
1949	25.6	1.9	2.3	5.1	16.4	14.6	2.9	21.6	2.1	3.7	3.8	100.0
1950	21.0	1.7	2.4	5.0	16.5	14.9	3.3	25.1	2.2	3.8	4.1	100.0
1951	16.1	1.3	2.5	4.9	16.4	16.8	3.3	28.3	2.4	3.8	4.2	100.0
1952	14.0	1.0	2.4	4.8	16.3	18.7	3.3	29.0	2.6	3.7	4.2	100.0
1953	12.5	0.7	2.6	4.7	16.3	19.7	3.3	29.7	2.6	3.7	4.2	100.0
1954	10.7	0.5	3.1	4.5	16.0	20.0	3.9	30.7	2.7	3.7	4.2	100.0
1955	9.5	0.4	3.0	4.3	15.5	20.1	4.0	32.6	2.9	3.6	4.1	100.0
1956	7.9	0.4	3.1	4.0	15.1	20.6	3.7	34.4	2.9	3.7	4.2	100.0
1957	6.9	0.3	3.1	3.8	15.1	21.5	3.3	34.8	3.1	3.8	4.3	100.0
1958	6.7	0.3	3.3	3.6	14.8	21.8	3.8	34.4	3.1	3.9	4.3	100.0
1959	6.0	0.3	3.7	3.3	14.5	22.1	4.0	34.5	3.2	4.1	4.3	100.0
1960	5.4	0.3	3.8	3.1	14.0	22.4	4.2	34.9	3.1	4.4	4.4	100.0
1961	4.9	0.3	4.0	2.8	13.4	22.6	4.9	34.9	3.2	4.5	4.5	100.0
1962	4.6	0.5	4.0	2.6	13.0	23.1	4.7	35.2	3.1	4.1	4.5	100.0

Source: *Life Insurance Fact Book* Institute of Life Insurance (1963), 65.

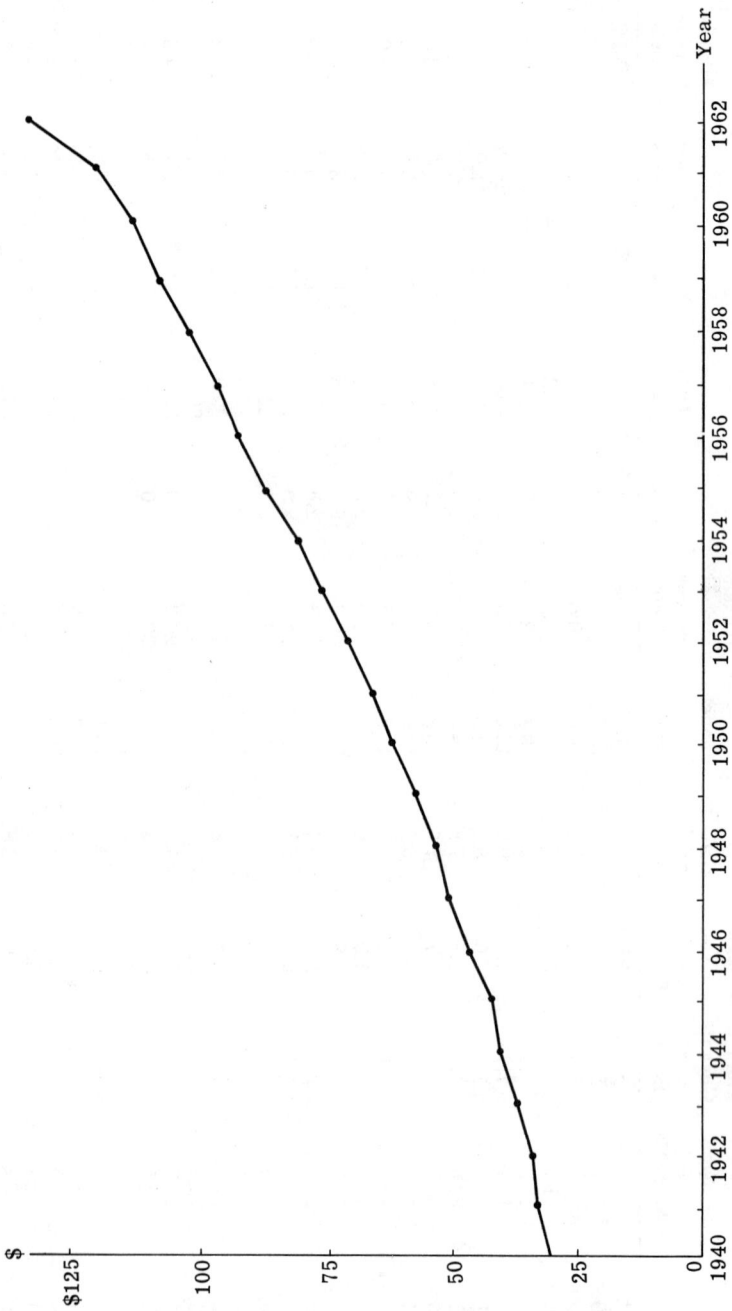

Figure 8-4 Total U.S. Life Insurance Companies' Assets, 1940–1962 (in Billions). *Source: Life Insurance Fact Book,* 1963.

and stock holdings are analyzed. It is interesting to note that slightly more than 67 per cent of the total invested industrial bonds was invested in those of manufacturing firms while the remainder was invested in those of nonmanufacturing firms. In the final analysis then, life insurance companies are extremely important to business firms because they constitute one of the major purchasers of securities issued by business firms. Many of their purchases are of new securities.

Typically, commercial banks finance business firms by means of short-term loans. For this reason they are usually discussed under the topic of money markets, although they do on occasion enter into term loans (loans having a duration of a year or more, but usually less than ten years).

From Table 8-6 it can be seen that at the end of 1963 commercial banks in the aggregate had loans and investments of slightly over $254 billion, of which only about 21 per cent were in commercial loans and less than 2 per cent were in the form of securities other than those of federal, state, or municipal agencies. Substantial portions of the total were invested in

Table 8-6
Distribution of Commercial Bank Assets, 1963
(Millions)

	Amount	Percentage of Total	Percentage Composition of Total Loans	Percentage Composition of Total Investments
Loans:*				
Commercial†	$ 52.9	20.8	33.9	
Agricultural	7.5	3.0	4.8	
To financial institutions	13.1	5.2	8.4	
For purchasing or carrying securities	7.9	3.1	5.1	
Real estate	39.1	15.4	25.1	
Individual	34.6	13.6	22.2	
Other	4.0	1.6	2.6	
Total loans	$156.0	61.4		
Investments:				
U.S. government securities	$ 63.2	24.9		64.3
Nonfederal governmental units	29.8	11.7		30.3
Other	5.2	2.0		5.3
Total investments	$ 98.2	38.6		
Total loans and investments	$254.2			

* Figures are shown gross of valuation reserves.
† Including open-market paper.
Source: Federal Reserve Bulletin (June 1964), 740.

the securities of various governmental agencies, both federal and local, in real estate and in personal loans.

Of the total loans made, slightly less than 34 per cent were commercial loans while about 25 per cent were invested in real estate loans and about 22 per cent in individual loans. Of the total investments, about 64 per cent were in United States government securities.

From this brief exposition it can be seen that only about one fifth of commercial banks' investable funds are made available to businesses. These are usually of a short-term duration, designed to provide temporary funds for seasonal or unusual needs.

Also of significance in the decade of the 1950's has been the phenomenal rise in importance of *private pension funds*. Some of these funds are administered by the firms themselves. Many firms, however, have commercial banks administer their funds in the form of personal trusts. Both of these are referred to as *noninsured pension funds*. The total assets of noninsured corporate pension funds at the end of 1963 amounted to $46.5 billion. Some pension funds, however, are administered by life insurance companies in the form of annuities; these are called *insured pension funds*. The reserves in these types of plans at the end of 1963 amounted to over $23 billion. Thus, the grand total of private pension fund resources totaled about $70 billion.[14]

The investment policies of pension funds are less uniform and less well-known than those of other financial institutions. In general, about 40 per cent of the investments of noninsured funds are in corporate stocks, 42 per cent in corporate bonds, and the rest are committed to cash, government securities, mortgages, leaseholds, and other investments. The allocation of resources among various investment outlets for insured funds is that of the life insurance company. Commercial banks tend to be more conservative in the administration of funds than the firms themselves. Thus there is the tendency for them to place most of these funds in high-grade bonds and better-grade stocks. Nevertheless, of all financial institutions, they have become the largest net purchasers of common stock. Most of their stock holdings are in the so-called blue chips. Pension funds also hold a great deal of their resources in high-grade corporate bonds, many acquired through private placements. Other types of investments are relatively less important than the commitments in corporate securities.

It is not clear how much new cash is provided to business firms by pension funds. In 1961 the additions to the stock holdings of pension funds were 43 per cent of net additions to stock issues outstanding. In 1963 their purchases of stocks far exceeded the net additions to issues outstanding.[15]

[14] U.S. Securities and Exchange Commission, *Statistical Bulletin 23* (June 1964), 33.
[15] *Ibid.*, 34.

In the past several years they have consistently brought to the market about $2 billion for the purchase of stocks and $1.4 billion for the purchase of corporate debt obligations. Thus their importance to the corporate securities markets lies in the fact that they have purchased about $83.4 billion of corporate securities over the past several years. To the extent that their purchases provide new funds for business firms, capital formation may result directly; to the extent that they purchase existing securities, they facilitate capital formation indirectly.

The Impact of the Financial System on Capital Formation

From our standpoint, the importance of securities markets lies in their ability to promote capital formation, thereby promoting the economic welfare of society. Thus another way by which securities markets can be differentiated is according to their impact on capital formation.

In the primary market, capital formation may or may not take place as the result of an economic unit's securing new cash. Whether or not capital formation takes place depends on what is done with the funds that are so acquired. If they are used to retire other forms of securities, there is no capital formation. For example, a million-dollar bond issue may be sold by a firm in order to pay off another million-dollar bond issue that is coming due. Similarly, because of price inflation, a firm may have to sell more securities to raise enough funds to replace assets coming due or to maintain the same absolute level of inventories. In neither case would there be any net real capital formation. Measurable capital formation, as defined in earlier chapters, takes place only when there is a net increase in the physical goods used to produce other goods and/or inventories— that is, when there is an increased ability to produce goods. If capital formation is to take place at all through the securities markets, however, it will be accomplished only in the primary market. Because transactions on secondary markets provide no new cash for business firms, they cannot result in the direct formation of new productive machinery or in the increase of inventories. These transactions are merely exchanges of already existing financial obligations for cash or credit. No new cash flows to those business firms or economic units whose securities these obligations represent. Consequently, no capital formation can take place directly as a result of transactions in the secondary markets.

The importance of the secondary markets is not to be minimized, however. As we have seen, the existence of secondary markets makes it manifestly easier to sell securities in the primary market, for the buyers of new securities then know they can sell them to other buyers if and when they choose to do so. Secondary markets thus increase the marketability of existing securities, a feature most investors find attractive if not necessary. As a consequence, securities are most easily sold on the primary markets because of the existence of the secondary markets and, other things being equal, allow for lower-cost capital funds to the firms that issue these securities. The limited-liability feature of corporate shares and the availability of a secondary market assuring liquidity of security holdings has made possible the growth of the small shareholder, who need not therefore participate in corporate management. This type of financing has been a contributing force to the growth of the large, efficient producer in many industries. Nonliquid, permanent physical assets are thus financed by liquid, intangible assets. Thus, to the extent that primary flotations can be sold more easily because of the existence of a secondary market, organized securities exchanges—as well as secondary transactions in the over-the-counter market—tend to facilitate capital formation.

SUMMARY

The importance of the financial system lies in its capacity either to promote capital formation directly or to facilitate it indirectly through various institutions and intermediaries. Complex as the system may be, all securities markets can be differentiated in several different ways. The type of market was seen to be an important characteristic of securities markets: each market deals either in new issues or in existing issues. The duration of issues, either short-term or long-term, is a second major characteristic. The location of transactions is a third useful way of differentiating securities markets; the vast majority of all transactions take place in the over-the-counter markets vis-à-vis the organized securities exchanges.

The institutions that have a most important bearing on financing business were also explored. Not all of those set forth in Table 8-1 were covered; only such institutions as investment bankers, private pension funds, life insurance companies, and commercial banks were discussed for these have a greater bearing on financing business. The final—and, from the standpoint of the entire economy, the most important—aspect of securities markets, their impact on capital formation, was also discussed.

SUGGESTED READINGS

ANDREWS, VICTOR. "Pension Funds in the Securities Markets," *Harvard Business Review*, 37 (November–December 1959), 90–102.
————. "The Supply of Loanable Funds from Noninsured Corporate, State, and City-Administered Employee Pension Trusts," *The Journal of Finance*, 16 (May 1961), 328–50.

BOGEN, JULES I. "Trends in the Institutionalization of Savings and Thrift Institution Policies," *Conference on Savings and Residential Financing, 1960 Proceedings.* Chicago: The United States Savings and Loan League, 1960.

CALVERT, GORDON L. *A Primer on State Securities Regulation.* Washington, D.C.: Investment Bankers Association of America, 1960.

COHAN, AVERY B. "Yields on New Underwritten Corporate Bonds, 1935–58," *The Journal of Finance, 17* (December 1962), 585–605.

CONKLIN, GEORGE T. "Direct Placements," *The Journal of Finance, 6* (June 1951), 85–118.

COOKE, GILBERT W. *The Stock Markets.* New York: Simmons-Boardman Publishing Company, 1964.

COREY, E. RAYMOND. *Direct Placement of Corporate Securities.* Cambridge, Mass.: Harvard University Press, 1951.

EDMONDS, S. "Financing Capital Formation," *Harvard Business Review, 28* (January 1950), 33–41.

FREUND, WILLIAM C. "An Appraisal of the Sources and Uses of Funds Approach to the Analysis of Financial Markets," *The Journal of Finance, 13* (May 1958), 275–94.

FRIEND, IRWIN, G. WRIGHT HOFFMAN, and WILLIS J. WINN. *The Over-the-Counter Securities Markets.* New York, McGraw-Hill Company, Inc., 1958.

GOLDSMITH, RAYMOND W. *Financial Intermediaries in the American Economy Since 1900.* Princeton, N.J.: Princeton University Press, 1958.

GUTHMANN, HARRY G. "Prospects for Private Financial Institutions," *Harvard Business Review, 4* (March–April 1962), 151–69.

HALLERAN, THOMAS A., and JOHN N. CALDERWOOD. "Effect of Federal Regulation on Distribution of and Trading in Securities," *George Washington Law Review, 28* (October 1959), 94–118.

HARBRECT, PAUL P. *Pension Funds and Economic Power.* New York: Twentieth Century Fund, Inc., 1959.

HICKMAN, W. B. *The Volume of Corporate Bond Financing Since 1900.* Princeton, N.J.: Princeton University Press, 1953.

INVESTMENT BANKERS ASSOCIATION OF AMERICA. *Investment Banking.* Englewood Cliffs, N.J.: Prentice-Hall, Inc., 1949.

KUZNETS, SIMON. *Capital in the American Economy.* Princeton, N.J.: Princeton University Press, 1961.

LEFFLER, GEORGE L., and LORING C. FARWELL. *The Stock Market,* 3rd ed. New York: The Ronald Press Company, 1963.

MCFERRIN, J. B. "The Structure of the American Capital Market," *Southern Economic Journal, 21* (January 1955), 247–260.

MILLER, EUGENE. "Trends in Private Pension Funds," *The Journal of Finance, 13* (May 1961), 313–27.

NAVIN, T. R. "Investment Banking Since 1900: An Unexplored Field in American Financial History," *Business History Review, 27* (March 1953), 60–65.

ROZEN, MARVIN E. "The Changing Structure of Financial Institutions," *The Quarterly Review of Economics and Business, 2* (November 1962), 69–80.

SOLDOFSKY, ROBERT M. "The Size and Maturity of Direct Placement Loans," *The Journal of Finance, 15* (March 1960), 32–44.

U.S. SECURITIES AND EXCHANGE COMMISSION. *Special Study of Securities Markets.* Washington, D.C.: Government Printing Office, 1963.

The Commission on Money and Credit has sponsored a number of monographs which bear on topics contained in this and other chapters. Among the more important ones for our purposes are:

AMERICAN BANKERS ASSOCIATION. *The Commercial Banking Industry.* Englewood Cliffs, N.J.: Prentice-Hall, Inc., 1962.

FRIEND, IRWIN, HYMAN P. MINSKY, and VICTOR L. ANDREWS. *Private Capital Markets.* Englewood Cliffs, N.J.: Prentice-Hall, Inc., 1964.

HORVITZ, PAUL M., *et al. Private Financial Institutions.* Englewood Cliffs, N.J.: Prentice-Hall, Inc., 1963.

LIFE INSURANCE ASSOCIATION OF AMERICA. *Life Insurance Companies as Financial Institutions.* Englewood Cliffs, N.J.: Prentice-Hall, Inc., 1962.

QUESTIONS

8.1 Is capital more likely to be formed as the result of transactions in the primary money market or in the primary capital market? Explain.

8.2 In the primary market, capital formation may or may not take place as the result of an economic unit's securing new cash. Explain.

8.3 How do financial institutions support the acts of saving and investing?

8.4 (*a*) Explain how the secondary capital market facilitates capital formation. (*b*) What is its impact on and relation to the primary capital market?

8.5 Why may a syndicate be formed to underwrite an issue of securities?

8.6 In what way is the investment banker an intermediary? How does his function differ from that of a commercial banker?

8.7 As a financial manager, would you prefer to use internal or external sources of funds for new plant expansion? What would be your main considerations in this analysis?

8.8 Examine and discuss the trends in the placement of corporate securities as portrayed in Table 8-3.

8.9 What factors appear to have influenced the rise in private placement of securities?

8.10 How do financial intermediaries contribute to capital formation? How do they affect it?

8.11 Do funds held as currency by individuals detract from the well-being of society by not being invested? Does your answer apply equally well to demand deposits? Explain.

8.12 Commercial banks receive funds from savers in the community, pay them a rate of interest, pay their own expenses, and allocate the funds to local enterprises, and grant stockholders a return for their funds and risk-taking. Comment on and criticize this process.

8.13 What relationship do you see between (1) the differentiation of securities markets as set forth in Table 8-1 and (2) the risk and expected rate of return? Discuss fully.

8.14 If there were no secondary market for securities, what would you expect the shape of the CMC to be like? Explain.

8.15 What influence would you expect institutional investors to have on the CMC? Explain.

PART II   FINANCIAL ASPECTS
OF THE FIRM

Chapters 9–13 compose Part II of this text. These chapters are devoted essentially to the study of the financial aspects of firm behavior. Whereas the emphasis of Part I was on the financial environment of the firm's behavior, Part II focuses upon the firm environment of the financial manager. We shall reserve for Part III the decisions facing the operating financial manager.

CHAPTER 9   THE NATURE
OF BUSINESS ENTERPRISE

The purpose of this chapter is to give a general picture of the economic objective of business enterprise (generally considered the maximization of profits), the noneconomic objectives of the firm, the general limitations on the pursuit of these firm objectives, and the organizational aspects of the firm that arise from the pursuit of these goals. There is no one generally accepted concept of the firm; many concepts (economic, holistic, organizational) exist.[1] The primary goal of this discussion is to present the basic influences that bear on the making of financial decisions.

GENERAL

It is essential to recognize that the business firm and the persons who direct its operations cannot be disassociated. Too often we tend to think in terms of the "firm" doing this or that without recognizing that the decisions of the firm are made by individuals. Entrepreneurial functions are carried out by individuals and cannot therefore be regarded exclusively in economic terms. The increased interest of the behavioral scientists in business administration reflects the current thesis that business managers are motivated not only by economic considerations but also by a host of other factors, some of which will be explored more fully in this chapter. Man is not only an economic creature, but a political and social one as well. All these aspects need to be recognized in a study of business. Thus, as we shall see, the business firm and the decisions it makes are no better than the amalgamation of ideas generated by persons within the enterprise. And such decisions, as well as the success of the firm, must necessarily reflect the personalities involved.

To a greater or lesser extent, the firm is a vehicle for all individuals participating. The lowest employee combines with the highest decision-maker in activity which is essentially economic in motivation. The employee is seeking a wage to contribute to his satisfactions; the manager may be seeking a salary. They also usually derive social satisfaction and

[1] Joseph W. McGuire, "The Concept of the Firm," *California Management Review*, 3 (Summer 1961), 64–88.

perhaps political satisfactions as well. Their rewards, however, tend to be in proportion to the effectiveness with which they contribute to the maximization of returns to owners. The greater the separation of the owners from the management of the firm, however, the less sensitive the managers may be to this goal in the short run. This lack of sensitivity may present a modern-day danger to large corporate efficiency. Yet, as long as the managers and other participants receive gains for the achievement of this goal, they will tend to be motivated to coordinate their actions to that end.

Moreover, the firm is a dynamic unit in a dynamic environment. Change is everywhere. Hence actions within the firm reflect attempts to adjust the firm's position to internal or external changes in order to achieve the firm's objectives as these are seen by the decision-makers of the firm. These continuous adjustments are efforts to reach an equilibrium (a position from which there is no tendency to change), which itself is constantly shifting. Thus a change in the cost of capital will call forth a chain of reactions within the firm in order to adjust to a new position more in keeping with the firm's goals. From a financial point of view, for example, it can be stated that all the items listed on a balance sheet, and their interrelationships, can be viewed as having one ideal or optimum state, any deviation from which should set in motion a series of actions designed to return the firm to that state. Because we lack complete understanding, precise measurement techniques, and adequate information, it is impossible to say what that optimum state is for any firm at any given point in time. Presumably the economic optimum state would be that mix and total sum of resources which maximizes the present worth of future income to the owners of the business enterprise.

It has been seen that a high standard of future material welfare depends, in part, upon a high level of present capital formation. The business firm is also the major vehicle through which economic capital is formed in a capitalistic society.

OBJECTIVES OF BUSINESS ENTERPRISE

One objective of business enterprise is survival; both in the short run and in the long run, maintenance of the firm's solvency is essential. Solvency is a requirement for maximizing profits or the present worth of future profits for the shareholders.

The objectives of shareholders are as diverse as their personalities. Some people buy shares with the expectation of receiving a reasonable dividend income. Price appreciation may be the goal of others. Prestige, "keeping up with the Joneses," the urge to try to "make a killing," and hundreds of other reasons may be proffered as possible explanations for stock purchases. The returns to stockholders can take the form either of price appreciation or of dividend income. For this reason we define profits from the shareholders' point of view: as *changes in the value of ownership claims plus dividends (but less any items that detract from this income stream, such as cash purchases of new stock)*. Also for this reason we establish this as the long-run goal of financial management. In pursuit of this goal we can view the business enterprise [2] as bringing together various factors of production, presumably in an efficient manner, in order to produce certain economic goods or services. This is its basic strategy, its over-all plan for action, its *raison d'être*. These factors of production (land, labor, capital, and management) are either bought outright or hired.[3] In order to hire or purchase various factors of production, money or credit is needed. The enterprise is the unit or legal form of organization through which production is carried on; through the entrepreneurial or managerial function, the firm's activities are directed, coordinated, and controlled. Managerial activity involves the making of decisions that ordinarily involve expectations concerning future economic and noneconomic conditions; therefore, they must include uncertainty and risk considerations. It is important for the financial manager to recognize that his enterprise operates in a state of uncertainty, for the implications of this fact are far-reaching. The decisions made by managers may be less than perfect in an *ex post* sense; hence errors are to be expected.

It has been stated that the underlying economic motivation of a business enterprise in a free, capitalistic society is the acquisition of profits. Thus the economic objective of a business enterprise is to maximize the economic welfare of the owners of the firm (with economic welfare being expressed as profits, as previously defined). In order to maximize profits, business managers attempt to choose from alternative courses of action those they believe will result in the greatest excess of revenues derived from factor outputs over the expenses—explicit and implicit—of factor inputs. *Explicit costs* are those usually involving outlays by the firm and are recorded by the accounting system; they are clearly measurable. *Implicit costs* do not involve outlays, yet they exist in a nonmonetary form; in the long run they must be covered by revenues in order for the firm to sustain its present status and to expand.

---

[2] The term *firm* is used interchangeably with the term *business enterprise*.

[3] Obviously, labor cannot be bought outright (although in a sense the lifetime contracts used in certain sports and entertainment fields are an attempt to do this, at least in part).

Although it may very well be argued that other factors, such as the desire for self-edification and independence, may condition efforts to maximize profits, it nevertheless appears that in even the largest corporations profit maximization is the dominant objective of firm behavior. Business enterprises may pursue other objectives which may in fact conflict with the profit objective. Indeed, it is recognized that other objectives, to be discussed more fully later, may be as important as the profit objective at some time. Nevertheless, profit maximization over extended periods of time still appears to be the fundamental objective of business firms. That is, the firm attempts to maximize its income streams, utilizing its resources so as to maximize the present worth of the income stream that may extend into perpetuity. This "present worth" concept will be elaborated in the next chapter.

But the pursuit of maximization of short-run profits may act against achievement of prospective long-run profits. Accordingly, it is widely presumed that business corporations attempt to seek their long-run economic welfare, *long-run* being a composite of the time horizons of the decision-makers of the firm. For example, immediately after World War II the demand for automobiles was well in excess of their supply. Under these conditions, the automobile manufacturers could have set their prices considerably higher than they did. They did not, however, so that shortages existed. It is widely believed that the reason for not raising prices arose, for the most part, from the manufacturers' desire to promote the long-run economic welfare of their enterprises. To have set prices at the highest obtainable level (which was apparently quite high, as can be seen from the under-the-table or black-market dealings in automobiles at that time) could very well have incurred the ill-will of the public and the government for years to come—a situation that might have proved inimical to the pursuit of the firms' long-range profit objective.

Furthermore, part of the strategy of firms may be such as to avoid making unusually high profits of a short-lived nature for fear of attracting new firms into the industry—which, in time, might tend to reduce the long-run average revenues of firms presently in the industry, and for fear of incurring restrictive or punitive governmental action.

THE CONCEPT OF PROFITS

In light of the foregoing discussion, the concept of profits as an economic goal needs to be explored briefly. *Profit,* as we use the term generally throughout this text, was previously defined as the *change in the value of ownership plus nonwage distributions to owners* during some time period. Accounting profits are the excess of net revenues over explicit costs, including depreciation and taxes. From a traditional economic point of view, however, profits are a residue—something left over, something in excess of implicit and explicit costs of operating the firm. The nature of profits is treated in detail in the next chapter. Here we are concerned primarily with the sources of such profits as economists have described them. Among the leading sources of economic profits are: imperfections in the market, innovations, and changes in expectations (uncertainty).

The importance of the sources of economic profits is to be found in the fact that most firms try to achieve them. Indeed, in a sense they must. Because all investment opportunities that lie on the *CMC* represent pure returns to capital (the pure rate of interest) plus a return for the risk of employing that capital in various ways, these investment returns can be viewed as being normal, reasonably expected ones; they are average, run-of-the-mill returns. Parenthetically, it may be stated at this point that many of the limitations on the pursuit of economic profits (a point to be discussed more fully later) are designed to eliminate or overcome the so-called imperfections.

Much of the profit realized by business enterprises today is a result of imperfections in the market: there is not perfect knowledge concerning opportunities and technology in an industry; there is not perfect mobility of factor resources; there is not perfect knowledge on the part of consumers concerning the outputs (products) of an industry; and there is not perfect knowledge of firms regarding the prices, quantities, and qualities of factor inputs. Not everybody, for example, has a perfect knowledge of the profit opportunities in, say, the electrical industry; not many would possess the technological information necessary to make such profits. Also, it seems self-evident that resources (with the possible exception of money capital) do not move easily from one geographical location to another. Skilled labor cannot easily be moved from New England to operate textile plants in the southern states. Nor can a great deal of skilled labor be moved easily from the Detroit area to produce automobiles in California. These labor shifts may take place in time, but it may take several years—if not decades—to accomplish such a change. As a result, there may be a substantial excess labor supply in Detroit, making it feasible for firms located there to pay lower wage rates—which is tantamount to underpaying the factors of production. Similarly, it is not always possible, feasible, or even desirable (because of relocation costs) for managerial talent to seek out its "opportunity wage." If the president of some large firm is receiving a salary of $200,000 a year while he could get $500,000 (his best opportunity wage) at another firm, he is—in effect—being underpaid to the extent of $300,000. This amount will accrue to the benefit of the owners as a residual profit. The same reasoning can be applied to other resources as well, and for the other market imperfections.

All these forces tend to contribute to varying degrees of monopolistic competition depending on the extent and intensity to which each of them exists. As a result of the imperfections higher average prices for outputs can be charged on the one hand and lower average compensation for factor inputs may be paid on the other. In both cases profits will tend to be in excess of what they would have been had there been perfect knowledge of opportunities and perfect mobility of resources.

Another imperfection in the market, somewhat akin to those discussed above, is that of limited entry into an industry. As long as a firm's average implicit and explicit costs are less than its average revenues and the entry of new firms into the industry is effectively barred, this firm will reap profits. Patents, trademarks, large capital resources needed to establish an enterprise, technical superiority unknown to others, and unusual managerial talent are typical effective barriers to the entry of new firms into an industry. For example, the past success of certain companies arises, no doubt, from the fact that entry is effectively restricted, not so much by overt acts on the part of these companies as by patents and technical considerations. Given the technical superiority of these companies, their patents, and managerial talent generally, the efforts of other firms to compete—much less to enter the industry—are fraught with innumerable difficulties. All these factors tend to bar other firms from entering the industry and make competition by existing ones difficult. As a consequence, the profits of firms so situated will tend to exceed what they might have been had there been easy entry into the industry.

Economists have long recognized the importance of innovations in creating profits. Innovations essentially are new products, new ways of doing old things, new technologies, or new ideas designed either to improve the production process or to stimulate consumption. These factors tend to create, at least temporarily, a monopoly position for the innovating firm. Also, firms seek—through advertising, variations in packaging, and other marketing devices—to produce differentiated products and to persuade consumers of the desirability of one product as opposed to those of competitors. These latter factors also tend to create certain monopolistic powers for the firm and tend to generate greater profits. Thus the firm that innovates, that brings out new products, or that improves its productive machinery will gain the rewards of such production. A firm with a new product has a monopoly on this one product, albeit only a temporary one; but as long as it has this monopoly, it could maintain prices well above costs. Subsequently, however, other firms will probably introduce substitute products and tend to reduce the profits by taking away a share of the market.

Similarly, new techniques which result in more efficient production will tend to lower the average costs of the firm that innovates, and hence will tend to raise its profits. This advantage, too, may be only temporary in nature.

Thus, it can be seen that bringing out new products, improving established products, improving technology, and attempting to change consumer preferences by various marketing devices all tend to generate profits for a business enterprise. But these profits may be only temporary in character, depending on the degree of "insulation" the innovating firm has from other firms that might imitate its techniques.

All these considerations are similar in nature. In each instance the profits arise from the partially or full monopolistic position of a firm with respect to hiring the factors of production, introducing innovations and product differentiation, or effectively barring entry of other firms into the industry. However, there is another source of profits which needs to be discussed: changes in the expectations of a firm in an environment of uncertainty surrounding business decisions.

Unexpected changes in production costs or in the demand for a firm's products not arising from any of the factors mentioned above are in the nature of windfalls and constitute a source of profits for the firm. For example, an unexpected decline in the price of raw materials will tend to increase profits beyond original expectations. Similarly, an unexpected shift of consumer demand to a firm's product not directly attributable to predictable causes would also constitute a source of windfall profits.

It is obvious that it does not usually matter whether the resources for profit-making are owned or hired; it is the services of these resources which are consequential to the acquisition of profits. These services, properly combined, will provide future revenue to the firm—which, if in excess of future implicit (including opportunity costs) and explicit costs, result in economic profits. Were there perfect markets and free entry, revenues would tend to equal implicit (including opportunity costs) and explicit costs and there would be no economic profits.

Marginal Analysis

Marginal analysis, as traditionally used by economists, is helpful in the understanding of profit. Simply put, marginal analysis of firm behavior indicates that an enterprise will undertake certain activities as long as their marginal revenues exceed their marginal costs. That is, it will undertake any activity that *adds* more to anticipated total revenues than it does to anticipated total costs. By doing this the enterprise will be seeking its maximum profits (if all true costs are included). Theoretically, it will continue to take on such activities as long as the opportunities to do so continue to exist. Economists suggest that, theoretically, firms will continue to do this up to the point where the difference in added anticipated revenue between two projects is equal to the difference in added anticipated cost associated with the particular project. This notion is an important one for financial managers to understand and appreciate for it establishes some guideposts for decision-making.

NONECONOMIC OBJECTIVES OF BUSINESS ENTERPRISES

In addition to the economic goals that bear on the behavior of business enterprises, there are noneconomic objectives of which financial management should also be aware. These have to do with the so-called human element. These considerations tend to add other dimensions to the strategy of the firm and to require an extension in the scope of thinking of the financial manager.

The advent of the application of behavioral sciences to the study of business administration reflects the fact that economic objectives, in and of themselves, are not the sole goals of managers of business firms and therefore do not fully explain the entire behavior of business firms. Indeed, some studies[4] indicate that noneconomic considerations may sometimes dominate the decision-making process of certain firms and that business objectives appear to be an amalgamation of economic, political, social, and ethical factors that reflect the personalities of and conflicts among the persons of the firm—especially those who direct or manage the firm's resources.

Such goals as good personnel relations, duties and responsibilities to the local community, and apparent obligations to consumers—although erringly offered as noneconomic goals—are exhibits of economic behavior insofar as attainment of these objectives contributes to long-run profitability. The awareness of the influence of such factors on profitability is a relatively recent development in the study of business enterprises. Along these same lines financial management has become increasingly aware of the importance of providing information to the investing public—an objective which should contribute to a more proper evaluation of securities and,

[4] See, for example: Martin Shubick, "Objective Functions and Models of Corporate Optimization," *The Quarterly Journal of Economics*, 65 (August 1961), 345-75.

consequently, affect the cost of capital. To the extent that such actions affect a firm's cost of capital, they also affect its long-run profitability.

Other individual motives, such as the desire for power and creativity, find expression in the operation of the firm and are part of the noneconomic aspects of firm behavior. Other objectives of business managers include the desire to build a business empire and to increase the firm's share of the market—either of which might be considered economic or noneconomic, depending upon management motivation.

Despite these factors, profitability is still the measure by which we usually judge the success of business firms. This is true both from an economic and legal point of view as well as from the point of view of society. Profits are typically viewed as long-run phenomena and they are the overriding motive for most business enterprises today, notwithstanding the existence of other motives at any point in time. In sum, profits tend to measure the success of management; they are essential for growth. Noneconomic goals—for the most part—can usually be pursued only to a limited extent and for a relatively short period lest the financial integrity of the firm be impaired in the long run and legal failure result.

RESTRAINTS ON THE PURSUIT OF THE OBJECTIVES OF THE FIRM

Although it is desirable to set forth the goals of business firms, it is equally important to recognize that there are limitations to the pursuit of these goals. These limitations are both public and private in nature. The following discussion is not intended to be an exhaustive review; rather, it is intended merely to suggest the general limitations involved.

In general, public legal restraints on the behavior of firms in the pursuit of their goals are designed to protect the relatively unorganized public from business practices, whether tacit or not, which are considered inimical to the welfare of society as a whole.

This is the social aspect to the pursuit of profits. Profits have long been recognized as a directing force in the allocation of society's resources where alternative uses obviously exist. Society, through the dollar vote, has to a considerable degree determined which schemes it will or will not support. Those firms enjoying comfortable profits are doing so with the approbation of society (assuming that there is reasonably fair competition). The uneven distribution of income among members of society that results from profit maximization can be and is partially mitigated by income tax policies (another restriction on the pursuit of profits). There are, however, serious social defects in the unfettered pursuit of profit maximization. Some of these are well-known and scarcely bear repeating here. Dishonest business practices as well as seemingly unquenchable desires for concentration of financial resources and power has led, or has threatened to lead, to an allocation of resources not in the best interest of society as a whole. For example, as nineteenth-century capitalism blossomed in the United States, the rule of the age was to let businessmen be completely free to pursue maximum profits, their consciences being the guide to the promotion of social welfare. As students of American economic history, we are aware that this system was defective. Consequently, the government established constraints in the forms of taxes and legislation; these tended to establish the framework within which businesses could pursue maximum profits and, at the same time, attempted to redirect resources in a manner designed to promote the social welfare. An alternative would have been to let the government own and operate all or some of the material means of production. This system (socialism) has not been popular as a *modus vivendi* in the American society. We have been equally dissatisfied with allowing businessmen to decide for themselves how best to serve the social welfare.

Businessmen generally have also learned that long-run profit advantages are to be found in the avoidance of such practices. And, although each of these aspects is prevalent in our society, it is the compromise between them that characterizes most economic activity in the United States. The government establishes constraints on business enterprises in order to pursue the social welfare of society. It also takes part in the production of goods and services, but only in areas in which the profit motive presumably is not sufficient to offset risk. Social welfare is determined by a consensus of government officials, politicians, and voters. In a way, it can be said that there is a degree of specialization with respect to national goals. The economic goals of the nation include a high level of employment, rising standards of material well-being, and relatively stable prices. Businessmen work within the social framework set by government and, through it, they attempt to achieve maximum profits. For this reason, although we tend to stress the profit motive of business firms in this book, we do so in the realization that it is constrained by the rules set forth by society. The notion underlying this system of economic activity is that the good of the whole (i.e., society) transcends the good of any individual or firm. As seen in Chapter 7, profits are extremely important as a means of allocating the resources of our economy to their most productive uses. But our system is less than perfect; profits do not perfectly allocate resources; firms are run by fallible men; some business decisions, intentionally or not, are inimical to the social welfare as determined by a consensus of society; and restraints on business enterprises are necessary in order to promote the economic well-being of society.

Legal Restraints

Accordingly, the individual state governments have certain powers to regulate the activities of corporations, those state-sanctioned associations of persons. In brief, the state can dictate the kinds of powers the corporations may have. For example, there are incorporation statutes and more specific constraints and powers as spelled out in the charter of corporations in the various states. There are also so-called incidental powers of a corporation; these are the powers necessary for the achievement of the expressed rights mentioned in the charter. These are not explicitly stated, and there are considerable differences among authorities concerning which powers are incidental and which are not. These differences arise from subjective interpretations of what a corporation can or cannot do and the assumption that such powers derive from the very existence of the business corporation. Among some of the more important powers are the right to contract, the right to sue, the right to be sued, and the right to disburse earnings. Finally, there may be acts which are outside the powers of the corporations. These are called *ultra vires* acts—i.e., beyond the scope of expressed or implied powers of the corporation's charter.

There exists a whole body of law interpretative of the rights of the corporation. For our purposes, among the most notable interpretation of the law governing the operation of business corporations is the common law precedent established by the decision in *Wood v. Dummer*.[5] In this decision United States Supreme Court Justice Story determined that the capital stock of a business enterprise is like a trust fund, to be administered for corporate purposes and for the protection of creditors. According to this doctrine the capital stock constitutes the basic proprietary dedication that must be left intact and unimpaired to serve as a buffer between business losses and creditors; hence it cannot be lessened by dividend disbursements. Today no dividends can be paid out of legal capital (defined as the common and preferred stock at par or stated value).

There are also various state laws and regulatory commissions with which financial managers must contend. Most states are very active in regulating public utilities that operate within their territories, although various other commissions may also be established to deal with the additional regulatory problems of a given state. Perhaps no state enactments are more controversial than the so-called blue-sky laws. These were enacted by state legislatures to protect their residents from fraudulent sales of securities made within the state. Their effectiveness depends on the state's enforcement procedures. Most states are relatively inactive in en-

[5] *Wood* v. *Dummer*, 3 Mason (Maine) **308** (1824).

forcement. Later the federal government entered the field of securities regulation. As a result of proved abuses in the securities markets prior to the stock market crash of 1929, several federal statutes regulating the interstate offering of securities to the public were created.

On the federal level many statutes have been enacted which tend to constrain the unfettered pursuit of firm profits. Regulatory commissions are set up to administer the statutes, to establish order within a given industry, or to regulate various business practices. The regulation is accomplished through various administrative decrees as set forth by the various commissions. Thus, for example, the Securities and Exchange Commission is responsible for administering the Securities Act of 1933, the Securities and Exchange Act of 1934, the Public Utility Holding Company Act of 1935, and other federal statutes. The Federal Trade Commission is responsible for administering the Federal Trade Commission Act of 1914. The Federal Power Commission is responsible for administering the activities of firms coming under the jurisdiction of the Federal Power Commission Act. The Interstate Commerce Commission is charged with the duty of administering the Interstate Commerce Act of 1887. Obviously, each of these statutes, as well as the commissions created to administer them, bear most importantly on businesses associated with the public interest and are designed to promote the public welfare. For example, the Securities Exchange Commission administers the Public Utility Holding Company Act of 1935 which, in effect, bars the stratification of public utility holding companies to a total of three levels and requires the operating companies controlled to be adjacent. The Securities Act of 1933 requires disclosure of as much relevant information to prospective investors as is deemed prudent. Interstate offerings of new issues of securities must be preceded by a registration statement filed with the Securities and Exchange Commission and a prospectus which divulges relevant information regarding not only the security but also the corporation. Such a prospectus must be given to each prospective buyer of the security.[6]

Public corporations send proxies to stockholders in order to secure their votes. Proxies enable stockholders who cannot attend stockholders' meetings to vote on a single slate of directors and on certain important factors which materially alter the legal structure of the firm or have a significant bearing on their position as legal owners. The matters on which they are to vote often dictate the future over-all performance and objectives of the business enterprise. The effectiveness of this proxy system is often seriously questioned. It is generally believed that most proxies are, for the most part, a rubber stamp for the incumbent directors and the wishes of existing management.

[6] Certain interstate offerings are exempt from these and other regulations.

Nonlegal Constraints

In addition to the legal restrictions, there are certain nonlegal restraints that need to be considered. For example, business enterprises are frequently constrained by the value system in which they operate. Although this changes from society to society and from time to time, it may modify the goals of the firm. For example, public opinion and morality, whatever they may happen to be in a pluralistic society, will tend to circumscribe and influence the operations of the business firm. It is unquestionably true that many larger firms find it necessary to be public-relations conscious and try to act in a fashion consistent with what they envision as public opinion and public morality. Firms may also attempt to project a favorable corporate image. The extent to which a body of public opinion and morality regarding the pursuit of a firm's objectives really exists is, of course, subject to debate. Nevertheless, it seems that business enterprises are constrained by what they interpret as public opinion and morality, perhaps because they fear an adverse public reaction that might ultimately lead to even more legal restraints.

In addition, pleasant working conditions for employees, provision of long-run material security (perhaps through a pension plan), awareness of the import of their decisions on the community, minimal levels of honesty, and the consciences of individual managers all may tend to constrain the firm in its pursuit of maximum profits. Yet, the desire of professional managers and other participants in the firm to provide for their individual welfare and security with the minimum necessary regard for the welfare of other parties, especially in our largest, public corporations, may well impede the efforts of the firm to maximize profits in the traditional economic sense.

There is serious doubt, moreover, concerning the effective control which the legal owners of large corporations possess over the operations of their firms. In many large business enterprises, the ownership securities of which are publicly held, a severe cleavage often exists between the legal owners of the firm and those who control it. From a legal standpoint, the owners of a business are the stockholders. But because ownership of stock in most large corporations is so widely dispersed, actual control of these firms may reside in the hands of the board of directors and/or the top officers of the firm. In only a few cases will the preferred stockholders possess any voting rights at all, except under circumstances defined in the contract between them and the firm and in the statutes of the state of incorporation. Because of management's control over the proxy machinery, legal owners of corporations may exercise little direct control over the firm's behavior.

Because the objectives of these two separate groups may be at variance with each other, this phenomenon is significant. It is conceivable that corporate management would not pursue certain opportunities beneficial to the stockholders for fear of being wrong and thereby projecting a bad image to them, the rest of the business world, and the public, whereas it may very well be to the best interest of the legal owners and for society for management to take the risk. The rewards to management of the success of such a venture appear small in relation to the penalties of failure. Having large salaries, they benefit little from increased profits. The probabilities of the success of an innovation, say, in the nature of a new product, may not be large; yet the firm that aggressively pursues innovative practices, after thorough research and deliberation, may be maximizing the profits to the shareholders and contributing to the total welfare of society. In many cases stockholders do not have any significant control over the operations of large publicly held business enterprises and therefore are usually not interested in the control aspect of stock ownership. Important managerial decisions can be made to the exclusion of the interests or influence of the stockholders. Professional business managers make the typically entrepreneurial decisions, although they usually own very little, if any, of the stock of the firm. This does not mean that corporate management does not have a responsibility to stockholders. On the contrary, they have a crucial responsibility to them. The lack of responsiveness on the part of such management to the profit motive and to the interests of stockholders would have a crippling impact upon the functioning of a free enterprise system, and its ability to respond efficiently to consumer demands, to allocate resources properly, and to insure the growth of capital and therefore to raise society's standard of living.

THE STRUCTURE OF BUSINESS FIRMS

Organization

Business firms are presumably organized in such a manner as to facilitate the pursuit of their goals. Achievement of goals requires a decision-making process, which in turn implies the responsibility for making decisions among alternatives and the authority to effectuate them. Making the proper decisions requires information about alternatives and their expected results. In order to secure this information, the decision-maker may seek the aid of staff experts. The staff performs an advisory or supportive function and usually does not make any actual operative decisions. The judgment and support of the staff is required, however, to enable "line" personnel to make decisions. Personnel performing in "line" capacities are engaged directly in the profit-generating activities of the firm: production and distribution. Many firms have an extensive staff of experts whose competence is especially adapted to areas in which decisions of far-reaching importance are frequently made; outside consultants may be engaged when the problem is of such a specialized nature that the firm's staff advisers are not able to handle it. A typical organization chart is shown in Figure 9-1.

The large firm is so organized that broad policy decisions concerning such matters as goals, products, expansion, election of officers, securities flotations, and dividend policies are usually made by the board of directors or a committee of the board upon the advice of a group of experienced personnel whose judgment is well-acknowledged. The authority for these decisions resides in the board of directors, which is elected by the shareholders and the members of which may or may not be salaried. The board meets periodically to review the over-all strategy of the firm in the pursuit of its goals and to make new decisions for the future in light of current developments.

The actual execution of these policy decisions is delegated to the officers of the firm: the executives. The president or executive vice president customarily is delegated the chief responsibility for carrying out the overall policy objectives and coordinating the activities of subordinate officers who head various functional divisions. These officers are often designated *vice presidents* or some equivalent term. Below each of the various departments or divisions are various levels of managers with different degrees of authority and responsibility. Each level is empowered to make decisions up to a given magnitude. All decisions beyond that magnitude presumably will have to be referred to a higher authority. For example, the regional manager in charge of sales may be empowered to make individual capital expenditures (noncurrent expenditures) over a given period of time of up to $10,000 (decided by higher authority as the amount sufficient to handle routine requirements). Any expenditure decisions in excess of that amount must be made by, say, the vice president in charge of soap sales. In turn, the vice president may be empowered to make decisions concerning capital expenditures which do not require a sum in excess of $50,000. Any expenditures proposed beyond that amount must go to the president, who himself may be limited to decisions involving $100,000 or less. All those decisions involving over $100,000 are made by the board of directors.

In addition to these officers, there are two others who should be briefly discussed at this point: the treasurer and the secretary.

The treasurer of the firm is usually responsible for the receipts and

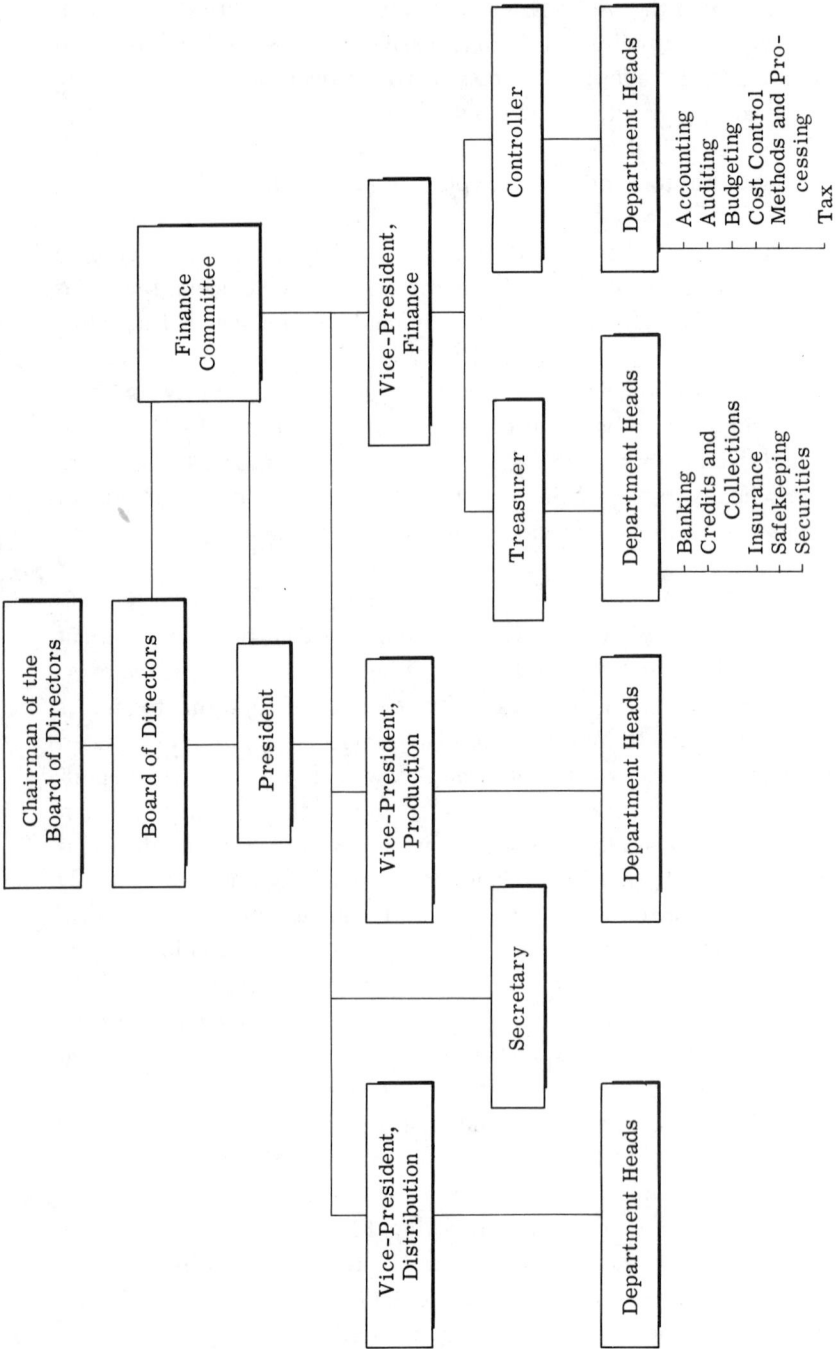

Figure 9-1 Company Organization Chart.

disbursements of the firm as well as for its securities and list of stockholders. Closely associated with this position is that of controller (comptroller). The controller normally has the responsibility of keeping the accounting records. The making of financial plans for future periods may be the responsibility of the controller, the treasurer, or the financial vice president. These plans for the future are called *cash and capital budgets* and are a systematic presentation of anticipated financial needs and resources.

The secretary is responsible for recording the minutes of the board of directors' meetings. He also will likely have the responsibility for sending out proxy statements, annual and periodic reports to shareholders, and notifications of special meetings.

Beyond the so-called top-management group, there is the middle-management group which consists primarily of persons heading various sections under each of the major divisions or subdivisions of the firm. The scope of middle managers' authority and responsibility is even more constrained than that of their superiors.

Finally, although the structure of large firms may differ in appearance from that of smaller firms, the same basic functions have to be performed in each. The titles will vary and the number of persons involved will be quite different among business firms. Indeed, the actual operations of a business—the lines of authority—whether the firm be large or small, a corporation, partnership, or proprietorship, a manufacturing or merchandising firm, or whatever, are not actually as clear as this discussion would imply. On the contrary, lines of authority and methods of operations are as diverse as the persons who operate enterprises.

Control

Control is the manipulation of firm resources in order to achieve the goal of the firm. Control of the enterprise, especially in the larger firms, is a most difficult, and at times seemingly impossible, task. It must be constantly exercised because of the dynamic state of the world in which the firm operates. Continuous measurement and feedback of information from firm activities necessitates changes in the planned activities of the firm in pursuit of its goals. Usually these data cannot be immediately processed so that some time lag inevitably is involved in adjusting the firm to changed circumstances. Data must be processed, summarized, and analyzed before valuable information is made available to management for control purposes. Elaborate summary forms and reports must be prepared periodically; these reports serve as the major basis for controlling a firm's operations. They should contain the information necessary for higher personnel to evaluate the performance of the section reporting. Thus closely allied with controlling the enterprise is the method of reporting information and the comparison of the measured results with the goals of the enterprise.

Communication

We will be concerned primarily with the communication of information, especially as it is related to financial matters. Communication of financial data customarily relies heavily on the use of certain accounting techniques and records. Only a general summary of them will be presented here.

To communicate with the general public, and with stockholders in particular, the annual report is extensively used. In the usual financial report there is generally a breakdown of the assets, liabilities, and net worth of the business enterprise, and a summary statement of the accounting profit picture for the recent period (usually one year). In addition, there is usually a message from the chairman of the board or the president (or both), a breakdown of the products of the firm, information concerning the prospects of the firm, and a summary of financial data for perhaps five to ten years past. They are frequently produced in four colors on high-gloss paper, which makes them very attractive (and expensive), but they often fail to convey enough financial data for present and prospective investors to make adequate decisions regarding the financial integrity of the firm. Too often they tend to obscure the essence of the operations of the firm. Companies that are doing well tend to exude enthusiasm for the performance of management. Those that are doing poorly generally blame factors other than the management for the poor performance.

Other means of communicating financial data to the public are various quarterly and semiannual reports of financial condition similar in nature to, but more abbreviated than, annual reports; prospectuses and registration statements filed with the Securities and Exchange Commission; and listing statements filed with the various national and regional securities exchanges. Obviously, these methods of communication are used by national or large business enterprises whose equity securities are held by the public. For smaller firms, there may be no effective means of communicating such data to the public except by newspaper advertisements similar to those used by banks. On the other hand, there may be no desire to communicate such information, as is the case with large, closely held firms.

For purposes of securing credit, either from trade sources, banks, or other financial institutions, small, nonpublicly held firms as well as publicly owned firms may be required to provide such items as internal statements of control, detailed income statements and balance sheets for several years past, projected income statements, and sales, cash, and other types of budgets. Personal interviews by potential creditors are often required as well.

Within the firm, the means of communicating financial data are varied and there seems to be no clear-cut way which can be considered "best." Obviously, the more information a business enterprise has with respect to its over-all internal operations, the more capable it is of being controlled. The question to be asked is: Will the additional information result in additional benefits exceeding the additional cost necessary to derive such information? Usually, no precise statement can be made regarding the acquisition of additional information. The problem is, however, one of trying to balance the additional benefits derived from having additional information against the additional cost of securing it. Presumably the additional benefit should exceed the additional cost in order to make it worthwhile.

Internal statements of control—such as budgets, projected income statements, and break-even data—often terminate on specific dates as, for example, during seasonal lows of business activity. They have usually proved to be a useful and effective means of communicating financial information within the firm. Usually these statements are of varying quality, cover very short periods of time (such as a month) and are designed as a means to plan for the future. Moreover, they may be expressed, in some cases, in either physical or monetary terms. Production, purchase and cash budgets, and their accompanying analysis are often the sole means of communicating the short-term financial data of the firm, for usually they are rarely cast for periods extending more than six to twelve months into the future. Their contribution lies in comparing the actual results with projections in order to analyze changes that are taking place; this allows management to adjust its expectations of cash and other requirements.

Projected income statements and balance sheets, as well as financial analyses, are also frequently employed. Projects requiring large expenditures, the benefits of which are not to be realized except over long periods of time, are typically described by means of a capital budget. These, as well as the shorter-term budgets mentioned above, are designed, of course, to "keep tabs" on the financial health of the enterprise. Usually it is not until many of them are taken together that a judgment concerning the financial integrity of the firm can be made. However, it can be stated that to a large extent short-run budgets facilitate the long-run goal of the firm —which, as we have seen, is to make profits. Usually, however, because of the uncertainty surrounding all business decisions, the planning horizon of most firms is relatively short, even for capital expenditures.

The role of the officer in charge of the financial matters of the firm respcting the communication of financial data is not precise. It is often not clear who he is and it is seldom clear to whom he reports. In many firms he will report directly to the president. In others he may report to the finance committee which may consist of, say, the president, the chairman of the board, a few other directors, and himself. Decisions are frequently made by the cooperative efforts of the representatives of the various departments or divisions of the firm who make up a decision committee.

SUMMARY

The pursuit of economic goals by business firms is directed at the maximization of the present value of the profits of the firm. At the same time it is recognized that other goals, typically short-run in character, as well as federal and state laws, temper the full realization of this goal. In another light, short-run objectives—which are usually an amalgamation of economic, philosophical, sociological, and psychological considerations—may be viewed as being intended, either objectively or subjectively, consciously of subconsciously, to maximize the long-run welfare of the individuals in the firm, the firm, and/or society. This is so whether the form of the business enterprise is a proprietorship, a partnership or a corporation. If one can abstract from the legal form of the business enterprise, the underlying essence of the firm's operations within its so-called restraints is to allocate relatively scarce resources among alternative uses with the view to maximizing the present value of future income.

SUGGESTED READINGS

ABRAMS, F. W. "Management's Responsibilities in a Complex World," *Harvard Business Review, 3* (May 1951), 29–34.

BALLANTINE, HENRY WINTHROP. *Ballantine on Corporations*, rev. ed. Chicago: Callaghan and Company, 1946.

BERLE, ADOLF A., JR., and GARDINER C. MEANS. *The Modern Corporation and Private Property.* New York: The Macmillan Company, 1932.

COPPOCK, JOSEPH D. *Economics of the Business Firm.* New York: McGraw-Hill Book Company, Inc., 1959.

DENNISON, H. S. "Decision-Making at the Top Executive Level," *American Economic Review, 41* (May 1951), 98–105.

DORIS, LILLIAN (ed.) "The Treasurer and the Controller," *Corporate Treasurer's and Controller's Handbook.* Englewood Cliffs, N.J.: Prentice-Hall, Inc., 1951.

EARLY, J. S. "Business Budgeting and the Theory of the Firm," *Journal of Industrial Economics, 9* (November 1960), 23–42.

———. "Marginal Policies of 'Excellently Managed' Companies," *American Economic Review, 46* (March 1956), 44–70.

EELLS, RICHARD, and CLARENCE WALTON. *Conceptual Foundations of Business.* Homewood, Ill.: Richard D. Irwin, Inc., 1961.

FIRESTONE, FREDERIC N. *Marginal Aspects of Management Practices.* East Lansing, Mich.: Bureau of Business and Economic Research, Michigan State University, 1960.

GORDON, R. A. *Business Leadership in the Large Corporation.* Washington, D.C.: The Brookings Institution, 1945.

HUNT, PEARSON. "A Program for Stockholder Relations," *Harvard Business Review, 35* (September–October 1952), 99–110.

MCGUIRE, JOSEPH W. *Theories of Business Behavior,* Englewood Cliffs, N.J.: Prentice-Hall, Inc., 1964.

NEWMAN, W. H. "Basic Objectives Which Shape the Character of a Company," *Journal of Business, 26* (October 1953), 211–23.

ROBERTSON, D. H. *The Control of Industry.* New York: Harcourt, Brace & World, Inc., 1923.

SHUBIK, MARTIN. "Approaches to the Study of Decision-Making Relevant to the Firm," *Journal of Business, 34* (April 1961), 101–18.

SIMON, HERBERT A. "New Developments in the Theory of the Firm," *American Economic Review, 52* (May 1962), 1–15.

———. "Theories of Decision-Making in Economics," *American Economic Review, 49* (June 1959), 253–83.

QUESTIONS

9.1 If a firm states its prime objective as survival, how would this affect the achievement of profits?

9.2 Is the desire to achieve maximum short-run profits in contradiction to the achievement of long-run profits? Discuss.

9.3 What factors contribute to the creation of economic profits?

9.4 What does marginal analysis mean to the firm that wants to pay a 5 per cent dividend every year, rather than just breaking even? Does marginal revenue allow for profit? Discuss carefully.

9.5 "It is essentially the corporate structure that necessitates having a financial manager as evidenced by the fact that most proprietorships and partnerships function without them." Discuss this statement.

9.6 Certain restraints (legal and nonlegal) are imposed upon the firm's pursuit of its profit objective. If the profit objective is an efficient resource-allocation system, why not eliminate the restraints?

9.7 Why is it so difficult to control a large business enterprise? What is needed to control effectively?

9.8 How is communication in the firm related to control?

9.9 With what parties do you think a financial manager would normally have to communicate.

9.10 How might noneconomic factors affect the achievement of maximum profits?

9.11 In what way or ways are the objectives of the firm and those who manage it interrelated?

9.12 In what way is the CMC and knowledge of its shape related to the economic objectives of the firm?

9.13 How might imperfections in a firm's markets, innovations or windfalls affect the CMC? Explain.

9.14 Set forth whatever other legal and nonlegal constraints on the pursuit of economic objectives you can think of that are not mentioned in this chapter.

9.15 Select an annual report of a company of your choice and make a critical evaluation of its content concerning the effectiveness with which the financial status of the firm is communicated to shareholders. Be sure to look for things that you, as a shareholder, would like to know in order to evaluate the firm.

CHAPTER 10   PROFITS AND VALUE

We have examined at some length the kinds of objectives that appear to be important to managers of firms. Although the average manager in a sense pursues many objectives, some of them conflicting with one another, there are a number of compelling reasons for focusing our attention primarily on one: the attainment of profits. We have indicated some of the sources of profits and suggested that the attempt to maximize profits constitutes one of the major elements of a pure, free-enterprise system. But we have not yet indicated the manner in which profits are measured—nor, for that matter, just what profits are. We will see that these are vexing questions deserving considerable attention. We attempt to answer them in this chapter.

PROFITS AS A REWARD TO OWNERS

Common usage identifies the term *profits* with ownership of a firm. One thinks of wages as the reward for labor, salaries as a reward for management and/or labor, interest as a reward for lending money, rent as a reward for providing land or buildings, and profits as a reward for bearing the risk associated with ownership. By and large, this concept of profits is a satisfactory one, and we shall generally associate the term with the ownership function. On the other hand, there are cases in which profits may accrue to some of the other participants in the activities of a firm; we shall consider such possibilities at the end of this chapter.

For present purposes, it will be useful to visualize the firm as an organization which makes relatively explicit agreements with its workers, creditors, landlords, and managers regarding the payments for their services. Such a situation leaves the ultimate risk associated with the business to be borne by the owners, the firm's *residual claimants*. The effects of the fortunes of the business on these owners we will call *profits*.

PROFITS AS A CHANGE IN VALUE

We measure wages as the amonut of money received by a worker per day, per week, per month, or perhaps per year. In any event, the measure is invariably in terms of some period of time. Similarly, we will define *profits* as a flow, the total amount of profit per quarter, or per year, for example. Traditional accounting measurements of profit are calculated in this manner. The profit and loss statement (also called the income statement) records all explicit items of revenue (or income) during a period and subtracts therefrom various explicit items of cost (or expense). The difference is considered the profit during this period.

Although it is useful to think of profit in this fashion, there are some advantages in considering it in a somewhat different light. For example, if we want to know how much water has been added, on a net basis, to a bathtub during a particular period of time, there are two ways of providing an answer. We might record the flow of new water through the faucet and subtract from that amount the flow through the drain (if any) during the period. This is similar in concept to the method used in preparing a profit and loss statement. A different way of providing the answer is somewhat more straightforward. We might merely measure the level of the water at the beginning of the period and then again at the end. The difference would, of course, be the net change.

The analogy between the bathtub example and the measurement of profit is simple to make. The profit and loss statement gives the inflow (income) and the outflow (expenses) of the firm. The difference represents the net change in the value of the firm. We may usefully begin our definition of profit with this concept: *profit should measure the change in the value[1] of a firm over some time period.* Needless to say, there should be no practical difference between such a concept and one stated directly in terms of the flow of profits. This will become clearer when the definition is developed fully.

PROFITS: DEFINITION

We have chosen to identify profits with ownership of a firm. Thus we should measure profits in terms of the impact of the activities of a firm on its owners' welfare. At the beginning of a period, ownership of a firm is "worth" some given amount to those who hold the ownership; at the end of the period, it is "worth" some (probably different) amount; finally, during the period, owners of the firm may have received something of value by virtue of their position vis-à-vis the firm. These three results of ownership give rise to profits (or their converse: losses).

At the beginning of a period, the owners of a firm have in their possession a (hopefully) valuable asset: the firm. At the end of the period, they

[1] The meaning of the word *value* is discussed in a subsequent section.

typically have that asset plus some additional assets (usually cash from dividends). During the period, they may, of course, have contributed some asset (often cash) to the firm. *If the value of their ownership of the firm at the end of the period plus the value of the assets received during the period (less the value of assets contributed) exceeds the value of their ownership at the beginning, they have made a profit (measured by the difference).* On the other hand, if the value of their ownership at the end of the period plus that of the net assets received during the period (less contributions) falls below the value of their ownership at the beginning, they have suffered a loss (again measured by the difference). To simplify the discussion, however, we can use the term *profit* to cover both possibilities, for losses can be viewed as simply negative profits. The total profit of a firm during a particular period is thus simply:

$$
\begin{array}{c}
\text{Profit} \\
\text{during} \\
\text{period}
\end{array}
=
\begin{array}{c}
\text{Value of} \\
\text{ownership} \\
\text{of firm} \\
\text{at end of} \\
\text{period}
\end{array}
+
\begin{array}{c}
\text{Value of} \\
\text{assets} \\
\text{distributed} \\
\text{to owners} \\
\text{during} \\
\text{period}
\end{array}
-
\begin{array}{c}
\text{Value of} \\
\text{assets} \\
\text{contributed} \\
\text{by owners} \\
\text{during} \\
\text{period}
\end{array}
-
\begin{array}{c}
\text{Value of} \\
\text{ownership} \\
\text{of firm at} \\
\text{beginning} \\
\text{of period}
\end{array}
$$

In later sections we will indicate that there are substantial differences between *profit* as we will choose to measure it and *profit* as measured in traditional accounting statements. (To keep these two measures separate, we will use the term *accounting profit* to refer to the latter.) The differences, however, are concerned not with the concept itself but with the measure of value utilized. This can be seen by rearranging the equality defining profits:

$$
\begin{array}{c}
\text{Value of} \\
\text{ownership} \\
\text{of firm} \\
\text{at end of} \\
\text{period}
\end{array}
-
\begin{array}{c}
\text{Value of} \\
\text{ownership} \\
\text{of firm at} \\
\text{beginning} \\
\text{of period}
\end{array}
=
\begin{array}{c}
\text{Profit} \\
\text{during} \\
\text{period}
\end{array}
-
\begin{array}{c}
\text{Value of} \\
\text{assets} \\
\text{distributed} \\
\text{to owners} \\
\text{during} \\
\text{period}
\end{array}
+
\begin{array}{c}
\text{Value of} \\
\text{assets} \\
\text{contributed} \\
\text{by owners} \\
\text{during} \\
\text{period}
\end{array}
$$

The difference on the lefthand side of this equation corresponds closely to the accountant's measure of the increase in surplus between the end of the previous period and the end of the current period (although, as indicated earlier, the valuation techniques differ). One possible source of such an increase is an additional contribution of assets by the firm's owners during the period. This source is indicated by the last item on the righthand side of the equation. The more common source of such increases comes from the profit and loss statement. The amount posted to surplus is typically found by computing profit and subtracting from it the amount of dividends paid out during the period. The first two terms on the righthand side of the equation represent this difference. Thus the basic concepts are indeed very similar.

ECONOMIC PROFITS

Although a great deal remains to be said about the measurement of profits, it is desirable that we preface this discussion with some consideration of a related but quite different concept: economic profits.

As we have defined the term, *profits* indicate the total reward to the owners of a firm. Although this measure will prove adequate for most purposes, it suffers from one major defect. We have chosen to identify wages with labor, rents with land, interest with capital, and profits with ownership. A division of the elements of return in a firm makes sense only if one division does not include portions of the other. But this is not the case with ownership. Owners of many firms may provide labor and land as well as capital. To hold strictly to the identification of reward with the type of service provided the firm, we need to attempt to divide the total reward to owners into components for land, labor, capital, and then some residual for ownership. The concept of economic profits provides this latter element.

Whenever a firm's owners provide something other than mere ownership, there is an implicit cost involved if they have not received explicit payment for their contributions. If the owner of a drycleaning shop provides labor, management, and capital to his firm, he is foregoing some income which he could have earned had he chosen to work elsewhere, manage some other establishment, and/or invest his capital otherwise. These rejected alternatives represent a real cost to him; if the firm's profits are just equal to such costs, he is really no better off than had he not chosen to own the firm in the first place. If profits are so low as to be less than the sum of these costs, he is actually worse off than he would have been had he not owned the firm. Only if profits exceed the sum of such implicit costs will he have gained from the choice. The *opportunity cost* is the proper manner for measuring such implicit costs.

The concept of economic profits provides a means of expressing the differential between profits and the implicit costs of ownership:

Economic Profits = Profits − implicit costs of ownership.

The implicit costs of ownership are calculated by estimating the earnings available under the next best available alternative. Thus the opportunity cost of labor is determined by assessing the market to find the highest wages which could have been earned in similar work. The opportunity cost of land and buildings is merely the best alternative rent which can be obtained. Finally, the opportunity cost of capital (its implicit interest cost) is the expected return from other investments of comparable risk.

Two facts about economic profits should be noted. First, they conform closely to a kind of profits often deplored by opponents of the free-enterprise system. When an individual makes an economic profit, he is, in effect, getting something for nothing, because he has been rewarded for all his opportunity costs. At first one might think that this is not so because the individual must be rewarded for bearing risk. But the opportunity costs are calculated to include a risk premium (the expected return on investments of comparable risk) so the element of risk-bearing is included in the opportunity costs. In industries characterized by competition, economic profits will arise as a result of chance forces, but so will economic losses. Only in noncompetitive situations can economic profits persist for substantial periods of time.

The second fact about economic profits concerns the difficulties of measurement. We will see that significant problems arise in attempting to measure profits. But to measure economic profits we must succeed in measuring profits plus a host of opportunity costs. The difficulties are thus magnified, and the answer depends to a major extent on subjective judgments as to just what constitutes "comparable conditions." Thus it is more than likely that even impartial and informed persons might disagree as to the specific economic profits sustained by a firm during any given period. The implications of such a possibility will command our attention later in the chapter. First, however, we will return to our initial concept of profits and the major problem involved in its measurement.

THE VALUATION OF OWNERSHIP

The key aspect of the measurement of profits concerns the value of the firm at the beginning and end of the period in question. Because the other elements of profits, the value of assets distributed to owners and/ or contributed by them during the period, usually take the form of cash, we need give little attention to their valuation, save to indicate that where noncash dividends are distributed the problems of valuation are virtually the same as those associated with valuation of the firm as a whole. Obviously, if we are to measure profits we must have some concept of the valuation of the ownership of the firm.

How much is a firm worth to its owners at any particular time? This is an extremely difficult question to answer in many cases, but a useful beginning can be made by determining the nature of the benefits associated with ownership of a business. First, we can generally dismiss the past history of the firm as being directly relevant in determining the value. Past history is, after all, just that; it is the future that is of relevance. No matter how splendid the past history of a firm, if its future is bleak, the owners have something of relatively little value. On the other hand, the value of an oil exploration company that has just discovered its first oil well is scarcely to be based on its record of consistent failures. To state the point explicitly: the present value of the ownership of a firm is related solely to the prospects for future benefits accuring to the owners. The past record of the firm is relevant only to the extent that it sheds light on the prospects for the future.

Thus far we have indicated that the present value of the ownership of a firm is related to the prospects for future benefits. But what is the nature of the relationship? The answer can best be seen by recalling that ownership of a firm is really an investment: one with prospects undoubtedly subject to some amount of risk.

To keep the discussion simple, we will follow the practice adopted in Part I, restricting our attention to an example in which the future benefits are all expected at the end of one year. In the present context, one might think of a firm which is scheduled to be liquidated in a year with one final payment to its owners and which plans to pay no dividends during the intervening year. How might one value the ownership of such a firm?

The first stage in the valuation process consists of forming estimates of the possible outcomes—in this case the liquidated value of the firm. As indicated in Part I, these estimates should encompass not only the expected outcomes but also the risk involved. Given these estimates (which in all likelihood contain a large element of subjective prediction), how can the value of the ownership be determined?

In our earlier discussion of the capital market, we concluded that at any particular time there is a general relationship between the expected return and the risk of good investments. Market conditions might, for example, be such that investments with a risk of ½ offer an expected return of 8 per cent. Now, assume that you have an investment opportunity of equal risk which has an expected return of $8. How much is it worth? If it were priced at $100, it would have an expected rate of return of 8 per cent—which we will assume is neither better nor worse than that prevailing on investments of comparable risk in the market in general. This, then, is certainly not worth more than $100. Or on the other hand, it is certainly not worth less than $100 (because presumably it could be sold for $100). This simple example indicates the proper technique for valuing an investment: *find the price which would make it give an expected rate of return equal to that prevailing among investments of equal risk in the market in general.*

In Part I, we faced a slightly different, but obviously related problem. We asked the following question: Given the expected outcome (*EO*) and the present cost of an investment, what was its expected rate of return (*ER*)? Recall that the calculation was simply:

$$\text{Expected Outcome} - \text{Present Cost} / \text{Present Cost} = \text{Expected Rate of Return}$$

Thus, for example, if a given project had two possible outcomes, $116 and $100, the cost of undertaking the project were $100, and the probability of realizing either outcome were .5, the expected outcome (*EO*) would be $108 and the expected rate of return (*ER*) would be 8 percent $\left(\dfrac{\$108 - \$100}{\$100}\right)$. In the present case, the situation differs only in what we wish to find, the present cost (or present value) which would make this investment have a given expected rate of return. Substituting more convenient notations and utilizing simple algebraic manipulations, we can rearrange the formula to provide this information directly so that

$$\frac{EO - PV}{PV} = ER$$
$$PV(1 + ER) = EO$$
$$PV = \frac{EO}{1 + ER}.$$

This latter formula gives the present value of any investment whose return can be expected to take place entirely one year hence; it is simply

$$\text{Present Value} = \frac{\text{Expected Outcome}}{1 + \text{Expected Rate of Return}}.$$

The expected rate of return to be used in this present value computation is that given by the *CMC*—that rate of return that can be reasonably expected on a given investment including a premium for risk. This formula enables one to calculate immediately that price which would make an investment yield a given expected rate of return. By using the expected rate of return given by investments of comparable risk in such a formula, we can determine the value of such an investment. This is the reason that present value constitutes such an important financial tool. Needless to say, most real cases involve somewhat more complex calculations because the returns from the investment are expected to take place over longer periods of time. We shall detail the methods used in such situations in the next chapter. For the present discussion, however, it should suffice to indicate that no new principles will be involved and that such methods, though often tedious, are readily applied.

We can summarize this discussion with a general definition: *The present value of anything offering prospects for future benefits is simply that price which would give an expected rate of return equal to that which can be presently obtained on investments of comparable risk.*[2]

MEASURING VALUE FOR THE PUBLICLY HELD CORPORATION

The foregoing discussion should indicate that the valuation of the ownership of a firm is a highly subjective process. The valuation is dependent upon subjective judgments about the firm's future (both expected outcomes and risk) as well as the conditions in the capital market in general. Thus one would scarcely expect to find a complete consensus concerning the value of the ownership of any given firm. Indeed in most cases there will be a whole range of opinions concerning a firm's value. All one can hope to find is some middle ground. Fortunately, in one important type of firm a figure is available on almost a minute-by-minute basis.

Because value is a subjective element, only when the ownership of a firm (or a portion thereof) is actually transferred for a money price do we have any solid evidence concerning people's feelings on the matter. For any transaction to take place, both parties must feel that they are benefiting. Thus if a firm is sold, we can infer that the buyer thought it worth more than the seller's estimate. We cannot tell how great the discrepancy was, but the recorded price does at least offer one consensus because we know that at least one person considered the firm worth more than that and at least one considered it worth less.

Fortunately we do not have to wait for the sale of the entire ownership of a firm to get information concerning people's valuations of it. Most large firms are owned by many people and the ownership privilege may be (and is) bought and sold in very small pieces. When such shares of ownership are widely held, a fairly active market is usually maintained.

[2] The exact technique for computing the present value is described in Chapter 11.

The prices at which shares change hands are recorded and publicized throughout the country. Thus if we read that a common stock sold for $54 a share during a particular day, we can be sure that a fairly large number of people felt that the proportion of the ownership represented by one share was worth more than $54—all the people who held on to their stock rather than selling at $54. On the other hand, an even larger number of people felt it was worth less than $54—all those who did not purchase that stock at $54.[3] Obviously $54 represents some sort of consensus as to the value of a particular proportion of the ownership of that company.

The existence of national security markets thus provides an extremely responsive measure of the public's valuation of the ownership of publicly held corporations. The best single measure of the total value of the ownership of such firms can be expressed by the formula

$$V = P \times S$$

where

V = the value of the firm
P = the market price per share of common stock
S = the number of shares of common stock outstanding

This fact is of the utmost importance. There is a persistent feeling in some financial circles that corporate management should not attempt to set its policy with an eye to the behavior of its stock on the national market—that such an attitude is somehow undignified. Such an attitude is hard to justify, for the price of a firm's stock provides a rapid and obvious indication of the reaction of the firm's owners to the activities of the management. Our whole notion of profit leads one to the obvious conclusion that a management activity in the interests of the firm's owners should pay close attention to the effects its policy may have on the price of the common stock. The management which attempts to maximize profit for its owners cannot disregard the national security market, where estimates of a major component of that profit are recorded. Needless to say, if there is not an active, well-regulated market for the firm's stock, some other method must be used to estimate the value of the firm. In

[3] As indicated elsewhere, tax considerations, market imperfections, and lack of information make it likely that some people will hold a security thinking it worth less than its market price while some will not buy a security even though they think it worth more. These are only minor factors, however, and do not invalidate the use of the market price as an indicator of a consensus of value.

most such cases the management will estimate the value using the present-value technique described earlier in this chapter, although in some cases they may consult the owners to determine their feelings.

EFFECTS OF DECISIONS ON PROFIT

Before we turn to the question of alternative measurements of profit, it is important that the full implications of our concept be understood. This can best be done with a simple example.

Assume that a firm begins its life with $900 cash and no obligations. Obviously, its value is $900. Assume that it is presented with an opportunity to purchase for $900 a machine that will last one year and provide an expected income of $1,100 one year hence. There is, however, some risk that the actual income may be more or less than the expected $1,100. Investigation of the conditions in the capital market indicate that investments of comparable risk give expected rates of return of about 10 per cent. The present value of the machine is

$$\frac{\$1,100}{1 + .10} = \$1,000.$$

If the price of the machine were $1,000, it would be neither especially good nor especially bad. If it were more, it would give an expected rate of return below that obtained from investments of comparable risk. But because the cost is less than its present value, it promises an expected rate of return above that generally available on investments of comparable risk and thus should be undertaken. In this case, the investment has an expected rate of return of 22 per cent $\left(\dfrac{\$1,100 - \$900}{\$900} \right) (100)$, far in excess of the 10 per cent offered by comparable investments.

After the calculations were completed, assume that the firm purchased the machine in question. As of that moment, it traded $900 for an asset worth $1,000. The value of the ownership of the firm jumped $100 practically overnight; that $100 would, according to our concepts, be considered profit and associated with the time the machine was purchased. Furthermore, because the period involved was very small (an instant of time), any opportunity cost for interest on the owner's $900 capital would be so small that the economic profit would be nearly $100 also.

Now, what happens during the remainder of the year? On the instant after the machine purchase, the ownership of the firm is worth $1,000. On the last day of the year, if the expected $1,100 materializes (and the machine is worthless), the value of ownership will be $1,100. Profit during the remainder of the year is also $100. But during the year $1,000 was tied up. Because the opportunity interest cost on this money might well have been $100, there would be no economic profit after the purchase of the machine.

The example is extreme, but it emphasizes an important attribute of our measure of profit. When a desirable decision is made, the results are attributed to the period in which the decision is made. By the same token, undesirable situations are also reflected at the time they become known. Anyone who follows the activities of the security markets will find this attribute familiar. He will also see the advantage of such a concept. A decision or outside event which makes the future prospects of a firm rosier than they had previously been benefits those who own the firm at the time the knowledge is disseminated, even though the events themselves take place much later. If the owners choose, they can sell their ownership immediately for its new, higher value. If they choose not to sell, of course, they can take the benefits themselves at any later time. In any event, new owners will receive only the usual (generally available) reward for investment, unless a similar situation arises after they purchase a portion of the firm.

The impact of decisions or outside factors on the value of the ownership of the firm is an extremely difficult subject, one to which we shall devote much attention in the remainder of this book. At present it might be well, however, to indicate the kinds of change in a firm's prospects that can raise and lower the value of ownership of the firm. To aid the reader in understanding the principles involved, examples of each category are given for all changes that will raise the value of the firm's ownership; the reader may supply examples to illustrate the changes that will lower the value of the ownership by reversing the examples given for raising the value.

(1) Changes that raise the value of the ownership:

(a) *A higher expected outcome with lower risk.*

Example: A firm had bid for a contract to supply goods held in a warehouse, an operation which would give it a net income of $1,000. Before the award was made, the prospects appeared fifty-fifty; thus the expected outcome was $500, and the risk was considerable. When the contract was awarded to the firm, the expected outcome jumped to $1,000 with no risk whatsoever, resulting in an increase in the value of ownership of the firm.

(b) *A higher expected outcome with no change in risk.*

Example: A firm has invested in a product given a fifty-fifty chance of acceptance by consumers. Initial estimates indicate that, if it is accepted, the firm's receipts will be $3,000; if not, only $1,000 will be received—giving an expected value of $2,000 with a fifty-fifty chance of having the outcome $1,000 more or $1,000 less than this expected value. A reappraisal of the product's prospects indicates that, if accepted, the product will yield $4,000; if not accepted, it will give $2,000. The expected value is now $3,000 while the risk is essentially unchanged, resulting in an increase in the value of the firm's ownership.

(c) *A lower risk with no change in the expected outcome.*

Example: A firm hoped to receive a government contract to make a new fighter airplane. Approximately 2,000 aircraft were to be built. One other company had bid on the job, and the prospects of the two companies appeared equal. The government was expected to have one firm build all 2,000 planes. Each company on this basis would have an expected outcome of 1,000 planes. To everyone's surprise the government decided instead to have each firm build 1,000 aircraft. Upon announcement of the award, the value of the ownership of the firm rose because it was now certain of having one half the contract work whereas previously it only had a fifty-fifty chance of receiving the entire contract.

(d) *A sufficiently higher expected outcome to more than compensate for an accompanying increase in risk.*

Example: A firm has a fifty-fifty chance of winning a contract. Initially it thought the contract was worth $1,000, giving the firm an expected outcome of $500. If the contract were won, however, there is also a fifty-fifty chance of realizing an outcome $500 above or $500 below the expected value ($500). A later re-evaluation of the contract indicates that it will be worth $2,000 to the firm and would require an investment of $200. After this information was obtained, the owners decided that the value of the firm to them was greater than before, because the expected outcome had risen to $900—a sufficiently large increase to more than compensate for the added risk (assuming that there is now a fifty-fifty chance of the actual outcome being either $2,000 or a minus $200).

(*e*) *A sufficiently lower risk to more than compensate for an accompanying fall in the expected outcome.*

Example: A firm had assessed its future and concluded that it had a fifty-fifty chance of making $1 million or going bankrupt —an expected outcome of $500,000 with considerable risk attached. New information indicates that this is not correct. Instead it is almost certain that the firm will make $490,000. Although this represents a slight decrease in the expected outcome, the great reduction in risk led the owners to conclude that the value of the firm had risen.

(2) Changes which will lower the value of the ownership:
   (*a*) *A lower expected outcome with higher risk;*
   (*b*) *A lower expected outcome with no change in risk;*
   (*c*) *A higher risk with no change in expected outcome;*
   (*d*) *A sufficiently lower expected outcome to more than offset the advantage of an accompanying decrease in risk;*
   (*e*) *A sufficiently higher degree of risk to more than offset the advantage of an accompanying increase in expected outcome.*

THE VALUATION OF INDIVIDUAL ASSETS

Thus far we have directed our discussion to the valuation of the ownership of a firm as a whole, with no attention to the valuation of its components. This approach is quite correct for the purpose of measuring profits. The value of the ownership of a firm depends on the prospects for the firm as a whole. Although in a physical sense the firm is merely the sum of its component parts, the value of the firm is scarcely likely to be equal to the sum of the values of its parts; any particular firm is a unique combination of assets (or at least it hopes to be). Any technique for valuing the ownership of such a firm by calculating values for individual assets and subtracting from their sum the values of the firm's liabilities will only by chance lead to the true value of the firm as a whole.

We shall deal with the problem of asset valuation in detail in the next chapter; however, a brief description of the method and its purpose will be valuable at this point. The concept of asset valuation, which is of importance to the financial manager, is one indicating the effect on the total value of the firm if the asset in question is removed from (or added fo) the firm. This figure provides the financial manager with the information he requires to decide whether or not to keep the asset in the firm, because if he can sell the asset for more than this amount he should sell it; if not, he should keep it. Without going into the ramifications and difficulties involved in applying this concept of asset valuation, we can immediately see that the sum of the recorded values of the assets of the firm is scarcely likely to equal the total value of the firm when measured in this manner. As a simple example, assume that a firm has a franchise to distribute the hot dogs of a small manufacturer. The franchise is a continuing one as long as the firm uses a delivery truck constructed and painted to resemble a hot dog. It has one such truck, valued on the books of the company at $4,500. Its other resources—including desks, filing cabinets, a safe, and certain other office equipment (the firm rents its office) —bring the total recorded value of the firm to $4,800. The firm does an annual business of $240,000 and generates from this a net profit (after taxes) of $2,400. What is the total value of this firm? If $4,800 were the value of the firm, the owners should be willing to sell it at that price. Most likely they would not sell at that price, which is only two times current earnings. If investments of equal risk yielded 20 per cent, the value to them would be $12,000 $\left(\dfrac{\$2,400}{.20}\right)$.

If the truck were sold, the value of the firm would fall to zero, for the franchise would be lost and earnings would fall to zero. Is the value of the truck then $12,000? If all the firm's office equipment—recorded on the books at $300—were sold, earnings and firm value would also fall, because of the resulting extreme inefficiency, to zero. Is the value of the office equipment also $12,000? Because the *total* value of the firm is only $12,000, certainly the value of the firm could not be $12,000 (the "value" of the truck) plus $12,000 (the "value" of the office equipment). It is readily apparent that the value of the individual assets cannot be computed separately. The assets so complement one another as to produce the total value of the firm. Nor is it proper simply to aggregate the recorded value of the assets to derive the value of the firm. Each individual asset is combined with all other assets to generate the earnings which, in turn, provide the basis for determining the value of the firm as a whole.

We have seen that the valuation of individual assets in a manner directly useful for the decisions required of a financial manager will not lead to a sum which, when liabilities are subtracted, indicate the value of the ownership of a firm. Is there some other method of asset valuation that will indicate this value? Let us briefly consider some alternative techniques.

One method would value each of the assets at the amount for which it could be sold individually. It is obvious that the sum of such amounts (minus the firm's liabilities) should be less than the true value of the ownership of the firm as a going concern. If it were more, the owners of the firm would be better off if the firm were to sell its assets at the indicated prices and go out of business; if it were the same, they would be as well off; only if it were less would they be better off staying in business. Owners of most firms obviously have a strong preference for keeping their firms in business, and we may conclude that in the majority of cases the true value of the ownership of the firm exceeds the amount obtained by this method.

An alternative method would value each asset at its *historical value*. Obviously, the sum of these amounts (minus liabilities) might diverge greatly from the true value of the ownership of the firm. The use of some sort of depreciation formula to adjust these values downward as the assets grow older may reduce the magnitude of the error, but the divergence may still be considerable. For example, in times of inflation, the value of the firm computed by such a method may be seriously understated.

A final method uses the historical costs of individual assets, adjusted according to some depreciation formulas, but adds one additional item to account for any difference between the sum obtained and the true value of the firm. The use of an account labeled *goodwill* for such a purpose was once widely accepted accounting practice and is still used when a firm purchases another firm for an amount exceeding the latter's recorded book value. In general, however, no such device is used in standard accounting procedure today.

To conclude this discussion, we may say that a valuation of the ownership of the firm cannot satisfactorily be made by assigning values to the individual assets (or even classes of assets), adding up these values, and subtracting the value of the firm's liabilities from their total. This is not to say that there are not purposes for which the assignment of individual values to assets is not desirable. Quite to the contrary, we will devote our attention to the valuation of assets for purposes of deciding whether to add them to the firm or to get rid of them. But the sum of such values would have questionable meaning and most certainly would not be equal to the value of the firm as it stands. This leaves open the issue of other purposes for which both the assignment of individual values and their summation may be reasonable.

ACCOUNTING PROFIT

In our discussion of profit and economic profit, we stressed the highly subjective nature of both concepts. Only when a firm's stock is widely traded can some objective measure of profit be obtained and in no case can a thoroughly objective measure of economic profit be found. This means that estimates of one or both concepts must, in the usual case, be based upon the informed judgment of one or more individuals.When such individuals are indeed informed and when no possibility of bias exists, the resulting estimates may have considerable value. But if these conditions are not met, the use of such subjective measures is fraught with hazard.

A situation in which grave possibilities of bias exist arises when the management of a firm is distinct from and reports to its owners. In such cases, there is every reason for management to tend (perhaps subconsciously) to overestimate profits. Under such conditions it is desirable to add to the subjective elements of profit, calculated in the manner indicated here, some more explicit objective data concerning the past operations of the company. Traditional accounting statements are designed to do just this.

No attempt will be made here to outline the nature of traditional accounting techniques; the reader is referred instead to any of the standard texts on the subject. Here we will illustrate the standard practice in one important area, indicating only one of the most important differences between the measurement of profit as outlined here and that provided in the usual accounting statements.

Traditional accounting methods summarize the operation of a firm during some period (usually a quarter or a year) in a profit and loss statement. This statement records items of income and items of expense, with the difference labeled *profit*. We shall use the term *accounting profit* to indicate the amount obtained in this manner. Included in the items of expense are certain depreciation charges, representing the amortization of some portion of the original cost of the firm's assets. These charges are typically determined separately for each of the firm's major assets. The usual technique involves fitting a standard pattern of depreciation to the historical cost of the item so that it will be fully depreciated at the end of some predetermined life. One of the most popular methods is the *straight-line method,* in which the amount of depreciation charged on the asset each period is the same. Figure 10-1 illustrates the resulting pattern of the undepreciated value of the asset. Notice that this value never exceeds the asset's historical cost—nor, for that matter, does it ever rise; it falls in every period until it reaches zero at the end of its estimated life. Moreover, the use of the same pattern for every asset means that the only manner in which the characteristics of an individual asset can be taken into account is through the estimation of the life of the asset (that is, the length of time before its expected undepreciated value reaches

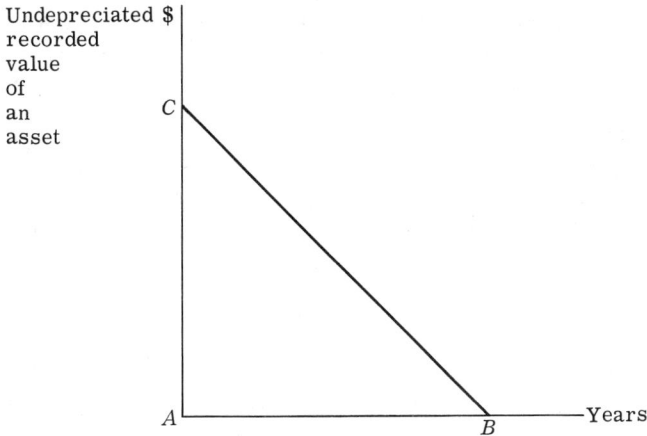

Figure 10-1 Straight Line Depreciation.

zero). Segment *AB* in Figure 10-1 marks off the estimated useful life of the asset. Finally, because this life is seldom changed after it is first estimated, there is usually no adjustment in the pattern after the initial purchase of the asset. Point *C* represents the initial cost of the asset (net of any estimated salvage value). The slope of Line *CB* represents the rate at which the asset is amortized.

This discussion indicates that the accountant is highly constrained in estimating accounting profit, because the figure is very much dependent on (among other things) the depreciation charges that must follow rigidly confined patterns. This leads to a seemingly reasonable degree of objectivity in the reported figure, but can cause great divergence between accounting profit and our concept of profit, which measures the change in the value of the ownership of the firm.

What is the relationship between depreciation charges in the accounting profit and loss statement and the concepts of valuation which underlie our measure of profit? One of the crucial elements of profit is the change in the value of the ownership of the firm. If the net change in the total value of all the firm's assets during the period is exactly equal to the total depreciation charged on the individual assets, then accounting profit will give results similar (with respect to this element, at least) to those obtained in measuring profits. This, however, is quite unlikely. There are two reasons for this. The first, indicated in an earlier section, is that the total value of a firm's assets can seldom be calculated by summing up the individual values of the assets, no matter how these values are derived. The same would hold true for changes in the total value. The second reason lies in the highly constrained methods by which the undepreciated values of the assets are determined. In many cases the real values of the assets to the firm will diverge considerably from the simple straight-line trend (although this method may be a good approximation for the average asset). As indicated earlier, the magnitude of this divergence can be considerable after periods of inflation.

This example should serve to illustrate one manner in which accounting profit, as usually measured, is quite unlikely to provide an adequate measure of profit for purposes of financial management. Another problem for financial management is the use of "the sale" as the point of realizing revenue. Obviously, sales are not the same as cash revenues and care must be taken, under some circumstances, not to treat sales as the receipt of cash. On the other hand, traditional accounting methods—based largely on fairly rigid rules—make it possible to determine the financial history of the firm with some accuracy. This information, in turn, can be used by the financial manager (or by the owners of the firm) to estimate earnings and/or to make required financial decisions, although it will often have to be supplemented with additional data. Needless to say, if accounting information is to be used to best advantage, the financial manager must understand the rules by which it was collected and summarized.

PROFIT AND OTHER PARTICIPANTS IN THE FIRM

At the beginning of this chapter we suggested that profit need not be solely associated with the owners of a firm. Profit arises under conditions in which an individual or individuals take risks and get more or less than they expected. Obviously, some individuals in a firm other than those normally considered owners might take some such risks and thus be subject to profits or losses (within the meanings we have assigned the terms). For example, workers who are not paid in advance subject themselves to some degree of risk. In general, however, such cases are likely to be of relatively minor importance, and we shall disregard them in this book.[4] On the other hand, the possibility of a profit or loss accruing to such people should not be completely overlooked in those cases in which it appears relevant.

SUMMARY

Three concepts of profit are important for the purposes of this book. *Profit* refers to the change in the value of the ownership of a firm during a given period plus the value of any assets distributed to its owners

[4] People may be viewed as income-producers whose economic value is based on the present worth of their future earnings. Investments in education are not riskless; they are made with the view of enhancing expected earnings.

during that period minus any additional investments by owners during the same period. *Economic profit* is profit less the opportunity costs foregone by the firm's owners as a result of their committment (if any) of capital, labor, land, or management skills to the firm. For purposes of measuring these first two types of profit, the relevant valuation technique is one which considers the firm as a whole. The value of the ownership in the firm at any particular time should be calculated by finding that price which, if paid for the firm, would give an expected return equal to that obtainable in the capital market from investments of comparable risk. The third type of profit, *accounting profit,* is similar to profit in its definition but the valuation techniques used are based generally on objective techniques applied to historical data. For purposes of management decision-making, the former two types of profit are more important than the latter. On the other hand, the practical necessity of having a generally agreed upon measure makes the determination of accounting profit essential.

SUGGESTED READINGS

American Institute of Accountants. *Changing Concepts of Business Income,* New York: The Macmillan Company, 1952.

BODENHORN, DIRAN. "A Cash-Flow Concept of Profit," *The Journal of Finance, 19* (March 1964), 16–31.

BUCHANAN, NORMAN S. *The Economics of Corporate Enterprise,* Chap. 8. New York: Henry Holt and Company, 1940.

EDWARDS, EDGAR C. and PHILLIP W. BELL. *The Theory and Measurement of Business Income,* Berkeley, California: University of California Press, 1961.

HAWTREY, R. G. "The Nature of Profit," *Economic Journal, 61* (September 1951), 489–504.

MAY, GEORGE O. "Concepts of Business Income and Their Implementation," *Quarterly Journal of Economics, 68* (February 1954), 1–18.

MOONITZ, M. "The Valuation of Business Capital: an Accounting Analysis," *American Economic Review, 41* (May 1951), 157–165.

STAUBUS, GEORGE. *A Theory of Accounting to Investors,* Berkeley and Los Angeles: University of California Press, 1961.

WESTON, J. FRED. "A Generalized Uncertainty Theory of Profit," *American Economic Review, 40* (March 1950), 40–60.

———— and NEIL H. JACOBY. "Profit Standards," *Quarterly Journal of Economics, 66* (May 1952), 224–250.

QUESTIONS

10.1 Define *profits* and list the computational components of profit.

10.2 How should the analyst proceed in trying to measure unrecorded implicit costs?

10.3 Compare *profits* with *economic profits*. What are the differences? What are the similarities?

10.4 Economic profits are undesirable from society's point of view. Comment.

10.5 What is the relation between the formula for the expected rate of return and the formula for present value?

10.6 Define *present value*. What data are needed for value computations?

10.7 If profits are created at the moment of decision, does this agree with your observations of changes in the values of individual securities? Explain your answer.

10.8 Why would an investment that lowers the risk of the firm cause profits?

10.9 Why is it that a going concern value may exceed the sum of the values of the individual assets?

10.10 What are the basic differences between *profits* and *accounting profits?*

10.11 At what point in the life of a firm is the value of the firm equal to book value (values recorded on a balance sheet)? Comment.

10.12 If the accounting methods do not satisfactorily measure profits or value, of what use are they? Discuss.

10.13 If accounting profits are zero, should the value of the firm be zero? Explain.

10.14 What rationale can be given to the measurement of profits by changes in the value of ownership plus nonwage distributions but less contributions made by owners to the firm? Discuss fully.

10.15 Is the concept of profits as defined in this chapter in any way related to the concept of present value? Explain.

10.16 Make a comparison and/or critique of *accounting profits, economic profits,* and *profits* as we have defined them. What is the justification for each of these definitions of *profits?*

PROBLEMS

10.17 If $100 is the expected outcome of an investment due one year hence, and investments of equivalent risk receive an 8 per cent return in the market, find the value of the investment.

10.18 Find the value of a large, publicly held company listed on the New York Stock Exchange (*Moody's Manual of Industrials* may be helpful).

10.19 Bacon Enterprises at the beginning of the year is worth $80,000 when capitalized at 10 per cent. At this time a decision is made to undertake an investment which would cost $5,000 and yield an expected outcome of $6,000 at the end of the year. Investments of comparable risk yield 10 per cent. (*a*) What is the value of the firm after the decision is made to accept the investment? (*b*) What then are the expected profits for the year and what is the expected value at the end of the year if no more capital than the $5,000 is added and no distributions to owners are made?

10.20 (*a*) If you can assume an expected outcome of $2,000 at the end of the year and investments of equivalent risk yield investors 10 per cent, what is the value of the asset at the beginning of the year? (*b*) If $1,500 must be paid for the investment, what is the profit immediately after the investment decision? (*c*) What is total profit by the end of the year?

10.21 The expected outcome at the end of the year of the Arbuckle Belt Buckle Company is $50,000. Investments of equivalent risk yield 10 per cent. (*a*) What is the value of the firm at the beginning of the year? What are the expected profits for the year? (*b*) If a reappraisal of the company's risk indicates it should yield only 8 per cent, what is the value of the firm at the beginning of the year and the expected profits for the year?

CAPITAL CONCEPTS

Before examining the nature of the demand for capital in the firm, we must understand some of the various meanings of the term *capital*.

Capital, even in the restricted context of the firm, has a variety of meanings. Earlier we rather broadly defined *capital* as resources over which the firm has control and which will be used in the creation of profit. This definition is adequate for our purposes, but it may be desirable for the reader to be aware of some of the more specific meanings frequently assigned to the term in the literature on the firm.

The capital of the firm, as we implied, consists of its fixed assets, raw materials, cash, receivables, and any other resources customarily recorded by accountants as total assets. But our definition also includes other profit-generating resources, usually intangible human capital. The former, more restricted use of the term applies only to the accountant's total assets. *Total assets* are occasionally equated with *total capital* in the finance literature.

Subdivisions of this total-asset type of capital are also referred to as *capital,* with some descriptive adjective affixed. *Working capital,* for example, is that part of capital which is circulating, changing its form (from cash to inventory to receivables to cash again) within a rather short period of time. Working capital generally is measured as the amount of current assets of the firm (cash and assets generally expected to be converted to cash within one year in the normal course of operating a business). Cash usually is first invested in inventories; these are then sold and become receivables, which, when collected, become cash again. (An illustration of this flow is shown on the inside cover of the book.) *Fixed capital* is that part of total assets which also circulates but only over a longer cycle, and in the accountant's view these would normally include machinery, fixtures, and buildings—objects that yield their services only over an extended period of time. These types of assets will lose their usefulness to the firm over a period of time through deterioration or obsolescence. But fixed assets also include land, which may yield services infinitely without loss in value and without the necessity of reinvestment to restore its usefulness.

Capital may also be viewed as the claims against the total assets of the firm. The total money value of the claims equals the total money value of the assets measured by "acceptable" accounting methods. This is subdivided into two categories: debt and owners' claims. These two categories are mutually exclusive and exhaustive. The owners' claims may consist of outstanding shares of common stock and preferred stock,[1] as well as *paid-in capital* and *undivided profits* in the case of the corporation or *total proprietor's* (or *proprietors'*) *claims* in the case of the noncorporate enterprise. Debt claims consist not only of outstanding creditor securities in the form of bonds and long-term notes; they also include short-term notes payable, term loans due within one year, accounts payable, and other accrued liabilities. Yet it is customary to include only the face value of the securities as the corporation's capitalization. *Face value* is the stipulated repayment value in the case of debt securities; it is the par value or stated value (stated value is used if the stock is a no-par stock) in the case of ownership securities. *Par value* has little to do with economic value, but refers to the monetary amount set on the corporate stock establishing the base for state incorporation franchise taxes. Without a stipulated amount for common stock, the par or stated value in many states is assumed for tax purposes to be $100 per share. Customarily, it is desirable to establish a low par or stated value in these cases. According to the "trust fund doctrine," par value also establishes a limit to the payment of dividends, for dividends cannot be declared and paid that would infringe upon the par or stated value of the stock.[2] The par value is stated in the corporate charter and may not be changed except by an amendment, and stock may not be legally issued for less than the par value. Par value is usually only part of the amount paid in by the stockholders. Amounts in excess of par or stated value are credited to an account such as Paid-in Capital. Par value carries no significance generally in the determination of market or other measures of economic value.

The following equity section of a balance sheet is illustrative of many industrial corporations. Note that the common stock has a $1 par value.

---

[1] See Appendix B for a description and discussion of common stock, preferred stock and debt securities. Not all claims, however, are represented by securities.

[2] State laws often require a stated value in the case of no-par stock to use as a tax base and as a limit to the payment of dividends.

Equity
Common stock ($1 par)

Authorized	1,000,000 shares		
Unissued	500,000 "		
Issued and outstanding	500,000 "		$ 500,000
Paid-in capital (also called capital surplus)			500,000
Undivided profits (or earned surplus)			397,262
Total Equity			$1,397,262

It could just as well have been a $1 stated value or a no-par stock. Interestingly, from the above example one would be inclined to suggest that the stock was sold for $2 per share, $1 being credited to Common Stock and $1 to Paid-in Capital although this may not necessarily have been the case. Also, although the state granting the charter bases its tax upon the par value of shares authorized, whether issued or not, unissued shares are available to the company for sale, exchange, or payment in the future and thereby provide some flexibility to the capitalization. Whether or not the cost of the tax paid on unissued shares is warranted depends on whether or not the additional benefits derived from the flexibility offset that cost; additional costs would be incurred when further increases in shares are desired. Additional authorized shares entail a charter amendment, and stockholder approval is therefore required. These expenses would be the major consideration in carrying unissued, but taxable, shares on the books.

Undivided Profits generally are the cumulative accounting profits retained by the company, less any dividends. Although other charges and credits may be made to this account, cumulative retained earnings usually predominate. These retained earnings probably have been accumulated over many accounting periods and are represented in numerous and untraceable investments on the asset side of the balance sheet. The difference between Undivided Profits at two points in time usually would constitute the accounting profits (losses) retained in the period. Total accounting profits would be higher than this by the amount of dividends paid during the period, because these are charged against the Undivided Profits account.

Often the term *capital* refers only to owners' claims and excludes creditors' claims. This adds to confusion in the use of the term. Accounting statements frequently refer to owners' claims as *capital* and to creditors' claims as *liabilities*. In our example, owners' claims are referred to as *equity*.

One may also find use of the term *raising capital*, and in this sense the phrase means securing new cash. This use of the term has the restrictive connotation of referring only to liquid capital. This is consistent with our meaning of the word, for cash is part of capital and any excessive cash at any moment will soon be expected to be used productively.

Thus the meanings of the term *capital* are many and varied. For our purposes, we shall retain our original definition of *capital,* and use some operational extensions of it such as *working capital* or *fixed capital.*

FACTORS INFLUENCING THE DEMAND FOR CAPITAL

There are many factors influencing the demand for capital in the firm. These can be represented by a schedule of demand. Ultimately the demand for capital depends upon the consumers' desires for the product or service, and in this sense it is often referred to as a *derived demand* for capital. Behind the simplicity of this statement, however, are such factors as the relative supplies and prices of other factors used in producing the good or service and the combination of these factors to produce the output (the production function). The precise amount of capital obtained and employed by the firm during a given period is also a function of the supply of capital to the firm for the same period.

Capital is sometimes referred to as an intermediate factor. It has, of course, been recognized that we can obtain a greater final product through the use of roundabout methods rather than through direct methods of production. The cost of "roundaboutedness" is time. Rather than trying to catch fish by hand, a stranded Robinson Crusoe may take time out to make a pole and hook; to do so, he must postpone present consumption. The rate of exchange of the present good for the future good reflects the net productivity of capital and is referred to very generally as the *rate of interest.*

Capital is a necessary ingredient for the operation of the firm. Labor working without the use of capital (if it embodied no human capital) would be akin to trying to start a fire without air. The factors are complementary. The optimal mix of factors in terms of relative quantities depends upon, among other things, the good or service being produced for sale. A less than optimal combination of factors in the firm results in a less satisfactory level of goal achievement; by the same token, profits could be increased by adjustments in the relative quantities of the factors employed. Firms generally attempt to achieve an optimal combination of factors and to make adjustments that move them toward their goal; but imperfect information, information lags, and the inability to make rapid adjustments prevent the achievement of the ideal mix.

If we were to hold the quantity of capital (physical and human) employed in a firm constant while increasing the quantity of labor, the profit per unit of labor would eventually decrease. As we know, employees always possess some degree of capital, so we could reduce the physical capital as we add employees to offset the additions of human capital or we could replace heavy-capital-endowed employees with a larger number of less skilled employees. The additional labor, although holding total capital constant, may add to total profits, but at some point the profit per unit of labor must diminish (the law of diminishing returns). A digression from the optimal combination of factors, such as employing more labor with a constant amount of capital, will increase output, but not most efficiently. The same increase in production could be had at lower cost. As labor is added, the average and marginal rate of return to labor (per unit) would fall. As capital is held constant, the increasing profits will cause the average and marginal rate of return to capital to rise. When management becomes aware of this, it will tend to add to that factor having the greatest rate of return and decrease (or halt additions to) the factor having the lowest return, thus working back toward the best combination of resources. Equilibrium would exist when the marginal rates of return to all factors were equal, as this would be optimum.[3]

For each level of output there exists an optimum or least-cost combination of factors of production. If the managers of a firm knew precisely both the best physical combination of the factors needed to produce goods or services and the prices of the factors, they would adjust the employment of factors to such an optimum. If they knew the least-cost combination of factors, they could proceed to draw up the demand for each factor at various levels of output. The specific demand for each factor, given price, would also depend upon knowing the optimum output—that which produces maximum profits. Traditional elementary economic analysis of the firm tells us that this output exists when marginal revenue equals marginal cost. If the firm can hire factors to achieve that output, it would tend toward that level of output. Frequently, however, factors cannot be expanded or contracted rapidly and the firm must be content with under and overcapacities in certain factors until correction is possible. Later we shall devote brief attention to multiple-product firms and the problem of allocation of capital to the different goods or services to be produced.

The Production Function

The physical correspondence between output and input is referred to as the *production function*. This may be simply illustrated by a pay-off

---

[3] From the firm's point of view (and not from the point of view of the factor owner), the aforementioned rates of return are net of the costs of the factor. The rate of return to capital would be net of the cost of capital. The rate of return to labor would be net of the cost of labor. (The wage payment is in part a payment for human capital and in part a payment for labor.)

Table 11-1

Production Payoff Matrix

		Number of Units of Labor				
		1	2	3	4	5
Number of Units of Capital	1	21	42	50	56	55
	2	25	50	68	73	71
	3	28	56	78	85	83
	4	30	60	87	93	90

matrix for two inputs, labor and capital, such as the one in Table 11-1. The payoffs in the body of the table represent output.[4] For example, the input of two units of capital and two units of labor results in an estimated output of 50. The reader should be able to observe the diminishing returns for either factor; if labor is held constant, the relative increments to product as a result of capital additions become smaller and smaller. The increments in output in Table 11-1 are also referred to as *marginal physical products*. The table could just as well have been labeled "Land and Labor" if one thinks in terms of the traditional economic factors, or "Equipment and Employees"; the concept would remain the same no matter how one happens to view the elements contributing to the production of economic goods.

The Marginal Physical Product of Capital

There would exist in most cases several combinations of factors (except in the cases of fixed proportions of the factors) that would produce the same output. The simple matrix above shows that 50 units of output could be produced by using either one unit of capital with three units of labor, or two units of capital and two units of labor. Given the prices of the factors, the least-cost combination can be determined; it exists when the marginal physical product received from the last dollar expended is the same for all factors. In other words, $\frac{MPP_1}{Price_1} = \frac{MPP_c}{Price_c}$. The price ($P$) of the factor is the cost of that factor to the firm and the price of one additional unit is the marginal cost (MC) and the marginal physi-

---

[4] A more frequently used production function for illustrative purposes is of the form, $O = .9L^{.25}C^{.75}$, where O is the output of the enterprise, L is units of labor, and C is units of capital. This function (Cobb-Douglas type) is most easily evaluated by the use of logarithms. By differential calculus, $MPP = .675C^{-.25}L^{.25}$. See: E. H. Phelps Brown, *The Framework of the Pricing System* (Lawrence, Kan.: University of Kansas, 1949), pp. 104–108.

cal product (MPP) times the marginal revenue (MR) per unit of output gives the marginal value product (MVP). An optimum output condition could be stated in terms of factor prices and the value of additional outputs. For example, if the MVP ($MPP \times MR$) is given or known, then the optimum level of output is achieved when the $MVP = MC$. This sort of analysis of firm behavior, although unrealistically ideal, does lead to some rules for optimal behavior, given the tentative prices and the productivity of the factors of production.

Changes in factor prices cause changes in the demand for capital. The price effects upon demand are customarily classed into two categories: the substitution effect and the output effect. Should the price of labor rise, one usually expects capital to be substituted for labor by the firm in order to maintain the least-cost combination for producing the output. This has the effect of reducing the demand for labor. Labor's demand may also be reduced because the higher total level of cost (even though still least-cost) will cause total output to be less; this lessening of demand is referred to as the *output effect*. The demand for capital therefore could be reduced for these two reasons because of the increase in the price of the factor.

ALLOCATION OF CAPITAL IN THE FIRM

Traditional economic theory does not deal extensively with the problem of choosing products to maximize profits; rather, traditional theory relies principally on the rule that the ratio of the marginal physical products to the price of the factors ought to be equal for all uses of the factors in the firm. For the factor capital, in producing A and B products, $\dfrac{MPP_{ca}}{P_c} = \dfrac{MPP_{cb}}{P_c}$; that is, the ratio of the marginal physical product of capital when used in the production of A to the price of capital ought to equal the same ratio as that for B. This is a necessary requirement for the optimum allocation of capital among products. This would suggest that the ratio of the marginal rate of return on A to the cost of capital should equal the ratio of the marginal rate of return on B to the cost of capital; in other words, the marginal rate of return on each product should be equal for optimum capital allocation. If there is a state of certainty regarding returns on proposed investments, the firm would invest capital until the marginal rate of return on each product equaled the cost of capital.

The optimum allocation for a firm with a multiple product line is the equality of the marginal rates of return which should produce theoretically correct results. Capital, however, usually is not invested in infinitely small increments, but only in nondivisible "lumps." Consequently, one could expect only a tendency toward such a theoretically optimum condition. We shall have more to say regarding the allocation of the firm's capital after a consideration of the conditions of supply and a more realistic analysis of a firm's schedule of demand for capital.

THE FIRM'S DEMAND SCHEDULE

A requirement for the efficient operation of modern firms is that they attempt to foresee problems before they arise and prepare for their optimum disposition. Such planning is necessary for potential nonroutine cash outlays to insure the achievement of the objective of the firm. The desire for profits usually brings many investment opportunities before the firm. To a large degree these opportunities constitute the schedule of the firm's demand for capital.

Opportunities arise in many different ways. Profit opportunities may arise through a formal generating process such as exists in some firms which have a department or division devoted to such exploration. The existence of research and development departments is a case in point. In other cases the opportunities may come to the attention of management through the comments of customers, employees, or almost any person who has some sort of communication with the firm. A good businessman is an opportunist; he has a "nose" for new ideas—for profit—and enjoys capitalizing on them. It matters little if the original source is the employee suggestion box or the research and development department; the firm must evaluate such opportunities and make decisions concerning its possible involvement. *Project evaluation* is a screening process in which each proposal must pass through successively more precise stages before it is finally accepted or rejected. Some will be rejected almost immediately; others, at a later point in the process. At each point in the screening process, the firm must weigh the cost of continued evaluation against the prospective rewards. At some point in this process, the rewards for certain proposals will appear too low and the projects will be discarded at that point. In other words, some projects will be eliminated before the evaluation process is over because the expected cost of further information concerning the expected return and risk exceeds the expected gain even with the expected reduction in uncertainty that results from more information.

Let us assume the results of this process produce a number of opportunities available to the company. With maximization of shareholders' return in mind, the firm in determining the acceptability of investment opportunities must behave in such a way as to achieve this goal. One such method used to achieve this goal is to rank the opportunities in order of their internal rates of return.

The Time-Adjusted Rate of Return

To compute such returns, an estimate of cash outlays required for the investment project and net cash inflows per period are needed. The net cash inflow is measured as the difference between the cash expenditures and cash receipts resulting from the investment project. Consider an investment in an apartment house costing $100,000. For the first year, rental receipts are $30,000 and the outlays for maintenance, taxes, and repair are $10,000; the net cash inflow is $20,000. At the end of the second year the apartment house is sold for $80,000 and, when this sum is added to the rental receipts of $30,000, the total is $110,000; deduction of expenses results in a *net cash inflow* of $100,000.

The data below summarizes the information presented by a hypothetical firm's staff on two investment opportunities.

	Investment A	Investment B
Dollar investment required (cash outflow) (time $t = 0$)	$1,000	$1,000
Dollar net cash inflow (time $t = 1$)	200	1,000
Dollar net cash inflow (time $t = 2$)	1,000	200

The entire cash outflow (investment required) is assumed in this case to take place all at time $t = 0$; the inflow, which is the net cash proceeds (cash receipts — cash expenditures) from the investment, is assumed to occur at precisely one and two years from $t = 0$. At the end of $t = 2$, no more cash inflow will be forthcoming. Although these are simplifying assumptions, they do not seriously detract from the practical application of the concept.

It should be noted that the simple average return in both cases, unadjusted for time, would be the same. The gain would be the net cash inflow less the investment requirement (cash outlay). To compute the return, the net cash inflows must be related to the investment. In both cases, the return would be

$$ER = \frac{\$1,200 - \$1,000}{\$1,000} = 20\%.$$

A simple average return per year would be 20%/2 or 10 per cent. However, this *average return* calculation is deficient, and for an important reason: it fails to take into account the time at which the net cash inflows are realized and *it makes a difference to the firm when the cash flows takes place*. Investment B is obviously preferable to A, for the firm receives $800 more for the first year from Investment B than from Investment A. This amount can be readily invested at least at the generally prevailing interest rate for rather riskless investments and thereby enhance the firm's profit by that amount, an amount which it would not have if it took on Investment A. Consequently, this measure must be refined to account for such timing differences.

The *time-adjusted rate of return* can be computed by finding the appropriate discount rate which would equate the present value of cash outlays (CO) for the investment and the present value of the net cash inflows (CI). This may be presented in the form of the following equation:

$$\sum_{t=0}^{n} \frac{CO_t}{(1+ER)^t} = \sum_{t=1}^{n} \frac{CI_t}{(1+ER)^t}$$

In the particular case at hand, all outlays are made at $t=0$, and the net cash inflows are expected to occur at $t=1$ and $t=2$. Consequently, for this specific case the equation becomes

$$\frac{CO_0}{(1+ER)^0} = \sum_{t=1}^{2} \frac{CI_t}{(1+ER)^t}$$

The problem is to find that value of ER which satisfies the equation. The equation cannot be solved directly for ER, so we must substitute probable values until the proper one is found.

For Investment A, suppose we try the simple 10 per cent rate.

$$\frac{\$1,000}{(1+.10)^0} = \frac{\$200}{(1+.10)^1} + \frac{\$1,000}{(1+.10)^2}$$

$$\frac{\$1,000}{1} = \frac{\$200}{(1.1)^1} + \frac{\$1,000}{(1.1)^2}$$

As the second cash inflow of $1,000 is two years away from receipt, it must be annually discounted once for the second year and again for the first year in order to derive a discounted value for the cash inflow two years away; consequently, the denominator in the second term on the right is squared in order to find the time-adjusted (annually) compounded rate of return. This is close to equality with the cash outlay, but we can

$$\$1,000 = \$181.82 \quad + \$826.45$$
$$\$1,000 = \$1,008.27$$

observe that some higher rate of discount would reduce the right side of the equation further. At 11 per cent the right side becomes $991.80. By rough interpolation, we would say the rate of return was 10.5 per cent for Investment A. For Investment B, the rate of return would be 17 per cent.[5] Because the $1,000 is received sooner, the return on Investment B exceeds that of Investment A.

This measure of the worth of potential investments suffers somewhat because the technique assumes that the funds received at the end of each year up to the end of the life of the project can be reinvested at the same rate of return. In Investment B it is implicitly assumed that the $1,000 received at the end of Year 1 can be reinvested at 17 per cent and that the benefits of the compounding effect is at that rate.[6]

The time-adjusted rate of return is subject to further criticism, at least from a theoretical point of view, in that it is possible that more than one rate of return can satisfy the equation. However, with additional analysis, a unique rate may be determined.[7] Nevertheless, the time-adjusted rate of return on investment opportunities gives the firm a reasonably satisfactory basis for the ranking of investments on the basis of profitability. Exceptions would exist where the net cash inflows change from positive to negative during the life of the investment project and where future rates of return may be expected to differ substantially from the rate computed. Assuming the firm developed a number of proposals and computed the returns in this fashion, a schedule such as that in Table 11-2 could be constructed. This schedule shows the demand for capital arranged in order of decreasing rate of return. This demand may be put on a cumulative basis as in Table 11-3 and graphed as a demand schedule in Figure

---

[5] The process of arriving at the 17 per cent rate of return on Investement B is left to the reader as an exercise.

[6] Our analysis, at this point, ignores risk as a consideration in selection; we shall look at this problem later on.

[7] If the equation is stated as

$$\text{Present Value} = \sum_{t=1}^{n} \frac{CI_t}{(1 + ER)^t}$$

and if $X = \dfrac{1}{(1 + ER)}$ is substituted, the equation becomes a polynomial of degree t, capable of having multiple roots. See: Eugene L. Grant and W. Grant Ireson, *Principles of Engineering Economy*, 4th ed. (New York: The Ronald Press Company, 1960), pp. 509–13.

Table 11-2

Schedule of Capital Demand for Year X

Expected Rate of Return	Dollars of Investments Proposed
50% and over	500
40 to 49.9%	1,000
30 to 39.9	2,500
20 to 29.9	3,000
10 to 19.9	5,000
0 to 9.9	7,000

11-1. This schedule represents expected returns for anticipated demands for capital in the coming year. It does not include demands in years beyond this one year, an important consideration when capital supply is limited. Figure 11-1 could be fitted for a smooth function, as in Figure 11-2.

Table 11-3

Cumulative Schedule of Demand for Year X

Expected Rate of Return	Dollars of Investments Proposed
Over 50%	500
40% and over	1,500
30% and over	4,000
20% and over	7,000
10% and over	12,000
Above 0%	19,000

Present Value

Present Value for One Period (One Year)

Another measure of the value of investment proposals is to use the present-value method. This method offers certain measurement advantages over the time-adjusted rate of return method and thereby avoids the criticisms made of that method. It assumes only that net cash inflows are reinvested at the discount rate which is the minimum attractive rate for investments of this risk. The minimum attractive rate (the discount rate) is the firm's cost of capital plus a premium for risk. Given, for example, a minimum attractive rate of return of 10 per cent, the present value of an expected return of $115 would then be computed as

$$PV = \frac{EO}{1 + ER_m} = \frac{\$115}{1 + .10} = \frac{\$115}{1.10} = \$104.55.$$

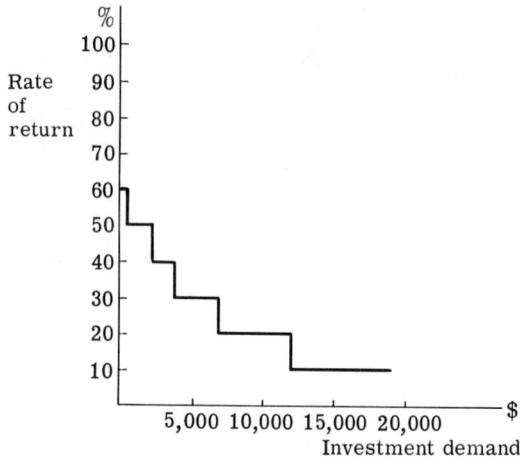

Figure 11-1   Cumulative Investment Demand.

The computations of present value above were restricted to one period. For one year, the present-value formula is

$$PV_1 = \frac{EO_1}{1 + ER_m}$$

where

EO_1 = expected outcome (of cash inflow or cash outflow) at the end of Year 1

ER_m = the particular minimum attractive rate of return above the firm's cost of capital for investments of equivalent risk for one year

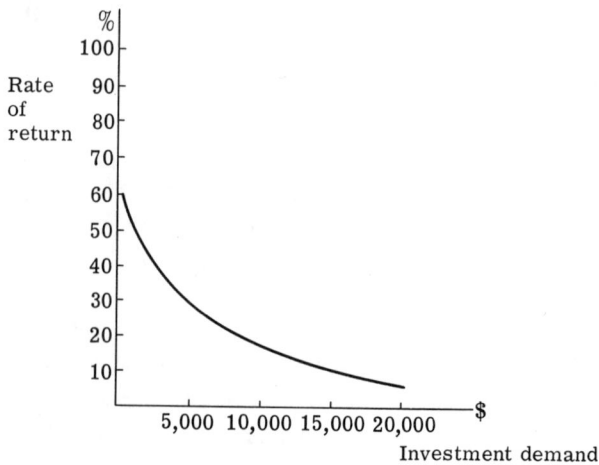

Figure 11-2   Curve of Cumulative Investment Demand.

Present Value For More Than One Period (More Than One Year)

For more than one year or period, the computation becomes only slightly more complex. If one assumes that there also exists not only an expected pay-off at the end of Year 1 but also an expected pay-off at the end of Year 2, one may determine the value of the expected pay-off of the second year in a similar manner.

The rate used to discount the expected outcome is stated in terms of a rate for one year only. In the case of the expected net cash inflow due at the end of Year 2, the pay-off should be discounted, in effect, at twice the annual rate to determine its present value. Consequently, the formula becomes

$$PV_2 = \frac{CI_2}{(1 + ER_m)^2}$$

where

PV_2 = the present value of the expected net cash inflow at the end of Year 2

CI_2 = the expected net cash inflow at the end of year 2

ER_m = the minimum attractive rate of return for investments of equivalent risk for *one* year

For the present value of the expected net cash inflow at the end of the third year, the formula is simply

$$PV_3 = \frac{CI_3}{(1 + ER_m)^3}$$

This extension may then be continued for as many times as there exist expected outcomes (net cash inflows).

The present value of all the future expected pay-offs is the sum of the discounted payoffs of the individual years:

$$PV = \frac{EO_1}{(1 + ER_m)^1} + \frac{EO_2}{(1 + ER_m)^2} + \frac{EO_3}{(1 + ER_m)^3} \cdots + \frac{EO_n}{(1 + ER_m)^n}$$

or, in other words,

$$PV = \sum_{t=1}^{n} \frac{EO_t}{(1 + ER_m)^t}$$

It should be noted in the use of these formulas that it is assumed that the pay-off will accrue at the end of the period. This may be true for returns on bonds, savings accounts, or similar investments, but in the case of many firms the returns accrue throughout the period.

For Investments A and B, assuming a minimum attractive rate of return of 10 per cent, the present value of the inflow is computed as

$$PV_A = \frac{\$200}{(1+.10)^1} + \frac{\$1,000}{(1+.10)^2}$$
$$= \$200 \,(.9091) + \$1,000 \,(.8264)$$
$$= \$1,008.22.$$

$$PV_B = \frac{\$1,000}{(1+.10)^1} + \frac{\$200}{(1+.10)^2}$$
$$= \$1,000 \,(.9091) + \$200 \,(.8264)$$
$$= \$1,074.38.$$

In both A and B the present value of the inflow exceeds the cost of investment ($1,000), the present value of the outflow. However, Investment B produces the greatest gain over the initial outlay of capital and must therefore be chosen over Investment A if only one of the proposed investments can be accepted.

RISK AND THE DEMAND FOR CAPITAL

A firm's decisions to select investment proposals on the basis of expected returns alone does not appear to coincide with its actual behavior. It is general knowledge that firms are unwilling to accept investment proposals expected to yield only a small margin above the estimated cost of their capital.[8] If the returns on all investment proposals were known with certainty, their decision problem would be simplified considerably. Risk, however, influences their demand for capital to a significant extent. It is to a discussion of this topic and its influence on investment decisions that we now direct our attention.

Risk was defined previously as the relative standard deviation of the investment's expected returns. We viewed risk as the standard deviation relative to its respective mean. In our earlier terminology, the SR/ER

[8] Richard C. Chewning, *An Investigation of Industrial Methodology Used for Determining the Cost of Capital when Making Capital Budgeting Decisions* (Unpublished D.B.A. dissertation, Department of Accounting, Finance and Statistics, University of Washington, 1963).

ratio accomplished this end. *ER* stands for expected (mean) return and *SR* stands for standard deviation of the return. The ratio *SR/ER* is referred to as the *coefficient of variation* in statistics.

Assume a particular $100 investment under consideration by a firm has an expected outcome (*EO*) of $115, and an estimated standard deviation of the outcome (*SO*) of $10. Transforming these into rates, *ER* becomes 15 per cent $\left(\dfrac{\$115-\$100}{\$100}\right)$ (100) and *SR* becomes 10 per cent $\left(\dfrac{\$10}{\$100}\right)$. The risk or coefficient of variation now becomes 2/3 $\left(\dfrac{SR}{ER}=\dfrac{10}{15}\right)$. For Investment A, with a standard deviation of 10 per cent and a 15 per cent expected return, the *SR/ER* becomes 2/3 and would appear as in Figure 11-3, for example (if the market were well informed concerning its risk).

As stated in Chapter 5, *risk* refers to variability and *uncertainty* connotes varying degrees of confidence in the variability estimates. A flip of an honest coin obviously has variability in its outcomes, only two of which are possible. The relative frequency of occurrence of each outcome in the coin case is known to be .5; this variability illustrates risk because the outcome is not a known fact. We are, however, perfectly confident in our variability estimates and, in this sense, no uncertainty exists. In other situations much less information about the pattern of variation may be available, therby giving rise to a lack of confidence in the outcomes. This lack of confidence in the variation of outcomes is known as *uncertainty*. In this light it is quite possible to have two investment alternatives with equal expected returns (*ER*) and equal risks (*SR/ER*), and yet

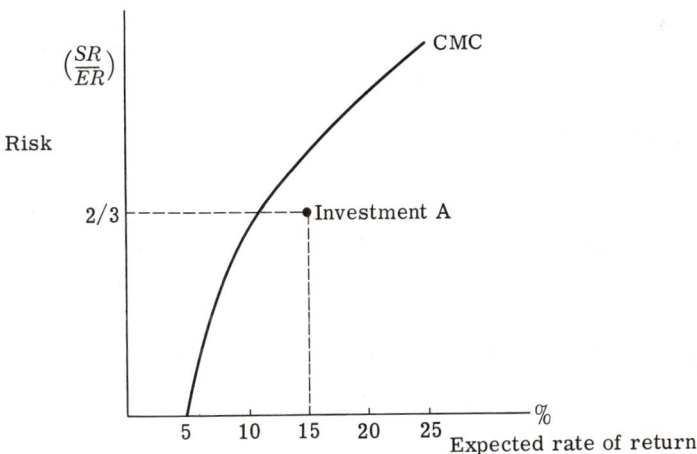

Figure 11-3 Capital Market Curve and Investment A.

prefer one alternative to another because of the greater confidence in one set of estimates as compared to the other. Quite often the decision-maker will illustrate such preferences when faced with decisions in which one alternative bases its return upon flows further distant in time than another. Time is one of the influences that tends to reduce our confidence in prediction and thus increases uncertainty.

Risk and Firm Size

Risk in individual investment projects affects the risk of the firm as a whole and may affect its cost of capital. Risk may also be considered as an outright threat to the firm's survival. Inability to survive is the antithesis of the firm's objective. Therefore, full recognition of risk exposure helps management to evaluate the desirability of various investment alternatives. For we shall see that because of risk and uncertainty firms cannot afford to act according to traditional theory in which the marginal revenue product of each factor equals the price of that factor at optimum output (for capital, the marginal return would equal its cost).

Let us begin by noting that many investment projects or alternatives involve a relatively fixed investment requirement and, because of the size of the firm, some projects may be attractive to some and unattractive to others. For example, firms in a particular industry are assumed to be plagued by a particular kind of accident. Let us assume that consultants have suggested a solution enabling firms to eliminate this cost. The cost is in the form of damage to a machine and usually amounts to $2,000 in repair and downtime.[9] The largest firm has twenty such machines in use and the smallest firm only three. The consultants estimate the cost of implementing the solution at $25,000.

The gross saving to the largest firm would amount to about $40,000 a year (20 × $2,000), as the damage seems to occur on the average at the rate of one machine per year. The smallest firm could save only $6,000 (3 × $2,000). Although it is apparent that such an investment alternative is attractive for the largest firm, it is not likely that the smallest firm could even consider such an investment. From this it can be seen that a firm's size may affect the demand for funds insofar as it affects the desirability of various investment alternatives. But firm size may affect the willingness to undertake investments in yet another way.

It may not be assumed that every investment project actually yields its expected rate of return or even turns out to be successful. We might consider, for example, the impact of the threat of failure upon the deci-

---

[9] Downtime cost is the cost to the firm of having the machine not in use, foregoing revenue thereby.

sions of firms. Any given investment opportunity involving a fixed dollar investment represents to the small firm a greater probability of failure of the whole firm than it does for a larger firm, a proposition we shall now substantiate. For this purpose we shall make certain assumptions to keep the model from becoming too complex and to emphasize the point of the illustration, although the kinship to reality can be readily inferred.

Assume an investment project's outcomes are two instead of many— a complete loss of the $10,000 investment at the one extreme and a profit of $10,000 at the other. We will assume all projects facing the two firms involve these amounts. Firm A is a small firm with total assets of $30,000 and Firm B is a large firm with total assets of $100,000. Now if the probability of success of the investment project (a profit of $10,000) were .6 and the probability of failure (a loss of the $10,000 invested) were .4 each time the firm committed itself, the small firm with $30,000 in assets runs a greater chance of bankruptcy than the large firm, as shown in Figure 11-4. The figures enclosed by the circles represent the state of each firm's total assets. The lines connecting these circles denote paths which the firm could follow on successive investment commitments. The probability of each path is written above it. Moving from left to right for successive investment commitments, we can note the possible paths a firm may take. At the outset, Firm A ($30,000) has a .6 chance of moving to $40,000 of total assets and a .4 chance of moving to $20,000 as a result of the first commitment, and so on. It can at least be intuitively observed that there exists a chance of failure of the small firm by the end of three investment attempts of the same magnitude and probability of success. The probability of failure for Firm A, $P(f_A)$, in three tries is $(.4)^3 = .064$ and for B, $P(f_B) = 0$. That is, Firm B could not possibly fail in this period, but Firm A would have over six chances out of 100 of "folding" after three investment commitments. In the long run the probability of "ruin" would be given as[10]

$$P(f) = (q/p)^z$$

where

$P(f) =$ the probability of failure in the long run,
$q =$ the probability of failure on a given try,
$p =$ the probability of success on a given try, and
$z =$ the total assets divided by the investment requirement per attempt.

[10] David W. Miller and Martin K. Starr, *Executive Decisions and Operations Research* (Englewood Cliffs, N.J.: Prentice-Hall, Inc., 1960), pp. 366–75.

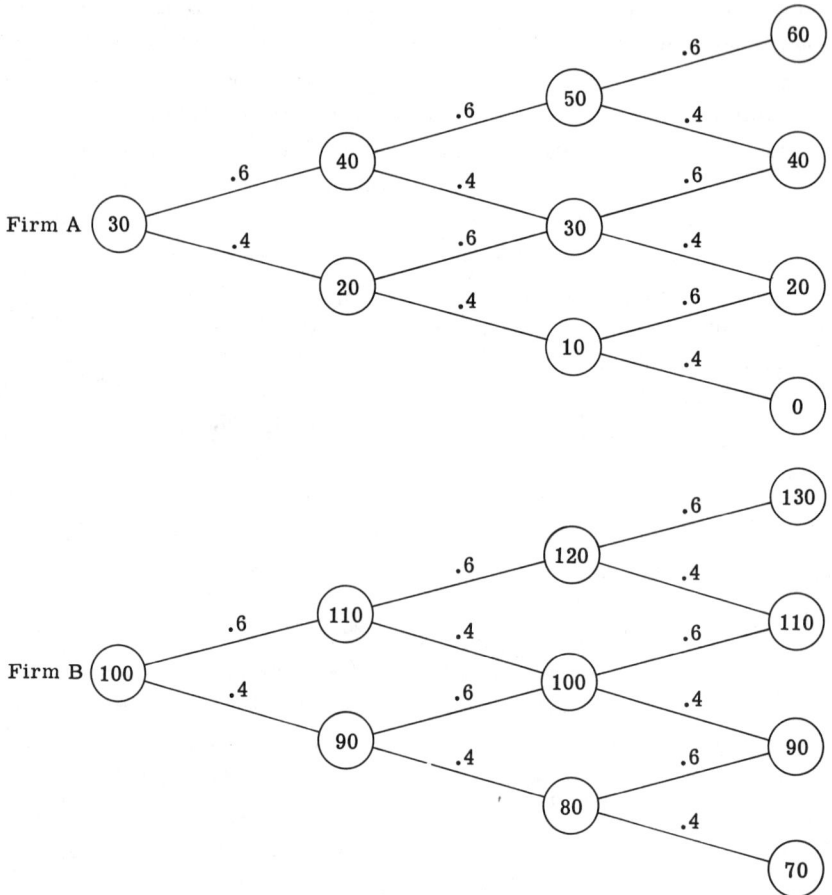

Figure 11-4 Impacts of Investments on Firms of Different Size.

In our example

$$P(f_A) = (.4/.6)^3 = .2963$$

and

$$P(f_B) = (.4/.6)^{10} = .0173.$$

It can be seen that two firms of different size facing the same individual risk proposition expose themselves to varying degrees of danger. All other things being equal, Firm A would probably avoid projects which require large commitments relative to its size, or projects where the q value was high. We know, however, that firms vary in their willingness to assume risk and the acceptance of a proposal depends upon the risk aversion(s) of the decision-makers. If we altered this case to one in which investment requirements were $15,000 instead of $10,000 for each investment commitment, z would equal 2 for the small firm and $P(f_A) = (.4/.6)^2 = 4/9 = .4444$. The probability of ruin now becomes very high.

The illustration here has been extreme in order to focus attention on this aspect of risk—not in the individual project but to the whole enterprise. It emphasizes the differential impact of the same investment upon firms of varying sizes and therefore tends to affect the firm's demand for capital.

Risk and Diversification

The business firm customarily produces more than one product or service. In evaluating the risk of a given investment proposal, the firm must weigh not only the possible enhancement of profit but also the impact of the particular proposal on the risk of the whole firm because the risk of the firm has an important bearing on its cost of capital which, in turn, affects the profitability of the firm to its owners.

To illustrate this point, view the firm as a diversified pool of investments. The nature of this pool affects the risk level of the firm for it is in the nature of diversification to bring the level of risk for the whole pool of investments below the average of the risks of the separate investments. Each individual investment could carry a risk and an expected return above that associated with the firm as a whole, but as a result of diversification the risk of the pool of investments (the firm) is less than the average of the individual risks.[11]

For example, the Wickman Company has restricted its operations to four profitable products which are listed below, along with their expected risk and returns. (Equal investment is made in each product.) Now, considering the firm as a whole, one can evaluate the expected return as 13 per cent, but the risk (as measured by variation in total return) of the firm should be, say, 3/4. The lower risk for the firm as a whole arises from the fact that the four investments are each affected by a different set of forces; they each possess a degree of independence of one

	Return	Risk (SR/ER)
Product 1: Fluidometers	11%	1
Product 2: Rocket belts	15	1
Product 3: Dehdramartinis	15	1
Product 4: Autodegrees	11	1
Average	13%	$4/4 = 1$

[11] Stephen H. Archer, "Diversification and Risk Reduction," *University of Washington Business Review*, 13 (April-June 1964) 19–25.

another. Certain events are not likely to affect all of them unfavorably all at once or in the same degree. Consequently, there is a reduced expected variability in returns for the firm as a whole.

Certain projects may be desirable for their effect upon the total risk faced by the firm. If a project can be added so as to maintain return but reduce the risk of the whole firm, the company's position would then improve with respect to its capital costs. As we shall discuss in Chapter 13, an informed market would then drive up the price of claims on the company in time and thus move down the cost of capital. The reduction in cost of capital, however, benefits the company only after an extended period because it takes quite a while to add new money and replace old security claims at lower rates than existed before. It benefits the owners of the company immediately because the value of their claims is now increased because of recognition by the market of the reduced risk of the enterprise. Profits are enhanced and the shareholder's position tends to be maximized.

Thus the risk of a particular investment project when viewed separately is likely to exceed the risk of the project when viewed as a part of a group of projects that are at least partially independent of each other —independent in the sense that the forces affecting the outcomes of the various projects affect each differently. In the last chapter, when considering the value of the firm, we noted that the value customarily exceeded the sum of the individual parts. By way of reinforcing that view, the preceding discussion indicates that the risk of the whole is likely to be less than the average risk of the parts. This is a major factor in understanding why a firm's value can exceed the sum of its parts. In short, risk reduction increases value.

Obviously, different combinations of individual projects contribute to the maximization of the firm's objective. On the other hand, individual investments involving desirable combinations of risk and return can be attractive because of their own merits. Suffice it to say for the present that the firm would tend to select individual projects as well as combinations of projects which reduce risk, increase return, or both.

SUMMARY

The term *capital* is used to mean many different things, although it is almost always associated with the generation of income. Often the expression *raising capital* means raising cash only; however, it is expected that all the money raised would soon be productively employed to generate income for the firm.

Many factors affect the firm's demand for capital, including the manner in which capital is combined with other productive factors to produce output and the prices and productivity of all the factors of production. The firm attempts to employ factors in combinations that involve the least cost to the firm for a given output level.

Investment proposals before the firm may be evaluated and ranked by a measure which orders them according to their desirability—such as the time-adjusted rate of return on investment and the present-value method. The more profitable the proposals before the firm, the more capital it will seek. A schedule can be constructed depicting the firm's demand for capital.

Risk also affects the firm's demand for capital. The expected rate of return on investment proposals is not a sufficient criterion on which to base the acceptance or rejection of the proposals. Proposals with high risk are less desirable than those with lower risk, given the same expected return. The size of the firm alone may affect its willingness to assume risks; small firms will tend to avoid large investment commitments with high risk even though the expected returns may be very high. Diversification of the firm's investments among many proposals is very likely to reduce the total risk exposure of the firm.

SUGGESTED READINGS

BENNION, EDWARD GRAHAM. "Capital Budgeting and Game Theory," *Harvard Business Review, 34* (November–December 1956), 115–23.

BREAK, G. F. "Capital Maintenance and the Concept of Income," *Journal of Political Economy, 62* (February 1954), 48–62.

BUCHANAN, NORMAN S. *The Economics of Corporate Enterprise.* New York: Holt, Rinehart & Winston, Inc., 1940.

CHENG, PAO L., and JOHN P. SHELTON. "A Contribution to the Theory of Capital Budgeting—the Multi–investment Case," *The Journal of Finance, 8* (December 1963), 622–36.

CUNNINGHAM, N. J. "Business Investment and the Marginal Cost of Funds," Parts I and II, *Metroeconomica, 10* (August and December 1958), 60–73, 155–81.

EISNER, ROBERT. *Determinants of Capital Expenditures,* Urbana, Ill.: Bureau of Business and Economic Research, University of Illinois, 1956.

GORDON, MYRON J., and ELI SHAPIRO. "Capital Equipment Analysis: The Required Rate of Profit," *Management Science, 3* (October 1956), 102–10.

HIRSHLEIFER, JACK. "On the Theory of Optimal Investment Decision," *Journal of Political Economy, 66* (August 1958), 329–52.

ISTVAN, DONALD F. "The Economic Evaluation of Capital Expenditures," *Journal of Business, 34* (January 1961), 45–51.

LATANÉ, HENRY ALLEN. "Criteria for Choice among Risky Ventures," *Journal of Political Economy, 67* (April 1959), 144–55.

LORIE, JAMES A., and J. LEONARD SAVAGE. "Three Problems in Rationing Capital," *Journal of Business, 28* (October 1955), 229–39.

LUTZ, FREDERICH, and VERA LUTZ. *The Theory of Investment of the Firm.* Princeton, N.J.: Princeton University Press, 1951.

MCLEAN, J. G. "How to Evaluate New Capital Investments," *Harvard Business Review, 36* (November–December 1958), 59–69.

MERRETT, A. J., and ALLEN SYKES. "Calculating the Rate of Return on Capital Projects," *Journal of Industrial Economics, 9* (November 1960), 98–115.

MEYER, J. R. and E. KUH. *The Investment Decision.* Cambridge, Mass.: Harvard University Press, 1957.

ROBERTS, HARRY V. "Current Problems in the Economics of Capital Budgeting," *Journal of Business, 30* (January 1957), 12–16.

SOLOMON, EZRA. "Leverage and the Cost of Capital," *The Journal of Finance, 18* (May 1963), 273–79.

SOLOMON, EZRA (ed.). *The Management of Corporate Capital.* New York: The Free Press of Glencoe, Inc., 1959.

TURVEY, RALPH. "Present Value Versus Internal Rate of Return—An Essay in the Theory of the Third Best," *The Economic Journal, 73* (March 1963), 93–98.

QUESTIONS

11.1 What accounts (items) are usually included in the capitalization of a company?

11.2 Is the par value of the stock likely to limit the market price of the shares? Explain.

11.3 Why would a company have authorized shares that they did not issue?

11.4 What condition expresses the least-cost combination of factors of production? Could this expression also be used for different forms of one factor such as capital? Or for different sources of funds?

11.5 An increase in the price of labor has what effects on the demand for capital? On output? Discuss.

11.6 What expression exhibits the condition of an equilibrium allocation of capital to the production of various products?

11.7 Does the simple average rate of return tend to overestimate or underestimate the time-adjusted rate of return? Explain.

11.8 Under what conditions is it desirable to avoid the use of the internal or time-adjusted rate of return as a measure of investment merit?

11.9 Why could certain investment proposals be attractive to large firms and not to small ones?

11.10 Why would certain investment proposals be profitable or attractive to some firms of the same size and not to others? Explain.

PROBLEMS

11.11 Compute the internal rate of return for the two investment proposals facing the Holmes Home Company. The net cash flows for an apartment house and acreage for development are listed below:

Time	Apartment House	Land Development
0	− $100,000	− $100,000
1	+ 27,000	+ 45,000
2	+ 27,000	+ 35,000
3	+ 27,000	+ 25,000
4	+ 27,000	+ 15,000
5	+ 27,000	+ 5,000

11.12 Compute the time adjusted rate of return for the three investment proposals facing the Huff Powder Company.

Time	A	B	C
0	− $50,000	− $100,000	− $50,000
1	+ 10,000	+ 10,000	+ 13,000
2	+ 10,000	+ 20,000	+ 13,000
3	+ 10,000	+ 30,000	+ 10,000
4	+ 10,000	+ 40,000	+ 13,000
5	+ 20,000	+ 30,000	+ 15,000

11.13 Prepare a schedule of demand for the combined proposals of Holmes Home Company and Huff Powder Company. Prepare a cumulative schedule as well.

11.14 The Bradish Radish & Vegetable Company was trying to decide whether to buy a new truck costing $5,000. The net cash inflow arising from savings in repairs and greater efficiency were estimated to be $800 in the first year, then $1,000, $1,200, $1,500, and $2,000 in successive years. It was assumed that the truck could be sold for $300 in the last year. Com- tion as to purchase. Assume a minimum attractive rate of return for this investment of 8 percent.

11.15 Refer to the investment proposals of the Holmes Home Company (**11.11**). Using 8 per cent as the minimum attractive rate required on in- vestments of equivalent risk, find the present value of both proposals. Has the decision on the two alternatives been altered? Discuss.

11.16 The management of the Goslin Goggle Company has a number of investment proposals facing it which involve considerably larger outlays than it had been accustomed to make up to this point. Each requires an outlay of about $50,000, whereas normally the firm's investment proposals required between $1,000 and $10,000. The company now employs about $50,000 in total assets. The new proposals would yield a gain of $50,000 if successful and a total loss if not. The probability of success is estimated at .7. Find the probability of ruin. What is the probability of ruin if the investments were only $25,000 in size?

CHAPTER 12   THE SUPPLY OF CAPITAL
TO THE FIRM

The phrase *the supply of capital to the firm,* implies that there exist sources of money or credit which the firm can utilize to hire the resources with which to generate income. These resources take many forms, ranging from very highly liquid ones (such as cash) to relatively illiquid ones (such as buildings and equipment). In rather rare circumstances the firm receives its supply of capital in the form of noncash assets. Ordinarily, firms receive their supply of capital in the form of money and in turn convert most of this into other assets operationally capable of achieving the goal of maximizing profits. In this chapter we shall discuss the supply of capital as a supply of money—always implying that money will be turned into other forms of capital.

Some experts in finance suggest that the righthand side of a firm's balance sheet represents sources of capital that the firm has already used. Although this is correct, it should be added that sources other than those indicated on the balance sheet may have been used in the past. A bond issue, bank loan, or preferred stock issue may have been used several years ago and subsequently retired. In other words the balance sheet is not an exhaustive list of sources. It does not indicate that other sources are in fact available to the firm. Only in a very restricted sense does it indicate the sources of capital supply. Indeed, the potential supply of capital to a firm can and does take many forms, only a few of which might be shown on the balance sheet. However, one way of utilizing a balance sheet to yield a rough indication of changes in a given firm's sources of supply between periods is to compare changes in the balance sheets of the periods under review. Table 12-1 illustrates this point. Over the period from 19x7 to 19x0, Company Q increased its total sources $2,000; it would appear that the firm retired bank loans and reduced some of its payables with earnings retained in the business and from the sale of bonds. This limited analysis of sources is unable to detect, of course, any changes that may have occurred within the period; it serves only to compare one period with another. Moreover, this information about the firm is historical and the important objective of the financial manager is to determine the supply of capital generally available now and in the future.

Table 12-1
Changes in Sources of Capital Between Periods

Company Q, Dec. 31, 19x7		Company Q, Dec. 31, 19x0		Changes
Creditors' and Owners' Claims		Creditors' and Owners' Claims		
Accounts payable	$ 2,000	Accounts payable	$ 1,000	− $1,000
Accrued expenses	1,000	Accrued expenses	1,000	0
Notes payable, bank	1,000	Bonds payable	3,000	+ 2,000
Preferred stock	2,000	Preferred stock	2,000	0
Common stock	2,000	Common Stock	2,000	0
Paid-in capital	2,000	Paid-in-capital	2,000	0
Retained earnings	3,000	Retained earnings	4,000	+ 1,000
	$13,000		$15,000	+ $2,000

THE SUPPLY SCHEDULE

There exists many different sources of capital for business firms. Any given source will have different dimensions characterizing it; we shall place these dimensions in three classes. First, *sources will differ as to maturity;* some have an infinite life (such as common stock and retained earnings) while others have a rather short life (such as accounts payable). Short-lived sources may need to be replaced frequently; long-term sources are typically difficult to alter because of their extended duration. Sources whose duration is too short to suit the needs of the business are unduly expensive because they must be refinanced frequently. This involves an expense in the form of replacement costs, to say nothing of the risk (in terms of cost) of refinancing the obligation on less favorable terms. If the maturity is long, the degree of flexibility in adjusting the sources of financing is less and considerable cost may be associated therewith. With this in mind we can say that the *cost of renewal* decreases as the maturity of the capital supply is increased and the *cost of inflexibility* increases as the maturity is lengthened. The behavior of these costs might be graphically depicted as in Figure 12-1. In that figure *total maturity cost* is the sum of renewal and inflexibility costs. There is no empirical evidence, however, to indicate the precise nature of such functions, and other costs, primarily monetary in nature, are likely to dominate the selection of sources of capital.

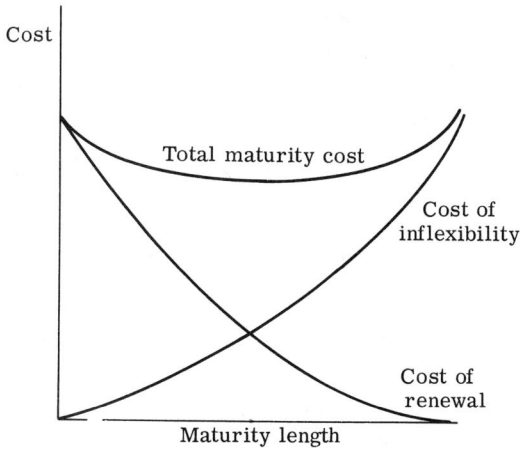

Figure 12-1   Non-Monetary Cost of Capital Curves.

Second, *sources will differ as to the control* they exert over the firm. The sale of an issue of common stock may carry the threat of complete or partial loss of control of the firm when enough of the firm's stock can be bought by a collective interest group. The sale of preferred stock may involve the possibility of losing control which usually is contingent on the future ability of the firm to meet preferred dividend requirements. The sale of a bond issue may involve immediate loss of some control as a result of indenture provisions restricting the range of a firm's behavior with respect to, say, dividend policies and working capital. It also involves the threat of losing some degree of control, if not all, should the firm be unable to meet interest and principal payment requirements.

Last, *sources will also differ as to monetary cost* to the firm. Whereas the costs arising from maturity and control are essentially implicit costs, this is an explicit cost of capital. Customarily, it is expressed as a rate per hundred dollars, or in other words, a percentage. This cost depends on the risk of investment loss as assessed by investors in the firm. In an informed market, the coordinates of the point reflecting risk and return of investment in the firm will lie on the *CMC*. The return is interpreted in two ways. First, it is a return to the investors; second, it is also a cost to the firm: the explicit cost of capital. We shall have more to say about the specific cost of capital to the firm in the next chapter. There we shall discuss the monetary cost of capital when the capital supply is a mix involving a variety of types of sources. There we are concerned with such problems as the nature and measurement of the cost of capital when the sources include retained earnings, sale of common and preferred stock, sale of bonds, and the use of short-term debt.

To proceed with our present analysis, however, we assume the firm is rational in its behavior and, consequently, is a profit-maximizing unit. In traditional microeconomic analysis, it is assumed that the firm—in attempting to maximize profits—strives to attain a least-cost combination of factors used in production. In microfinance as well, we must assume rational firm behavior; the firm is always tending toward a least-cost combination of sources of capital. As a result, the optimum combination of sources is one which, at each quantity of capital supply available to the firm, would be such that no other mix of sources could supply that quantity of capital at any lower total cost to the firm. Combinations may well exist which are equal in cost but, for this optimum or least-cost position to prevail, none may have a lower cost. For the sake of simplicity, let us consider a hypothetical firm with a given risk as having only two sources of supply available to it. Sources A and B offer quantities of capital to the firm at the schedule of prices given in Table 12-2. For illustrative purposes only, we have used discrete $1,000 units. Given these data, the firm could proceed to construct a combined schedule of supply in the follow-

Table 12-2

Capital Offerings by Sources, 19x8

	Source A			Source B	
Units of Capital	Cost per Annum Per $1,000	Cumulative	Units of Capital	Cost per Annum Per $1,000	Cumulative
1st $1,000	$50	$ 50	1st $1,000	$ 65	$ 65
2nd $1,000	50	100	2nd $1,000	55	120
3rd $1,000	50	150	3rd $1,000	50	170
4th $1,000	50	200	4th $1,000	40	210
5th $1,000	60	260	5th $1,000	40	250
6th $1,000	70	330	6th $1,000	50	300
7th $1,000	no offering		7th $1,000	60	360
8th $1,000	”		8th $1,000	80	440
9th $1,000	”		9th $1,000	110	550
10th $1,000	”		10th $1,000	150	700
11th $1,000	”		11th $1,000	250	950

ing manner. If the firm wanted only $1,000, it should take it from Source A, where the cost is only $50; if the firm needed $2,000, it would get it from A also, and for the same reason. If $5,000 is needed, however, it should be secured from Source B because the combined cost of five $1,000 doses of capital in that case is $250 as opposed to $260 in the case of Source A. To see this more clearly, the combined schedule of $1,000 units of capital and total costs at various levels is shown in Table 12–3. For our

Table 12-3
Combined Schedule of Capital Offerings (Sources A & B), 19x8

Capital Offered	Source	Total Cost	Average Cost	Marginal Cost
$ 1,000	A	$ 50	5.0%	5.0%
2,000	A	100	5.0	5.0
3,000	A	150	5.0	5.0
4,000	A	200	5.0	5.0
5,000	B	250	5.0	5.0
6,000	B	300	5.0	5.0
7,000	6B + 1A, or			
	5B + 2A	350	5.0	5.0
8,000	6B + 2A, or			
	5B + 3A	400	5.0	5.0
9,000	6B + 3A, or			
	5B + 4A	450	5.0	5.0
10,000	6B + 4A	500	5.0	5.0
11,000	7B + 4A, or			
	6B + 5A	560	5.1	6.0
12,000	7B + 5A	620	5.2	6.0
13,000	7B + 6A	690	5.3	7.0
14,000	8B + 6A	770	5.5	8.0
15,000	9B + 6A	880	5.9	11.0
16,000	10B + 6A	1,030	6.4	15.0
17,000	11B + 6A	1,280	7.5	25.0

purposes we assume that at each level of capital offered, no other combination of sources is available at any lower cost. Notice that, as more and more doses of capital are taken on, the price structure of capital forces the firm seeking funds to shift from Source A to Source B. However, as the magnitude of the need increases, a combination of the two sources is utilized in order to obtain the least-cost combination of capital available to the firm so that, for example, at the $12,000 capital requirement level five $1,000 units of capital costing $250 are secured from Source A and seven $1,000 units costing $360 are secured from Source B for a total cost of $620.

The graph of this schedule is shown in Figure 12-2 and reflects the

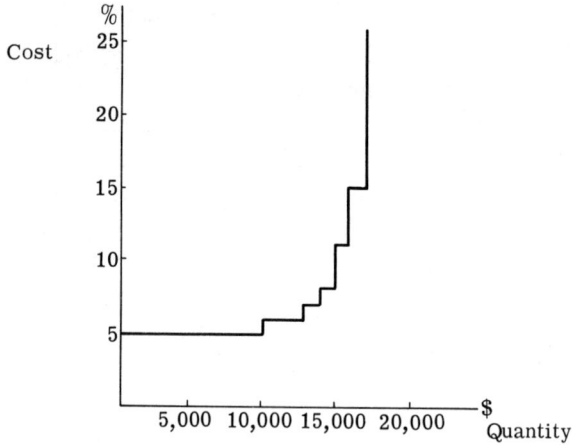

Figure 12-2 Supply Schedule of Capital.

supply of capital offered at various levels of explicit monetary cost (in per cent) to the firm. One may at least theoretically fit a smooth curve to approximate the function. But it is important to recognize that the supply function should also include the implicit loss of control, renewal, and/or inflexibility costs. Although we cannot be sure of the precise shape of the supply function, it may be relatively flat for a significant range. Figure 12-3 merely suggests the possible nature of such a function. The total cost (TC) is a function of monetary cost (C_1), maturity cost (C_2), and control cost (C_3), so that $TC = f(C_1, C_2, C_3)$. The inclusion of these three costs as variables implies that there is a significant functional rela-

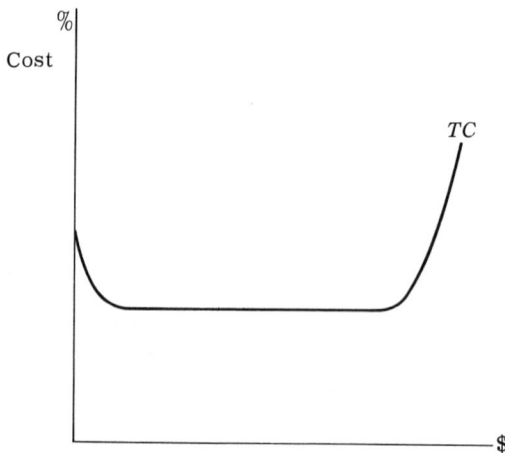

Figure 12-3 Smoothed Supply Schedule of Capital.

tionship between monetary cost and quantity, between maturity cost and quantity, and control cost and quantity. It is suggested at this point that the monetary cost will increase as the quantity of capital increases. As the quantity supplied to the firm in any fixed period increases, the cost of capital should eventually increase. It may be a matter of conjecture as to which mix of sources provides the cheapest capital; yet at some point, the quantity of capital supplied in a period may become so large relative to the existing size of the firm that the risk of investment increases greatly, as we saw in the example of the risk exposure to chance (stochastic) happenings facing the large and small firms (see Chapter 11). At some point the firm will not be able to employ additional doses of money at profitable rates, which would decrease the expected return, reduce the value of the firm to the investor, and increase the cost of capital. We could scarcely expect a firm to triple its size every year indefinitely without considerable sacrifice in returns. It can also be expected that the employment of other factors such as management or labor could not keep pace with an excessively rapid rate of increase in capital employment and diminishing returns to capital could thus be anticipated. The market is aware of this danger and alters its supply schedule accordingly to compensate for the increased risk.

It can also be anticipated that the expected cost of loss of control would increase as the total quantity supplied increased. In order to secure more capital, greater sacrifices are likely to have to be made in control of the business. After a certain point additional money might not be forthcoming unless suppliers are given some control over managerial decisions. Control costs would not be involved in the case of internal sources, but after the use of these is exhausted control costs are involved. If more capital is supplied than the firm can profitably employ at reasonable risk levels, then the expected control costs increase because, for example, the probability of preferred stockholders receiving a vote through failure to meet dividends or the probability of creditor control increases; the expected variability in future earnings is increased so that the total risk of the enterprise is enhanced.

The case of maturity cost is less obvious. One's first inclination is to estimate that the cost would be independent of quantity. As quantity increases, however, some supply alternatives (such as retained earnings) are no longer available. Such a reduction in alternatives must eventually bring about increased cost. In other words, the reduced availability of sources is likely to prevent the firm from achieving its lowest maturity cost, as illustrated in Figure 12-1. This cost, along with monetary and control costs, makes up the total supply function.

VARIABLES AFFECTING THE SUPPLY OF CAPITAL TO THE FIRM

We do not have sufficient empirical evidence to establish the precise influence of various variables on the position and shape of a firm's supply schedule of capital. We can, however, discuss those variables that are thought to be associated with changes in supply. We shall classify these into two broad categories: those variables over which the firm has some control and those over which the firm has no significant influence.

Variables Subject to Firm Influence

Sources of supply making up part of the supply function are the flow of revenue-covered depreciation charges and the earnings retained in the business. The term *earnings,* in this context, refers to accounting profits. It is fairly obvious that the firm can influence both to some degree. Its choice to pay cash dividends or not directly affects the earnings retained. However, the decision to reduce dividends naturally may affect the cost and supply of capital from the sale of common stock. The ability to choose a depreciation policy for tax purposes will also affect the supply function. For example, Firm A and Firm B are identical in all respects save one: the depreciation method employed. Because of allowable variations in depreciation of assets for income tax purposes, it can be seen

	Firm A	Firm B
Sales	$1,000,000	$1,000,000
Cost of goods sold (excluding depreciation or depletion)	600,000	600,000
Expenses (excluding depreciation)	200,000	200,000
Depreciation	100,000	200,000
Net income (before taxes on income)	100,000	0
Income taxes (50%)	50,000	0
Net income, after tax	50,000	0
Total estimated capital available to the firm (depreciation plus net income after tax)	$ 150,000	$ 200,000

that "depleciation" (depreciation and depletion) can reduce the government's drain (taxation of income) on the supply of capital available to the firm. Increased taxes, however, would have to be paid at a later time when depreciation charges decline. Even at that, it is generally desirable to depreciate assets at the fastest rate allowable because of the opportunity cost of the additional cash inflow now as opposed to that realized in a subsequent period. That is to say, the additional cash realized can be invested to return at least the yield on United States Treasury Bills and thereby should tend to maximize shareholders' profits.

The firm can also indirectly enhance the available supply by reducing existing noncash assets. In other words temporary asset reduction may also be used as a source of capital. A firm, for example, could delay additional purchases of inventory; if sales out of inventory continue, cash will flow in without a corresponding outflow, resulting in larger holdings of cash. This same result could be accomplished by a direct sale of inventory. The reduction of inventory may result, however, in lost sales through stockouts (inability to make sales because of lack of stock). If that is the case, the costs of this source can become quite high. Sale of nonoperating assets (those not needed in the operation of the business), sale of accounts receivable, or any other asset for that matter may contribute to the supply of money and thus be available for new investments. Sale of operating assets can also provide cash, but then the firm usually will not be able to continue operations for long. Such assets must be replaced (a permanent arrangement for sale of receivables, however, is sometimes employed), unless such a sale is the result of a deliberate policy of contracting the firm's scale of operations. If they are excess assets, then their disposal could be considered a permanent source of capital.

In an extreme sense, the firm may consider the disposal of all of its noncash assets. This available source may be shown in the supply schedule; in most cases it would be an extremely high-cost source. The cost of this source would be the profits given up by the firm.[1]

The external market's view of the risk of the firm can be altered by the firm so that the firm is not penalized for an uninformed view of risk inherent in it. The firm may even be able to convince the market that it is a lower risk investment than it actually is because the market is not a perfect judge or all-knowing. Moreover, the market's view of the risk of a particular firm may cause the elimination of whole areas of potential capital supply. The market's view of risk may be measured by a whole host of factors which suppliers traditionally use to gauge the risk level of the firm. These factors are not used by all suppliers, but probably all

---

[1] If the profits given up were not substantial, it may pay the firm to dispose of the assets so that, depending on the demand schedule, they may be re-employed more profitably. If the firm appears unable to employ them profitably, it may at least invest them in securities of other firms (becoming an investment company) or distribute all the cash to their securities holders who can re-employ the cash themselves. The latter case is referred to as voluntary liquidation; it usually follows that the firm (if a corporation) will relinquish its corporate charter (dissolve) and disappear (winding up).

suppliers external to the firm use some of them as an aid in determining an over-all level of risk. These include a whole host of ratios, such as the current ratio, times-interest-earned, inventory turnover, receivables turnover, quick-asset ratio, debt to net-worth ratio, as well as such things as industry descriptions and evaluation, credit ratings, age of firm, and previous credit experience.[2] The size of the firm is also believed to be associated with risk; one can well understand such a judgment in view of the previous exposition on the "chance" exposure of small firms to business failure. At this point of the text, we shall continue to emphasize our over-all appraisal of risk as the relative variability in returns. In this regard, risk itself can be affected by the firm's choice of investment projects. Projects whose return variabilities are rather uncorrelated with other returns tend to reduce firm risk and stabilize over-all returns.

Through the investment project selection process, the firm also influences the level of returns to investment and likewise the trend of earnings to the firm over time. Realized and expected high rates of growth in earnings and dividends resulting from efficient selection of investment projects may have marked effects on the over-all supply of capital. For example, in the lopsided 1961–62 common stock market, the expected upward trend in earnings seemed to have a significant impact on the saleability of issues.[3] New companies sold large amounts of common with little more than a promise or hope of being a "growth" (growth in earnings and price per share) company.

Variables Not Subject to the Influence of the Firm

Many other variables, external to the firm, affect the supply function. The variables affecting interest rates in the economy are variables affecting the supply of capital to the firm. On the supply side, factors that affect the saving of businesses, individuals or government and the money-creating activities of the banking system affect the supply of capital in the economy. A firm is also affected in its competition for capital by the demands in the capital market of consumers, governments, and businesses. Variations in the demands for supplies of capital in the market exert forces tending to alter costs of capital in different segments of the market at different times. We shall look next at the various sources of supply of capital available or potentially available to the firm.

[2] Further elaboration of these factors is to be found in Chapters 21 and 22.

[3] See especially: U.S. Securities and Exchange Commission, *Statistical Bulletin* (June 1964), 12; John A. Gorman and Paul E. Shea, "Capital Formation, Saving and Credit," *Survey of Current Business, 44,* (May 1964), U.S. Department of Commerce, Office of Business Economics (Washington, D.C.: Government Printing Office), 14.

SHORT-TERM SOURCES

The most important sources of capital available for short periods are loans from commercial banks, interbusiness open accounts, sales of commercial paper in the open market, and "loans" from finance companies and "factors." These loans are frequently self-liquidating in that the source of payment of the loan is the collection on sales financed by the loan. A listing of most short-term capital sources is provided below.

Short-Term Sources

(1) Interbusiness credit (trade credit)
    (a) Open account
    (b) Notes and trade acceptances
(2) Commercial Banks
    (a) Unsecured promissory notes
    (b) Loans secured by endorsement (co-signer)
    (c) Loans secured by receivables or installment paper
    (d) Loans secured by inventory
    (e) Loans secured by collateral such as cash value of life insurance, stocks and bonds
    (f) Bankers' acceptances
    (g) Discounted notes and trade acceptance of clients' customers
(3) Commercial paper
(4) Finance companies and factors
    (a) Loans secured by receivables or installment paper
    (b) Loans secured by inventory
    (c) Sale of receivables
(5) Temporary asset liquidations
(6) Advances from customers
(7) Small loan companies, industrial banks, credit unions and pawn shops
(8) Loans from friends, relatives, stockholders, officers, and directors

Short-term sources, by our definition, provide capital for periods up to one year.

Interbusiness Credit on Open Account

Interbusiness credit on open account is the most important form of short-term credit in the United States and is often referred to as *trade credit*. Although trade credit is not a source of money directly, the credit given for purchase obviates the necessity of securing money elsewhere;

consequently we view it as a source of capital. Supplying firms may also lend to their customers for a longer term, but this occurrence is rather unusual. Trade credit arises out of the selling process and is represented only by bookkeeping entries on the records of the buyer and seller. When a sale is made, it is usually a "charge" and not for cash or a COD. When it is "charged," it becomes an account receivable to the seller and an account payable to the buyer.

The essence of trade credit (and all forms of credit) lies in deferred payment. Credit allows the firm to secure the benefits of goods and services immediately; payment is deferred until a more convenient time—a time, for example, when sufficient cash is accumulated to extinguish the obligation. Even if a firm has enough cash on hand to meet its obligations upon receipt of a bill, it may choose to defer payment until the specified due date because of the opportunity cost associated with a present outlay of cash as opposed to an equivalent cash outlay at some future time. That is to say, if trade credit is available, it is advantageous for the firm with ample cash to take on the credit for the period during which no charge is made for it and invest its available cash even in, say, United States Treasury Bills, thereby increasing the income of the enterprise. Deferring the payment of bills tends to increase the firm's liquidity and reduces the probability of running out of cash to handle unexpected events. Moreover, even though some firms pay their bills upon receipt, they may find it necessary to delay payment at times. Even if payment were not purposely delayed, a large amount of trade credit will arise in the normal course of business simply because of the time lag between shipment of goods and receipt of payments. Clearly, the use of trade credit is an especially convenient, perhaps necessary, way of carrying on business in highly developed economies.

The *credit terms* given by the seller are an important factor in the supply of this type of capital. Variation in terms affects the supply function of the potential debtor. Credit terms on a net sixty days rather than a net thirty days permit the doubling of credit by the buyer. If a firm buys an average of $10,000 of goods per month, on the average it will have $10,000 on account, if the credit terms are net thirty. If terms are changed to net sixty, the firm can delay payment another thirty days and purchase another month's supplies to run its bill up to $20,000.

Frequently, the credit terms of sales permit a *cash discount* for accelerated payment of the account. Such terms as 2/10, n/30 permit the buyer to deduct 2 per cent from the bill if payment is made within ten days of the invoice date. If the firm does not pay within this ten-day period, it must give up the cash discount and pay, in effect, 2 per cent for the use of the capital for the twenty days between the eleventh and thirtieth days. On a per annum basis, this amounts to 36 per cent ($360/20 \times 2$ per cent), a monetarily expensive source when viewed in per annum rates.

Trade credit is frequently granted to firms which might be turned down for credit by other sources. This is partly because a hundred dollars of trade credit involves less than a hundred dollars of risk, especially if the selling firm is operating at less than full capacity. In the first instance, the profit margin in the sale price of the additional goods allows such a firm to accept a higher loss ratio than a moneylending institution could prudently accept (the latter has no such margins to buffer its losses). This is also true if the additional sale tends to reduce the total cost per unit of output. If the additional goods sold to "marginal" credit risks make some contribution to overhead—that is, cover all their variable costs and part of their fixed costs—extension of trade credit is a feasible policy. The seller is also likely to know well the nature of the buyer's business and can better evaluate the risk of default. Credit restraints on the sellers usually limit the total supply of trade credit available and hence the extent to which they can take on "marginal" debtors from this source.

Short-term Loans of Commercial Banks

Commercial banks are in business to lend, to provide credit for the development of the community of which they are a part. Their business is to make loans whenever such loans can be worked out without seriously endangering the security of the bank. Most banks aggressively compete for loans as well as for deposits. And most bank loans are represented by promissory notes which, when signed by an authorized individual of a firm, represent the debt of the firm. These loans are next to trade credit in importance in the short-term supply field. The notes may have a duration of almost any length, although typically they mature in one, three, or six months. Payment is expected at the end of the term and continuous renewal is frowned upon. Other loans may be made where repayment is made in monthly installments, especially if the source of repayment is more suited to this method.

Bank loans, along with trade credit, customarily expand according to the seasonal needs of the firm's customers and during periods of expansion and prosperity. Loans tend to decline during off-season activity and during recessions.

Many loans are secured only by the general credit of the firm. Other loans of higher risk are secured by the pledge of assets of the firm or by the firm's principals. Because the corporation has limited liability, on some occasions the bank may request a personally wealthy officer to guarantee payment. In other cases other parties with an interest in the firm's well-being may "endorse" the notes. Other forms of security may involve the assignment of stocks and bonds, cash values of life insurance, accounts receivable, installment paper, other notes, or inventory. As one might presume, a majority of bank loans are secured in some form. Frequently, larger loans can be obtained only if they are secured, thereby reducing the cost of the loan to the relatively questionable borrower. Banks may also purchase notes and acceptances of trade customers of a firm on a discount basis. They may advance short-term credit through the use of bankers' acceptances.[4]

Firms with seasonal needs find it particularly desirable to obtain borrowing authority prior to the actual need. This authority, or *line of credit,* provides the firm with the flexibility to increase or decrease bank debt whenever necessary (within the specified limits of the line). The line establishes the limit above which total bank debt is not to extend; it gives the firm a source to be relied upon in advance of need. As the firm's experience proves its credit worthiness, the firm may be able to increase its line. However, a single bank is limited in its lending to a certain percentage of its capital (usually 10 per cent). Thus, other banks may participate in making a loan if the needs of the firm require larger amounts and the firm appears well able to handle such a loan.

The *unsecured, noninstallment* commercial bank loans are about as cheap a source of capital for many firms as can be found. Only the sale of commercial paper, restricted to larger, well-known firms with excellent credit standing, would be cheaper in terms of monetary cost to the borrower. Relatively, firms that are good credit risks can borrow on an unsecured, short-term basis at a cost which is usually not far above the prevailing rates on United States Treasury bills. Firms of greater risk to the bank typically do not qualify for unsecured credit at prime bank rates and can be accommodated only on some other basis. In order to make these riskier loans feasible to banks, some form of security may be required, or installment repayment may be required, or both. These adjustments reduce the risk of the lender to an acceptable level; unfortunately these methods of reducing risk involve higher processing and handling costs, forcing the bank to charge an effective rate of interest significantly above the unsecured loan rates. Such secured installment loans made to

[4] A banker's acceptance is a bill of exchange (an unconditional written order drawn by one on a bank to pay a third party a sum of money) drawn on a bank and accepted by it. "In this manner the bank guarantees the payment of the accepted bill at maturity and enables its customer, who pays a commission to the accepting bank for this accommodation, to secure financing readily and at a reasonable interest cost. Banker's acceptances are used to finance the movement or storage of merchandise, principally commodities, and to finance dollar exchange transactions." *Short-Term Investments,* 6th ed. (New York: Salomon Brothers & Hutzler, 1964), 20.

poorer risks often run about as high as the rate on loans by the bank to individuals acting as consumers.[5]

Effective interest costs may not be easily recognized by the borrowing firm. Lines of credit usually require *compensating balances* of at least 10–20 per cent of the line or the loan amount outstanding. That is, the borrowing firm may be required to keep, say, 20 per cent of the amount borrowed on deposit. This required deposit, in effect, increases the cost of the source. For example, if a firm is given a line of $100,000 at 6 per cent and is required to keep a demand deposit of a least 20 per cent of the loan outstanding, then when the line is fully used, the effective amount lent is $80,000, but interest is paid on $100,000. The cost is 7.5 per cent (.6 × $100,000/$80,000) rather than 6 per cent.

One form of commercial bank loan is the *discounted note*. When a $1,000 note at 5 per cent is discounted, the effective amount lent is $950 [$1,000 − ($1,000 × .05)]. The effective rate is 5.3 per cent ($50/$950). A straight loan of $1,000 at 5 per cent carries an effective rate of 5 per cent ($50/$1,000).

If the loan were to be paid in equal monthly installments, the effective rate would be approximately double the stated rate. The stated rate is applied to the original balance, but the principal is repaid in parts over the full life of the note so that the average loan for the period is about half the original loan. For example, if a one-year $1,000 loan at 4 per cent were to be repaid in equal monthly installments, the effective amount lent would be a little over $500 and the total interest cost charged would be $40 (.04 × $1,000). The effective rate would be approximately 8.0 ($40/$500) per cent.

Sale of Commercial Paper

Unsecured promissory notes sold by commercial or industrial firms on the open market through commercial paper dealers or privately sold

---

[5] At the time of this writing the prime lending rate of large city banks (mainly those in New York, Chicago, and Los Angeles) was 4.5 per cent, a figure which had not changed since August 23, 1960. At the same time (March 1965) the Federal Reserve discount rate was 4 per cent, rates of prime finance company paper of a 30–59-day duration were 4–4⅛th per cent, prime commercial paper rates were 4⅛th per cent and 30–90-day banker's acceptances were 4⅛th per cent (*Interest Rates* [New York: Irving Trust Company, July 8, 1964]). Interestingly, short-term rates on small loans, for example, in the $1,000–$100,000 class, rarely carry the prime rate; in fact in recent years the vast majority of loans falling in this class have carried a rate of 5 per cent or more with about 60 per cent of all loans in the $1,000–$10,000 class averaging a rate of 6 per cent or more. On the other hand, a substantial number of loans falling in the $100,000 and over class carried the prime rate. For loans of $200,000 or more, about 60 per cent carried the prime rate. In all classes rates lower than 4.5 per cent were highly uncommon. See: Board of Governors of the Federal Reserve System, *Bank Rates on Short-term Business Loans* (Washington, D.C.: Government Printing Office, various statistical releases, October 4, 1961 to September 30, 1964).

by the issuer to commercial banks, life insurance firms, business firms, and finance companies are referred to as *commercial paper*. These notes run for a period of six months or less and constitute one of the cheapest external sources of short-term capital available to the firm. Commercial paper avoids the compensating balance requirement of bank loans and is easily issued in large sums to one or two buyers with practically no negotiation. About one third of the commercial paper is sold through the dealers who resell it throughout the country; the remaining two thirds are privately placed with financial institutions.

Only the large, nationally known firms of high credit standing can avail themselves of this source. A large New York financial institution could hardly be expected to purchase the promissory notes of a small manufacturer in Big Lake, Minnesota. To say the least, the firm's financial condition must be generally known in order to find a ready market for the paper.

Capital from Finance Companies and Factors

Firms in this category are engaged mainly in making *loans secured by receivables or inventory*. This is done through the selling or pledging of receivables or the pledging of inventory to various institutions. These transactions may provide a constant source of credit depending on the desires of the parties involved. Although finance companies and factors are the chief forces in this market, for purposes of our present discussion we shall also group in this category institutions similar to finance companies, such as commercial credit or discount companies. Commercial banks are also heavily involved with loans secured by receivables and inventory and hence will be included at this point.

Loans Secured by Accounts Receivable

Accounts receivable are customarily the most liquid asset, aside from cash itself, of most firms. This trade credit of the seller arises out of sales and may be assigned to finance companies (or commercial banks) as security for loans. Usually the clients of the firm assigning the receivables know nothing of the assignment. Should clients fail to pay their accounts, the finance company would have recourse to the borrowing firm. It is then up to the borrowing firm to collect on the defaulted receivables to the extent that it can do so. If it cannot collect in full, it absorbs the loss arising out of nonpayment or partial payment. The finance company still is entitled to repayment of its loan in full from the borrowing firm. The limit to which a borrowing firm can draw credit is established by the amount and quality of the receivables accepted by the finance company.

Furthermore, now blocks of receivables may be discounted with a finance company as they are received. The costs of administering the collateral as well as the higher average risk of the borrowers causes this form of financing to have comparatively higher costs; they can be as high as 18 per cent per annum.

Sale of Receivables

Receivables may also be sold outright to *factors* or finance companies. Factors are specialized institutions that purchase accounts receivable. In this case the purchaser of the receivables has no recourse to the seller. Aside from buying receivables outright, factors also perform the services of credit investigation, lending, collection, and risk-taking. As a result, a business could conceivably eliminate its credit department altogether. In factoring receivables, the firm receives the money from their sales immediately, less the appropriate discount that covers the cost of the four functions the factor performs for the firm. The factor customarily also holds back a part of the cash on a sale as a reserve to cover bad debts and other problems that may be encountered in collecting the receivables.

The cost of factoring includes two elements, an interest charge and a commission charge. The interest charged ordinarily is 6 per cent per annum of the face amount of the factored receivables. The commission charge is typically around 1–2 per cent per month, depending on the size of the invoices, the volume of sales, the nature of the business, the length of the credit terms, and the competition among factors. The purpose of the commission is to cover the costs of collection, credit investigations, and possible bad debts. Because the factored accounts of any given firm may turn over as many as six or seven times a year, the cost of factoring could be as high as 20 per cent [6 per cent + (2 per cent × 7)]. Obviously, not all of this "cost" is an interest expense as such. Much of it will reflect the cost of the services of the factor. For factoring to be profitable, however, the expected gains from such services would have to exceed the expected cost.

Loans Secured by Inventory

Firms may also borrow from finance companies and banks using inventories as security for the loans. Although not all products make acceptable inventory collateral, many nonperishable products can be used. The cost of this form of credit runs about 1 per cent higher than loans secured by accounts receivable. The financing of automobile dealers' inventories is a form of inventory-secured financing, but it generally involves special arrangements. Chattel mortgages, field-warehouses (warehouses for hire), and trust receipts provide security arrangements enabling the institutions to take the inventory as security for loans.

Miscellaneous Short-term Sources

Other short-term sources include loans from relatives, friends, stockholders, officers, and directors; negotiated loans, loans from suppliers in addition to trade credits; loans from small-loan companies, industrial banks, credit unions, or pawnshops; temporary asset reductions; advances from customers on contracts; and government agencies such as the Small Business Administration and municipally sponsored industrial banks. These sources are less important in terms of volume than the ones discussed above. Nevertheless, they are relatively important to new and other high risk firms. The costs of these sources of capital vary greatly. The costs of borrowing from a small-loan company or pawnshop are sure to be relatively high and the amounts available rather limited. Very large firms typically do not resort to these sources. Smaller firms may find they constitute important sources of credit.

SOURCES OF INTERMEDIATE-TERM AND LONG-TERM CAPITAL

The length of time covered by the intermediate and long term is not precise for it is impossible to state categorically where the short term ends, the intermediate term begins and then leaves off, and the long term begins. Having defined the short term as one year or less, we can conveniently and arbitrarily define all durations of one year or more as long-term. In general, the intermediate-term class includes those sources which involve maturities of one to ten years. But in this discussion we are also interested in longer-term debt securities which, for our purposes, will be confined to those possessing finite maturity dates on the order of ten to fifty years. The major intermediate- and long-term sources of capital include term loans, industrial equipment financing, bonds, and lease financing. A listing of these is set forth below.

Intermediate- and Long-Term Sources

(1) Term loans
    (a) Commercial banks
    (b) Life insurance companies
    (c) Government sources
(2) Industrial and Commercial Equipment Financing
(3) Bonds
    (a) Debenture bonds (unsecured bonds)
    (b) Mortgage bonds

(c) Collateral trust bonds
(4) Lease financing
    (a) Equipment leasing
    (b) Sale-and-leaseback financing

In the intermediate- and long-term financing area, repayment more frequently than not is made on an installment basis rather than in a lump sum at maturity. Even bonds frequently require sinking funds as payment on the principal or gradual reduction in the principal amount of the debt outstanding through other methods. Bonds generally are expected to be retired on or before maturity dates. Because of the length of time that the supply of capital is involved, risk is more closely related to longer-run factors such as profitability and size of cash flow than to the current liquidity of the firm which is more important in short-run supply.

Term Loans

The term loan generally involves maturities of one to ten years. Only infrequently would they run longer. Four times out of five, the loan requires monthly, quarterly, semiannual, or annual payments that amortize the total principal over the life of the loan. On some occasions there may be a "balloon" payment at maturity. That is, the installment payments during the life of the loan are not enough to cover the principal completely at maturity. In this event the remainder, which is greater than the installments, is payable at maturity; this is the final "balloon" payment. The repayment schedule can be tailored so that the loan is repaid out of the cash flow (approximated by the sum of earnings and depreciation, if any) generated by the investment. More often than not, the term loan is secured. Often the security is in the form of a chattel mortgage on plant, equipment, or other assets purchased by the loan. Customarily, the loan contract provides protective provisions for the lender. These are designed to prevent deterioration of liquidity and net worth and to direct the earnings of the company toward the liquidation of the loan. Prepayment of the loan, in whole or in part, generally is allowed without penalty.

Commercial banks that make term loans prefer shorter maturities than life insurance companies, and large, unsecured loans for working capital purposes are more commonly made by insurance companies than by bankers. On installment loans the effective annual interest rate charged by commercial banks in 1957 was 8.7 per cent, whereas the rate on short-term bank loans was almost 5 per cent. In that same year, term loans accounted for about 38 per cent of their total business loans.[6]

---

[6] Carl T. Arlt, Jr., "Member Bank Term Lending to Business, 1955–57," *Federal Reserve Bulletin,* 47, 4 (April 1959), 353–60.

The Small Business Administration (SBA) will also make loans in participation with local banks that may not, legally or from a risk point of view, be able to advance the full amount of funds needed by the small firm (under 1,000 employees). The SBA may make the loan on its own if private sources are not available. The loans, on the average small, are secured by the pledge of assets and carry a competitive charge.

Industrial and Commercial Equipment Financing

Although industrial and commercial equipment may be financed by term loans from banks, insurance companies, the SBA, or even by many other financing alternatives, a rather specialized method deserves comment. A manufacturing firm may decide to finance its equipment sales directly by holding the notes itself. Ordinarily, the terms of the agreement are such that the notes may not in turn be discounted with a financial institution such as a bank or finance company. This type of financing is used in a great variety of instances, ranging from those involving transportation equipment and baking equipment to those involving oil and restaurant equipment. Customarily, the firm makes a down payment of a third to a fifth of the purchase price and the remainder is paid in installments over a period up to three years (for rolling stock of railroads purchased on this basis, the repayment period is usually fifteen to twenty years). The note is usually secured by a conditional sales contract or chattel mortgage and the effective interest cost is, on the average, a little higher (1–3 per cent) than the average term loan (except in the case of railroad financing, in which—because of the peculiar resalability of the asset pledged—the monetary cost is invariably lower than on other forms of available financing). Some manufacturers set up separate subsidiaries to carry the installment loans. The loan, if discounted to an institution, may be with or without recourse to the manufacturing company. If a loan is discounted without recourse, the institution must absorb any losses as a result of loan delinquencies; if recourse exists, the institution may recover its loss from the firm discounting the note.

Sale of Bonds and Notes

Bonds are certificates of indebtedness and, when sold, are a source of funds issued with a typical maturity date of ten years or more. Corporate notes are like bonds in all respects (except length of life) and typically run less than ten years. The security provisions for these instruments vary considerably depending upon the issuer's credit standing, the types of assets held by the issuer, and legal restrictions on the company resulting from previous debt financing.

The *debenture bond* is an unsecured bond. It is unsecured in the sense that there are no specific assets of the firm which serve as physical collateral and on which such bonds have a lien in the event of failure. Instead, the safety of the principal and interest of these bonds rests on the general credit of the firm. For this reason, and others, the firm will probably be required to agree to a number of provisions designed to protect bondholders from any deterioration in their security. These protective provisions are similar to those frequently required in a term loan. They would probably outline the conditions under which any additional bonds of equal or senior claim on the company could be issued, if at all. The provisions would probably prevent any pledging of company assets unless the debenture holders shared equally and rateably in the pledged assets in the event of liquidation. Invariably, debentures would include provisions for redemption and retirement. The retirement of the issue may take place in part, if not *in toto,* before the maturity date. The specific manner in which the bonds are typically retired by the maturity date is through a sinking-fund provision. This provision usually requires a certain percentage or amount of bonds to be retired each year before maturity and at specified prices (usually at face value or market price, whichever is lower).

A *subordinated debt*[7] represents a firm's unsecured obligation whose claim against the company in case of default—such as failure to meet interest requirements, principal payments, or any other provisions of the contract—is subordinate to other, defined senior debt. To understand when this form of debt might be used, consider the following example. When a bond issue is prepared for sale, the contract or agreement, called an *indenture,* stipulates what is required of the company. One of the provisions may prohibit the issuance of long-term debt having an equal or senior claim on the assets of the firm. Under these conditions, firms may find it necessary, if not desirable, to sell subordinated debentures, especially as an alternative to preferred stock, because of the lower effective cost to the company (interest is tax-deductible); yet the interest cost would certainly be higher than nonsubordinated debt. Obviously not all firms possess the credit standing to market such bonds with success.

Bonds secured by the pledge of a firm's physical assets are called *mortgage bonds.* They may be secured by all the assets in general (a blanket mortgage), or they may be secured by specific assets (usually certain types of fixed assets). In the case of railroads and public utilities, in particular, a company may also issue bonds with a junior claim (second

[7] Robert W. Johnson, "Subordinated Debentures: Debt That Serves as Equity," *The Journal of Finance 10* (March 1955), 1–16.

mortgage) on fixed assets already pledged. If the company should fail, the claim of the junior bond is second in line on the specific assets pledged and, of course, has equal claim with other secured but unsatisfied creditors on the remaining unpledged assets (along with the general creditors).

Customarily some provision is required for the retirement of bonds. There are two basic methods of accomplishing this. The first is the sinking-fund provision which requires the company to put aside money each year in a fund for retirement; in most cases these funds are used to purchase the company's own bonds. In the absence of a sinking fund, a second method of gradually retiring long-term debt issues before maturity is to construct the indenture so that part of the total issue comes due serially (that is, every year). Debt possessing such a provision is called *serial debt*.[8]

Corporate bonds may be sold to a single investment banker or to a syndicate. In either event the risk of selling the issue is lifted from the issuing company. If the issue has been well priced (by the firm and banker), there will be no difficulty in selling them. This *underwriting* sale frequently involves less than a full day.

The bonds may also be sold directly to an institution or group of institutions, with or without an investment banker acting as an intermediary. When the investment banker is not used as an intermediary in placing bonds directly with these large buyers, the firm may be engaged as a consultant. The importance of private placement of bonds is borne out by the fact that they account for over half of corporate bond sales. Privately placed bonds differ only slightly from term loans and although a life insurance company may sell the bonds it holds much more easily than a loan of equal size, to provide the same flexibility term-loan provisions often provide for replacement of the note with bonds upon request.

The cost to the firm of this form of debt is relatively quite low. The explicit monetary cost would be the interest payment as a percentage of the net proceeds to the company. The net proceeds would be the price to the bond buyer less the underwriter's fee and the firm's costs in preparing the issue for sale, including the prospectus required by federal law for publicly distributed securities issued on an interstate basis or through the mails. The Securities and Exchange Commission passes on the prospectus to make certain there are no omissions or misrepresentations of the facts surrounding the issue. Total percentage costs of flotation decrease as the size of the issue increases. The cost is 1.2 per cent of the sale price to the public for a debt issue over $50 million; 1.5 per cent for an issue from

---

[8] Additional detail describing bond characteristics may be found in Appendix B.

$10–$20 million; and 3.8 per cent for an issue of $2–$5 million.[9] Private placement would eliminate most of these flotation costs.

Small firms that desire to tap capital markets for long-term funds may turn to Small Business Investment Company (SBIC) which are federally chartered and supervised by the Small Business Administration. Because these institutions are looking for opportunities for capital gains, most of their investments are in firms with growth prospects using convertible debentures (bonds exchangeable for stock under stipulated conditions) as vehicles. These bonds yield about 6–8 per cent. In time, obviously, the SBIC anticipates eventual profitable conversion to the common stock of the company.

Lease Financing

The Lease of Assets

Realistically, the lease of assets would not be considered a source of money; it is, however, a vehicle for securing capital and hence is included at this point. If the company were to sell assets and then lease them, this procedure would then provide a source of funds.[10]

Lease provisions vary, but they do have a number of traditional features. The lessee pays the costs of maintenance, taxes, and insurance, and similar direct expenses, as if he owned the leased asset. In some cases he is given an opportunity to buy the asset upon the expiration of the lease. A renewal option is frequently available, especially if the term of the original lease did not exceed the economic utility of the asset.

The ownership of assets may reside with the equipment manufacturer (as in the case of electronic computers), a life insurance company or other type of institutional investor (as in the case of real estate), or a trust (as in the case of railroad rolling stock and some airline equipment). In the latter case, the trust holds the title to the equipment, leases it to the transportation company, and sells certificates of beneficial interest in the trust to investors.

The lease arrangement enables many firms to secure assets at reasonable costs which they might not otherwise be able to do. Smaller firms may not have financing alternatives to secure enough favorable financing. In cases in which no deposit is required, leasing could be viewed as 100 per cent debt financing.

A firm engaged in leasing buys the assets, holds title to them, and

---

[9] U.S. Securities and Exchange Commission, *Cost of Flotation of Corporate Securities, 1951–55* (1957).

[10] Disposition of assets as a source was discussed earlier in this chapter.

leases them. As a result it may have a less risky investment than would be the case if it were to lend the money outright under a mortgage loan or bond. In case of delinquency, the lessee retains ownership; under a loan arrangement, creditors would have to undertake rather lengthy and expensive legal proceedings to secure the asset pledged.

The firm that leases is able to avoid the restrictive protective provisions usually found in term loans and bond issues. It also avoids the creation of an explicit liability on its financial statement, even though the lease commitment may require equal financial responsibility for meeting payments. Despite these advantages, the firm has little flexibility in adjusting its methods of securing capital later, for lease agreements run for many years.

The lease payment includes the cost of amortizing the value of the equipment plus a stipulated rate for "financing." If a deposit is required, the effective rate is higher than the stipulated rate. If the company could estimate some positive expected residual value of the asset at the expiration of the lease, then its lack of title also increases the cost of this source. On the basis of stipulated rates alone, however, this does not appear to be as cheap a source as the term loan or other arrangements. These rates are typically 1–2 per cent higher than bank sources.

Sale and Leaseback

One technique of financing that has become more important in recent years has been the sale and leaseback. A firm using this technique negotiates with an institution for the sale of an asset, equipment, or commercial or industrial real estate (land and/or buildings); the institution simultaneously enters into an agreement with the selling firm for the long-term lease of the asset which was sold. This arrangement provides the firm with an amount of cash equal to the assets' fair market value. (If the firm were to borrow against the asset, it could expect to secure as a loan no more than 70 per cent of the fair market value.)

Whereas a loan against an asset necessitates the creation of a liability on the company's books, the sale-and-leaseback method produces no such debt with the restrictive provisions customarily found in the indenture. The lease agreement, however, may require lease payments which are just as binding on the firm as debt commitments would be. Consequently, although the firm's balance sheet may give a better immediate impression of the firm's financial position because of the absence of debt under the lease arrangement, the firm usually is just as committed to periodic payments as it would be under a loan agreement. Because the institution does not have a creditor's claim on the firm, however, it expects very little in the way of compensation for the failure of the company to meet the lease payments if the firm fails and goes into bankruptcy.

If the firm had already taken the original cost of the asset as a deduction for the determination of its income taxes through depreciation, it could sell the asset (presumably at a fair market price considerably above its book value—cost less accumulated depreciation) and now use the lease payment as a deduction for tax purposes. It would be obliged, however, to pay taxes on the capital gain.

The cost of lease financing is probably not cheaper than many other alternatives, but it is difficult to generalize; it is dependent upon tax factors as well as the existence of any residual value of the asset once the lease is terminated. The residual value, particularly in the case of real estate held during inflationary periods, may be a significant amount which the firm does not obtain unless a special provision is made in the lease agreement for the firm to repurchase the asset at a price set by the agreement. On the other hand, the firm avoids the risk of obsolescence. Also, when it does not own the equipment, the firm need not renew its lease if the asset is no longer efficient.

As part of the cost, a firm must consider the loss of flexibility that prevails until the lease agreement expires. If a firm owns an asset rather than leases it, it may be able to sell it and buy more useful equipment when conditions warrant such action. Under a lease arrangement, however, the firm is usually tied to the leased property and the agreed-upon lease payments until the termination of the lease.

SOURCES OF PERMANENT CAPITAL

The permanent sources of capital are often the hardest for a firm to obtain when needed and in the desired quantities. This is particularly true for the very small firm, which usually has little access to the investment banker's sale of stock or other securities in the markets for long-term capital. The list below outlines the permanent sources.[11]

(1) Sale of preferred stock.
(2) Sale of common stock.
(3) Sale of assets.
(4) "Depleciation."
(5) Retention of earnings.

[11] Appendix B provides a more detailed description of securities.

Sale of Preferred Stock

Preferred stock of the firm may be sold to secure additional capital. If any significant amounts are to be raised in this manner, the selling organization of an investment banker is usually necessary in order to tap a sufficiently large number of possible investors to raise the required money. Assuming the issue is underwritten, the capital needs can then be virtually assured.

Preferred stock customarily provides for *voting power* only in the event the firm fails to pay the stipulated preferred dividend on one or several successive dividend dates. The control given preferred stock may be one vote per share and thus they would still compete for control with common votes; it may be that they are given the right to elect a certain minority portion of the board of directors; or they may be given full power of control—that is, the right to elect the full board of directors. This presents a contingent loss of control only. Preferred stocks which are convertible into common stock, of course, may also represent a potential threat to control if the votes so secured are significant enough to gain representation on the board of directors.

In case of corporate liquidation, holders of preferred stock (which invariably have a stipulated preference in liquidation) usually have a claim on the firm's assets superceding that of the common stockholders but subordinate to that of all legal creditors. This *preference as to assets,* as this provision is often called, is equal either to the par value or to the stipulated value of the preferred stock or to a stipulated liquidation value (a sum in excess of the par or stipulated values). This group is also entitled to preferential treatment with respect to any dividend arrearages. In the absence of a preferred-as-to-assets provision, preferred shareholders participate proportionately with common shareholders.[12] Failure to vote preferred dividends, of course, does not constitute a breach of contract, but such a passing of dividends produces enough financial complications for the firm as to make it almost mandatory that a firm meet these dividends to maintain its credit standing and continue smooth operations.

In many cases, preferred stock *protective provisions* may require their gradual repayment through a sinking-fund provision. Failure to meet these provisions does not constitute default, however. Frequently, the amount of such sinking-fund payments is a variable dependent upon earnings.

---

[12] Henry Winthrop Ballantine, *Ballantine on Corporations,* rev. ed (Chicago: Callaghan and Company, 1946), 507–509.

Other provisions usually provide for protection against issuance of securities of equal or senior claim on the firm's assets, such as bonds; this provision may be waived if two thirds or three quarters of the preferred shares so approve. Provisions may also require the maintenance of a certain ratio of current assets to current debt, retention of earnings, or a limit on the ratio of debt to preferred shares. Invariably the firm retains the right to redeem the preferred at its option, and, if financially able, thereby regain its freedom and flexibility in financing.

The market is not always receptive to preferred issues. Such issues enjoy neither the legal status of bonds nor (for almost all preferreds) the possibility of participating in residual earnings (their income rate is limited by contract) such as common stock. As a result a public offering can be accomplished usually only by reliable and well-established corporations. Furthermore, even in these cases the cost of preferred as a source of funds is greater than the sale of bonds. The additional yield must compensate for the contingent nature of the payment to the investor, while the relatively inferior legal and financial status of the stock, to say nothing of the nondeductibility of dividends for tax purposes, is a distinct disadvantage to the firm.

Sale of Common Stock

Most companies have only one class of common stock; but some of them, in their desire to maintain control of the firm, will issue a voting class held by the management and a nonvoting class sold to outside investors. This works reasonably well in many situations as most external investors care very little about running the company. They are in the venture to make a profit. If their expectations are not realized, they sell and take their loss (if necessary). A new group of investors buys the shares in hope of profit, and so on. Customarily, the issues are alike in all respects except voting power.

The common shareholder, being the *residual owner* in the company, presumably needs no protective provisions; he expects that the managers —in their desire to benefit themselves as officers and/or shareholders—will maximize the stockholders' position. Stockholders do, however, generally possess certain rights. They have the right to vote (unless a class of stockholders specifically is denied that right), the right to sell their evidence of ownership (the certificate), the right to inspect the corporate books (within reason), and the right to share in the residual assets upon liquidation. They elect the directors, amend the charter and bylaws, and approve mergers and sales of assets.[13]

[13] In some cases, they may have the pre-emptive right, which is the right to participate in proportion to their holdings in any new offerings of shares by the company.

The cost of issuing common stock, consisting of underwriting and other expenses, is higher on the average that that of issuing preferred stock or bond flotations. As shown in Table 12-4, a common stock issue in

Table 12-4
Costs of Issue, 1951–53–55,
Registered Issues Offered to the General Public

Size of Issue (Millions)	Bonds, Notes, and Debentures	Preferred Stock	Common Stock
$ 0.5 to 0.9	11.49%	12.63%	21.76%
2.0 to 4.9	3.78	4.88	9.97
10.0 to 19.9	1.52	2.92	4.66
50.0 and over	1.19	2.51	—
Median	1.49	4.34	10.28

Source: U.S. Securities and Exchange Commission, *Cost of Flotation of Corporate Securities* (1951–55, 1957).

the $10–$20 million category costs on the average of 4.7 per cent of gross proceeds; for issues of $2–$5 million the costs are 10 per cent; for those of $0.5–$2 million, the costs jump to 21.8 per cent.

Small firms desiring to sell small issues normally find considerable difficulty in obtaining an investment banker willing to underwrite them. The sale of common shares of a small and/or unknown company usually entails greater risk than the sale of those of a large, well-established firm. This makes it difficult for the investment banker to gauge the public acceptance of the issue. If no underwriting is possible, a less satisfactory arrangement for the firm is to arrange for the investment banker to distribute the issue on a *"best efforts"* basis—that is, on the basis that he will do the best he can to sell as much as he can. Moreover, substantial costs in preparation of informational material are spread over a relatively small issue, and commission fees must be large enough to stimulate the merchandisers to "crank up" and place the issue with their clients.

A firm with some established record of sales and profits, preferably one of growth, and a reasonable over-all financial position can float an issue much more successfully than a firm not possessing these characteristics. Such a firm will receive a fair price for sharing its income and control. If it is an issue above $1 million, it can expect the costs of flotation to be reasonable in relation to the proceeds.

Sale of Assets

The sale of certain or all assets of the firm is yet another source of cash. The cash, in turn, can be expended on assets designed to generate profit. This source of capital, then, is just replacing capital with capital in other forms. If the assets being sold were employed in a relatively unprofitable fashion, then such a source may be considered. For such a procedure to be profitable, the value of the firm after such reemployment of assets must increase; that is, the present value of all expected cash flows as a result of new commitments must exceed the present value of all expected cash flows as a result of the present commitments, with due allowance for the greater uncertainty in the former case.

"Depleciation" Covered by Firm Sales

"Depleciation" (i.e., depreciation and depletion) is not, as accountants will argue, really a source of capital to the firm. The source, they would say, is sales. Unfortunately, sales are not a source either unless they are consummated on a cash basis. Few firms, except those engaged in merchandising, realize a large portion of total sales in cash. Rather, their sales take the form of credit extensions and are accounted for as receivables. These must be collected, sold, or assigned. Because in most cases the firm is likely to generate sufficient sales and collect all but a very small percentage of total receivables to cover all costs of the firm, including "depleciation," we shall refer to it as a source (implying the assumptions already made).

One may next ask why this source was included as a permanent one, when it would appear that it should usually be classed in the intermediate category. It should be in the intermediate- or long-term category, it is argued, because the asset will eventually need to be replaced. Indeed, depleciation charges may be viewed by many as a method to assure that the recovery of an asset's original cost would be realized over its estimated useful life. Nevertheless, in most cases, depleciation provides a permanent source of capital.

Let us start with a new firm which buys machines at $1,000 each. For the sake of simplicity, let us assume the following: the life of each machine is ten years; there is no salvage value; the firm uses the straight-line depreciation method; and the purchase price of each machine does not change in subsequent years. The firm starts out using its original capital and purchases ten machines for $10,000. Assume further that at the end of the first year the firm's profit is zero. In this case, operating revenues just cover all operating expenses, including the cost of goods sold and the depreciation on ten machines of $1,000. This $1,000 is realized as cash, and the firm uses this amount to buy another machine. It now has eleven machines. At the end of the second year, profit is zero but all the expenses mentioned are fully covered by operating revenues. Then, the firm has $1,100 to spend and buys another machine. And so on. Table 12-5 illustrates the eventual effect of this process. It can be seen that deplesiation has provided a source of capital for the purchase of seven or eight additional machines; in this sense, it is a permanent source.

Table 12-5
Depreciation as a Source of Capital

Year	Number of Machines Owned Beginning of Year	Original Cost of Those Owned	Cash Realized Through Depreciation Each Year	Unspent Amount Accumulated
1	10	$10,000	$1,000	$ 0
2	11 (+ 1)	11,000	1,100	100
3	12 (+ 1)	12,000	1,200	300
4	13 (+ 1)	13,000	1,300	600
5	14 (+ 1)	14,000	1,400	——
6	16 (+ 2)	16,000	1,600	600
7	17 (+ 1)	17,000	1,700	300
8	19 (+ 2)	19,000	1,900	200
9	21 (+ 2)	21,000	2,100	300
10	23 (+ 2)	23,000	2,300	600
11	15 (+ 2 − 10)	15,000	1,500	100
12	16 (+ 2 − 1)	16,000	1,600	700
13	16 (+ 1 − 1)	16,000	1,600	300
14	17 (+ 2 − 1)	17,000	1,700	——
15	18 (+ 2 − 1)	18,000	1,800	800
16	17 (+ 1 − 2)	17,000	1,700	500
17	18 (+ 2 − 1)	18,000	1,800	300
18	18 (+ 2 − 2)	18,000	1,800	100

Retained Earnings

Accounting profits of the firm not paid out in cash dividends are a source of capital to the firm, although one might again consider the true source to be collections on sales after the deduction of all costs, expenses, income taxes, and cash dividends. Retained accounting profits are an approximation of this source of capital. If the firm made sales which were not collected, this approximation would be incorrect. A firm with rapidly growing sales may find itself automatically committed to a policy of reinvesting capital in accounts receivable and, perhaps, inventory to support the increasing sales. The sales themselves thereby preempt the use of recorded retained earnings.

It may be difficult for the firm to determine the precise amount that will be made available from this source at any point in time. All those factors influencing accounting profits, plus the firm's dividend policy, affect the magnitude of this source. Thus there exists some uncertainty surrounding this element in the firm's supply function.

Cash flow is a term generally used to mean the difference between cash receipts and cash expenditures over a given period. If sales can be presumed to be collected during a given period (a good assumption, except in the case of a rapidly growing firm where an adjustment must be made for the increase in accounts receivable), then the difference between sales and all costs and expenses may be assumed to be the cash flow. Because some of the costs and expenses deducted from sales to arrive at income do not require cash outlays (depleciation primarily), these amounts should be added to profits after taxes to arrive at the proper approximation of cash flow.

Retained earnings, however, do have a great advantage over most other sources. Like depleciation and the sale of assets, the firm need suffer no direct actual or potential loss of control as a result of the use of these sources.

The cost of retained earnings is not an explicit cost. The cost of the use of retained earnings is the next best alternative use to which they could be put, typically measured by the benefits foregone by shareholders (those of not receiving higher dividends). In general, the return that stockholders could average with the use of the extra dividends after personal income taxes would be the cost of this source of capital.

SUMMARY

The supply of money to a firm may be theoretically represented as a schedule. The cost of capital supplied in any time period is a function of the quantity demanded and the relative amount available. These costs include the monetary outlays of the firm, cash payments plus the cost of expected control loss, and maturity cost. Most sources involve some potential threat of loss of control; some loss of control may be evident in the restrictive provisions of the financing agreements. Maturity costs involve the cost of renewal plus the cost of inflexibility in financing.

The sources of money are many and varied. They have been grouped as to maturity—short-term, intermediate, long-term, and permanent sources of capital.

SUGGESTED READINGS

BECKHART, BENJAMIN HAGGOT. *Business Loans of American Commercial Banks.* New York: The Ronald Press Company, 1959.

CAHN, B. D. "Capital for Small Businesses: Sources and Methods," *Law and Contemporary Problems, 24* (Winter 1959), 27–67.

COHEN, ALBERT H. *Long-Term Leases: Problems of Taxation, Finance and Accounting.* Ann Arbor, Mich.: Bureau of Business Research, University of Michigan, 1954.

DAVIS, RICHARD G., and JACK M. GUTTENTAG. "Are Compensating Balance Requirements Irrational?" *The Journal of Finance, 17* (March 1962), 121–26.

FERGUSSON, D. A. "Recent Developments in Preferred Stock Financing," *The Journal of Finance, 7* (September 1952), 447–62.

FOULKE, ROY. *The Story of the Factor.* New York: Dun & Bradstreet, Inc., 1953.

HELLWEG, DOUGLAS. "A Note on Compensatory Balance Requirements," *The Journal of Finance, 16* (March 1961), 80–84.

JACOBY, N. H., and R. J. SAULNIER. *Term Lending to Business.* New York: National Bureau of Economic Research, 1942.

MOORE, CARROLL G. "Factoring—A Unique and Important Form of Financing and Service," *Business Lawyer, 14* (April 1959), 703–27.

PHELPS, CLYDE WILLIAM. *Accounts Receivable Financing as a Method of Securing Business Loans,* 2nd ed. Baltimore: Commercial Credit Company, 1961.

———. *The Role of Factoring in Modern Business Finance.* Baltimore: Commercial Credit Company, 1956.

SEIDEN, MARTIN H. *The Quality of Trade Credit.* New York: National Bureau of Economic Research, 1964.

SEIDMAN, W. S. *Accounts Receivable and Inventory Financing.* Ann Arbor, Mich.: Masterco Press, Inc., 1957.

QUESTIONS

12.1 Does the right side of the firm's balance sheet list all the sources of capital supply to the firm? Explain.

12.2 What are the control "costs" involved with the use of a bond issue as a capital source? (Appendix B may be helpful in answering this question.)

12.3 Why would costs of capital increase when a firm seeks successively larger amounts of capital funds in the market?

12.4 Do larger than "normal" depleciation charges save the firm income tax payments? Explain. How does depleciation affect retained earnings?

12.5 How would you compute the cost of capital to a firm considering the sale of an asset as a source?

12.6 Do credit terms affect the supply of trade credit? What are the costs to the firm of delaying payment beyond the due date?

12.7 Why is trade credit easier to obtain than bank credit?

12.8 It is often said that unsecured loans from commercial banks are cheaper than secured loans. How can this be? Discuss.

12.9 Why is the sale of commercial paper available only to large, well-known businesses? In what respects is commercial paper like a short-term bank loan?

12.10 Why should industrial or commercial equipment financing be easier to obtain than term loans? Explain.

12.11 Why might a firm be interested in a sale-and-leaseback method of financing? Discuss.

12.12 What control costs are associated with the sale of preferred stock?

12.13 What costs are included in flotation costs?

12.14 Is depleciation a source of funds to a firm? In what sense? Discuss.

12.15 What sources of funds are not realistically available to small businesses, such as a grocery or filling station?

12.16 What sources of funds are not realistically available to the new, relatively unknown, closely held company?

PROBLEMS

12.17 If a cash discount is offered with terms of 1/10, n/30, what is the cost to the firm of trade credit for the twenty days after the discount period? What is the cost when the discount terms are 1/10, n/60 for the fifty days?

12.18 Select a company of your choice and analyze the changes in its sources of supply by examining its balance sheets for the past five years.

12.19 Construct a schedule of capital offerings for the Blair Corporation and graph it given the following three independent sources of supply:

Blair Corporation: Source of Funds

Units of Capital		A Costs per Year per $1,000	B Costs per Year per $1,000	C Costs per Year per $1,000
1st	$1,000	$40	$ 70	$35
2nd	1,000	40	60	35
3rd	1,000	40	50	40
4th	1,000	40	40	40
5th	1,000	60	35	40
6th	1,000	60	35	
7th	1,000	60	35	
8th	1,000	60	35	
9th	1,000	80	50	
10th	1,000	80	100	

12.20 Comment on the reality or lack thereof of the graph in Figure 12-1. Can you think of any way in which you might prove or disprove the graph?

12.21 Compute the effective monetary costs for the following bank loan arrangements for the Clark Shoe Service Company. Which loan do you recommend and why? (*a*) A $10,000, one-year loan at 5.5 per cent with a 10 per cent required compensating balance; (*b*) A $10,000, one-year loan discounted at 6 per cent; or (*c*) A $10,000 unsecured installment loan at 4 per cent for three years. Assume $10,000 as an initial amount will be required.

12.22 A company engaged in the production of goods for the military is often allowed to amortize some or all of its fixed assets over a sixty-month period for tax purposes. For our purposes, assume the Loyal Lumber Company's entire production is for the military. Assume that it now has $500,000 of assets to be amortized in one year, $1 million in two years, $1.5 million in three years, $2 million in four years, and $2.5 in five years; that there is no estimated scrap value of any of these assets; all other fixed assets are to be amortized over a ten-year period. The company's abbreviated income statement and lefthand side of the balance sheet for last year is as follows:

Net revenues	$25.0 Million
Cost of goods sold	10.5
Depreciation	2.5
Other operating expenses	7.0
Net income before taxes	5.0
Taxes (50%)	2.5
Net income after taxes	$ 2.5

Cash	$ 4.0
Receivables	3.0
Inventories	2.0
Fixed assets (net)	16.0
	$25.0

(a) Set forth the company's income statement for the succeeding five years, assuming there are no changes in revenues, cost of goods sold, other operating expenses, receivables, or inventories. (b) What is the cash flow out of operations for each of the six years? (c) Set forth the company's lefthand side of the balance sheet at the end of the fifth year, assuming there are no changes during the period except those indicated by the above data. (d) If the company had amortized all these assets over a ten-year period, what effect on cash flows would the rapid amortization have? (e) On the basis of your answers above, what specific advantages and disadvantages do you see to rapid amortization of assets for tax purposes?

12.23 You need the full use of $60,000 for three months. How much would it cost, expressed as an annual rate, under each of the following arrangements? (a) Borrow from a bank at 6 per cent discounted without a compensating balance. (b) Borrow from a bank at 5 per cent, not discounted but with a 20 per cent compensating balance. Your normal bank balance is $8,000. (c) Borrow on a warehouse receipt with terms of: (1) 7 per cent per annum; (2) the loan equal to 80 per cent of the value of the goods pledged; (3) a flat fee of $500; and (4) a fee of 1 per cent of inventory warehoused. There is ample inventory to pledge.

CHAPTER 13 THE FIRM'S COST OF CAPITAL

In order to arrive at decisions concerning commitments of capital, the cost of the capital must be considered. This cost may have an important bearing on the acceptance or rejection of particular capital investments (long-term investments) when the firm is a going concern. It should even affect decisions regarding the liquidation (sale of all assets) and the dissolution (termination of legal existence) of the firm. No matter what method is actually employed to judge the desirability of various investment proposals, the cost of capital must enter into the decisions. It should be obvious at the outset that the basic rule is that no project should be undertaken if its expected rate of return does not exceed the expected cost of capital by some factor or if its present value of net cash inflow does not exceed the required investment.

INTRODUCTION

The cost of capital to the firm may be viewed in different ways. One is to view it in the aggregate sense as the measure of the sacrifice that must be made on the part of the economy (or suppliers of capital) to create the capital. The rate at which present goods are exchanged for future goods is the price of such exchange: the cost of capital. This approach emphasizes the cost as a disutility, or the sacrifice of current consumption necessary to create capital which delivers goods for future consumption in an amount not equal to that sacrificed but also with something added as a reward for sacrifice, which reflects the productivity of capital. Although one may be satisfied with such a statement, by itself it does little to explain the determinants of the cost of capital.

In Chapter 6, we examined the general determinants of the rate of interest in the economy. The cost of capital was determined in the classical sense both by the supply of funds being offered in the money and capital markets and by the demand for these dollars generated by individuals and organizations wishing to borrow from future consumption for present consumption and those wishing to enhance future consumption by the creation of capital. In another case, the cost of capital was determined by the interaction of the quantity of money and the liquidity preference function (the demands for holding money at various interest rates). The explicit introduction of risk required the use of a *CMC* to portray capital costs, and generally the same forces at work in the loanable funds and liquidity preference cases were at work in determining the shape and location of the *CMC*.

The determinants of the rate of interest provide much of the understanding necessary for the financial manager to interpret change or to forecast changes in the cost of capital in the economy. These are not, however, a sufficiently satisfactory explanation of the determinants of capital costs under risk conditions to the particular firm. In order for financial management to achieve the lowest cost of capital for the firm (to maximize the firm's objective), it needs to be aware of the elements affecting the cost of his firm. The financial manager also finds it necessary to measure the cost to his firm if decisions are to be made concerning the proper amount of capital to employ in the firm relative to other factors of production, the total level of all factors to employ, and the allocation of the capital.

AN APPROACH TO THE DETERMINATION
OF THE FIRM'S COST OF CAPITAL

The first step in approaching this complex problem is to study the determinants of capital cost under a simplified model similar to the aggregative model of Chapter 6. The firm can, as shown in the last chapter, develop an estimate of its supply schedule of capital for some given period of time. The supply schedule in the last chapter illustrated hypothetical offerings of capital to a firm at various rates. In Chapter 11 we saw how a firm's demand for capital could be established as well. We can now overlay the demand function on the supply function and depict the results as in Figure 13-1. This figure indicates that the intersection of these two functions takes place at Point *E*, at which the cost of capital and the return on it are 8 per cent and the quantity supplied and demanded are $14,000. It cannot be overemphasized, however, that in order for this model to operate properly, the risks of proposed investments are necessarily not only equal to each other but are also at such a level as not to alter capital suppliers' views regarding the risk of the firm as a whole. This intersection (*E*) is the point at which the cost of the last dollar supplied is exactly equal to the expected return on the last dollar to be invested. In other words, the marginal cost equals the expected marginal return at this point—an optimum decision point for the firm under these

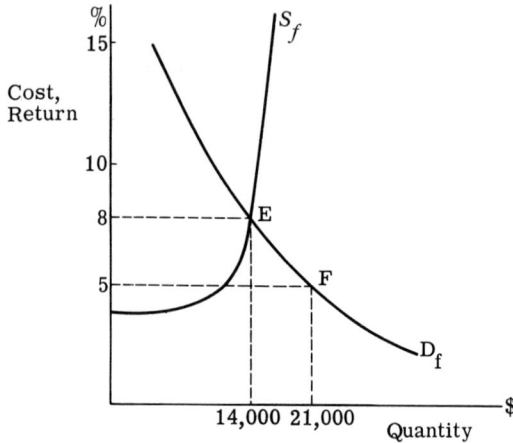

Figure 13-1   Simple Determination of the Firm's Cost of Capital.

conditions. As we shall see later, however, this is not a proper choice for the firm.

The cost of capital at the point of intersection is the cost of the last dollar supplied and not the cost of all offerings. Under the simple structure of the model and given the continuity of the demand and supply functions, this marginal cost of capital should be used to determine how much capital should be secured. If the firm were to use instead the average cost (5 per cent) as its guide for determining which investment projects should be selected and which should not, it would hire an excessive amount of capital. It would hire an amount equal to Point F (or $21,000). The firm's profits would be lower as a result than if it used marginal cost because the lowest priority investment project would yield a return lower (5 per cent) than the cost of the last dollar of capital secured (8 per cent). Consequently, under these conditions, marginal cost is the proper cost for decision purposes in this rudimentary model.

This model reflects conditions of demand and supply covering a period of time long enough for us to assume that the variables remain constant for analytical purposes. If the supply of capital in a particular decision period is not independent of the supply in other periods, misallocations of capital over time may result under a $MC = MR$ *decision rule*. For example, if as a result of securing a given quantity of capital in the current period, capital will be offered only at higher costs in the next period, in the second period the firm would reject investment proposals with a higher return than many which were accepted in the first period. This is, in reality, quite likely to be the case, especially if too short a period is selected. Often a particularly attractive source of capital used this year may not be available on such favorable terms next year because of its recent use; the use of debt financing last month may prevent the use of it next month unless equity financing is expanded. We shall find the resolution of this complex problem unnecessary when we confront the problem in an operational sense and hence will not pursue it further here. It is, however, an interesting topic for the mental exercise and reflection of the student.

The determinants of the cost of capital in this case have been shown to lie in the determinants of the demand and supply functions themselves. Cost is a function not only of the offering schedules of the sources of supply but also of the amount of capital demanded. Realistically, the offering schedules, however, are no doubt affected by the suppliers' (investors in the firm) views of the risk of investment in the firm and the risk of the investment by the firm in capital proposals, both of which certainly affect the quantity of capital demanded. It needs to be emphasized that the $MC = MR$ rule should not be used by the firm to determine the level of investment because, although the last additional cost is likely to be certain, the marginal revenue is uncertain and comparison of the two is both unwise and invalid. Because of these uncertainties as well as others, one is compelled to proceed to a model which incorporates risk explicitly in order to understand more fully the cost of capital to the firm.

RISK AND THE COST OF CAPITAL

The cost of capital to a particular firm is, as we indicated in Part I, dependent upon general market conditions. The market attempts to evaluate the risk of investment in the firm in relation to other general, run-of-the-mill investments. These generally available market opportunities are reflected in the CMC. This curve represents an aggregative model reflecting the investment returns from investments at various risk levels. These generally known opportunities should tend to be near the CMC as shown in Figure 13-2. They may not fall exactly on the curve, for the market is not a perfect market; yet the buying and selling interactions in the market should cause these to drift towards the CMC. Figure 13-2 may be viewed as a scattergram of investments for suppliers as well as demanders of capital. The CMC is a curve of best fit for these investments, and each point in Figure 13-2 reflects the combination of estimated risk and return for an investment.

One might be inclined to question such a portrayal of returns to investors on the grounds that current dividend yields on growth stocks

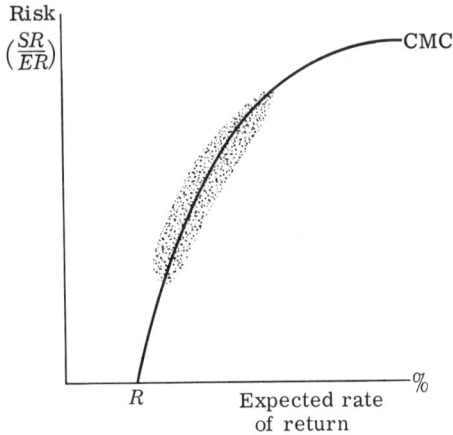

Figure 13-2   Market Capital Costs.

are typically extremely low and yet these investments are not riskless. However, profit to the common shareholders is not only the amount of dividend received; it also includes increases in the value of ownership. Consequently, the expected return to owners of the International Business Machines Corporation (IBM) include not only the expected dividends but also the expected gain in the value of ownership.[1]

The market price of the security being offered in the general market is a function of profit, as we have defined it, and a capitalization rate. This rate of return (k) is the rate which investments of this risk should secure in the market, so that

$$\text{Market Price} = \frac{\text{Profit per Share}}{\text{Capitalization Rate}}$$

[1] If within one year potential investors in IBM common stock expect a capital gain of $50 and dividends of $5, the total expected return would be $55. If, moreover, the risk (SR/ER) were 1 and intersected the CMC at a return of, say, 10 per cent, investors should be willing to pay $550 ($55/.10) for the common stock. If the estimates of risk and return can be accepted and the price were not $550, then the investment would be represented by a point away from the CMC. Presumably, however, the market would not let it stray too far. Less highly publicized investments could reasonably be expected to stray further from the CMC for longer periods. An investor purchasing an undervalued security (a point to the right of the CMC) will not stand to gain significantly if most investors do not recognize its underevaluation and do not, therefore, drive the price up to the point where the yield corresponds to its risk on the CMC. It should be remembered that not all investments on or near the CMC are equally attractive to each investor; the CMC is a general consensus. The particular combination of risk and return attractive to a specific investor depends upon the nature of his indifference to risk and return. The average investor will select that investment on the CMC which is tangent to his indifference curve. Obviously, if investment opportunities exist to the right of the CMC and an investor knows of these opportunities, he will go as far to the right of the CMC as his indifference map will take him. Choices of investments known to be to the left of the CMC are irrational.

Profit was defined as expected dividends plus the change in present value of expected returns. The ratio of expected profit per share (EO) to current market price per share (P) would yield the expected return (k); this ratio is a rough measure of the cost to the firm of new equity capital. The relationship is

$$k = \frac{EO}{P}$$

By inference

$$EO = P \times k$$

If the market underestimates profit or risk—or both—the market price of common shares would be low and the cost of capital (return to the investors) would be higher than it would be if the market accurately evaluated risk and profit. The opposite would be equally true. Hence, our measure of the cost of capital secured by the sale of common stock is the ratio of expected profit (EO) to the market price (P) of common stock outstanding. That is, it is the market-determined capitalization rate (k). The cost of a new issue of common stock usually assumes that the new funds received will be able to earn a return on funds equal to that earned in the past for outstanding shareholders unless information exists to the contrary, in which event the new expected profit and price determine cost. The price (P) used to compute this cost should be net of flotation costs—the costs necessary to sell the issue (underwriter fees as well as the costs incurred by the firm to place the issue on the market). The cost of capital obtained through the sale of preferred stock is determined by dividing the annual dividend payment by the expected net proceeds to the company (expected selling price to the public less flotation costs).

In addition to the sale of common stock and preferred stock, the firm sells a variety of debt securities. Given the *CMC*, each type of claim offered carries with it a certain risk to the investor—which, at the same time, corresponds to the appropriate cost of the particular source of capital. To be more precise, however, there does exist a margin of difference between the yield to the investor and the cost of capital to the firm; this difference is due to flotation costs. The net proceeds to the firm from the sale of a 5 per cent bond to an investor at $1,000 will be less than $1,000 by the amount of the flotation costs. Consequently, where the expected yield to the investor may be 5 per cent, the cost of capital to the firm may be, for example, 5.1 per cent. Later in this chapter we shall return to this point and develop more fully the methods of computing a firm's cost of capital. But for purposes of general analysis we shall continue to speak of the yield to the investor and the cost of capital as one and the same.

Each alternative instrument sold by the firm to finance its investments involves both an expected return and risk to the investor. The risk in the case of each instrument is evaluated by those buying and selling in the capital market. The risk facing the investor in an instrument issued by the firm may be quite different from the risks facing the firm internally. The firm directs itself to maximizing profits—the return to the owners of the firm. An investor in a bond obligation of the firm is interested in maximizing his income, given his aversion to risk. The risk, returns, and aversion to risk of the firm are all likely to be different from those of the bond investor. The internal rates of return on investments by the firm customarily exceed the returns on many of the individual obligations of the firms. Because the expected return to the investor (the denominator in the SR/ER ratio) is different from the expected return to the firm on its investments, risk—as measured by the ratio of the standard deviation of expected returns to the expected return—is likely to be different also.

Consequently, although in a general way the risks facing the firm are similar to the risks facing the investor and affect the total risk of the investor's portfolio, the degree of risk can be expected to differ depending on the security. The yield to the investor is viewed as the cost of capital to the firm, qualified by flotation expenses and, in the case of debt, the tax deductibility of interest. Consequently, it is worthwhile to examine briefly the nature of risk facing the investor. To do this, however, we must assume the attitude of a potential or present investor in a firm's securities. Fundamental to this, it ought to be recognized that the investment industry breaks down the yield concept into a variety of components. Principally, these components include the riskless, pure interest rate, the risk premium for business risk, the risk premium for financial risk, the premium for purchasing power risk, and the risk premium for money risk and for market risk. Certain other variations in the particular contractual provisions of the instrument may cause certain additional (usually minor) variations in the yield to the investor.[2]

Investment Risks[3]

Business Risk

From the standpoint of investors, business risk depends upon the nature of risk in the firm that causes variability in the returns on the

[2] For a more thorough discussion of the elements of yield to the investor, see: Harry Sauvain, *Investment Management,* 2nd ed. (Englewood Cliffs, N.J.: Prentice-Hall, 1959), 87–172.

[3] That part of a yield attributable to the pure rate was discussed in Chapter 4 and need not be discussed again at this point.

investments the firm has made, and the firm's ability to reduce the total risk to the firm through diversification—that is, by investing in various relatively uncorrelated firm investments. The premium in yield to the investor for business risk relates the expected variation in returns relative to the expected return of the particular instrument under consideration. A 5 per cent bond obligation which sold for $1,000 might well have an expected distribution of returns to investors such as in Figure 13-3. Because of the contractual liability of the payments, failure of the business to meet the payments to Bond A would normally be expected to involve at least a partial loss to the owners of the bond. The probability of a return less than 5 per cent (the current yield to maturity) in the case of most bond issues would be exceedingly low. The existence of a probability of a return in excess of 5 per cent would presumably arise from the prospects of a premium to be paid in the event the bond were redeemed by the company before maturity. The risk (SR/ER) involved in such an investment (Bond A) would apparently be low.

A more unusual case would involve a distribution such as that shown in Figure 13-4, where the investor exhibits less confidence in the expected return of Bond B. In this case, the 5 per cent coupon bond sells at a discount (a price less than face value) to yield 7 per cent (assuming the bond will be retired at maturity). The risk (SR/ER) would obviously be greater for Bond B than for Bond A.

Financial Risk

Investment literature does not always distinguish financial risk from business risk. When they are not used synonomously, financial risk refers to the risk arising from the style in which a firm is financed. In the case

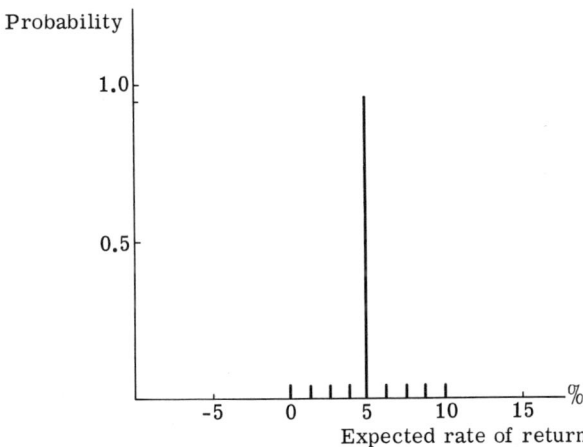

Figure 13-3 Estimated Probability Distribution of Returns for Bond A.

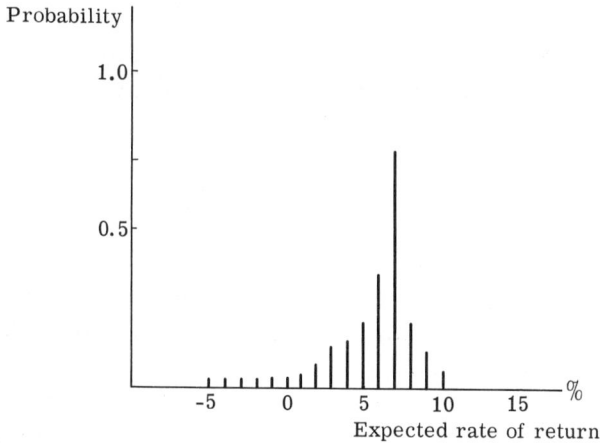

Figure 13-4   Estimated Probability Distribution of Returns for Bond B.

of evaluating the risk to investors in preferred stock, for example, the existence of the prior claim of debt increases the risk to preferred stock investors above the existing business risk because the likelihood of not being paid is greater. The point here is that the financial risk of a particular instrument depends upon the use of sources of financing with a prior claim on the firm.

The use of such prior claim financing is commonly referred to as *leverage* or *trading on the equity*. It is used in an attempt to increase returns to owners. Invariably it increases the risk of return to the owners. This risk is the financial risk.

In this brief treatment of business and financial risk we have done little to spell out the process by which an analyst arrives at the risk of investment. In the case of the risks discussed above as well as other risks of investment, the techniques which investors use in analysis are many and varied. Many factors lie behind the estimates of returns and, consequently, risk; these include analysis of a whole host of factors that presumably contribute to the uncertainty of the investment outcome. This type of study is traditionally the subject of financial analysis, which is a topic to be discussed in Part III. There we will find that evaluation of risk and return, as presently carried out, appears to be almost an art rather than a science.

Purchasing Power Risk

The premium in yield to the investor for the assumption of purchasing power risk will vary over time as prospects for changes in prices of goods and services alter. The risk at any point in time is determined by the prospects for price stability and therefore the real returns to the investor of a particular instrument of investment. If the anticipations of investors suggest instability in future prices of goods and services, the investor in a preferred stock, for example, will be less certain in his estimate of real returns. The preferred stockholder holds a promise of a fixed money income and, should the value of money be expected to change, so will the expected real returns. If, instead of increasing uncertainty about price stability, it becomes quite evident that prices are going to rise, then the value of existing preferred shares must fall in order to maintain the existing level of expected real return; an investor would need a discount from face value to make the fixed money income equal to a compensatory real return.

Common shareholders may or may not require a premium for purchasing power risk. If a firm's monetary assets (assets whose dollar value would not be expected to rise in inflation) exceed their monetary liabilities (claims on the firm which are fixed in dollars), the firm is referred to as a *net-monetary creditor;* if the monetary liabilities exceed the monetary assets, the firm is referred to as a *net-monetary debtor.* Kessel has suggested that net-monetary debtors gain during inflations and net-monetary creditors gain during deflations.[4] A firm with monetary assets equal to its monetary liabilities should require little, if any, premium for purchasing power risk for its common shareholders.[5]

Money Risk

The risk premium in the yield to the investor for money risk depends upon expectations concerning the stability in the interest rate. Changes in this rate arise from economic forces discussed in Chapters 4 and 6. When these changes do occur, the *CMC* shifts to the right or left.[6] The shifts of the *CMC* may cause roughly parallel shifts in the whole structure of rates, so that a change in the pure interest rate eventually brings about a change in other rates. The change may be in the order of a shift in the *CMC* to a position approximately parallel with the old *CMC* position.

A shift of the whole *CMC* would tend to cause changes in the prices of all instruments of investment, for yield is directly related to price. For example, assume a bond, preferred, or common stock is expected to pay

---

[4] See: Reuben A. Kessel, "Inflation-Caused Wealth Redistribution: A Test of a Hypothesis," *American Economic Review, 46* (March 1956), 128–41.

[5] For a discussion of investment results in shares of common stock in different industries, see: Stephen H. Archer, "Common Stocks as an Inflation Hedge," *Financial Analysts Journal, 16* (September–October 1960), 41–45.

[6] Changes in the *CMC* may also arise from another factor: namely, variations in the willingness of investors to asume risk. An increase in risk aversion by the investors would reduce the general slope of the *CMC*.

income (EO) forever and the yield necessary to compensate the investor for the pure rate and for the assumption of risk is k. The market price (P) would be simply the ratio of EO to k.

$$P = \frac{EO}{k}$$

It is also true that $k = \frac{EO}{P}$. In most cases, however, the income (EO) is not assumed to be paid forever nor is it necessarily expected to be the same amount in all periods of the future. If the income is constant, like an annuity, the price (or present value) would be:

$$P = EO \left[\frac{1 - \dfrac{1}{(1+k)^n}}{k} \right]$$

where n is the number of periods for which EO is expected to be paid. Where EO is not expected to be constant,

$$P = \sum_{t=1}^{n} \frac{EO_t}{(1+k)^t}$$

where EO_t is a subscripted variable standing for income in the tth period. The income used in the equations is a general expression standing for interest, dividends, gains, or other returns on invested capital. The point to be emphasized here is that in all cases k appears in the denominator and any change in k affects P. An increase in k tends to decrease P and a decrease in k tends to increase P. Consequently, shifts in the CMC tend to cause changes in prices of the outstanding instruments of investment. These possible variations in price create uncertainty about prospective returns. To illustrate: if a twenty-year bond were issued at $1,000 a year ago with a 4 per cent coupon and new nineteen-year bonds, alike in all respects, were being issued at $1,000 with a coupon of 5 per cent, the value of the old bond already outstanding would fall to $878.30, even if no further increases in interest rates alter the returns (*ex-post*) to the investor. The investor in the 4 per cent bond would have received $40 in interest, lost $121.70 in capital losses, producing a net loss of $81.70—a return for the year of minus 8 per cent. If the investor instead held the bond to maturity, the return for the whole period would be 4 per cent; the return on the nineteen-year bonds would be 5 per cent if there were no further changes in interest rates or if the investors held the bonds to maturity.

Issues closer to redemption permit little variation in price, which minimizes the money risk. Reinvestment costs do increase, however, if the investor must replace his investment at short intervals. If the same 4 per cent bond had only one year left to maturity when general interest rates changed to increase the yield on one-year issues to 4.5 per cent, the effect on price would be small. As the bond will pay $1,000 in one year it will sell to yield the short-term interest rate, 4.5 per cent, for the year. If the one-year interest rate for this risk security were 4.5 per cent, the bond should sell for $995.20, yielding 4.5 per cent at maturity (ignoring any tax preference for capital gains).

For common stockholders, a shift in the *CMC* for risks of that particular level would cause changes in the price of their shares. The prospects for such variations in return to the common shareholder increase his risk of investment.[7]

Market Risk

One need only lift the phone to call a broker and within a few minutes he will have sold his 100 shares of American Telephone and Telegraph Company common stock at the prevailing market price. If, however, the asset to be sold were a car, real estate, or machinery, so quick a disposal would usually involve a substantial discount from the prevailing market price. In order to sell these assets at or near the prevailing market prices a considerably longer period would be needed. Because of this risk—that is, the risk of not being able to sell an asset quickly without incurring an appreciable discount from current market price—one would usually expect a small additional premium to exist to compensate the investor for lack of liquidity. This is known as the *market risk* of an investment.

COST OF CAPITAL: THE FINANCIAL STRUCTURE

Modigliani and Miller have suggested that a firm's cost of capital at a point in the supply function is essentially independent of its mix of debt and equity sources of capital, assuming perfect markets and the use of personal leverage as a substitute for the absence of leverage in the firm.[8]

---

[7] It frequently happens that the rise in interest rates coincides with prosperity and, sometimes, inflation. Prosperity increases effective demand and the expected internal rates of return on firms' investments. Inflation in the case of many common stocks also increases real returns. Consequently, although higher interest rates may tend to deflate security values, in the case of common stocks this tendency will often be offset by such other forces as increasing returns of firms. Money risk also generally plays a relatively smaller role in the total risk of investment in common stocks and consequently has less influence on the total k and, therefore, on price.

[8] Franco Modigliani and Merton H. Miller, "The Cost of Capital, Corporation Finance, and the Theory of Investment," *American Economic Review*, 48 (June 1958), 261–97.

Income taxes are viewed, as an exception, however, and their existence gives rise to some optimum (or range of optimum) mix of debt and equity.[9] Others argue that the over-all cost of capital to the firm is affected by the financial structure.[10] To understand these two positions more fully, let us briefly discuss the possible impacts of the financial structure upon the various investment risks.

The money risk as a whole might be expected to be affected by the method of financing. Financing methods that involve a short period to maturity involve little more risk. The longer the maturity, the more the price (and consequently return) is affected by interest rate changes. The shorter the maturity, however, the greater the renewal costs. Greater risk premiums must be paid for assuming greater money risk, which may or may not be offset by other risks.

The studies of Kessel were cited in the discussion of purchasing power risk. Given the monetary assets of a firm (which are customarily determined by the nature of the business), the purchasing power risk assumed by the common shareholders—and thus the cost of capital—is affected by the proportions of monetary liabilities used in the financial structure. It has been suggested that the Kessel theory may contradict the Modigliani-Miller hypothesis.[11] A contrary position could be presented and would run somewhat along the following lines. If the existence of an excess of monetary liabilities over the monetary assets permits gains to common shareholders in inflation, the holders of the monetary liabilities (investors) lose during inflation. Expectations concerning instability in the price level may create purchasing power risk, but it does not appear that a highly leveraged capital structure permits a lower cost of capital, for the cost of capital through the use of monetary liabilities would rise as price instability prospects increase.

The business risk of the firm as a whole would be unaffected by the financing method. This risk is inherent in the variability of returns to the investments of the total enterprise and the degree of diversification. Indeed, to the extent debt securities are used, the contractual nature of the obligations requires the firm to avoid default. However, this risk is to a large extent passed on to common shareholders who must bear almost all

[9] Franco Modigliani and Merton H. Miller, "The Cost of Capital, Corporation Finance, and the Theory of Investment: A Reply," *American Economic Review, 49* (September 1959), 655–69; and Franco Modigliani and Merton H. Miller, "Corporate Income Taxes and the Cost of Capital: A Correction," *American Economic Review, 53* (June 1963), 433–43.

[10] For a discussion of the arguments pro and con, see: Myles S. Delano, "Some Comments on Capital Budgeting and the Cost of Capital," *University of Washington Business Review, 22* (October 1962), 5–15.

[11] J. Fred Weston, *Managerial Finance* (New York: Holt, 1962), 257.

the potential inconstancy of returns to the business after the deduction of the fixed payments to senior securities. The variation becomes relatively greater when borne by a smaller base of common shares than would exist if the entire structure were financed by the owners.

Let us assume the absence of any other risks of investment except business and financial risk. Assume a firm expects earnings of $100,000 (ignoring taxes) and a standard deviation of $50,000, so that risk ($SR/ER$) is 1/2. Also assume that the CMC in such a case requires a 10 per cent rate of return on the 100,000 shares of common stock which finance the entire firm's operations (an all-equity firm). The price of common should be $10 ($1/.10). The cost of capital is also 10 per cent (ignoring flotation costs). If the same firm were to arrange its capital structure to include 50 per cent bonds with a risk of 1/4 so that the cost of debt capital were 5 per cent, the mean expected earnings available to common shareholders would be $75,000 (assuming total earnings before interest remain at $100,000). As a result of financial risk the standard deviation in profit now becomes, for example, $75,000 and the risk ($SR/ER$) to common becomes 1. The CMC requires a yield of, say, 15 per cent and, based upon 50,000 shares of common, the earnings per share would be $1.50. The price of common remains at $10 ($1.50/.15). But the expected yield on common is 15 per cent. The average weighted cost of capital in the latter case is 10 per cent [(50 per cent debt × 5 per cent) + (50 per cent equity × 15 per cent)].[12]

This example makes it appear that the cost of capital attributable to business and financial risk *could* remain the same no matter what the mix between debt and equity. Indeed, except for the effect of debt on after-tax earnings, it becomes difficult in theory to refute the argument that the cost of capital is unaffected by the degree of leverage used by the firm under the assumption of perfectly operating capital markets.[13]

---

[12] Methods of computing the cost of individual sources of capital are treated subsequently and the rationale for using the weighted average cost of capital is reserved for a later section of this chapter.

[13] One line of argument against such a conclusion may lie in the nature of profits and the construction of statistical measures. If firm profits are to exist, the time-adjusted rate of return or yield to the firm on its investments must exceed its cost of capital. If the mean returns to the firm must be different from mean returns to investors to create profit and risk can be measured as the relative variation from the mean, then risks to investors for all securities of the firm must average greater than the risks of the firm because of the lower denominator. The average or mean is also heavily affected by extreme values and a highly leveraged company's common stock would involve a high risk requiring a high return; this high cost of capital would pull the mean up to a high level. Consequently, one might expect the average cost of capital to vary according to the method of financing because of the manner in which the mean and relative standard deviation are here constructed. Aside from these technical considerations, it becomes difficult to refute the Modigliani and Miller posi-

In contrast to the Modigliani and Miller position is the more traditional position of business finance, which holds that there is some optimum debt-equity ratio that minimizes the cost of capital but that, in
most cases, the cost appears to be unaffected to any significant extent
over a wide range of variation in this ratio. Weston has likened the change
in cost of capital with changes in the debt-equity ratio to a "saucer" (see
Figure 13-5).[14] A high debt-equity ratio increases risk to common shareholders who do not feel sufficiently compensated in increased return, such
that the cost of capital increases on the whole as the cost of debt financing
increases.[15]

However, the debt-equity ratio is not the only variable in the determination of the optimum mix of capital although it may be the important
factor. Short-term sources must be prudently managed. The firm must be
informed enough to seek out the lowest-cost sources and avoid the more
expensive forms. The firm may also lower its cost by the efficient use of
funds (as by taking care of seasonal demands with short-term sources,

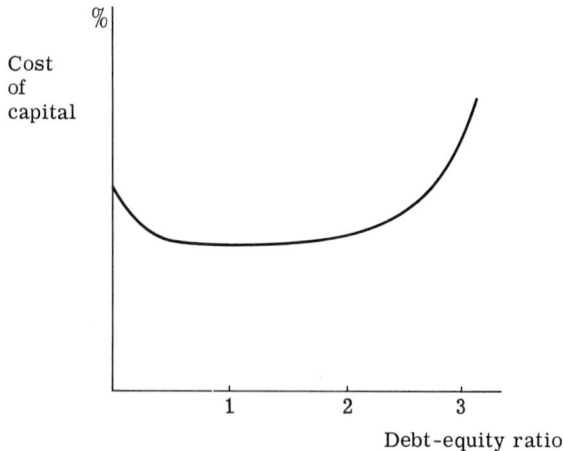

Figure 13-5   Saucer-shaped Cost of Capital Relationship.

tion, although one may question the premises leading to their conclusion. For a challenge of the assumptions underlying their position, see: Myron J. Gordon, *The Investment, Financing, and Valuation of the Corporation* (Homewood, Ill.: Irwin, 1962)
103–108; and David Durand, "The Cost of Capital, Corporation Finance, and the
Theory of Investment: Comment," *American Economic Review,* 49 (September 1959),
639–55.

[14] Weston, *Managerial Finance* (New York: Holt, 1962), 257.

[15] Durand arrives at approximately the same result in his conclusion that the curve
is saucer-shaped—perhaps more steep at the extremes and flat in the middle. He be-
lieves, however, that there is not an optimum mix over a wide range and only his
belief in the imperfect nature of the markets causes him to disagree with Modigliani
and Miller (Durand, *op. cit.*).

a subject to be discussed further in Part III). In general, however, we shall assume there exists some combination of sources that minimizes the cost of capital to the firm.

MARGINAL COST OF CAPITAL MEASUREMENT

In the case presented early in this chapter, marginal cost was the appropriate cost of capital to be used in determining the acceptance or rejection of investment alternatives as long as marginal revenues were forthcoming with certainty. There it was pointed out that the optimal point for the firm occurred when the cost of the last additional dose of capital equilibrated the additional expected return of the last investment alternative accepted as long as marginal revenues are certain. If they are uncertain, a risk premium must be added to marginal cost.

The marginal cost in this analysis was based upon the cost of the mix of sources. The mix of sources is assumed to be an optimum mix (least-cost combination) at all points along this curve of marginal costs. We shall now turn our attention to the measurement of the cost of capital at any point along the curve, which is measured as the weighted average of the costs of the various sources in the mix at this point. The measurement of the cost of capital leads to the question of whether we should use the cost of the capital to be raised in the current period or whether one should consider the cost as future cost. The cost of capital of previous financing is obviously irrelevant for present investment decisions. Estimated future costs, however, have occasionally been suggested as the appropriate cost of capital. Future costs, it is argued, should be matched with the future revenues which are to be received on investments made in the present period. The commitment for those future capital payments, however, is made in the present period and the payments tend to be matched against the revenues to the expectation of which the firm in a sense commits itself in the present period. Therefore, it is only consistent that the *present* costs of capital should be matched with present investment alternatives.

One further modification needs to be made. In any decision period, such as a year, the firm will not find it economical to raise capital from all its sources. Costs of raising capital (flotation cost in the case of securities) are not proportional to the amount of capital secured at one time. Some of these costs are fixed. Consequently, it would not be advantageous to sell a small stock issue as well as a small bond issue at the same time in order to maintain the assumed proper mix of capital. It would be more appropriate to sell a large bond issue in this period and a large stock issue in the next period, or vice versa. From a practical point of view, the cost of capital is best approximated for the current period by using weights reflecting the long-run desirable mix of capital sources. In other words, the cost of capital in the *current* period should be weighted by the relative expected mix of future sources of capital the firm intends to use. But before we demonstrate the methodology of computing the weighted average cost of capital, let us turn to the methods employed to compute the cost of the various sources of capital.

COMPUTING THE COST OF VARIOUS SOURCES OF CAPITAL

The Cost of Bonded Debt

In determining the cost of bonds, much will depend on the current market price. If the bonds are currently selling above or below their face value, then the *effective yield* will be greater or less than their coupon or nominal yield. Ordinarily, bond tables would be used to establish what the yield to maturity of the bonds would be in such cases.[16] But there is a longhand method which can be used to make a rough approximation of a bond's yield to maturity. The formula for such a computation when bonds are selling at a discount (that is, at a price below face value) is

$$k_b = \frac{I + D/n}{\frac{P + MV}{2}}$$

where

k_b = yield to maturity of bonds (gross cost of debt issue)
I = Interest income
D = the amount of the discount (face value—market price)
n = the number of years to maturity
P = the current market price of the bond
MV = the maturity value of the bond.[17]

---

[16] If the bond were selling on the market at face value, its yield to maturity would be equal to the coupon rate. Because bond prices fluctuate inversely with changes in interest rates, the likelihood of a bond selling at exactly face value after its issuance is very slim.

[17] Ordinarily the maturity value of a bond will be assumed to be its face value and the amount of discount as well as the number of years to maturity will be based on that figure and the maturity date. In some cases a firm may anticipate retiring the bonds some time before maturity. It can ordinarily do this at its option but usually at a price above face value. Under these circumstances the "call price" of the bond then becomes MV, and n will be measured from the present to the call date. As a result k_b will be different from what it would otherwise be because the magnitude of n and MV changes.

If, for example, a $1,000 face value bond with a coupon of 5 per cent were to mature in ten years and were selling at 90,[18] its yield to maturity could be calculated as follows:

$$k_b = \frac{\$50 + \$100/10 \text{ years}}{\dfrac{\$900 + \$1,000}{2}}$$

$$= \frac{\$50 + \$10}{\dfrac{\$1,900}{2}} = \frac{\$60}{\$950} = 6.32 \text{ per cent.}$$

What this formula represents can be demonstrated by two approaches. The first is that it relates the average amount of income received over the ten-year period ($60) to the average amount we have invested ($950). The interest income of $50 is taken directly from the provisions of the bond contract, which obligates the firm to pay 5 per cent each year on each $1,000 bond. But, because the bond is selling for $900 and because a purchaser of this bond will get back $1,000 were he to hold it to maturity, then, in effect, his average yearly income is increased by $10 ($100 ÷ 10 years) with the result that his average income is $60 ($50 interest income + $10 amortized discount).

The average invested amount arises from the nature of the discount problem also. The initial amount invested is $900. The amount received at the end of the ten-year period is $1,000. This averages out to $950. It can be assumed (if no further interest rate changes take place) that the price of the bond should increase by about $10 in each of the years it has left to maturity. At the end of the first year, the price of the bond will be about $910; at the end of the second year, about $920; and so on, so that the average price of the bond for the period is $950. What yield to maturity would the firm need to pay were it to sell ten-year bonds at this time? It could probably not do better than the yield on debt securities already outstanding—that is, 6.32 per cent. The gross cost of the debt issues of the firm is assumed to be 6.32 per cent, even though flotation costs are not included in this case. If they were, the results would be little different. Because interest expenses are deductible for tax purposes, this gross figure needs to be adjusted for the tax rate of the firm. If the tax rate is 50 per cent, the net cost of this debt to the firm would be 3.16 per cent [6.32 per cent (1 − tax rate)].

[18] Bond prices are typically quoted in points where each point represents $10 for a $1,000 bond. A $1,000 bond selling at 96¾ has a market price of $967.50. Certain bonds are quoted in terms of yields rather than price.

The Cost of Preferred Stock

Computing the *cost of preferred stock* is somewhat less complicated than the computation of the cost of debt. The main differences between this computation and that for bonds are that dividends on preferred stock, although limited in nature (like interest on bonds), are presumed to be payable into perpetuity, for there is no maturity date for preferred stocks, and such dividends are not deductible for tax purposes. The formula for the cost of preferred is

$$k_p = \frac{EO}{P}$$

where

EO = income to preferred (the dividend payment)
P = present market price
k_p = cost of preferred capital

The cost of capital is equal to the ratio of annual dividend income per share to the current market price of the preferred stock. This ratio is often called a current *dividend yield*. Because dividends on stock are not deductible for tax purposes, the yield (k_p) resulting from our calculations is not adjusted as it was in the case of bonds.

To illustrate the above case, let's assume a firm has a 5 per cent, $100 par value preferred stock outstanding. Let's further assume that the market price of the preferred stock is $90 per share.[19] The dividend yield on these preferred stocks and hence their cost is

$$k_p = \frac{EO}{P}$$
$$= \frac{\$5 \quad \text{(5 per cent of \$100 par)}}{\$90}$$
$$k_p = 5.56 \text{ per cent}$$

The Cost of Common Stock

Computation of the cost of capital from the sale of common stock is similar in nature to that of preferred stock. Like preferred stock, common stock is issued in perpetuity. The income used is the firm's current dividends per share plus expected capital gains. These profits are likewise

[19] Unlike bonds, preferred stock prices are quoted in actual dollar amounts, where one point is $1.

presumed to persist into perpetuity. The basic formula for the cost of capital for the sale of common stock is

$$k_c = \frac{EO}{P}$$

where

EO = income (estimated current dividends per share plus expected capital gains)

P = current market price per share

k_c = cost of common capital

The present market price per share presumably represents a rough consensus of investors regarding the future profits of the firm even though many shareholders evaluate it higher than the actual market price and many nonshareholders evaluate it lower. This ratio of EO to P is called a *profits-to-price ratio* or a *profit yield*. Like all other yields we have discussed thus far, it relates some concept of income (expected profits) to market price. Profits are not deductible by the company for tax purposes, and no adjustment of the profit yield is made as was done with bonds.

Assume that a firm's common stock is selling for $50 per share and that its estimated profits (expected dividends and capital gains) are $5 per share. The cost of common stock in this event would be 10 $\left(\frac{\$5}{\$50}\right)$ per cent.

The Cost of Retained Earnings

Computation of the cost of retained earnings is similar in nature to the computation of the cost of all other sources of funds. But before we explore the mechanics of this computation, we need to set forth the rationale for computing the cost of retained earnings in the first place.

Many businessmen, and we are sure most students, feel there is no cost to the business when earnings are retained. If by this is meant there are no explicit, tangible costs of earnings retention, there can hardly be any argument. There are, however, opportunity costs associated with earnings retention. Theoretically, the cost of retained earnings is the investment opportunity (or opportunities) foregone by stockholders because of such retention. What kind of investment opportunity would be foregone? It should be an investment opportunity equal to the average risk and expected return found in the firm itself. Because there is, in fact, no investment opportunity of precisely the same kind and quality as the firm that retains the earnings, we use the firm itself to determine the opportunity foregone. The retention of earnings in a firm is actually an investment in the firm just as all other items on the righthand side of a balance sheet represent sources of funds for previous investments. The cost of these retained earnings is computed in the same manner as the cost of common stock; that is, the *profit yield* is used to compute this cost If, as in our example of the cost of common stock, expected profits are $5 per share and the current market price is $50 per share, the cost of retained earnings is $10 \left(\dfrac{\$5}{\$50} \right)$ per cent.

It may be argued that the cost of retained earnings should be computed as above, but taking into account the marginal tax rate on the common stockholders' ordinary income. The argument for this runs along these lines. The cost of retained earnings is measured by the *opportunities foregone by the stockholders.* Now if the retained earnings were paid out to stockholders to do with as they please, then the additional income they receive will involve an increase in their tax. Because it is assumed that the earnings received are reinvested in the common stock of the firm whose stock they already own, then the investment of the disbursed earnings in these stocks should take into account the additional tax that the stockholders must pay. And any calculation of cost of retained earnings must likewise account for this. For example, assume there are $5 per share accounting profits, all of which are paid out, and the marginal tax rate of all the recipients is, say, 30 per cent. Then the amount available for reinvestment by the stockholders in this stock after taxes would be $3.50 [$5 − ($5 × .30)] or [$5 (1 − .30)]. As the stockholder still has to pay capital gains tax on the gains in price per share due to profitable reinvestment, the difference in taxability is perhaps only one half the marginal tax rate inasmuch as capital gains (long-term) are taxed at half the rate on ordinary income. That is, the adjustment of EO for income taxes for the average stockholder at rate T overstates the tax saving because he pays a capital gains tax (eventually), so the tax saving by reinvestment is only about one-half T (or $T/2$). Relating this adjusted outcome to the current market price per share will bring a cost of retained earnings to $8.5 \left(\dfrac{\$4.25}{\$50.00} \right)$ per cent. The formulation for this calculation is

$$k_r = \frac{EO\,(1 - T/2)}{P}$$

where

$T =$ the estimated average marginal tax rate of stockholders

P = the current market price

k_r = the cost of retained earnings (the yield of disbursed
earnings reinvested by stockholders in the firm)

Because of the difficulty of assessing the marginal tax rate of stock-holders (at best a firm could come up with only an average marginal tax rate), any exact determination is precluded. Beyond that it is question-able whether such further refinement in the method of calculation will add that much to the analysis. The determination of cost of retained earn-ings by the firm was based on its (stockholders') opportunity to invest in the company's equity position. Because the earnings are retained, the loss of opportunity on the part of the stockholders to reinvest in their own business, if they choose, is an illusion. If the welfare of the firm and that of the stockholder are presumed to be identical, and if there are no simi-lar opportunities available to the stockholder except purchases of more of the firm's stock, then retention of earnings is really more beneficial to him than distribution. Consequently, in computing the cost of retained earnings, it is probably more realistic to employ the same methodology used to compute the cost of common stock capital, which was, as you will recall, expressed by the relationship, EO/P.

Cost of Depleciation

The cost of this source is again an opportunity cost. The alternative use of the funds is the repayment of capital supplied in previous periods. Such repayments would include bond retirement or the payment of non-taxable capital dividends to stockholders. If we assume that long-term and permanent sources of capital were secured for the purchase of fixed assets, then the opportunity cost should be the average of costs of such past sources. Such a weighted past cost could be computed. In the inter-ests of easy computation, however, let us assume the cost to be the same as the weighted average of current costs of the long-run future mix. This assumption would mean that we would compute the weighted average cost, excluding depleciation, and then assume the cost of the depleciation source to be that cost, ignoring tax adjustments. Inasmuch as such a cost would have no computational impact on the weighted average cost of capital, it is usually left out of such computations.

Costs of Other Debt Sources[20]

The method of measuring the cost of corporate notes (longer than one year) is identical with that used in determining the cost of corporate bonds.

[20] See pages 255–57 for the cost of trade credit.

The measurement of the cost of various types of installment debt is frequently very confusing because of the declining outstanding loan balance. Assume a firm borrows $1,000, repayable in equal quarterly installments over a period of five years. Although the quoted rate is 6 per cent, the lender multiplies it by the original balance of $1,000 to secure the total interest dollars to be paid. The result is

$$.06 \times 5 \text{ (years)} \times \$1,000 = \$300.$$

The before-tax effective cost to the firm is computed by the formula,

$$k_i = \frac{2m \ C_l}{A(n+1),}$$

where

$n =$ number of payments
$m =$ number of payments in one year
$C_l =$ dollar cost of capital for the entire loan
$A =$ amount of the loan
$k_i =$ the effective cost of installment debt capital

In our example, $n = 20$, $m = 4$, $C_l = \$300$, and $A = \$1,000$. Therefore

$$k_i = \frac{2 \times 4 \times \$300}{\$1,000 \times 21} = \frac{\$2,400}{\$21,000} = .1143 = 11.43 \text{ per cent.}$$

The before-tax effective cost is over 11 per cent. Adjusted for a 50 per cent income tax, the effective cost to the firm is 5.7 per cent. Any additional special charges involved with the credit should be added to the $300.

For loans which have a "balloon" payment as the terminal one, a more lengthy process is required to determine the cost. The method to be used is the same as that used in Chapter 11 to determine the rate of return on investment expenditures. Instead of cash inflows, however, cash outflows are used and the rate that discounts these flows so that their sum equals the amount of the loan is found.[21]

Costs of short-term bank credit vary with the credit arrangement. If the firm borrows $1,000 for three months and pays $1,015 at maturity, the cost is 6 per cent, the quoted rate, or 3 per cent after taxes. If the firm's note is discounted, it receives $985 ($1,000 − $15) and pays $1,000 in three months. The cost to the firm is 6.1 per cent $\left(\frac{\$15}{\$985} \times \frac{12 \text{ months}}{3 \text{ months}} \right)$,

[21] See pages 257–59.

The Firm's Cost of Capital 303

an annual rate above the quoted 6 per cent annual rate. After taxes the rate would be 3.05 per cent. If the firm is required to carry a compensating balance in its deposit account of, say, 20 per cent of its loan, the effective cost increases. Assuming it might carry a near-zero balance at some time during the year, then the whole 20 per cent is an imposition on the firm and the principal amount of the loan would have to be increased to allow for this balance. In fact, given these conditions, the firm would have to borrow $1,250, the before-tax cost of which would be 7.5 per cent $\left(\dfrac{\$18.75}{\$1,000} \times \dfrac{12}{3}\right)$. After taxes it would be 3.75 per cent. The $18.75 is a product of the annual rate (6 per cent) times 1/4 a year × $1,250, the amount of the note. As these seasonal sources are normally used only, say, one fourth of the year, the *weight* of their cost in computing the over-all firm cost of capital should be only one fourth of the amount borrowed.

Other current liabilities normally include accruals for taxes, wages, interest, and accounts payable. These are sources of capital to the firm and are presumed to be cost-free (with the possible exception of accounts payable). The cost of the payables is zero if they do not extend beyond the payment period (or cash discount period, if it exists). If the firm does not pay when payables are due, it must incur some implicit cost in terms of the deterioration of its credit standing, a factor that will probably affect the availability of future credit. If the firm fails to take cash discounts, the cost was earlier observed to be prohibitively high. The appropriate weight for this zero cost source as well as the others is the average expected usage through the year.

MEASUREMENT OF THE WEIGHTED AVERAGE COST OF CAPITAL

The weighted average cost of capital, in theory, would be found by determining the total risk to investors of each of a firm's obligations and equities. Given the risk of each source, the cost of capital of each type of security could be obtained from the current *CMC*. Using the *CMC* in Figure 13-6 as the one depicting currently prevailing market yields to investors, a firm with an estimated capital structure such as that shown in Table 13-1 could then compute its weighted average cost of capital after taxes in the manner demonstrated. The average after-tax cost works out to be 7.4 per cent.[22]

[22] An alternative method for computing the weighted average cost of capital after taxes is to weigh each source in the capital structure and multiply the several results by the appropriate rates. For the example above, the result would be as shown in Table 13–2.

Table 13-1

Weighted Average Cost of Capital

Source	Amount	×	Percent-age Cost	×	Tax Ad-justment	=	After-Tax Cost
Bonds	$ 2,000,000	×	4%	×	1 − .50	=	$ 40,000
Preferred stock	2,000,000	×	5	×	none	=	100,000
Common equity	6,000,000	×	10	×	none	=	600,000
	$10,000,000						$740,000

$$\frac{\text{Total After-Tax Costs}}{\text{Total Capital}} = \frac{\$740,000}{\$10,000,000} = .074 = 7.4\%$$

It should be recalled that this manner of estimating the cost of capital does have a slight downward bias in that the yields to the investor will run a little lower than the cost to the firm because of flotation costs and other costs to the firm in servicing the source once the capital has been secured. The cost of capital to the firm is different from the yield to investors because of the tax adjustments made for the fact that interest payments are deductible before applying the corporate tax rate. Given average explicit flotation costs on a $15 million bond issue of about 1.5 per cent of gross proceeds, for a twenty-year bond issue this would amount to 1.5/20 or .075 per cent; even if sinking-fund payments were one twentieth the amount of the issue each year, making the average loan $500 per bond instead of $1,000, the average annual flotation costs would amount to only .15 per cent (15/100 of 1 per cent). For a common stock issue of

Table 13-2

Weighted Average Cost of Capital

Source	Per Cent of Total Capital	×	Percentage Cost	×	Tax Adjustment	=	After-Tax Cost
Bonds	$\dfrac{\$\,2,000,000}{\$10,000,000}$ =		20% × 4%	×	1 − .50	=	0.004
Preferred stock	$\dfrac{\$\,2,000,000}{\$10,000,000}$ =		20 × 5	×	1	=	0.010
Common equity	$\dfrac{\$\,6,000,000}{\$10,000,000}$ =		60 × 10	×	1	=	0.060
							0.074 = 7.4%

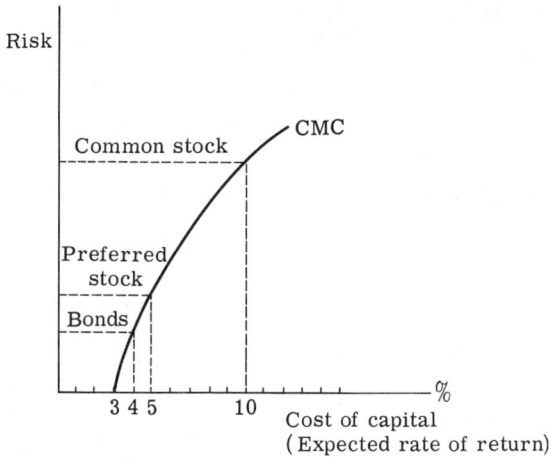

Figure 13-6   Market Costs of Capital.

the same size, the cost of flotation costs allocated over twenty years would amount to only about .25 per cent.

In an operational sense, the firm's over-all cost of capital is measured as the after-tax cost of the individual sources in the total mix of sources expected to be used in future financing weighted by the expected long-run proportions felt by the firm to minimize the cost of capital at the level of capital needs anticipated. The costs of the individual sources must be the current after-tax costs. This can be accomplished usually in the case of notes, bonds, preferred stock, common stock, and commercial paper by computing the market yield to the investor, adjusting wherever possible by the amount of (or estimate of) the costs of securing the capital (flotation charges) and, in the case of debt, for the tax-deductibility of interest expenses.[23] Where the current market yield is not available, it must be estimated. In the case of nonpublic sources such as negotiated term loans and privately held common stock, rates prevailing on competitive market issues will provide approximate current costs. This approach to measurement is satisfactory only as long as the firm can be assumed not to be on the rising portion of its marginal supply curve. As long as it is demanding reasonable amounts of capital in the "flat" region of the sources of supply schedule, this method of measurement will operate satisfactorily. If, however, it is considering larger additions and facing a rising cost of capital curve, it must compute an average cost for each level of capital considered. For our purposes we will presume that most firms

[23] The student should bear in mind that there may be additional costs of capital— those implicit costs to secure the capital and to service the payments. Normally these are relatively insignificant and for most purposes may be ignored.

lie somewhere within the "flat" region of the supply of capital curve. The measurement should use the market values of outstanding securities rather than par or face values. Consider the following rather realistic example. Assume that the Pipeline Company plans only one adjustment in its current mix of sources of capital. The mix of the sources outstanding is given below. The adjusted long-term expected mix of sources (undertaken to

Source	Current Market Value or Estimated Market Value	Percentage of Total Sources
Installment term loans (ten years to final payment)	$ 5,000,000	12.50
Debentures (ten years to maturity)	14,500,000	36.25
Common stock (and retained earnings)	20,500,000	51.25
Total	$40,000,000	100.00

minimize the cost of capital) consists of the following: installment loans, 12.5 per cent; debentures (ten years to maturity), 18.75 per cent; debentures (twenty years to maturity), 18.75 per cent; and common stock plus retained earnings, 50.0 per cent. The cost of twenty-year debentures must be estimated. The after-tax weighted average cost of the adjusted capital structure is computed for the company below. The over-all cost of capital for the Pipeline Company is approximately 4.9 per cent. However, rarely

Source	Cost (per cent)	Proportion of Mix	Cost × Proportion
Installment notes	4.4	0.1250	0.5500
Debentures (ten years)	2.0	0.1875	0.3750
Debentures (twenty years)	2.5	0.1875	0.4688
Common stock and retained earnings	7.0	0.5000	3.5000
Total		1.0000	4.8938

is the adjustment of a firm's capital structure a once-and-for-all proposition as in the illustration. Indeed, the desirable mix for the company may be constantly changing. Should prices in the common stock market move generally upward in relation to profits, the current proportion of the common stock source would tend to increase because the cost of this source would decrease as the price of its stock advances, and it may be desirable to tend toward proportions involving higher relative amounts of common and less of, say, installment notes. The student should be able to answer the question: "What might happen to a business firm's mix of sources if bond prices increased?"

SUMMARY

The cost of capital is an important figure for the firm and is used to help determine the desirability of committing capital to investment proposals. The intersection of a firm's supply and demand schedules would, in theory, determine the investment proposals to accept. The revenues, however, are usually less certain than costs and such considerations detract from the usefulness of the theoretical analysis.

The cost of capital of any particular instrument sold by the firm to investors would be the yield to the investors, with a usually small adjustment for flotation charges. The yield is a function of the risk to the investors and the current position of the *CMC*. The risks to the investors include business, financial, purchasing power, money and market risks. The *CMC* shifts as the supply of and demand for loanable funds shifts and the general slope of the curve may change over time as investors alter their willingness to assume risks.

The cost of capital may be independent of the firm's mix of debt and equity capital. Although one may present a reasonably strong case for this position, most information seems to indicate that certain mixes of sources cause the cost of capital to rise. Perhaps, then, there is, in an operational sense at least, some optimum financial structure which minimizes the cost of capital to the firm.

After securing the current market costs of the various sources, the weighted average cost may be computed. The weights used should be the expected long-run proportions of the various sources which are anticipated to minimize the cost of capital to the firm at a given level of capital demand.

SUGGESTED READINGS

ALLEN, F. B. "Does Going into Debt Lower the 'Cost of Capital'?" *Financial Analysts Journal*, 10 (August 1954), 57–61.

BARGES, ALEXANDER. *The Effect of Capital Structure on the Cost of Capital.* Englewood Cliffs, N. J.: Prentice-Hall, Inc., 1963.

DELANO, MYLES S. "Some Comments on Capital Budgeting and the Cost of Capital," *University of Washington Business Review*, 22 (October 1962), 5–15.

DURAND, DAVID. "The Cost of Capital, Corporation Finance, and the Theory of Investment: Comment," *American Economic Review, 49* (September 1959), 639–54.

———. "Costs of Debt and Equity Funds for Business: Trends and Problems of Measurement," *Conference on Research in Business Finance.* New York: National Bureau of Economic Research, 1952.

MODIGLIANI, FRANCO, and MERTON H. MILLER. "The Cost of Capital, Corporate Finance and the Theory of Investment," *American Economic Review, 48* (June 1958), 261–97.

———. "The Cost of Capital, Corporation Finance, and the Theory of Investment: A Reply," *American Economic Review, 49* (September 1959), 655–69.

SOLOMON, EZRA (ed.). *The Management of Corporate Capital.* New York: The Free Press of Glencoe, Inc., 1959.

SOLOMON, EZRA. "Measuring a Company's Cost of Capital," *Journal of Business, 28* (October 1955), 240–52.

———. *The Theory of Financial Management.* New York: Columbia University Press, 1963.

WESTON, J. FRED. "A Test of Cost of Capital Propositions," *Southern Economic Journal, 30* (October 1963), 105–12.

QUESTIONS

13.1 Should the firm use the average cost or marginal cost of capital for its investment decisions? Explain.

13.2 Under a certainty assumption as to costs and revenues, up to what point should the firm accept investment projects? Is this also true in the case of risk? Explain.

13.3 Is the cost of capital to the firm the same as the expected return to the investors? Explain.

13.4 What are the components of the yield to an investor? Explain them.

13.5 A shift of the *CMC* to the right has what impact on the cost of capital to the firm? Explain.

13.6 Fill in the blanks. (*a*) A decline in yield means price has ———. (*b*) A rise in price means yield has ———. (*c*) A rise in yield means price has ———. (*d*) A decline in price means yield has ———.

13.7 Rank the following according to market risk: (*a*) A 1966 Mustang convertible, (*b*) a share of Boeing Airplane Company stock, (*c*) a custom-made table, and (*d*) a U.S. Treasury bill.

13.8 Would a variation in the ratio of debt to equity cause changes in the cost of capital to the firm? Discuss.

13.9 Should the past or present capital costs be used for decision purposes or should the expected costs of the future be used? Explain.

13.10 (*a*) How is it possible for the prices of high-grade bonds to vary from their face values? (*b*) What impact on a firm's cost of capital do these market price variations have? (*c*) In light of your answers above, what impact will these variations have on the acceptance or rejection of invest-ment proposals? (*d*) In light of your answers above, and any other con-siderations that come to mind, what impact do these variations have on the aggregate present value of the entire firm and the aggregate present value of the ownership commitment?

13.11 In the computation of the cost of common stock, discuss the merits and shortcomings of each of the following: (*a*) the use of current market price; (*b*) the use of average market price over the past year; and (*c*) the use of estimated market price over the economic life of the investment opportunity under review.

PROBLEMS

13.12 Using the data and schedules of Problem 11.13 and multiplying the sources of Problem 12.19 by factors of 10, graphs the resulting schedules. Determine the intersection of the supply and demand functions. How does this affect the investment decision of this case?

13.13 Find the yield to maturity of a 5 per cent bond selling at $980 and maturing in two years, and that of a 5 per cent bond selling at $980 but maturing in five years.

13.14 Calculate the monetary cost of capital of the following sources: (*a*) A $5.50 preferred stock issue that can be sold to the public at $96. The firm must pay a dollar to the investment bankers and thus would net $95. (*b*) Retained earnings when the firm's common stock is selling at $30 a share. The stock pays $1 out of $2 earned in dividends and expected appre-ciation due to reinvestment is $1.25 per year. The average marginal tax rate for shareholders is 30 per cent. Assume company tax rate of 48 per cent.

(c) Depreciation. (d) A ten-year, $1 million term loan which can be obtained at a rate of 4 per cent and which is to be retired in equal annual installments beginning at the end of Period 1.

13.15 The Mueller Mining Company has the sources available as listed in Problem 13.14. Although it does not expect to use all sources in the current year, it feels that its least-cost combination of capital can be secured if it maintains the following capital structure proportions in the future:

Preferred stock	12.5 per cent
Term loan	25 per cent
Common stock and retained earnings	62.5 per cent

Compute their weighted average cost of capital.

13.16 Compute the cost of capital as of July 1, 1967 for a firm having the following capital structure.

Subordinated Debentures, 4½%, due July 1, 1980	$ 5,000,000
Debentures, 5%, due July 1, 1989	10,000,000
Bank Loans, 6%, 3 months duration	10,000,000
Accounts Payable	5,000,000
Accrued Wages	2,000,000
Provision for Income Taxes	3,000,000
Preferred Stock ($100), 5½%	15,000,000
Common Stock ($50)	20,000,000
Paid-in Capital	5,500,000
Reserve for Plant Expansion	10,000,000
Retained Earnings	14,500,000

The Subordinated Debentures were issued on July 1, 1960 and are selling at 97. The Debenture 5's were issued on July 1, 1959 and are selling at 100. The bank loan has a 15 per cent compensating balance requirement. The preferred stock, issued twenty years ago, is selling at $105. Estimated per share earnings for the common stock are $5.40, and current earnings per share are $3.60. The current dividend payout on the common is 60 per cent of available earnings and is expected to be reduced to 40 per cent in the future. The common is currently selling at 64¾. The company's income tax is 50 per cent. Assume the desired capital mix is the present mix and the expected capital gain on common stock is $7.

PART III   FINANCIAL MANAGEMENT

The habit of searching for truth and of energizing it, of marshalling facts in logical order and of extracting a principle, of seeing where that principle can be applied and of applying it, is the real goal of education. Ladling science, Laputa-wise, into the brain of a student to save time is as harmful as ladling soup into his gullet to save teeth. To save teeth we must use them; to know truth we must find it; to win in the long struggle of life we must struggle until we love the struggle. All these seeming paradoxes are equally true. Education should not—indeed cannot—be made easy.[1]

This passage from Gerstenberg typifies well the intent of much of the preceding two parts of the book. But it serves even better to characterize this, the third and final part. Hopefully, by now a sufficient awareness of the importance of capital—both in a real, economic sense and in a liquid (funds), financial sense—has been gained. The two are indeed inextricably intertwined, for the fabric of finance and financial decision-making is not very meaningful until it is related to economic capital. On the other hand, economic capital has little appeal or luster until it takes on some operationally meaningful characteristics, which the study and practice of finance try to give it. Hopefully, the student will have grasped the conceptual framework and the financial aspects of the firm that will enable him to analyze the problems of financing business enterprises, for it is now time to "energize" what we have studied in a logical, systematic way. It is now time to utilize principles already discovered and to extract new ones so that all of them may be applied to the solution of the financial problems of business firms.

---

[1] Charles W. Gerstenberg, *Materials of Corporation Finance* (Englewood Cliffs, N.J.: Prentice-Hall, 1915), vii. Note from *Webster's New Collegiate Dictionary: Laputa:* "In Swift's *Gulliver's Travels*, a flying island whose inhabitants are philosophers, devoted to mathematics and music."

311

This section of text, then, deals with the subject of financial management. We shall be concerned with problems facing the financial decision-maker. In this respect managerial finance is the operation by which sources of capital are secured and applied so as to maximize profits. The operations may be day-to-day or episodic in nature. The day-to-day operations emphasize the problems of providing cash to meet the needs of the firm and the management of sources of supply and the application of funds to maximize profits. The more episodic activities include such events as merger, sale of stock, and retirement of securities.

In theory, firms are assumed to maximize returns to owners. This would be accomplished if a firm's expected marginal costs equaled its expected marginal revenue—unless the commitment is so large relative to the firm's resources that it constitutes a significant threat to survival or there exist varying degrees of risk in estimated marginal costs and marginal revenues, which is almost certainly the case in practice. Up to this point we have discussed only the major aspects of the environment of the business enterprise and the general aspects of firm behavior—those which pertain most importantly to the management of a firm's finances. Most of the discussion has been couched in relative and general terms with little concern for the informational limitations or operational requirements of the enterprise. It was designed to establish a conceptual framework within which operational financial decisions can be made and to expose the structure of the myriad forces impinging upon the financial decision-maker's problems.

Part I dealt primarily with aggregate theoretical and descriptive material pertinent for financial managers. Part II was a narrowing of Part I in that aggregative discussions were abandoned and the focus of attention was on general, theoretical, and descriptive aspects of financing business enterprises. Part III is much more specific in character. It deals with the more concrete methods and techniques used (as well as the reasons for their use) or recommended to be used under varying circumstances. It is an extension of the last two sections in that it concentrates largely on the implementation and integration of the principles and concepts set forth there.

CHAPTER 14

THE SCOPE AND NATURE
OF FINANCIAL
DECISION MAKING

Before we can discuss the what and how of financial decision making within the context of Parts I and II, it is necessary to delineate the scope of authority and the responsibility of the person or persons traditionally implementing these financial tasks. It is to this subject that the present chapter directs itself.

THE FINANCE FUNCTION

The finance function is but one of the important functions that must be performed in a modern, large business. The financial manager's functions and activities cannot be entirely divorced from others in the pursuit of the goals of the firm, predominant among which is maximizing profit. We can conclude the operational function of the financial officer is likewise to promote these profits. But we have also seen that business firms do not operate in a vacuum; rather, they function within a dynamic social and economic environment in which various institutional arrangements bear significantly on business decisions and in which noneconomic considerations may well temper the pursuit of profits.[1]

Based on these few generalizations, the functions of the financial decision-maker can be described.

As mentioned above, paramount among these financial activities is the concerted effort to achieve an optimum financial scheme of things for the firm so as to maximize the welfare of common shareholders. This welfare has been defined as the maximum price of their shares combined with the maximum dividend income less their contributions to the firm consistent with their risk-aversion characteristics. Operationally, this involves decisions regarding the optimum structure of assets and the optimum style of financing; that is, we will be concerned with the best available methods by which capital is secured, allocated, and adjusted. The optimum structure of assets is a matter of economic as well as technologi-

---

[1] In other words, a firm and the persons who perform the tasks of operating it may have other goals and objectives. Although a firm may have such subgoals, its central task is generally and ultimately to enhance profits.

cal considerations. It may be viewed in part within the theory of asset choice in which decisions are based on the expected benefits to be received from various asset choices, the costs of such actions and the feelings of decision-makers regarding these two factors as well as their subjective estimate of risk. In part, the optimum asset structure is dictated by technological constraints necessary for efficient operations. The latter point is a matter of engineering knowhow and the state of the arts. But it is also concerned with the allocation of resources in the firm according to their expected benefits taking into consideration the decision-makers' risk aversions. The optimum style of financing, on the other hand, hinges on economic and institutional considerations. This aspect is concerned with such things as sources of capital, their cost, the mix between debt and equity, attitudes of capital suppliers, and the risk aversions of the decision-makers.

Although these aspects, and others, are to be studied shortly, the basic operational goal of the firm is profit (as previously defined). Some would suggest that survival is the basic goal of the enterprise. In our earlier discussion of this point, we established that, for our purposes, this is a parameter of the financial decision-making process. The question facing us from a managerial point of view is: How can we maximize profits?

Recall, however, that the objectives of business enterprise (and hence that of the financial manager) are derived from the nature of the business enterprise itself. That is to say, the business enterprise in our capitalistic system is so constituted that it is designed to bring together various factors of production in an efficient manner in order to generate outputs of goods and/or services with the ultimate objective of seeking profits. In pursuit of this goal certain institutional arrangements must necessarily be contended with or reconciled. One of the most important of these is the legal form of business and the way in which it affects the form and nature of the contractual relationships of the firm. For the present, a major practical legal aspect of this devolves into a matter of determining the likelihood that a firm will pay its bills on time, the alternative to which may be legal failure. Thus, implicit in the profit objective is a need to maintain the solvency of the firm—to generate sufficient cash with which to meet maturing legal obligations. In an extended sense, dividend requirements on preferred stock may also be considered as falling under the purview of the total obligations of the firm because failure to meet them could seriously impair the firm's credit standing although this would not precipitate legal failure. By the same token, failure to meet dividends on common stock may frequently impair the credit standing of a firm although it will have no adverse legal implications. The essense of the principle suggested here is that capacity to meet all the firm's future "requirements"—legal and nonlegal—is necessary to maintain the continued success of the firm. Profits in themselves are not enough to sustain the firm over long periods; all claims on assets, earnings, and control of the firm have also to be met or serious repercussions may result. The generation of sufficient cash to meet these claims is often referred to as the *liquidity objective* of the firm. *Liquidity*—defined as cash, and resources that can be turned into cash within a relatively short period without an appreciable concession over original cost upon liquidation— is desirable for two major reasons. First, as described above, there are the legal (and credit-standing) consequences of inability to pay bills. Second, uncertainties requiring cash will arise in the future; the firm has little, if any, direct control over these, but it can guard against them by maintaining liquid balances. Even the former objectives, however, can be viewed in the context of profit maximization, because legal failure would preclude the continued pursuit of profits in the long run. Thus the necessity to maintain solvency requires careful cash budgeting and an emphasis on cash flows as conditions precedent to the pursuit of the ultimate goals of the firm: profits. In a sense, then, the financial officer is an "economist," attempting (as he does) to allocate scarce resources among alternative uses so that the marginal expected rate of return to resources devoted to reducing the cost of insolvency equals the marginal expected rate of return to resources used for revenue-producing activities.

In a restricted sense, however, the twin objectives of liquidity and profitability may be viewed as antithetical propositions, because the more liquid the firm's resources are (especially cash), the lower is the percentage of total resources devoted to revenue-producing activities. Yet although the liquidity objective is usually gained only at the expense of the loss of some revenue, a proper allocation of resources among such activities maximizes the profit objectives. This latter point of view implies that investment in cash can be viewed as being productive in and of itself. From the standpoint of a firm, the existence of cash—the proper amount of cash (whatever this may happen to be)—enables it to produce more profits in the long run. This can be done, for example, by having cash on hand to take advantage of purchase opportunities if and when they arise. Also, a certain minimum amount of cash is necessary to maintain the credit position of the firm. Maintenance of a sound credit position should tend to reduce future costs of capital. Hence, maintenance of a "sound" liquidity position may enhance profits, provided that the established liquidity level harmonizes with the nature of the enterprise. Furthermore, in a sense, liquidity is a very short-run proposition whereas profits are a long-run proposition. But, as we know, a series of short-run propositions tend to phase into a long-run proposition, and it is in this time perspective that we ought to view the function of the financial manager; that is, his allocation of and preoccupation with cash resources on a day-to-day basis is with the view to promoting his primary goal of profit maximization in the long-run. By keeping his short-run position secure, he is able to plan for profitability in the long run. In this sense, liquidity is not competing with profitability; rather, it is a means toward the end: profits. And, if capital is viewed as any resource which a firm controls and which will generate income (as previously defined), the liquid assets of the business enterprise can be viewed as promoting profits. The test of capital procurement and administration lies in the efficient utilization of these resources to enhance the value of the enterprise.

The finance function, then, ideally involves efforts to derive a financial scheme that will tend to maximize returns to common stockholders while making provision for solvency. Moreover, viewing liquidity and revenue-producing objectives as essentially complementary propositions, financial management must maintain a proper balance between the two. Providing capital to pay bills when they come due and providing the best returns possible when using capital promotes the maximum welfare of common shareholders. To this end the allocation and control of all financial resources of the firm is essential. These aspects of financial management and control will be discussed in the ensuing chapters.

FINANCIAL MANAGEMENT—AN OVERVIEW

Having postulated maximum welfare to residual shareholders as the prime objective of financial management, a question would then naturally arise: How will this goal be achieved? Central to the achievement of this goal is the investment decision-making process and the means of financing those investments selected. All costs other than those associated with financing the enterprise are assumed to be minimized in a rational way. Many general considerations contribute to profit maximization. Such things as limited entry into an industry, technical superiority, innovations, and favorable changes in expectations all tend to promote profits. They all tend to alter either expected rates of return or risk magnitudes or both. In addition to these considerations, normal rates of growth in the typically exogenous variables of microeconomic analysis will likewise generate changes in the value of the ownership of a firm. These variables—technology, population, incomes, tastes, and conditions of ownership of the factors of production—are held constant in static, microeconomic analysis. This is not altogether unrealistic either, for these are uncontrollable variables from the standpoint of the firm and ordinarily do not have a significant influence on the firm in the short run because meaningful changes in them usually take place only over extended periods of time. The *CMC* summarizes the investment conditions—supply *and* demand—that prevail in the market, taking into consideration both risk and expected rate of return. Because the *CMC* represents a convergence of aggregate investment opportunities, the "normal" rates of change in the exogenous variables of static, microeconomic analysis affect the whole of the capital market and nearly all firms (investment opportunities) will experience changes in the values of ownerships. None of these changes would necessarily move any firm to the right of the *CMC*, however, but because changes brought about by changes in the exogenous variables will not affect each firm in the same way, some firms will experience more than normal changes in their operations, tending to move them to the right of the *CMC*, at least for the short-term, and others will experience less than normal changes, moving them to the left, even though these changes will have a rather uniform effect on the whole of the *CMC*.

Efforts to find investments that lie to the right of the *CMC* are usually couched in such economic terms as *innovations, differentiated products, limited entry,* and other imperfections in the market—problems with which the financial manager needs to be intimately concerned. Many of the physical activities associated with these concepts, however, when formulated as operational policies, typically fall outside the realm of his specific purview. His involvement arises when capital is needed to promote certain objectives that fall within these categories. The financial manager's efforts should be directed to allocating capital to investments which would be located to the right of the *CMC* through superior management of financial resources and taking into account the needs of these other internal as well as external requirements that impinge upon his enterprise. It is this latter point and the techniques used to obtain these results that will be our concern in the rest of the book.

We can also postulate that the financial manager's concern is with the composition of at least some of the firm's assets, the composition of the sources of capital used to finance these assets, and the methods used to adjust these sources. The size of the firm is a matter of firm objectives. The financial manager's involvement in these decisions is a continuous one, for it entails decisions to expand, methods by which expansion is to take place, determination of the profitability of various ways to expand —as well as decisions to contract the firm's scale of operations, to change the method of operations, to continue present operations or to replace them with more efficient ones, and to abandon certain aspects of the operation of the firm.

Furthermore, any given business operation that is to be run efficiently must bring together the best physical combination of the economic factors of production. Efficient operation of an automobile plant dictates a minimum level of operations. This is a physical constraint to automobile production; it says nothing about the style of the automobiles to be sold, the distribution system to be used, or the promotional program necessary to market the automobiles. The efficient operation of a grocery store requires display racks, shelves, freezer cabinets, refrigeration units, checkout counters, cash registers, and storage facilities. In each of these examples due weight must be given to the amount and/or quality of each of the considerations mentioned. What is the proper amount of advertising for automobile producers? What is the proper size refrigeration unit for a grocery store? What combination of available floor space and display shelves will assure a smooth flow of customer traffic and still provide ample shelving for merchandise displays? And what number of employees should either the automobile manufacturer or the grocer hire? How many should be skilled and what skills should they possess? How many should be supervisory and what degree of supervisory competence do they need? Where shall the automobile plant or the grocery store be located? Should the plant be rented, or bought outright? What about the grocery store? Should the land be rented or purchased? Would it make any difference if the plant or the store were rented?

Obviously, the questions could go on. And the answer to any one question would probably always include the words *it depends* or their equivalent. That is to say, the answer to any one of the above questions would "depend on" the answer to a number of the other questions posed. To break the endless circle posed by this dilemma, one might rank these considerations according to the amount of cash outlay they will require and consider only the top three or four cash outlays at one time. If a decision as to plant location, say, will materially affect the size and quality of the labor force as well as shipping costs (part of the distribution system), then a different combination of these three considerations might result in different solutions to the problem. In effect, any one of these variables, assuming close interdependency, could be more dominant than others under a given scheme. The object is to derive that combination of variables that will provide the best solution to the over-all problem. In short, the engineering requirements (the best combination of economic factors of production) are such that they dictate the scale and location of operations necessary for efficiency. The financial manager has little direct control over these engineering requirements. He does have a role in the decision-making process, however. It arises when estimates concerning the profitability and costs of a given scheme of factor combinations is proposed. Based on his estimates will be the decisions as to which combination to accept or reject.

Another problem area to be explored more fully is that of asset composition—the problem of determining that level of various asset investment required to operate the enterprise profitably. Existing assets represent past investment decisions, presumably efficient compositions when the investment decisions are made. The essential guide in this process is the *potential profitability* of the existing and proposed investments. In our discussion of this topic we will view all the elements typically found on the lefthand side of a balance sheet as investments. That is to say, a firm makes investments in cash and receivables and as well as in inventories and fixed assets. We are interested in the means used to determine the amount of investment that must be made in each of these to maximize profits. Coincidental to this determination we may employ a budget. A *budget* is a written plan of a firm's expected activity and, as such, serves as a guide for action. To determine working-capital investments, we will use a budget covering a limited time period (usually no more than a year). A short-term budget of considerable importance in finance is the *cash budget,* which summarizes the inflow and outflow of cash during a given period based on forecasts of sales, inventory, and receivables.

Discussion of longer-term capital investments (usually more than a year in duration) falls under the category of *capital budget.* This process entails the determination of the profitability of current cash outlays (and ones that will be made in the future) relative to the present value of the future cash benefits to be derived from the outlay.[2] In this discussion of long-term investments we will also consider the purchase of other companies. As part of the determination of long-term investments we will also see that consideration of replacement of assets is important, as well as decisions concerning disposal of assets and extinguishment of debt and equity sources of capital.

Finally, consideration of the composition of financing, or the style by which the firm is financed, will eventually take us to a discussion of financial analysis. External financial analysis will present the conceptual framework which outsiders (more appropriately, suppliers of capital) typically use to evaluate the financial integrity of the firm. At that point it will become apparent that the methods and procedures employed by

[2] The current cash outlay required for long-term investments of this sort is incorporated into the cash budget when the outlay is made.

segments of this outsider group are woefully inadequate for purposes of financial management. Having already discussed working-capital investments, long-term commitments, and their analysis, we will find that these considerations serve as the basis for internal financial management. We will discuss and analyze the procedures for selection of various courses of action based on internal needs. Because the conditions under which a firm operates may change considerably over time, we will also discuss the methods used or to be used to adjust financial resources and the conditions under which such adjustments may be appropriate.

SUMMARY

Managerial finance may be characterized as being concerned with the systematic assembly, presentation, and analysis of qualitative and quantitative considerations on which financial managers as well as suppliers of capital will base judgments concerning the short-run and long-run financial integrity of the firm under review and which will enable them to assess and enhance the value of the enterprise. Determining the scale of operations of the enterprise, the composition of its assets, and the style in which the assets are financed are primary considerations. The techniques employed to achieve the goals of the enterprise must be as efficient as possible in order to minimize the cost of operations and/or maximize revenues. To pursue these long-run goals, firms must maintain their legal solvency over the short run, thus emphasizing the need for liquidity.

SUGGESTED READINGS

American Management Association. *The Financial Executive's Job.* New York: The Association, 1952.

——. *The Financial Manager's Job.* New York: The Association, 1964.

ANTHONY, ROBERT N. "The Trouble with Profit Maximization," *Harvard Business Review,* 38 (November–December 1960), 126–34.

DAUTEN, CARL A. "The Necessary Ingredients of a Theory of Business Finance," *The Journal of Finance,* 10 (May 1955), 107–20.

The Duties of Financial Executives. New York: National Industrial Conference Board, 1952.

GORDON, MYRON J. "Security and a Financial Theory of Investment," *Quarterly Journal of Economics,* 74 (August 1960), 472–92.

MOLLER, GEORGE. "The Financial Executive: His Role in Over-all Planning," *The Controller,* 30 (January 1962), 17–18.

ROBBINS, SIDNEY, and EDWARD FOSTER, JR. "Profit Planning and the Finance Function," *The Journal of Finance,* 12 (December 1957), 451–67.

SCHWARTZ, ELI. "Theory of the Capital Structure of the Firm," *The Journal of Finance, 14* (March 1959), 18–39.

SHUBIK, MARTIN. "Objective Functions and Models of Corporate Organization," *Quarterly Journal of Economics, 75* (August 1961), 345–75.

WESTON, J. FRED. "The Finance Function," *The Journal of Finance, 9* (September 1954), 265–82.

QUESTIONS

14.1 Why is solvency important to the firm's stockholders?

14.2 Define *liquidity?* What firm assets contribute to liquidity?

14.3 What is the cost to the firm of not meeting requirements for preferred dividends?

14.4 How does the liquidity objective conflict with the profitability objective? Are the two really in conflict?

14.5 Comment on the statement "Cash is productive."

14.6 What are the important functions of the financial manager in the modern business?

14.7 Why are the decisions of a financial manager so important to the firm?

14.8 Define *budget.* Differentiate between *cash budget* and *capital budget.*

14.9 It has been stated that the primary function of the financial manager is to have enough cash on hand to pay bills. Comment on the reality or lack thereof of this position.

This chapter is concerned with the liquidity problem facing financial managers. The central question to which we will seek answers is: What types (and how much of each) of the current assets are proper in order to maximize the returns to the owners of the firm? Too much cash, receivables, and inventory result in excessive capital investment—and excessive capital costs reduce the rate of return to shareholders; yet restrictive credit policies or stockouts increase the chances of insolvency and the amount of lost sales. It is the task of financial management to strike a near-optimum mix and quantity of current assets so that there is neither too much nor too little working capital.

WORKING CAPITAL

Working or *circulating capital* was defined as capital circulating into cash over an operating cycle. Customarily, working capital is equated with all the current assets. Although one year is the period frequently assumed to cover the operating cycle of a firm, in fact it may be four months or sixteen months—and, for certain purposes, these operating cycles are more useful analytical periods.[1] The illustration on the inside cover of the text depicts the typical flow of such an operating cycle. This represents a short cycle—"short" in the sense that only the current assets are shown. A long cycle consists of capital circulating into cash over a time interval long enough to include the cash recovery of fixed assets—that is, the gradual recovery of original cash expenditures on fixed assets through collections on sales (assuming prices cover costs including depleciation). A short cycle is also depicted in Figure 15-1. A long cycle is shown in Figure 15-2.

Before proceeding further, however, it is important to emphasize the distinction between stocks and flows. The balance in the cash (checking) account measures the stock of cash. The flow may be an inflow or out-

---

[1] An operating cycle is the time required for cash to make a complete cycle— from cash to inventory to accounts receivable and into cash again. For an elaborate discussion of the use of the operating cycle, see: Colin Park and John W. Gladson, *Working Capital* (New York: Macmillan, 1963).

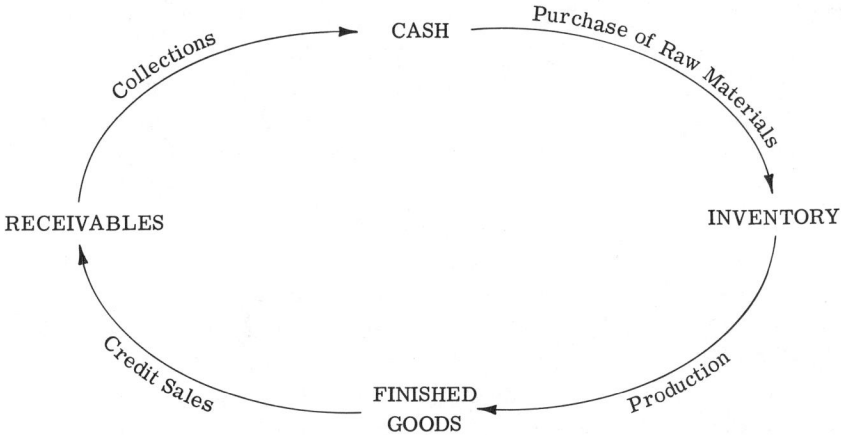

Figure 15-1   A Short Cycle for Generating Cash. *Source:* Adapted from Jules I. Bogen (ed.), *Financial Handbook* (3rd ed.). (New York: The Ronald Press Company, 1952), p. 711.

flow. If the inflow exceeds the outflow, the stock will rise (and vice versa). The *stock* is measured at a point in time such as that reflected on a balance sheet. A *flow* must be measured as a rate per period of time—such as income per year (for example, the income statement) or cash inflow per month. Both stocks and flows of this sort are of prime interest to the financial manager because the absolute amount of cash as well as the rate

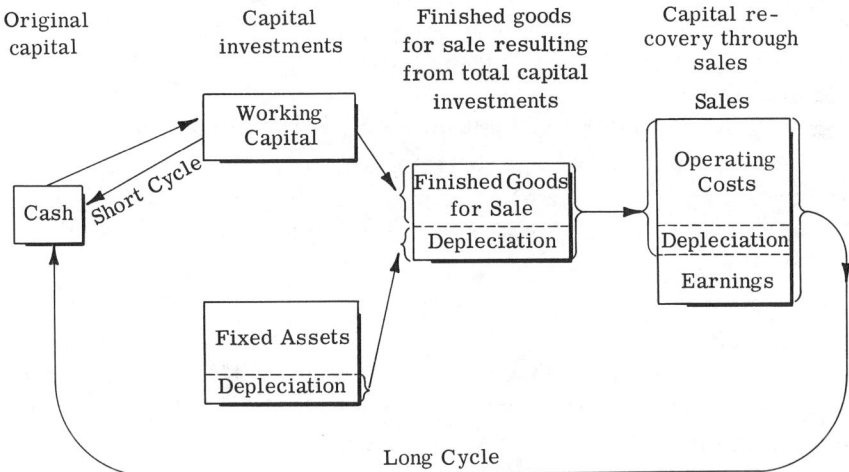

Figure 15-2   A Long Cycle for Generating Cash. *Source:* Adapted from: Arthur H. Winakor, "Maintenance of Working Capital of Industrial Corporations by Conversion of Fixed Assets," *University of Illinois Bulletin XXXI*, 21 (Urbana, Illinois: University of Illinois, Bureau of Business Research, January 23, 1934), p. 8.

at which it flows through the business as a result of operations determines to a large extent the ability of the firm to pay bills, to take on new capital projects, to pay dividends, and to make a host of other financial decisions. *Cash flow* or *net cash inflow* arising out of operations are interchangeable terms used to describe the difference between the inflows and the outflows but excluding capital expenditures and capital distributions, debt repayments, and dividends or other nonoperational flows. These net flows obviously may also take on negative values. Without capital expenditures or capital distributions, the net cash inflow would describe the rate of increase in the level of the cash balance—the stock of cash. The stock of cash, accounts receivable, and inventory are indicated in the cover illustration by tanks. Working capital is the sum of the dollar amounts in these tanks. The flows are illustrated by the pipes.

Net working capital is defined as the difference between *working capital* and *short-term liabilities*. It is that portion of working capital that should be financed by long-term and permanent capital sources. As a general rule of thumb, net working capital should equal the difference between the minimum amount of current liabilities and current assets at about the lowest level of a "normal" operating cycle. Current asset needs above this amount are used only at special times of the year and, as a general rule, can be more cheaply financed by short-term lending sources than by long-term debt or ownership investments. *Minimum current liabilities* are the amount of accruals and accounts payable in existence at the lowest level of the normal operating cycle and ordinarily cannot conveniently be further reduced. They involve no explicit cost of capital to the firm.

We shall now return to methods of working-capital financing. For the present, it is sufficient to state that there should be a level of working capital and net working capital that maximizes profits. It is the job of the financial manager to determine and seek these levels.

INSOLVENCY

Inasmuch as this discussion involves liquidity, it also involves firm survival; thus the nature, degrees, and types of business failure need to be examined briefly at this point. We shall refer to *technical insolvency* as the inability of the firm to meet cash payments on contractual obligations. The lack of cash to meet payments of accounts payable, wages, taxes, interest, and debt retirement will constitute technical insolvency even though the enterprise may have a substantial and adequate dollar value of assets. When assets are plentiful, it is usually not difficult for the firm to plan ahead and arrange for sufficient cash through various sources to prevent any embarrassment. In most cases, any temporary lack of liquidity can be overcome by borrowing or through the planned liquidation of certain assets (especially short-term ones). A sound, profitable business should have no difficulty in this regard, and reasonably intelligent planning would ward off the danger. If the firm is in difficulty because of successive losses or insufficient original investment in working capital, lenders will be less willing to place funds at its disposal. The firm should be aware of the potential variability that exists in the availability of funds. The "willing" lender is often less willing during periods of "tight" money, great financial uncertainty, or panic.

Legal insolvency exists when a firm's recorded assets amount to *less than its recorded liabilities.*[2] This condition arises when successive losses create a deficit in the owners' equity account, rendering it incapable of supporting the firm's legal liabilities. The firm may be liquid and paying its current bills, but it can be legally insolvent. For many types of financial institutions, legal insolvency forces the firm into immediate bankruptcy status. In other cases, the insolvency casts enough doubts about the ability of the firm to pay its obligations that its creditors might all insist on payment of their claims as soon as possible. Such a situation usually leads to technical insolvency and bankruptcy. A firm that runs out of cash, even though profitable and not legally insolvent, will usually be forced into bankruptcy.

Consider the following hypothetical case of the very profitable Stevenson Indian Sales Company. The firm went broke because it had too little cash, even though its earnings were substantial. The company manufactured a very popular new gun. The gun cost $7.50 to make and sold for $10. Stevenson followed the policy of keeping an anticipated thirty-day supply of guns on hand—that is, of producing an inventory in one month sufficient to take care of its projected sales for the succeeding month. The sales manager predicted an increase in sales of 500 units each month beginning in March. The terms of sale were n/30 and all receivables were collected at the beginning of the month following the sale. The company's policy was to pay its bills promptly. The company also leased all its fixed assets and its total costs of production were equal to the total cash outlays shown in Table 15-1. From this table it can be seen that as of January 1, 1865, the company had a working capital position consisting of $10,000 in cash, $7,500 in inventory, and $10,000 in accounts receivable. Table 15-1 also illustrates the changes in the firm's liquidity and profitability. The lower portion of the table indicates the month-to-

[2] Under some state laws, however, insolvency is the inability to pay bills.

Table 15-1 Stevenson Indian Sales Company, 1865

	January	February	March	April	May	June
Cash (beginning of month)	$10,000	$12,500	$11,250	$ 6,250	$ 2,500	$ 0
Receivables 1st of month (preceding month's sales)	10,000	10,000	10,000	15,000	20,000	25,000
Inventories 1st of month (for next month)						
Dollars (@ $7.50 per unit)	7,500	11,250	15,000	18,750	22,500	26,250
Units	1,000	1,500	2,000	2,500	3,000	3,500
Production (for next month)						
Dollars (@ $7.50 per unit)	7,500	11,250	15,000	18,750	22,500	26,250
Units	1,000	1,500	2,000	2,500	3,000	3,500
Sales						
Dollars (@ $10 per unit)	10,000	10,000	15,000	20,000	25,000	30,000
Units	1,000	1,000	1,500	2,000	2,500	3,000
Accounting costs (75% of Sales)	7,500	7,500	11,250	15,000	18,750	22,500
Monthly profits	2,500	2,500	3,750	5,000	6,250	7,500
Cumulative profits	2,500	5,000	8,750	13,750	20,000	27,500
Cash inflows:						
Cash on hand	10,000	12,500	11,250	6,250	2,500	0
Receivables (preceding month's sales)	10,000	10,000	10,000	15,000	20,000	25,000
	20,000	22,500	21,250	21,250	22,500	25,000
Cash outflows:						
Production (current month)	7,500	11,250	15,000	18,750	22,500	26,250
Net cash flow	$12,500	$11,250	$ 6,250	$ 2,500	$ 0	($ 1,250)

month cash flow. (Of course, there were no income taxes in 1865.) Notice that the firm's cash position eventually was reduced to zero—which, presumably, rendered it incapable of paying its bills as they came due (that is, it became technically insolvent). The requirements for increased investments in inventory and receivables were so demanding because of the rapid expansion of sales that all the available cash at the beginning of the period as well as the net cash inflow resulting from operations were inadequate to meet all the firm's needs—all of this in spite of the firm's seemingly good earnings status. This extreme example demonstrates a fact often unrecognized by some financial managers: the rapid growth of a firm frequently results in the painfully late realization of the necessity for additional financing to maintain liquidity.

It is not unusual for a financially embarrassed firm to avoid bankruptcy by some sort of "workout" arrangement with its creditors. The creditors may not wish to sue for satisfaction if it appears that they would recover a smaller proportion of their claim by so doing. The workout requires the agreement of all creditors and the loss of some or all management control by the owners. Frequently, small creditors may try to hold up an agreement to a workout and thus force the major creditors to advance enough funds to pay off the recalcitrants in full or in proportions greater than those received by other creditors. If the workout is successful, in time major creditors will be able to look forward to full satisfaction of their claims and will avoid bankruptcy proceedings and its attendant court costs (including foreclosure or reorganization costs). Cash and liquidity management, then, can have rather ominous ramifications which could be unprofitable to shareholders. Obviously, desirable levels (stocks) of cash and rates of cash flow are important in this regard, and our discussion now turns to these topics.

THE NEED FOR THE STOCK OF CASH

The same *motives for holding cash* in the economy also exist in the firm; these are, as you will recall, transaction, precaution, and speculation.[3] If the cash inflow equaled cash outflow at all times, there would be no necessity to hold cash for transaction purposes. The two, however, are usually not perfectly synchronized. Even if they were *expected* to be synchronized perfectly, the firm faces considerable uncertainty about the synchronization being realized. Such uncertainty requires most firms to hold cash for precautionary purposes should the expected inflow lag behind the expected outflow. On occasion the firm will hold cash in expecta-

[3] *See* Chapter 6.

tion of price declines in items to be purchased. Traditionally, however, businesses are ill advised to attempt to profit by such speculative activities; their function is customarily to produce a good or service, not to speculate.

Planning for a stock of cash at a point in time for transactions and precautionary purposes involves a study of cash inflows and outflows from operations. A firm might well plot its cash flow for a typical month, as is shown in Figure 15-3. Curve CO, in which the discrete daily points have been connected for visual presentation, represents cash outlays. Points A, A', A", A''' on the curve represent peaks caused by weekly wage payments; Point B represents the peak of cash outlays for payment of accounts payable. Curve CI represents cash inflows. From the 1st to the 4th of the month the cash outflow exceeds the cash inflow and the stock of cash on Day 1 must be sufficient to cover this transactions gap of $19,000. As of the first of the month, $19,000 was the expected cash needed for transactions purposes. From Point C to D there is no need for a cash balance for transactions purposes, but by Day 17 the cash balance should be $36,000 ($17,000 plus $19,000 for the beginning of the next month). In this example there were assumed to be twenty-two business days and each succeeding month would be like the preceding ones. Payments for interest, dividends, or capital expenditures are nonoperating cash outlays and separate consideration must be made for them. A business with seasonal activity will likely need separate cash analysis for nonnormal months. If the estimates are not accurate, more or less than the estimated needed cash will be required. Moreover, the amount of cash needed by a firm generally does not grow proportionately with sales.

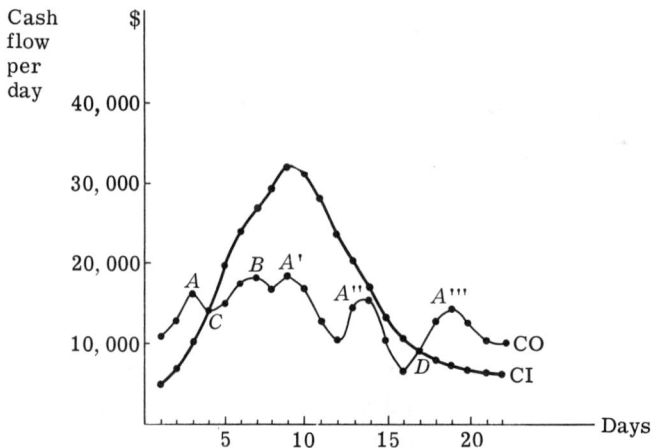

Figure 15-3   Cash Flows for One Month

For precautionary purposes, additional cash should be available, especially during the first five days and the last five days. Point A'' is a little too close to being equal to cash inflows not to allow for an additional margin as well. To establish the addition to cash balance for the precautionary motive, the firm should consider plotting a number of such charts, or one depicting just the *net* cash flow. Figure 15-4 illustrates a typical firm's precautionary analysis through the plot of many months. This gives a firm a good impression of the expected variability in net cash flows. It could then proceed to tabulate these, compute a mean for each day, derive its cash balance for transactions purposes, and compute a measure of variability (such as the standard deviation). If the sample of months were large enough so that the mean and the standard deviation could be considered a reliable estimate of the true mean and variability in the population, and if the deviations from the mean are normally distributed, management may decide what likelihood of running out of cash it is willing to accept. If it wishes to bear the risk only one time in 10,000, then it ought to add to the transactions cash balance an amount equal to about 3.7 times the standard deviation (which is found by finding the standard deviation corresponding to .4999 in a table of areas under one half the standard normal curve). For example, if the standard deviation for the cash balance required on the first day of the month is $2,000, then the firm should add $7,400 (3.7 × $2,000) in order to avoid assuming a magnitude of risk greater than one chance out of 10,000 of having a cash stockout. In this case the firm would need a cash balance of about $26,400 on the first day of the month. A lower balance would mean that the firm

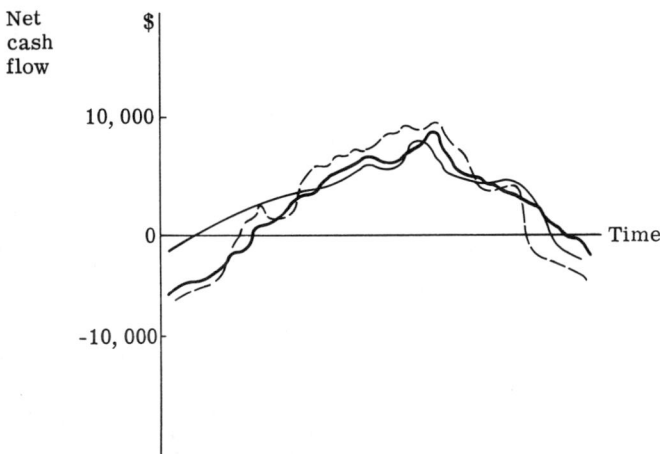

Figure 15-4   Net Cash Flows for an Extended Time Period

runs a greater risk. Any desires for holding cash for speculative purposes should be added to this balance. It is obvious from the foregoing that seasonal and nonroutine cash analysis requires rather detailed planning.

THE CASH BUDGET

A *cash budget* provides detailed, short-term cash planning, predicting all inflows and outflows of cash and the expected shortage of cash at points over a period of six to twelve months. The cash budget is an important tool for the financial manager in maintaining liquidity and will tend to point out any occasions when the cash on hand is insufficient to meet the needs of the firm or periods when there is an excess of cash above that needed by the firm. Inasmuch as this budget is concerned with cash, it ignores the noncash items a profit-and-loss statement includes. Monthly periods constitute a convenient length of time for measuring the cash flows into and out of the firm because they are short enough to indicate seasonal variations in cash needs.

The information necessary for the preparation of the budget includes a sales forecast by months, in order to estimate collections on receivables and to estimate variable cash costs. There exist numerous methods of estimating sales. It is not our purpose here to go into forecasting methods, but regression and time-series analysis[4] are among the more useful tools employed for this purpose. Sales of appliances, for example, may be estimated by a multiple-regression model including such independent variables as disposable income, rate of household formation, and data on the replacement cycle. These estimates may be subjectively modified by the management staff for variables not considered in the statistical analysis. Statistical estimates may be adjusted for information from the sales force about new competitive forces or new products, for example. Armed with sales estimates, selling credit terms, and experience data on the collection of receivables, cash receipts can be estimated. For example, if January sales are estimated to be $20,000 and the firm sells on ordinary terms of $n/30$, it could examine its previous collection experience to determine that 90 per cent ($18,000) of January sales are collected in February, 9 per cent ($1,800) are collected in March, and 1 per cent are not expected to be collected at all.

From the sales predictions and the current level of inventory, the

[4] For the use of time-series analysis in forecasting see: John Neter and William Wasserman, *Fundamental Statistics for Business and Economics,* 2nd ed. (Boston: Allyn, 1961), 671–708; for the use of regression analysis in forecasting, see: Robert Ferber and P. J. Verdoorn, *Research Methods in Economics and Business* (New York: Macmillan, 1962), 91–101.

firm may plan its production rate; this will enable it to compute cash outlays for purchases of materials and labor. The purchases have to be ordered early enough to assure delivery by the time the material is needed for production (a stock of such materials will be planned for an inventory if there is uncertainty in the time lag between sales and delivery or in the production rate) and the invoice data can be estimated from previous experience which, when used with purchase credit terms, can be used to determine a payments schedule on accounts payable. A lead time of 30 days would generally require that orders for materials for January production be made in December, delivered in January, and paid for in February (assuming credit terms received were *n*/30). In a seasonal business, the decision as to whether the firm should seek level production with lower per unit costs and larger inventories or fluctuating production with small inventories depends upon such variables as inventory carrying costs, cost of obsolescence risk, overtime rates, and employment and discharge costs. An analytical model for this problem has been developed; although it is not perfect, it arrives at reasonable decisions.[5] To simplify the following analysis, the more common cash expenditures and cash receipts can be enumerated as follows:

Cash Receipts:

Cash sales
Collection on accounts receivable
Sales of securities
Loans
Sales of assets

Cash Outlays:

Accounts payable
Wages and salaries
Income taxes
Insurance
Advertising
Utilities
Interest on bonds and notes
Dividends or withdrawals
Retirements of loans or securities
Capital expenditures

These may be organized into a worksheet such as that illustrated in Table 15-2. As inferred in the preceding paragraph, it is assumed that purchases of materials and supplies are ordered a month ahead of production, delivered at the beginning of the month of production, and paid for at the beginning of the month following production. It is also assumed that 90 per cent of sales are collected in the first month following sale and 9 per cent in the second month. It is further assumed that Accounts Receivable outstanding on January 1 are $20,000 and Accounts Payable

[5] Charles C. Holt, *et al., Planning Production, Inventories, and Work Force* (Englewood Cliffs, N.J.: Prentice-Hall, 1960).

Table 15-2   D. Johnson Beverage Sales Company Cash Budget Worksheet, 1967

		January	February	March	April	May	June
I.	Sales	$20,000	$26,000	$35,000	$50,000	$40,000	$30,000
II.	Receipts:						
	Collections	19,800	19,800	25,200	33,840	48,150	40,500
	Other						2,000
	Total receipts	$19,800	$19,800	$25,200	$33,840	$48,150	$42,500
III.	Purchases (delivered, net of cash discount)	13,000	17,500	25,000	20,000	15,000	15,000
IV.	Payment on purchases	10,000	13,000	17,500	25,000	20,000	15,000
	Wages and salaries	3,000	3,500	5,000	4,000	3,000	3,000
	Utilities	300	350	500	400	300	300
	Security payments or retirements (Term loan)		1,500			1,500	
	Other outlays	100	450		200		
	Income tax payments			5,000			4,000
	Dividends	2,000			2,000		
	Capital outlays	5,000	500	1,500		16,000	
	Total expenditures	$20,400	$19,300	$29,500	$31,600	$40,800	$22,300
V.	Net cash inflow (Loss)	(600)	500	(4,300)	2,240	7,350	20,200
VI.	Cash balance would be (End of month, assuming no loans)	3,000	3,500	(800)	5,240	10,350	28,990
VII.	Loan balance	—	—	3,800	—	—	—
	Repayment	—	—	—	2,240	1,560	—
VIII.	Actual cash balance (End of month, including loans and repayment)	$ 3,000	$ 3,500	$ 3,000	$ 3,000	$ 8,790	$28,990

as of that date are $10,000. Other assumptions are self-evident in the data. It has been estimated that a beginning-of-the-month cash balance of $3,000 is necessary to take care of intramonth transactions as well as to provide a "cushion" for variation in the expected receipts and expenditures pattern. The initial cash balance on January 1 is $3,600. Basing its decision upon these estimates, the firm should plan to borrow $3,800 in March, and to repay it in April and May. If it were not for projected capital expenditures in January, the firm would not have to borrow. Knowing when cash deficiencies will arise, however, enables the firm to seek out sources of capital to fill the gap well in advance of need. By contrast, managment, in viewing the extra-large predicted cash balances in May and June, should consider alternative uses of these funds so as to maximize profits. If all the cash is not needed for dividends or capital expenditures immediately, consideration should be given to investing the funds in short-term securities or, perhaps, to repaying outstanding liabilities (which is just another form of investment). Funds could be used, for example, to repay a short-term or term loan and, when needed later in the year, a loan could be recreated. Decisions to move into and out of short-term investments, whatever their nature, must also account for the attendant transactions costs involved to determine the feasibility of the investment.

The foregoing discussion indicates that the cash budget is extremely useful as a planning tool—planning for new borrowing or replacement of existing debt, for dividend payments, for cash outlays, for capital expenditures, or for any cash flow. Obviously, the cash budget is based on estimates and the further a period is from the present the more uncertain are the estimates. And the more subjective the estimates the more likely it is that they will be subject to the biases of optimistic salesmen and managers. The concern over long-run liquidity must be approached in a similar but more generalized manner.

MANAGEMENT OF CASH

The financial manager must make certain that the investment in cash is efficiently used. The need for a precautionary balance within the month may often be reduced if the availability of other sources of funds is a certain and sufficiently reliable source of support to the company in the case of need. A "rich uncle" may be the best and cheapest precautionary reserve to the maximizing nephew. Long-term, good relationships with banks customarily make for a good precautionary reserve; their cooperation and availability needs to be counted upon. It has been said that more care should be used in selecting a bank than in selecting a wife.

In order to minimize *cash "leaks,"* the firm should establish some sort of control system over incoming cash. If the receipt of such funds can be broken up into two or three steps and responsibility for each assigned to different employees, the ability to embezzle is greatly reduced. Collusion between two or more people is usually difficult to achieve. Petty-cash funds should also be under a tight control system. Checks made in payment for bills received also should be made out under a strict control system to assure that checks are paid for materials actually ordered and received.

Checks received should be quickly deposited in order to speed the collection process and maximize the cash balance. Such reductions of "float" (checks in the process of collection) tend to increase the cash balance, reduce receivables and reduce the risk of holding uncollectible checks. Another way of increasing the cash balance—or, in other words, to make efficient use of the cash resources—is to delay payment on bills until the end of the no-cost period. Early payment reduces cash needlessly. If credit terms are 1/10, $n/30$, the payment should be delayed to the tenth day. Disbursement delays may also be accomplished by using drafts (an order by the firm to the bank to pay the supplier). In this case the draft is mailed to the supplier on the tenth of the month; he then has his bank present it to the firm's bank, and only then does the firm need to provide the cash for payment of the draft. Such a cash saving may involve some fees paid to the bank for the service.

Temporary excess cash balances may be invested to earn some return. Such idle funds should be invested only in United States bills, high-grade commercial paper, short-term municipal bonds, or certificates of deposit.[6] These low-risk investment outlets may also be used for the precautionary portion of the firm's cash balance.

LONG-RUN LIQUIDITY

The firm may also be interested in the maintenance of long-run liquidity, a flow of liquid assets needed to meet long-run cash commitments. *Variable* cash costs are likely to be covered by collections on sales in a rational business operation and the problem of this sort of liquidity

[6] Certificates of deposit represent deposits of funds with a bank but are negotiable. Their maturities vary in length but are never longer than one year. Since their inception in 1961, they have become a very popular and important investment medium for investors seeking short-term, high-grade opportunities. In 1964 the total amount outstanding aggregated almost $14 billion. See: Richard Fieldhouse, *Certificates of Deposit,* "Bank Study Series" (Boston: Bankers, 1962); and "Negotiable Time Certificates of Deposit," *Federal Reserve Bulletin, 49* (April 1963), 458–68.

is not significant for long-run analysis. *Nonvariable* cash outlays, however, are of general concern. No matter what the level of operations is, these bills must be met. These include such items as property taxes, interest on bonds, dividends on preferred stocks, term-loan payments, sinking-fund payments required by bond indentures, other debt retirement and nonvariable lease payments.

In cases in which fixed cash outlays must be paid for a number of years into the future, the current stock of cash becomes rather inconsequential. The size of the expected net cash flow is the best general measure of a firm's long-run ability to meet the fixed cash payments. The firm may compute average annual net cash flow based upon the past experience in receipts and expenditures. Or, more accurately, it estimates future operating receipts and expenditures based upon estimates of future sales and costs.

Long-run net cash flow can be approximated rather well as the sum of net income after taxes plus any noncash charges made against revenue in the determination of net income. These noncash charges usually take the form of depreciation, but there may occasionally be other noncash charges under various amortization schemes or appropriations to equity reserves from income which should be included. Consequently, the figure for long-run liquidity would be the sum of net income after taxes plus all noncash charges made against revenue in determining the income. Moreover, generation of cash over extended periods of time can be enhanced by minimizing tax expenditures. For example, the use of accelerated depreciation wherever possible increases the total amount of depreciation deductible for tax purposes and reduces the tax burden (cash outlays) during the period of use. And, although it cannot be denied that such rapid amortization of facilities defers the tax burden to future periods and that the same aggregate amount of tax will be paid (if there are no reductions in tax rates), it must be remembered that a dollar today is worth more than a dollar tomorrow because it can earn interest during the period involved. In effect, the government provides an interest-free loan.

In general, adjustments will have to be made in the net cash flow estimate before it can be related to such outlays as interest and lease payments. Because interest may be deducted as a cost before determining taxable income, the net cash flow should be adjusted by using net income before income taxes. We shall keep in mind, however, that the dollars for preferred dividends or term-loan payments must be earned after the federal income tax deduction. Another adjustment in the net cash flow is the addition, to the net cash figure, of the payments for the interest itself. The adjusted net cash flow may now be compared to the fixed cash outlays. For purposes of illustration we shall use the following information from the statement (assumed to be representative of future statements) of A. Olson, Inc. The net cash flow would be computed as the sum of net income after taxes ($3,000) plus depleciation ($10,000) plus amortization of patents ($4,000), or $17,000. The adjusted net cash

A. Olson, Inc.
Income for the Year Ended February 30, 1918

Revenues	$100,000
Cost of guns manufactured	50,000
(exclusive of depleciation and lease charges)	
Depleciation	10,000
Lease of plant	5,000
Administrative expenses	20,000
Selling expenses	1,000
Amortization of patent	4,000
Interest	5,000
Net income	$ 5,000
Income taxes	2,000
Net income after taxes	$ 3,000

flow would be $17,000 plus income taxes ($2,000) plus the fixed lease payment ($5,000) plus interest ($5,000), or $29,000. The adjusted net cash flow may now be related to the fixed cash payments of $5,000 (lease payment) and $5,000 (interest). The ratio of adjusted net cash flow to these payments is 29/10; these payments are expected to be covered 2.9 times. Under these conditions, adjusted net cash flow could fall to almost one third its present amount and these payments would still be covered.

If preferred dividends, term-loan repayments, or bond sinking-fund requirements must also be met, further computations should be made. Let us assume that a term-loan payment of $3,000 and preferred dividends of $100 must also be paid. The term-loan payment has a prior claim on the company, so the coverage of this payment should be computed first. As the cash for this payment must be made available on an after-tax basis, we are interested in how many dollars of adjusted net cash flow must be available before taxes to cover a $3,000 after-tax payment. The number of dollars necessary is computed in the following formula in which T = the tax rate:

$$\text{Pretax Dollars Required} = \frac{\text{After-Tax Payment}}{1 - T}$$

In the present example the pretax dollars required would be $5,000 $\left(\frac{\$3,000}{1-.4}\right)$. The coverage of this $5,000 term-loan payment plus the previous fixed cash costs amounts to $29/15 = 1.93$. The pretax dollars required for the preferred is equal to $167 and the coverage for the preferred dividends is 1.91. The student might be inclined to deduct the prior claims from the adjusted cash flow and then compute the preferred dividend coverage; such a procedure, however, will tend to produce misleading conclusions. For example, under this method $14,000 ($29,000 − $15,000) is available to cover (on a pretax basis) the $167 preferred dividend, which is covered 83.8 $\left(\frac{\$14,000}{167}\right)$ times. It would appear from the high coverage ratio that the preferred dividend is more secure than any of the payments with a prior claim on the company. Obviously, this is not so. To correct for such misleading tendencies, all charges should be included in the denominator.

MANAGEMENT OF ACCOUNTS RECEIVABLE

Credit sales arise out of previously accepted capital-expenditure proposals, part of which investment could reasonably be expected to be in working capital (cash, inventory, and receivables). Thus credit sales in part reflect the success of such projects. The accuracy of the estimates of the investment requirements presumed the sound judgment of management in setting credit terms, selecting accounts for credit, and prudently minimizing losses and delays in receipt of payment through the use of credit insurance and/or proper collection procedures.

Through the manipulation of the length of credit period, the cash discount, expenditures on collections, the credit line, and its criteria for selecting customers, the firm manages its level of accounts receivable. An increase in the length of the period may increase demand but may also increase the likelihood of delinquencies. An increase in the cash discount would tend to increase demand and decrease credit delinquency and bad debts. Raising the criteria for acceptance of accounts reduces demand but decreases delinquencies and bad debts. Increasing the line of credit increases demand but also increases delinquencies and bad debts. Increasing expenditures on collections reduces bad debts and delinquencies but reduces demand. A change in any one of these methods requires that the other variables be examined because of their joint impact on the final result.

Establishing the Credit Terms

The terms of sale could be a highly influential factor in determining the volume of sales of the firm. The terms of sale, however, are usually standardized within a line of business and the nature of competition for many lines is such that it would be suicidal to offer any less favorable terms than those generally accepted; sales would tend toward zero. To grant more favorable credit terms only invites equal action by competing firms. If a firm is in a more protected competitive position, it may be able to deviate from traditional terms in order to improve its receivables position.

In determining the terms of sale, a number of considerations (other than those mentioned above) need to be taken into account. For example, a limited amount of available net working capital tends to restrain the size of the accounts receivable and would restrict sales because of the shorter credit terms that would have to be imposed (to speed up the collection period) or the firm could not grant the credit. Furthermore, credit terms are affected not only by the type of product or service sold, the traditional terms of the line of business, the firm's competitive position, and the limits on the firm's capital, but also by the available unused productive capacity of the firm. In considering its credit terms, the firm may be able to stimulate more sales by lengthening its credit. Although such action will tend to pick up sales to less credit-worthy customers, the firm needs to collect only a fraction of them to break even on the marginal sales. If variable costs are 60 per cent of total selling price, for example, the firm needs to average only a little better than a 60 per cent collection rate in order to add to its profits. When general business conditions improve to the point where sales to preferred accounts utilize almost all capacity, the firm can tighten up terms again to minimize its investment in accounts receivable. Reduction in the length of the credit period not only would reduce receivables but would also tend to cause some customers to move elsewhere. However, this policy must be used with caution, for a firm's customers tend to take the credit terms as a fixture and expect consistent treatment.

Cash discounts produce a powerful stimulant to quick payment of bills, thus tending to reduce delinquencies and bad debt losses, permitting reductions in collection expenses, and allowing the firm to relax its criteria for the selection of accounts or to increase its credit line. The cash discount unfortunately does cost, for it effectively reduces the dollars received from sales. The question to be resolved is whether the effectively reduced sales price is compensated for by reduced expenses of handling accounts receivable. The additional lost revenue from a lower sales price must be equally offset by additional reductions in costs of credit sales to break even.

Selecting Accounts

During periods of poor business, when the firm has excess capacity, it could profitably accept accounts possessing greater risk of loss than most of its existing accounts. It would tend to be profitable for the firm to accept accounts to the point where the expected revenue (probability of collection × the credit balance) equals the variable cost of the goods or services sold plus the cost of financing for the expected time that credit is to be outstanding. The expected revenue per dollar of sales can be plotted against the sales volume to illustrate the nature of customer conditions facing the firm. Figure 15-5 illustrates such a state for Sprouse Enterprises, Inc., under relatively good and poor business conditions, when variable costs are 60 per cent of total costs. The best sales level in good times is at capacity; in bad times it is at Point A. Unfortunately, the objective information necessary for such analysis is extremely limited and the financial manager would have to depend heavily upon the subjective judgment of qualified credit personnel after a review of whatever information is available.

Certain sources of information are traditionally available to the credit investigator, who must establish the acceptance or rejection criteria of accounts, determine the limit of the credit line, and estimate not only the probability of collection but also the time needed to collect the account. One of the most valuable of the sources of information is the firm's past credit experience with a particular customer.

Especially for new accounts, information must be secured from other sources. The most commonly mentioned reference source is the Dun & Bradstreet, Inc., *Reference Manual,* which lists businesses' estimated financial strength and a general composite credit appraisal. A subscribing firm may also secure a full credit report on the potential customer upon request. Specialized credit services are also available, such as the National Credit Office (in the textile field). The National Association of Credit Management has available a credit interchange service whereby local credit bureaus agree to exchange information on firms' account-paying habits. When an inquiry is made, the local credit bureau secures current reports from the suppliers of the firm being investigated. Another source of information may be the firm's bank, which can contact a bank in the potential customer's city and secure information as to its loan experience with that customer. The potential customer may agree to submit

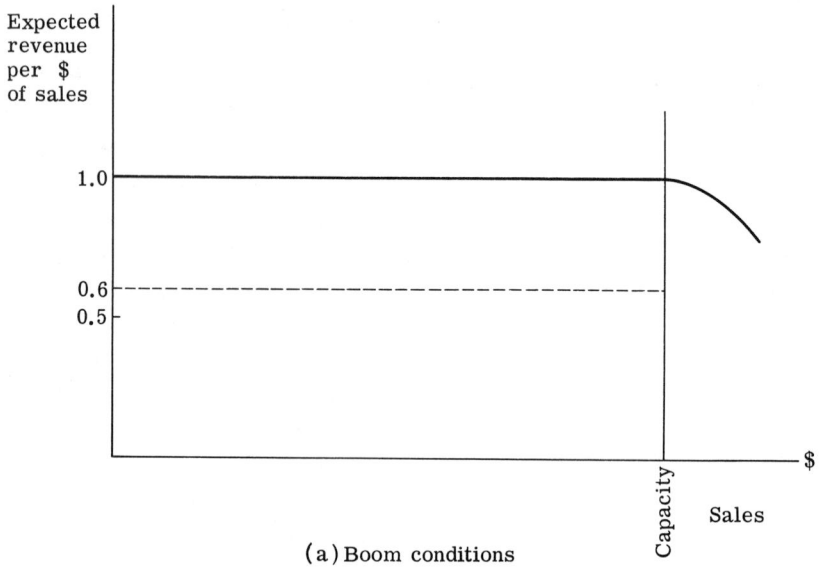

(a) Boom conditions

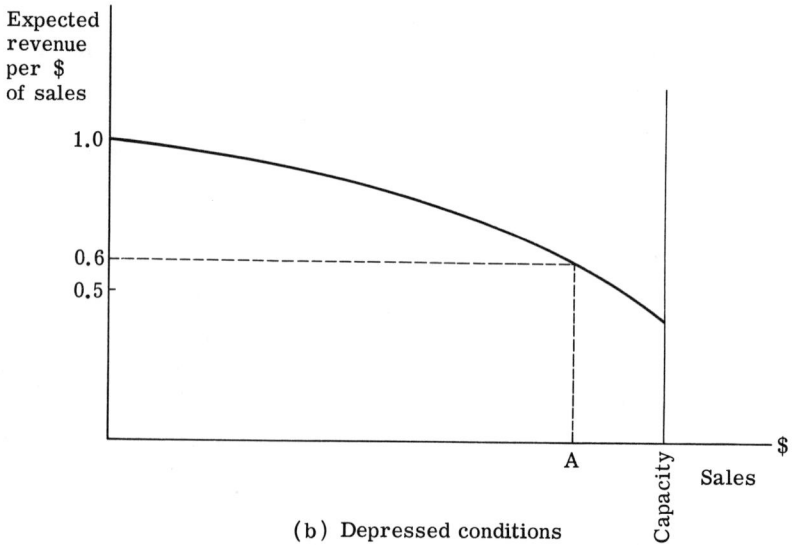

(b) Depressed conditions

Figure 15-5 Expected Revenues from Sales to Customers

copies of his financial statements or to be interviewed by the firm's credit representative. If financial statements are available, the firm may be able to get some indication of the client's paying habits by computing the ratio of his accounts payable to his annual purchases. A ratio of 1/12 would indicate the firm pays its account on the average every thirty days based on the statements submitted at this time of year, for about 11/12ths of its annual purchases remain to be paid. The local salesman may also be able to add or secure information, although his report would certainly be expected to be biased (in favor of the sale).

Adjustments up or down in the credit line (the maximum a customer can charge) influence the demand for credit. During periods of poor business, the firm may decide to increase its credit line to pick up additional business. In fact, the company may encourage customers by notifying them of available credit.

Occasionally, a customer needs credit beyond the normal credit period. In these cases, the firm could continue to finance the customer. Or, if it did not want to finance the account beyond the full collection cycle, it could aid in the location of other suitable financing. Arrangements for an installment loan may be set up with the local bank or other financial institutions, for example. Only in extreme cases would foreclosure be sought.

Collection on Accounts

Proper management of the investment in receivables implies the existence of a collection function. A collection department takes over the responsibility of receivables management after the credit has been granted. The collection department's objective is to insure the earliest possible payment on receivables without any customer losses through ill will. Prompt collection or payment tends to reduce the investment required in receivables and its associated capital costs and tends also to reduce the rate of losses in accounts receivable investment. The longer a receivable remains outstanding, the longer the firm exposes itself to possible loss. The firm may even lose sales; a customer will not be so inclined to reorder from a supplier to which it owes money. Ideally, any collection pressure from the collection department should be gentle and subtle enough to prevent any loss of customers. On the other hand, it must also be firm.

An important aspect in the minimization of working capital investment within the firm itself is to *bill* one's *customers as quickly as possible* so that payments can be received quickly. Such a policy reduces the required investment in receivables. If a company has average daily credit sales of $60,000 ($15 million a year) and invoices are sent out one day later than they could be, the firm is losing $2,400 a year in interest income foregone (assuming the funds could be collected one day sooner and invested at 4 per cent).

Another internal way to use cash more efficiently is to *centralize* certain functions. It may be desirable to bring together all elements of an enterprise that process cash receipts and disbursements so as to cut down the "handling" time between the initial receipt of checks in the business, their processing, and their deposit at the bank. Even billing functions and collection functions should be carefully integrated to minimize receivables and maximize profits. Often it is wise policy for a nationwide organization to regionalize its territories in order to speed up cash turnover. There are several methods used to accelerate collection. One entails the establishment of bank relationships in various marketing areas, determined, say, on the basis of dollar volume of business. Customers then are instructed to remit their payments to these regional banks. Because most of the checks deposited to the company's regional bank originate in that region—chances are many of them originate in the very city in which the bank is located—the time it takes to clear the checks is considerably reduced. With a company doing $60,000 a day of credit billing the interest income of the "extra" cash would amount to $7,200 (3 × $60,000 × .04) a year, assuming a 4 per cent rate. Any cash not needed by regional offices can be drawn down, by a wire transfer, to the company's main bank. All of this can be arranged for in advance with the several regional banks, each of which can be instructed to allow the company's deposits to reach a certain upper limit and to transfer additional cash, by wire, to the firm's main bank.

Another method used to accelerate collection provides for regional sales offices to make collections from customers, deposit them daily in a regional bank, and wire a daily report of deposits to the home office. The home office can then order funds transferred by wire from one bank to another, as they are needed, or order their investment in short-term outlets. The latter method is more suited to the firm that makes a large number of small collections daily, the former method is more suited to a company that has large and numerous collections.

Another method of cash management that has become popular in recent years is the use of the *lock box*. Under this procedure, the marketing area of a firm is geographically subdivided and customers in each region are instructed to make their remittances to a post office box (instead of a regional office). These payments are picked up by the firm's regional bank and the process of clearing the checks begins almost immediately. The use of a lock box can speed up the availability of funds by about three days, depending on the size of the region served by one box and the swiftness with which the bank operates. To justify the use of a lock box, however, a large volume of collections is necessary. In such a case, the lock box procedure would reduce not only a firm's accounts receivable balance but also the number of personnel and the amount of space, overhead, and equipment necessary to process incoming checks to make them ready for deposit.

None of these regional banking arrangements is without disadvantages (i.e., costs). In the first instance, the various banks may require a rather substantial compensating balance to cover the cost of processing the checks remitted to them, or charge a processing fee for each check. Another disadvantage is the partial loss of control over credit extensions. For example, it may be several days longer than "normal" before a firm finds out it has a delinquent account.

In some cases a firm may decide to secure credit insurance to guard against the possibility of unusual losses in accounts receivable. Banks frequently require such credit insurance before agreeing to make a loan to a firm. Customarily, it is a deductible form of insurance very much like the deductible provisions in automobile collision insurance. Under this arrangement the firm bears the average or expected loss on receivables. Only when the losses exceed that average amount does the insurance company share (coinsurance) in the losses. If average or expected losses are $50,000 and the firm in one period experienced losses of $80,000, the insurance company would pay the firm $24,000 [($80,000 − $50,000) × (.8)], assuming a 20 per cent coinsurance by the firm. The credit insurer also customarily limits the coverage on individual accounts according to the credit rating of the client. If at some later time a bad debt were collected, the funds would be distributed pro rata to the insurance company and the firm according to the proportion of their losses. The cost of credit insurance is on the average about .1 per cent. Credit insurance reduces the risk of loss to the firm and might be particularly valuable for a firm selling to a small number of large accounts. When a firm sells to a large number of small accounts, this in itself generally reduces the risks involved and the firm can undertake to insure itself. This is known as *self-insurance*. If past experience is sufficiently long, the firm may be able to determine the loss distribution it faces. For example, in Figure 15-6 dollar losses on accounts receivable for the past 100 months of the L. Heath Company, manufacturer of snowshoes and related equipment, are put in the form of a relative-frequency distribution. The average loss was about $22,000. To the extent that these data reflect expected future performance, expected losses are also $22,000. But the distribution indicates that it is possible for the loss to double, so the firm must weigh

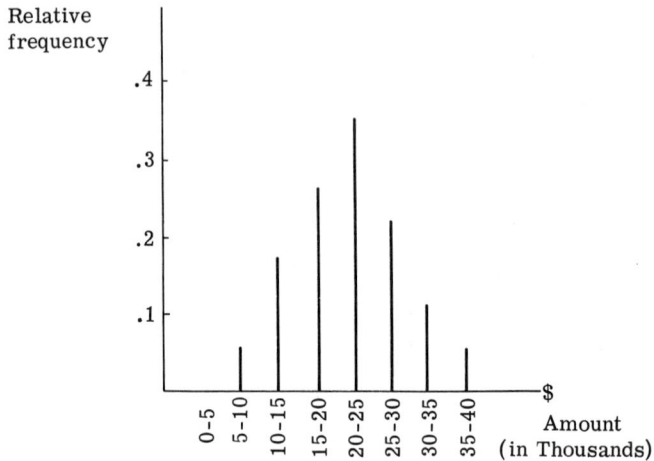

Figure 15-6 L. Heath Company, Relative Frequency Distribution of Monthly Losses in Accounts Receivable

the cost of insurance against such events with the cost to the firm that such a threat to its survival imposes. Insurance may also permit them to carry less precautionary cash reserves and involves less financial disruption when unusual losses occur. These savings are then weighed against insurance costs in order to arrive at a decision on whether or not to insure. A small number of large accounts would presumably be expected to cause a greater variability in the distribution facing the firm. Sale of receivables to factors or sales finance companies customarily also transfers such risks.

Reasonable attention to securing prompt payment of bills does the customer a favor by keeping him from acquiring sloppy bill-paying habits, a factor which may impair his credit standing. On the other hand too much pressure may incur his wrath, and the firm may lose an otherwise good account. Marginal customers will probably feel free to order more merchandise from the supplier with which it has a paid-up account than from the supplier with which it has a delinquent account.[7] Because some customers are always on the margin and even though a firm will find it difficult to isolate them, the possible lost sales may so impair profitability that a policy of liberal (not generous) but firm (not harsh) collection procedures is called for to curry favor with customers.[8]

[7] The use of a type of analysis involving the understanding of the Markov Chain Process and matrix multiplication may give good information to the firm regarding expected loss rates by age category and a steady state age distribution of accounts. It will also produce an estimate of the proper allowances for doubtful accounts. *See:* R. M. Cyert, H. J. Davidson, and G. L. Thompson, "Estimation of the Allowance for Doubtful Accounts by Markov Chains," *Management Science, 8* (April 1962), 287–303.

[8] For an extensive discussion of this and other topics contained in this chapter, see: National Association of Credit Men, *Credit Management Handbook* Rev. ed. (Homewood, Ill.: Irwin, 1965).

INVENTORY MANAGEMENT

The purpose of inventory is to prevent the loss of sales either to a competitor or through a long delay in filling an order. From the standpoint of securing capital, inventory is substantially less liquid (further away from cash) than receivables and therefore is usually a less desirable form of collateral for bank loans. If it is used as collateral, the loan is usually more expensive.

The management of inventory (supplies, raw materials, work in process, and finished goods) is not customarily undertaken by financial managers. More often than not inventory management is carried out by the purchasing department. Its function is that of balancing the cost of lost sales and frequent reordering costs involved in smaller inventories with the carrying costs (capital costs, warehousing costs, service costs, and risks of holding stock) of larger inventories. Numerous quantitative models have been developed to find the cost-minimizing or optimum level of inventory,[9] but inasmuch as the function of inventory management generally lies outside the scope of financial management, we shall not pursue the topic further.

SUMMARY

This chapter discussed the liquidity problem facing the financial manager. Working capital is the capital circulating into cash over an operating cycle. Net working capital is working capital net of short-term liabilities. Working capital generally consists of cash, marketable securities, accounts receivable, and inventory. Traditionally the financial manager has been directly concerned with the balances in all these accounts— except inventory, which is usually the province of a purchasing department.

The need for a cash balance is based upon the knowledge that firm receipts and expenditures are not perfectly synchronized (transactions demand), that there exists uncertainty in the estimates of net cash flow (precautionary demand), and that on some occasions cash may be held to take advantage of expected price changes (speculative demand). Technical insolvency and possible business failure result from inadequate attention to the management of cash. Close study of the pattern of net cash inflow can be helpful in determining the desirable stock of cash. The

[9] See, for example: C. West Churchman, Russell L. Ackoff, and E. Leonard Arnoff, *Introduction to Operations Research* (New York: Wiley, 1957), 199–278; and Alan S. Manne, *Economic Analysis for Business Decisions* (New York: McGraw, 1961), 116–54.

cash budget is an invaluable tool for planning the efficient use of cash. It helps determine how much cash will be needed and when the firm will have excess cash. Excess cash balances, if temporary, may be placed in temporary investments to reduce the cost of maintaining liquidity.

Longer-run considerations are little concerned with the current stock of cash. When extended periods of time are considered, it is more important to study the size and variability of the cash flow in relation to the fixed cash requirements.

The management of accounts receivable involves the manipulation of credit periods, cash discounts, criteria for account selection, credit lines and collection costs—all in order to maximize profits. Each of these variables tends to have an impact on the level of sales, delinquencies, bad debts, and business costs. Furthermore, these variables are not independent of each other. Obviously, there are numerous methods by which the financial manager may achieve great flexibility in altering the accounts receivable balance as well as the rate of cash inflow.

SUGGESTED READINGS

ARGYRIS, C. "Human Problems with Budgets," *Harvard Business Review,* *31* (January–February 1953), 97–110.

DAVIDSON, SIDNEY, GEORG A. SORTER, and HEMU KALLE. "Measuring the Defensive Position of a Firm," *Financial Analysts Journal, 20* (January–February 1964), 23–29.

EARLEY, JAMES S. "Business Budgeting and the Theory of the Firm," *Journal of Industrial Economics, 9* (November 1960), 23–42.

Economic Order Quantity, 2nd rev. ed. Washington, D.C.: Government Printing Office, 1961.

EDWARDS, E. O. "Funds Statements for Short- and Long-run Analysis," *Journal of Business, 25* (July 1952), 156–74.

How to Build Profits by Controlling Costs. New York: Dun & Bradstreet, Inc., 1959.

JACOBS, DONALD P. "The Marketable Security Portfolios of Nonfinancial Corporations: Investment Practices and Trends," *The Journal of Finance, 15* (September 1960), 341–52.

MASON, PERRY. "Cash Flow Analysis and Funds Statement," *Journal of Accountancy, 221* (March 1961), 59–72.

MUELLER, F. W., JR. "Corporate Working Capital and Liquidity," *Journal of Business, 26* (July 1953), 157–72.

PATON, WILLIAM A., JR. *A Study in Liquidity.* Ann Arbor, Mich.: Bureau of Business Research, University of Michigan, 1958.

PHELPS, CLYDE WILLIAM. *Commercial Credit Insurance as a Management Tool.* Baltimore: Commercial Credit Company, 1961.

ROBBINS, SIDNEY M. "Getting More Mileage Out of Cash," *N.A.A. Bulletin,* 42 (September 1962), 65–74.

SAGAN, JOHN. "Toward a Theory of Working Capital Management," *The Journal of Finance, 10* (May 1955), 121–29.

SCHABACKER, JOSEPH C. *Cash Planning in Small Manufacturing Companies.* Washington, D.C.: Small Business Administration, 1960.

SOLDOFSKY, ROBERT M. *Lectures in Financial Management.* Iowa City, Iowa: Iowa Supply Company, 1958.

Terms of Sale Generally Used in 90 Lines of Business Activity. New York: Dun & Bradstreet, Inc., 1957.

VATTER, W. J. "Fund Flows and Fund Statements," *Journal of Business, 26* (January 1953), 15–25.

WALTER, JAMES E. "Determinants of Technical Solvency," *Journal of Business, 30* (January 1957), 30–43.

WESTON, J. FRED. "Forecasting Financial Requirements," *The Accounting Review, 33* (July 1958), 427–40.

QUESTIONS

15.1 Define *working capital, net working capital,* and *operating cycle.*

15.2 What would be the impact upon working capital if the operating cycle were reduced or increased (in length of time)?

15.3 Which is more important to the short-term lender—the stock of cash or the flow of cash? Explain.

15.4 The stock and flow of cash can be related to a bathtub of water with the faucet on and the drain open. Explain.

15.5 How is the stock of cash related to the net cash flow?

15.6 Is it possible in modern business to operate with no current liabilities? Explain.

15.7 A statement has been made that money is related to technical insolvency and profits to legal insolvency. Does the avoidance of one type of insolvency solve the concern over the other?

15.8 A firm can be assured of avoiding technical insolvency by holding all cash. Comment.

15.9 Why does a firm with increasing sales and profits need to concern itself with technical insolvency?

15.10 Under what conditions could an operating firm get by with a zero cash balance at all times? Under what conditions could it plan a cash balance with no allowance for precautionary balances?

15.11 Set forth the informational requirements for the estimate of cash receipts and cash expenditures.

15.12 Is it always a wise policy to reduce as far as possible the level of minimum current liabilities? Comment.

15.13 What types of cash outlays are almost invariant with the level of operations?

15.14 Comment on the validity of the approximation of net cash flow by the use of the sum of earnings after taxes and the noncash charges against revenue. Include in your answer the assumptions implicit in the use of such an approximating technique.

15.15 The size of the accounts receivable balance can presumably be manipulated by management by the control of certain variables. What are these and what is the nature of their influence?

15.16 What information would you want before setting the credit terms for your firm? Where would you look for such information?

15.17 Would you permit salesmen to set the terms of credit sales?

15.18 What are the advantages to the firm of exerting some pressure upon customers for collection?

15.19 What can be done to minimize the level of accounts receivable without adjusting the terms of sale or using methods that might reduce sales?

PROBLEMS

15.20 Given the following balance sheet information, (*a*) Determine the amounts of working and net working capital, and (*b*) Assuming minimum current liabilities of $20,000, what amount of net working capital would normally be recommended?

Purdy Goods, Inc.
Balance Sheet, 1966

Cash	$ 10,000	Accruals	$ 10,000
Receivables (net)	40,000	Accounts payable	30,000
Inventory	25,000	Total current liabilities	$ 40,000
Total current assets	$ 75,000	Common stock	20,000
Fixed assets	25,000	Surplus	40,000
Total assets	$100,000		$100,000

15.21 The Page Water Company has the following data on its operating cash inflows and outflows:

Day	1	2	3	4	5	6	7	8	9	10	11	12	13
Inflow	$500	500	400	300	0	0	600	700	800	800	0	0	1,500
Outflow	400	400	500	600	0	0	500	800	1000	600	0	0	300

Day	14	15	16	17	18	19	20	21	22	23	24	25	26
Inflow	$600	300	300	300	0	0	400	300	300	300	300	0	0
Outflow	300	300	200	600	0	0	300	300	300	300	600	0	0

Day	27	28	29	30
Inflow	$300	300	300	300
Outflow	400	400	400	500

(*a*) Disregarding nonoperating cash flows, what cash balance would you recommend for the 1st-of-the-month transactions purposes (assuming this pattern was representative of all months)? (*b*) How much of the cash balance on the 13th could be paid in dividends and yet provide enough cash until the 13th of next month?

15.22 If the cash balance needed on the 1st of the month by the Page Water Company in 15.21(a) varied randomly because of irregularities in cash flows, and if such a balance could be considered an expected value of a normal distribution with a standard deviation of $100, how much of a precautionary balance should be carried on the 1st of the month if management does not wish to run short of cash more than twenty-three times in 1,000? (Use Table C-3 in Appendix C.)

15.23 As financial manager of Jensen Stores you are asked to plan for the cash needs or discover any expected cash surpluses in the next six-month period beginning July 1st. Any needs are to be provided by short-term bank loans. The sales forecast has been made by your market analyst as follows:

Month	Sales
July	15,000
August	30,000
September	25,000
October	30,000
November	30,000
December	20,000
January	15,000
February	10,000

The following additional information may be useful. (*a*) This past May and June sales amounted to $10,000. (*b*) All sales are on credit and, based upon the credit terms and previous experience, only 10 per cent will be received in the month of sale, 60 per cent in the following month, and the remaining 30 per cent in the second month after sale. (*c*) The cost of goods sold amounts to 75 per cent of sales. Purchases are ordered a month before sales and are paid in the same month of purchase. (*d*) Inventory at the end of June is expected to be $15,000, which includes the delivery of purchases ordered in June. (*e*) Wages and salaries are $1,500 plus 5 per cent of sales in the current month. Accruals of wages and salaries and other current miscellaneous current liabilities are the same at the end of each month. (*f*) Depreciation amounts to $300 per month, rent $400 per month and other expenses involve outlays of 2 per cent of sales per month. (*g*) The company plans no new capital expenditures, nor will it pay dividends in this period. (*h*) The firm's desired beginning-of-month cash balance is $5,000 but $7,000 is the expected stock of cash on July 1st.

Prepare the firm's plans and arrange any necessary borrowing. Assume an effective 7 per cent interest cost on all loans and assume that such loans are made only on a discount basis.

15.24 Given the following income statement of the Goldstrucker Silver Company, estimate the net cash flow:

Goldstrucker Silver Company
Income statement, 1885

Income:	
Net sales	$131,000,000
Other income less other deductions	1,000,000
	$132,000,000

Costs and expenses:

Cost of goods sold	103,000,000
Depreciation	4,000,000
Depletion	1,000,000
Selling, general, and administrative expenses	18,000,000
Interest expense	1,000,000
Income taxes	1,000,000
Net income	$ 4,000,000

15.25 The Goldstrucker Silver Company above has a $32 million debt, $3 million of which must be repaid annually. What can be said about the longer-run view of the firm's liquidity?

15.26 Thompson Stores, Inc., is presently operating at about 50 per cent of capacity with sales of $10 million. Bad debts are estimated at only 1 per cent. Costs of producing another $10 million of sales would run about $6 million. The firm has estimated the additional sales could be made to successively inferior classes of credit risks. These are given as follows:

Class	Sales Potential	Expected Percentage of Bad Debts
I	$2,000,000	10%
II	3,000,000	20
III	4,000,000	30
IV	5,000,000	50

How would you advise management on its selling policy?

15.27 The following statements have been prepared by the Zulauf Corporation:

The Zulauf Corporation
Comparative Balance Sheets

	1966	1965
Cash	$ 2,000	$ 5,000
Accounts receivable	10,000	6,000
Inventories	24,000	29,000
Property and plant (net of accumulated depreciation)	85,000	80,000
Other assets	4,000	2,500
	$125,000	$122,500

Accounts payable	$ 9,000	$ 14,000
Accrued liabilities	3,000	3,000
5% bonds (due 1972)	13,000	13,000
	25,000	30,000
Stockholders' equity:		
Common stock	75,000	75,000
Retained earnings	25,000	17,500
Total liabilities and stockholders' equity	$125,000	$122,500

The Zulauf Corporation
Income Statement
For the Fiscal Year Ended September 30, 1966

Net sales		$210,600
Operating expenses:		
Variable:		
Cost of goods sold	$105,300	
Selling expenses (cash outlay)	30,000	
General and administrative expenses (cash outlay)	22,650	157,950
Margin		$ 52,650
Fixed:		
Depreciation on plant	$ 15,000	
General and administrative expenses (cash outlay)	17,000	$ 32,000
Net operating profit		$ 20,650
Fixed interest expense on bonds		650
Net income before income taxes		$ 20,000
Less federal income taxes (these taxes have been paid)		10,000
Net income		$ 10,000
Dividends paid in cash to common stockholders during year		$ 2,500

On September 30, 1966, you were elected to the position of Finance Manager for Zulauf Corporation, which has just completed its fiscal year and paid its income taxes. Your old job paid more, but you feel this new opportunity will provide you with a challenge to your liking. Assume that you meet the following *unrelated* situations (except that they use the common background given above) in the first few days on your new job. (*a*) One of the first things you are concerned about is the cash flows which make it possible to pay the bills on time. You ask one of your employees for a statement of cash receipts and cash disbursements for the fiscal year just ended. The assistant replies that none has been prepared, and that he does not know how to prepare this report, but he is anxious to learn if you will show him how. You agree to prepare the report as a guide for your employee in the future. (*b*) You are informed by the sales manager that competitors are starting to make credit sales allowing their customers 60 days to pay, rather than the thirty days which have been customary for Zulauf and the industry. The sales manager asks for your reaction to lengthening the period granted by Zulauf. (*c*) Prepare a cash budget for October and November: (1) assume sales will be $20,000 and $30,000 respectively; (2) assume all sales are collected in the month subsequent to the month of sale, and all sales are on credit; (3) assume inventory at the end of any month should not be less than $20,000; (4) assume inventory purchased in one month is paid for in the next; (5) assume all other variable expenses are paid currently in cash assuming that accrued liabilities are maintained at a constant amount of $3,000; (6) ignore accrued income taxes; (7) assume cash payment of fixed costs in October and November amount to $1,600 in each month; (8) ignore interest costs on new short-term debt; and (9) assume September sales were $10,000.

CHAPTER 16   INVESTMENT MANAGEMENT

Decisions to invest or not to invest are among the most important to the firm because its success in the maximization of profits (the change in the value of ownership plus nonwage distribution to owners less their contributions) is dominated by such decisions. Many investment decisions whose original commitment will not be recovered for a considerable period also carry ⌐ long-lasting impact upon accounting profits. Therefore, the methods of making such decisions are important and it is to this matter that we now turn our attention.

INFORMATION FOR INVESTMENT DECISIONS

Investment decisions are based upon the prediction of outcomes, the confidence in those expected outcomes, the estimate of the required outlays, and an estimate of the cost of capital to the firm. The methods used to secure such information vary widely: some are quite primitive while others are highly sophisticated. In some situations the uncertainty about these values may be so great as to make the techniques of evaluating investment proposals appear too sophisticated for the quality of information secured, and management may desire to rely upon crude subjective judgments. In other cases, however, reasonable estimates of the four elements mentioned above may be secured, at least in part, and as a general rule the utilization of such information tends to improve the decision-making process. A structured format for investment decisions also tends to lend some objectivity to many decisions and knowledge of the underlying theory or variables that make one investment more attractive than another can improve even subjective decisions.

The data used in making estimates is different from that customarily used by accountants. Accountants concern themselves with past costs and revenues and their allocation. Investment decisions require estimates of future costs. In fact, investment decisions are based upon future cash outlays (including income taxes) rather than past costs, and cash receipts rather than past revenues. Frequently, cost data must be obtained from experimental studies, not from accounting records. And investment de-

354

cisions add still another variable to investment decision-making not included in accounting measurement: the time value of money.

The past is essentially irrelevant for current decisions. Errors made in the prior periods should not affect current decisions except as they contribute to the knowledge of the basis for the error. Investments made in prior periods may be considered for liquidation, however. Consider, for example, the decision to continue to use a truck purchased two years ago for $10,000. The truck is used for hauling peat moss to markets. The nature of the market for peat moss has changed since the purchase, and, instead of four loads a week, demand for the haul of only two loads exists. The net cash flow fell from $3,300 last year to $1,500 this year and the expected net cash flow is $1,500 per year for the next five years. If the owner feels he needs a 10 per cent return to cover 8 per cent capital costs plus an increment for uncertainty in returns, the present value of these cash flows is

$$PV = \sum_{t=1}^{5} \frac{\$1,500}{(1+.10)^t} = \$5,686.50$$

If he could now sell his truck for $6,000, it would pay him to do so even though the undepreciated cost of the truck on the books is $7,140 (seven-year life, straight-line depreciation, assuming no expected salvage value). From an accounting point of view a loss on the sale of the truck of $1,140, ignoring tax saving, would have to be charged off against common stock equity. But the important variables in the decision to sell are (1) the realizable sale value related to (2) the expected net cash flow resulting from continued operation. Once the decision to purchase the truck was made, the cost became a "sunk" cost and it is no longer relevant to the current decision. Sunk costs and past costs generally are irrelevant for investment decisions, except as they affect the cash flow through income taxes.

Most investment proposals, if accepted, would have some impact upon existing firm operations and information regarding these tangential effects is necessary to evaluate properly the proposal under review. Investment requirements and cash inflows and outflows of a proposed project may be affected favorably or unfavorably when considered in conjunction with total firm operations. Some present facilities, for example, may be used for the proposed project so that the estimates of cash outlays are lower than they would be if the proposal were completely independent of current operations. Or a new product being proposed may cut into revenues of existing products. Consequently, the measurement of investment requirements as well as the net cash flow must be *incremental* in nature. The proposal must be evaluated by using incremental investment outlays and incremental outcomes. This tends to make measurement more difficult, but failure to evaluate the proposal in this fashion leads to erroneous results.

Once an investment outlay is proposed, it usually goes through numerous phases of evolution before it is accepted or rejected. The research and development department may develop what appears to be a very salable item. Staff members must attempt to evaluate the market for the item, under certain pricing assumptions. Other members of the staff attempt to estimate investment requirements and operating costs. Rough estimates may be then consolidated to give a crude measure of the desirability of the project. At this point, if the project appears hopelessly unprofitable, it should be dropped; if it appears extremely profitable, it may be accepted without further expense of evaluation. In most cases, however, a search for more information will continue and will take the form of refinements in original estimates and re-evaluations. During such a sequential state of evaluation, the firm faces a series of decisions centering on acceptance or rejection, or the securing of more information. The structure for making optimal decisions of this type has been formalized,[1] but the full presentation of such a model at this stage of its development and in this text is not warranted.

Risk measurements also improve the quality of evaluation of investment proposals. If a sample "population" existed, we could obtain reasonably reliable approximations of the mean value and a measure of the variability of the sample mean (standard deviation in this case). In the case of future values, however, such sampling is impossible; there is no such objective experience upon which the decision-maker can rely. Estimates of the possible variation in values must be made both with the knowledge that the interplay of the variables will create a return which is considered to be the best estimate, and with the knowledge that other outcomes, in view of the lack of knowledge about the behavior of variables which do in fact determine the return, might result. Schlaifer and others have suggested that the decision-maker, even though relying upon judgment, ought to formalize his decision-making process by constructing a subjective probability distribution.[2] The subjective probabilities of the possible outcomes can be estimated by using the best judgment of the

[1] James B. MacQueen, "Optimal Policies for a Class of Search and Evaluation Problems," *Management Science, 10* (July 1964), 746–59.
[2] Robert Schlaifer, *Introduction to Statistics for Business Decisions* (New York: McGraw, 1961), 13–22; and Pierre Massé, *Optimal Investment Decisions* (Englewood Cliffs, N.J.: Prentice-Hall, 1962), 219–34.

estimators as to the various states or sets of conditions under which the investment will be operating. The internal consistency of these probability estimates can be improved through the use of a lottery procedure similar to the standard gamble technique.[3] Such a distribution would take the form such as that in Figure 16-1. The distribution might more conveniently be drawn as a continuous function. It has as its mean the value of $50. The subjective distribution cannot be assumed to have the same attributes as an objectively derived distribution. The objective distribution permits us in most cases to estimate objectively the possible errors involved in relying upon it; this is not true with such a subjective distribution. Unfortunately, different individuals will be likely to express different subjective distributions for the same outcome. If many such subjective estimates by experts could be combined, one could reasonably expect the reliability of the "pooled" distribution to increase and become more valuable. The increased reliability of "pooled" distributions has been examined in a limited number of cases and such distributions have been found to behave very satisfactorily as an approximation of the true values in the population.[4]

It is to be expected that such distributions, particularly if "unpooled," will reflect the personal bias of the estimator. This is, of course, true with all of the required estimates. The averaging of such estimates should

[3] Robert Schlaifer, *Introduction to Statistics for Business Decisions* (New York: McGraw, 1961), 13, 14.

[4] Larry E. Richards, *A Study of Pooled Subjective Distributions Toward Approximation of the Objective Distributions.* Unpublished M.B.A. Research Paper, Department of Accounting, Finance and Statistics, University of Washington, 1963.

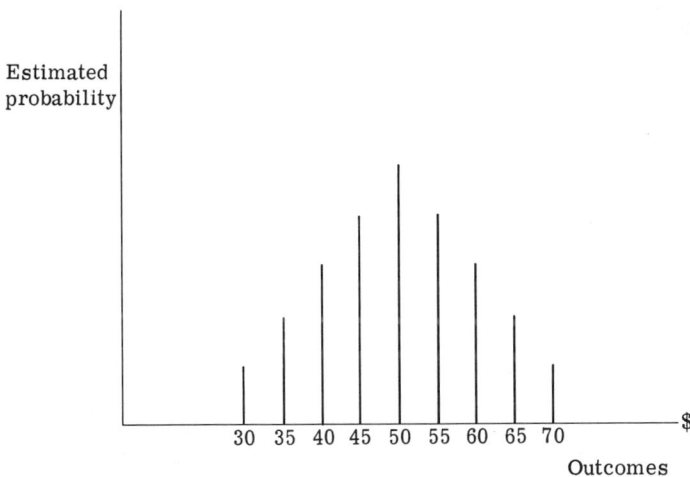

Figure 16-1 Subjective Probability Distribution

tend to improve reliability. It also may be useful to conduct postaudits of the results of the estimators to evaluate their efforts and disclose any upward or downward biases in their past estimates.[5]

THE DISCOUNT RATE AND THE CUTOFF RATE OF RETURN

Up to this stage we have assumed as our discount rate, the minimum attractive rate of return. This rate (ER_m) customarily should exceed the average cost of capital (k). We know that firms, in actual practice, will not accept a proposal that promises a rate of return only equal or slightly above capital costs, because they are unwilling to accept in exchange a *certain cost of capital* for *uncertain returns*. Also, there is some uncertainty in their estimates of capital cost. The firm consequently must establish a minimum attractive rate of return in excess of the cost of capital. This rate becomes the cutoff point for projects evaluated on a rate-of-return basis and it also becomes the discount rate in present-value analysis. For simplicity's sake, let us refer to this rate as d rather than ER_m. The discount rate (d), or the minimum attractive rate of return should be used in the analysis of all projects. This rate reflects a degree of risk equivalent to the average for the firm. In other words, if the project is expected to have no significant effect on the business risk of the enterprise, the rate should be used. If the project will either lower or raise the risk of the firm, a smaller or greater discount rate should be employed. A question naturally arises: What should this rate be? The analysis should proceed along these lines.

Management should be presented with a set of alternatives. One of the alternatives should be the cost of capital to the firm (management could also invest in their own sources of capital). They may then be asked to point out sets of equivalence between a certain return and an uncertain return. For example, consider the Meyers Company, whose capital costs are estimated at 8 per cent; the risk (SR/ER) of the firm for its operations as a whole is 1/2. Mr. Meyers and the other major stockholders were faced with a choice of a $100,000 investment with an 8 per cent certain return or an investment of $100,000 with a risk ($SR/ER$) of 1/2 and a return of 9, 10, 11, or 12 per cent. The feeling of shareholders toward the various combinations of risk and expected returns is as follows:

---

[5] An alternative procedure may be to set up a probability distribution for each element affecting the outcome, and then—using analytical or simulation techniques—generate a probability distribution for the outcome as a whole. See: David B. Hertz, "Risk Analysis in Capital Investment," *Harvard Business Review, 42* (February 1964), 95–106.

Stockholder	Number of Shares	Choice of Return
Meyers	50,000	10%
Alexis	15,000	9
Saposnick	15,000	10
McCarthy	10,000	12
Remington	10,000	11
Total shares	100,000	

The total number of shares outstanding is 100,000 and the weighted average of their choices is 10.15 per cent. The $100,000 is the average investment commitment of the firm. In a similar manner the rates could be chosen for numerous combinations of investment sizes and risks. These may be portrayed as in the illustration in Figure 16-2. Consequently, for

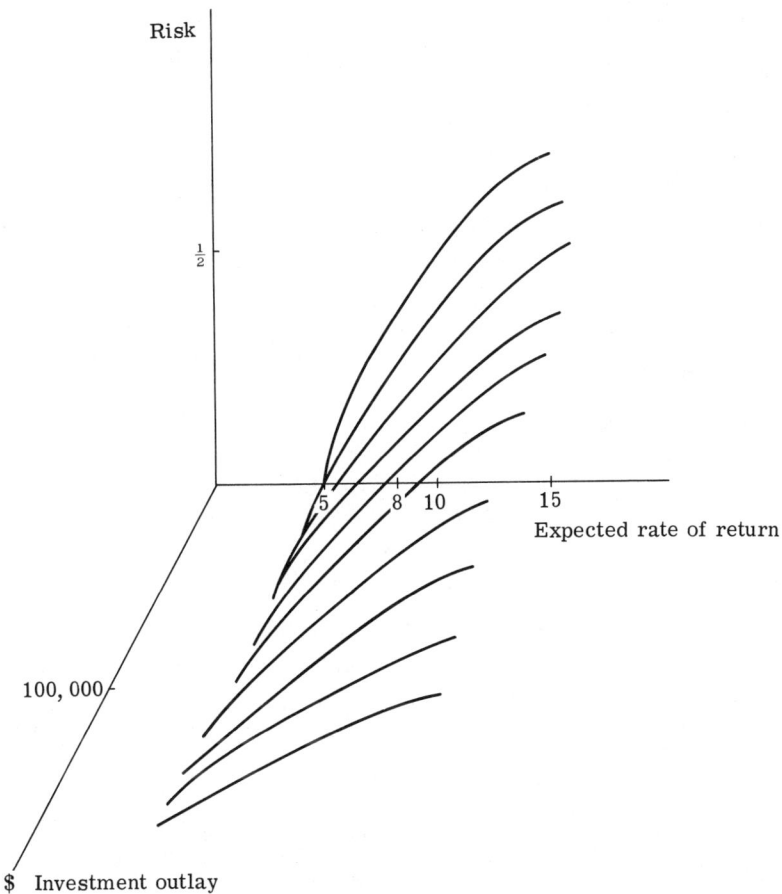

Figure 16-2   Management Return Requirements

the average investment of $100,000 and a risk equivalent to 1/2, a discount rate of 10.15 per cent should be used. For situations in which it appears from the subjective probability distributions that the risk is definitely greater than 1/2, a greater discount rate should be selected. In large corporations, of course, such a poll of stockholders would be impractical. The risk-aversion characteristics of the firm would then have to be those of management—those, in other words, of the individuals who make the decisions on capital expenditures.

TECHNIQUES OF MEASURING INVESTMENT MERIT

There exist a number of methods to measure the attractiveness of investment proposals. The simple average return, the time-adjusted rate of return, and the present-value methods were introduced in earlier chapters. Other methods, such as payback and the annual-cost method, are also available. Payback will be examined here, but the annual-cost method will not.[6]

Payback

The *payback* system is a widely adopted method of measuring investment merit. It has the attribute of simplicity and costs less to use than most methods. The payback period is the length of time required for the project to return, in net cash inflows, the amount of investment outlay. Consider the net cash flow displayed in the following diagram:

Net Cash Outflow

$10,000				
0	1	2	3	4
0	$3,000	$4,000	$3,000	$5,000

Net Cash Inflows

The diagram indicates a net cash outflow of $10,000 at time $(t = 0)$, and net cash inflows in succeeding later periods. After the first year, $3,000 is recovered; after the second, $7,000; after the third, $10,000. The payback period would therefore be 3.0 years. But even if all the $10,000 had been

---

[6] The annual-cost method has general attributes somewhat like those of the present-value method. It is somewhat more difficult to use in cases in which the outcomes are variable. Under this method the cost of investment outlay, adjusted for the time value of money, is allocated to the periods which the proposal is expected to cover. For an excellent discussion of this method and the others, *see:* Eugene L. Grant and W. Grant Ireson, *Principles of Engineering Economy,* 4th ed. (New York: Ronald, 1960), 76–136.

recovered in the third year, the payback period would still be 3.0—a very important fact, because this method fails to take into consideration such varying distributions of cash flow even though the $3,000 received in the first year and the $4,000 in the second could have been reinvested at some rate of return. This method also fails to consider any receipts after the payback period, no matter how great they might be. Despite these very significant criticisms, payback continues to be the most frequently used method for making investment decisions.[7]

Some of its advantages may warrant its use. First, the firm may use the payback system as a crude device early in the screening process to eliminate those proposals which obviously would not be attractive under any measure. The Greiner Gym Company, for example, eliminates all proposals having a payback period in excess of twelve years. They have judged that any proposal with a greater payback period, in a business as volatile as trampolines, could not be desirable under any more sophisticated measure.

When the uncertainty surrounding the outcome estimates is great (as in military contracts), a prime—if not the most important—consideration is the speed of capital investment recovery. Firms in industries subject to rapid technological changes (and thus to great obsolescence risks) would also be inclined to favor the payback method.

Firms under severe capital constraints, in which liquidity or the turnover of capital are dominant considerations, would also use payback. Obviously, for small expenditures it would be impractical to use more sophisticated methods. And finally, a particular division might have investment proposals of about equal life and risk; payback would work well in evaluating such proposals.

The Time-Adjusted Rate of Return

Infinite Life

The rate of return for projects assumed to be perpetual can be computed simply when the expected outcome is constant. The formula for this computation is

$$ER = \frac{EO}{PV_o} \tag{1}$$

[7] Chewning's study amply demonstrates this for the oil, chemical, and paper industries. *See:* Richard C. Chewning, *An Investigation of Industrial Methodology Used for Determining the Cost of Capital When Making Capital Budgeting Decisions.* Unpublished D.B.A. dissertation, Department of Finance and Statistics, University of Washington, 1963), 215–17.

where PV_o is the present value of the investment outlay. If the net cash inflow (EO) is not constant, a more elaborate formula must be used. The formula determines the rate of return (ER) which equates the sum of future payments to present investment outlay (PV_o). The formula for this is

$$PV_o = \sum_{t=1}^{\infty} \frac{EO_t}{(1+ER)^t} \tag{2}$$

As t becomes large, the denominator becomes large, making the fraction small. Consequently, the return may be approximated by computing with a large value for t, as distant net cash flows add little to the sum.

Finite Life

The rate of return for proposals with finite lives can be computed by using either an annuity formula or tables, if the outcomes are predicted to be a constant value. If we use the formula

$$PV_o = \frac{EO}{ER} \left[1 - \frac{1}{(1+ER)^n} \right] \tag{3}$$

or Table C-2 in Appendix C, the rate of return (ER) of a $10,000 investment returning a net cash inflow (EO) of $2,000 per year for six years is about 5.4 per cent.[8]

If the life is finite but the net cash flow is uneven, we must rely on the more lengthy basic formula (2), modified for the finite life. As an additional illustration, consider the computation of the return on a bond which costs $900 and pays a nominal rate of 4 per cent ($40) to maturity five years hence, when $1,000 will be paid. This uneven distribution has a "balloon" payment at the end of five years.

Net Cash Outflow

$900					
0	1	2	3	4	5
0	$40	$40	$40	$40	$1,040

Net Cash Inflows

The reader may verify the yield as 6.4 per cent.[9]

[8] This is computed directly from the table by taking the ratio PV_o/EO, which is $10,000/$2,000 in this case, and using the row for six years to find the closest value to PV_o/EO in the body of the table. The rate of return heading in that column can then be easily read.

[9] Recall that the use of the time-adjusted return method may give unreliable results when the value of EO fluctuates from period to period. *See:* D. Teichroew, A. A. Robichek, and M. Montalbano, "Mathematical Analysis of Rates or Return Under Certainty," *Management Science, 11* (January 1965), 395–403.

The rate-of-return method assumes that funds received before the termination of the project are reinvested at the derived rate of return. This assumption may not hold true for proposals computed to yield a greater than average internal rate of return to the firm. Neither of the reservations concerning the use of the rate-of-return method, however, is a serious obstacle to the practical application of the method.

The Present-Value Method

The most reliable method and the most sophisticated method for determining investment worth is the present-value method. The present-value method yields a unique result and assumes that funds received before the termination of the project are reinvested only at the discount rate used. If the present value of the future sums (EO) exceeds the present value of the outlays (PV_o), the project is considered profitable.

Infinite Life

Investment assumed to have a perpetual existence can be valued by the formula

$$PV = \frac{EO}{d} \tag{4}$$

When the expected outcomes are estimated to be variable rather than constant, the valuation must use the basis formula

$$PV = \sum_{t=1}^{\infty} \frac{EO_t}{(1+d)^t} \tag{5}$$

In a practical sense, however, we would never be finished with such a computation and some practical way out of the dilemma is necessary. We are aware of the fact that as t becomes large the denominator becomes large and distant outcomes add little to the present value total. When the values to be added become small enough (an arbitrary accuracy decision), the summation may be discontinued. In other words, from an operational point of view distant outcomes will make little difference in the present value of investment proposals. For example, the present value of $100 received fifty years from now is worth nine cents at a discount rate of 10 per cent. The present value of $100 per year for fifty years is $991.50, when discounted at 10 per cent. The last year added nine cents to the $991.50. Relative to the total present value additional $100 values further out in time can be ignored for practical purposes. Moreover, it is also true that the higher the discount rate the less significant do distant outcomes become.

For example, if $100 were received each year for thirteen years, the present value would be $322.33 when discounted at the 30 per cent rate. For a twenty-five-year period this $100 annual cash flow has a present value of $332.86. The inclusion of the additional twelve years added only $10.53 to the results, an amount equal to slightly more than 3 per cent of that derived for the thirteen-year period. It can be seen from this example that it may be impractical to calculate present worth values beyond, say, thirteen years when discount rates are high; little is added to the final results. When the cash flows beyond thirteen years are roughly equal in amount to one another, they may be capitalized and then discounted back to present value.

Finite Life

If the net cash inflow is constant over a finite period, the present value can be computed from the annuity formula

$$PV = \frac{EO}{d} \left[1 - \frac{1}{(1+d)^n} \right] \qquad (6)$$

The value may also be computed by use of an annuity table.[10]

Again, if the net cash inflow is not constant, the present value should be computed from the more basic formula given as

$$PV = \sum_{t=1}^{n} \frac{EO_t}{(1+d)^t} \qquad (7)$$

In *any* case, the latter formula (7) gives accurate results.

When two competing proposals are expected to have different lives, they may still be compared but one must assume the proposal with the shorter life to be repeated until its span equals that of the longer-lived proposal. For example, consider the problem facing Brosky and Olson Blower Manufacturing, Inc., which must choose between two machines. The Delano machine lasts ten years, costs $10,000, and generates a net cash inflow of $1,500 per year; the Jolivet machine has an expected life of five years, costs $5,000, and has an expected net cash inflow of $1,400 per year. Using a discount rate of 6 per cent, the present value of the Delano machine is $11,040 (7.3601 × $1,500) which is $1,040 above the present value of the outlay of $10,000. The Jolivet machine has a present value of $5,897.36 (4.2124 × $1,400), $897.36 above the investment outlay. At this point it would appear that the Delano machine is the pre-

---

[10] *See:* Table C-2, Appendix C.

ferred machine for it adds more to total present value but less on an annual basis. However, let's examine the two alternatives under an assumption of a common life span. To make them comparable we need to assume repeated replacement of the assets to some common multiple of the lives of the two machines. Fortunately, in this case a common multiple is one life of the Delano machine. Reinvesting $5,000 at the end of the fifth year gives a present value of the *outlay* of $3,735 (.747 × $5,000). This, added to the initial $5,000, makes a total outlay of $8,735. The present value of the net cash inflow of $1,400 for ten years is now $10,304 (7.3601 × $1,400), or $1,569 above the present value of the outlay. The results now illustrate that the Jolivet machine is to be preferred, which is the correct conclusion. The Jolivet machine permits the company to delay a $5,000 investment to the end of the fifth year. This illustration highlights the impact of *deferred investments* on the attractiveness of investment proposals.

SELECTION OF DIFFERENT TYPES OF PROPOSALS

The measurement of the attractiveness of investment proposals to this point has been relatively straightforward. A number of questions arise, however, regarding the techniques to be employed to measure the value of investment projects when demand is expected to grow, when prices are expected to change, when there are deferred investments, or where there are alternatives with different capacities for service. Each of these must now be examined.

Investment Alternatives with Different Service Capacities

A problem in analysis of investment proposals frequently occurs when management must consider two competing investment alternatives which have different capacities for service. The East Mask Company considered two machines—one capable of molding ten masks per day (2,000 per year) and costing $2,000 and another injection-molding machine costing $10,000 but capable of producing ten times the number of masks as the other machine. The problem was resolved when the sales of this mask were estimated at fourteen per day (or 3,000 per year). The masks sold for $1 a piece and the incremental net cash inflow from production and sale is anticipated to be $700 per year. Two of the smaller machines costing $4,000 could be used and—if we assume the machines have the same ten-year life—the expected rate of return would be about 12 per cent. The expected rate of return would be negative if the larger machine were to be purchased. Clearly the different service capacities present no ana-

lytical problem; the sales forecast determines the relative desirability of
the proposals. The company, however, should consider the alternative of
lower price and higher volume.

The Impact of Expected Growth in Demand and Price Changes

Expected Growth in Demand

Occasionally, analysts become somewhat concerned about their analysis when the demand for the product is expected to grow rapidly. Planning for extra capacity is normally worthwhile, especially when the costs
of the addition may be high. The larger initial outlay and the larger
maintenance and operating costs must be considered in the decision-making process. This situation creates no unusual problem for analysis, however. The alternative investments to consider are (1) low capacity now
with its lower initial outlay and lower operating and maintenance costs,
but with its associated costs of additions later on and (2) full capacity
now, all in view of a given forecast of demand. In fact, a whole range of
capacities could be considered to find the one which maximized the
profit. The important concept to be grasped here, however, is that the
time value of money tends to make lower-capacity alternatives more
attractive, for the addition to capacity involves a *deferred investment*.

For example, in 1932 the Welke Brewing Company was going to add
another bottling line. Short-term demand seemed to suggest the need
for a less than full capacity even though estimated growth in demand
made full capacity an eventual need. The choice then becomes one of
investing (1) $300,000 now to take care of long-term needs or (2) $200,-
000 now and $200,000 ten years from now when the additional capacity
is needed. Because both involve a $200,000 cash outlay now, the problem
is to decide whether it is worthwhile to pay out an extra $100,000 now or
$200,000 ten years from now. The alternatives may be compared by find-
ing the present worth of the $200,000 ten years away, using an appropri-
ate discount rate of, say, 8 per cent; the answer is $92,640. This makes the
deferred investment—the lower-capacity plan—more attractive when
compared to the additional $100,000 needed now. But this conclusion
ignores the additional costs of operating and maintaining the full-capacity
line for the first ten years. To correct for this we can find the present
value of these outlays of, say, $5,000 per year for ten years at 8 per cent;
this adds a cost of $33,550 to the full-capacity line, making for a total cash
outlay whose present worth is $133,550. Thus the deferred investment is
made even more attractive. The prediction of ten years as the point at
which additional capacity will be needed was based upon expected de-

mand; when converted to expected net cash inflows, it indicated that at this point in time it would be profitable to add to capacity.

Expected Price Changes

Additional complications in analysis may arise from *expectations of changes in price levels*. These should be incorporated into the analysis. The anticipation of a price rise may alter the investment decision. For example, an expected increase in the selling price of the proposed product may make some proposals more attractive. On the other hand, if the rise in price increases costs and cash outlays relatively faster than it does selling prices and cash receipts, it may make some investments less attractive. The prospect of rising prices may make the longer-lived investments relatively more attractive than shorter-lived investments and present investments more attractive than deferred investments. In the previous example, if price-level increases are assumed to have no impact on net cash flows (selling-price increases offset increased costs) but would involve an investment of $300,000 in ten years rather than $200,000, the decision would be altered in preference to the full-capacity line investment now. The present value of the $300,000 at 8 per cent is $138,960, which is a greater cost than the total of $133,550.

The Case of Exponentially Increasing Demand

In some cases growth in demand for a prospective product is expected to increase at a constant rate per annum. This may be the motive behind some new product proposals or when one firm is considering buying another. In this case the present-value formula can be amended to include a constantly increasing expected outcome by adding a progression factor to the numerator. Our basic formula (7) can be expressed as

$$PV = \sum_{t=1}^{n} \frac{EO\,(1+g)^{t-1}}{(1+d)^t} \qquad (8)$$

In this formula the expected outcome (EO) is the first year's expectation; thereafter the numerator will increase exponentially, reflecting a constant rate of growth (g). If the rate of growth exceeds the discount rate, additions to the present value sum will be increasing with time rather than, as customary, decreasing.[11] This increase in EO normally would be expected

[11] In the case of a perpetual investment, the present value would explode to an infinite value when $g>d$. Normally, however, the growth rate is not anticipated to increase infitely. Even if it were, the increasing uncertainty of such distant outcomes would require an increasing discount rate because of the increased spread of the subjective distributions (increased risk). A factor should be added to the denominator,

to continue for a limited period (m years) after which the outcome could be expected to be constant and the total expression would be

$$PV = \sum_{t=1}^{m} \frac{EO\,(1+g)^{t-1}}{(1+d)^t} + \sum_{t=m+1}^{n} \frac{EO\,(1+g)^{m-1}}{(1+d)^t} \quad (9)$$

Consider the case in which a new product was introduced by the Parks Corporation. It is expected that with the present value of total outlays of $100,000, the firm could handle all needs for their product in the coming years. The growth in net cash inflow is expected to take place at 50 per cent for the first five years after the initial year's net cash flow of $5,000. Thereafter sales are expected to level off so that the net cash flow would be $25,000 for the following five years, at the end of which time (it is assumed) obsolescence will eliminate the product. The net cash inflows and the present values are shown as follows:

Year	Net Cash Inflow	Present Value ($d = 10$ per cent)
1	$ 5,000	$ 4,545
2	7,500	6,198
3	11,250	8,452
4	16,875	11,525
5	25,312	15,716
6–10	25,000	58,825
	Total	$105,261

The present value of $105,261, less the present value of the outlays of $100,000, adds $5,261 to the value of the firm and therefore should be undertaken.

Investments to Reduce Risk

Reductions in risk exposure may be as valuable to the firm as proposals promising high dollar returns on new products or cost-saving investments. Many risk exposures can, of course, be transferred to various insuring firms. One type of decision is whether or not to purchase insurance. The

---

it has been argued, assuming a constant rate of increase in risk such that $d + v$ (for uncertainty) exceed g to limit the present value to a finite value. In such a case

$$PV = \sum_{t=1}^{\infty} \frac{EO\,(1+g)^{t-1}}{(1+d+v)^t}$$

See: Philip Kotler, "Elements in a Theory of Growth Stock Valuation," *Financial Analysts Journal*, 18 (May–June 1962), 35–44.

Wickman Company estimated that a flood of the river adjacent to its plant would cause damage in any year according to the probability distribution in Figure 16-3, and the expected cost would be

$$
\begin{aligned}
.90 \times \$ \qquad 0 &= \$ \qquad 0 \\
.01 \times \quad 40,000 &= \qquad 400 \\
.02 \times \quad 60,000 &= \quad 1,200 \\
.05 \times \quad 80,000 &= \quad 4,000 \\
.02 \times \quad 100,000 &= \quad 2,000 \\
\end{aligned}
$$

Expected Cost Per Year $7,600

An insurance company will offer a policy in which it will pay 80 per cent of all losses (coinsurance) for an annual premium of $6,180. The firm's expected cost would then be $7,700 [$6,180 + (.20) $7,600]. Under the scheme whereby the firm insures itself, the expected cost is $7,600. Although at first it would seem desirable to avoid the extra $100 expected cost, this conclusion ignores the value of the reduced risk to the firm. The firm can exchange a situation in which it might lose up to $100,000 for a situation in which the possible loss could vary only between $6,180 (the cost of insurance) and $26,180 (the case of $100,000 flood damage). Should the flood occur and the firm have no insurance, a large financial loss could bring about the failure of the firm and thus the loss of the total value of the enterprise. The Wickman Company took out the insurance policy from Williams Insurance Company.

Several months later the Hall Insurance Company offered to insure the plant at a premium of $1,500 per year if the Wickman Company

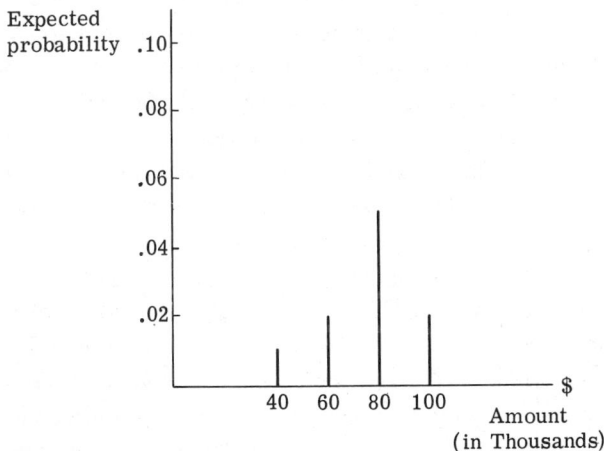

Figure 16-3   Estimated Frequency and Cost of Flood Damage per Year

would construct a spillway to carry off flood waters. The probability of overflowing such a spillway and causing damage to the plant is estimated at .035 and the overflow could cause about $40,000 in damages (including, of course, the cost of lost production time). The expected loss under self-insurance would be $1,400 ($40,000 × .035) + ($10 × .965), the possible losses being 0 or $40,000. Under the insurance plan, the possible loss would be $1,500 or $9,500 [$1,500 + (.20 × $40,000)] with an expected loss of $1,780 [$1,500 + .035 (.20 × $40,000)]. The spillway could be completed in a year and the savings in insurance premium costs would be $4,680 ($6,180 − $1,500) per year and the saving in expected loss (20 per cent of the expected loss) would be $1,240 ($1,520 − $280), or a total expected saving of $5,920 ($4,680 + $1,240). This saving would continue for the remaining life of the plant—twenty years. At an 8 per cent discount rate, the present value of the saving is $59,173. The cost of the spillway was $40,000, so the firm went ahead with construction and changed its insurance policy. This decision also contributed to the lessening of uncertainty about the potential losses and therefore would stabilize the firm's income and net cash inflow. A flood could not cause a financial loss of more than $8,000 (.20 × $40,000), whereas prior to the construction of the spillway the plant could have suffered a loss as great as $20,000 (.20 × $100,000).

The Impact of Investments Upon the Risk of the Firm and Capital Costs

It is conceivable that certain investments may so affect the over-all risk of a firm as to alter its capital costs. Consider, for example, the Meier Company, whose average risk of investment to investors of ¾ (SR/ER) requires an 8 per cent yield. This is the average cost of capital (k); its capital structure is half debt (yielding investors 3 per cent for a risk of about ½) and common stock equity (yielding investors 13 per cent for a risk of 1). The expected outcome of the firm is $120,000 per year.

The company has been producing air conditioners for many years. The sales of air conditioners are closely related to the heat of the summer. This, plus the fact that sales vary with the level of economic activity, contributes to the relatively high level of risk for this firm. The firm is currently considering the production of a new line—a new type of gas heater that creates its own supply of gas from a concentrated chemical tablet. These heaters are expected to sell reasonably well but sales would be related to the coldness of the winter. Some of the firm's equipment and facilities can be used for the new line so that the *additional* investment would require a present outlay of $300,000. Subjective probability distributions of expected outcomes yield a mean expected outcome of

$30,000 and the standard deviation of $20,000 produced a risk ($SO/EO$) of ⅔. The firm feels that the minimum attractive rate of return for an investment of this risk and size is 10 per cent. The expected outcome is expected to continue perpetually so that the present value is $300,000 ($30,000/.10), adding nothing to profits.

However, an important element was left out of the analysis. Although the new product's impact upon the net cash inflow and the investment outlays on the firm were evaluated properly on an incremental basis, its effect upon the variability in returns for the firm as a whole was not considered. The proper approach would be to revalue the whole firm with the added investment. The value of the firm before the investment was $1,500,000 ($120,000/.08). With the addition of the new line, the expected net cash flow totals $150,000. The new standard deviation of the expected outcomes obtained from the subjective probability distribution about the mean of $150,000 is equal to $100,000, and the risk is then ⅔. This narrowing of the range of variability relative to the mean is caused by diversification effects (for cold winters in this area are poorly correlated with hot summers). The lessened relative variability will enable the firm, in time, to secure capital at an average cost of, say, 7.5 per cent based upon the risk of ⅔. The value of the firm would then be about $2,000,000 ($150,000 ÷ .075). The gain in the value of the firm and hence the value of ownership would be $500,000. The value of the proposal becomes $500,000 ($2,000,000 − $1,500,000); the net present value is $200,000 ($500,000 − $300,000). This example illustrates the importance of giving consideration to the impact of the investment upon the risk of investment in the firm.

Replacement Decisions

If an asset is replaced by another asset performing the same service, a replacement decision must be made. Sometimes the replacement means disposal of the old asset, but it may mean the old asset is kept to perform other services (such as a standby role). Replacement decisions fall into two categories, depending on their nature. Some assets, for instance, deteriorate with time and fail gradually while others deliver full service to the end of their life—their length of life being, however, somewhat unpredictable. The latter type of problem involves a decision as to whether the firm should make replacements as the items fail or replace all items regularly even though most have not failed. The replacement of light bulbs is typical of this type of replacement decision. Although this is a profit-maximizing type of problem, it is of little concern to the financial manager for it involves no capital-expenditure analysis or time-preference analysis. An analytical solution for this type of problem has been developed, however.[12]

The replacement decision for items that fail gradually, however, does involve the time value of money and customarily becomes part of the capital budget of the firm. In replacement decisions the cost of an old machine (based on the present value of operating and maintenance costs) must be less than the expected cost of a proposed new machine (on the basis of its investment outlay plus operating and maintenance costs) to warrant its continued use. The undepreciated portion of the old asset, its original cost, and its annual depreciation are irrelevant except as they affect cash flow through income taxes. The realizable value or salvage value, however, involves cash and must be incorporated into the analysis.

In considering the replacement of an old asset by a new asset, the *savings* in operating and maintenance costs must be sufficient to make the new investment (less the salvage value) worthwhile. Operating and maintenance (including repairs) costs of deteriorating assets increase with time, so that the older the asset becomes the more profitable it will probably be to replace it. A gradually deteriorating old asset has a relatively short expected life and must be compared with a new asset with a longer expected life. This fact introduces complications in replacement analysis. Ideally, only investments of equal lives should be compared. The cost savings of the possible new asset could be figured for a time equal to the life of the old asset combined with some other alternative. For example, the old asset plus its replacement should be compared for a life span equal to that of the net asset. It will probably be necessary to compare cost savings under different assumptions to find the most favorable policy. Different assumptions, based upon increasing operating and maintenance costs, can be used for comparison—including some based upon the major alteration or overhaul of the old asset. The proposed replacement's cost saving may be based upon the continued use of the old asset and its replacement by a new asset, say, one year hence. In all cases the service assumptions must be equated. If a better replacement is anticipated in each of the later years, each of the alternative combinations of use of the old asset plus a later new asset should be considered. Unknown future proposed replacements are likely to be difficult to evaluate in a quantitative sense, but the estimates of their performance (based upon qualitative information) may be incorporated into analysis with greater uncertainty factors, involving larger discount rates. The expected economic life

---

[12] C. West Churchman, Russel L. Ackoff, and E. Leonard Arnoff, *Introduction to Operations Research* (New York: Wiley, 1957), 477–516; and Pierre Massé, *Optimal Investment Decisions* (Englewood Cliffs, N.J.: Prentice-Hall, 1962), 42–83.

of the proposed new asset is a problem involving a considerable amount of judgment. If the rate of obsolescence is high, a full physical life should not be used. Yet, requiring a very short payback period has the effect of continuing the service of old assets beyond their useful period.

The use of mathematical models in replacement decisions has been relatively well developed.[13] These models incorporate the problems described above. For example, a factor of rapidly decreasing salvage value of a new machine builds into the model the obsolescence impact on the life of the proposed investment. Even at that, however, lack of adequate data may hinder the application of such models. Many of the problems of replacement analysis can be seen in the following case.

About ten years ago Faerber and Hugon Manufacturing installed a data-processing system costing $12,000 and capable of handling the firm's needs except that a change in income taxes and some other methods of reporting expenses required that it rent another piece of equipment at $690 per year. For tax purposes, the firm had used the straight-line method, assuming a twenty-year life. The equipment was not expected to have any salvage value at the end of the twenty years. After the company's purchase of another firm, its needs will about double; additional equipment could be added to the existing system but the addition to rental costs would be quite high. A number of plans were proposed by the data-processing department:

System 1. Add rental equipment costing $5,010 per year, thereby not requiring additional investment.

System 2. Install another system like the present one which would double total capacity and involve only one rental unit of $690 per year. This system, however, would require $15,000 in new investment.

System 3. Sell the existing system for $4,000 and replace it with a new Sorensen system requiring a $24,000 investment and rental costs of $970.

System 4. Sell the old system for $4,000 and replace it with a system requiring a $30,000 investment but rental costs of only $510 per year.

The company expects any selection to be almost completely obsolete in ten years and any new equipment purchased now could be sold for one third its original cost at the end of the ten-year period. Annual property taxes are 1 per cent of original costs; operating and maintenance costs are about the same for all systems. The company assumes a 50 per cent corporate income tax rate; financial management suggests 6 per cent as the appropriate discount rate for this low-risk investment.

[13] *See*, for example: Edward H. Bowman, and Robert B. Fetter, *Analysis for Production Management*, rev. ed. (Homewood, Ill.: Irwin, 1961), 365–95; and George Terbough, *Dynamic Equipment Policy* (New York: McGraw, 1959).

The relevant costs for tax purposes for these plans are property taxes, rental costs, and depreciation. These are calculated as

	System 1	System 2	System 3	System 4
Property taxes	$ 120	$ 270	$ 240	$ 300
Rental costs	5,700	1,380	970	510
Depreciation (SL)	600	1,600	1,600	2,000
	$6,420	$3,250	$2,810	$2,810
Extra taxable income over System 1		$3,170	$3,610	$3,610
Income tax (50%) over System 1		$1,585	$1,805	$1,805

The book value of the present system is $6,000 and, because it can be sold for only $4,000, the loss of $2,000 is a tax-deductible expense which reduces current taxes by $1,000. Thus the realizable cash value of System 1 is $5,000 ($4,000 + $1,000). This $5,000 reduces the investment requirements of Systems 3 and 4 by $5,000. Ten years from now realizable salvage values for Systems 2, 3, and 4, respectively, are $5,000, $8,000, and $10,000. The net cash flows for the three systems over System 1 are shown below:

Year	System 1	System 2	System 3	System 4
0 (net investment outlay)	$0	−$15,000	−$19,000	−$25,000
1	0	+ 2,585	+ 2,805	+ 3,205
2	0	+ 2,585	+ 2,805	+ 3,205
3	0	+ 2,585	+ 2,805	+ 3,205
4	0	+ 2,585	+ 2,805	+ 3,205
5	0	+ 2,585	+ 2,805	+ 3,205
6	0	+ 2,585	+ 2,805	+ 3,205
7	0	+ 2,585	+ 2,805	+ 3,205
8	0	+ 2,585	+ 2,805	+ 3,205
9	0	+ 2,585	+ 2,805	+ 3,205
10	0	+ 2,585	+ 2,805	+ 3,205
10	0	+ 5,000	+ 8,000	+ 10,000

Systems 2, 3, and 4 show yearly net cash savings above System 1 of $2,585, $2,805, and $3,205, respectively. For example, System 1 costs $5,820 ($120 + $5,700) per year and System 2 costs $3,235 ($270 + $1,380 + $1,585), so that the cash savings of System 2 over System 1 are $2,585. System 1 involves no annual savings over the other systems, so that if System 2, 3, or 4 has a positive present value, it will be preferable to

System 1. The net present value can be computed by summing the negative outlay with the positive value of net cash flows and the present value of the salvage value. The net present value of System 2 is $7,753 (− $15,-000 + $19,961 + $2,792); the net present value of System 3 is $7,090 (− $19,000 + $21,659 + $4,431); the net present value of System 4 is $5,286 (− $25,000 + $24,748 + $5,538). The analysis indicates that System 2 would maximize profits.

The assumptions made in this case for purposes of simplicity should be noted. The analysis assumed a comparative life for all systems of ten years, assumed no additional superior systems would be forthcoming soon, and assumed straight-line depreciation with the 50 per cent tax rate. The use of accelerated depreciation and investment tax credit along with the 48 per cent rate would have reduced income taxes in the early years more than in the later years and hence would have tended to make Systems 3 and 4 more favorable. The interested student may wish to apply his tax and analytical skills to determine whether the decision would be altered.

CAPITAL BUDGETING

From among all the possible investment proposals submitted, the firm must choose those that will maximize profits. It must bring together in a budget the requirements for capital outlays and the availability of funds to supply those needs. Some of the investment proposals may be competing or even mutually exclusive. Other projects may be completely independent of each other and investment in one has no impact at all on the profitability of others. In yet other cases two or more investments may be complementary, in that the profitability of one or more exists only if the other(s) is undertaken. More than likely there will also be proposals which are partially independent, having partially competing or partially complementary impacts on other projects.[14]

The choice of a particular set of investment proposals depends in part upon the policy set down by management with respect to the supply of funds. Management may consider that the supply of funds available to it for the coming year is fixed. Such a policy tends to be restrictive of the maximizing ability of the firm. Nevertheless, such conditions may exist, although they are more likely to exist for the departments and divisions within the firm than for the enterprise as a whole. Usually, however, only expenditures above a certain dollar figure must secure capital budget approval and small expenditures can be approved by middle- and lower-

[14] For a more detailed discussion of this point, *see:* Neil R. Paine, "Uncertainty and Capital Budgeting," *The Accounting Review*, 39 (April 1964), 330–32.

management personnel who have only a limited budget for such expenditures.

The limitation of funds does not alter the basic nature of the problem. It is like the unlimited budget except that, after a certain quantity of funds has been used, the cost of funds are assumed to be infinitely high.

The solution to the budget problem is to find that combination of proposals which maximizes profit. The Miki Shopping Center, Inc., has a *capital limit* (set by the board of directors) of $250,000 and the following set of *independent* investment proposals:

Investment	Net Present Value	Investment Requirement
A	$17,000	$ 50,000
B	50,000	200,000
C	14,000	160,000
D	20,000	100,000
E	7,000	50,000
F	29,000	150,000

There exist many possible combinations, such as A alone, B alone, AB, ABE, and so on, some of which exceed the capital limit. There are sixty-three combinations to consider.[15] Twenty-three of them conform to the capital constraint. In this case the answer appears rather obvious; the combination of A and B adds $67,000 to the value of the firm. It was assumed in this case that all these proposals had no impact upon the firm's existing operations and that variations in uncertainty were accounted for in the choice of discount rates in the computation of the various present values.

In cases in which the firm can assume independence, the selection could be made by taking the ratio of net present value to the investment requirements. Such a ratio has been referred to as a *profitability index*. These would be as follows:

A	.34
B	.25
C	.14
D	.20
E	.14
F	.19+

[15] $_nC_r = \dfrac{n!}{(n-r)!\,r!}$ where $n = 6$ and r equals first 1, then 2, then 3–6; when $n = 1$, $C = 6$, and, respectively, $C = 15$, $C = 20$, $C = 15$, $C = 6$, $C = 1$. The total is 63.

Normally they would then be ranked as follows:

A	.34	$ 50,000
B	.25	200,000
D	.20	100,000
F	.19+	150,000
⌈C⌉ (or)	.14	100,000
⌊E⌋	.14	50,000

A line could then have been drawn (the cutoff point) where the cumulative investment requirements equaled the capital constraint. Problems would exist, however, if the cutoff point hit the middle of one project. Then a search process like the one used would be required.

When the independence (of other proposals and of the firm) assumption is removed, net present values must be computed for all combinations of projects based upon incremental cash flows, investments, and the impact upon risk of the firm as a whole. The process is obviously tedious when done by hand, but it is less of a problem for the computer to calculate such values and search for the combination of proposals that maximizes the value to the firm (and thus the value of ownership, assuming the proportion of nonownership capital is not altered). The evaluation may also take into consideration the size of the total budget upon costs of capital and when the size becomes large enough to reach the rising portion of the cost of capital curve, the marginal cost encountered there must be used for those levels of capital demand.

Mathematical models to the solution of the budgeting problem exist, but are helpful only under certain assumptions.[16] Both dynamic and linear programming methods have been applied to some such allocation problems. Given the firm's existing resources and a number of alternative equipment choices, that combination of inputs that maximizes profits can be found. The particular equipment, when combined with the other resources that maximize the objective, is automatically selected.[17]

It can be seen that when the assumption of independence of the various proposals from each other exists and when all proposals are assumed to have no impact upon existing costs and expectations, the analysis is not too difficult. These assumptions are not likely to hold true for the majority

[16] See: Joel Cord, "A Method for Allocating Funds to Investment Projects when Returns Are Subject to Uncertainty," *Management Science*, 10 (January 1964), 335–41; H. M. Weingartner, *Mathematical Programming and the Analysis of Capital Budgeting Problems* (Englewood Cliffs, N.J.: Prentice-Hall, 1963); and N. Charnes, W. W. Cooper, and M. H. Miller, "Application of Linear Programming to Financial Budgeting and the Costing of Funds," *Journal of Business*, 32 (January 1959), 20–46.

[17] Pierre Massé, *Optimal Investment Decisions* (Englewood Cliffs, N.J.: Prentice-Hall, 1962), 84–197, 373–92.

of the proposals before the firm. Under such circumstances, it is better to approach the budgeting problem from the point of view of the value of the firm. This approach was suggested earlier in this chapter in the Meier Company illustration, when the proposed investment resulted in a reduction in the risk of the firm and caused a decline in capital costs, thus increasing the value of the firm. The value of the firm, prior to the acceptance of the proposal, was $1,500,000 ($120,000/.08). The addition of the project reduced the standard deviation of the possible outcomes (the possible *ex post* values of the firm) and permitted a reduction in the discount rate such that the capitalized value became $2,000,000 ($150,000/.075). Under this approach each of the possible combinations of proposals with the existing firm operations would be computed to find the value-maximizing combination.

SUMMARY

Decisions to invest determine the underlying profitability of the enterprise, whether profitability is measured in terms of profits or accounting profits. The information upon which the investments are based are estimates of outcomes, investment requirements, and an appropriate discount rate based upon estimates of the cost of capital to the firm and the estimated risk inherent in the particular project. Past errors, "sunk" costs, and accumulated depreciation are all irrelevant for purposes of investment decisions except to the extent that they influence the taxability (therefore cash flows) of the firm. Estimates of cash outflows and inflows must be incremental in nature, for many proposed investments may have an impact on the firm's existing operations. Subjective distributions will be required to determine the confidence in the estimates of expected outcomes. Generally, project evaluations go through successive phases, during each of which the firm must make a decision regarding the acceptance or rejection of the project or the securing of more information at some cost.

There exist several methods by which to measure the attractiveness of investment proposals. The *payback* method involves the length of time required for the project to return in net cash inflow the amount of the investment outlay. Payback fails to consider any time distribution of cash flows and, even though widely used because of its simplicity, it ignores any cash flow beyond the payback period. The *time-adjusted* (or *internal*) *rate-of-return* and the present-value methods are much more precise in their evaluations. The time-adjusted rate of return, however, assumes funds received from cash flow are reinvested at the derived rate of return and can give unreliable results when the estimated outcomes vary from period to period.

Firms are generally unwilling to exchange a certain cost (the cost of capital) for uncertain returns and consequently require a return in excess of cost. This is borne out by the observation that the realized internal rate of return of operating firms usually exceeds the cost of capital. As a result, firms use a cutoff rate above the cost of capital. The discount rate or cutoff rate should be raised or lowered as the risk of the proposal deviates from the average for the firm; it would also tend to be adjusted to the proposal's size relative to the business wealth.

Investment proposals of different lengths of life should be compared on an equal-life basis (established by finding a common multiple of the life of the alternatives). Expected increases in prices may make deferred investments attractive sooner or larger-capacity investments more attractive unless an expected decrease in the net cash inflow (caused by increased costs) makes the project unattractive. It is conceivable that certain investments may so affect the over-all risk of the firm that capital costs are altered. In such cases, the value of the entire firm is affected. An investment with relatively low returns may be attractive if it tends so to reduce risk that capital costs can be significantly reduced too.

After the final stage of evaluation, projects remaining for consideration must be studied in relation to each other and to the supply of funds. Some investments are mutually exclusive, others are independent and some are complementary in nature. Consequently, some proposals, when combined, may have a differing impact upon the value of the firm. All feasible combinations of proposals should be examined to find the maximizing combination satisfying the capital constraint. If no constraint exists, successively larger combinations requiring more capital must be evaluated, using increasing discount rates to reflect rising capital costs. It will pay to add projects up to the point where the value of the firm is not increased by the addition of the last project.

SUGGESTED READINGS

American Management Association. *How the DuPont Organization Appraises Its Performance.* New York: The Association, 1950.

————. *Tested Approaches to Capital Equipment Replacement,* New York: The Association, 1954.

BIERMAN, HAROLD, JR., LAWRENCE E. FOURAKER, and ROBERT K. JAEDICKS. *Quantitative Analysis for Business Decisions.* Homewood, Ill.: Richard D. Irwin, Inc., 1961.

————, and SEYMOUR SMIDT. *The Capital Budgeting Decision.* New York: The Macmillan Company, 1960.

DAVIDSON, SIDNEY, and DAVID F. DRAKE. "Capital Budgeting and the 'Best' Tax Depreciation Method," *Journal of Business, 34* (October 1961), 442–52.

DEAN, JOEL. *Capital Budgeting,* New York: Columbia University Press, 1951.

————. "Measuring the Productivity of Capital," *Harvard Business Review, 32* (January–February 1954), 120–30.

DERMAN, CYRUS. "Optimum Replacement and Maintenance under Markovian Deterioration with Profitability Bounds on Failure," *Management Science, 9* (April 1963), 478–81.

DILBECK, HAROLD K. "Capital Budgeting: Applied Aspects of Theory," *Public Utilities Fortnightly, 73* (March 26, 1964), 19–23.

DOBROVOLSKY, SERGI P. "Depreciation Policies and Investment Decisions," *American Economic Review, 41* (December 1951) 906–14.

DOMAR, E. D. "Depreciation, Replacement, and Growth," *Economic Journal, 63* (March 1953), 1–32.

DOUGALL, HERBERT E. "Payback as an Aid in Capital Budgeting," *The Controller, 24* (February 1961), 67 ff.

EISEN, M., and N. LEIBOMITZ. "Replacement of Randomly Deteriorating Equipment," *Management Science, 9* (January 1963), 268–76.

GANT, DONALD R. "Illusion in Lease Financing," *Harvard Business Review, 37* (March–April 1959), 121–42.

GORDON, MYRON J. *The Investment, Financing and Valuation of the Corporation.* Homewood, Ill.: Richard D. Irwin, Inc., 1962.

GORT, MICHAEL. "The Planning of Investment: A Study of Capital Budgeting in the Electric-Power Industry," Parts I and II, *Journal of Business, 24* (April 1951), 181–202.

HAYNES, W. WARREN, and MARTIN B. SOLOMON. "A Misplaced Emphasis in Capital Budgeting," *The Quarterly Review of Economics and Business, 2* (February 1962), 39–46.

HEDGES, BOB A. "Modifying the Business Financial Plan to Reduce Static Risk Management Costs," *The Journal of Finance, 19* (May 1964), 340–48.

LITTLE, L. T. "Historical Costs or Present Values?" *Economic Journal, 62* (December 1952), 848–71.

MEIJ, J. L. (ed.). *Depreciation and Replacement Policy.* Chicago: Quadrangle Books, 1961.

MERRETT, A. J., and ALLEN SYKES. *The Finance and Analysis of Capital Projects.* New York: John Wiley & Sons, Inc., 1963.

REUL, R. "Profitability Index for Investments," *Harvard Business Review,* 35 (July–August 1957), 116–32.

SHILLINGLAW, GORDON. "Guides to Internal Profit Measurement," *Harvard Business Review,* 35 (March–April 1957), 82–94.

———. "Profit Analysis for Abandonment Decisions," *Journal of Business,* 30 (January 1957), 17–29.

SMITH, VERNON L. "Depreciation, Market Valuations, and Investment Theory," *Management Science,* 9 (July 1963), 690–98.

SOLOMON, EZRA (ed.). *The Management of Corporate Capital.* New York: The Free Press of Glencoe, Inc., 1959.

SOLOMON, EZRA. *The Theory of Financial Management.* New York: Columbia University Press, 1963.

TERBOUGH, GEORGE. *Business Investment Policy.* Washington, D.C.: Machinery and Allied Products Institute, 1958.

WALTER, JAMES E. "A Discriminant Function for Earnings—Price Ratios for Large Industrial Corporations," *Review of Economics and Statistics,* 41 (February 1959), 44–52.

WELLISZ, S. "Entrepreneur's Risk, Lender's Risk and Investment," *Review of Economic Studies,* 20 (February 1953), 105–14.

QUESTIONS

16.1 How do the data requirements for investment decisions differ from the data made available through accounting records?

16.2 Are all past outlays for resources irrelevant for investment decisions? Explain.

16.3 How does an anticipated salvage or realizable sale value enter into an investment decision?

16.4 Why is it important to deal in incremental flows of cash?

16.5 Why should firms not be expected to invest in proposals expected to return the cost of capital or a little better? How can firms be expected to behave in their investment decisions in the face of such conclusions?

16.6 What are the advantages and disadvantages of the payback investment-selection method?

16.7 What implicit assumptions are present when the time-adjusted rate-of-return method is used as a measure of investment desirability?

16.8 What is the impact of deferred investments on the value of an investment alternative?

16.9 What peculiar problems are raised for the investment decision-maker when a growth in demand is anticipated? Explain.

16.10 Explain the consequences for valuation techniques when the rate of growth of cash flow exceeds the discount rate.

16.11 Why may it be beneficial to the firm to invest to reduce its risk?

16.12 Differentiate between *mutually exclusive, independent,* and *complementary* capital-expenditure proposals.

PROBLEMS

16.13 The Henning Ranch is considering the purchase of a new hay-baler. If it can be purchased for $8,000, savings in labor and storage costs are anticipated, as well as a larger amount of usable hay because of the greater efficiency of the new machine. The incremental cash flows are as follows:

$t = 0$	−8,000
1	+2,000
2	+2,000
3	+2,000
4	+2,000
5	+4,000

The fifth-year flow reflects the desire of Henning to sell the machine at the end of five years for $2,000. Find: (*a*) the payback period; (*b*) the rate of return; and (*c*) the present value ($d = .10$).

16.14 Refer to the data on the Zulauf Corporation in Problem 15.27. The advertising manager wants an appropriation budget of $30,000 for the current fiscal year, which will increase sales (in his opinion) by $80,000. (*a*) In discussing the profit-planning aspects of this proposal, what figures will you use? Assume that this year's fixed costs will be the same as last year's. (*b*) If the average cost of capital were 8 per cent, comment on the desirability of the proposal.

16.15 A government bond of Great Britain promises to pay £50 per year perpetually. (*a*) If investments of equivalent risk in the market yielded

5 per cent, what value would you place on such an issue with no maturity? (*b*) If investments of equivalent risk sold to yield 4 per cent, what value would you assign? (*c*) If the market yield should be 6 per cent, what value should you assign? (*d*) What is your rate of return if you pay £2,000? (*a*) If capital costs you 5 per cent and the bond sold in the market to yield 5 per cent, would you buy it? Explain.

16.16 A 4 per cent bond of the Hoogstraat Glass Works, Inc., has four years to maturity and has a face value of $1,000. (*a*) What is the rate of return if it can be purchased at $980? (*b*) What is its value if investments of equivalent risk are selling to yield 5 per cent? (*c*) Find a table of bond values and compare your answers.

16.17 The Pigott Car Company is considering an investment in a piece of equipment costing $150,000. It is expected to yield an incremental net cash flow of $17,000 per year for ten years. (*a*) Compute the rate of return using Table C-2 in Appendix C. (*b*) Find the present value first by the annuity formula (6) and then by the use of Table C-2, Appendix C, if management feels an appropriate discount rate for this investment is 12 per cent. (*c*) Is this investment a desirable one?

16.18 A law student is considering an investment in a Master of Business Administration degree. He feels he must have a 10 per cent yield to compensate for capital costs and uncertainty. His outlays will be $2,000 in each of the two years needed to complete the program and he estimates he will forfeit two years' income at $6,000 per year. He estimates the income to him with and without the degree to be as follows:

Year	Without MBA	With MBA
3	$ 6,000	$ 7,000
4	7,000	8,000
5	8,000	9,000
6	8,000	10,000
7	9,000	11,000
8	9,000	12,000
9	10,000	13,000
10	10,000	15,000
11–15	12,000	20,000
16–20	12,000	25,000
20–30	12,000	30,000
30–40	15,000	30,000

(*a*) What is the net present value of the incremental negative and positive cash flows? Figure only for first 25 years. (*b*) What should be his decision?

16.19 The Hubbard Fuel Company owns two chain saws bought a year ago at $225 each. A third saw is being rented at $5 a month. One saw, damaged and not insured, is expected to cost $60 to repair. The Rosenthal Sales & Service Company suggested that Hubbard sell the two saws to Rosenthal for a total price of $270 and rent two more at $5 a month. The service company buys them wholesale and services the saws themselves and thus it should cost Hubbard less. The annual renting cost for two saws would be $120 (12 × $10) less depreciation cost saved by the sale of $30 ($270/9) or $90 according to Rosenthal. Rosenthal estimates the annual cost to Hubbard of owning the two saws as follows:

Repair	$ 60
Depreciation	45 ($450/10)
Taxes	14 (3 per cent of original cost)
Servicing costs	20
	$139

Evaluate the Rosenthal analysis and make your recommendation, assuming capital yields 8 per cent to Hubbard. Assume $60 repair is an annual expected expense for two saws. Ignore income taxes.

16.20 Five years ago the Mitchell Manufacturing Company installed a new furnace for $9,600. A salesman for the Brown Heating Company recommended that it be replaced with a new heat pump. The Brown salesman estimated an annual saving in fuel cost of $2,000 and no other differences in costs or service. The cost of the heat pump is $12,000, but $1,000 will be allowed on the old furnace. The old furnace was fully depreciated with no salvage value. It is, however, still capable of providing several more years of service. The new machine would be depreciated by the sum-of-the-digits method over five years with zero expected salvage value. The effective corporate tax rate is 48 per cent, with 24 per cent on capital gains. The management's discount rate for this analysis is 10 per cent after taxes. State your assumptions and make the investment decision. Support your conclusion. Assume old furnace can operate five more years.

16.21 Buckley Industries is considering an investment in a new product developed by its research department. The investment required is $100,000, and the estimated incremental cash flow to the company is $5,000 the first year and will increase at the rate of 10 per cent per annum. The company's required return for this risk and size of investment is 8 per cent. (a) If the life of the new line is infinite, what is the decision; what is the approximate net present value? (b) What problems are encountered in the analysis and how may they be overcome?

16.22 The Allen and Smith Corporation is confronted with a number of investment proposals. The firm's funds are limited to $200,000 and as long as any proposal has an investment requirement between $10,000 and $100,000 and a risk between ¼ and ¾ the discount rate used is 10 per cent. There is no impact on the firm's capital costs. The following investment proposals are available:

Proposal	Present Value Outlay (10%)	Present Value Net Inflows (10%)
A	$30,000	$ 35,000
B	70,000	100,000
C	50,000	60,000
D	90,000	100,000

(*a*) What proposal(s) should be accepted? (*b*) Assume that, if B were undertaken, the present value of net inflows of C is zero or, if C were undertaken, the present value of net inflows of A is zero. What proposal(s) should be accepted in each of the two events? (*c*) Assume that, if A were undertaken, the present value of net inflows of D would increase to $120,000. Which proposal(s) should be accepted?

16.23 The Burke Candy Company has agreed on the following discount rates, given its weighted average cost of capital of 8 per cent and business risk of ½:

Size of Investment \ Risk	¼	½	¾	1	
$1 to $9,999	8	9	10	11	
$10,000 to $49,999	9	10	11	12	Rate
$50,000 to $99,999	10	11	12	13	
Over $99,999	11	12	13	14	

The following net cash flows are expected for the four investment proposals:

Proposal \ Time	0	1	2	3	4	5
A	−$15,000	+$2,000	+$2,000	+$2,000	+$2,000	+$2,000
B	− 40,000	+ 2,000	+ 8,000	+10,000	+10,000	+10,000
C	− 70,000	+ 5,000	+15,000	+15,000	+15,000	+20,000
D	−140,000	−10,000	+20,000	+30,000	+30,000	+30,000

Proposal \ Time	6	7	8	9	10	Risk
A	+$2,000	+$2,000	+$2,000	+$2,000	+$4,000	½
B	+10,000	+10,000	+10,000			1
C						¼
D	+30,000	+30,000	+30,000	+30,000	+50,000	½

The proposals are all independent of one another. (*a*) Compute the net present value and profitability index of each. (*b*) What should be their decision (1) if unlimited funds are available; or (2) if only $120,000 in funds is available at the 8 per cent cost?

16.24 If in the Burke Candy case above another $100,000 in funds could be secured at an average cost of 10 per cent, which would raise the required return (discount rate) by two percentage points in each case, what would be the proper investment decision?

CHAPTER 17   EXPANSION AND CONTRACTION

Firms may expand by a variety of methods, but two common ways are (1) growth from within through retained earnings or sale of securities, and (2) the acquisition of other business units or parts of units by holding companies, purchases of assets, mergers or consolidations. Expansion may be vertical, horizontal, complementary, or diversified. Vertical (the acquisition of the firms of customers or suppliers), horizontal (the acquisition of the competitor firms), and complementary (the acquisition of a company that can use at least some of the existing facilities of the firm) expansion are presumed to have favorable impacts on the firm, especially upon earnings. Diversified expansion (the acquisition of business whose demand is unrelated to existing business) has an impact primarily upon the reduction of risk in the firm.

The *motives* for expansion are to increase the value of the firm through risk reduction or increased net cash inflow, or both. Horizontal expansion, for example, presumes that larger size will decrease unit costs of production. Often, however, the economies of scale do not justify the degree of horizontal or vertical expansion achieved. Other motives of management—such as security, power, and prestige—may become more relevant in such decisions.

INTERNAL EXPANSION

Growth by internal expansion is attractive to many firms, for it permits them to expand gradually without the initial losses customarily involved in absorbing another concern. It also avoids the issuance of securities either for the acquisition or for cash, thereby enabling the firm to rely only upon internal sources and avoid any possible loss of control. In fact, many small businesses find it difficult to sell securities of any kind, so internally generated capital becomes the only source for expansion. Internal sources depend principally upon funds provided by noncash depleciation charges against revenue and retained earnings. As depleciation sources can normally be expected to be reinvested, the primary source which is a variable under control of the firm is retained earnings.

The retained earnings are directly affected by the dividends paid by the firm. It is to the policy of the firm toward dividends that we shall now direct our attention.

Dividend Policy

As a general rule, stockholders have no *right* to receive dividends. The power to declare dividends is in the hands of the board of directors. In accordance with the articles of incorporation or the bylaws, the directors specify the amount and form (cash, stock, or other property) of the dividend, the class of stock affected, the stockholders of record, and the date of payment. The stockholders of records are determined about two weeks prior to the payment. This is called the *record date;* it is the date on which the list of stockholders to whom dividends are to be paid is made up. When the board has declared a dividend, the stockholders have a right to receive it and it becomes a liability of the corporation payable to the individual stockholders (now creditors). Although even preferred stockholders depend upon the board of directors for their dividends, the board usually recognizes the significance of maintaining the corporation's credit standing through the continuance of dividends, to say nothing of their awareness of a common provision for a shift in voting control when a certain number of preferred dividend payments have been bypassed.

Questions concerning the legality of various dividends are very complex because of the varying laws of the different states. In about one third of the states the law stipulates that no dividend may be paid when the firm is insolvent or when payments would result in insolvency; in most states, no dividend may be paid unless the value of the assets after payment exceeds the liabilities and legal capital (par or stated value of the stock). In a few states no dividend can be paid unless an earned surplus (retained earnings) exists. In most states, then, dividends cannot impair the legal capital, the par or stated value of outstanding shares. If a dividend has been illegally paid, many states require stockholders to return it. Generally, directors are not liable for the illegality as long as they relied on audited financial statements. In other cases the penalty, when imposed, generally calls for recovery of the illegal dividend from directors, who then become personally liable. Often bond, loan, or preferred stock contractual provisions may restrict dividends only to the earnings retained after issuance of the security or require the maintenance of a working capital or net working capital position which may render it impossible to make cash dividend disbursements. These provisions are intended to preserve, if not enhance, the cash position of the firm so that it is better able to meet interest or dividends as well as principal payments on the securities and is an example of a *control cost* the firm often must assume when using this source of capital.

Stock dividends on common stock are fairly usual. A *stock dividend* is the payment of the stock (common stock usually) of the firm as a dividend; as in the case of cash dividends, a charge is made against retained earnings. Instead of reducing cash, however, a stock dividend increases the common stock account. In some cases stock dividends are large relative to existing shares. The purpose of the stock dividend in this case may be to raise the "legal" capital in order to qualify the company for a greater volume of business (as in the case of a financial institution). In other cases large stock dividends may be paid to reduce the price of the shares in the market in order to make them more marketable to a larger group of investors or to reduce market risk.

A stock dividend may also be paid as a substitute for a cash dividend. When used for this purpose a stock dividend is customarily relatively small. Because a firm does not have to part with any cash, stock dividends can be a distinct advantage if cash is needed by the firm. Such dividends also tend to satisfy stockholders, for those who wish a cash dividend can sell their additional stock (although there are selling costs involved and the stockholders dilute their proportionate equity in the firm by so doing). If the selling stockholder holds the stock six months or more, the proceeds from the sale are taxed as capital gains. On the other hand cash dividends are taxed as ordinary income. A disadvantage for the firm and thus for stockholders is the expense of issuing the new certificates and handling fractional shares (sometimes paid in cash). All of these advantages and disadvantages notwithstanding, once it has been decided that reinvestment of earnings is in the stockholders' best interests, there appears to be little constraint on the size of stock dividends issued as a substitute for cash. However, a stock dividend whose value (measured by its equivalence in market value per share) exceeds current earnings would tend to mislead stockholders into believing that the whole stock dividend is income and not a liquidation of capital, as part of it must be in such cases.[1]

Once investment projects have been selected, the role of dividend policy is to determine just how much of the investment, if any, must be financed by external sources. The size of the cash dividend is usually determined by a number of factors—especially the past and current accounting profits after taxes, depleciation and other noncash charges against revenue, anticipated accounting profits, the state of firm liquidity, changes in sales, business confidence, and the firm's record of dividend payments. The size of the dividend tends to vary *inversely* with the change

[1] The topics of stock splits and stock dividends are discussed further in Chapter 20.

in sales but directly with the other variables.[2] This certainly suggests that financial expediency—as indicated by the liquidity measure, cash flow— is an important determinant beyond legality.

There are still other factors which tend to make firms rely more heavily upon retained earnings for financing investments than for distributing cash dividends. For some firms securities may be difficult to sell. In some cases the owners or management may want to avoid losing control and will not sell voting stock. (This would be especially true of smaller, more closely held firms.) High marginal income tax rates on shareholders' ordinary income tend to make dividend payments a less attractive form of stockholder income. Finally, the nature of the securities markets at the time equity financing is needed may be such as to make the sale of securities unattractive.

As a general observation the dividend policies of most mature firms without great investment demand for capital can be classified in one of two ways. Some firms, especially those with more stable accounting profits and cash flows, attempt to pay a *regular dividend* to be maintained even in less prosperous periods. In prosperous periods, the firm may declare "extras" which are not to be considered to be regular dividends. This type of policy tends to elevate the respectability of the stock toward the so-called blue-chip circle. Blue-chip firms have an established record of meeting regular dividends and will not increase the dividend unless prospects are excellent that the higher regular dividend can be maintained. Such a policy tends to disburse ownership and appeals to more conservative investors desiring dividend income. Once this type of investor following is established, any dividend failure may cause considerable stock liquidation—accompanied, of course, by a decline in stock price. In fact, to many, the payment of the established dividend may even be considered important to the credit standing of the company.

The second kind of dividend policy—that of paying a *relatively constant percentage of earnings* (accounting profits)—generally does not allow a firm to move into the blue-chip class but does tend to avoid excessive market repercussions of changing dividends as earnings change. In this case the investor following is conditioned to a relatively constant dividend policy. Growth firms also tend to favor this policy, only their investment following is the type which expects a low dividend ratio and presumably is interested in capital gains rather than in cash dividends. These rapidly growing firms tend to gather an investor following that

[2] Paul G. Darling, "The Influence of Expectation and Liquidity on Dividend Policy," *The Journal of Political Economy*, 55 (June 1957), 209–24.

prefers capital gains, and the stock does not tend to sell any more cheaply than that of firms following other dividend policies.

As the objective of the firm is to maximize profits, the firm is looking for that combination of capital gain in shares plus dividends which is greatest. Unless the firm already has an established dividend, profits may be maximized by retaining 100 per cent of earnings (if these can be reinvested at an internal rate of return equal to or above the cost of capital plus the appropriate risk premium for the proposals).[3] This policy suggests that dividend policy, if not already established, should not call for cash disbursements unless the firm's profitable investment demand is insufficient to use all the cash generated. Thus a dual policy of paying dividends and selling common stock also appears theoretically unrealistic, for the dividends should not be paid when obviously the investment demand is such that stock must be sold to raise additional capital. But because at some stage in the life of the firm it may pay to sell some of the ownership and attract more investors, a dividend policy—however meager at first—needs to be considered. Also, a firm's equity capital requirements might not be totally satisfied by retained earnings and hence resort to the equity markets may be necessary. In this event, the sale of stock with an acceptable dividend policy or the prospects for one may be greatly facilitated and the firm's cost of equity capital may be lower than it would have been in the absence of the dividend.

METHODS OF EXTERNAL EXPANSION

The greater risk of investment in small firms tends to make them seek greater security by becoming a part of a large enterprise; studies of the 1931–46 period illustrated the point that the rate of return on ownership was more volatile for smaller firms than for larger units.[4] Expansion can be achieved more rapidly through external means, although it may be difficult to assimilate large additions to the firm quickly and economically. The methods of acquisition or combination used vary according to the particular circumstances. Quite often tax, legal, and control considerations dictate the particular method used. The methods we shall briefly examine

[3] For a general formulation of a mathematical model to determine a presumably optimal dividend payment, *see:* David W. Miller and Martin K. Starr, *Executive Decisions and Operations Research* (Englewood Cliffs, N.J.: Prentice-Hall, 1960), 328–34.

[4] Richards C. Osborn, "The Relative Profitability of Large, Medium-sized, and Small Business," *Accounting Review,* (October 1950), 402–11; and (by the same author) *Effects of Corporate Size on Efficiency and Profitability* (Urbana, Ill.: University of Illinois, Bureau of Economic and Business Research, 1950).

include merger by sale of assets, merger by holding company and dissolution, statutory merger, and consolidation.

Examination of these methods does not constitute a complete examination of all forms of control or combination. Certain informal "arrangements" allow cooperation among firms designed to enhance the profits to shareholders of both firms.[5] These combinations usually take the form of trusts (little used today) and holding companies. A *holding company* is a firm that owns controlling stock in other holding companies or operating corporations. This involves the purchase of stock to acquire control and allows the controlled company, called a *subsidiary*, to act as a legally independent unit while it is, in fact, part of a functionally coordinated whole. The decision to purchase stock and become a holding company is similar to any other investment decision. The returns from the investment (capital gains plus dividends) are presumably expected to be high enough to warrant the investment. The coordination of the units may cause the *parent company*, the company that owns the shares in other companies (subsidiaries), to expect considerably larger subsidiary earnings and thus dividends and capital gains. The buying company may purchase the stock in the open market (public market) or by offering *tenders* to existing stockholders.[6]

Combination may also be secured through the lease of all the properties of another company. This *combination lease* may permit profitable combination without the outright purchase of needed assets. This method is quite common in the real estate, mining, and oil industries and is not uncommon in the rail, public utility, and chainstore fields. For the buyer, the lease has the advantage of avoiding large cash expenditures or issues of securities. For the securityholders of the leased company, the lease increases the reliability of payment on the security but reduces the potential residual gain. In effect, the securities of the leased company become guaranteed securities—guaranteed by the leasing firm. Generally, this

---

[5] These include "gentlemen's agreements," pools, association agreements, cartels, communities of interest, purchase and sales contracts, and interlocking directorates. *See:* Harry G. Guthmann and Herbert B. Dougall, *Corporate Financial Policy*, 4th ed. (Englewood Cliffs, N.J.: Prentice Hall, 1962), 517–19.

[6] A tender is an offer to buy a stipulated number of shares at a given price. It usually involves the same offering price to all shareholdings, contingent, however, upon the buying company's securing enough shares to command control. The tendered price is typically above recent market prices, thereby making it attractive to stockholders. The management of the selling company may or may not give the offer its blessing. The buyer may discriminate in its offerings in order to maximize the control at least cost, although in most cases the same offering is made to all shareholders. The tender is often used to gain control of other firms and to avoid purchase of shares in the open market, an action which would probably force up the market price of the sought-after stocks.

method is simple and quick; only the approval of the shareholders of the lessor is required.

Purchase of Assets

A firm may buy all or part of the assets of another firm. The purchase will probably exclude cash and securities, however. After the purchase, the selling company may simply distribute its liquid assets to shareholders and dissolve the firm or it may retain the assets as a holding company or investment company. When all the nonliquid assets are being sold, the combination may be referred to as *merger by sale of assets.*

Under this merger method, the buyer need not secure the approval of its shareholders unless new securities must be authorized to pay for the assets. The selling stockholders must approve the proposal; depending upon the state law, the holders of a majority to four fifths of the shares must approve.[7] Under a cash purchase, creditors of the selling company must be paid by the selling company from the receipts of sale. The purchaser must give creditors notice of the intent to buy—otherwise the buyer may be held liable for the seller's debts. Usually, however, the buyer will take over and assume long-term debts of the seller. Liens on fixed assets go with the property unless these debts are paid at the time of the purchase with cash or securities of the buyer. Otherwise, the buyer becomes liable for these debts of the seller up to the value of the assets purchased. The buyer may pay off these debts in cash or assume them.

A valuation, like those made regarding any other investment, must be made by the buyer to determine what he is willing to pay in cash or securities. The buyer must estimate the expected increment to its cash flow and apply the appropriate discount rate. Should the addition tend to reduce the acquiring firm's business risk, the total value of the combined firm based upon the lowered capital cost presumed to prevail after the fusion must be determined. A comparison of the value of the combined firm with that of the firm before the acquisition will yield an indication of the value of the acquired firm.

To illustrate a merger by purchase of assets, let us examine the case of the Molander Drug Company, which recently purchased Rosen Chemical Corporation. Rosen Chemical had the following balance sheet:

---

[7] Dissenting stockholders may attempt to arrest the sale on statutory or fraudulent considerations, but they could also sue for compensation if they can establish misappropriation of their investment by directors. If they object to the value received for their shares, they can seek appraisal of the shares' value under the appropriate state laws governing this case. Awards of extra payment to dissenters reduce the payment to approving stockholders.

L. Rosen Chemical Company
December 31, 1966
(in thousands of dollars)

Assets			Liabilities and Capital		
Current assets:			Current liabilities:		
Cash	$10,000		Accruals	$ 3,000	
Marketable			Payables	12,000	$ 15,000
securities	10,000		trade		
Receivables					
(net)	30,000		Long-term Debt:		
Inventory	20,000	$ 70,000	Term Loan	20,000	20,000
			Total liabilities		35,000
Fixed assets:					
Plant &			Common equity:		
equipment			Common		
(net)	50,000	50,000	stock ($1)	10,000	
			Paid-In		
			capital	40,000	
			Retained		
			earnings	35,000	
			Total common equity		85,000
Total		$120,000		Total	$120,000

The average earnings after taxes over the past five years were $12 million, a 10 per cent return on assets. Depreciation charges were the only non-cash deduction from revenue and averaged $4 million. Thus the average cash flow amounted to an estimated $16 million. Molander estimated that the purchase and operation of all assets except cash and marketable securities would not reduce or increase the business risk of the firm sufficiently to anticipate any significant change in the cost of capital, which is estimated to be 8 per cent. When the firm is combined with Molander Drug it is expected that $17 million can be added to cash flow per year; Molander will have to add $5 million to its cash balance, however, for transactions purposes. The cash flow can be expected to continue indefinitely. To keep the cash flow intact, however, outlays for plant and equipment will have to be made over the years. These would reduce the positive net cash flow in certain years; as a rough estimate they would *average* $4 million per year, the amount of depreciation charges. Although it is imprecise, let us make a simplification by using average net cash flow in perpetuity of $13 million, the amount of the net *addition* to after-tax earnings of Molander (before deducting interest cost on the term loan). As the Rosen Chemical stock was not traded on the open market, the value of the assets to Molander was best estimated by finding the present value of the expected cash flow. For this risk and size of investment the minimum attractive rate of return has been stated by management to be

12.5 per cent, producing a valuation of $104 million ($13,000,000/.125). Molander wanted to purchase the assets at less than this to make a significant net addition to the value of his firm.

The seller, Rosen Chemical, computed the book value of the assets to be sold at $100 million and figured Molander could generate about $12 million additional earnings per year. Rosen capitalized these at 12.5 per cent to produce a value of $96 million. But Rosen also estimated its assets could be replaced by Molander at $120 million. Allowing for the fact that the fixed assets were depreciated at an amount equal to $20 million, Rosen decided on a selling price of $100 million, or replacement cost less accumulated depreciation. Molander made an initial offer of $100 million for the assets ($65 million in stock and the assumption of the $35 million term loan). But the directors of Rosen Chemical felt this offer was less than Molander was willing to pay, so they countered with $103 million. They finally negotiated a sale for $102 million ($67 million in stock in Molander Drug and the assumption of the $35 million term loan). Creditors were notified and all stockholders approved the sale. Rosen sold its marketable securities (United States Governments), paid off accruals and accounts payable of $15 million, distributed $67 million in stock and $5 million in cash to its stockholders, and dissolved. The use of stock for the purchase made the flotation of stock by Molander unnecessary (saving flotation costs), and Rosen stockholders—who would have otherwise received cash for the sale of their assets—were thus able to postpone an income tax on the capital gain from the sale.

Expansion by Holding Company

Rather than make an outright purchase of assets, an interested buyer may find it desirable to purchase enough stock to gain control over another company. This delays the final fusion, postpones part of the required outlay, and allows the buyer more time to assess the profitability of a final merger. The subsidiary stock might be acquired by purchases in the open market, but most likely not enough stock can be secured in this manner at reasonable prices. The holding company would more likely offer tenders to stockholders or negotiate the purchase or exchange of significant blocks of shares. If the combination later appears attractive, it is a relatively simple matter to merge the subsidiary through sale of assets or statutory merger and dissolve the subsidiary. If the combination does not appear attractive, the holding company must locate a buyer for its block of stock or arrange for an investment banker to distribute it to the public.

Statutory Merger and Consolidation

Under statutory merger or consolidation complete fusion takes place automatically under the procedures set up by the statutes of the various states. A merger leaves intact the corporate structure of the surviving firm; the consolidation eliminates the old corporate charters and brings a new one into being. All liabilities are assumed by the new or remaining corporation and all liens on assets remain unaffected. The precise procedures differ from state to state and stockholder approval of all corporations involved is required. The plan of merger or consolidation filed with the state includes the arrangement for the exchange of securities. The securities of the surviving corporations are issued directly to the stockholders of the dissolved corporation. Again settlement must be made with any dissenting stockholders as was the case in the merger by sale of assets. The earned surplus or retained earnings of consolidating corporations must be set up in the new corporation as part of the stock or paid-in capital—which, in effect, freezes previously accumulated earnings of both companies, a feature not present with a merger, and which may render a consolidation unattractive. A merger freezes the earned surplus of the nonsurviving corporation(s). Consolidation does have the advantage of permitting the formation of a new corporate structure through a new charter. Notwithstanding the above, the basis for the exchange of shares is the most significant problem to be resolved in the agreement to combine.

Stockholders of both combining companies expect to gain by the combination. Presumably the earning power of the combined operation will be higher than that of each firm individually as a result of such factors as economies of scale and other cost reductions. This enables both groups of stockholders to gain from the combination. If the issues are publicly traded, the measure of that increased wealth is the market value of the securities after consolidation. Obviously, stockholders will not care to witness a decline in market wealth. The extent to which each group gains depends on many things, not the least of which is a valuation of the exchange itself. But in the final analysis the allocation of the total increment to wealth will depend upon the relative bargaining power of the parties to the consolidation or merger.

The following case illustrates the complexity of the problem. A promoter by the name of Reed observed that the Hartley Moving Company, mover of household goods, could benefit by combining with an oil sales firm. After considerable study, he found a likely candidate in the Ferreira Oil Company. Reed felt that the summer peak activity of the movement of household goods would complement the winter peak activity of fuel oil sales so that considerable cost savings could be obtained. Ferreira was an old, family-held firm, but with no provision for management succession; Hartley's stock had a local active market. Reed presented the idea to both firms, received tentative agreements, and proceeded with a plan of statutory merger in which Hartley was to be the surviving corporation. The year-end balance sheets of the two corporations are set forth in Table 17-1. The average total earnings before interest and after taxes amounted to $17,000 for Hartley and $7,000 for Ferreira. The combined earnings of the two companies were estimated at $35,000, and a reduction in business risk for Hartley was anticipated.

The market value of Hartley stock was $14 and this was concluded to be a fair market price by Reed. This made the market value of the Hartley claims on assets equal to

Stock	$140,000	($14 × 10,000)
Debt	30,000	
	$170,000	

Table 17-1
Balance Sheets of Hartley Moving and
Ferreira Oil Before Merger
December 31, 1964

	Hartley Moving Company		Ferreira Oil Company	
Assets				
Current assets:				
Cash	$15,000		$ 5,000	
Receivables (net)	10,000		15,000	
Inventory (LIFO)	5,000	$ 30,000	20,000	$40,000
Fixed assets (net):				
Furniture and fixtures	$ 3,000		$ 2,000	
Trucks and equipment	30,000		20,000	
Land and buildings	36,000	69,000	17,000	39,000
Other assets	$ 1,000	1,000	$ 1,000	1,000
		$100,000		$80,000
Liabilities				
Current liabilities:				
Accruals	$ 1,000		$ 1,000	
Payables	9,000		9,000	
Bank loan	——	$ 10,000	10,000	$20,000
Long-term debt:				
Term loan	$10,000	20,000	$10,000	10,000
Common equity:				
Common stock	$10,000*		$30,000†	
Paid-in capital	20,000		10,000	
Retained earnings	40,000	70,000	10,000	50,000
		$100,000		$80,000

* $1 par value.
† $100 par value.

The market value of claims of $170,000 suggests the earning power on the Hartley market value of assets of 10 ($17,000/$170,000) per cent. Reed thus figured the capitalized value of Ferreira to be $70,000 ($7,000,-/.10). However, the combined operations warranted a valuation of $350,-000 ($35,000/.10),[8] if the 10 per cent capitalization rate is used. A new capital structure was agreed on. It included 13,600 ($1 par) shares. Ferreira stockholders received 3,600 shares in Hartley, a rate of exchange of 12 for 1 (3,600 new shares ÷ 300 old shares). Ferreira shareholders appeared to receive a value of $50,400 ($14 × 3,600) for their 300 shares equity with a book value of $50,000 and earning power valued at $40,000 ($70,000 − $30,000). The new balance sheet, as shown in Table 17-2,

Table 17-2
Hartley Moving Company
Pro Forma Balance Sheet
March 31, 1965

Assets			Liabilities		
Current assets:			Current Liabilities:		
Cash	$20,000		Accruals	$ 2,000	
Receivables			Payables	18,000	
(net)	25,000		Bank loan	10,000	$ 30,000
Inventory	25,000	$ 70,000	Long-term debt:		
			Term loan	30,000	30,000
Fixed assets (net):			Common equity:		
Furniture and			Common		
fixtures	5,000		stock	$13,700	
Trucks and			Paid-in		
equipment	50,000		capital	71,800	
Land and			Retained		
buildings	53,000	108,000	earnings	40,000	125,500
Other assets:					
Prepaid					
expenses	2,000				
Goodwill	5,500	7,500			
		$185,500			$185,500

appeared with $5,500 goodwill, a conservative upward valuation in assets, considering expected earning power.[9] Hartley Moving Company estimated

[8] A consolidation would permit a new capital structure of $350,000 including $60,000 of assumed debts and $290,000 in stock. The $290,000 would have to be either Common Stock or Paid-In Capital. The promoter could likely allocate himself a fair "slice" of the new stock. Such a high capitalization would require the inflation of assets by goodwill or some other means. Should the expected potential not be realized, the decline in stock values would likely hinder later financing.

[9] Reed received 100 shares for his promotional efforts. Within two years the firm achieved an earning power of about $34,000 and the stock sold at $25 per share. Ferreira's holdings were then worth $90,000.

it could have paid a considerably higher price. This did not enhance Ferreira's bargaining position, however, because other oil firms were obtainable at equally attractive prices. A problem could have arisen in this case if the merger involved a substantially larger number of shares; Hartley could find himself out of control of the combined firm. In such cases a new preferred stock issue might have been used in the exchange.

CONTRACTION

The point of view of the buying firm has been presented in the preceding discussion. The decision to discontinue a line, sell a division, or sell all the assets presumes that the selling firm increases its value to its shareholders by such action. If the present value of the loss in cash flow, discounted appropriately (including the impact on business risk and thus capital cost), is less than the price offered by the buyer, it pays the seller to sell. The cash received may then be disbursed to shareholders if opportunities for reinvestment do not exist. Such liquidating or capital-disbursing dividends are generally tax-exempt. If all that remains of the corporation is an assetless shell, it should be dissolved.

A firm considering the sale of part of its assets usually has some advantage in evaluating its worth. Because the firm has had experience with the operation, the uncertainty involved with the estimates of cash flow or earnings is likely to be less than in cases in which a firm is considering a new line.

Take the case of the Bridenstine Publishing Company, which made an offer to the Olson Printing Company to purchase a magazine that had a regional following. The Olson Company estimated the loss in earnings after taxes as a result of the sale to be $20,000 per year. The depreciation on certain special plates to be sold was not significant, so a net cash flow of $20,000 was assumed to be accurate for analytical purposes. Because this figure was rather predictable, the firm capitalized the value at 10 per cent, a rate considerably less than that ordinarily used for considering new capital expenditures. This produced a value of $200,000 ($20,000-/.10), which was less than the Bridenstine offer of $230,000. The offer was accepted and—because Olson had not had many attractive internal investment opportunities in recent years and there were no acceptable opportunities at the present—the money was distributed to stockholders.

SUMMARY

Firms may expand by growth from within or by the acquisition of other businesses. Internal expansion may be less rapid, but it allows surer, more gradual growth. Expansion by combination may require several years before the combined firms can be fully integrated and co-ordinated. Internal expansion is often hindered or aided by the nature of the dividend policy followed, particularly if public security markets are largely unavailable to the firm.

With respect to dividend policy, firms with relatively low business risk may be inclined to embark upon a regular dividend policy which hopefully enhances the value of the stock, maximizes the position of shareholders, and aids in achieving a least-cost combination of capital. Other firms cannot afford such a policy and need to rely upon a relatively constant-percentage-of-earnings payout policy. Frequently a firm may successfully issue a stock dividend instead of a cash dividend (when cash is short) and at the same time satisfy investor's desires for some sort of disbursement. Rapidly growing firms will be maximizing profits by reinvestment of earnings, thereby precluding the establishment of much in the way of a dividend policy. As a general rule, as long as the earnings can be employed more profitably by the firm than by stockholders, retention of earnings is profitable. However, to mollify shareholders and their desires for disbursements, some dividend policy—no matter how small —is often necessary.

External expansion involves the purchase of some or all of the assets of another firm, statutory merger, or consolidation. The firm may become a holding company by purchasing stock in another company before instigating a more permanent type of fusion. If the securities of the company to be purchased do not have a market price, the value of that firm is established by the same methods used to establish the values of individual assets. The present value of future earnings becomes the basis for bargaining by the buyer and the seller. Usually the combination is expected to generate sufficient cash savings or other benefits so that the value of the combined firms is greater than each operating independently. This gives the negotiators or promoters a margin of profit for all parties concerned.

Contraction involves similar considerations. When the present value of the lost earnings is less than the offering price, it pays for the firm to sell. If there exist no profitable investment opportunities in the firm, the funds should be distributed to stockholders.

SUGGESTED READINGS

BERANEK, WILLIAM. *Common Stock Financing, Book Values and Stock Dividends: The Theory and the Evidence,* Madison, Wisc.: Bureau of Business Research, University of Wisconsin, 1961.

BOSLAND, CHELCIE C. "Stock Valuation in Recent Mergers: A Study of Appraisal Factors," *Trusts and Estates, 94* (June, July, and August 1955), 516–24, 583–90, 663–69.

BOTHWELL, J. C., JR. "Periodic Stock Dividends," *Harvard Business Review, 28* (January 1950), 89–100.

BRITTAIN, JOHN A. "The Tax Structure and Corporate Dividend Policy," *American Economic Review, 54* (May 1964), 272–87.

BUCHANAN, NORMAN S. *The Economics of Corporate Enterprise.* New York: Holt, Rinehart & Winston, Inc., 1940.

DOBROVOLSKY, S. "Capital Formation and Financing Trends in Manufacturing and Mining, 1900–1953," *The Journal of Finance, 10* (May 1955), 250–65.

———. "Economics of Corporate Internal and External Financing," *The Journal of Finance, 13* (March 1958), 35–47.

HARKAVY, OSCAR. "The Relationship between Retained Earnings and Common Stock Prices for Large, Listed Corporations," *The Journal of Finance, 8* (September 1953), 283–97.

JACOBY, NEIL H., and J. FRED WESTON. "Factors Influencing Managerial Decisions in Determining Forms of Business Financing: An Exploratory Study," *Conference on Research in Business Finance.* New York: National Bureau of Economic Research, 1952.

LINTNER, JOHN. "The Cost of Capital and Optimal Financing of Corporate Growth," *The Journal of Finance, 18* (May 1963), 292–310.

———. "Distribution of Incomes of Corporations Among Dividends, Retained Earnings, and Taxes," *American Economic Review, 46* (May 1956), 97–113.

MCLEAN, J. G., and R. W. HAIGH. "How Business Corporations Grow," *Harvard Business Review, 32* (November–December 1954), 81–93.

MILLER, M. H., and F. MODIGLIANI. "Dividend Policy, Growth, and the Valuation of Shares," *Journal of Business, 34* (October 1961), 411–33.

ORTNER, ROBERT. "The Concept of Yield on Common Stock," *The Journal of Finance, 19* (May 1964), 186–98.

SUSSMAN, M. RICHARD. *The Stock Dividend.* Ann Arbor, Mich.: Bureau of Business Research, University of Michigan, 1962.

ULMER, MELVILLE J. "Long-term Trends in the Financing of Regulated Industries, 1870–1950," *The Journal of Finance, 10* (May 1955), 266–76.

WALTER, JAMES E. "Dividend Policies and Common Stock Prices," *The Journal of Finance, 11* (March 1956), 29–41.

———. "Dividend Policy: Its Influence on the Value of the Enterprise," *The Journal of Finance, 18* (May 1963), 280–91.

WESTON, J. FRED. *The Role of Mergers in the Growth of Large Firms.* Berkeley, Calif.: University of California Press, 1953.

QUESTIONS

17.1 What advantages exist for the firm that is able to satisfy its investment requirements from internal sources over the firm that must use external sources? Are there disadvantages?

17.2 What are the two dominant factors that determine whether or not a corporation can declare a dividend? Explain.

17.3 What are the advantages and disadvantages of a stock dividend versus a cash dividend (*a*) to the company; (*b*) to the stockholder?

17.4 What differences would you expect between the dividend policy of a small, privately held young company and the policy of a mature, publicly held large firm? Why?

17.5 A company that has had a regular dividend policy pays cash dividends and yet sells common stock to meet its investment needs seems to be contradicting itself. Explain.

17.6 How are creditors protected when the assets of one firm are sold to another for cash? Explain.

17.7 What factors determine the price of the assets of one firm sold to another?

17.8 How might a consolidation affect the dividend policy of a firm? Explain.

17.9 Why might a buying firm prefer a statutory merger (*a*) to a consolidation or (*b*) to a sale-of-assets merger?

17.10 What advantages accrue to the buyer and seller when securities rather than cash are used for payment?

17.11 What happens to the creditors of an acquired company under a statutory-merger arrangement?

17.12 How can a firm determine when it may be desirable to sell a portion of the assets of a company? Explain.

17.13 In 1956 the New York Central Railroad distributed its holdings of common shares in United States Freight Company to its shareholders on the basis of one United States Freight Company share for twenty-three shares of New York Central. Fractional shares were paid in cash, which—based on then-current quotations for United States Freight—amounted to $1.33 for each share of New York Central held. The central also said this distribution would take the place of the company's regular $.50 quarterly dividend. Is this a stock dividend or a property dividend?

PROBLEMS

17.14 Examine the dividend payout over the past ten years by a number of companies selected by your instructor and indicate the nature of the dividend policy each of them appears to be pursuing.

17.15 The Simpson and Walker Timber Company was interested in the purchase of the Orton Lumber Company, a smaller firm whose assets consisted primarily of mills and timber holdings. Orton's balance sheet showed the following:

Orton Lumber Company
Balance Sheet
December 31, 1899

Assets			Liabilities		
Current assets:			Current liabilities:		
Cash	$ 1,000		Accruals	$ 1,000	
Receivables			Payables—		
(net)	2,000		trade	2,000	$ 3,000
Inventory	3,000	$ 6,000	Mortgage		17,000
Fixed assets:			Common equity:		
Mills and					
equipment			Common		
(net)	25,000		stock	30,000	
Timber					
rights	69,000	94,000	Surplus	50,000	80,000
		$100,000			$100,000

The average annual earnings of Orton after taxes were $9,000. Depleciation annually averaged $6,000. Simpson and Walker estimate the purchase of inventory, mills, equipment, and timber rights would add $18,000 to their annual cash flow for the coming fifteen years when the expected cash flow would fall to zero. Simpson and Walker require a 10 per cent return on investments of this risk. (*a*) What is the book value of the assets at this time? (*b*) If Orton common stock sells in the market at ten times earnings after taxes, what is your estimate of the value of the assets? (*c*) According to the information available, how do you evaluate the prospects for sale to Simpson and Walker? Support your case.

17.16 The Hill Casket Company was negotiating with the McLelland Body Company for a merger. The Hill Casket Company was to be the surviving firm. Hill Casket common stock was currently selling at $12 a share on average earnings per share of $1 and dividends of $.50. McLelland Body Company was selling at $10 per share on average earnings of $.95 cents with a $.10 dividend. Hill agreed to assume all debts and offered one share of Hill Casket for each share of McLelland Body. (*a*) Is this offer fair to Hill stockholders? (*b*) Why should Hill be willing to exchange on a one-for-one basis? (*c*) How would McLelland shareholders fair in the merger? Explain carefully.

17.17 The Sutton Bustle Company was offered $500,000 for its undergarment division, which included the sale of trademarks, a plant, and certain equipment. Stehman Dress Corporation estimated that, at the $500,000 figure, the division would so complement its other operations that substantial profits could be added to the firm. Sutton had been producing an old line which ran counter to current trends in the industry so that the decrease in its permanent cash flow as a result of the sale would amount to only $50,000 per year. The risk in this type of venture was considered quite high and Stehman felt the offer ought to yield a 15 per cent return on investment. Should Sutton sell? Explain.

18 FINANCING DECISIONS

Financial management faces the responsibility of providing the firm with funds when needed. If net cash flow is positive but insufficient to meet the dividend requirements desired by management, the contractual payment requirements on securities, and approved capital expenditures, the financial officer seeks ways of supplementing the firm's sources to meet such needs. Which of the many possible sources available to him should be chosen? The answer is: that combination which maximizes profits. Generally, this may be restated as that combination of sources that provides the needed capital at minimum cost—cost being broad enough to include direct, indirect, and implicit costs. This concept of cost should also include the impact of the particular combination chosen on capital costs in the future.

In an earlier chapter we discussed the cost of capital to the firm. Our general conclusion was that, under conditions of perfect markets and no income taxes, the cost of capital may be insensitive to changes in the proportion of debt to equity, although this issue is by no means settled. The fact is that investors do not seem to accept this position and traditionally accepted debt levels prevent the operation of perfect markets. This, combined with the income tax impact favoring debt, produces a somewhat saucer-shaped cost of capital, in which there exists at least some range of the ratio of debt to equity which is optimum from a cost standpoint. Implicit in this statement is the fact that, whether debt or equity is being secured, the least-cost combination of sources is being used.[1] We shall now turn our attention to the rationale and problems facing the financial manager in the actual choice of sources of capital supply. Unless stated otherwise, it will be assumed that costs in the current period of analysis are independent of future periods.

SHORT-TERM FINANCING

As a rule of thumb it was stated that short-term credit should not be used beyond the minimum level needed for seasonal purposes. Generally

[1] For purposes of the investment decision, the establishment of cutoff points and discount rates depend upon the marginal cost of capital.

it is cheaper, if credit is needed for only a small portion of the year, to borrow for that period rather than use permanent or long-term sources the costs of which would have to be paid for the whole year, even though they could be offset by earnings on short-term investments for the balance of the year. The longer the expected portion of the year that the funds are likely to be needed, the more likely it is that long-term or permanent sources should be used.

There are other occasions when the financial manager will use short-term sources. If a firm is growing, needs beyond those supplied internally may be temporarily financed by short-term sources until arrangements for a more satisfactory source of supply can be obtained. Short-term sources may also be used for many other temporary requirements. In yet other cases such sources are used by firms when cheaper alternatives do not exist. The small firm, for example, may not be able to secure capital from public markets at any reasonable cost and consequently its needs, beyond those cared for by internal sources, have to be supplied through term loans (if available) and even short-term credit at times.

Essentially short-term financing centers on commercial banks, sales finance companies, and factors. Trade credit beyond the free period results in high costs because of the loss of the cash discount and/or the cost of credit deterioration. Under a continuing agreement, a factor assumes the credit-and-collection function for the firm and buys its accounts receivable as they are created, with no recourse for credit losses. Surprisingly, the firm may also secure almost complete credit service from the factor—including inventory loans, loans on fixed and other assets, and open unsecured credit. When he factors receivables, the financial manager not only receives, in effect, a high cash value from the sale of receivables, but he also saves costs of credit and collection. The outright sale of receivables also leaves his current liability position clear of debt, something which a loan secured by receivables would not accomplish. Such a "healthy" current position may make other borrowing more feasible. It also tends to reduce any uncertainty regarding costs of credit and collection, including the incurrence of bad debts. The firm can assure itself that its costs of doing credit business are set at a known percentage of its net credit sales. Because the factor specializes in this credit function, it may not pay for the firm to create its own credit and collection department. The firm should compare the total net costs of factoring, after deducting savings arising from the elimination of the credit and collection department, with other capital sources. In arriving at a decision, we must also consider that the balance sheet remains clear for further financing and the uncertainty in costs is reduced.[2]

Although the sales finance companies engage primarily in the purchase of automobile and appliance dealers' installment-sales contracts, and thus provide financial support to these retail dealers, they customarily also provide loans on inventory. One such loan is referred to as *floor planning,* which entails financing of retailers' wholesale purchases from manufacturers. The purchase of retailers' installment-sales paper performs a function for these businesses similar to that performed by a factor for businesses granting open-account credit. Because of the length of life of this paper, the amount the dealer would have to invest to carry his own contracts plus his "floor" inventory represents a substantial amount of capital. Specializing in this type of financing, sales finance companies have developed an almost complete line of financing for such dealers, thereby competing with commercial banks for dealers' accounts. Although there may be some advantage in the economies associated with dealing with one financial institution, the competitive relationship that may be created between a bank and a sales finance company may benefit the dealer by lowering credit costs. The cost comparisons between a sales finance company and a bank are different, for the finance company may provide a group of related services—including credit and collection service, insurance, and sales promotion assistance—which may not be provided by banks. However, the dealer must be able to evaluate these differences as well as the reliability of the source in making his decision on which supplier or suppliers of such funds to use.

For the majority of firms and for general, short-term needs, the commercial bank can be the firm's "best friend." Banks compete with one another for deposits and for investments. As with other purchases, the purchase of bank services involves comparing service with price. Depending upon prices and banking conditions, most firms prefer to maintain a continuing relationship with one bank rather than to "hop" between banks. A customer not receiving adequate service from one bank may use the threat of competition from time to time to correct the matter. Often this is not just an idle threat. A medium-sized, old line commercial bank had been servicing the needs of a medium-sized automotive chemical company since its inception. When the chemical firm had embarked on an extensive promotional campaign, its production and shipments were

---

[2] For a more thorough discussion of this topic, *see:* Clyde William Phelps, *The Role of Factoring in Modern Business Finance,* Studies in Commercial Financing No. 1 (Baltimore: Educational Division, Commercial Credit Company, 1958).

increased substantially. The company asked the bank to double its line of credit. The bank investigated the matter and refused the application. The chemical firm said it would seek other banking relationships, and ended up with a line of credit three times larger than the previous one and at a rate .25 per cent cheaper. In most cases, the firm would prefer to maintain continuing relations with the same bank. As a general rule the build-up of experience in dealing with one bank should result in benefits over time in the convenience of securing credit, in the size of the credit that can be obtained, and in the reliability of a lending source even during periods of "tight" money. However, in order to maintain top service, including loans, the bank will probably encourage the maintenance of relatively significant deposit balances.

Although we have previously mentioned that the firm's need for a cash balance is based upon transactions and precautionary requirements, other purposes often advanced for carrying a cash balance are related to bank activity. Firms often carry deposit balances in excess of that necessary to take care of their transactions and precautionary needs in order to maintain goodwill at a bank. This may be viewed on an indirect payment for bank services, including transactions activity. If a low balance were maintained, the bank would base its service charges on demand deposit activity.[3] The firm will also normally carry some "excess" balances to cover "float" (checks in the process of clearing). Although float, service, and goodwill may be additional reasons for holding cash balances, essentially transactions and precautionary needs determine the size of these balances. If a firm can be sure its bank will accommodate it whenever necessary, it may be able to eliminate precautionary balances. To insure such accommodation, however, a compensating balance may be required and a greater balance is needed in either event. A comparison must be made between the size of the compensating balance required for certainty of loan accommodation and the size of needed precautionary balance.

Several arrangements may be established with a bank to facilitate the borrowing process. Rather than negotiate an individual loan when the need arises, the officers of the firm may feel more comfortable if they have discussed with the bank their current financial position and expected needs. The firm can then obtain from its bank an impression of the extent to which the bank may be willing to accommodate these needs and the terms under which loans would be granted. Such an understanding between the bank and its clients may evolve through continued dealing

---

[3] The rate of return on funds left on deposit to reduce service charges, however, generally amounts to less than 1 per cent.

with one another. A firm, however, may desire a more explicit arrangement and may periodically review its financial position and needs with the bank in order to prearrange financial support with given terms up to agreed limits (if conditions remain constant). Such an understanding is referred to as a *line of credit*. In order to secure the line of credit, the firm is often required to maintain a certain average level in its deposit account.

The cost of the line of credit includes the cost of making the arrangement and the cost of keeping average deposit balances in excess of what the firm otherwise would maintain. For example, if the Blythe Company customarily kept an average deposit of $10,000 in the Palmer National Bank, and the bank agreed to extend a $100,000 line of credit (available for the coming year) only if Blythe agreed to maintain a 20 per cent average balance, under an 8 per cent cost of capital to the firm the costs of the line would be $800 {[(.20 × $100,000) − $10,000] .08} plus the costs in time and expense of arranging the credit estimated at $250. The interest charges for any outstanding loan were additional costs incurred at the annual rate of 5 per cent. As might be expected, Blythe Company borrowed the $100,000 for three months for a cost of $1,250. The total cost for the funds amounted to $2,300 ($800 + $250 + $1,250). Without the line of credit the firm could have saved the cost of the compensating balance of $10,000 or $800, but there would have been greater uncertainty both in securing the credit and in the magnitude realized. Blythe considered an alternative to this arrangement, which was to borrow $90,000 through the sale of bonds at 6 per cent after flotation costs. The firm could have invested the $90,000 in United States Government bills at 3 per cent for nine months of the year. The total cost using this source would be $3,375 [(.06 × $90,000) − (.03 × $90,000) × ¾]. The use of the line of credit enabled them to save $1,075 per year.

If a firm feels it needs greater certainty in its borrowing ability, it may request a *loan commitment* from the bank. The loan commitment eliminates almost all uncertainty in obtaining credit. Some financial managers may feel such assurances are necessary for various reasons. In some cases a firm may not be able to bid on a contract without an assurance of the financing needed to carry out the contract. In other circumstances the credit guarantee of the loan commitment may be worth the additional cost if the firm were to fail if no cash could be guaranteed quickly.

The loan commitment usually is more costly than the line of credit. In addition to arrangement costs, the firm may be expected to carry compensatory deposit balances. But a loan commitment may also require higher balances and/or a charge for the unborrowed portion of the loan commitment. This charge would usually be about .5 per cent for the period of the commitment.

As a general rule, the firm should finance seasonal needs with short-term capital. If, however, the funds were needed, say, nine months of the year, the bank might not wish to finance the firm over that long a period. The cost of using long-term bonds would be little different and perhaps less (depending on interest rates). The idle funds could be invested in bills for three months.

LONG-TERM DEBT FINANCING

The use of long-term debt in the form of term loans, mortgages, and bonds implies that the firm has a need for funds beyond just temporary requirements. These needs can be satisfied by long-term debt or equity funds, or both. There are many reasons why debt should be used, but one stands out: interest is tax-deductible. Because interest payments are deductible from revenues before computing income taxes, the use of debt may effectively reduce the average cost of capital to the firm. If the investment industry has traditionally accepted a certain level of debt for firms in given industries, it is probable that a firm not utilizing the accepted debt limits is not maximizing profits for the owners. Within the degree of debt acceptable by the market, a lower average cost of capital can be achieved because the low effective after-tax rate on debt does not proportionately increase the cost of equity capital. It thus behooves management to consider the use of debt capital.

Debt may be sold privately or publicly.[4] The term loan, the mortgage, and privately placed bonds are available even to the smaller firms that do not have access to the public securities markets. If the alternative to issuance of debt is the sale of common stock, the smaller business may prefer debt to loss of control for debt can be privately placed whereas common stock generally cannot. The disadvantages of debt are that the debt *must* be repaid and the contractual restrictions or protective covenants of the indenture may be awkward for the firm and involve some control cost.[5]

Inasmuch as debt issues require repayment, the timing of such repayment is of the utmost importance and must be agreed upon by both the creditor(s) and the firm. Whereas the firm would like to have both a long repayment period with its attendant small annual requirements and the

[4] For a discussion of capital markets and investment banking, see Chapter 8.
[5] See Appendix B for a description of covenants customarily found in bond contracts.

ability to accelerate payment without cost, the lenders—in order to reduce their risk exposure—prefer shorter periods and higher payments, with less flexibility on the part of the firm to make advance payments or retire the issue. These are all matters subject to negotiation, but other factors besides the negotiating ability of the two parties contribute to the maturity and repayment decision; not the least of these is the ability of the firm to handle future outlays and expected needs.

If physical assets are used as security for the debt, the economic life of the asset will serve as an outer limit to the maturity; this tends to act as a limit on how slowly the firm may be able to repay the debt. Also the balance of debt outstanding should never exceed the economic value of the asset pledged. Should the lender find it necessary to foreclose on a secured term loan or mortgage bond, he would expect the liquidating value of the pledged asset to be sufficient to cover his debt. As a result of this and because of the uncertainty surrounding estimates of decline in value, creditors will ordinarily require that the estimated value of the pledged asset well exceed the debt and that the debt will be repaid before the value of the asset declines to zero. Also, rarely will they lend a firm an amount equal to the full value of the asset pledged. The maturity of the loan will also be affected by the nature of the business of the lender. Commercial banks require more liquidity than insurance companies and generally impose a more rapid repayment schedule.

The ability to retire debt ahead of schedule with little penalty depends upon the state of the market. If institutions are hard-pressed for funds and interest rates are high, the borrower may have no alternative but to accept terms which reduce his flexibility. If, on the other hand, the institutions are in strong competition for investment outlets and interest rates are relatively low, the flexibility provisions may be greatly enhanced by the debtor.

The anticipation of movements in interest rates and general credit conditions by the anticipation of aggregate economic activity and monetary and fiscal policy should be a key element in the financial manager's decision-making. Preferential terms may be secured six months or a year hence, if credit conditions change. Often, however, the need for capital is sometimes so pressing that it is impossible to defer financing.

The nature and restrictiveness of the protective covenants depend upon traditional expectations of lenders as well as on the competitive conditions of the market. If possible, the borrower under a mortgage bond will try to provide greater flexibility for future financing if he can obtain an open-end mortgage which permits the sale of more bonds of equal claim position at some later date. A provision frequently included in a blanket mortgage supporting the mortgage bond is the after-acquired-property clause which automatically places under the mortgage all real property acquired later, so that new assets cannot be debt-financed. The use of a lease may be one way of securing equipment when financing is restricted by such a clause. Another method is to create a subsidiary to buy new property and incur the debt to finance it. Another alternative is to buy the equipment with a mortgage already attached by the seller of the property.[6] In this way the firm acquires equipment which has been financed by external sources but which also circumvents the after-acquired clause. One way to eliminate this restrictive clause, or any other undesirable provision for that matter, is to refinance the debt. (The financial feasibility of doing this is discussed in Chapter 19.) In any case, the financial manager needs to exert care in the acceptance of restrictive provisions incorporated into bond indentures.

THE USE OF THE FINANCIAL LEASE

From the viewpoint of the financial manager, the lease may be considered an alternative to purchase and it may be used as an alternative to borrowing. The decision to lease or to buy is essentially an investment decision. Customarily in such decisions an operating lease is used—one cancellable by the lessee (the operating firm). Operating leases do not involve long-fixed future commitments and would be used by the firm in those cases in which the risk of ownership is high. Operating leases are expensive but, if it is not known how the asset will contribute to the profitability, such a lease may be the best way to reduce the uncertainty. Operating leases may also be used when the firm estimates the risks of obsolescence significantly higher than the lessor. The services provided by the lessor also reduce the uncertainty to the firm in estimating costs of operation. The investment problem of lease or buy is the problem of determining whether or not the savings realized from owning the asset will be enough to justify the risk of ownership. Our concern here is not with the lease-or-buy decision involving operating leases, but with the lease-or-borrow decision involved with financial leases.[7]

The *financial lease* is a device for permitting the purchase of an asset without a large immediate cash outlay. There is no question as to the desirability of the services of the asset, the question is: How should it be financed? Financial leases are not cancellable by the firm; the firm agrees

[6] Such a mortgage is referred to as a purchase-money mortgage. See Appendix B for a further discussion of these points.

[7] For an excellent discussion of leasing, *see:* Richard F. Vancil, *Leasing of Industrial Equipment* (New York: McGraw, 1963).

to a stream of lease payments that will recover the investment and a rate of return for the lessor. On some occasions the arrangement may take the form of sale-and-leaseback, in which one firm sells assets already owned, receives the proceeds of the sale, and leases back the sold property. In this way the services of the sold asset are received while new capital is secured. As in all lease decisions, the issue is to determine whether the financial lease is a desirable financing alternative.

It has been suggested that funds provided by financial leases normally cost at least .5 to 1 per cent more than the cost of debt financing.[8] This might be explained in part by the observation that lease obligations are generally less attractive than secured debt securities because of the lower priority of claim on the corporation in case of bankruptcy and because lease obligations are less marketable should the investor wish to sell before maturity. This would seem to suggest that the firm should avoid the use of lease financing in favor of debt financing.

When a firm has already extended itself to the limit of traditionally acceptable debt levels, however, exploring a new source of financing may be cheaper than pushing debt beyond acceptable limits. A class of lenders often hesitates to lend too much to one firm and the firm that is willing to deal with multiple sources can probably raise more funds at lower cost. The effect of using such multiple sources is to broaden the credit pool available to the firm.

Under the financial lease, the lessee (the hiring firm) assumes all the auxiliary operating costs of the equipment—that is, the same costs the lessee would incur if it owned the equipment. The decision to secure the equipment is one of capital expenditure; once it has been made, the firm must choose the financing method. The financial lease is an alternative much like debt, for it involves a fixed obligation in the form of lease payments—just as would be expected under a sinking-fund arrangement for debt repayment. After management has decided in favor of financing by fixed-cost capital rather than equity capital, the issue becomes one of choosing among debt, preferred stock, or the financial lease. The choice of financing method should be based upon the minimization of capital costs. A simple example may serve to illustrate the considerations involved in the decision. McGuire Sports Equipment, Inc., decided that the purchase of a new piece of equipment costing $1,000 would be profitable for the firm. The equipment was expected to last five years and to have no salvage value. The firm was in reasonably sound financial condition and considered that investment alternatives of average risk and size should

[8] Donald R. Gant, "Illusion in Lease Financing," *Harvard Business Review* 37 (March–April 1959), 121–42.

yield a 12 per cent rate of return to cover adequately capital costs and allow for risk. The 10 per cent weighted average cost of capital rate, however, was used for this investment decision because of the certainty of the payment estimates.

The firm had broken down the financing problem to a choice between a term loan with the Parker National Bank and a financial lease with the Elbing Insurance Company. McGuire uses the sum-of-the-digits method of depreciation for tax purposes and has an effective income tax rate of 48 per cent. The bank, under a term-loan arrangement, wanted five payments of $237 a year beginning at the *end* of the first year; the Elbing Insurance Company wanted a declining schedule of payments totaling $1,080 over five years, with payments to be made at the *beginning* of the year. Table 18-1 shows the analysis for the bank plan and Table 18-2 gives the cost results for the financial lease. The present value of the outlays under Table 18-1 amounts to $440, whereas under the lease plan the present value of the outlays equals $542. In this particular example the lease was not advantageous. The lease usually becomes more valuable to a firm when other sources of financing become available only at higher costs because the firm exceeds the acceptable debt levels imposed by suppliers of capital.

THE SALE OF STOCK

The sale of stock may involve the sale of preferred or common. The considerations involved with the sale of preferred stock are similar to those involved in the sale of bonds although, because of tax considerations, debt capital is usually cheaper if the market will permit additional debt. The responsibility to meet preferred dividends is not as strong as that of debt interest or principal payments, but the passing of preferred dividends places a burden on the operation of the firm in the form of possible restrictions on common dividends, impairment of credit standing, and contingent voting power.

If the preferred is convertible into common stock, quite frequently they are offered to existing stockholders before they are sold to the rest of the public. There are two reasons for this. First there may be legal compulsion in the form of so-called pre-emptive rights. The pre-emptive right is a legal doctrine which establishes that a firm offering new ownership securities either directly through the sale of stock or indirectly through the form of a conversion privilege has to offer them to its present stockholders before it can sell them to the rest of the public. In some cases these rights are required by the state of incorporation. In others

Table 18-1
Financing Under Loan with
Parker National Bank

End of Year	Payments On Debt	Interest Implied (6%)	Tax (48%) Saving on Interest	Sum of Digits Depreciation	Tax (48%) Saving on Depreciation	Total Tax Savings	Net Cash Outflow	Present Value of at 10% Cash Outlays
0	0							
1	$ 237	$ 60	$29	$ 333	$160	$189	$ 48	$ 44
2	237	49	24	267	128	152	85	70
3	237	37	18	200	96	114	123	92
4	237	26	12	133	64	76	161	110
5	237	13	6	67	32	38	199	124
Total	$1,185	$185	$89	$1,000	$480	$569	$616	$440

they are presumed to be nonexistent unless explicitly stated in the charter. If neither of these conditions exist, a firm may decide to sell its convertible securities to existing stockholders anyway. This could be particularly advantageous if there is a rather substantial stockholder interest, thereby providing a ready market for new securities and hopefully reducing the selling effort involved.

The sale of common stock to present stockholders is referred to as a *rights offering* or as a *privileged subscription.* Whether or not such a sale is made to present shareholders is a matter of legal compulsion and/or discretion. The pre-emptive right may require the sale of new common stock to existing shareholders. As we saw in the case of convertibles, this provision allows the existing shareholders the opportunity to maintain their proportionate interest in the assets, earnings, and control of the firm. Perhaps more importantly, but only accidentally, the pre-emptive right also allows shareholders to maintain their proportionate interest in the market value of the firm.

The discretionary aspect of offering new shares to existing shareholders arises because these holders constitute a readymade market for a company's shares and thus it may be cheaper to sell the new shares in this way. Regardless of the motivation, many offerings of new common shares are offered to existing shareholders.

To make a rights offering effective, new shares are sold to existing shareholders at a price below prevailing market prices. This offering price, called the *subscription price,* provides a stimulus to stockholders to purchase the shares to which they are privileged. For example, the Latousek Company may decide to sell new shares to existing shareholders. The current price of its stock is $40 a share. In order to make the issue

Table 18-2
Financing Under Lease with
Elbing Insurance Company

End of Year	Payments on Lease	Tax Savings (48%) End of Year	Net Cash Outflows	Present Value at 10%
0	$ 370	$ 0	$370	$370
1	270	178	92	84
2	200	130	70	58
3	150	96	54	41
4	100	72	28	19
5	0	48	(48)	(30)
Total	$1,080	$524	$614	$542

attractive for potential buyers, its price should be less than the prevailing market price. Clearly, a price greater than the prevailing market price is out of the question: the outstanding shares could be bought more cheaply. If the offering price is equal to the prevailing market price, it would not make any difference to present shareholders whether they bought the new shares or shares already outstanding; thus the firm runs the substantial risk of not selling the issue. Even if the offering price is set fairly close to the prevailing market price, downward variations would tend to make the sale of the issue tenuous. Because of these considerations, the offering price is set sufficiently below the market price to allow for reasonably expectable downward variations in market price. But to insure against the possible failure of the sale, the company would be well advised to make an arrangement with an investment banker whereby he would be ready to buy up the unsubscribed portion of the offering and support the existing market until the sale was completed. This is known as *standby underwriting*. In consultation with the underwriter, the company may set the offering price of the new stock at $35 a share. For convenience, let us assume there are two million shares already outstanding and that the company is offering an additional 500,000 shares to present shareholders. These new shares will be apportioned among stockholders whose names appear on the records as owners of shares as of a specified and predetermined date, called the *record date*. The rate at which the *stockholders of record* are then entitled to subscribe to the new issue is determined by the ratio of the number of "old" shares to the number of "new" shares, so that

$$SR = \frac{S}{S_n}$$

where

SR = subscription rate, or the number of existing shares needed to subscribe to one new share

S = number of existing shares

S_n = number of new shares offered

In the case of the Latousek Company, the subscription rate is

$$SR = \frac{2,000,000}{500,000} = 4:1$$

Thus it takes four "old" shares to subscribe to one "new" share.

To simplify our discussion, several additional concepts must be introduced. The first is the concept of *rights*. When a new offering is being made, each shareholder will receive a warrant stipulating the extent to which he may participate in the offering. In our example, a holder of eight shares of stock would have the right to buy two new shares at the privileged price of $35; and a holder of ten shares would have the right to subscribe to 2.5 shares. In other words, each existing shareholder has the right to subscribe to as many new shares as his proportion of "old" shares to "new" warrants. Each share has the right to subscribe to the new issue. It is from this concept that the term *right* is derived. If there were two million shares outstanding, as there are in our example, then two million rights will be sent to existing shareholders whose names appear on the books of the corporation as of the predetermined (although not necessarily preannounced) record date. Prior to the record date the stock is said to be selling *cum rights* (or *with rights* or *rights on*). That is, a sale of the stock before the record date carries with it the right to sub- scribe to the new issue. If Charlie D. buys four shares of Latousek com- mon from David A., he will also receive the rights to subscribe to the new issue when they are sent out, which is very shortly after the record date. Usually the time allotted for subscription to the new issue is no more than thirty days, at the end of which time the right to subscribe expires. This terminal date of the subscription period is known as the *expiration date*. In the period beginning just prior to the record date and extending to the expiration date, the stock is said to be selling *ex rights*—that is, during this period purchases and sales of the stock do not carry with them the right to subscribe to the new issue. If David A. were now to buy four shares of Latousek common from Charlie D., he would not receive any rights entitling him to subscribe to the new issue.

Because we are interested in the welfare of shareholders, especially in terms of the market value of their shares, and because a rights offering tends to dilute these market values, we are interested in the approximate value of such subscription rights. Because four "old" shares—each having a market value of $40—are required to purchase one "new" one at $35, the aggregate value of all five shares immediately after the sale is $195 [($40 × 4) + ($35 × 1)]. The average market value of each share then would be $39 and we would say that the market price of the stock was diluted by $1 a share as a result of the privileged offering. A simple alge- braic formula is used to determine the extent to which dilution takes place:

$$V_R = \frac{P_1 - P_s}{SR + 1}$$

where

V_R = the extent to which dilution will occur once the issue is sold (the value of one right)

P_1 = the market value of existing shares selling with rights

P_s = the subscription price of new shares

SR = the number of old shares needed to subscribe to one new share[9]

V_R in this formula refers to the value of one right; SR refers to the number of rights required to buy one new share. These are the same as the definitions given above for all practical purposes. The reason the denominator has a +1 in it is because the value of any one right is functionally related to the spread between the market price (P_1) of the shares outstanding and the subscription price (P_s), the number of old shares needed to subscribe to one new share (SR) and the one new share to be added (+1). Because market price reduction will not take place until just before the record date when the stock is selling ex rights, the value of the right, cum rights, is

$$V_R = \frac{\$40 - \$35}{4 + 1} = \$1$$

After the ex rights date the formula for computing the value of the right is

$$V_R = \frac{P_2 - P_s}{SR}$$

The +1 has been dropped because shares traded after the record date do not carry with them the right to purchase one new share. What would we expect the market price (P_2) of the shares to be after the record date? Because they do not carry the right to subscribe to the new shares, we would expect the market price to drop by the value of one right. In other words, the market price ought to be $39. Using the ex rights formula for determining the value of a right, we get

$$V_R = \frac{\$39 - \$35}{4} = \$1$$

Other things being equal, the value of the right does not change.

What happens to a firm's cost of capital when it sells new issues of common stock? Obviously, the first implication is that the denominator in

[9] Stephen H. Archer, "The Theoretical Value of a Stock Right: A Comment," *Journal of Finance, 11* (September 1956), 363–66.

the calculation of cost of capital is reduced. But there will be a proportionate change in the earnings per share, so that—aside from flotation costs—the cost of this increment of capital remains unchanged.

The sale of stock to investors that are not existing stockholders may be accomplished with an underwritten issue if a suitable investment banker can be found to buy the issue at reasonable flotation costs. If the banker does not wish to take the risk except at very high cost, he may agree to distribute the issue on a "best-efforts" basis that does not guarantee to the firm the sale of the entire issue. Smaller, less well established firms frequently are forced to accept such an arrangement, or they attempt to sell the issue themselves (which is usually difficult because of their lack of investor contacts).

Not only may flotation costs or the lack of underwriting support hinder the decision to sell common, but for a small firm control may also be an important factor. A public distribution by an investment banking group, however, usually provides a reasonably wide disbursement of the stock issue. The firm may also hesitate to issue common stock because it may feel that the current price does not adequately reflect its value and that to invite new shareholders into ownership at such low prices would only operate to the disadvantage of existing shareholders. A sale at such times would dilute the earnings position of the existing owners. The retention of earnings may be the only manner in which smaller firms can reasonably build up the equity portion of its capital structure.

FREQUENCY OF FINANCING

A model has been proposed to determine how often the firm should go to suppliers for cash. The model is taken from the economic order quantity model used in the standard inventory situation. The firm could go to its suppliers frequently, but fixed costs of securing capital each time may be so high that it pays to go to the sources less frequently and carry a larger balance to "carry" the firm between "trips" to the market. The problem is one of weighing the cost of going to the market against the costs of carrying the inventory of cash. If Q is the optimum order size then Q is determined as

$$Q = \sqrt{\frac{2CB}{k}}$$

where

$C = $ the average fixed cost of securing cash from a supplier

B = the demand for cash in the period analyzed (such as a year)
k = the cost of carrying the inventory of cash[10]

If the cash is secured above immediate needs, the excess can be invested in short-term marketable securities; thus k should be computed as the difference between the supply rate and the rate received on short-term investments. In a practical sense, C is not completely fixed. The model can be expanded to cover cases of uncertainty in demand (B), uncertainty in length of time to replenish cash, and the cost to the firm of running out of cash.[11] Consider an example of the certainty model in which the Jaedicke Salmon Packing Company estimated it needed $1 million per year, the difference between the cost of capital (k) and the return on short-term securities is 2.5 per cent, and the average fixed cost of securing capital is $20,000. Q in this case would be

$$Q = \sqrt{\frac{2 \times \$20,000 \times \$1,000,000}{.025}} = \$1,264,911.$$

The firm would go to the market about every 1.264911 years, raise $1,264,-911, and invest temporary excess cash in temporary short-term investments, withdrawing the cash as it needed funds. The firm could use the same formula to determine how much to withdraw at one time from short-term investments, using the short-term interest rate as the cost of carrying cash. If the Jaedicke Salmon Packing Company were giving up the 4 per cent short-term rate by taking funds out of certificates of deposit, how much should be taken out each time if it costs a flat $50 to remove any funds? The answer is

$$Q = \sqrt{\frac{2 \times \$50 \times \$1,264,911}{.04}} = \$56,214.$$

Withdrawals of $56,000 would mean the firm would make a withdrawal about every three weeks ($1,264,911/$56,000). The more uncertain the firm is about its needs, the more marketable should be its temporary holdings. As a general rule, the firm should make investments with a maturity sequence that would coincide with its expected use of funds. In

[10] William J. Baumol, "The Transactions Demand for Cash: An Inventory Theoretic Approach," *Quarterly Journal of Economics*, 63 (November 1952), 554–56. *See also:* William Beranek, *Analysis for Financial Decisions* (Homewood, Ill.: Irwin, 1963), 345–96.
[11] For an illustration of the computation of the level of cash balances which should optimally signal the "reorder" of cash, *see:* Harold Bierman, Jr. and Alan K. McAdams, *Management Decisions for Cash and Marketable Securities* (Ithaca, N.Y.: Cornell University, Graduate School of Business and Public Administration, 1962), 58–61.

this case about $56,000 should mature about every twenty-three days. This would tend to reduce withdrawal costs and reinvestment costs and minimize losses arising from interest-rate risk (losses in value caused by changes in interest rates). Longer maturities, however, present higher yields and, if the firm cares to speculate that interest rates will decline, substantial capital gains could be realized. If the level of interest is expected to rise, short maturities should be held to minimize losses.

SUMMARY

Financial management has the responsibility of providing the needed capital at least cost—the term *cost* being used in a broad enough context to include direct monetary costs as well as indirect and implicit costs. Only such a least-cost combination will maximize firm profits. The fact that the interest cost on debt is deductible before determining income taxes tends to favor the use of debt financing, but the traditionally acceptable levels of debt tend to force higher costs on firms that exceed such limits.

Short-term credit, as a general rule, should not be used to finance the permanent or long-term needs of the firm. For a small business, however, there may be little alternative because of the prohibitive costs of other forms of credit or lack of access to the public securities markets. For temporary needs and for seasonal needs, short-term capital is ideal. The major short-term sources beyond the automatic or minimal level of current liabilities (which includes accruals and trade credit) are factors, sales finance companies, and commercial banks. Generally, short-term credit needs are predictable within limits and, in order to reduce the uncertainty of supply, it may be desirable to negotiate a line of credit or a loan commitment.

Long-term debt, consisting essentially of term loans, mortgages, and bonds may be used when the firm has financing needs beyond short-term requirements. The firm generally would prefer arrangements with long, low payments, no restrictive provisions, and permission to accelerate the debt retirement without cost. The lenders, however, are likely to force repayment of the debt as rapidly as the firm is able to handle the charges through its cash flow. If the debt is secured, the economic life of the pledged assets in the outer limit of the maturity.

A financial lease is similar to debt in that it requires an obligation to make a fixed payment to the lessor so that principal and interest may be recovered. In general, financial leases are not cancellable. Once the use of the particular piece of equipment has been determined profitable and the choice of debt financing over equity has been made, lease financing becomes an alternative to borrowing. The use of such multiple sources of borrowing may broaden the credit "pool" from which the firm may draw. Lease financing may be especially attractive when the firm is "loaned up" by investor standards.

The sale of stock results in an increase in the equity of the firm's capital structure. Common stock must be offered to existing stockholders if the pre-emptive right exists. Even if it does not exist, the firm may prefer to offer new stock to existing shareholders first. Such a privileged offering involves the grant of rights to shareholders in order that they may exercise their purchase. Small firms may find difficulty in securing the underwriting services of an investment banker and may have to be content with a "best-efforts" sale. The sale of stock to new shareholders should not occur at a time when it would dilute the earnings position of existing shareholders.

In discussing the frequency with which a firm should "go to the market" for funds, it was seen that a high fixed cost of capital procurement tends to decrease the frequency with which a firm seeks capital and increase the magnitude of funds sought on each "trip" to the market. On the other hand, a high carrying cost tends to increase the frequency with which a firm seeks capital, decrease the amount sought on each "trip," and decrease the balance carried. Although an analytical model can be used to determine this frequency, lack of confidence in estimated needs may preclude its use.

SUGGESTED READINGS

DONALDSON, GORDON. *Corporate Debt Capacity*. Boston: Harvard University Press, 1961.

GORDON, MYRON J. *The Investment, Financing, and Valuation of the Corporation*. Homewood, Ill.: Richard D. Irwin, Inc., 1962.

———. "Optimal Investment and Financial Policy," *The Journal of Finance,* 18 (May 1963), 264–72.

MILLER, D. C. "Corporate Taxation and Methods of Corporate Financing," *American Economic Review,* 42 (December 1952), 839–54.

SMITH, DAN THROOP. *Effects of Taxation on Corporate Financial Policy*. Boston: Graduate School of Business Administration, Harvard University, 1952.

SOLOMON, EZRA. *The Theory of Financial Management*. New York: Columbia University Press, 1963.

STEVENSON, HAROLD W. *Common Stock Financing*, Ann Arbor, Mich.: Bureau of Business Research, University of Michigan, 1957.

WESTON, J. FRED. "Toward Theories of Financial Policy," *The Journal of Finance, 10* (May 1955), 130–43.

QUESTIONS

18.1 How should the seasonal capital needs of a firm be financed? Explain.

18.2 What factors contribute to a firm's use of short-term debt beyond the automatic (minimum needed) level of current liabilities?

18.3 What are the various costs involved in a firm's arranging a line of credit? How would these be expected to differ from the costs of arranging a loan commitment?

18.4 Comment on the following statement: "It is bad business for a firm to go into debt to finance its investments." (Consider this comment in the broad context of Parts I and II.)

18.5 Why should a firm use long-term debt at a 6 per cent cost when short-term debt is available at 5 per cent?

18.6 What factors influence the length of repayment of debt?

18.7 Distinguish between *operating lease* and *financial lease*.

18.8 Does the use of the financial lease enable a firm to secure more capital in the long run? Discuss.

18.9 For what reasons should a firm consider a rights offering rather than a public sale of stock?

18.10 Is there such a thing as an optimal combination of sources of funds? What would be its necessary ingredients? Discuss.

PROBLEMS

18.11 Refer to the Zulauf Company's financial statements in Chapter 15. A new bank has been established in the neighborhood and you meet the loan officer to establish a line of credit. Set forth your presentation to him.

18.12 The Jones Press Company needs $80,000 for one month and $50,000 for two months. It normally has a $5,000 cash balance. The Hardin Bank & Trust will grant a loan commitment for the required amount at 5 per cent if Jones will carry an average balance of 20 per cent of the commitment during the loan period and pay .5 per cent for the whole year on the size of the commitment. What is the cost of this source of capital?

18.13 The Robinson Data Processing Company is considering a line of credit. It needs $40,000 for a six-month period. It normally carries a $3,000 cash balance. The Scott Bank will grant the line of credit needed if Robinson Data Processing will carry 20 per cent of the line as an average balance during the entire year. The rate on the loan is 5 per cent and the costs to Scott of arranging and setting up the line of credit and loan amount to $100. What is the cost of this source if the company expects to have no excess funds to put into its cash balance during the year?

18.14 As an alternative, Robinson Data Processing Company, in talking with the Seyfried Investment Company, finds that it could raise $40,000 by arranging a private placement of bonds to a local insurance company. The bonds would be 6 per cent bonds, the net proceeds to the company to be at face value. Robinson would have to pay Seyfried $500 for its service and incur another $500 in costs in setting up the sale. The bonds would have a duration of twenty years and would contain provisions that are no more restrictive than the line of credit. Each year the company could use the $40,000 for its six-month seasonal needs. During the portion of the year in which the funds are not needed, they could be invested to yield 3 per cent. Comment on this proposal in comparison to the proposal for the line of credit from the Scott Bank.

18.15 In June of 1959 Noma Lites, Inc., offered its entire holdings of D. Kaltman & Company, Inc., common stock to its existing shareholders at $4 per share. The subscription rate was 1.9 shares of Kaltman for one share of Noma. In 1956 Noma had distributed 225,000 shares of Kaltman to its shareholders. (*a*) Was the distribution in 1956 a stock dividend or a property dividend (a distribution of resources owned)? (*b*) Is the offer to purchase the shares a privileged subscription in any sense of the term or is it an offer to purchase what shareholders already own?

18.16 In 1962 Ling-Temco-Vought, Inc., offered its existing common and preferred shareholders the right to buy the company's holdings of 1,166,-000 shares of Information Systems, Inc. The subscription price was $3.30

a share. (*a*) In what sense, if any, can this be viewed as a "privileged" subscription? (*b*) As a shareholder of Ling-Temco-Vought, would you be able to argue that the stock of Information Systems was already owned by the shareholders and that the company was actually selling you what you already owned? If so, how would you argue the case? If not, on what basis would you refuse to take this position?

18.17 Compute the value of the rights for the Thompson Company, whose stock is selling with rights at $38. The subscription price is $35 and stockholders can buy new stock at the ratio of one share for each ten held.

18.18 The Long Hardware Company owns a chain of stores. The firm is incorporated and Long owns 900 of the 1,000 shares outstanding. The remaining shares are distributed equally among his ten store managers. Long receives a salary of $2,000 a month; he pays his managers $1,000 per month. The following balance sheet is the most recent:

Long Hardware Company
December 31, 1967 (in thousands of dollars)

Assets			Liabilities and Equity		
Cash	$ 50		Payables–trade	$ 30	
Receivables	100		Bank loans	230	
Inventories	250	$400	Accruals	20	
Fixed assets	100	$100	Current		$280
			Mortgage		60
			Total liabilities		$340
			Common stock	100	
			Surplus	60	
			Total equity		$160
		$500			$500

Current assets and current liabilities are seasonally high. Bank loans decline to about $130,000 at the lowest point in annual activity. Most of his stores are leased under a financial lease arrangement. (*a*) Comment on his current status of financing. (*b*) What financing alternatives do you feel are realistically available to him? (*c*) Do you have any general recommendations? Discuss.

18.19 The Klempel Company has estimated that it needs new cash at the rate of $2 million per year. It can secure funds at an average capital cost of 8 per cent and invest in short-term securities for 3 per cent. If it costs an average of $6,000 every time the company secures capital—no matter how much—how often should it "go to the market"?

18.20 The Kester Mining Company has $2 million invested in United States bills yielding 3 per cent per annum; this will satisfy the firm's need for funds during the coming year. If it costs $50 to sell these, regardless of the amount, how much should be withdrawn at a time?

18.21 The Quick Sink Boat Company plans to issue 10,000 shares at $50 a share to the holders of its outstanding 60,000 shares. On May 20 the stock sold for 53-1/2. At what price would you expect the stock to be on May 21, the record date, providing other things remain unchanged?

18.22 The Alvord International Company decided to issue 200,000 shares of common stock to existing shareholders. At the time it announced the offering, that is on November 20, shareholders of record as of November 1, who held a total of 1,200,000 shares, were given the privilege of subscribing to the new shares at $20. The market price on November 19 was 24-1/2. At what price would you expect the common to sell on November 21?

CHAPTER 19   ADJUSTING CAPITAL SOURCES

Because the conditions or management under which a business operates may change, changes in the mix between debt and equity funds or in the nature of the covenants that are typically found in most securities agreements may be necessary. In a dynamic world these changes are almost certain to take place. The firm has little control over some of the changes; others may be a result of the firm's instigation. As a result of the dynamic influences on business enterprise, one of the most interesting and fascinating aspects in the study of business finance centers on adjustments of the various sources of capital in order to bring them in line with realized or expected changes in the environment in which the firm operates. To the extent that firms continuously seek some least-cost combination of capital sources, such adjustments appear to be almost continuous.

Often business firms are not aware of what adjustments will be necessary at some future date. To provide for future flexibility, however, the first "line of defense" lies in the proper preparation of the various securities contracts. This will protect the firm against adverse business developments which may necessitate adjustments in the contracts of the firm's creditors and/or owners. Some of these adjustments can originate with the firm itself. Some may be initiated by creditors. Others will be imposed by the courts or regulatory agencies.

In Chapter 8, as you will recall, it was mentioned that any security[1] is essentially a marketable contract consisting of a number of provisions. These provisions are often called *covenants*. This package of covenants will vary from firm to firm, from industry to industry, and over time. Sometimes it will reflect the whims of the investment market, a factor over which the issuing firm has very little control. Sometimes it will reflect the customs of the trade—as, for example, in the case of trade credit, another factor over which the firm may have little or no control. Most often this package of covenants will reflect the basic business risks of the issuing firm.

But direct negotiations between a firm and potential suppliers of cap-

---

[1] A *security* is broadly defined as any claim on the assets, earnings, or control of the firm. These would include, for example, mortgage bonds and common stock.

ital do not ordinarily take place. In a public offering of debt securities, for example, the services of an investment banker are often engaged. Because of his experience and sensitivity to current and prospective market conditions, he will, in effect, negotiate a given package of covenants with the corporation for the creditors. His own best interests would dictate that this package be attractive to potential buyers so that he may be able to sell the securities quickly and at a profit. The interests of the firm, however, must also be considered and in some cases they conflict with those of the investment banker. As a result, a compromise takes place. Hence the package of provisions resulting from these negotiations will reflect various compromises and may not be completely satisfactory either to the firm or to the investment banker (working on behalf of creditors). Many of the covenants contained in this long-term package, however, are fairly standard.[2] Some of them are somewhat unusual. Others are used in specific industries and under particular conditions. The securities contracts negotiated directly with creditors are, for the most part, similar to those in which the services of an investment banker were employed. We will discuss the most typical provisions at some length, allude to the more specific, and for the most part ignore the highly specialized.

ADJUSTING LONG-TERM SOURCES

The adjustment of capital sources involves changes, either minor or radical in character, in either or both of the two basic classes of sources of capital for a firm: creditors and owners. This broad topic has been referred to as *refinancing,* which means that a firm's financing scheme is being changed. Refinancing can take many shapes and forms, the most extensive of which, for example, may be a complete recasting of the financial structure as a result of bankruptcy or reorganization. Or it may consist of rather simple changes in one of the provisions of an original securities contract. The reasons for these changes should reflect management's efforts to achieve some least-cost combination of capital sources. From a stockholder's point of view, the changes should result in an eventual improvement in profits—that is, an improvement in the value of the enterprise.

Of all the various adjustments that may take place, adjustments in long-term sources are the easiest and, in many respects, the most convenient with which to start out our discussion. In this chapter we will concentrate on adjustments of the creditorship sources of capital. These adjustments usually take the form of *conversion* or *redemption.* Under the category of redemption, three factors will be considered. First there

---

[2] For a brief summary of these covenants, the student is referred to Appendix B.

is *refunding*, defined as the replacement of one creditorship claim by another. The security replaced is typically called in, paid for with the proceeds of another issue, and cancelled. In cases in which securities are refunded before their maturity date, the security issued in its place usually has a maturity date later than the original issue; in many respects it is similar to a loan renewal. Second, we will discuss *sinking funds*, which are defined as periodic allocations of cash designed to retire part or all of the long-term debt prior to maturity. In many respects sinking-fund allocations are similar to installment financing. And third, we will discuss *serial redemptions*, which are redemptions of debt having a series of specific maturity dates. These, too, are similar to installment payments. In Chapter 20 we will take up the adjustment of short-term credit sources and ownership sources.

Conversion

Often securities include a provision which allows the owners of these securities to exchange them for other securities, usually common stock, at some future date under certain given conditions. This is referred to as the *conversion privilege*.[3] For example, a firm may issue a number of bonds each having a $1,000 denomination and, among a number of other covenants, a provision allowing the owners of these bonds to convert them into common stock in the next, say, five years, at the rate of twenty-five shares of common stock for each $1,000 bond. Although this is a common way of stating the *terms of conversions*, they could have been stated differently in the contract. For example, the contract may have stated that the holder of the $1,000 bond is entitled to convert it during the next five years at a price of $40. By dividing the face value (FV) of the bond by the *conversion price* (P_c), that is, $40, the resultant will be the *conversion rate* (CR)—in this case, twenty five shares. There is no one universal way of stipulating the rate at which bonds are converted into common stock. Both are used, but if the formula below is utilized, the student of business finance should have no trouble in going from the conversion price to a conversion rate:

$$CR = \frac{FV}{P_c}$$

where

CR = conversion rate
FV = face value or par value of the convertible security
P_c = conversion price

[3] The present discussion of conversion centers on bonds, but the principles apply to convertible preferred stocks also.

Using the above information, we get

$$CR = \frac{\$1,000}{\$40} = 25 \text{ shares}$$

Alternatively, we could have worked from the conversion rate to the conversion price. In that case we would get

$$25 \text{ shares} = \frac{\$1,000}{P_c} = \$40$$

Conversion Parity

In determining the extent of conversion, some mechanical aspects of convertibility must first be considered. Actually, the *conversion security* is the one into which another security is convertible. The *convertible security* is the one which can be exchanged for another security, either senior, junior, or equal to it in claim on assets, earnings, or control. Almost invariably, convertible securities are convertible into junior securities. Only in very rare instances have they been convertible into securities of equal or senior claim. In our example, the junior security (common stock) is the conversion security and the senior security (bond) is the convertible security. If the stock is selling at $40 per share (other things being equal), one would expect the bond to sell for $1,000 given the conversion rate of twenty five shares of common stock for each convertible security held. The principle involved here is that the value of the convertible security should tend to equal the aggregate value of the conversion security, provided that the market price per share is equal to or greater than the conversion price. In this case the conversion price is $40 ($1,000/25 shares), and the value of the convertible security upon conversion into the conversion security is $1,000 ($40 × 25 shares). If the market price of the junior security were to increase to, say, $50 per share, what would one reasonably expect the senior security to be selling for? You would probably say that it would have to sell at a price equal to the converted value of the junior security, and you would be correct. But what price is that? If it has to be at least equal to the converted value of the junior security, it would be worth $1,250 ($50 per share × 25 shares). When the value of the convertible security is *equal* to the aggregate value of the conversion security, *conversion parity* is said to exist. If we consider market values only, this represents a point of indifference to conversion from the standpoint of the convertible security holder. On the other hand, if the value of the convertible security is greater than the aggregate value of the conversion security, there will be no conversion. If the value of a convertible security is less than the aggregate value of the conversion security, however, there may be conversion. In practice, the student will find that convertible securities and conversion securities have aggregate values which tend to be about the same when the market price of the latter is greater than the conversion price. This is so because any upward movements in the price of the common stock beyond the conversion price should tend to push up the bond price. Thus, in our example, the $1,000 (face value) convertible bond was assumed to be selling at $1,000 because the price of the junior security was $40 per share. If our hypothetical junior security were selling for $35 per share and the price of the bond remained at approximately $1,000, however, the value of the bond would clearly be greater than the converted value of the stock (25 shares × $35 = $875). Its value in this case is supported by the interest payment and the maturity value rather than by the conversion value of common. On the other hand, if the market price of the stock were to go up to $60 a share, the aggregate value of the stock would then be $1,500 (25 shares × $60). If it could be hypothesized that the market value of the bond did not change—that is, it remained at $1,000—then it would behoove any individual to buy the bond at $1,000, convert it into the junior security having an aggregate value of $1,500, take the $1,500 and buy another bond, again convert it, and continue this process until such a time as it was no longer profitable to do so—that is, until conversion parity is established. Common stock price changes rarely take place so abruptly, and even if they did these opportunities for *arbitrage profits* would not go begging.[4] Investors would be quick to recognize that such an opportunity is available, and sufficient demand for the bond will materialize, which will tend to drive up its price. Also, upon conversion of a number of bonds, the market price of the stock would tend to decrease, providing the demand for the stock stays the same, decreases, or increases at a rate less than the increase in the supply of stock. Thus there are two forces that come to bear on the equilibration of the aggregate values of both the convertible and conversion securities. First, on the demand side there is the upward pressure on bond prices. Secondly, on the supply side, the increase in the number of shares of common stock tends to push down the market price of the shares, other things equal. Thus, there is this tendency for the aggregate value of both the senior and junior securities to be essentially the same.

Some Considerations in the Use of Convertible Securities

A question naturally arises: Why and when is a conversion feature used by a firm? Perhaps the three outstanding uses of a conversion feature are

---

[4] Arbitrage is the process of buying and selling the same security in different markets in order to take advantage of unwarranted differentials in prices.

(1) that it tends to "sweeten" an issue, (2) that it tends to put off or defer the sale of common stock and prevent current dilution of common stock earnings, and (3) that it tends to scale down the long-term debt of the firm and increase its equity capital. It is widely believed that the existence of a conversion feature will tend to make it easier to sell a bond than it would have been had there been no such provision. The reason for this is that investors think that they can have the benefit of a bond investment, while having a potential claim on common stock earnings. If the earnings per share of common stock go up in, say, the next five years, the market price of the stock presumably would also rise and holders of the convertible bonds would be able to participate in the capital gains arising from the increasing earning power of the company. Because of this, it is widely argued that the sale of bonds possessing a conversion feature tends to lower the interest rate on the issue. That is to say, the conversion covenant itself is sufficiently appealing to investors that, given two bonds, alike in all regards except that one has a conversion covenant and the other does not, they will be willing to pay more for the former than for the latter, which is equivalent to saying that the *direct* cost of this increment of capital is less with the covenant than without it.

Interestingly, the second purpose for which conversion features are included in bond contracts is to sell common stock indirectly or on a deferred basis. Often a firm in need of more capital may not be in a position to sell common stock directly because of poor market conditions, a temporarily adverse earnings position at the time the capital is desired, a rather poor cash dividend policy, or the relatively unknown nature of the firm. Under these conditions the sale of common stock at reasonable prices directly to present stockholders or even other investors may be effectively precluded. Nevertheless, management may feel confident that earnings of the common stock will improve substantially in time, or that market conditions will change, or that the company and its stock will become more widely known—all of which should have the beneficial effect of increasing the price of the common stock to a point at which it would become desirable to convert the senior security. Thus, because the firm wishes to expand or improve its present operations but capital is not readily available through the sale of common stock, an issue of bonds containing the conversion feature may be very appropriate. If the anticipated increase in earnings materializes, if dividends increase, if market conditions improve, or if the investment merits of the stock is more widely recognized—if any of these things occur, chances are that the market price of the stock will rise at some subsequent date. If the market price does rise, then once again chances are good that conversion of the bonds into the stock may take place. This, in effect, is deferring the sale of stock to some subsequent, more favorable date.

One of the advantages of the conversion feature lies in the *reduction of senior claims* once the option is exercised by the holders. In essence what conversion does to the financial structure is to reduce the amount of senior claims and increase the amount of junior claims, thereby changing the mix of debt and equity. This tends to improve the firm's credit position, allowing (other things being equal) for subsequent use of more debt. But the exercise of the conversion option has two side effects, the full implications of which are difficult to assess. First, there is a presumed tendency to dilute the common stock position with respect to dividends, earnings, and market price, as a result of conversion into common stock. How serious this is depends on the rate at which the senior securities are converted and the size of the senior issue to be converted relative to the size of the common issue previously outstanding. If market prices of common securities are reduced, then profits (as we have defined them) likewise are reduced. Second, there is the effect on the firm's weighted average cost of capital. By conversion of debt securities the firm loses the tax advantages of deducting interest expenses for tax purposes. Other things being equal, this would normally tend to raise a firm's weighted average cost of capital, a factor which *may* be partially offset by the higher valuation of common stock because of market aversion to prior claims. On the other hand, an expense is reduced and the aggregate common stock earnings will be enhanced, although per share earnings are likely to decline. Perhaps the stock price will adjust to the point at which the new price-earnings ratio (the reciprocal of the earnings yield) is just equal to the old one, in which case the weighted average cost of capital will increase. However, if the risk of investment in the common stock is reduced significantly, its market price may tend to change to a point at which the new price-earnings ratio is higher than the old. In that event, depending on the extent of the increase, the cost of equity capital could be kept the same or reduced. Obviously, it is difficult to estimate what will happen under such conditions.

To illustrate some of the complex dilutionary and cost of capital implications associated with the use of convertible bonds[5] Table 19-1 is useful. In that table seven different "states" or sets of circumstances are utilized to depict the varying possible impacts on expected earnings per share of common stock and the weighted average cost of capital. All

---

[5] The basic concepts apply as well to the use of convertible preferred stocks, except that several adjustments would be in order, the most notable of which involves income taxes.

Table 19-1
Dilutionary and Cost of Capital Effects of Convertible Securities

	State I			State II			State III			State IV			State V			State VI			State VII		
	Before The Sale of Convertible Bonds			Before the Conversion of the Bonds and With a 10% Increase in Net Revenues									After the Conversion of the Bonds and With a 10% Increase in Net Revenues								
				No Change in PER			Change in PER Needed to Maintain Original Market Price			Change in PER Needed to Maintain Original Cost of Capital			No Change in PER			Increase in PER To 12			Change in PER Needed to Maintain Original Cost of Capital		
	Per cent of Total Capital	After-Tax Rate	Cost	Per cent of Total Capital	After-Tax Rate	Cost	Per cent of Total Capital	After-Tax Rate	Cost	Per cent of Total Capital	After-Tax Rate	Cost	Per cent of Total Capital	After-Tax Rate	Cost	Per cent of Total Capital	After-Tax Rate	Cost	Per cent of Total Capital	After-Tax Rate	Cost
Capital structure Mix																					
Short-term debt	20%			17%			17%			17%			17%			17%			17%		
Convertible debenture bonds, 4%				17%			17%			17%											
Mortgage bonds, 5%	20%			17%			17%			17%			17%			17%			17%		
Common stock	40%			33%			33%			33%			50%			50%			50%		
Surplus	20%			17%			17%			17%			17%			17%			17%		
Total	100%			100%			100%			100%			100%			100%			100%		
Weighted average cost of capital																					
Short-term debt	20	0.0	0.000	17	0.0	0.000	17	0.0	0.000	17	0.0	0.000	17	0.0	0.000	17	0.0	0.000	17	0.0	0.000
Convertible debenture bonds, 4%				17	2.0	0.340	17	2.0	0.340	17	2.0	0.340									
Mortgage bonds, 5%	20	2.5	0.500	17	2.5	0.425	17	2.5	0.425	17	2.5	0.425	17	2.5	0.425	17	2.5	0.425	17	2.5	0.425
Common equity	60	10.0	6.000	50	10.0	5.000	50	11.2	5.600	50	11.5	5.750	67	10.0	6.700	67	8.5	5.695	67	9.06	6.070
Total			6.500			5.765			6.365			6.500			7.125			6.120			6.495
Earnings per share	$6.20			$7.00			$7.00			$7.00			$6.26			$6.26			$6.26		
Price-earnings ratio	10			10			8.90			8.7			10			12			11		
Market prices																					
Convertible debenture bonds, 4%				$1,000			$1,000			$1,000											
Mortgage bonds, 5%	$1,000			$1,000			$1,000			$1,000			$1,000			$1,000			$1,000		
Common stock (rounded)	$62			$70			$62			$61			$63			$75			$69		

these states represent the R. W. Mayer Company's capital structure before, during, and after the use of convertible bonds. The data set forth under each state include the company's expected capital structure mix, its weighted average cost of capital, and market price data for its outstanding securities. Throughout this analysis it is assumed that the company's expected earnings and capital structures are as shown in each state. In order to compute the cost of common stock capital, we should make various assumptions about expected price changes and dividend changes. Unfortunately these assumptions increase the complexity of the example considerably. Consequently, here we shall assume that expected price change plus dividends are approximated by earnings and the cost is the earnings yield.

The R. W. Mayer Company's long-run expansion program calls for successive increases in total assets. To finance this program, several issues of securities will have to be floated during the ensuing expansion period. In an effort to be consistent with these long-run needs for outside capital and to maintain flexibility, management has decided to change the firm's long-run financial policy. This change involves a change in the capital structure mix from that shown in State I (which represents the status of the firm before any expansion). But because of an anticipated reduction in the variance of expected earnings, management feels a new capital structure mix, containing a greater proportion of debt and a smaller proportion of equity, is called for and would more nearly approach what they feel is optimal for the firm. This desired capital structure mix is set forth in States II, III, and IV and is expected to be their choice for the indefinite future. Convertible bonds are intended to be a permanent feature of the new capital mix. That is, the firm intends to utilize convertible bonds on a regular and recurring basis in the years ahead because it feels this type of bond will be easier to sell than other types or forms of securities, and these bonds at the same time provide—through the conversion feature—an increase in the dollars of equity financing, a desirable result in light of the anticipated outside capital requirements. Once converted, additional convertible bonds (larger issue) will be issued to maintain the mix assumed to be optimal. If no expansion were to take place, State I would represent what management regards as an optimal capital structure.

The current phase of the expansion program requires a cash outlay of $1.5 million, $.5 million of which the firm has in excess cash, the other $1 million of which it will secure from the sale of convertible debenture bonds. Each $1,000 bond is convertible into fifteen shares of common stock. The firm at State I has 100,000 shares of common outstanding. Before the expansion (State I) earnings per share are $6.20 and the shares sell at ten times those earnings, so that the market price per share of common is $62.

State II represents the results of financing the first phase of the expansion program and the change in financial policy. The capital mix has changed; it now contains more debt and less equity. Expected earnings per share are assumed to increase to $7.00 as a result of the expansion. If we can assume that the price-earnings ratio (*PER*) stays the same, the market price of common stock shares will be $70. In this state the weighted average cost of capital decreases from 6.5 per cent (State I) to 5.8 per cent. Whether or not this is realistic is subject to debate, but some decline in the cost of capital arising from the tax-deductibility of interest is to be expected. If the firm has not achieved its least-cost combination of debt and equity because it has not taken on "enough" debt (as established by market-determined acceptable debt levels), then the addition of $1 million of convertible bonds (a change in the mix) should lower the cost of capital. On the other hand, we should think that the additional debt would create additional risk to shareholders so that higher rates of return on their investments would be required by common stockholders. In this event we would expect them to require greater earnings for the same price (a higher yield) or a lower price for the same earnings. States III and IV depict both situations. In State III the market price of the common stock is assumed to stay the same while more earnings are required to achieve it than was the case in State I, all because of the issuance of the additional debt; the market now assumes a higher risk and a lower price-earnings ratio results—in this case it is 8.9 ×'s ($62/$7). Taking the reciprocal of this figure to derive the earnings yield, we get 11.3 per cent. When this figure is used for the common equity portion of the weighted average cost of capital, k becomes 6.4 per cent.

In State IV, if we assume the cost of capital remains as it was in State I (that is, 6.5 per cent), the market price of the common stock must drop to $61 per share or a price-earnings ratio of 8.7. In this event the *unweighted* cost of common equity is about 11.5 per cent, as opposed to 10 per cent in State I.

Which of the states—II, III, or IV—is likely to occur? The answer to this question is at best conjectural. Because of the tax-deductibility of interest, the cost of capital could be expected to decline in any event. If we assume that the price-earnings ratio will decline because of the added risk, the question is: How far must it decline to keep our cost of capital the same as it was previously? We saw in State IV that the stock could decline to a price which is 8.7 ×'s expected earnings. A decline beyond that point would raise the cost of capital and render the use of convertibles imprudent. If a firm has not exceeded "proper limits"[6] of debt financing, the issuance of convertible bonds should have some of the effects illustrated in State II. That is to say, the tax-deductibility of interest in itself should reduce the firm's cost of capital. Also, the increased earnings resulting from the expansion program should increase the market value of the shares. If the market's assessment is such that the quality of the issue is unchanged, then State II will prevail. If the quality of the issue is thought to have declined, then something similar to States III and IV will result.

States V, VI, and VII depict the company's financial status after the bonds have been converted. But in these three states we assume that the use of convertible bonds is regarded as a "once-and-for-all" method of financing. That is, the management did not foresee any continuing need to finance with convertibles in the future and wanted to return to approximately the mix of State I. But the impact of conversion is to produce a mix as shown in States V, VI, and VII, assuming the amounts of short-term and mortgage debt do not change.

State V indicates what might happen when conversion takes place and the price-earnings ratio is unchanged afterward. The effect of this occurrence is to raise the cost of capital and reduce the market price of the common shares. The latter phenomenon is referred to as *dilution* and results because more shares—15,000, to be exact—are added to the existing 100,000 shares of common stock but no change or a less than proportionate change in total earnings has taken place. That is, a greater number of shares now divide up the same or a slightly larger "pie" as a result of conversion. Although aggregate earnings available for common shareholders increase because the convertible debt interest expense is eliminated, the increase in these earnings is ordinarily slight after taxes relative to the increase in the number of shares resulting from conversion. Working back from our knowledge that there were 100,000 shares outstanding before conversion and the earnings per share were $7, then the net income available to common must have been $700,000. We also know the firm issued $1 million of debt at 4 per cent. Because only half of the interest expense of $40,000 results in a tax saving, once the bonds are eliminated this half accrues to the benefit of the common shareholders. In this case the amount is $20,000 so that after complete conversion of the bonds there are $720,000 available for common shares. But conversion of the shares also involves an addition to the total number of shares outstanding. In this case the amount added is 15,000 shares, which—when

---

[6] Discussion of "proper" debt limits as viewed from the market is deferred until Chapters 21 and 22.

combined with the 100,000 shares already outstanding—results in 115,000 total shares. Dividing the income available to common stockholders ($720,000) by the number of shares outstanding (115,000) we get a new earnings-per-share figure of $6.26, a decrease of slightly more than 10 per cent from the previous $7 level. If the *PER* remains at 10, the market value of the shares will decline by slightly more than 10 per cent also (from $70 to $63). Whether or not this is a likely event is subject to debate. If the firm was at a least-cost combination of debt and equity, once conversion takes place the resulting relationship between the two is less than optimal and we could expect the cost of capital to increase because relatively high-cost capital (common stock) is substituted for relatively low-cost capital (bonds). On the other hand, a reduction in debt may result in less risk to common shareholders, in which event they may be willing to pay a higher price for the diluted earnings (say, 12 × 's earnings, as in State VI), especially if a broader market is secured. In State VII, we depict a situation in which the cost of capital after conversion of the bonds equals the cost of capital before the bonds were even issued (State I). In that case the price-earnings ratio would have to increase from 10 to 11 ×'s and the market price of the stock would be $69 per share.

We have dwelled on the dilution and cost of capital of convertible securities because of their importance to business financing. It should be apparent that no definite answers are available to questions concerning the impact of convertibles on a firm's cost of capital. In has been argued that the convertible feature allows a firm to issue securities at a lower coupon rate than if there were no conversion privilege. Although this would seem to be logically correct, there are no adequate studies to prove this assertion. For companies with good credit, however, the likelihood of receiving much of a concession on the coupon rate would seem to be small.[7] For less credit-worthy firms, this appears to be a tenable proposition.

To illustrate the dilution effects further, let us turn again to the R. W. Mayer Company. Let us assume it sold its convertible bonds to existing shareholders at a rate which would protect their proportionate interest in earnings, assets, control, and market price. That is, it offered its $1 million of convertible debentures to existing stockholders at the rate of one $1,000 bond for each 100 shares of common held, and all shareholders were able to—and did—purchase their respective proportionate interest. Upon conversion of the bonds, dilution (in the strict sense of the word)

[7] For the impacts on American Telephone & Telegraph's convertibles, *see:* Charles A. D'Ambrosio, *Use of Convertible Debenture Bonds by A.T. & T., 1946–1956.* Unpublished M.S. thesis, Department of Finance, University of Illinois, Urbana 1958.

would take place, provided that everything else remains the same. For example, in State I a stockholder owns 100 shares of stock having an aggregate market value of $6,200, and he purchases the $1,000 bond to which he is entitled. In State II, the aggregate market value of his common holdings increases to $7,000 (100 shares × $70). On conversion he has 115 shares of stock, each share having a market value of $63 (State V), so the aggregate value of his holdings is $7,245. In this sense then, no dilution in market value has taken place and the stockholder has not lost value. To see the dilutionary effects, we have to include with the original $6,200 (100 shares × $62), the $1,000 paid for the bond. In that case, the aggregate value of the investment is $7,200 whereas, as we have seen, the final value is $7,245 (115 shares × $63). But just prior to conversion the aggregate investment of one shareholder consisted of $7,000 in common stock (100 shares × $70) and $1,050 (15 shares × $70) in the bond for a total of $8,050. The $805 difference between the two figures is accounted for by the decline in price of $7 per share on 115 shares. In this illustration the dilution is clear.

Methods to Stimulate Conversion

It may happen that conversion of senior securities is not forthcoming even though conditions may warrant it; or at least the holder of the convertible security may be indifferent with respect to conversion. Armed with the basic notion of conversion parity, we shall see that there are several ways to stimulate conversion, if and when it is feasible but not forthcoming. One of these methods is to *call the bonds for redemption.* Invariably, a call feature is included in a convertible bond issue which provides the firm the option of retiring part or all of its outstanding bonds. An important provision typically allows the firm to call the securities for redemption in whole or in part on thirty to sixty days' notice. Obviously, one of the chief merits of this feature is the flexibility it provides for future financing. If conditions are such as to make conversion particularly attractive, calling the convertible securities for redemption would be one way to stimulate conversion. For these conditions to exist, the value of the convertible security on conversion must exceed the call price. For example, if conversion parity is $1,250—that is, the bond is selling for $1,250 and the aggregate value of the junior security upon conversion is also $1,250 (25 shares × $50 per share)—and the bonds are called for redemption, it would be logical to expect a rash of conversions by the holders of these bonds. Why? Because their alternative to receiving $1,250 in value upon conversion is to receive the call price—that is, the stipulated rate at which the bonds may be called by the firm. For example, the call price may be 106. Because bond prices are quoted as a percentage of face value, this means that the amount that will be realized by bonds redeemed under the call will be $1,060—$190 less than if the bonds had been converted. It is easy to see why, under such conditions, a call for redemption will stimulate conversion.

Another method of stimulating conversion is to include an *acceleration clause* in the conversion agreement. In essence, this provision decreases the conversion rate over a period of years. For example, although the bonds may be convertible at $40 in the first two years they are outstanding, in the next two-year period they may be convertible at $45, then at $50. In each of these cases the conversion rates would be 25, 22.222, and 20 shares respectively. Presumably if the price of the junior security is increasing throughout this period, the lower conversion rate should be attractive and should stimulate conversion before a change in the rate takes place. For example, in the case cited earlier, the price of the bond was $1,250, the price of the common stock was $50 per share, and the conversion rate was twenty five shares. Now, if a change in the conversion rate to 22.222 shares were imminent (because of the acceleration clause), it is likely that a substantial conversion of the senior security would take place. The reason for this lies in the disadvantage of holding the senior security in light of the acceleration clause, for to do so would be to incur a loss of $139; the value of the junior securities before the change in the conversion rate is $1,250; their value after the initiation of the acceleration clause would be $1,111 (22.222 shares × $50). Thus, by this method, conversion can be stimulated. It should also be pointed out that this provision tends to reduce the dilutionary effects of conversion. (We leave it to the reader to verify this.)

A third possible way to stimulate conversion indirectly is to *increase the dividend rate* on the common stock. This action would have a twofold effect. First, it would probably have a favorable effect on the market price of the conversion security. In addition, it would tend to increase the amount of dividend income on a junior security. Whether or not this would generate conversion of senior securities depends on income differentials and the bondholders. If the value of the senior and junior securities are at parity and the senior security is selling close to face value, a differential in yield of each security (assessing the greater income attached to the junior security) could induce conversion. On the other hand, holders may not be willing to convert even if the return on the converted junior securities is greater than that on the senior one. The reason for this lies in the fact that a legally superior claim on assets, earnings, and control would have to be given up for a legally inferior one. Moreover, holders of high-grade convertible securities may feel they can "have their cake and eat it too" because there is effectively no upper limit on the price of the convertible security—but there is an effective *lower* limit. The only effective constraint on the upward trend is set by the price of the junior security into which it is convertible. On the other hand, the effective "floor" is established by the interest rates prevailing on bonds of similar quality and is independent of the conversion feature.

An illustration may be helpful at this point. Let us refer to the earlier example of the convertible bond which was selling at $1,250 and convertible into common stock at $40. Let us assume that this bond is rated Aaa and that the yield on similarly rated, nonconvertible bonds is 4 per cent. Let us further assume that the coupon rate on the convertible issue is also 4 per cent. From the data given, we can know that the price of each share of stock into which the bonds are convertible is $50. But what if the price of the common stock dropped to $40 per share? What would be the price of the bond? Even if we disregard the yields on each of the securities, the value of the aggregate junior securities would be $1,000 (25 shares × $40). If the price of the stock dropped to, say, $30, the answer is not so clearcut. We do know this, however: the price of the bond will probably not fall below its "intrinsic value"—that is, its value based on its merits as a bond alone. If all other Aaa bonds are selling to yield 4.0 per cent, as we have assumed, the price of this bond should be $1,000 and should not deviate significantly.

Antidilution Covenant

Often included in a convertible security is a so-called *antidilution clause*, a provision designed to protect the position of the convertible bondholder. This feature provides for an adjustment of the conversion price of a convertible security (or conversion rate, if no price is given) in the event that existing common stock is split up, a stock dividend is declared, or any other major change in the number of common shares outstanding takes place. It is designed to enable convertible bondholders to maintain their proportionate interests in the assets, earnings, control, and market price of the firm and its claim to junior securities. Without this provision, their position could be seriously impaired. For example, a $1,000 bond convertible into common stock at $40 has a claim on twenty-five shares of stock. Because a holder of the bond has a claim on the firm's shares, we can also suggest that he has a claim on the earnings of the stock, the assets that might accrue to stockholders, the control of the firm that might reside with common stock ownership, and the value of the stock. Hence, any actions that tend to dilute these claims are inimical to the interests of convertible bondholders. To cite a specific instance, let us take the case of the 4 per cent debenture convertible into common stock at $40. We saw that if the market price of the common stock is $50 per share, the price of the bond will tend to be $1,250 ($50 × 25 shares). If the company decided to split its stock on a two-for-one basis, the effects of such action on the common stock would be extremely important. The effect of this proposed action would be to double the total number of outstanding shares and decrease the earnings per share, the market price, and the claim on assets by one half. In this event, the market price of the stock after the stock split theoretically would be $25 per share. If earnings per share and book value per share prior to the split were $5 and $10, respectively, then afterward they would be $2.50 and $5. If no adjustment were made in the claim of the holders of convertible bonds respecting common stock, the market value of the bond would drop to a price supportable by its own investment merits: $1,000. Also, the bond-holders' claims, through stock, on residual assets, earnings, and control will be cut in half. In all these cases their over-all claim to common stock and its benefits are said to have been diluted. Thus the value of the common stock upon conversion at this rate would be $625, or exactly half the previous value. In order to protect the convertible bondholders against this and other inequities that might arise because of stock splits or other changes in the total number of shares outstanding, the conversion price would also have to be adjusted—in this case to $20, so that the conversion rate would double to fifty shares. In this event the holders would have a claim on an aggregate market value of common stock exactly equal to that which existed before the split—that is, $1,250 (50 shares × $25). The same would be true of the claim on assets, earnings, and control. This, in essence, is the nature of antidilution provisions.

The Call Provision

Another method of adjusting creditorship claims involves a provision to call in the claim at the option of the firm within specified time periods at specified prices. This feature provides flexibility in the financing or refinancing of a business firm. On balance, the call feature is perhaps one of the most important provisions a firm may incorporate in senior securities. So desirable is it that the firm might be willing to concede other types of provisions in its contract with investors in order to include this particular covenant. An important characteristic of the call feature is that is allows for the elimination of provisions in the contract which may have been appropriate when the issue was originally sold, but which are no longer desirable.

Typically, a call feature is particularly desirable for bonds issued when interest rates are relatively high. When interest rates go down, and if the firm is at all capable, the potential savings in interest expenses resulting from calling in the existing issue and selling another in its stead will be matched up against the costs involved in doing so. If there is a net advantage in the process, the call feature will allow for its execution. Moreover, in this event, it should be noted that reduction in the amount of interest expense will tend to reduce the risk of the shareholders. If the risk to shareholders declines, then common shareholders should be willing to pay more for the common stock and the value of ownership will tend to increase. The analysis in Table 19-1 with reference to convertible bonds could be applied, in part, to the analysis of the impact a call will have on profits and cost of capital. One need only assume the convertible bonds were regular debenture bonds which were called in, and then trace the impact of the call through various states as we did once the bonds were converted. In part, however, this analysis will be deficient because it fails to take cognizance of the cost of the call itself. In part, the analysis suffers from the fact that no change in equity capital will presumably take place because of the call. Even at that, however, the use of Table 19-1 can lead to some general tendencies that should prevail.

Usually, however, the privilege of being able to call in the securities is not without cost. The call provision can be a disadvantage to the investor, especially when bonds are sold at high interest rates. The investor runs the risk of having the bonds called in when interest rates fall, thereby losing a source of relatively high income. If such bonds are called, their holders must reinvest their funds at lower levels of interest, thereby reducing their income. In addition, there is the bother and expense (trading costs) to the investor of reinvesting the funds received because of the call. Two methods of compensating the investor for this disadvantage have been used extensively. One is of somewhat recent origin. The other has been in existence for a number of years.

The Call Premium

The older of the two is the provision of a *premium call price*. Although a bond may very well have a call privilege, usually there are a series of prices in excess of face value at which it will be called. For example, a bond may be callable, say, at 106. Because bonds usually have face-value denominations of $1,000, a bond having a denomination of $1,000 and callable at 106 is, in effect, callable at $1,060. The difference between the face value of the bond ($1,000) and the call price (in this case, $1,060) amounts to $60 and is the *call premium,* a provision usually incorporated into callable bond contracts. The *call prices,* as they are called, are usually graduated downward, the highest being that closest to the date of issuance, and the lowest that closest to the date of maturity. The premium will decrease to zero sometime before the bond reaches maturity. Presumably the *call premium* compensates the investor for the sacrifice of the investment he now holds for one that will probably give him a smaller return.

In recent years, with a general rise in interest rates, large investors in bonds (typically institutions) have required that firms issuing such debt instruments provide that the bonds not be called in for at least several years after they have been issued. Not unusual would be a provision stipulating that the issuing firm could not call in its bonds within, say, five years after their issuance. This provision is designed to circumvent the refinancing of bonds at lower interest rates at an early date. This provision is referred to as a *deferred-call* feature because it effectively defers (bars) the issuing company from calling in the securities before some specified date. On the other hand, bonds callable for sinking-fund purposes usually are callable at face value; if they are callable at a premium, the premium is usually not as great as it would be if they were callable for nonsinking-fund purposes. Obviously, if a firm wishes to retire its debt, and the market price is below the call price, rather than call in the securities, the firm will buy them in the open market.

The Feasibility of the Call: Management's Point of View

But most of this discussion has been mainly from the standpoint of the investor, who usually has very little control over the refunding of a bond issue. From management's point of view the critical issue is whether or not such an operation will reduce the cost of capital and/or increase the welfare of shareholders. The basic approach to this problem is identical to the analysis of investment projects as discussed in Chapters 11 and 16, for the proceeds of the new issue are "invested" in the old issue; the present value of the cash benefits of retiring the old issue is compared with the present value of the cash outlays required for such refundings. To illustrate such a refunding decision, assume the data presented in Table 19-2. Note that the unamortized bond discount as well as unamortized flotation costs are included as pertinent data. Their importance arises because they, along with the premium for the call, are tax-deductible in the year of refunding. Had these bonds remained outstanding for the remainder of their life (that is, twenty years), the discount (or premium) and flotation expense would have to have been amortized over that period. It is also assumed that duplicate interest will be paid for a period of

Table 19-2
Comparative Date for PMV Company's Refunding Operation

	Debenture Bonds to be Refunded	Debenture Bonds to be Issued
Principal amount	$1,500,000	$1,500,000
Coupon rate	6%	4.5%
Years to maturity	20	20
Unamortized bond discount	$75,000	
Unamortized flotation costs	$5,000	
Call price	105	
Proceeds to corporation		$1,500,000
Flotation expenses		$40,000

sixty days, during which the new bonds will be issued and the old bonds called and retired. But because interest is tax-deductible, we will need to include only one half the duplicate interest in our cash-flow analysis (assuming a 50 per cent tax rate). This expense can be reduced even further if we assume that the proceeds of the new issue are invested in United States Treasury Bills at 3 per cent for a period of thirty days. However, only one half of this income is available as an offset because the income is taxable. With this in mind, we can turn to Table 19-3, which sets forth the net cash outlays of the refunding operation. Table

Table 19-3
Net Cash Outlays Required by PMV Company's Refunding Operation

	On the Books of the Company	Actual Cash Outlays
Retirement of 6% bonds		$1,500,000
Call premium [(105% − 100%) × $1,500,000]	$ 75,000	75,000
Flotation expenses of new issue		40,000
Duplicate interest*		5,625
Unamortized bond discount of retired bonds	75,000	
Unamortized flotation costs of retired bonds	5,000	
Total book expenses	$155,000	
Gross cash outflow		$1,620,625
Tax savings (50% of $155,000)	77,500	77,500
Net book expenses after taxes	$ 77,500	
Net cash outflow		$1,543,125
Proceeds of new issue		1,500,000
Net cash outlay needed to refund		$ 43,125

* See table 19-4 for this calculation.

Table 19-4
Calculation of Duplicate Interest Expense

(1) Annual interest expense (6% × $1,500,000)	$90,000
(2) Monthly interest expense	7,500
(3) 60-day duplicate interest before taxes	15,000
(4) 60-day duplicate interest after taxes (50% × $15,000)	7,500
(5) Annual interest income from Treasury Bill investments (3% × $1,500,000)	45,000
(6) Monthly interest income from Treasury Bill investments before taxes	3,750
(7) Monthly interest income from Treasury Bill investments after taxes	1,875
(8) Net 60-day duplicate interest [(4) − (7)]	5,625

19-4 contains the calculation of the duplicate interest incurred. It can be seen that the net cash outlay required by this refunding operation is $43,125. Table 19-5 sets forth the net cash benefits to be received from refunding. Note that two values are used to derive the net cash benefits. These are the yearly net cash outlay required on the 6 per cent bonds

Table 19-5
Annual Net Cash Benefits Resulting From the PMV Company's Refunding Operation

	On the Books of the Company	Actual Cash Outlays
Annual cash outlays required on 6% bonds:		
Interest expense (6% × $1,500,000)	$90,000	$90,000
Amortization of bond discount $\left(\dfrac{\$75,000}{20\text{ years}}\right)$	3,750	
Amortization of flotation costs $\left(\dfrac{\$5,000}{20\text{ years}}\right)$	250	
Total book expenses before taxes	$94,000	
Taxes (50%)	47,000	47,000
Total book expenses after taxes	$47,000	
Actual annual cash outlay		$43,000
Annual cash outlays required on 4.5% bonds:		
Interest expense (4.5% × $1,500,000)	$67,500	$67,500
Amortization of flotation expenses $\left(\dfrac{\$40,000}{20\text{ years}}\right)$	2,000	
Total book expenses before taxes	$69,500	
Taxes (50%)	34,750	34,750
Total book expenses after taxes	$34,750	
Actual annual cash outlay		$32,750
Annual cash benefits resulting from refunding		$10,250

had they not been retired, and the yearly cash outlays required on the 4.5 per cent bonds. From Table 19-5 it can be seen that the yearly cash benefit expectable from refunding amounts to $10,250.

The next step is to decide whether or not it is desirable to refund the 6 per cent bonds. To do this there are several methods we can employ. First we can take the present value of the annual cash savings for twenty years and compare the results with the required cash outlay computed in Table 19-3 ($43,125). The discount rate would be the weighted average cost of capital, as this investment is essentially riskless to the firm. Assuming the PMV Company's cost of capital to be 8 per cent, and using Table C-1 of Appendix C, we get $PV = 9.8181 \times \$10,250 = \$100,636$ the present value of the net cash benefits. Inasmuch as the present value of the net cash outlay is $43,125, it is clearly profitable to refund this issue.

As an alternate method of computing the desirability of refunding, the internal-rate-of-return approach could have been used. We ask ourselves: What rate of return is necessary to equate our annual cash benefits to the required cash outlay? We can use the annuity table factor (because net cash benefits are constant from year to year). This is found by dividing the required cash outlay by the annual cash savings:

$$\frac{PV_o}{EO} = \frac{\$43,125}{\$10,250} = 4.2073$$

Using Table C-2 of Appendix C and looking across the twenty-year row, we see that the rate of return of the refunding operation is between 23 and 24 per cent.[8] As long as this rate of return exceeds the cost of capital after taxes, it is desirable to refund.

Sinking Funds

Another adjustment in the sources of capital is the use of the sinking fund. A sinking fund is a method of periodically retiring debt either in whole or in part over the life of the issue; it is an allocation of cash designed specifically to retire creditorship (including preferred stock) claims either in whole or in part before maturity. Ordinarily, the appropriations of cash are used by a trustee, usually a large bank, to purchase the bonds. Although callable features are almost universally included in creditorship claims, when a sinking fund is also included, the bonds are callable either at face value or at a schedule of premiums substantially less than the call premiums which prevail when the bonds are called other than for sinking-fund purposes. The rate at which the bonds are retired through

[8] For discussion purposes, this is a sufficiently precise answer. A more exact answer can be had through interpolation.

the sinking fund varies from security to security, and from firm to firm and ordinarily two sets of call prices on a given bond can be found: a sinking-fund call price (which could be either at face value or at a premium), and the regular call price (which goes into effect after the maximum amount of bonds have been retired through the sinking fund).

The funds so appropriated by a sinking fund are given to the trustee, who in turn will either call in the bonds at the redemption price or buy up the bonds in the market. If the market price (plus trading costs) of the bonds is less than the call price, the trustee will buy them in the market. Otherwise, the trustee will call a number of bonds, usually picked at random, in order to satisfy the sinking-fund requirement.[9]

The functional utility and essence of a sinking fund is really quite simple: it is easier to appropriate a certain amount of cash to retire a certain amount of debt each year than it is to come up with the total sum necessary to retire the entire debt at maturity. Consequently, sinking funds are extremely popular in bond contracts.

Sinking funds are used most frequently by industrial firms, although railroads now are required to have sinking funds in all newly issued bonds. Public utilities, particularly electrical utilities, use a sinking fund less frequently because in general they tend to refund their creditorship claims rather than retire them. That is to say, public utilities typically maintain about the same relative proportion of debt to total resources year after year. As a consequence, they have no need for a sinking fund because they have no intention of reducing the proportion of debt financing.

Sinking funds tend to increase the risk to the shareholders because such funds require a commitment of cash and must be provided for by the financial manager in his cash budget. The firm will probably draw on its regular net cash inflow for this purpose. On the other hand, although the obligation to retire the debt in the short run would tend to increase risk, in the long run—because the debt is reduced and interest charges are pared down—the risk is reduced.

[9] If the sinking fund is obligatory in nature, there is a definite promise to appropriate the cash and retire the debt. This is the nature of most sinking funds. Failure to appropriate the cash and retire the debt could precipitate legal failure, just as failure to meet the interest on other legal obligations could precipitate bankruptcy. There appears to be no case on record in which a firm, having failed to meet sinking-fund requirements but having paid the interest on the debt, has been forced into bankruptcy. The trustee, acting under the so-called *prudent-man rule*, would do more harm to the bondholders by forcing the company into bankruptcy if the firm did not meet the sinking-fund payments on its debt while still being able to meet its interest. There are times in the course of a firm's business operations when cash shortages will arise. The rule seems to be that, as long as the interest is paid on the debt, a trustee should not foreclose on the corporation for failure to meet an obligatory sinking fund.

There is also an optional type of sinking fund and, as the term implies, the corporation has the option of retiring debt as, if, and when it chooses to do so.

A further implication of the sinking fund arises when the appropriated cash is used to retire the outstanding debt. The use of the cash to retire debt creates a demand for the securities beyond that which would exist were there no sinking fund. As a consequence, there would be a tendency to drive up the price of the bonds—and this is equivalent to reducing their yield. In computing a firm's cost of debt capital, the lower yield adjusted for taxes should tend to result in a lower total cost of capital to the firm.

The payment of debt through the sinking fund tends to reduce the relative proportion of debt to equity. In this event, the risk to the shareholders would be reduced, although it is problematical that the total cost of capital will be altered. The reason for this seeming paradox lies in the fact that it is not likely that the price of the common stock will increase enough to cause the cost of the enlarged common equity to be reduced so far as to offset the cost of the debt capital retired. The thinking processes applied in the cost of convertible bonds and their impact on cost of capital and market value of common shares and as set forth in Table 19-1 apply here as well.

It may be thought that a sinking fund is inimical to the operations of a conversion feature. This may appear so because of the cash required by a sinking fund, a cash appropriation which could impair the dividend-paying capacity of the firm and thereby have deleterious effects on the market price of the equity securities. This could detract from the appeal of the conversion feature. A study made of the use of sinking funds showed that 48 per cent of convertible issues had sinking funds; 48 per cent of convertible issues had no sinking funds; and 4 per cent of convertible issues had sinking funds that went into operation after the expiration of the conversion privilege.[10] Thus, in practice, there is no clearcut preference or usage and in many respects the argument for including or excluding a sinking fund with a conversion feature seems to be largely an academic one. A sinking fund, as we know, is designed to retire debt. A conversion feature, on the other hand, is designed to substitute one form of securities for another. If a sinking fund is administered properly —that is, by retaining earnings in the business equivalent at least to the average of the sinking-fund payments—then, in effect, equity capital is being substituted for debt. And, of course, this is the purpose—at least in the long run—of using the conversion feature. Thus both provisions can achieve the same long-run objective. But if the company fully expects conversion to take place during the conversion period, then there is no

[10] C. James Pilcher, *Raising Capital with Convertible Securities* (Ann Arbor, Mich.: Bureau of Business Research, School of Business, University of Michigan, 1955), 54–56.

need for a sinking fund. For example, American Telephone & Telegraph convertible bonds have been issued in the past in such a way as to render conversion overwhelmingly attractive. Let's examine, for example, the American Telephone & Telegraph Convertible Debenture 4¼'s, due 1973. These bonds were sold to the then existing stockholders in various denominations in January 1958. The face amount of the entire issue was $718,313,000—of which all but $2,073,600 was bought by shareholders. The remainder was sold in the open market at $1,342.50 for each $1,000 debenture. Each bond was convertible into one share for each $100 of debentures with the payment of $42 per share at the time of conversion. Thus, in effect, each new share cost $142. During 1958 the price range of American Telephone & Telegraph common was $168–$227. Obviously, under these conditions it was attractive to convert this issue and no sinking fund was required. So attractive was this conversion feature that the bond contract prohibited conversion for a period of five months immediately after issuance. Even at that, a little over six months after the date of issuance slightly less than 76 per cent of the issue was converted. A year and six months after issuance, all but a little more than 1 per cent was converted. The remainder of the issue, about $5.5 million, was called in August 1964 at 105.90.[11]

On the other hand, if the company does not expect conversion to take place, either wholly or in part, and it can foresee no way of forcing it, then inclusion of a sinking fund is a tenable proposition. In fact, there usually is little to be lost by its inclusion, especially if the provision is a discretionary one. If the firm does not know whether conversion will be forthcoming, it should use a sinking fund.

For companies owning so-called *wasting assets,* such as those in the coal, forest, and oil industries, a sinking-fund provision is almost a necessity. Ordinarily the amount of sinking fund to be appropriated is dependent on the amount of minerals used up. For example, a sinking fund for a coal company could be established in such a manner that the amount of cash allocated for sinking-fund purposes would be contingent upon the amount of coal (expressed in tons or dollars, preferably the former)

---

[11] One may wonder why the convertible issue was used at all. There are several reasons for this but the three outstanding ones are: (1) institutional investors can buy these bonds, thereby broadening the market; (2) with the deferred-conversion feature included, relatively low-cost capital is utilized while facilities are being constructed and telephone-rate adjustments are secured, and later the invested capital is capable of carrying the cost and dividends applicable to the common stock; and (3) the ability of the equity markets to absorb issues of this magnitude is questionable. For further discussions of this, *see:* Charles A. D'Ambrosio, *Use of Convertible Bonds by A.T. & T., 1946–1956:* Unpublished M.S. thesis, Department of Finance, University of Illinois, Urbana, 1958; and C. James Pilcher, *Ibid.*

extracted and sold. Moreover, part of the revenues derived from the re-sources sold represent a return of capital, the cash derived from which should be used to retire the debt secured by these assets.

Some reasons for using the sinking fund lie in the fact that the future obviously is difficult, if not impossible, to predict. Consequently, a firm may not be in a position later either to retire its debt when it comes due or to refund it. Also, the firm's business risk may change and prudence would suggest providing for such a contingency. Another reason for the use of the sinking fund lies in the fact that investors favor such securi-ties. Hence the presence of a sinking fund may allow a firm to issue bonds more cheaply in terms of both the cost of flotation and the effective in-terest rate.

Insofar as the sinking fund is an appropriation of cash, however, it could impair the dividend-paying capacity of the firm. If the dividend-paying capacity is reduced, the market price of common stock and pre-ferred stock may change also, and this may tend to increase the cost of each of these sources of capital. We say it "may" tend to do this be-cause other balancing forces, such as changes in risk, may tend to offset this effect. Again, we refer to Table 19-1 for the implications for risk and cost of capital of changes in the capital structure. Even though the increase in the cost of common and preferred capital is realized, it may be offset by the tendency for the cost of debt capital to decrease.

Serial Debt

Serial bonds may be viewed as another way in which the firm may retire its debt. A serial bond issue is one which matures periodically over the life of the issue but differs from the use of the sinking fund in one very important respect: part of the entire serial bond issue comes due on a specific maturity date every year after the issue has been outstanding for a certain period. That is to say, although there are no specific ma-turity dates on the various bonds issued when a sinking fund is used, with a serial issue each bond has a specific maturity date and only a few of them will normally be due at the termination of the issue. When serial bonds come due, failure to meet them can precipitate legal failure. By contrast, as long as it meets interest payments on sinking-fund bonds— even obligatory ones—the firm which is unable to meet its principal pay-ments will probably be able to avoid bankruptcy. Hence, in this respect, a serial bond tends to carry with it a greater degree of risk, at least in the short run, than a sinking-fund arrangement. A maturing serial bond *must* be paid. Obviously, a rather predictable and stable income flow is ordi-narily necessary in order to be able to handle a serial bond. Oddly enough, the most extensive use of serial securities today is to be found in equipment trust obligations, which are most extensively used in the railroad industry. The special nature of equipments obligations, however, makes the serial feature especially adaptable in this case.

In general, the same objectives achieved through the use of sinking funds can be achieved through the use of serial bonds. That is, they provide for the use of debt while equity capital is accumulated through retention of earnings. Moreover, by using a serial retirement feature, the average cost of the whole issue may be less because those parts of the issue which are close to maturity sell at lower yields than those parts with more extended durations. Call premiums are also avoided. These, in turn, should have a favorable (though probably small) influence on the total weighted average cost of capital. The change in the firm's capital structure resulting from this debt retirement would be similar to the speculations discussed in Table 19-1 with reference to convertible securities.

Note: A discussion of other methods of adjusting capital sources is contained in Chapter 20, and the summary to those topics as well as the ones discussed in this chapter, will be found at the end of Chapter 20.

SUGGESTED READINGS

BROMAN, KEITH L. "The Use of Convertible Subordinated Debentures by Industrial Firms, 1949–59," *The Quarterly Review of Economics and Business,* 3 (Spring, 1963), 65–75.

The Calculation of Savings in Bond Refunding, New York: Irving Trust Company, 1962.

GUTHMANN, HARRY G. "Dilution and Common Stock Financing," *Harvard Business Review,* 23 (Winter, 1945), 246–52.

———. "Measuring the Dilution Effect of Convertible Securities," *Journal of Business, 11* (January 1938), 44–50.

HESS, A. P., and W. J. WINN. *The Value of the Call Privilege,* Philadelphia: University of Pennsylvania Press, 1962.

MERRILL, EUGENE S. "A Guide to Bond Refunding," *Public Utilities Fortnightly, 70* (September 27, 1962), 385–94.

PORTERFIELD, JAMES T. S. "Dividends, Dilution and Delusion," *Harvard Business Review,* 37 (November–December 1959), 56–61.

WILSEY, H. L. "The Use of Sinking Funds in Preferred Stock Issues," *The Journal of Finance,* 2 (October 1947), 31–42.

WINN, W. J., and ARLEIGH HESS, JR. "The Value of the Call Privilege," *The Journal of Finance, 14* (May 1959), 182–95.

QUESTIONS

19.1 Recently issued callable bonds and preferred stocks prohibit the issuing corporation from calling them for a stipulated number of years after their issuance if the coupon rate of securities issued in their place are less than the coupon rate of the called issue, unless they are called for sinking-fund purposes. What merit do you see in this provision, viewing it both from the standpoint of the security holder and that of the firm?

19.2 What advantage to the firm, if any, is there to including each of the following covenants in a convertible debt security: (*a*) callable, (*b*) sinking fund, (*c*) first mortgage?

19.3 "Because life insurance companies cannot invest a very large proportion of their assets in equity securities, they are not very interested in the purchase of bonds convertible into common stock." Comment on this statement.

19.4 In what way or ways can the following long-term debt adjustments be related to both shareholders' profits and risk as these are defined in this book: (*a*) conversion of the debt to common stock; (*b*) a sinking-fund provision in a debenture issue; (*c*) a callable provision in a debenture issue; (*d*) serial retirement of a debenture issue?

19.5 In what way or ways, if any, is a convertible bondholder protected against the issuance of additional common shares? Is this protection necessary?

19.6 In the convertible bond issue discussed on page 451, what was the total amount realized by American Telephone & Telegraph after all the bonds were converted?

19.7 One of the purported reasons for using a convertible feature is to make a security containing this provision easier to sell. Because the security is easier to sell, the cost of this form of capital may be lower with the feature than without it. How might one evaluate whether a convertible issue is easier to sell (cheaper) than one without the convertible covenant?

19.8 Of the three methods used to stimulate conversion, which is likely to be most effective? Explain. Does it make any difference whether the conversion security is selling below, at, or above the conversion price? Explain.

19.9 What influence might a minimum net working capital requirement in a senior debt indenture have on each of the following: (*a*) conversion; (*b*) sinking fund; (*c*) serial retirement?

19.10 Is it reasonable to construct an antidilution clause so that adjustments in the terms of conversion are not made when minor changes in the total number of shares occur such as might result from the exercise of stock options or employee benefit plans?

19.11 Comment on the argument that the call premium is designed to compensate bondholders for the loss of future income on the called security as well as for the expense and bother of buying other securities.

19.12 It is often said that it does not pay to call in one bond issue and replace it with another one unless a gross savings of about .75 per cent is realized. Can you see any merit to this rule of thumb? Explain.

19.13 At one time the Illinois Glass Company had an outstanding bond issue which contained a mandatory sinking fund but provided no call provision. Discuss the ramifications of such a situation.

19.14 Why might investors prefer bonds without sinking funds to bonds with sinking funds? Explain.

19.15 Why might investors prefer bonds with sinking fund to bonds without sinking funds? Explain.

19.16 Is a sinking fund more desirable for bonds or notes than for preferred stock? Explain.

19.17 What rationale do you see for the provision that when bonds are called for sinking-fund purposes the call price is frequently the face value of the security whereas when they are called for any other reason they are callable only at a premium?

19.18 In the spring of 1963 American Telephone & Telegraph sold $250 million of debentures, the proceeds of which were used to retire an equal amount of 5 per cent debentures due in 1983. The debenture 5's were sold in 1957. The new issue was to mature on May 1, 1999, and was to carry a coupon rate roughly equal to that of the issue to be retired. What possible reason could explain refinancing at this time?

19.19 A board member suggests that the Mythical Company's 5 per cent bonds payable should be redeemed. What factors and figures should be taken into account in making this decision?

PROBLEMS

19.20 If a $50 par value preferred stock is convertible into common stock at $35 and is selling in the market at $162 per share, at what price must the common stock be selling to maintain conversion parity?

19.21 The C. N. Henning Company planned to issue $10 million of convertible subordinated debentures. Each $1,000 bond was to be convertible into twenty-five shares of common stock. The common stock was selling in the market at $42 a share. During the past twelve months the price of the common fluctuated between $40 and $73. Mr. Pigott, financial vice president, recommended the twenty-five-share conversion rate but also argued for a *deferred convertibility feature* which would stipulate that the bonds could not be converted for at least six months after their issuance. He also recommended that the conversion covenant contain a provision whereby an additional $50 in cash per bond would be required at the time the bonds are converted. (*a*) What is the effective conversion price of the bonds as proposed by Mr. Pigott? (*b*) What value to the firm is there to deferring convertibility? (*c*) At what price should the common sell before you would expect conversion? (*d*) Assuming all the bonds are converted within two years after their issuance, what would be the total gross proceeds derived from the sale of the convertible issue? (*e*) What merit, if any, do you see to requiring the bondholders to come up with $50 additional cash at the time of conversion?

19.22 If a $1,000 bond is convertible into common shares at $62.50 and the shares are selling at 89¼, at what price would you expect the bonds to be selling?

19.23 The BIG Publishing Company issued a 5.24 per cent callable preferred stock several years ago. Since then, interest rates have turned down and the preferred is currently selling at $131 and has varied slightly from that price for the past several months. The preferred is callable at 105 plus accrued dividends. A local investment banking firm has approached the firm and is promoting the idea of refinancing the existing preferred issue. The total costs of refinancing are estimated at $50,000, although the investment banker is willing to take the issue only on a "best-efforts" basis. The balance sheet and income statement for the firm is given below. The common stock is selling at twelve times its current earnings. The president of the company asks you, as its financial vice-president, whether it is desirable to call the preferred issue and float another in its place. He wants specific answers to the following questions (assume a 50 per cent tax rate); (a) Based on the data available, should we refinance the present preferred issue with another preferred issue alike in all regards except coupon rate? If so, how profitable will such refinancing be? (b) What impact on the firm's cost of capital will refinancing the preferred issue with another preferred have vis-à-vis a bond issue? (c) What influence does the "best-efforts" underwriting agreement have on your conclusions above? (d) Would any of your answers above be different if the preferred stock were callable for sinking-fund purposes at par and that your estimate of future cash flows indicate that an average of $500,000 a year for the next twenty years would be available from current operations to retire the issue in full?

BIG Publishing Company
Balance Sheet
December 31

Current assets:		
Cash	$1,234,567	
Receivables (net)	2,468,024	
Inventory	3,297,409	$ 7,000,000
Fixed assets:		
Plant (net)	$5,500,000	
Equipment (net)	9,500,000	$15,000,000
Other assets:		3,000,000
		$25,000,000
Current liabilities:		
Wages	$1,166,667	
Taxes	533,333	
Accruals	1,800,000	$ 3,500,000
Preferred stock ($100):		10,000,000
Common equity:		
Common stock ($10)	$2,500,000	
Surplus	9,000,000	11,500,000
		$25,000,000

BIG Publishing Company
Income Statement
December 31

Net revenues	$37,500,000
Operating expenses	33,750,000
Net operating income	3,750,000
Income taxes (50%)	1,875,000
Earnings available for preferred	1,875,000
Preferred dividends	529,000
Earnings available for common	$ 1,331,000

19.24 Assume: (1) a 5.5 per cent $1,000 convertible subordinated bond due in ten years is rated Baa; (2) other Baa bonds of the same class are selling to yield 4.5 per cent; (3) the conversion rate is thirty shares of common; and (4) the common is selling at $35 a share. (a) At what price could you expect the bond to sell? (b) According to the information given, would you recommend calling in the bond at a call price of 104? Explain.

19.25 The G. O'Callaghan Brewing Company, originator of Thirsty Thirteen, a beer of incomparable quality which must pass thirteen rigorous tests before it is sold to the public, wished to refinance its 4.77 per cent prior preferred stock issue with a 4.5 per cent, twenty-year debenture bond. The current market price of the preferred stock is 106. Underwriters have told the company that there is a high likelihood of selling the new bond issue at a premium so that the net proceeds to the company would be the full amount of the issue (that is, $15 million). The president of the company thought it looked like a profitable refinancing operation. He has asked you, as the financial manager, to determine exactly whether or not it would be profitable and to what extent. In addition to the above information assume the following: (1) flotation expenses are $50,000; (2) the bonds are sold at a premium so that the net proceeds to the company are $15 million; (3) the preferred issue aggregates $15 million and is callable at 103½; (4) the company is in a 50 per cent tax bracket; and (5) assume the overall cost of capital for the firm is 10 per cent.

19.26 Assume that a $1,000 convertible debenture bond having a 4.50 coupon rate is convertible into common stock at $65. (a) To how many shares of common stock is the holder of these bonds entitled? (b) If the price of the stock were $83 per share, what would you expect the price of the bond to be? (c) If the bond is rated Aa, other Aa bonds are selling to yield 4.75 per cent, and the price of the common stock were $59 per share, what would you expect the price of the bond to be?

CHAPTER **20** ADJUSTING
CAPITAL SOURCES
(Continued)

Having discussed at length methods of adjusting some long-term sources of debt capital, it is now in order for us to discuss adjustments of short-term sources, adjustments of ownership sources, and other forms of adjustments that are more radical in nature than the rest.

ADJUSTING SHORT-TERM SOURCES

Adjustment of short-term creditorship claims is much less precise in nature than the adjustments of long-term claims. Short-term claims can be adjusted by means of provisions for periodic repayment, say, for example, every month rather than a lump sum terminal payment. This is very similar in nature to a sinking fund, but is used more for so-called intermediate-term debt than for short-term debt. Another way of adjusting short-term debt is to refinance it with the proceeds from the sale of other claims or by retention of earnings. Quite often it may happen that a firm experiences a sizable increase in the amount of short-term debt it has on hand and is not capable of meeting maturing payments without considerable strain on the financial resources of the firm. This may come about for any number of reasons such as rapid expansion and the use of short-term capital to finance the beginnings of long-term projects. Neither of these is intended to imply mismanagement of a firm's finances. On the contrary, firms may embark on either one of these policies fully apprised of their implications. For example, the Consolidated Edison Company of New York has on several occasions resorted to the use of short-term loans to implement a substantial construction project. As part of this same policy, the firm had in each instance issued long-term securities, usually bonds, several months later, the proceeds of which were used to retire the short-term loans. The intent of this policy is to use relatively cheap short-term capital while facilities are being constructed and to replace this source of capital with long-term funds once the facilities are constructed and capable of contributing to the earnings of the firm.

Another example of this swelling in the amount of short-term debt a firm has is that often found in a rapidly growing enterprise. If the growth of the firm is especially rapid, substantial increases in receivables and inventories would not be uncommon and would probably be accompanied by decreases in cash. If the expansion is of a permanent nature, then permanent financing is called for. The best form of this financing would be retained earnings or the sale of common stock. But both of these may be inappropriate at the time expansion is taking place; the former because it provides "too little, too late"; the latter because of adverse market conditions—too much of future earnings will have to be given up to sell the issue, thereby raising the firm's cost of capital. Also, expansion plans usually require implementation rather quickly after they have been finalized, and the slowness of securing many forms of long-term creditorship claims may preclude their timely use. Hence often the fastest and sole recourse for a firm faced with this situation is to seek short-term funds. A concomitant of securing these short-term funds is to provide for their refinancing on a long-term basis at some subsequent date.

Still a third way of adjusting short-term sources of capital is to seek modifications in the obligation. If there is a bank note coming due, it may be refinanced on the same basis as the existing note but with an extended maturity date. Firms doing this may be no more capable of meeting the note, say, six months from maturity than they are at the time it falls due. Cases may arise, however, in which some fortuitous event renders a firm incapable of meeting the note when due and an extension is required. Assuming a satisfactory banking relationship, the note can probably be renewed.

ADJUSTING LONG-TERM OWNERSHIP SOURCES

Adjusting Preferred Stock

Adjustments of preferred stock issues, as alluded to in our discussion of debt adjustments, frequently take the form of conversion, sinking funds or calling in the stock. But since they have no maturity date, there is no legal need to redeem the preferred stock at all if the firm chooses not to do so. More and more in recent years, however, firms have been making efforts to retire their preferred stock through the use of sinking funds. This action would seem to give explicit recognition to the implicit nature of all businesses—namely, that conditions of a firm may so change as to warrant retirement of the preferred stock. When preferreds do have a sinking fund, typically they also have a callable feature and a series of call prices similar to those contained in bonds.

Another form of adjustment of preferred stockholders' claims that may be of consequence has to do with the disposition of dividend arrearages. Often holders of preferred stock may have their dividends passed in one or more periods. This may be caused by any number of reasons. These past dividend accumulations are called *arrearages*. Frequently, a firm will wish to eliminate these arrearages in order to be able to pay dividends on its common stock. By law, as long as preferred dividends are not paid, or as long as there are arrearages on preferred stock, dividends on the common stock cannot be paid.[1] But there are times when a firm which, for example, is unable to pay its preferred dividends may wish to secure more equity capital through the sale of common stock, and would find it necessary—or at least desirable—to eliminate the arrearages on its preferred stock in order to make the potential sale more feasible. There are several ways of making this adjustment, but one that seems to be employed frequently is that which entails sending out notifications to preferred stockholders soliciting an amendment to their agreement in order to eliminate the arrears in exchange for stock or other concessions and thereby (hopefully) improve the credit position of the firm. In any event some sort of incentive is usually necessary in each case. Among the more typical inducements in addition to partial cash payment are (1) higher coupon rates, (2) convertibility, (3) the issuance of new preferred with favorable covenants to preferred shareholders, or (4) the issuance of common stock along with the new or amended preferred. But, unless the firm will be more profitable in the future than it has in the past, none of these would be particularly attractive. Preferred shareholders may have little alternative, however, for they are not in a position to force anything on the firm. If any one of these adjustments is made and the newly acquired capital is successfully employed in the enterprise, such adjustments should have the effect of increasing the market price of the common stock. Also, such an adjustment eliminates a potentially sizable burden on the firm's working capital.

Adjusting Common Stock

Financial management may find it desirable to adjust the common stock position of the enterprise for certain internal reasons or in order to adjust the market for its stock. The chief means of accomplishing these objectives are the stock dividend and the stock split.

Stock Dividends

As the term implies, a *stock dividend* is a dividend distribution to present stockholders in the form of more stock. It is usually stated as a

---

[1] This assumes, as is almost uniformly true, that the preferred does have the cumulative feature. See Appendix B for further elaboration.

percentage of the amount of shares already outstanding. For example, the management of the Bowlin Company may decide to declare a stock dividend of 4 per cent. This means that the stockholder possessing 100 shares of Bowlin stock is entitled to receive four more shares from the corporation. Obviously, this increases the number of shares outstanding as well as the aggregate amount of the par or stated value of the common stock account. Where does this increase in bookkeeping amounts come from? It comes from the surplus account. Section A of Table 20-1 is useful in illustrating this point.

Table 20-1
Effects of a Stock Dividend on the Bowlin
Company's Common Stock

	Before Stock Dividend	After a 4% Stock Dividend
A. Balance sheet effects		
Common stock ($20)	$20,000,000	$20,800,000
Surplus	30,602,194	29,802,194
	$50,602,194	$50,602,194
B. Income statement effects		
Earnings available for common	$ 5,602,194	$ 5,602,194
Earnings per share	5.60	5.38
C. Market effects		
Price-earnings ratio	10.00	10.00
Market price per share	$ 56.00	$ 53.80

Although simple accounting is involved, awareness of the *purpose* of a stock dividend is important. It may be to give explicit recognition to the fact that earnings have been retained in the business in the past, and have been permanently invested in the resources of the firm and cannot be distributed to stockholders. The formal recognition of the permanent nature of these previously retained earnings is known as a *capitalization of surplus.*

Obviously, there may be a serious impact on market price of the outstanding shares depending on the magnitude of the stock dividend. Stock dividends which are very small in magnitude—that is, only a few percentage points of total stock outstanding—probably will have little recognizable impact on market price, although theoretically one can trace the impact of the effects by the change in the total number of shares.

This is done in Table 20-1, Section B. There the Bowlin Company declared a 4 per cent stock dividend, which had the effect of increasing the total number of shares from 1 million to 1.04 million. The effect of this increase in shares on the earning per share of the firm is to reduce them by twenty-two cents. If the price earnings ratio stays the same, the market price of the stock should fall from $56 to $53.80.[2] Thus the impact on the market value of shares of a small stock dividend should be negligible.

If the stock dividend is sizable, however, it will tend to lower significantly the market price of the stock. This effect may be quite desirable, aside from achieving the purpose of capitalizing a sizable portion of the surplus. It has long been presumed that there is a range of market prices considered desirable for the favorable trading of securities. The bounds of this range are not precisely known, but it is suggested that investors prefer a price somewhere between $10 and $60. Securities selling at prices outside this range are presumed to have a more limited market. It has traditionally been argued that securities selling for prices well in excess of, say, $60 per share should be adjusted to a more favorable trading range so that more individual investors could purchase them. With the emergence of more institutional investors, it would seem that some of this argument has lost its stature, for these investors can and do buy without respect to the market price itself; their resources are so large they can afford to buy a hundred shares, say, of a stock selling at $500 a share, whereas relatively few individuals are able to do so. Moreover, institutional purchases of common stocks have become increasingly important in recent years so that, although more studies need to be made, based on the available information regarding their capacity and inclination to purchase equities on a regular basis with apparent disregard for the magnitude of the market price (but not the value of the stock), the argument for placing a security on a more favorable trading basis loses some of its force. To the extent that a stock dividend does reduce market prices per share and broadens the ownership base by allowing more persons to buy its stock than would otherwise do so, this purpose is served. However, as we shall see later, a stock split can achieve the same end, and it is less expensive.[3]

Actually, the important question is what impact the stock dividend has on the firm's cost of capital and the profits (changes in market value and disbursements) of shareholders. To the extent that the price-earning ratio remains the same, there is no change in the firm's cost of capital, because no change in market price relative to earnings per share takes

---

[2] Actually, the market price would have to be either $53.75 or $55.875 (or 55¾ or 55⅞), because shares are usually traded in eighths in American securities markets.

[3] Robert W. Johnson, *Financial Management* (Boston: Allyn, 1962), 516–517.

place. If the stock dividend is large enough to affect market price so as to put it in reach of a substantially larger number of prospective purchasers and there is, in fact, an influx of purchasers desiring to buy the stock so that the market price is driven up relative to earnings per share, then the cost of common equity should decline as well, and so will the weighted average cost of capital.

By the same line of reasoning, the profits of shareholders (as we define them) would be affected in a similar way. As a result of the 100 per cent stock dividend, shareholders holding 100 shares receive another 100 shares. But if aggregate firm earnings and price-earnings ratios are unchanged, then the aggregate value of the stockholders' shares is likewise unchanged, as demonstrated by the example below:

	Before the 100 Per cent Stock Dividend	After the Dividend
Aggregate firm earnings	$5,602,194	$5,602,194
Earnings per share	5.60	2.80
Price-earnings ratio	10	10
Market value per share	56	28
Number of shares held	100	200
Aggregate value of shares held	$ 5,600	$ 5,600

We leave it to the student to speculate on the possibility of how the market value of the shares may be increased, thereby reducing the cost of capital.

Stock Splits

A second change in the common stock of a firm can come from a stock split. A *stock split* may be defined as a *division of an existing number of shares* into a greater number but without capitalizing any of the accumulated surplus. Recently stock splits have been very popular both with corporate financial managers and the public, because they place the stock within a buying price range more favorable to the investor.

The terms of the split are expressed as the ratio of the number of total shares after the split to the number of old shares held, such as "a two-for-one split." A stock split does not increase the amount of legal capital; it divides the same legal capital into a larger number of smaller units. For example, the Faerber Company and Karchtner, Inc., had essentially the same equity structure:

Faerber Company		Karchtner, Inc.	
Common stock		Common stock	
($100 par)	$1,000,000	($100 stated value)	$1,000,000
Paid-in capital	200,000	Paid-in surplus	500,000
Retained earnings	3,800,000	Earned surplus	3,500,000
	$5,000,000		$5,000,000

Both companies obviously have 10,000 ($1,000,000/$100) shares outstanding and have a *book value* of $500 ($5,000,000/10,000 shares) per share. The Faerber stock is selling at $140 per share in the market and Karchtner, Inc., is selling at $200.[4] The Faerber Company declared a 200 per cent stock dividend and Karchtner, Inc., has asked stockholders to approve a three-for-one split. After the stock dividend and the split, the equity section of the balance sheets appeared as follows:

Faerber Company		Karchtner, Inc.	
Common stock		Common stock	
($100 par)	$3,000,000	($33⅓ stated value)	$1,000,000
Paid-in capital	200,000	Paid-in surplus	500,000
Retained earnings	1,800,000	Earned surplus	3,500,000
	$5,000,000		$5,000,000

The number of shares of both companies has increased to 30,000 and both have reduced the price per share.[5] In both cases, the accounting profits of the company were unaffected and stockholders were not better off unless the market price of the stock rose or the market risk tended to be reduced. Notice also that, in the case of Karchtner, Inc., the amounts of both the common stock and the retained earnings accounts were unaffected by the split. The stated value, however, was reduced and the number of shares outstanding was tripled.

As a final point, it should be mentioned that without lower market prices it would be difficult to sell new shares of some firms and a split of its stock is often a necessary first step in broadening the firm's market.

It sometimes happens that a firm's stock is selling below the minimum

---

[4] The Faerber stock is not necessarily regarded by investors as being a cheaper stock, for cheapness depends upon the ratio of price to earnings. The price-earnings ratio for Faerber is 38 (140/$5); for Karchtner, Inc., 20 ($200/$10). Faerber stock is the "dearer."

[5] After the dividend and split, the price of the Faerber stock was $47 and Karchtner, Inc., traded at $67.

limit of our $10–$60 acceptable trading range. There are many reasons for this, but usually the primary one is lack of earnings. By a *reverse split*, a firm can boost the market value of its shares. A two-for-one reverse split of the Diomar Company would have the effects shown in Table 20-2.

Table 20-2
Reverse Split of the Diomar Company's Common Stock

	Before the Split	After the Split
A. Balance sheet effects		
Common stock par value	$ 5.00	$ 10.00
Common stock account	5,000,000	5,000,000
Number of shares outstanding	1,000,000	500,000
Surplus	6,535,251	6,535,251
B. Income statement effects		
Earnings available for common	1,000,000	1,000,000
Earnings per share	1.00	2.00
C. Market effects		
Price earnings ratio	10.00	10.00
Market price per share	$ 10.00	$ 20.00

OTHER ADJUSTMENTS OF CAPITAL SOURCES

Often it is necessary to take more drastic steps to adjust the sources of capital. The methods already discussed are considered rather "routine" operations, engaged in almost every day by some firm or another. But even with the existence of provisions to adjust the sources of business capital, a firm may not be able to accommodate itself to a changed operating environment, and resort to more radical action is sometimes called for to correct situations of extreme financial stress. The usual proximate cause of a firm's financial plight and, hence its inability to adjust its sources of capital, is a deficiency of liquid working capital. Ordinarily, the ultimate cause may be found in a number of other considerations, not the least of which is poor management. This issue is more than just a moot point because, in the adjustments to be discussed subsequently, the question of whether or not an incumbent management is to be perpetuated is often an important consideration.

Nonbankruptcy Adjustments

When a firm's financial difficulties are adjudged by all interested parties to be of a temporary nature, arrangements can often be made to relieve the financial strain without going to court. Sometimes creditors will agree to an *extension* of the maturity date of a loan which, at the moment, appears rather ominous. Although this does not correct a more fundamental disorder, it does give the firm more "breathing room;" it allows the firm to make other adjustments in its financial management without the burden of repaying the principal of the loan. An extension is not given without cost, however. Restrictions on a firm's dividends may be imposed; major owners of small firms may be asked to put up more money; or future borrowings are precluded except on a subordinated basis.

Composition is yet another form of adjustment of capital sources. This method involves recomposing the debt of the firm in such a way that the creditors receive partial payment for their claims—say, $.60 to $.80 cents on $1. Creditors may find it more expedient to follow this route than to take the troubled firm to court to seek full satisfaction. Under the latter procedure, they run the risk of not receiving as much or—if they do receive as much or more—they have legal costs to meet, which may more than offset the possible gains achieved by going to court.

A third nonbankruptcy method of adjusting capital sources involves the operation of the enterprise by a group of creditors, called a *creditors' committee*, until such time as there is sufficient liquid capital to meet the impending claims or until an acceptable composition is found.

In all these cases there is no legal compulsion for any creditor to accept the attempted adjustment. Any creditor not satisfied with the proposal of the majority (or minority) to relieve the financial burden of the firm can refuse the arrangement, insist that his claim be met in full and, if not, take the firm to court to be liquidated or reorganized. Sometimes creditors (especially small ones) will create a *nuisance value* by being unwilling to participate in the modification; they will be paid off in full with the approbation of other creditors. The recalcitrant creditors, however, run the risk of having their bluff called and they may receive less satisfaction once the firm is put under the mantle of the courts than if they had agreed to the proposed settlement.

Bankruptcy Adjustments

When "routine" adjustments and even the more severe ones such as composition and creditors' committees cannot relieve the financial plight of a firm, the next and final resort is the courts. Because this step is so drastic, the situation must be very severe before it is taken. But, inasmuch as this topic is so broad in scope, so specialized in character, and so penetrating in its implications, a book of this orientation cannot give full justice to it. Accordingly, the paragraphs that follow merely sketch some of the more common elements of bankruptcy adjustments.[6]

Reorganization of a firm's capital structure under the mantle of the courts is a more severe adjustment of capital sources than any we have discussed so far. There are many variations in this legal process. We will discuss only two. The first one, *Chapter XI reorganizations,* applies basically to smaller firms that only have unsecured debts. In this provision, the debtor company can petition the court for an *arrangement* of its debts. If a majority of creditors (both in number and in amount) and the court approve the reorganization plan, it becomes binding on all creditors. This aspect in itself is a major step from the composition or extension in which objecting creditors did not have to abide by a proposed plan.

The second, and the one in which we are primarily concerned, is the so-called *Chapter X reorganization,* which applies to large firms with more complex capital structures. Under this section of the United States Bankruptcy Act, one of three parties may file a petition in the Federal District Court, prevailing upon it to declare a corporation bankrupt. This may be done by the management of the firm,[7] the trustee of a bond issue, or at least three creditors whose aggregate claims on the corporation total at least $5,000. Upon declaring the corporation bankrupt, the court appoints a trustee (1) to administer the affairs of the firm for the benefit of all claimants, including shareholders; (2) to make a valuation of the resources of the firm and an inventory of the claims upon it; and (3) to submit either (a) a plan for the financial reorganization of the firm (made up in consultation with creditors and shareholders) or (b) a recommendation to liquidate the assets, dissolve the firm, and wind up its affairs. A plan for financial reorganization is proposed if the trustee feels there is a chance of maintaining the firm as a going concern provided adjustments in the debt obligations are made. At the time the plan is submitted to the court, all interested parties can have their say. Inasmuch as the essential financial difficulty facing a firm whose affairs have reached this stage is poor profitability, the proposed recasting of the financial structure is usually so designed as to be supportable by the expected earnings of the financially reconstituted firm. The court must seek the advice of the

---

[6] Extensive discussions of this topic are to be found in Arthur Stone Dewing, *The Financial Policy of Corporations,* 5th ed. (New York: Ronald, 1953), II, 1, 228–1,496; Harry G. Guthmann and Herbert E. Dougall, *Corporate Financial Policy,* 4th ed. (Englewood Cliffs, N.J.: Prentice-Hall, 1962), 607–71; and *Vanderbilt Law Review,* 15 (December 1961).

[7] If the management files the petition, it is called a *voluntary reorganization;* the others are *involuntary reorganizations.* It may be wise for management to seek the reorganization for the simple reason that by such a move it may tend to perpetuate itself while gaining relief from some of its financial burdens. This would more likely be accomplished in Chapter XI reorganizations.

Securities and Exchange Commission if total liabilities are greater than $3 million; in other cases it has the option of seeking consultation. The Securities and Exchange Commission tries to determine whether the plan is fair, equitable, and feasible for all parties concerned. So must the court. If the court deems the proposed reorganization satisfactory, it is submitted to creditors and shareholders for approval. If two thirds of the creditors and a majority of shareholders approve the plan, it is accepted by the court and becomes effective.[8] Once the plan is approved, even minority shareholders must go along; there is legal compulsion to effect the reorganization.

If the firm cannot be preserved as a going concern, liquidation will ensue. In determining whether or not to liquidate a firm, the question is: Is the firm worth more alive than dead? This question is resolved by answering the question discussed in Chapters 16 and 17: Is the present value of the liquidated parts of an enterprise greater than the present value of the firm as a going concern? If the answer is "yes," liquidation is called for and sale of the assets should proceed. Once the sale of assets begins, it usually becomes painfully clear that few, if any, assets except cash bring their balance sheet value. Indeed, a significant shrinkage in asset values is to be expected. Because of this, not all claims on these assets will be satisfied in full: there simply will not be enough cash available. In this event, whatever cash is available must be allocated and the method by which this is usually done under Chapter X is called the *absolute priority of claims.* This rule suggests that certain claims are to be satisfied prior to the satisfaction of other claims. The priority of claims in liquidation typically takes the following order:

(1) *Special current debt,* such as trustee expenses, unpaid wages earned in the last six months preceding bankruptcy but not to exceed $600 in any one case, and taxes.

(2) *Secured creditors,* such as the holders of mortgage bonds and collateral trust bonds, but only to the extent of the liquidating value of the pledged assets.

(3) *General creditors,* consisting of unsatisfied secured creditors and all unsecured creditors, but only to the extent of their proportionate interest in the aggregate claim of this class.

(4) *Subordinated debt.*

(5) *Preferred stockholders,* to the extent provided in their contract plus dividend arrears.

(6) *Residual legatees* (common stockholders).

---

[8] Shareholders have no say in a reorganization plan if the firm's liabilities exceed its assets (that is, if it is insolvent).

Let us examine briefly the case of the Connery Metal Works Company, which filed a bankruptcy petition and, on the advice of the trustee and the order of the court, is in the process of liquidation. The cash proceeds from the liquidation of all assets are shown in Table 20-3; the claims on those assets are shown in Table 20-4. Notice that upon liquidation the firm received $29 million in cash from the sale of $70 million in book value of assets. In other words it received about 41 per cent of book value in liquidation. Let us now examine a number of other ramifications of this case.

Table 20-3
Connery Metal Works Company,
Cash Proceeds from Liquidation

Assets	Book Value	Cash Proceeds From Liquidation
Cash	$ 1,500,000	$ 1,500,000
Receivables	3,000,000	2,900,000
Inventories	8,000,000	4,000,000
Plant A	10,000,000	3,500,000
Plant B	15,000,000	5,000,000
Other fixed assets	30,000,000	11,000,000
Other assets	2,500,000	1,100,000
	$70,000,000	$29,000,000

Table 20-4
Connery Metal Works Company,
Claims on Assets and Cash Proceeds from Liquidation

Current Liabilities		
Bank loans	$ 6,500,000	
Wages payable	1,000,000	
Accounts payable	3,500,000	
Taxes payable	1,000,000	
Other current liabilities	500,000	$12,500,000
Long-term Debt		
First mortgage bonds, on Plant A	$ 5,000,000	
First mortgage bonds, on Plant B	12,000,000	
Convertible debentures	8,000,000	
Subordinated debentures	5,000,000	30,000,000
Common Equity		
Common stock	$37,500,000	
Surplus	(10,000,000)	27,500,000
		$70,000,000

First of all, assume both Plant A and Plant B are pledged as collateral under two separate bond indentures, the bank loans are payable to the Mawicke First National Bank of Heffernan, Texas; and the inventory was pledged as collateral for the note. Assume, for simplicity, that none of the wages payable was accumulated in the preceding six months and that the claim of the subordinated debentures, which are held by the Lyman Investment Company, come immediately after the satisfaction of the general creditors.[9] The disbursement of the cash proceeds would be as shown in Table 20-5. Notice that special current claims were satisfied in full and that each secured claim received the full amount realized from the sale of the pledged assets. The remainder of the claim was treated equally with those of the general creditors. After the special creditors and secured claimants were satisfied, the remaining cash was apportioned among the general creditors according to the proportion of their respective claims to the total claims of the general creditor class. Thus, for example, the unsatisfied First Mortgage, Plant B bonds, which constitute one third of the total claims of the general creditor class of $21 million, were entitled to receive one third of the $15.5 million available to that class. The same procedure was used to allocate the cash to the other claimants of this group. Note that the subordinated debentures and the common stock received nothing in liquidation, a not unusual event. Table 20-6 has the allocations received by each group of claimants.

The absolute priority doctrine is also applied in cases of *reorganization*. Among the factors to be taken into account in the reorganization plan are the following. The capital structure must be recast to bring it in line with the projected earnings of the revamped firm. Clearly, no more senior debt should be issued than can be comfortably handled over the foreseeable future. In fact, sufficient leeway should be made for the issuance of debt securities in the future if the need arises. Because of this necessity, fixed charges are to be avoided and contingent-charge securities (such as preferred and common stock or income bonds) are used in their stead.[10] The total value of the securities to be issued is determined by capitalizing the expected future income of the firm at a rate consistent with the business risk, a statement easy to make but typically very difficult to implement. The next step is to issue the new securities to the old claimants under the absolute-priority doctrine. Typically, the recast capital

[9] Usually, subordinated debt claims in liquidation are specified in the contract. Ordinarily, these claims are subordinated to all other forms of long-term debt and often to short-term bank debt, but rarely to other short-term claims.

[10] Income bonds are bonds the interest on which is dependent on the achievement of a certain, specified level of earnings. If the earnings are achieved, interest is paid; if the earnings are not achieved, interest does not have to be paid.

Table 20-5
Satisfaction of Claimants on Liquidation of the Connery Metal Works Company

Claims (In Order of Priority)	Amount of Claim	Percentage Of Total Class Claims	Amount Realized in Liquidation	Amount Available for Distribution to Classes
Total cash available				$29,000,000
Special current debt:				
Taxes payable	$ 1,000,000			1,000,000
Amount available for next class				$28,000,000
Secured creditors:				
First mortgage, Plant A	5,000,000		$3,500,000	
First mortgage, Plant B	12,000,000		5,000,000	
Bank loans	6,500,000		4,000,000	12,500,000
Amount available for next class				$15,500,000
General creditors:				
Unsatisfied secured creditors:				
First mortgage, Plant A	1,500,000	7.1		1,100,500
First mortgage, Plant B	7,000,000	33.3		5,161,500
Bank loans	2,500,000	11.9		1,844,500
Unsecured creditors:				
Convertible debentures	5,000,000	23.8		3,689,000
Wages payable	1,000,000	4.8		744,000
Accounts payable	3,500,000	16.7		2,588,500
Other current liabilities	500,000	2.4		372,000
Amount available for next class				0

Table 20-6

Final Allocation of Cash Proceeds of
Liquidating the Connery Metal Works Company

	Amount of Claim	Amount Realized	Per Cent of Total Claim Realized
Current liabilities			
Bank loans	$ 6,500,000	$ 5,844,500	89.9
Wages payable	1,000,000	744,000	74.4
Accounts payable	3,500,000	2,588,500	74.0
Taxes payable	1,000,000	1,000,000	100.0
Other current Liabilities	500,000	372,000	74.4
	$12,500,000	$10,549,000	84.4
Long-term debt			
First mortgage Bonds, Plant A	5,000,000	$ 4,600,500	92.0
First mortgage Bonds, Plant B	12,000,000	10,161,500	84.7
Convertible bonds	8,000,000	3,689,000	46.1
Subordinated bonds	5,000,000	—	—
	$30,000,000	$18,451,000	61.5
Common equity	$27,500,000	—	—
Totals	$70,000,000	$29,000,000	41.4

structure will wipe out the junior claimants such as subordinated debt, preferred stock and common stock.

Although the rule to be followed in reorganizations is absolute priority, vociferous arguments have been made for the doctrine of *relative priority*, whereby each of the claims, including stock, is scaled down but none is eliminated (as would usually be the case under absolute priority). The extent to which this doctrine may be applied appears to be based on expediency, for in reorganizations in which junior claimants might ordinarily be wiped out, if new cash is needed, these junior claimants may be allowed to participate in the reorganization provided they put up more capital. Even beyond that, the doctrine of absolute priority is not as rigid as it seems. As one authority puts it: "The doctrine of absolute priority acts as a guide and a check on obvious inequity, but the actual distribution of securities among the different groups is still determined by a bargaining process.[11]

SUMMARY

There are all sorts of ways to adjust capital sources. Whenever a security is sold to the public, regardless of its duration, the purchaser and seller are essentially agreeing to a given package of covenants including the return under the then-prevailing business environment of the issuing firm. To hedge against untoward and unpredictable future events, provision for adjusting capital sources should be made at the time the issue is sold. Some such provisions are conversion, sinking funds, callability, and serial retirement. Their desirability is to a large extent analytically determinable within the construct of attempts to minimize capital costs while maximizing profits.

Sometimes provision for adjusting capital sources does not have to be made explicit. Stock dividends and stock splits fall into this category.

Often, a firm might have to prevail on the sources of capital supply for modifications of its capital structure not provided for by contract provisions. Extension of loan maturities and adjustment of preferred stock arrearages are cases in point.

When a firm's financial plight becomes so severe that it can no longer remedy the situation by the use of security covenants or by simple modifications agreed to by one or more capital sources, then resort to more drastic measures is necessary. Attempts to recast a firm's capital structure by a reorganization involves scaling down the debts of the firm and usu-

[11] Richards C. Osborn, *Corporation Finance* (New York: Harper, 1959), 591.

ally eliminates the old shareholders altogether. If reorganization is not feasible, then liquidation is in order. In both events the doctrine of absolute priority is the basic guide to the allocation of assets or claims on assets.

As mentioned, in all these adjustments the effort is to minimize the cost of capital and maximize the value of ownership. Even reorganizations and liquidations can be viewed in this context, inasmuch as the former tends to reduce capital costs and the latter tends to keep them at a minimum; the latter also precludes the continuation of more losses.

SUGGESTED READINGS

BARKER, C. A. "Are Stock Dividends Effective?" *Harvard Business Review, 38* (July–August 1958), 99–114.

———. "Effective Stock Splits," *Harvard Business Review, 34* (January–February 1956), 101–106.

BATES, JOHN M., *et al.* "Symposium on Bankruptcy," *Vanderbilt Law Review, 15* (December 1961), 1–239.

BILLYOU, D. F. "Priority Rights of Security Holders in Bankruptcy Reorganizations: New Directions," *Harvard Law Review, 67* (February 1954), 553–90.

BUCHANAN, NORMAN S. *The Economics of Corporate Enterprise.* New York: Holt, Rinehart & Winston, Inc., 1940.

CALKINS, FRANCIS J. "Corporate Reorganization under Chapter X: A Postmortem," *The Journal of Finance, 3* (June 1948), 19–28.

———. "Feasibility in Plans of Corporate Reorganizations Under Chapter X," *Harvard Law Review, 61* (May 1948), 763–81.

———. "Liquidation and Bankruptcy," and "Involuntary Reorganization," *Essays on Business Finance.* Ann Arbor, Mich.: Masterco Press, 1963.

DEWING, ARTHUR STONE. *The Financial Policy of Corporations.* 5th ed. New York: The Ronald Press Company, 1953.

FERGUSSON, DONALD A. "Preferred Stock Valuation in Recapitalization," *The Journal of Finance, 13* (March 1958), 48–69.

HOLZMAN, R. S. "Spinoffs, Splitups and Splitoffs," *National Tax Journal, 5* (September 1952), 277–78.

UDELL, GILMAN G. (compiler). *Bankruptcy Laws of the United States.* Washington, D. C.: Government Printing Office, 1960.

WATSON, E. T. P. "Distribution of New Securities in Sec. 77 Reorganizations," *The Journal of Finance, 5* (December 1950), 337–67.

QUESTIONS

20.1 The Monahan Surgical Supply Company recently found that its predicted cash flow for the impending three months would fall far short of that needed. The financial manager, Al Monahan, felt that an extension of a substantial bank note coming due in this period was necessary to relieve the strain. He approached the senior loan officer with his proposition for an extension, and explained that its refusal would put the firm under extreme financial strain and the possibility of bankruptcy would be quite high. (*a*) How would you present the case for an extension of time to the loan officer? (*b*) If you were the loan officer, what factors would you consider important to this case?

20.2 The Kearney Company, manufacturers and distributors of typing paper and carbon paper, was founded several years ago essentially as a "garage and backyard" operation. So successful has the firm been, however, that it moved to new quarters two years ago. The vice president for marketing estimates an average increase in sales of 23 per cent per year for the next five to seven years. The production manager feels an increase in physical production capacity of at least 100 per cent is warranted under these conditions and a doubling of inventory space is likewise needed. Because of rapid past growth, aggregate short-term indebtedness increased from 10 per cent of total capital to 50 per cent, the major share of which consists of short-term bank loans, and the strain on the firm's cash position (according to the financial vice president, Mr. D. Henderson) was becoming oppressive. As a result, he suggested funding most of the short-term debt through the issuance of bonds. (*a*) In light of the information given, the knowledge you have acquired to this point, and the information contained in Appendix B, what provisions would you suggest this bond contract contain? Explain fully. (*b*) Is there any other information you deem necessary to your analysis? If so, what? If not, why not? (*c*) How would your answer to (*a*) differ if this additional information were available?

20.3 Early in 1963 officials of the American Can Company announced it would buy its shares on the open market whenever it was capable of doing so and the opportunity existed. (*a*) On what basis might a decision to follow this policy be made? (*b*) What implications does this policy have for: (1) the firm's cost of capital; (2) the firm's risk; and (3) its dividend policy?

20.4 In mid-1962 the president of the Independent Telephone Corporation announced that the company would buy its shares in the market from time to time when the market price fell below the book value of the stock. Another company official said such action would serve the best interests of stockholders and the company. (*a*) What relation between book value and market value exists? (*b*) How does this action serve the best interests of shareholders? Of the company?

20.5 The president of the Hardbeck Instrument Company announced in a recent annual report that the company is instituting a regular policy of issuing stock dividends each year so as to conserve cash. In his words, "The stock dividend is a substitute for cash." A college coed whose father gave her twenty-seven shares of Hardbeck stock upon graduation from high school wrote the president and said that as far as she could see a stock dividend is a rearrangement of the common equity whereas a cash dividend is an appropriation out of current earnings and that conceptually the two are not, strictly speaking, interchangeable. The president has delegated you the responsibility and authority to reply to this acquisitive shareholder. What response would you make?

20.6 You hold seventy-five shares of the Hot and Cold Insulation Company. The directors declare a 6 per cent stock dividend with cash being paid for fractional shares. On what basis do you think the cash-for-fractional-shares exchange should be decided?

20.7 What effect, if any, does a stock dividend have on a firm's cost of capital? On its risk? Would your answer be any different if a stock split were involved?

20.8 In 1959 the privately held Cascade Natural Gas Company First Mortgage 4⅝ per cent bonds were modified as follows: (*a*) all sinking-fund payments from October 1, 1959 to October 1, 1962 were to be waived; (*b*) the coupon rate was to be increased from 4⅝ per cent to 4⅞ per cent; and (*c*) a sinking-fund provision was incorporated in the modified indenture providing for retirement of $200,000 of the bonds on April 1, 1963, with an increase of $5,000 each year thereafter.

Under what conditions might you, as the holder of these bonds, agree to such modifications? Are there any other modifications you might require?

PROBLEMS

20.9 In 1962 Virginia-Carolina Chemical Corporation (which has since been acquired by Socony Mobil Oil Company) proposed a plan to eliminate arrears of $96 per share on its preferred stock. The plan called for conversion of the 213,000 6 per cent $100 par value preferred shares and accumulated arrearages into 1.3 shares of 5 per cent $50 par value prior preferred stock and one share of $50 par value 5 per cent convertible preferred which had a conversion rate of 1.1 shares of common. For the year ended June 30, 1962, the company earned $4.4 million and the prospects for earnings to persist at or above this level were considered by many to be excellent. On July 2, 1962, the price of the 6 per cent preferred was $115. The price of common at the time the plan was announced was $140. (a) What purpose or purposes are served by this adjustment? (b) Inasmuch as two thirds of the preferred shareholders had to approve the plan before it could be effective, how would you vote your 100 shares of preferred? The following information on the 6 per cent preferred may be helpful in your analysis.

(1) Dividend record:

1928 $3.00	1946 $5.00
1929 $2.00	1947 $11.50
1930–36 nil	1948 $12.00
1937 $1.50	1949 $10.00
1938–40 nil	1950–58 $6.00
1941 $1.00	1959–61 nil
1942 $5.00	1962 $3.00
1943–45 $3.00	

(2) Liquidation rights: Has preference over common to $105 plus dividends, if voluntary, and $100 per share plus dividends if involuntary.

(3) Callable on sixty days' notice at 105 plus dividends.

(4) Cumulative.

(5) Participating with common share-for-share after common has received $3.00 a share in any fiscal year.

(6) Net income before dividends but after taxes:

1954	$3,618,198
1955	2,409,063
1956	1,379,016
1957	946,380
1958	1,665,244

1959	1,351,990
1960	2,105,719
1961	2,525,627
1962	4,438,831

20.10 If a company declares a 5 per cent stock dividend and you hold twenty shares selling for $43 a share, at what theoretical market value should each share sell after the dividend?

20.11 Progressive Paper, Pencil, and Pen, Inc., wishing to share its recently achieved prosperity arising out of increased school enrollments, declared a 25 per cent stock dividend on the morning of October 1st, payable on October 15th to shareholders of record September 15th. On September 30th the stock was selling at $40 a share. (*a*) If the stock dividend were the only influential factor, at what price would you expect the stock to be selling at the close of trading on October 1st? On October 15th? (*b*) If there were two million shares of $2 par value outstanding before the dividend and the earned surplus was $17 million, set forth the common stock and earned surplus sections of the balance sheet giving effect to the dividend. (*c*) If the earnings per share were less than $10, would you seriously question the merits of the stock dividend? If so, why? If not, why not?

20.12 The Tina Mining Company struck a particularly profitable lode, precipitating a rather substantial rise in the market price of the firm's stock; within six months of the day the discovery was announced, the stock rose in price from 16¾ to 95⅞ and the average daily volume of trading in the stock increased sevenfold. The management decided that certain advantages would accrue to the company as well as to shareholders were the firm to list its securities on a regional stock exchange, whereupon it made application for such listing. As a condition precedent to listing, the directors announced a stock split of five-for-one. The company's equity section of the balance sheet prior to the split consisted of 1.5 million shares of $10 par value common, $1 million of paid-in capital, and $14 million of earned surplus. (*a*) What price should result from the split, at least theoretically? (*b*) Set forth the common stock and surplus sections of the balance sheet giving effect to the split. (*c*) What benefits might accrue to the company and its shareholders as a result of having their shares traded on a stock exchange?

Eight months after the stock was split and listed, it was discovered that the lode was in fact a very small one and that only a very small portion of the ore was of high enough quality to mine commercially. After four years from the date of listing, during which time the lode was mined for its profitable ore and further explorations were made in the area with the hope of finding more high-grade ore, the company was notified by the regional exchange that its stock was being considered for delisting because of its very low price—it was selling for only 10 per cent of its after-split price. The board of directors met and decided that the listing of its stock was still desirable and that it would effectuate a reverse split so as to place the stock in a more favorable trading range. (a) What magnitude of reverse split would you recommend were you a director of this firm? Why? (b) Taking into account the fact that the company lost $7.5 million in the past four years, set forth the firm's common stock and surplus sections of the balance sheet giving effect to the reverse split. (c) Based on your recommendation, at what price should the common be selling after the reverse split? (d) Why might the directors continue to feel that a listing of its shares on a stock exchange is desirable? Would the average daily volume of trading in the stock make any difference?

20.13 Last year the Lemon Automobile Company announced its intention to liquidate its assets, dissolve the corporation and wind up its affairs. This decision was made when the sales of its compact car, the Lemonette, proved to be a sour, last ditch effort to turn a profit. The company since then has disposed of all its assets and is in the process of determining the distribution of cash. Set forth the allocation you think should be made based on the following information. Assume the only special current debt consists of taxes and advances on government contracts.

Lemon Automobile Company, Cash Proceeds of Liquidated Assets

Assets	Book Value	Cash proceeds from liquidation
Cash	$ 10,000,000	$ 10,000,000
Receivables	15,000,000	14,000,000
Inventories	25,000,000	17,000,000
Big G plant	30,000,000	18,000,000
Big C plant	20,000,000	10,000,000
Big F plant	10,000,000	4,000,000
Big 3 plant	60,000,000	42,000,000
Other fixed assets	50,000,000	15,000,000
Other assets	15,000,000	9,000,000
	$235,000,000	$140,000,000

Lemon Automobile Company, Claims on Assets

Current liabilities		
Bank loans, unsecured	$ 6,500,000	
Wages payable	3,500,000	
Account payable	7,500,000	
Taxes payable	2,500,000	
Advances on government contracts	5,000,000	$ 25,000,000
Long-term debt		
First mortgage bonds, Big G plant	$ 20,000,000	
First mortgage bonds, Big C plant	12,000,000	
First mortgage bonds, Big 3 plant	30,000,000	
Second mortgage bonds, Big 3 plant	15,000,000	
Subordinated note	15,500,000	92,500,000
Common equity		
Common stock	$100,000,000	
Surplus	17,500,000	117,500,000
		$235,000,000

CHAPTER 21

FINANCIAL ANALYSIS:
THE CAPITAL SUPPLIER'S
POINT OF VIEW

THE IMPORTANCE OF THE CAPITAL SUPPLIER'S POINT OF VIEW TO FINANCIAL MANAGEMENT

In Chapter 13 we suggested that the cost of capital was influenced by what investors in the firm's securities felt about the risk and expected rate of return of the firm. If there were perfect knowledge and rational behavior on the part of the firm as well as on the part of investors in its securities, then the risk and expected rate of return for any one firm would be evaluated in exactly the same manner by both. Taken in conjunction with all other firms and investors any given firm, viewed *in toto* as one investment, would lie on the *CMC* (as would all other firms in the economy). Furthermore, the risk and expected rates of return of each firm in the economy would be such that investors would be equally satisfied with this particular firm or any other firm on *CMC* (which is, as you recall, the economy's indifference curve toward combinations of risk and expected returns) possessing the same combination of risk and expected returns.

But, as we have also seen, there is not perfect knowledge of opportunities, either for the firm or for investors. Indeed, knowledge can be so imperfect at times as to render reasonable decisions impossible. We are particularly interested at this point in the ways investors, long- and short-term, attempt to use the knowledge or information available to them in order to appraise the firms' securities. The importance to financial managers of being aware of this process of appraisal lies in the fact that the market price, explicit monetary cost and/or implicit costs of securities may be affected. To the extent that these are affected by investor behavior, the cost of capital is affected. And, insofar as the cost of capital contributes to long-run (and short-run) investment decisions which affect profits, this analysis assumes even greater importance.

THE POINT OF VIEW OF CAPITAL SUPPLIERS

The basic methodology utilized by investors to appraise a firm's financial condition is financial analysis, and the chief component of this approach has traditionally been called ratio analysis. The function of financial analysis is to determine in a qualitative and quantitative way the future over-all credit standing (risk) of the firm under review, based on present and past information—or, more specifically, to derive some notion of a firm's ability to meet its obligations. From the viewpoint of the outside investor, this is at best a difficult and hazardous task. Nevertheless, financial analysis is employed for this purpose and because businessmen, creditors, and owners often require the existence of some sort of minimum financial status before extending credit at all (much less on the most favorable of terms), efficient financial management must concern itself with this problem. The reason for this interest on the part of investors is to be found in the firm's desire for cash with which to maximize profits through investments. But cash is also needed to pay interest and principal on debt and dividends on stock. Cash is needed to pay wages. It is needed to take care of contingencies—uncertainties that are likely to arise but which cannot be anticipated with respect to time or magnitude of occurrence. Cash is needed to accommodate increases in output, whether they be temporary or permanent in nature. Inasmuch as internal sources of capital are not always adequate to meet all these needs for cash, investors are often relied on to supply what cash may be lacking. But investors do not supply capital unless the firm demonstrates some bill-paying capacity. Moreover, there is one general class of capital supply—common stockholders—which looks for something more than just bill-paying capacity. Indeed, in a sense, dividend payments on common stock, particularly if they are "regular" dividends, may be viewed by shareholders as the equivalent of a bill to be paid. But, as we have emphasized, common shareholders also look for increases in the market value of their shares. Without getting into the complex factors that may influence the growth in the value of shares, it is generally conceded that it is the expectations of increased profitability that increase the value of common shares. And, of course, among investments of equal risk, investors in common stocks tend to purchase those whose expected increase in market value (plus expected cash distributions) are greatest relative to cash outlays required to secure them.

The essence of financial analysis, from the point of view of both present and potential suppliers of capital as well as financial management, then, lies in the derivation of an estimate of a firm's potential risk as well as its expected returns. But financial analysis—from the standpoint of present or potential suppliers of funds—varies from the analysis that is necessary and useful for financial management. As a result, two elements of this methodology exist because the point of view of and the data available to both suppliers of capital and financial management are only partially the same. But one cannot ignore the other in making decisions; rather each must take the other into consideration as a variable in their decision. Indeed, a few aspects of financial analysis are common to both prospective suppliers of capital and to financial management of a firm as well, even though these common elements may be put to different uses by each. The one is quite traditional in nature and consists primarily of computation of a series of relationships. This *ratio analysis,* as it is called, is used by suppliers of capital, although, as we shall see, financial management may also find its occasional use necessary. This approach, because it is used primarily by outsiders, is referred to as the *external approach* to financial analysis. It consists of a fundamental core of relationships that have been traditionally used by suppliers of capital in their efforts to measure the expectations of the firm. These ratios are based primarily on data taken from balance sheets and income statements of the firm. Although there is no special magic in ratio analysis per se, since it is used extensively by external suppliers of capital and will be so used in the foreseeable future and since the suppliers of capital can influence a firm's cost of capital significantly, the student ought to be apprised of the fundamental concepts and relationships involved and financial management must be aware of what suppliers of capital regard as important and act accordingly.

On the other hand, ratio analysis, although essentially an external approach to the financial analysis of a firm, being used (as it is) primarily by suppliers of capital, will be used to some extent by financial management itself before it either seeks or extends credit. But for purposes of internal control, ratio analysis is usually woefully inadequate. The chief shortcoming of ratio analysis lies in its inability to project the dynamic, everyday operations of the firm and long-run profitability. For these purposes other techniques are required in order to determine the timing as well as the magnitude of the flow of capital into and out of the firm. This is referred to as the *internal approach* to financial analysis. This approach would also be useful to suppliers of capital were the data available to them. In some cases (such as short-term bank loans) cash budgets, a typical tool of internal financial management, may be provided by management. But capital budgets, another tool of internal financial management, usually are not available to capital suppliers. The internal approach, which yields a much clearer picture of a firm's near-term bill-paying capacity and long-run profitability, is reserved primarily for internal planning and control purposes. Because we have already discussed most of the important considerations necessary for internal financial analysis, our attention at this point will be on the tools of external financial analysis and the uses to which suppliers of capital (investors) put them.

To illustrate what we have in mind when we speak of the influence of suppliers of capital on a firm's capital structure and cost of capital, take the case of the firm that has "too much" debt, a situation that may be inimical to sound lending practices of either banks or insurance companies. If the firm has "too little" debt, this may be a dissatisfactory state from prospective stockholders' point of view. We will not go into the explanation of what constitutes "too much" or "too little" debt, but either situation may occasion a firm's cost of capital above that which would be maximizing. Indeed traditionally established proportions of debt, which will be discussed in the following chapter, may permit the procurement of capital on a limited basis only—that is, on a magnitude less than that desired by management. Or capital may be had only at adverse costs. These costs may be explicit or implicit in nature. Higher interest rates (explicit costs) may have to be paid for borrowed funds. Greater maturity or control costs may have to be met by the firm, increasing the implicit cost of capital to the firm. Or some part of the control of the firm may have to be given up. Restrictions on management policies may be imposed. These are some of the problems that may arise from an "improper" (in the investment sense) combination of debt and equity capital. They all manifest a degree of underlying fear that the firm will be unable to meet adequately its future obligations on debt and that increases in the market value of ownership either will not be forthcoming or will be so small relative to alternatives as to render the purchases of common shares imprudent. This ability ultimately devolves into a matter of having sufficient cash on hand when obligations come due and enhancing the over-all profitability of the enterprise so as to promote increases in the value of its common shares.

Furthermore, the existence of credit rating agencies such as Dun & Bradstreet, Inc., attest to the significance creditors, especially short-term ones, put on "adequate" credit standing. Short-term trade creditors may feel so strongly about a firm's unsatisfactory financial position that they may require cash before delivering goods or performing services. Less stringent but equally reflective of a firm's adverse "credit position" would be COD billing. On the other hand, firms with good "credit positions" need not want for reasonable amounts of credit, and on a long-term basis capital may be had at more favorable rates and with less restrictive contract provisions. Banks may be inclined to extend greater amounts of credit than before, or similar amounts of credit but at lesser explicit and implicit charges; or a combination of these may result. Obviously, advantages accrue to a firm possessing what suppliers of capital consider to be a sound financial condition.

At this point the student may also wonder what constitutes "generally accepted" standards and how they are derived. What do suppliers of capital regard as important? What norms do they use? What factors do short-term creditors regard as important? What factors are considered in evaluating a firm's financial condition? When ratios are used, to what standards, if any, can they be compared? And what about long-term suppliers of capital? Do they look for the same things that short-term creditors do? Does the duration of their claims have anything to do with the information they seek? Do the standards or norms apply "across the board?" If not, when and under what conditions might there be variations from such standards? Answers to some of these questions as well as others will be sought in the immediately ensuing chapter. Often the answers will seem quite reasonable. Sometimes they will be vague, or too general to be meaningful in the context presented. Hopefully, however, they will provide guidelines for a healthy skepticism of (1) financial analysis as used by suppliers of capital in general (and ratio analysis in particular), (2) the data used to elicit the answer, and/or (3) the reasoning processes used by suppliers of capital.

AN OVERVIEW OF CAPITAL SUPPLIER'S FINANCIAL ANALYSIS

Financial analysis, as it pertains to internal financial management as well as to external suppliers of capital, can be viewed analogously in terms of concentric circles. Figure 21-1 may be helpful in illustrating this point. When profits are defined as changes in the value of the ownership net of cash disbursements to and receipts from owners, and it is suggested that such changes in ownership value be measured by changes in the market value of the firm, estimates of what that market value is and how it can be improved are necessary. Accordingly, the core of these concentric circles applies most appropriately and immediately to internal financial management because here lies the value of the proprietary (owners') interests and because determination of proprietary value and methods to improve it, to achieve an optimum, are central to the task of financial management and analysis.

From the previous discussion it should be clear that a financial manager needs to be cognizant of investor behavior and the techniques the investor uses to evaluate a firm in order to make a satisfactory appraisal of ways in which the financial manager may improve the value of the ownership commitments. Once again, because investors rely so heavily on ratio analysis to appraise a firm, this is a necessary consideration for the financial officer who is attempting to minimize capital costs. This, along with internal financial analysis, constitutes the essence of the second con-

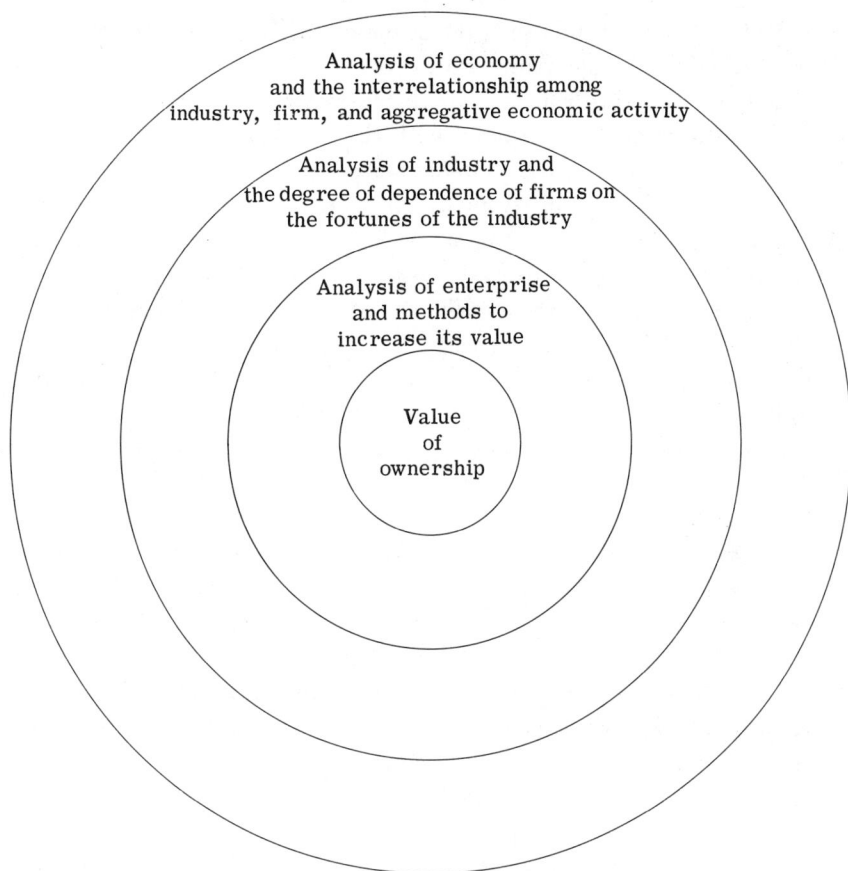

Figure 21-1   Interrelationships of Financial Analysis

centric circle of Figure 21-1: "Analysis of Enterprise and Methods to Increase Its Value."

In this regard, however, the analysis to determine the value of the firm cannot be disassociated from an analysis of the industry of which it is a part—the third concentric circle of Figure 21-1. Usually forces at work in the industry are at work on a firm within the industry. Hence an analysis of industry status—taking into account current trends in sales, technology, and other relevant factors, as well as the likely actions of one's competitors—typically is of the utmost importance. Comparison of a firm's performance to the industry's may shed some interesting insights for consideration.

Moreover, industry analysis per se is not very fruitful until it is related to the cyclical and secular aspects of the economy as a whole (the fourth concentric circle of Figure 21-1), because the fortunes of the industry are inextricably linked with those of the economy. Many firms will experience depressed activity in sympathy with cyclical downturns in the economy, although not necessarily to an equal degree. It is also true that many a firm's performance is associated with the performance of the industry in which it operates. The more closely a firm's product and/or service mix resembles that of the industry in which it operates, the more likely it is that it will act in unison with that industry. It may be, however, that some firms and industries are relatively insensitive to changes in aggregate, cyclical economic activity whereas others are highly sensitive to it. Many of our public utilities typify the former class. Manufacturers of producers' durable goods are examples of the latter. It is also true that firms may be more or less tied to the secular movements of the economy. A growth in total consumption as a result of changes in population or a shift in the pattern of consumption because of changes in income levels and/or the distribution of income, for example, can be expected to influence the industry and hence the firm. Food chains display these particular characteristics. Thus, a firm's performance is often related to that of its industry, and an industry's well-being may be uniquely related to the level of aggregative economic activity. Accordingly, the basic framework for financial analysis, both from an internal and from an external point of view, involves relating the value of ownership to the value of the enterprise (and ways to improve it), relating the enterprise to the welfare of the industry, and relating the industry to the economy.[1]

ESSENTIALLY QUALITATIVE CONSIDERATIONS FOR ANALYSIS

It is now in order for us to turn to the factors that might be considered in any given financial analysis. For the remainder of this chapter we will direct our attention to the two outer circles of Figure 21-1, as well as to a discussion of risk. (The discussion of the two inner circles is reserved for Chapter 22.)

Analysis of the Economy

Analysis of the economy usually centers on an estimate of present and prospective aggregative economic conditions. Only the very largest firms, however, have trained economists on their staffs that make forecasts of aggregate economic activity and relate such forecasts to the firm's operations. Reliance for their data is usually made on such sources as *The Sur-*

---

[1] With the advent of multilateral trade arrangements and with the movement toward a more and more cosmopolitical and cosmoeconomic world environment, the financial officer will be called upon to reconcile international developments to a much greater extent in the future than he is today.

vey of Current Business and *The Federal Reserve Bulletin.* Regional economic developments can be gleaned from district Federal Reserve Bank monthly letters and the business reviews published periodically by many state universities. Because this part of financial analysis is so complex and is covered in other books specializing on this topic, we do not intend to delve into it. It is enough to say that such an estimate is usually necessary for a complete analysis. Of particular importance may be the influence of aggregate economic factors on the *CMC* which affect the cost of capital to the firm and the value of the firm itself. These would take the form of monetary and fiscal policies. Also, those segments of aggregate economic activity most closely associated with the firm's industry will be more closely scrutinized by the economist or by management.

Analysis of the Industry[2]

We do not intend, in this short discussion, to present all the factors necessary for a comprehensive analysis of an industry. We are interested in emphasizing the importance of industry analysis and will suggest briefly only some of the relevant points that might enter such analysis.

Analysis of an industry can be centered basically on four factors, the first of which is its *economic structure.* This aspect of the analysis is primarily concerned with the structure of economic competition—that is, its composition along oliogopolistic, monopolistic, or other lines. Other things being equal, the more purely competitive the industry, the smaller the profit potentials. Factors to be considered in this analysis are: (1) the major producers of the industry, and their respective shares of the market; (2) the trend of their shares of the market over the years; and (3) the ease of entry and rate of exit of firms.

The second aspect of industry analysis, although not entirely separate from the first, centers on *economic character.* Briefly, this entails an investigation of the industry's stability or instability—the seasonal and/or cyclical nature of the industry—and is usually based on historical quantitative data (when these are available). Moreover, the nature of the output of the industry is important. For example, the income elasticity or inelasticity of demand of the goods or services produced might be considered. That is, what happens to consumption of a firm's product as national income fluctuates? Other considerations would be: (1) the extent or degree of price competition, if any; (2) the extent or degree of any form of nonprice competition; (3) the nature of the firm's product (con-

---

[2] *Industry* is rather loosely defined as a group of firms producing essentially similar products or services, where the cross-elasticity of demand for the products of the firms in the group is relatively high.

sumer durable, producer's durable, or consumer nondurable); and (4) the extent to which the industry is regulated.

The third area to investigate is the *secular trend* of the industry. Such factors as population growth and trends, technological changes, research and development outlays and the success of these projects, potential substitutes for the product, per capita income, per capita consumption of the product, and a host of other factors might be considered.

The fourth area of analysis is what might be called the *financial character* of the industry. In this we shall include examination of certain of the industry's financial ratios (the basic ones will be discussed in Chapter 22). Unusual patterns of development should be investigated. In some cases interindustry comparisons may prove valuable. These industry ratios may also be used as standards by which individual firms may compare themselves.

Analysis of the Enterprise with Particular Emphasis on Risk

Both from an internal and from an external point of view, analysis of a firm may begin with an investigation of the *nature of the business.* Chances are that this analysis will not produce substantial additional information over that elicited from the industry analysis. On the other hand, industry classifications are frequently crude and serious and significant deviations from the stated dimensions of the industry are often encountered and hence need to be cited and explored further. Many firms may not even be classifiable according to any of the generally accepted industry descriptions.

The immediate focus of our analysis is the enterprise's business risk, which has been defined as the expected variability of its expected profits. Because an approximation to business risk can be derived by the variation in past profits, analysis of those factors that generate profits and their stability is of the essence for future projections. The smaller the variance in profits, the smaller the degree of business risk (other things being equal). Obviously, the greater the variability the greater the business risk. Analysts typically concentrate their efforts on accounting profits rather than on profits as we have defined them. In view of this, we must also deal with accounting profits, or *earnings,* as the long-run approximation to profits.

The analyst's attention is focused on the factors underlying the supply of and demand for a firm's output as well as on the factors influencing the demand for and supply of inputs to a firm. The output of the firm may be analyzed from a number of viewpoints. For instance, are the firm's products luxury goods or necessities? Necessities usually exhibit greater earnings stability and tend to grow with population. What is the price elasticity of demand for the products? Firms whose products are essentially price inelastic—for example, cigarettes—typically have greater stability in earnings than those whose products are essentially price elastic. Firms whose earnings are relatively insensitive to changes in national income —for example, electric utilities—will exhibit greater earnings stability than firms whose earnings are influenced by changes in national income— as, for example, appliance manufacturers. There are a host of other factors that might be considered, such as governmental regulations, substitutes for the firm's output, labor relations, diversification, distribution channels, reliance on leisure time, disposable income, population growth (nationally and regionally, if necessary), or gross national product, to name a few. The student, after some reflection, ought to be able to make some judgment regarding the importance of each of these factors for the analysis of business risk.

A number of factors may also be considered in analyzing the supply of factor inputs. What, for example, is the proportion of fixed costs to total costs? Of variable costs to total costs? The higher the proportion of fixed costs to total costs, the higher the operating leverage of the firm and the higher the business risk (other things being equal), because the greater will be the relative variance in earnings over extended periods of time. *Operating leverage* refers to the extent to which total operating costs vary with changes in operating revenues. Obviously, only variable costs can be readily changed in the short run because, by definition, these costs vary directly with the level of output whereas fixed costs are constant regardless of the level of output.[3] Examples of the former are wages, selling expenses, and raw materials. Examples of the latter are salaries, insurance, and depleciation. Because of the impact that changes in operating revenues can have on profit margins, we are interested in the proportions of fixed and variable costs to total costs. If 80 per cent of a firm's total costs are fixed in nature at a given level of operations, for example, and a firm has a profit margin of 10 per cent at this level, it would not take much of a decline in total operating revenues to wipe out the profit margin. On the one hand an increase in operating revenues would tend to result in a greater than proportionate increase in the profit margin. On the other hand, if another firm's fixed costs were 30 per cent of total costs at a given operating level and it, too, had a 10 per cent profit margin, its over-all profit picture would be less affected by an equivalent change in operating revenues. The first firm's earnings would be more volatile than the second's and we would say that it has a greater degree of business risk (other things being equal).

To illustrate further the implications of what has just been stated, the

[3] In the long run all costs are variable.

distribution of fixed costs and variable costs may be used by management to determine the firm's hypothetical breakeven point—that is, the point at which revenues just cover all expenses. A great difficulty in the practical application of such *breakeven analysis*, as it is often called, is that many costs are not neatly classifiable as either completely fixed or entirely variable. In fact, most costs are often semivariable. Nevertheless, awareness of the concept may be useful.

The data for the two firms mentioned in the preceding paragraph are set forth, along with other information, in Table 21-1.

Table 21-1
Breakeven Data, Firms A and B

	Firm A		Firm B	
Net sales		$5,000,000		$5,000,000
Operating expenses				
Fixed	$3,600,000		$1,350,000	
Variable	900,000	4,500,000	3,150,000	4,500,000
Operating income		$ 500,000		$ 500,000
Margin		10%		10%

If both firms were to experience a 10 per cent decline in operating revenues, their respective income statements would look like those in Table 21-2. But Firm B would fare much better than Firm A because it could contract its costs much more easily.

Table 21-2
After a 10 Per Cent Decline in Revenues

	Firm A		Firm B	
Net sales		$4,500,000		$4,500,000
Operating expenses				
Fixed	$3,600,000		$1,350,000	
Variable	810,000	4,410,000	2,835,000	4,185,000
Operating income		$ 90,000		$ 315,000
Margin		2%		7%

On the other hand, a 10 per cent increase in operating revenues would favor Firm A's margin more than Firm B's. We leave it to the student to verify that the margins of Firms A and B after the increase of 10 per cent in revenues would be 16.5 per cent and 12.5 per cent, respectively.

Without belaboring this point, computation of the break even point can be done with the formula

$$BE = \frac{FC}{FC/NR + NOI/NR}$$

where

$\qquad BE$ = breakeven point in terms of operating revenue
$\qquad FC$ = fixed costs in dollars
$\qquad NR$ = net operating revenues in dollars
$\qquad NOI$ = net operating income in dollars

It is important to recognize in this breakeven analysis that heavy fixed costs tend to make for high degrees of business risk, and vice versa. But exceptions to this abound. Electric utilities have rather substantial fixed costs, for example, but their business risk is not considered great. We shall see why in the next Chapter.[4]

Third, some idea of the over-all operating position of the firm under review relative to the rest of the industry is customarily considered desirable. Is it a leading producer? The smallest? A high-cost producer? A technically superior producer?

As a result of answers to these questions and similar ones some qualitative impression concerning the degree of business risk is gained. The degree of business risk is not measured on some arithmetic scale, however. It cannot be said, for example, that one firm has a business risk of 1.0 while another's business risk is 1.5. The real world just does not have perfectly satisfactory methods of quantifying a basically subjective concept such as risk. Statistically, however, attempts to approximate it can be made by using some quantitative measure to rank them, such as the expected relative standard deviation (SO/EO), which relates the standard deviation of the outcome (SO) to the expected outcome (EO). In

---

[4] Many business finance books stress breakeven analysis much more extensively than we choose to do. The student is invited to explore these texts, especially: Pearson Hunt, Charles M. Williams, and Gordon Donaldson, *Basic Business Finance*, rev. ed. (Homewood, Ill.: Irwin, 1961), 331–38; and Robert W. Johnson, *Financial Management*, 2nd ed. (Boston: Allyn, 1962), 112–22. For some further insights, *see:* Joel Dean, *Managerial Economics* (Englewood Cliffs, N.J.: Prentice-Hall, 1951), 326–41; Joel Dean, *Methods and Potentialities of Breakeven Analysis* (London: Sweet & Maxwell, n.d.), reprinted from *The Australian Accountant*, 21 (October–November 1961); Roy A. Foulke, *Practical Financial Statement Analysis*, 5th ed. (New York: McGraw, 1961), Chap. 20; and Edmund Whittaker, *Economic Analysis* (New York: Wiley, 1956), 246.

Chapter 5 we computed the expected outcome (*EO*) and the standard deviation of the expected outcome (*SO*), relating them in order to derive a more meaningful measure of variability. That was the basic conceptual framework. This same framework may be used in practice, but on a more intuitive basis. For example, after an expert (the financial officer) reviews the various qualitative considerations mentioned above, as well as others, he might sum them up and represent them on a numerical scale, giving more weight to some considerations than to others. This would be a numerical representation of qualitative estimates of business risk—or, in other words, a subjective evaluation of business risk represented on a numerical scale so that the relationship between *SO* and *EO*, the expected relative standard deviation of the outcome, could then be determined. This would be a numerical representation of his qualitative judgment made after having reviewed the nature of each venture. For example, what might one estimate the business risk of the following business venture to be? A firm is organized to build a restaurant which will have unusual exterior designs and unusual interior features, will be located in a part of town which consists mainly of warehouses, and will cater mainly to evening diners and the "late-late crowd." Using this and other information too lengthy to include at this point, let us hypothesize an estimate of the firm's distribution of expected outcomes. Based on a review of all quantitative and qualitative data in this case and in all cases similar to it, the distributions of the expected outcomes might be shown as in Figure 21-2. The distribution has a mean expected return (*ER*) of 7.5 per cent and a standard deviation of the expected rate of return (*SR*) of 5 per cent.

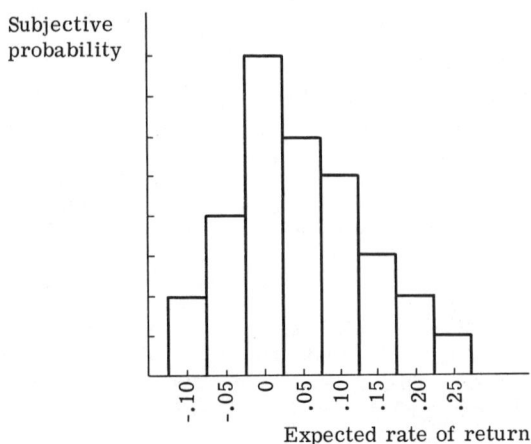

Figure 21-2 Probability Distribution of Expected Rates of Return for a Restaurant Venture

The expected relative standard deviation (SR/ER) is 2/3 (5 per cent/ 7.5 per cent). Is this high or low, good or bad? The answer to this would hinge on the risk aversion of the decision-maker and upon the investment returns generally available in the market (the CMC) for this risk level. If he can find opportunities with an ER of 7.5 per cent and an SR of 3 per cent, he would be better off to take such a CMC investment. Nevertheless, knowing this datum, he can place this general market investment on a scale ranging from zero on up. He can take other general market investment opportunities and do the same thing, arraying all possibilities in terms of expected outcome (ER) and expected relative standard deviation (SR/ER). He is now in a position to make a more informed judgment regarding the investment merits of the proposal.

As we suggested in Chapter 5, as far as we know businessmen do not make computations such as these. They do, however, go through a thinking process very similar to the ones used here, though not nearly so formally structured. They would usually ask a series of rather subjective questions such as the following: What are the chances for the success of this venture? (And how do we measure success?) How successful will it be over the years? How many years are relevant? Who would be the patrons of such a place? Will the enterprise generate revenues in excess of its explicit and implicit costs? (It has to, to stay in business in the long run.) Will its fascination wear off or will the entry of other firms wipe out possible profits realized at first? Moreover, what volume of business can this establishment hope to generate? How large is this "late-late crowd?" Would its demand be high enough and consistent enough over extended periods of time? Should the restaurant be open only on weekends: If so, the business of two days would have to carry the fixed costs (for example, rents or mortgage payments and overhead on fixtures) and variable costs (for example, heat and electricity) of seven days. If the business is to be open on week days, variable costs would probably go up considerably. And what volume of business would be needed to handle these total costs? The line of investigation could go on and on.

This example should seem familiar to the student; it is very similar to the example used in Chapter 5, where the estimated returns as well as the chance of these outcomes occurring were set forth in a statistical manner. The procedure invariably followed by most businessmen would be some intuitive estimate based on their knowledge of the qualitative characteristics of the venture and the possible monetary outcomes, and would mirror the statistical approach elaborated above as well as in Chapter 5.

This discussion may still leave the student with some reservations concerning his ability to estimate business risk. This is not at all unusual: such an estimate requires experienced judgment based on whatever data appear relevant. As difficult as it is, decisions of this sort need to be made before other financial analyses are made. In other words, for other aspects of financial analysis (especially ratio analysis) to seem meaningful for investment analysts they must be related to an intuitive estimate of business risk.

SUMMARY

This chapter introduces the basic rationale for external financial analysis. The need for such analysis, primarily by suppliers of capital (persons and institutions *external* to the firm) but in some cases by financial management as well, arises because of the lack of adequate knowledge available to suppliers and demanders of capital. The importance of external financial analysis to financial management lies in (1) the necessity of using the same data to meet minimum requirements expected by suppliers and (2) the effect the financial condition of the firm, as reflected in such analysis, has on its cost of capital. Qualitative considerations generally considered necessary for a thorough financial analysis include analysis of the economy, analysis of the industry and analysis of the firm. Subjective evaluation of business risk is crucial to the entire process. Quantitative considerations typically employed to derive an indication of business risk are taken up in Chapter 22.

SUGGESTED READINGS

BADGER, RALPH E., HAROLD W. TORGERSON, and HARRY G. GUTHMANN. *Investment Principles and Practices*, 5th ed. Englewood Cliffs, N.J.: Prentice-Hall, 1961.

BELLEMORE, DOUGLAS H. *Investments*. 2nd ed. New York: Simmons-Boardman Publishing Corporation, 1960.

CLENDENIN, JOHN C. *Introduction to Investments*. 3rd ed. New York: McGraw-Hill Book Company, Inc., 1960.

DOWRIE, GEORGE W., DOUGLAS R. FULLER, and FRANCIS J. CALKINS. *Investments*. 3rd ed. New York: John Wiley & Sons, Inc., 1961.

GARDNER, F. V. "Breakeven Point Control for Higher Profits," *Harvard Business Review*, 32 (September–October 1954), 123–30.

HAYES, DOUGLAS A. *Investments: Analysis and Management*. New York: The Macmillan Company, 1961.

LINTNER, JOHN. "Dividends, Earnings, Leverage, Stock Prices and the Supply of Capital to Corporations," *The Review of Economics and Statistics, 44* (August 1962), 243–69.

SOLDOFSKY, ROBERT M. "Accountants vs. Economists Concepts of Breakeven Analysis," *N.A.A. Bulletin,* (December 1959), 578.

U. S. Department of Commerce. *Guides for Business Analysis and Profit Evaluation.* Washington, D.C.: Government Printing Office, 1959.

WESTON, J. FRED. "Norms for Debt Levels," *The Journal of Finance, 9* (May 1954), 124–35.

———, and NEIL H. JACOBY. "Profit Standards," *Quarterly Journal of Economics, 66* (May 1952), 224–50.

Note: Questions and problems for this chapter have been deferred until the student has finished Chapter 22.

CHAPTER 22   FINANCIAL ANALYSIS: A CORE OF RATIOS

Despite the inadequacies of ratio analysis for internal control, we indicated in Chapter 21 that financial management nevertheless has to be sensitive to the needs and ways of thinking of potential as well as present suppliers of funds because of the influence of their actions on the firm's cost of capital; they must be aware of the processes by which outsiders appraise their firm. As a result, in this chapter we shall present the factors which outsiders generally use to evaluate a firm, bearing in mind that these factors may be imperfect in nature and must be used with caution and understanding. And, although our approach to this topic will assume the point of view of suppliers of capital, wherever appropriate we shall indicate the uses to which financial management may put the various relationships and their variations.

THE NATURE OF RATIO ANALYSIS

Ratio analysis of business enterprises centers on efforts to derive quantitative measures or guides concerning the expected capacity of the firm to meet its future financial obligations or expectations. To do this, present and past data are used and whatever extrapolations appear warranted are made to provide an indication of future performance. The financial obligations involved typically take the form of interest and preferred dividend expenses, and payment of the principal amount of debt or preferred stock at maturity.[1] Accordingly, ratio analysis centers to a large extent on historical data; through such data the expected ability of the firm to pay its interest and preferred dividends and the principal on all its obligations is judged. In this regard, the frequency with which capital funds come due may be important because large, short-term maturities may be oppressive to the firm whereas long-term obligations of, say, twenty years duration have a less ominous bearing on the current financial status of

---

[1] Technically, preferred stock has no maturity date. When a sinking-fund provision exists, however, the firm assumes required repayments, and failure to make them may seriously impair its credit standing and force down the price of the security, thereby resulting in an increase in the firm's cost of capital.

the firm. The more distant maturity date allows for gradual debt retirement over the years, albeit interest expenses would need to be met, probably semiannually. And because suppliers of capital are typically classed as short-term or long-term, ratio analysis can be broken down into these two categories.

The purpose of such analysis by suppliers is to aid them in their efforts to derive an estimate of the risk of providing funds to the enterprise. As we saw in Chapter 21 and elsewhere, this is essentially a matter of subjectively estimating a firm's ability to meet its obligations. In this regard, two basic types of risk are encountered. The first is *business risk,* a judgment about which is likely to be derived by analysis of qualitative factors influencing the variability of earnings in the absence of financial capital costs—that is, without regard to the mode by which a firm is financed. Then there is *financial risk,* a judgment about which is probably derived by comparing the amount of resources (both assets and cash flow) and their variability with creditor or owner claims on these resources. It should be stressed that some estimate of the totality of risk associated with a given security, derived from the *nature of the business itself* (busines risk) and the *manner by which it is financed* (financial risk), must be made.

A warning is in order at this point, however. There are many *pitfalls* in ratio analysis and in many respects it is more important to recognize these than to know the mechanistic processes of deriving results. Among these are the *illusionary* aspects of accounting data—illusionary in the sense that they lend an air of accuracy to the arithmetic results because the input data are numerical in nature. Actually, as most accountants agree, the data are at best usually estimates. Estimates have to be made concerning (1) the life of an asset, (2) the proper rate of depreciating assets, (3) provisions for doubtful accounts, and so on. Consequently, the analyst should not feel very comfortable with the results of his calculations, even though, based on the data available, they constitute the best basis for decision-making from an investor's point of view, especially if data over a long period of time are involved. Without the advantage of a time perspective, however, changes could not be noted nor trends elicited. Even at that, however, the dangers of using historical data for present and future decisions are always present. For some firms these dangers may not be so ominous; the average of their past performance will be a representative guide to the average of their future performance. For other firms past performance will have little bearing on future performance and financial analysis in these cases bears little fruit.

THE CORE OF RATIOS USED FOR ANALYSIS

Ratio analysis is a logical extension of the qualitative investigations considered in Chapter 21. Most creditors and investors attempting to evaluate a possible commitment in a firm will turn rather naturally to a series of relationships because people prefer to work with data which appear to be concrete in nature (even though the data only give the illusion of being so). Judgements seem to be made more easily when one can rationalize them with numbers. Suppliers of capital have for a long time[2] relied (and still do rely) upon the seeming security attached to quantitative data. And the simpler these data are, the better. Over the years these suppliers have developed a series of relationships in which they believe and in which they often place a high degree of confidence. It is to these relationships that we now turn our attention. At the outset, however, several prefatory comments are in order.

Quantitative relations of the type typically used in ratio analysis are not an end in themselves: they are a means to understanding a firm's financial position. Because it is an art rather than a science, quantitative ratio analysis is not capable of providing precise answers to the questions a financial manager (remember, financial managers may and do use ratios) or potential funds suppliers may have. Financial analysis is essentially a methodology, the core of which is a qualitative analysis of business and financial risks augmented by an analysis based on a series of mutually interdependent ratios (no one of which is meaningful in and by itself) and other financial statements that may be available. It is usually not until several ratios, often related to one another, are computed that the whole of ratio analysis takes on any meaning for suppliers. Ratio analysis, then, is a means to an end which is, properly speaking, a decision concerning some financial aspect of a business enterprise. The stature of ratios is partly derived, therefore, from the analyst's capacity to quantify available data in a systematic manner. In order to reach a decision based on such analysis, he must use some norms concerning the financial stature of the firm under review; a given firm's financial status, depicted by a series of ratios, must be compared to some standard and deviations from them explained.[3] These norms cannot be used as an objective for a

[2] Sister Isadore Brown, *The Historical Development of the Use of Ratios in Financial Statement Analysis to 1933*, "The Catholic University of America: Studies in Economics," Abstract Studies, Vol. 22 (Washington D.C.: Catholic U. of America Press, 1955).

[3] Efforts to crystallize norms for various types of enterprises are to be found in Paul M. Van Arsdell, *Principles of Corporation Finance* (Champaign, Ill.: Stipes, 1958), Chaps. 16, 17, 19, 21, and 22; Benjamin Graham, David L. Dodd, and Sidney

firm to achieve, however, because they are often averages and therefore have no relevance to the firm under review. They are dynamic in nature, constantly in flux, adjusting hopefully to the prevailing economic circumstances of the firm, the industry, and the economy—in short, to the conditions of their environment. They must be used with considerable caution and judgment and must be tempered to meet whatever extenuating circumstances might arise. Bearing the foregoing in mind, we need only to point out here that there is a *core of relationships* customarily used for the ratio phase of financial analysis and other ratios are, for the most part, a modification or extension of this core.

Profitability Ratios

Over-all Profitability Ratios

Generally, over-all profitability ratios relate to the firm's efficiency as presented in various financial statements. They attempt to give, from the historical pattern of income, some idea of the over-all rate of return on total reported assets (*RTA*).

Turnover Ratio. The first of these ratios is the *turnover ratio* (*TR*). It is computed by relating the net revenues (*NR*) of the enterprise to the total assets (*TA*) used to generate these revenues. Thus, the turnover ratio is NR/TA. In many respects the net revenues can be viewed as a firm's net outputs (expressed in monetary terms) and the total tangible assets (expressed in monetary terms) as the total recorded resources used to generate these outputs. Obviously, this total resource concept ignores physical assets already amortized and even more important human capital. As long as no satisfactory means is available to recognize these serious omissions in a monetary way, this ratio will tend to be overstated. The importance attached to this ratio in practice is that it represents an attempt to derive an idea of the turnover of recorded corporate assets. In other words, the business enterprise is viewed as an organization designed to bring together various factors of production in an efficient manner in order to produce goods and services. In the production of goods and services assets need to be used or "turned over." With the data contained in Tables 22-1 and 22-2, the turnover ratio for Firm A on Table 22-3 is $1(NR/TA) = \$150,000/\$150,000$.

Cottle, *Security Analysis*, 4th ed. (New York: McGraw, 1962), Chaps. 23–25, 37, 38; J. Fred Weston, *Managerial Finance* (New York: Holt, 1962), Chap. 4. Dun & Bradstreet also publishes data for selected industries. *See: 14 Important Ratios for 72 Lines of Business, 1965* (New York: Dun & Bradstreet, 1966).

Table 22-1   Comparative Balance Sheets of Three Firms

Recorded Resources	Firm A		Firm B		Firm C	
Current Resources:						
Cash	$10,000		$ 7,000		$ 6,000	
Marketable Securities	10,000		12,000		13,000	
Receivables (Net)	10,000		14,000		16,000	
Inventories	30,000	$ 60,000	27,000	$ 60,000	25,000	$ 60,000
Fixed and other Resources:						
Plant and equipment (Net)	80,000		80,000		80,000	
Other assets	10,000	90,000	10,000	90,000	10,000	90,000
Total assets		$150,000		$150,000		$150,000
Creditors' and Owners' Claims on Resources						
Short-term creditors' claims:						
Accounts payable	2,000		1,000		1,500	
Taxes payable	4,000		3,000		3,500	
Notes payable, 4.5%	6,000		5,000		5,500	
Accruals	8,000	$ 20,000	7,000	$ 16,000	7,500	$ 18,000
Long-term creditors' claims:						
Mortgage bonds, 4%	25,000		25,000		7,000	
Subordinated debenture bonds, 5%			25,000		25,000	
Preferred stock, 6%	25,000	25,000	25,000	50,000	25,000	57,000
		45,000		66,000		75,000
Residual owners' claims:						
Common stock	55,000		55,000		55,000	
Paid-In capital	15,000		10,000		5,000	
Reserve for contingencies	10,000		7,000		4,000	
Retained earnings	25,000	105,000	12,000	84,000	11,000	75,000
Total creditors' and owners' claim on assets		$150,000		$150,000		$150,000

Table 22-2
Comparative Income Statements of Three Firms

	Firm A		Firm B		Firm C	
Net sales		$150,000		$150,000		$150,000
Cost of goods sold		100,000		100,000		100,000
Gross income		$ 50,000		$ 50,000		$ 50,000
Operating expenses:						
General and administrative	$5,000		$5,000		$5,000	
Selling	4,750		4,750		4,750	
Wages	7,000		7,000		7,000	
Depreciation	2,000	18,750	2,000	18,750	2,000	18,750
Net operating income		$ 31,250		$ 31,250		$ 31,250
Other income		1,500		1,500		1,500
Total income		$ 32,750		$ 32,750		$ 32,750
Other expenses:						
Interest on notes payable	$ 270		$ 225		$ 238	
Interest on mortgage bonds					280	
Interest on subordinated bonds		270	1,250	1,475	1,250	1,768
Income before taxes		$ 32,480		$ 31,275		$ 30,982
Taxes (50%)		16,240		15,638		15,491
Income after taxes		$16,240		$ 15,637		$ 15,491
Preferred dividends		1,500		1,500		1,500
Income available for common (Residual income)		$ 14,740		$ 14,137		$ 13,991
Common dividends		$ 8,000		$ 8,000		$ 8,000

Table 22-3

Comparative Ratios for Three Firms

Ratio	Formulation	Results for Each Firm		
		A	B	C
A. Profitability ratios:				
(1) Turnover (*TR*)	$\dfrac{\text{Net revenues}}{\text{Total recorded assets}}$	$\dfrac{\$150,000}{\$150,000} = 1{:}1$	$\dfrac{\$150,000}{\$150,000} = 1{:}1$	$\dfrac{\$150,000}{\$150,000} = 1{:}1$
(2) Operating (*OR*)	$\dfrac{\text{Net operating income}}{\text{Net revenues}}$	$\dfrac{\$31,250}{\$150,000} = 20.83\%$	$\dfrac{\$31,250}{\$150,000} = 20.83\%$	$\dfrac{\$31,250}{\$150,000} = 20.83\%$
(3) Return of total assets (*RTA*)	$\dfrac{\text{Net income after taxes but before interest}}{\text{Total recorded assets}}$	$\dfrac{\$16,510}{\$150,000} = 11\%$	$\dfrac{\$17,112}{\$150,000} = 11.4\%$	$\dfrac{\$17,259}{\$150,000} = 11.5\%$
(4) Return in common equity (*RCE*)	$\dfrac{\text{Earnings available for common}}{\text{Common equity}}$	$\dfrac{\$14,740}{\$105,000} = 14.0\%$	$\dfrac{\$14,137}{\$84,000} = 16.8\%$	$\dfrac{\$13,991}{\$75,000} = 18.9\%$
B. Short-term ratios:				
(5) Current (*CR*)	$\dfrac{\text{Current assets}}{\text{Current liabilities}}$	$\dfrac{\$60,000}{\$20,000} = 3{:}1$	$\dfrac{\$60,000}{\$16,000} = 3.8{:}1$	$\dfrac{\$60,000}{\$18,000} = 3.3{:}1$
(6) Acid-test (*ATR*)	$\dfrac{\text{Cash and receivables}}{\text{Current liabilities}}$	$\dfrac{\$30,000}{\$20,000} = 1.5{:}1$	$\dfrac{\$33,000}{\$16,000} = 2.1{:}1$	$\dfrac{\$35,000}{\$18,000} = 1.9{:}1$

(7) Absolute-liquidity (*ALR*)	$\dfrac{\$ 20{,}000}{\$ 20{,}000} = 1{:}1$	$\dfrac{\$ 19{,}000}{\$ 16{,}000} = 1.2{:}1$	$\dfrac{\$ 19{,}000}{\$ 18{,}000} = 1.1{:}1$
	Cash / Current liabilities		
(8) Inventory-turnover (*IT*)	$\dfrac{\$ 100{,}000}{\$ 30{,}000} = 3.3 \text{ times}$	$\dfrac{\$ 100{,}000}{\$ 27{,}000} = 3.7 \text{ times}$	$\dfrac{\$ 100{,}000}{\$ 25{,}000} = 4 \text{ times}$
	Cost of goods sold / Average inventories		
(9) Receivables-turnover (*RT*)	$\dfrac{\$ 150{,}000}{\$ 10{,}000} = 15 \text{ times}$	$\dfrac{\$ 150{,}000}{\$ 14{,}000} = 10.7 \text{ times}$	$\dfrac{\$ 150{,}000}{\$ 16{,}000} = 9.4 \text{ times}$
	Net credit sales / Receivables		
(10) Cash-turnover (*CT*)	$\dfrac{\$ 150{,}000}{\$ 10{,}000} = 15 \text{ times}$	$\dfrac{\$ 150{,}000}{\$ 7{,}000} = 21.4 \text{ times}$	$\dfrac{\$ 150{,}000}{\$ 6{,}000} = 25 \text{ times}$
	Net sales / Cash		

C. Long-term ratios:

(11) Debt-to-equity (*DE*)	$\dfrac{\$ 45{,}000}{\$ 105{,}000} = .43{:}1$	$\dfrac{\$ 66{,}000}{\$ 84{,}000} = .79{:}1$	$\dfrac{\$ 75{,}000}{\$ 75{,}000} = 1{:}1$
	Debt / Owners' equity		
(12) Interest-coverage (*IC*)	$\dfrac{\$ 32{,}750}{\$ 270} = 121 \text{ times}$	$\dfrac{\$ 32{,}750}{\$ 1{,}475} = 22 \text{ times}$	$\dfrac{\$ 32{,}750}{\$ 1{,}768} = 19 \text{ times}$
	Total income / Interest expenses		
(13) Preferred-dividend-Coverage (*PDC*)	$\dfrac{\$ 32{,}750}{\$ 1{,}770} = 19 \text{ times}$	$\dfrac{\$ 32{,}750}{\$ 2{,}975} = 11 \text{ times}$	$\dfrac{\$ 32{,}750}{\$ 3{,}268} = 10 \text{ times}$
	Total income / (Interest exp. + Preferred dividends)		
(14) Common-dividend-Coverage (*CDC*)	$\dfrac{\$ 14{,}740}{\$ 8{,}000} = 1.84 \text{ times}$	$\dfrac{\$ 14{,}137}{\$ 8{,}000} = 1.77 \text{ times}$	$\dfrac{\$ 13{,}991}{\$ 8{,}000} = 1.75 \text{ times}$
	Earnings available for common / Common dividends		

For manufacturing firms in general, this ratio will average between 1:1 and 2:1. For public utilities it will average about .25:1 to .33:1 a year. An unusually high *TR* might indicate that the physical capacity of the firm is too small. An unusually low *TR* might indicate that the physical capacity of the firm is too large.

Operating ratio. The second ratio under the topic of over-all profitability is the *operating ratio* (*OR*). This ratio expresses the relationship between net operating income (*NOI*) and net revenues. It is calculated, then, from the ratio, *NOI/NR*. For Firm A, Table 22-3, it is 20.83 per cent (*NOI/NR* = $31,250/$150,000). The operating ratio can be used as a partial index of over-all profitability, because it represents what is commonly referred to as the *margin of profit* derived from revenues. In other words it indicates the percentage of each dollar of revenue available to the firm before payments for income taxes and for service of prior capital claims (that is, claims on income ranking before those of the residual claimants). The specific standards to which to compare this ratio, like all ratios, are comparative industry data. In general, however, one would expect this ratio to be about 15–25 per cent for manufacturing firms and much higher, about 25–50 per cent, for public utilities.

Return on Total Assets. Just as the turnover of assets and the margin of profitability can be expressed in ratio form, so too can the *over-all profitability* (in an *ex post* sense) of a business enterprise be quantitatively expressed. One quantitative expression is called the *return on total assets* (*RTA*). This ratio relates the net income (*NI*) of the business enterprise to its total tangible assets and measures the *return on total recorded assets* employed by a firm. Its formulation is *NI/TA*, where net income (*NI*) is the total means less income taxes but before interest. For Firm A this ratio is 11 per cent. The standard for manufacturing firms is 8–12 per cent. For public utilities it is 5–7 per cent. This ratio is a function of both the turnover of assets and the operating ratio (profit margin per dollar of revenues).

Over-all Profitability and Business Risk. Over-all profitability and its relation to business risk can be illustrated by reference to Tables 22-1, 22-2, and 22-3 above. Note that each of the three firms has the same dollar amount of total assets, that each turns over these resources to the same extent, and that each has the same profit margin (operating ratio) per dollar of revenues. Were we to compute the returns on total assets of each of these firms on a before-tax basis (using, say, net operating income as the numerator) each would be the same. The student may wonder why income before taxes is used in our computations. The reason for this lies in the fact that interest is a tax-deductible expense, and income after taxes in each of these cases is different, depending on the amount of interest a firm must pay. Moreover, taxes on income are not considered operating costs. The tax-deductibility of interest then would tend to distort the basic relationship between *TR* and *OR*. With before-tax data and given the same amount of net revenues and total assets for each firm, the return on total assets and operating ratios are coincidentally the same. With this simple illustration a very important point can be made, namely, that over-all profitability is the result of both the use of recorded assets as well as the operating margin or ratio, and that variability in either or both will result in variability in earnings. The greater the variability in earnings, the greater the business risk (and vice versa). What this suggests is that sales alone will not generate earnings; nor just assets; nor just the margin on sales. The relative stability of sales and cost is vital to a determination of business risk based on historical data. To the extent that the future mirrors the past, these data provide a rough guide to expected performance.

If, ignoring income taxes, we were to take the operating ratio (*OR*) and multiply it by the number of times we turn over our assets (*TR*), we would get our over-all return on total assets before taxes (*RTA*):

$$RTA_{BT} = OR \times TR$$

Return on Total Assets before taxes = Operating Ratio × Turnover Ratio

Put another way:

$$\frac{\text{Net Operating Income}}{\text{Total Assets}} = \frac{\text{Net Operating Income}}{\text{Net Revenues}} \times \frac{\text{Net Revenues,}}{\text{Total Assets}} \text{ or}$$

$$\frac{NOI}{TA} = \frac{NOI}{NR} \times \frac{NR}{TA}$$

Some other interesting relationships are brought out when the effects of various turnover ratios and operating margins and their impact on the rate of return on total assets are considered. The chart below is helpful in this discussion.

	Case 1	Case 2	Case 3	Case 4
Turnover Ratio (*TR*)	High	High	Low	Low
Operating Ratio (*OR*)	Low	High	Low	High
Return on Total Assets (*RTA*)	Average	High	Low	Average

Case 1 suggests that an extremely high turnover factor coupled with an exceedingly low operating ratio (margin) will generally result in an average rate of return on total assets. Many merchandising firms fall into this particular category. As illustrated by Case 2 on the other hand, a high turnover of assets coupled with a very high margin will result in a very high rate of return. Many firms exhibit these characteristics, particularly those with new products which are in high demand. Case 3 depicts a situation in which there is a low turnover factor combined with a high margin and a low (possibly even negative) rate of return. Many of the nation's stagnant or declining industries bear witness to this. Finally, Case 4 represents a firm with a low turnover combined with a high operating ratio. The result of this combination, generally, will be an average rate of return. Many of our public utilities fit into this particular category.

It is important to note that these particular relationships have nothing to do with the manner in which a firm is financed. That is, regardless of how the various financial resources are derived, given both the turnover of assets and the operating ratio, the over-all rate of return before taxes would be the same.

Return on Common Equity

A second aspect to be considered in the analysis of profitability is the rate of return on common equity (RCE). This ratio relates the earnings available to common stockholders (EAC) to the recorded claims of these residual claimants—including common stock, surplus, and all appropriations of surplus—that is, the total common equity (CE). In the example of Table 22-3, RCE is 14 per cent for Firm A ($EAC/CE = \$14,750/\$105,000$). This ratio is a function primarily of the over-all return on total assets, the explicit cost of prior capital claims, and the amount of prior capital claims.[4] It is used to compare the performance of a given company's equity investments with those of other companies. If two companies are alike in quality (risk), are equally well-known and achieve different rates of return on common equity and there is no indication that the future will be any different from the past, the company with the higher RCE will be favored by investors and a greater market valuation of the firm will result. For manufacturing firms a standard for RCE is 10–15 per cent; for public utilities, 6–10 per cent.

Trading on the Equity

The return on common equity should exceed the return on total assets in "normal" times. This is so because of the favorable results of *trading*

[4] *Prior capital claims* refer to all those claims on assets and earnings prior to those of the residual claimants—namely, the common stockholders.

on the equity. Trading on the equity occurs when capital other than that of the residual owners is employed in the enterprise. By this is meant the use of both long- and short-term debt and all classes of preference stock. The essence of trading on the equity is the use of these funds either at no explicit cost or at a limited explicit cost while their employment in the enterprise yields an explicit return in excess of the explicit cost. For example, if a firm can borrow other people's funds for, say, 4 per cent, and if it can use these funds productively in the enterprise at, say, 8 per cent, it is obvious that if it were to borrow $100, this sum, when employed, would earn $8 but have an explicit cost of $4, so that $4 remains "left over." The $4 that is "left over" accrues to the benefit of the residual claimants: the common stockholders. As a consequence, their return is enhanced by trading on the equity. Tables 22-1, 22-2, and 22-3 further illustrate this concept. Note that Firms A, B, and C have the same amount of total assets but that each has been financed in different ways. It was assumed above that the business risks of all three firms are essentially of the same kind and quality. All the firms may be said to be trading on their equity, but each generates a return on its residual claimants' commitments in varying magnitudes depending on the extent to which prior capital claims are employed in the enterprise and the explicit cost of these prior capital claims. These rates of return on owners' claims demonstrate the extent to which prior claim commitments tend to magnify rates of return to residual claim commitments. Notice that in each case the return on total assets after taxes (but before interest) is different. This is because interest expenses are tax-deductible. Notice, also, however, that *RCE* exceeds *RTA* in each case but in varying degrees, depending on the extent to which a firm is trading on its equity. Case A has the least amount of financial leverage (as trading on the equity is often called); its ratio of prior capital claims to owners' capital is the smallest. As a result, its *RCE* is also the smallest. As their degree of financial leverage increases, the *RCE*'s of Cases B and C also increase.

This magnification of owners' returns explains why firms are lured to trade on the equity. The nature of trading on the equity, however, also explains why firms hesitate to assume "too much" financial leverage. Indeed, the hoped-for benefits of trading on the equity can be a real problem if earnings fail to measure up to expectations. To illustrate, let us assume that in each of the three cases presented above net sales decline by 10 per cent. This sales picture can emerge either because prices decline while the quantity of goods sold remains the same, or because the quantity sold declines while prices stay the same, or both. In this case we will assume that the number of units sold remains the same and that the decline in net sales revenue results from a decrease in price. Thus we can assume further that the cost of goods sold remains the same and that the other variable operating expenses have not yet been adjusted. The results are shown in Table 22-4. Notice that in all three cases RCE declined. But notice also that the degree of decline was greatest for the more heavily levered firms. This phenomenon is caused by the fixed nature of the claims on income of the prior claim commitments. These fixed claims tend to act as a lever by which changes in income available for these claims are magnified many times over in the return on the owner's commitment.

Notice, however, that if the explicit cost of prior capital claims, measured as a percentage of the total prior claim commitment, is less than the return on total assets after taxes but before interest, trading on equity ceases to be advantageous. It is disadvantageous because the firm has paid more on the average for the use of funds (other than the residual claimants) than they effectively earned after taxes.

For example, in Table 22-4, although it is true that the relative decline in the return on common equity in Cases B and C is greater than that in Case A from what they had been in Table 22-3, trading on the equity continued to be profitable in all cases because the average cost of prior capital claims was less than the average return of these funds when employed in the business. Moreover, the cost of prior capital claims varied from firm to firm.[5] Some prior capital claims do not carry any explicit cost in the sense that no dollar sums are expended for their use. Some of a firm's short-term liabilities are of this nature. Thus the cost of prior capital claims will probably be considerably less, on the average, than the explicit rate of interest or dividends on other nonzero-cost forms of prior capital claims. As long as the expected average RTA_{BT} exceeds the expected average explicit cost of prior capital claims, it would appear advantageous to continue trading on the equity. (This conclusion, however, ignores the possible increase in risk which we have considered in other discussions.) In the case of Firm A, the average, explicit cost after taxes, but before interest and preferred dividends of all prior capital claims, is 3.63 per cent, and is calculated as follows:

$$\text{Explicit Cost of Prior Capital Claims} = \frac{\text{Explicit Costs of Prior Capital Claims (After Tax)}}{\text{Total Prior Capital Claims}}$$

---

[5] The student should recognize that we are discussing explicit costs—that is, the dollar payments that need to be made to command the use of certain dollar resources. These are different from opportunity costs, which usually relate to losses realized whenever a possible course of action is not pursued and from other implicit costs—those borne, but not incurred as dollar costs.

Table 22-4
Comparative Income Statements of Three Firms, After a 10 Per Cent Decrease in Net Sales

	Firm A	Firm B	Firm C
Net sales	$135,000	$135,000	$135,000
Cost of goods sold	100,000	100,000	100,000
Gross income	35,000	35,000	35,000
Operating expenses	18,750	18,750	18,750
Net operating income	16,250	16,250	16,250
Other income	1,500	1,500	1,500
Total income	17,750	17,750	17,750
Interest expense	270	1,475	1,768
Income before taxes	17,480	16,275	15,982
Taxes (50%)	8,740	8,138	7,991
Income after taxes	8,740	8,137	7,991
Preferred dividends	1,500	1,500	1,500
Earnings available for common (Residual earnings)	$ 7,240	$ 6,637	$ 6,491
RCE	$ 7,240 / $105,000 = 6.9%	$ 6,637 / $ 84,000 = 7.9%	$ 6,491 / $ 75,000 = 8.7%
Explicit Cost of prior capital claims (after tax) $\left(\dfrac{\text{Cost of prior capital claims}}{\text{Prior capital claims}}\right)$	$ 1,635 / $ 45,000 = 3.62%	$ 2,238 / $ 66,000 = 3.39%	$ 2,384 / $ 75,000 = 3.18%

or

$$k_e = \frac{\$1,635}{\$45,000} = 3.63 \text{ per cent}$$

The numerator of the equation is derived by multiplying the total explicit cost of interest expense by $(1 - \text{income tax rate})$ and adding the resultant to the amount of the preferred dividends. Taking Case B as an example, we get

$$\begin{array}{ll} \text{Explicit Cost of Prior} \\ \text{Capital Claims} \end{array} = \begin{array}{l} [\text{Interest Expense} \times (1 - \text{Income Tax Rate})] \\ + \text{amount of preferred dividends} \end{array}$$

or

$$k_e = \$1,475 \ (1 - .50) + \$1,500$$
$$= \$738 + \$1,500$$
$$= \$2,238$$

Relating this dollar amount to the dollar amount of total prior capital claims, we get

$$k_e = \frac{\$2,238}{\$66,000} = 3.39 \text{ per cent}$$

The explicit cost of prior claim capital is 3.39 per cent; for Firm C it is 3.18 per cent.

If we measure the degree of trading on the equity (financial leverage) by relating total prior claim capital to total capital so that

$$L = \frac{PCC}{TA}$$

where

$L = \text{leverage}$
$PCC = \text{prior claim capital}$
$TA = \text{total assets}$

and multiply each of the computed costs of levered capital by their respective L factors, we get the minimum rate of return required on total assets necessary to equal a zero per cent rate of return on common equity —a breakeven rate. Any rate of return earned on total capital beyond that would result in positive returns to the common equity; rates earned on total capital less than these breakeven rates would result in negative returns. For example, in Case B $k_e = 3.39$ per cent, $L = 44$ per cent ($66,000/$150,000), and the minimum rate required on total assets to yield a zero per cent return on common equity (RCE_{B-E}) is 1.49 per cent, or

$$RCE_{B-E} = k_e \times L$$
$$= 3.39 \text{ per cent} \times 44 \text{ per cent}$$
$$= 1.49 \text{ per cent}$$

where the subscript, $_{B-E}$, refers to breakeven. For Case A this rate is 1.086 per cent (3.62 per cent $\times$ 30 per cent) and for Case C it is 1.59 per cent (3.18 per cent $\times$ 50 per cent).

Short-term Ratios

Analysis of a firm's short-term position from an external point of view traditionally has centered on the computation of a series of ratios such as those, or variants thereof, presented in Table 22-3, Section B, "Short-term Ratios." Once again, those ratios are typically relied upon by creditors rather than by financial management. Heavy reliance on this core of short-term ratios is necessary for creditors because in many instances all the financial information they have available is contained in a firm's balance sheet and income statement which thus form the basic data for analysis. Credit rating agencies, such as Dun & Bradstreet, Inc., also base their judgments to a large extent on publicly available data which typically take the form of balance sheets and income statements.

The *purpose of ratio analysis of the short-term position* by potential or present suppliers of capital is to derive a picture of the capacity of a firm to meet its short-term obligations out of its short-term resources— that is, to estimate the risk of supplying capital to the firm. A core of short-term ratios has arisen over the years which, when viewed *in toto* and with respect to risk, is expected to yield a rough approximation of this bill-paying capacity.

Current Ratio. The first ratio typically used in short-term analysis is the current ratio (CR). This relates the sum of the firm's current assets (CA) to the sum of its current liabilities (CL). Included in the current assets are cash, and all items that are expected to be turned into cash within one year in the normal course of operations. These typically include cash, marketable securities, trade accounts receivable, and inventories. Current liabilities consist of all recorded debt coming due in the short term—that is, in a year or less. Items typically included in this category are wages, interest, accounts, notes, and taxes payable. For most manufacturing firms a ratio of 2:1 has traditionally been considered a benchmark of adequate liquidity. For public utilities this ratio is not very important. A satisfactory current ratio for any given firm is difficult to judge. For the three firms in Table 22-3, the respective current ratios were 3:1 ($60,000/$20,000), 3.8:1 ($60,000/$16,000) and 3.3:1 ($60,000/$18,000) which, when measured against the 2:1 standard, makes them appear to have adequate short-term assets from which to meet the short-term liabilities. Remember, however, that this ratio, as well as many others, relies only on balance sheet data which, as we know, are a statement of conditions at a particular moment of time. The balance sheet is static in nature and its data represents stocks rather than flows. What, for instance, will be the relation of current assets to current liabilities tomorrow? When will these short-term debts be coming due? All at once? Or gradually over the year? And what about preferred dividend payments? Surely, the firm regards these as obligations but, because of their legal nature (legally they are always viewed as part of the ownership), no provision is made for them in the short run (or in the long run for that matter) on a balance sheet. Provisions for these disbursements, and others that might not be found on a balance sheet under the category of short-term debt (such as bond retirements by means of a sinking fund), are made in the cash budget. Also, can all the current assets really be converted into cash at these recorded values? Perhaps not. The quality of the short-term assets would be a pervasive factor in this analysis. Moreover, end-of-the-year financial statements can always be made to "look good." That is to say, the current ratio as well as all other short-term position ratios can be manipulated so that varying results will ensue. For example, a firm having the following short-term position on December 28th has a current ratio of 1.5:1 ($75,000/$50,000). Now, to satisfy

Current Assets		Current Creditors	
Cash	$10,000	Account payable	$10,000
Account receivable	40,000	Notes payable	40,000
Inventory	25,000		
	$75,000		$50,000

the holder of the $40,000 note (say, a bank), the company decides to sell off its $40,000 in accounts receivable to a factor. (Let us ignore, for purposes of this illustration, the costs of selling the receivables and the time and terms required to consummate the transaction.) If the firm takes the proceeds of the sale and pays off the note on December 31st, the day on which the balance sheet is made up, the current position would be as follows:

Current Assets		Current Liabilities	
Cash	$10,000	Accounts Payable	$10,000
Inventory	25,000		—
	$35,000		$10,000

The current ratio then would be 3.5:1 ($35,000/$10,000). The provisos presented here regarding the current ratio obviously apply as well to other short-term position ratios and tend to point up some of the inherent dangers of relying too heavily on ratios alone.

Acid-Test Ratio: The current ratio was developed many decades ago as a means of deriving a rough idea of the liquidity of a firm.[6] Because some question might arise regarding their possible value in the event of liquidation, the typically least liquid of all the current assets, inventories, is often dropped from the numerator. The result—the ratio of the sum of cash, marketable securities, and receivables to current liabilities— is often presumed to be a better guide to the short-term debt-paying capacity of a firm. Actually this ratio does not entirely supplant the current ratio; rather it partially supplements it and, when used in conjunction with it, tends to give a better picture of the firm's ability to meet its short-term debt out of short-term assets. The acid-test ratio (ATR), as this relationship is often called, for Firm A is 1.5:1 ($30,000/$20,000). The traditional standard for this ratio is 1:1.

A variant of this ratio, which can be useful for financial management and should be more meaningul for creditors (especially short-term ones), is the number of days needed to generate cash out of operations to cover current liabilities. We can use some of the data given in Tables 22-1 and 22-2 to illustrate this point. Assume that in all these cases everything remains the same except the composition of current assets. Suppose instead of the current assets shown in Table 22-1, the distribution of current assets for each firm is as follows:

	Firm A	Firm B	Firm C
Cash	$ 4,000	$ 7,000	$ 2,000
Marketable securities	6,000	5,000	4,000
Receivables (net)	8,000	3,000	6,000
Inventories	42,000	45,000	48,000
	$60,000	$60,000	$60,000

[6] Brown, *op. cit.,* 13.

Also assume from the given income statements of Table 22-2 that the funds generated from operations consist of earnings available for common less common dividends but plus depleciation—that is, the difference between net sales (assuming they represent collected funds) and all cash expenses during the period. In this event, the cash generated from operations for each firm will be as follows:

	Firm A	Firm B	Firm C
Earnings available for common	$14,740	$14,137	$13,991
Common dividends	8,000	8,000	8,000
Income available for retention	6,740	6,137	5,991
Depleciation	2,000	2,000	2,000
Net cash generated from operations	$ 8,740	$ 8,137	$ 7,991

If we relate the cash generated by operations, a flow concept, to the stock concept of the difference between current liabilities and the quick assets (cash, marketable securities, and receivables), a notion of the number of days of operations that are necessary to take up the slack in these two figures is had. The formula is

$$RD = \frac{CL - QA}{CGO} \times 360 \text{ days}$$

where

RD = number of days required to cover current liabilities net of quick assets

QA = quick assets

CGO = annual cash generated from operations (after dividends)

Solving for Firm A, we get

$$RD = \frac{\$20,000 - \$18,000}{\$8,740} \times 360 \text{ days}$$
$$= \frac{\$2,000}{\$8,740} \times 360 \text{ days}$$
$$= 82 \text{ days}$$

It will take Firm A eighty-two days to generate enough cash out of operations to take care of the deficiency of quick assets to current liabilities. For Firm B it will take forty-four days; for Firm C, 27 days.

This, of course, assumes that preferred dividends and common dividends will continue to be paid (at the end of the year instead of quarterly, which is typical). In reality, under financial stress these distributions of cash will probably cease and hence the cash generated from operations will be augmented by these sums. Adding $9,500 to each of the firms' previous totals of $8,740, $8,137, and $7,991, we get $18,240 for Firm A, $17,637 for Firm B, and $17,491 for Firm C. (The verification of each of the calculations is left to the student.) With the new *CGO* figures, the number of days required for Firm A is now thirty-nine; for Firm B, twenty; for Firm C, 123.[7]

Absolute-Liquidity Ratio. As a logical consequence of the concept of eliminating inventories as a liquid asset in the acid-test ratio because of their questionable value in liquidation, another step is taken in an effort to derive a still more meaningful measure of liquidity. Although receivables are generally more liquid in nature than inventories, there may be doubt concerning their liquidity also. By eliminating receivables and inventories another measure of liquidity is had by relating the sum of cash and marketable securities to the current liabilities. Because 50 per cent is an acceptable standard for the absolute-liquidity ratio (*ALR*), Firm A's 1:1 ratio ($20,000/$20,000) appears to be adequate. This ratio, too, is not designed to supplant entirely either the current ratio or the acid-test ratio. It is often used in conjunction with them as well as with the ratios discussed later.

Inventory-Turnover Ratio. Determination of the rate at which various short-term assets are converted to cash has often been a concomitant of short-term ratio analysis. One of these ratios is the inventory-turnover ratio (*IT*). This ratio relates the cost of goods sold during a given period to the average amount of inventory outstanding during that period. It is computed by the formula[8]

$$\frac{\text{Cost of Goods Sold}}{\dfrac{\text{Beginning Inventory} + \text{Ending Inventory}}{2}}$$

For Firm A the turnover of inventory during the year is 3.3 times ($100,-000/$30,000). This ratio establishes the average yearly rate at which

[7] Obviously, the analysis used to determine the number of days needed to generate cash out of operations to cover current liabilities net of quick assets can be used in a similar fashion for all the current assets. It can also be used for just the cash assets. For a more complete treatment, *see:* Harold Bierman, Jr., "Measuring Financial Liquidity," (Ithaca, N.Y.: Graduate School of Business and Public Administration, Cornell University, n.d.), reprinted from *The Accounting Review*, 35 (October 1960).

[8] For convenience, Dun & Bradstreet, Inc., uses the ratio of net sales to inventories to compute *IT*.

inventories are turned into sales, which are later converted to cash. By itself, this ratio may indicate the extent to which inventories have been used in the enterprise. One might be led to believe that (other things equal) the higher the ratio the better, because it will indicate greater sales with the same inventory or the same level of sales with less investment in inventory, or both. But how about the sales that are lost because of the maintenance of low inventories or even periodic stockouts? Is the date on which the balance sheet is made up a time when inventories are seasonably low, thus distorting the ratio? And what about all the costs incurred as a result of frequent reordering or production runs? Or the costs of storing large accumulations of inventory out of one large production run? Obviously, these questions are serious and need to be answered before the value of this ratio in the analysis can be established. Unlike the current ratio and acid-test ratio there is no generally accepted standard for the inventory ratio, but comparison with other firms in the industry may provide a clue as to whether Firm A's *IT* is relatively good or bad.

Receivables-Turnover Ratio. The receivables-turnover ratio (*RT*) relates the net credit sales of a firm to recorded receivables. For Firm A the receivables turnover is fifteen times ($150,000/$10,000) (assuming sales are credit ones). This ratio indicates the rate at which cash is generated by the turnover (or collection) of receivables. This is not immediately apparent from the receivables-turnover ratio itself, however. Consequently, a variant of it is often employed. This is known as the *average collection period* (*ACP*) and can be found by dividing 360 days by the receivables turnover (360/*RT*). The result would then indicate the yearly average number of days receivables are outstanding, or the yearly average number of days it takes to convert a firm's receivables into cash. For Firm A the average collection period on receivables (*ACP*) is twenty-four days (360/15). This would indicate that the firm was collecting its receivables on the average of twenty-four days during the year. There are no special standards by which to gauge either of these relationships, although comparison with industry averages may prove useful.

When compared with a firm's terms of sales, however, this kind of information can serve as a rough guide to the efficiency of the credit and collection system of the firm. On the other hand, a high *RT* or low *ACP*, both ordinarily considered desirable, may indicate several other points that would detract from these apparently good signs. For example, a firm may be too strict in its credit policies, taking only the highest-quality credit risks. This would most assuredly produce a high *RT* relative to the terms of sale. Low-credit risks, as a class, take their discounts and/or pay their bills when due. Thus the *ACP* relative to the terms of sale under these conditions will be quite short. But what of the sales the firm misses because of this strict credit policy? Might it not be possible to increase the earnings of the firm (and hence the value of the ownership) by extending credit to other customers? The additional sales will generate earnings for the firm as long as the additional revenues derived from them exceeds the additional cost incurred as a result. The contribution to overhead that additional sales make may be another reason to relax existing strict credit standards.

As an adjunct to these two relationships, *aging of accounts receivable* is often done to gauge the adequacy of credit and collection policies. This is an array of the amount of receivables due in each of several time periods. The trend in the age of distribution of accounts receivable may provide information useful in credit or collection evaluation. The data in Table 22-5 may help to illustrate this point. Assume the company bills its customers on a 2/20, *n*/60 basis.

Table 22-5
Age of Outstanding Accounts Receivable

	Date				
	Jan. 1, 19x6	April 1	July 1	Oct. 1	Jan. 1, 19x7
1–20 days	30%	32%	35%	40%	40%
21–60 days	45%	45%	44%	45%	45%
61–90 days	20%	19%	17%	13%	12%
91 days and over	5%	4%	4%	2%	3%

In this situation it is apparent that some changes have occurred which are probably not just random or seasonal in nature. Based on what we know of the terms of trade (2/20, *n*/60), we can suggest that this firm's customers are not taking advantage of their cash discounts as we would expect them to. Also we can see that 25 per cent of trade customers were delinquent in the first period. Through various promotional devices, however, this firm was able to increase the total percentage paid within the sixty-day period. Continued efforts by the firm along these lines may be called for, but not without risk. If its credit policies become more stringent and it refuses to sell to delinquent accounts except on a COD basis, for example, it may lose some sales. The question is: Is the additional loss in sales sufficiently offset by the savings resulting from smaller investments in receivables? When the aging information is combined with the average collection period data, a firm has a rough guide to the health of its outstanding receivables. For example, Dun & Bradstreet, Inc., suggests: "The average collection period should be no more than one-third greater than the net selling terms of a particular business enterprise that normally sells its merchandise on open-book account."[9] The recommended average collection period in our example would be

$$ACP = 60 + (1/3 \times 60) = 80 \text{ days}$$

and, by this standard, when this average is exceeded or not met our credit collection policies should be reviewed.

Long-term Position Ratios

The beginning of an external analysis of a firm's long-term position begins with an analysis of a firm's profitability (as discussed earlier in this chapter). Those profitability ratios will not be duplicated here, although their importance for long-term analysis cannot be ignored. Bearing this in mind, let us turn our attention to the other long-term ratios.

Debt-to-Equity Ratio. This ratio relates all the recorded creditors' claims on assets, to the owners' recorded claims. The creditor category for our purposes includes all debt, whether long-term or short-term. The ratio could also be computed with preferred stock classed as a creditor rather than an ownership claim. For our purposes the owners' claim will consist of common stock at par or stated value plus all surplus items (such as capital surplus and retained earnings) and designations of surplus items (such as reserve for contingencies and reserve for plant expansion).

The treatment of preferred stock as a creditor claim may cause students to look askance, because prior to this time they were accustomed to regarding preferred stock as an ownership commitment. Preferred stock *is* an ownership commitment, but only in the eyes of the law. Very few preferred stocks exhibit other characteristics of an ownership security. Because we are interested in the financial aspects of business enterprise, we should look to the financial nature of preferred stock to determine whether it would be treated as debt or as equity.

From a financial point of view, the treatment of preferred stock as a creditor claim or as an owner claim depends on the nature of the preferred stock and the purpose of the analysis. We must look at the various covenants incorporated in the preferred stock agreement, the relative

[9] *How to Control Accounts Receivable for Profits* (New York: Dun & Bradstreet, 1959), 28.

stature of its claim on assets, the relative adequacy of earnings to take care of preferred dividends, and the purpose of analysis. If, after reviewing these factors, the preferred stock more nearly resembles a bond, it ought to be treated as a creditor-type claim. On the other hand, if the covenants and other factors indicate that the preferred stock more nearly resembles common stock in nature, then it ought to be included as part of its ownership claim. In most cases preferreds are more closely related to bonds than to common stock and hence for most types of analysis it ought to be treated accordingly—that is, in most cases preferred stocks are merely a variant of a bond offering.[10]

The purpose of the debt-to-equity ratio (*DE*) is to derive an idea of the amount of capital supplied to the firm by the owners, and its obverse: the amount of asset "cushion" available to creditors in the event of liquidation. Fundamental to financing business enterprises is the notion that, under ordinary circumstances, the owners of an enterprise should assume most of the risk of an enterprise. This is done by common stockholders, who have the lowest priority on the assets and earnings of the firms. Firms with relatively low risk can afford to secure much, if not most, of their total capital requirements from creditors. This is illustrated in the case of public utilities, in which the relative variance in expected earnings is small. Firms with higher relative variance in expected earnings, must have larger equity contributions. Thus business firms as a group average about 65 per cent common equity, creditors being willing to assume, on the average, little of the risk of the enterprise.[11]

From Table 22-3, we can see that the debt-to-equity ratio (*DE*) for Firm A is .43:1 ($45,000/$105,000). (This was also the formula for computing the leverage ratio, *L*.) The lower this ratio is, the more of total capital are the owners supplying. Depending on the estimated evaluation of risk, a judgment concerning the "proper" level for this ratio can be made. The lower this ratio is, the more asset "cushion" do the creditors

[10] For a more thorough treatment of this topic, *see:* Paul M. Van Arsdell, *Problem Manual in Corporation Finance* (Champaign, Ill.: Stipes, 1958), 8–11; and Paul M. Van Arsdell, *Principles of Corporation Finance* (Champaign, Ill.: Stipes, 1959), 92, 241, 256.

[11] Owners of small business firms have to supply a much larger percentage of their total capital requirements (about 90 per cent) because of factors other than risk considerations. Lack of knowledge concerning sources of funds may be one factor. A second may be found in the general unwillingness of banks to accept "small business" loans of significant magnitude. Also there is the lack of adequate institutional arrangements to provide long-term capital. Small Business Investment Companies are a partial, although at times insufficient, answer to this problem. Despite these and other nonrisk considerations, however, most small business ventures are highly risky, and it is questionable how much smaller the owners' contribution to total capital would be in the absence of these nonrisk factors.

have for their claims. In the case of Firm A, for example, the liquidation value of assets could shrink 70 per cent before creditors would be impaired—(a variant of the debt-to-equity (DE) ratio was used: the ratio of owners' equity to total recorded assets). On the average a DE ratio of 1:1 is acceptable. For firms with relatively stable earnings, this ratio might be as much as 2.5:1. This might also be true of firms experiencing rapidly growing earnings. For firms with highly erratic earnings, this ratio should be no more than about .33:1, according to accepted standards, and most of the debt in that case should be short-term.

Coverage Ratios. The interest-coverage ratio (IC) is frequently employed in external financial analysis, especially by firms that rate bonds such as Standard and Poor's Corporation and Moody's Investor Service. The traditional method of computing this relationship has been to relate the total income of the firm to all interest expenses paid during a given period. From this, the analyst hopes to derive some indication of a firm's past ability to meet the interest expenses of a period (usually one year) out of that period's income. Indeed, perhaps no other ratio is watched more closely by external analysts than this one. From it they hope to glean an idea of the extent to which a firm's earnings can contract before it is unable to meet interest payments out of current earnings. Obviously, the implicit assumption here is that the average historical performance of the firm under review will be its average performance in the future. As we know, this may or may not be true. In the absence of evidence to the contrary, historical data will be used by suppliers of capital to make such judgments regarding the future. For Firm A, the interest-coverage ratio (IC) was 121 times ($32,750/$270), which would be considered more than ample because for most firms with highly variable earnings the accepted minimum standard is usually about 6 to 8 times. But the fact is that interest expenses, as well as all other expenses, are met out of cash. Hence, to get an idea of a firm's long-run liquidity position by which it will meet its interest expenses out of operations, the total cash flow for the period ought to be used. But in addition to interest expenses, a sinking fund is often required; this, too (unless it is a discretionary one), represents a fixed obligation of the firm. So to be more accurate the analyst ought to relate the annual cash flow before interest to the sum of interest expenses and sinking-fund payments. This is referred to as the *debt-cash-flow-coverage (CFC_D) ratio*. If there are long-term installment notes or serial bonds coming due in the period, they, too, would be included in the denominator. Assuming Firm B's Subordinated 5's provide for a required annual sinking-fund payment of 5 per cent of the amount outstanding, the total required sinking fund payment would amount to $1,250. Because the sinking fund payment is made after taxes and because we wish to derive a before-tax coverage figure, we have to adjust the amount of the sinking fund payment for this. This can be accomplished by dividing the payment by $1 - T$ where T is the tax rate. Doing this for Firm B, we get $2,500 ($1,250/1 - .50). Thus the denominator of this ratio consists of the interest expense incurred plus the tax-adjusted sinking-fund payment. For Firm B the denominator is $3,975 ($1,475 + $2,500). The numerator of the ratio is the firm's income before interest and taxes plus depleciation. In the case of Firm B, it amounts to $34,750 ($32,750 + $2,000). For Firm B, using the formula

$$CFC_D = \frac{CF}{I + \dfrac{SF_D}{1 - T}}$$

where

CFC_D = debt cash flow coverage
CF = annual cash flow, before interest and taxes
I = interest payments
SF_D = sinking-fund payments on debt
T = the income tax rate

we get

$$CFC_D = \frac{\$34,750}{\$3,975} = 8.7 \text{ times}$$

This is considerably less impressive than its interest-coverage ratio of twenty-two times, but also considerably more meaningful. Unfortunately, there are no standards yet developed for this ratio as there are for the IC ratio. We would suggest, along lines similar to those used for the IC ratio, that cash flow before interest and taxes should cover service of debt—interest and sinking funds—by at least an average number of times so that the charges are covered at least once even by the worst expected annual cash flow. Firms with great instability of earnings will need a larger coverage; those with highly stable earnings will require a smaller coverage.

For Firms A and C the cash flow coverage of their debt service is 129 times ($34,750/$270) and 8.1 times ($34,750/$4,268) respectively.

The *preferred-dividend-coverage ratio (PDC)* may be employed in those cases in which firms have preferred stock outstanding. It is similar in nature to (but does not supplant) the interest-coverage ratio. It is computed by dividing the total income by the sum of both interest expenses and preferred dividends. For Firm A the preferred-dividend-coverage ratio is nineteen times ($32,750/$1,770). The purpose of this ratio is to measure the firm's ability to meet a given period's interest expenses and preferred dividend distributions out of the income for that period (usually one year). The higher this ratio is, the greater the shrinkage in income can a firm experience before there is any threat that it will be unable to meet the income requirements of debt holders and preferred stockholders. For preferred stocks to achieve the same quality status as bonds, the standard coverage acceptable is six to eight times. But for the same reasons that the interest-coverage ratio was wanting, the preferred-dividend-coverage ratio, as traditionally computed, is inadequate. To correct for this, we use the *preferred-stock-cash-flow-coverage* (CFC_{PS}) *ratio.* To employ this ratio we must again use cash flow per annum before interest and taxes in the numerator. The denominator will consist of the interest expense, the total required sinking-fund payment, and the preferred dividend obligation. If we assume a sinking-fund payment for preferred of $1,250, the before-tax requirement would be $2,500 ($1,250/ $1 - T$). The preferred dividends also have to be adjusted to account for the fact that it takes more dollars before taxes to cover preferred dividends than to cover interest, because the former is not tax-deductible. Therefore, instead of the $1,500 preferred dividend obligation shown on the income statement, we should use $3,000 ($1,500/$1 - .50$) in our denominator for this class of securities. For Firm B, using the formula

$$CFC_{PS} = \frac{CF}{I + \dfrac{SF_D}{1-T} + \dfrac{PD}{1-T} + \dfrac{SF_{PS}}{1-T}}$$

where

CFC_{PS} = preferred stock cash flow coverage
CF = annual cash flow before interest and taxes
I = interest payments
SF_D = sinking-fund payments on debt
PD = preferred dividends
SF_{PS} = sinking-fund payments on preferred stock
T = the income tax rate

we get

$$CFC_{PS} = \frac{\$34,750}{\$1,475 + \dfrac{\$1,250}{1 - .50} + \dfrac{\$1,500}{1 - .50} + \dfrac{\$1,250}{1 - .50}}$$

$$= \frac{\$34,750}{\$1,475 + \$2,500 + \$3,000 + \$2,500}$$

$$= \frac{\$34,750}{\$9,475}$$

$$= 3.7 \text{ times}$$

For Firms A and C, cash flow coverage of preferred stock comes to 6.0 times ($34,750/$5,770) and 3.6 times ($34,750/$9,768), respectively, if we assume the same sinking-fund requirement for each firm.

Assuming that Firm C's mortgage bonds have a $1,000 per year sinking-fund requirement in addition to the other sinking-fund requirements on subordinated debt and preferred stock, we leave it to the reader to verify that the cash flow coverage of the preferred stock in this case is slightly less than three times.

Because the interests of management and those of legal residual owners may be at variance, and because a dividend policy—once instituted on a regular quarterly or yearly basis—takes on the characteristics of a "fixed" income claim of the holders of common stock, to measure the adequacy of past years' income to meet dividends disbursed in those years, an extension of this "coverage" concept has emerged in recent years. This extension is known as the *common-dividend-coverage (CDC) ratio* and relates the amount of income available to common stockholders to the amount of common dividends paid; it attempts to measure the extent to which a firm's earnings available for common stock are capable of meeting dividends paid during a given period. For Firm A, the common-dividend-coverage ratio (CDC) is 1.84:1 ($14,740/$8,000). But to be consistent with our cash flow coverage notions, we ought to relate earnings before interest and taxes to the sum of the capital claims on earnings in that period. If we are to do this, the dividends on the common stock ought to be adjusted to reflect the amount of earnings that have to be earned before taxes to meet the dividend requirement on an after-tax basis. The analyst uses the *common-stock-cash-flow-coverage (CFC_{CS}) ratio* to accomplish this end. For all the firms in our example, the adjusted common dividends amount to $16,000 ($8,000/1 − .50). For Firm B, using the formula

$$CFC_{CS} = \frac{CF}{I + \dfrac{SF_D}{1-T} + \dfrac{PD}{1-T} + \dfrac{SF_{PS}}{1-T} + \dfrac{CD}{1-T}}$$

where

CFC_{CS} = cash flow coverage of common stock

CD = common dividends (and all the other symbols have the same meanings as used in the preceding examples)

we get

$$CFC_{CS} = \frac{\$34,750}{\dfrac{\$1,475 + \$1,250 + \$1,500 + \$1,250 + \$8,000}{1-.50 \quad 1-.50 \quad 1-.50 \quad 1-.50}}$$

$$= \frac{\$34,750}{\$1,475 + \$2,500 + \$3,000 + \$2,500 + \$16,000}$$

$$= \frac{\$34,750}{\$25,475}$$

$$= 1.4 \text{ times}$$

For Firms A and C, cash flow coverage of common stock dividends is 1.6 times ($34,750/$21,770) and 1.3 times ($34,750/$27,768), respectively.

SUMMARY

This chapter covered a core of ratios extensively used by creditors, businessmen, bond-rating agencies, and other credit agencies. The importance of these ratios is derived from two factors. First, there is the stress that suppliers of capital and institutions and persons that influence these suppliers place on these ratios in their efforts to assess the risk of supplying capital to the enterprise. Second, there are the managerial uses to which some of these ratios may be put. To the extent that achievement of an optimum financial plan is influenced by suppliers of capital, financial management must be aware of the tools suppliers utilize to assess (1) over-all profitability or firm efficiency, (2) return on common equity, (3) short-term risks, and (4) long-term risks of supplying capital. And, although there are many limitations to ratio analysis, accounting data provide the best available approximation to reality and hence are used by analysts as a basis for evaluating risk. Unfortunately, ratio analysis can tell us little about expected rates of return on over-all performance or about the magnitudes of the various ratios that could reasonably be expected in the future.

SUGGESTED READINGS

BELLEMORE, DOUGLAS H. *Security Analysis.* New York: Simmons-Boardman Publishing Corporation, 1959.

BOWLIN, OSWALD D. "The Current Ratio in Current Position Analysis," *Financial Analysts Journal, 19* (March–April 1963), 67–72.

COTTLE, S. and T. WHITMAN. "Twenty Years of Corporate Earnings," *Harvard Business Review, 36* (May–June 1958), 100–14.

FOULKE, ROY A. *Practical Financial Statement Analysis,* 5th ed. New York: McGraw-Hill Book Company, Inc., 1961.

GRAHAM, BENJAMIN, DAVID L. DODD. and SIDNEY COTTLE. *Security Analysis,* 4th ed. New York: McGraw-Hill Book Company, Inc., 1962.

GUTHMANN, HARRY G. *Analysis of Financial Statements,* 4th ed. Englewood Cliffs, N. J.: Prentice-Hall, Inc., 1953.

HELFERT, ERICH A. *Techniques of Financial Analysis.* Homewood, Ill.: Richard D. Irwin, Inc., 1963.

HUNT, PEARSON. "A Proposal for Precise Definitions of 'Trading on the Equity' and 'Leverage,'" *The Journal of Finance, 16* (September 1961), 377–86.

LERNER, EUGENE M. *Readings in Financial Analysis and Investment Management.* Homewood, Ill.: Richard D. Irwin, Inc., 1963.

MAURIELLO, JOSEPH A. *Accounting for the Financial Analyst.* Homewood, Ill.: Richard D. Irwin, Inc., 1965.

MCCLOUD, B. G., JR. "Pitfalls in Statement Analysis," *Bulletin of the Robert Morris Associates, 39* (January 1957), 143–48.

ROBBINS, SIDNEY M. "Investor Guideposts in Comparing Income Statements," *The Journal of Finance, 7* (March 1952), 47–65.

ROBINSON, ROLAND S., and ROBERT W. JOHNSON. *Self-Correcting Problems in Finance.* Okemos, Mich.: R & J Press, 1963.

VAN ARSDELL, PAUL M. *Problem Manual in Corporation Finance.* Champaign, Ill.: Stipes Publishing Company, 1958.

QUESTIONS

22.1 In what way or ways can suppliers of capital influence a firm's cost of capital?

22.2 You are the financial vice president of a large aircraft manufacturing firm and have been asked to speak about the past, present, and future financial status of your firm before the New York Society of Security Analysts. What you say may have considerable influence on your firm's future financing capability. What factors would you consider important to present to this high-level group?

22.3 Set forth in an intuitive way those factors which you regard as impinging upon the business risk of (1) a manufacturing firm, (2) an electric utility, and (3) a merchandising firm.

22.4 As a supplier of capital to a firm doing about 50 per cent of its business in foreign countries, what factors would you want to know about this part of their operations in making a financial analysis of the firm?

22.5 What impact on net income and cash flow would each of the following depreciation methods have, as compared with the straight-line method: (1) sum-of-the-years digits; (2) double-declining balance?

22.6 Of what particular importance is the return on book common equity to common shareholders? To long-term creditors?

22.7 What advantages and/or disadvantages do these three ratios—cash flow coverage of debt, cash flow coverage of preferred diivdends, and cash flow coverage of common dividends—have over the interest-coverage ratio, the preferred-dividend-coverage ratio and the common-dividend-coverage ratio?

22.8 Prepare a critique of the merits and shortcomings of ratio analysis.

22.9 Discuss the merits and shortcomings of treating preferred stock as a variant of long-term debt.

PROBLEMS

22.10 (*a*) Pick an industry of your choice and make a comprehensive analysis of it bringing to bear on it those factors mentioned in the text as well as any other that may come to mind. (*b*) According to this analysis, how would you appraise the risk of firms in the industry in general? (*c*) Select a company in the industry and appraise its risk. (*d*) Would your appraisal of risk be different if you were: (1) the president of the company; (2) a shareholder; or (3) a large insurance company analyst who has to decide whether or not to make a rather substantial loan to the firm? If so, why? If not, why not? (*e*) Make a comprehensive financial analysis of this firm, taking into account information covering the last five years.

22.11 The latest year's sales level for the Osborn Company was slightly less than $7.5 million. Given the firm's present physical capacity, it is estimated that sales can be expanded to a maximum of $8.7 million. Total operating expenses at capacity would be 88 per cent of sales. Of these operating expenses, materials comprised 40 per cent; wages, 15 per cent; depreciation, 5 per cent; property taxes, 2 per cent; rentals, 10 per cent; selling and administrative expenses, 10 per cent; insurance, 2 per cent; and variable manufacturing expense, 16 per cent. (*a*) From the given information, set forth the company's income statement (assume a 50 per cent income tax). (*b*) Set forth the breakeven sales in both absolute amounts and as a percentage of capacity sales.

22.12 Two college students are thinking about setting up a wholesale and discount business to occupy their spare time while they are in college. They wish to avoid heavy overhead expenses so they decided to sell their merchandise both (1) by door-to-door calls on business firms that give gifts to their employees at Christmas time or as part of an incentive program, and (2) by use of a brief, mailorder catalogue. In this way they could avoid expensive showrooms and equipment; they would need only have a small portion of a warehouse to keep their inventory. Some of the more important policy decisions they made are as follows: (1) investment in inventory should be at a "minimum" (this decision was implicit in their capital constraint; they each had very little money for this kind of venture); (2) they will need to hire no one; (3) they will inventory only small, relatively inexpensive items and try to arrange to have access to larger and/or more expensive items through other dealers; (4) they will try to avoid small accounts; (5) they can arrange for an adequate line of credit with a local bank once they establish an earnings record.

(*a*) From this information how would you assess the risk of the venture? Explain. (*b*) Would your assessment be any different if you knew the expected rates of return followed the pattern below and had an equal chance of occuring? Explain.

$$-50\%$$
$$-10\%$$
$$5\%$$

27%
45%
75%

(c) If the probabilities of each of the expected returns were as shown below, how would your assessment vary? Explain.

Probability	Expected Rate of Return
.13	−50%
.12	−10
.10	5
.30	27
.28	45
.07	75

22.13 If a firm's total assets are $7.5 million, its operating margin 12 per cent, and its before-tax return on total assets 16 per cent, compute its (1) turnover ratio and (2) net sales.

22.14 If a firm's turnover ratio is 1.75 times and its operating margin (before taxes) is 17 per cent, what is its before-tax return on total assets?

22.15 The following is the creditors' and owners' side of the balance sheet of the Beatrice Foods Company as of February 1964 (in millions).

Accounts Payable	$13.3
Accrued Payrolls	2.0
Federal Income Taxes	1.3
Other Accrued Taxes	2.7
Deferred Federal Income Tax	3.9
Self-insurance Reserves	0.8
$4 Convertible Preference Stock ($100 par)	9.8
4½% Preferred Stock ($100 par)	7.7
Common Stock ($12.50 par)	47.5
Earned Surplus	80.8
Treasury Stock	3.8

The 4½ preferred stock contains the following major provisions: (1) preference as to assets, (2) preference as to dividends, (3) cumulative, (4) restriction on dividend payments to common shareholders or purchase of common stock by the company if as a result net current assets would fall below $100 per share for the 4½ preferred, (5) one vote per share,

(6) callable, and (7) no pre-emptive rights. The $4 convertible preferreds contain essentially the same provisions as the 4½ preferreds except the former are convertible into common at any time prior to redemption at $53.58. (*a*) Rearrange the given data in a manner suitable for analysis. (*b*) Compute the company's ratio of creditors to owners.

22.16 In 1963 the current assets and current liabilities of the Pittsburgh Plate Glass Company were as follows:

Current Assets (in Millions)

Cash	$ 42.5
U.S. government securities	16.8
Notes and accounts receivable (Net)	108.9
Inventories	148.6
	$316.8

Current Liabilities (in Millions)

Trade accounts payable	$ 46.9
Notes payable	24.0
Accrued taxes	35.3
Other short-term liabilities	39.5
Long-term debt (Current portion)	2.0
	$147.7

Compute the following ratios for this firm: (*a*) current ratio; (*b*) acid-test ratio: (*c*) absolute-liquidity ratio; (*d*) inventory turnover (cost of goods sold in 1963 were $517.6 million); (*e*) receivables turnover (net sales in 1963 were $778.5 million); (*f*) average collection period; (*g*) cash turnover; (*h*) the number of days required to cover short-term debt net of quick assets (cash generated from operations in 1963 was $40.6 million depleciation and $21.7 million of retained earnings for a total of $62.3 million).

22.17 Cascade Natural Gas Corporation was incorporated in the state of Washington in 1953 at which time and in subsequent years it acquired and consolidated a number of small gas companies. The company distributes natural gas in a number of communities in Oregon and Washington having an aggregate population of about 407 thousand. Operating revenues in 1963 were about 21 per cent residential, 19 per cent commercial and 60 per cent industrial. The company's consolidated statements are set forth on page 532.

Gross revenues	$18,272,077
Gas purchases	11,578,929
Operating expenses	1,881,161
Depreciation and amortization	859,431
General taxes	1,126,783
Net operating income	2,825,773
Other income	94,508
Gross income	2,920,281
Interest payments	1,552,816
Debt discount and expense	19,697
Interest charged to construction (cr.)	*166,049*
Miscellaneous expenses	15,161
Preferred dividends	187,500
Common dividends	140,346

Assets

Net fixed assets	$35,401,788
Construction in progress	2,942,511
Cash	633,589
Receivables	2,995,974
Materials and supplies	349,421
Prepayments	127,342
Debt discount and expense	854,627
Gas conversion expense	833,236
Deferred debits	789,192
	$44,927,680

Liabilities and Net Worth

$0.55 Preferred stock (332,023 no par shares)	$ 3,320,230
Common stock ($1)	1,122,769
Capital surplus	5,156,464
Retained earnings	1,055,705
First mortgage bonds, 4⅞'s, Series A, due 1976	8,460,000
First mortgage bonds, 4⅞'s, Series B, due 1978	592,000
First mortgage bonds, 6's, Series C, due 1978	2,000,000
First mortgage bonds, 5¾'s, Series D, due 1982	2,100,000
Subordinated debenture 5½'s, due 1983	6,000,000
Subordinated notes, 6%, due 1975	2,000,000
Convertible subordinated debentures, 5¼'s, due 1970	5,818,700
Other long-term debt, 6%, due 1982	730,000
	$44,927,680

The Sinking-fund requirements of the various bond issues are as follows:

First Mortgage 4⅞'s, '76	$220,000 on April 1963 increasing $5,000 annually thereafter
First Mortgage 4⅞'s, '78	none

First Mortgage 6's, '78	$71,000 semiannually beginning in 1962
First Mortgage 5¾'s, '82	$55,000 semiannually beginning in 1965
Subordinated 5½'s, '83	$300,000 annually, 1967–82
Subordinated Notes, 6's, 75	$160,000 annually, beginning in 1965
Convertible Subordinated Debentures	none
Other Debt	none
$0.55 Preferred Stock (no par)	2.5 per cent of shares outstanding on November 1, 1960 and 5 per cent of such shares thereafter, to begin on November 1, 1961, and continue through 1990. In 1960 there were 358,945 no par shares outstanding.

(*a*) Compute each of the following: (1) interest coverage; (2) preferred dividend coverage; (3) coverage of common dividends. (*b*) Compute each of the following: (1) cash flow coverage of debt; (2) cash flow coverage of preferred dividends; (3) cash flow coverage of common dividends. (*c*) Which of the sets of ratios is more meaningful? Explain.

APPENDIX A FORMS OF BUSINESS ORGANIZATION

There are three types of modern business organizations in which we are basically interested: individual proprietorships, general partnerships, and corporations. Our discussion of these three forms will be brief, however, for we wish only to refresh the student's memory of certain characteristics of each that are pertinent to a study of business finance.

THE PROPRIETORSHIP

The proprietorship is the earliest and simplest form of business organization. The ownership of such a firm consists of one individual: the proprietor. In general, he needs no formal documents or any special licenses to operate in this form. Inasmuch as he assumes all the risk of the enterprise, if it prospers, he receives all the benefits; if it fails, he personally absorbs all the losses. The life of this form of organization is coincidental with the life of the proprietor or the occurrence of bankruptcy, and dissolution would take place concurrently with his decision (or the court's in the case of a court-ordered dissolution) to quit business.

Under this form of organization, there are no bylaws, charters, or other legal documents attesting to the firm's existence, and there are no certificates of ownership. The proprietor is the complete authority in all decisions unless he decides to delegate decisions to some of his employees.

In case of legal failure, the creditors of the business may look to all the assets of the business for satisfaction of their claims. If their debts are not completely satisfied, however, they may also look to the personal assets of the individual; the proprietor's personal bank account, his securities, and his other personal assets may be attached for satisfaction of his business debts. This liability relationship is described as *unlimited liability* for business debts.

The profits of the business are merged with the personal income of the individual and taxed as such unless he elects and is qualified to be taxed as a corporation. (The Internal Revenue Code allows both sole proprietorships and partnerships to be taxed as corporations if they choose to and are qualified.)

534

THE PARTNERSHIP

The partnership, or *general partnership* more specifically, is a form of business organization in which two or more individuals act as co-owners of an enterprise. No papers attesting to its existence need to be drawn up. Each partner has an unlimited liability for the debts of the partnership and, in the absence of any other specified arrangement to the contrary, the business income is allocated equally without regard to the respective capital contributions of the partners. A partner's portion of the income of the partnership, whether or not distributed, is merged with his personal income for income tax purposes unless the partners elect to be taxed as a corporation.

For the legal protection of the several partners, it is desirable to draw up a partnership contract which sets forth, among other things, the contributions of each partner, the method and extent of distributing profits, and the responsibilities and salaries of each of the partners who assume managerial positions. Rules relating to general partnerships have been established by common law; however, most states have adopted the Uniform Partnership Act, which tends to promote general agreement throughout the country.

It is particularly noteworthy that each partner is a general agent for the business. Each one is able to make or enter into a contract that binds the whole partnership. For example, if one partner agrees to purchase a machine, all partners are responsible for the payment of the bill. As a result of this liability and responsibility, one cannot be too cautious in the selection of his partners.

The partnership is terminated when one of the partners withdraws, goes personally bankrupt, or dies—any one of which occurrences, in effect, forces a change in the firm. For example, if one of several partners dies, a new partnership must be created in order to perpetuate the business. Perhaps it will be formed only by the remaining partners, or new partners, or by some combination of both. In any event, existing partners cannot be forced to accept any newcomer into the partnership. Incidentally, the claim against the partnership of a withdrawing partner extends only to the value of his interest in the venture.

The liability of the members of a partnership is joint and several. Any creditors that are not completely satisfied out of a partnership's assets can look to the personal assets of the various partners for payment. Firm assets, however, must be completely extinguished before creditors can look to the personal property of partners. Even when unsatisfied creditors seek payment from partners' personal assets, their claims are subordinated to those of the various partners' personal creditors.

To avoid the unlimited liability of a general partnership, the *limited partnership* form of organization is sometimes used. A business becomes a limited partnership if one or more of the partners possesses limited liability for the activities of the firm and its partners and one or more of the partners is a general partner with unlimited liability. A limited partnership does not ordinarily come into being until a statement expressing the intention of the various partners is filed with the appropriate state official and, of course, in accordance with the governing state laws. Customarily, limited partners may not participate in the management of the business and their liability is limited to the amount of capital they have invested. The limited partner is a silent partner and his name does not appear in the name of the organization.

THE CORPORATION

The corporate form of organization accounts for only about 15 per cent of the total number of business firms in the United States, whereas individual proprietorships account for about 70 per cent. In the United States, however, corporations account for approximately 85 per cent of the sales in the economy. The nature of the corporation and the laws providing for it enable us to understand its popularity for large businesses requiring large amounts of capital.

The corporation, as distinguished from the partnership or proprietorship, is viewed as a separate entity, as if it were an imaginary being. Indeed, it is treated before the eyes of the law as if it were a person capable of entering into a contract in its own name and not in the names of individuals who own or control it. The various states authorize its existence and, depending on the charter provisions, its legal life continues indefinitely regardless of changes in ownership. It has only the powers given to it by the state in which it is incorporated. These powers are set forth in its *charter,* which evidences state sanction for its existence, statutes, and court cases.

The cost of incorporating is customarily not excessive and usually is as low as a few hundred dollars. Each year thereafter the state of incorporation requires payment of franchise taxes, which are typically based upon the par value of securities authorized under the corporate charter.

The granting of a charter customarily requires the provision of the name and address of the corporation, a minimum number (usually very small) of incorporators, the creation of certain officer positions, the submission of a purpose for which the corporation is created (which usually may be very general), and the securities authorized for issue. The initial par value and total amount of common stock of the corporation must, of course, be authorized at this time also.

The corporate form of business enterprise vests its ownership shares with certain characteristics which render them very popular with many investors. Not only are common and preferred stock certificates legally transferable, but they also possess limited liability and are easily transferred from one owner to another without affecting the corporate existence. The common stockholder's liability extends only to the limit of the par or stated value of his share of stock, his personal assets being insulated from creditors for mistakes, errors, and/or debts of the corporation. Consequently, many investors (stockholders) who do not wish to participate in the management of the firm but who would like to be somewhat akin to limited partners, entitled to participate in the profits and losses, may do so without assuming any additional personal liability beyond the par value of their securities. As shares today are sold at or above par or stated value, no liability attaches to them and a present or potential shareholder's loss is limited to the amount of his investment. This provision of limited liability gives the corporate form a distinct advantage over the partnership and the proprietorship.

Ordinarily, if more capital is needed, shares can be sold.[1] If enough shares have not been originally authorized, it is not difficult for the corporation to obtain an amendment of the corporate charter to provide for the issuance of more shares. Usually not all of the authorized shares are issued initially by the corporation, and shares authorized but not outstanding remain available for later issue by the corporation as the need arises.

Each corporation establishes a set of *bylaws* which contain rules binding the directors, officers, and stockholders respecting the operations of the business. The difference between the charter and the bylaws is that the latter are more detailed, although bylaws cannot expand the powers contained in the charter. A common feature of bylaws are rules governing the issuance and transfer of stocks. Also, they invariably contain the time and place for stockholder meetings, methods for calling stockholders' meetings, provisions for directors' meetings, and payment of and provision for special committees. The subjects of dividends and corporate finance are generally covered in the bylaws, the charter, and statutes of the state of incorporation. Obviously the corporation has the power to

---

[1] Obviously, the sale of additional shares is not accomplished as easily as this statement implies.

deal in business related to the purpose for which it was created. It has the power to borrow money, make ordinary contracts, execute notes, write checks, and engage in other financial acts involving the corporation.

A corporation that becomes bankrupt is governed by the bankruptcy laws of the state or federal government, which set down the principles for its liquidation or reorganization. As the owners have limited liability, the creditors of the corporation may not look to any personal assets (except in cases of fraud by directors or officers) of the stockholders, active or inactive, for the payment of the debt claims. Hence the stockholders are protected from any additional liability.

According to corporate law the stockholders of the firm are its legal owners and two primary ownership characteristics are found in most stocks. First, they usually have the right to vote on matters which may materially affect their interests. And second, they are entitled to share in the corporate profits. This is accomplished by declarations of dividends, which are made at the discretion of the board of directors chosen by stockholders. Unpaid profits are reinvested in the corporation. The profits of the corporation are subject to a federal income tax, which amounts to 22 per cent on the first $25,000 of corporate profits and 48 per cent on the profits above this amount. Consequently, for many large businesses the corporate income tax amounts to approximately one half of the profits of the corporation. If the remaining half of the profits are distributed to stockholders, they are subject to another tax by the federal government under the personal income tax.

CHOOSING A FORM OF ORGANIZATION

An individual faced with a choice among the various forms of business organizations must of necessity weigh certain important elements of each before deciding upon the one best suited to his needs. The corporation has a relative disadvantage in fees and franchise taxes and, perhaps, in the income taxes that must be paid. It has the advantage if the entrepreneur has a large amount of personal assets, because his investment in a corporation would then limit the extent of his liability. When personal assets are few, there is little to be lost by operating as an individual proprietorship for there are no personal assets for the satisfaction of business debts. The corporation also has the advantage of usually being able to secure additional amounts of capital more easily and at lower costs. The proprietorship or partnership, however, has the advantage of involving considerably less burdensome taxes unless individual income is very high. But very prosperous partnerships or proprietorships can reduce their tax burdens by electing to be taxed as a corporation (provided they are qualified to do so). For example, assume that in a very successful, two-man partnership the additional income beyond the salaries paid to the partners requires them to pay a marginal tax (on that additional income) of about, say, 65 per cent. By electing to be taxed as a corporation, the two partners would be subject to taxes on their salaries at the appropriate personal income tax rate, and the additional income of the enterprise would be taxed at the applicable corporate rate only. The remaining earnings could be reinvested for an indefinite period.

Or these same two partners, whose personal income is apparently rather substantial, may wish to incorporate in order to take advantage of the lower taxes applicable to corporations. They could see to it that no cash dividends—or, at best, only very small ones—are paid to stockholders (among whom they would be the controlling or dominant ones). In this way the tax upon the additional business income would be limited to the corporate income tax. Because little or no cash dividends would be paid, personal income taxes on this previously taxable income would either be reduced considerably or eliminated altogether. It should be noted, however, that the federal government looks askance at incorporation as a method of avoiding personal income taxes as evidenced by a tax statute permitting the government to levy an additional surcharge on corporate income if the firm is found to be withholding "unreasonable" amounts of profits in the firm. "Unreasonableness," however, is difficult to measure and, except in extreme cases, this law is difficult to invoke.

APPENDIX B MAJOR SECURITY FORMS AND COVENANTS

All forms of securities can be classified either as creditorship or ownership. The former class includes all forms of bonds and notes, long-term or short-term, as well as most preferred stocks. Although it is true that the preferred shares are always ownership claims from the point of view of the law, from the standpoint of financial management and the securities markets many preferred issues are a variant of long-term debt issues. From a legal point of view bonds and notes are promissory notes which promise to pay a certain sum, with interest, at some future specified date.

Ownership securities consist of both preferred issues and common stocks. A preferred stock, because of its nature or the quality of its protection, may resemble common stock more closely than a bond, in which event it should be treated as such. Common stock represents the residual claim on the resources and control of the enterprise. It is typically associated with the concept of "risk capital," although the common shares of some firms are less risky than the preferred shares or bonds of some other firms.

CREDITORSHIP SECURITIES

Bonds

As mentioned above, a bond is a promissory note. It usually runs for a duration of not less than ten years. Bonds may either be secured or unsecured. Secured bonds have a pledge of assets attached to them which can be used to satisfy creditors' claims in the event of reorganization or liquidation. Unsecured bonds are those without a pledge of assets but whose security rests on the general credit of the firm.

Secured Bonds

There are basically three types of secured bonds: the *mortgage bond,* which has a pledge of real assets to support the claim; the *collateral trust bond,* which usually has the pledge of other securities to support the claim; and the *equipment trust obligation,* which is supported by equipment leased to other firms.

540

Mortgage bonds have a claim, called a *lien,* on real assets. Aside from the pledge of assets, there are several other important provisions typically found in a mortgage bond agreement. A mortgage may be on specific, named assets, or it may be a *blanket* mortgage covering all real assets of the firm. An important provision under the blanket mortgage is the *after-acquired clause,* which stipulates that any real property acquired after the sale of the bonds is to serve as security for the issue. This provision is intended to enhance the asset security of the loan over the life of the issue. Because there may be an erosion in value of the original assets pledged, this clause—from an investor's point of view—may seem quite logical. From the firm's point of view, such a provision may hinder future financing, for any contemplated successive issue of bonds would be precluded from having the first claim on some specified asset of the firm (a first mortgage); rather the claim would be second in line to the pledged assets (i.e., would be second mortgages or third mortgages—also called, as a class, *junior liens*).

Because such a provision may preclude future mortgage bond financing (but not necessarily the issuance of debenture bonds), a firm may prefer to redeem such bonds and issue others to replace them. The firm may also prevail on bondholders to eliminate this provision through a bond indenture modification. This requires the approval of the proper proportion of bondholders needed to amend the bond contract.

If neither of these avenues is open, then the firm can resort to several *circumventions.* One of these is the *lease* of desired facilities or equipment. Another is the *purchase-money mortgage,* used when new property is acquired with a mortgage attached. This is equivalent to a vendor's lien in law and takes precedence over the after-acquired clause. A third way to avoid the after-acquired clause is to finance new plant and equipment through a *subsidiary.* For example, the R. Oppedahl Company may have a subsidiary corporation, the C. Brown Company, issue bonds on which the Oppedahl firm guarantees the payment of interest and principal. The Brown Company then proceeds to purchase new plant and equipment and, because of the corporate entity, the subsidiary is insulated (in most cases) from the claims of the Oppedahl firm's creditors.

The after-acquired provision is usually accompanied by an *open-end* feature. This provision permits the firm to issue more bonds under the existing mortgage. Under this arrangement, new bondholders would have the same rights and privileges as old ones. If an open-end feature accompanies an after-acquired clause, usually some constraints are placed on the extent to which new bonds can be issued. These constraints usually take the form of a limitation on the proportion of new bonds to newly acquired assets that can be pledged on the new bond issue. Sixty per cent is not an uncommon limitation. Or it may be that a limitation on the amount of new bonds that can be issued is expressed in terms of the maintenance of some minimum coverage of interest charges. This provision is typically found in all types of open-end features, whether or not an after-acquired clause exists.

In contradistinction to the open-end feature, there is the *closed-end* feature. Under this provision no more bonds can be issued on an existing lien.

There are some more commonplace provisions found in secured obligations. First, there is usually a provision enabling the issuing firm to call in part or all of the outstanding bonds at its option. This is known as a *callable feature* and is discussed at length in Chapter 19.

Second, usually a provision will be made to retire the issue either in whole or in part before the maturity date. One such provision is called a *sinking fund* and typically requires the company to set aside a specific sum of cash annually or semiannually. The cash is usually given to the trustee, who then either calls the required amount of bonds for retirement or buys them in the market. Obviously, he will not buy them in the market unless they are selling at a price less than the sinking-fund call price. The latter price is usually set at face value or at a slight premium —a price greater than face value.[1]

Often, a bond contract will include a provision requiring the issuing firm to maintain a *minimum liquidity* position. This may be expressed in terms of net working capital (which, say, must cover the face value of the bonds by 150 per cent). Or, the desired maintenance of liquidity may be expressed in terms of a minimum current ratio (the ratio of current assets to current liabilities).

Sometimes bond contracts provide for a restriction on *dividend payments* by "freezing" a stipulated portion of existing earned surplus and/or a given percentage of future earnings, thereby restricting dividend debits to an amount in excess of that stipulated.

Another type of bond requires collateral, usually stocks or bonds, to be pledged for the bonds to be issued. These are called *collateral trust bonds*. The collateral is usually held by a trustee, such as a bank, for the benefit of the bondholders. Collateral trust bonds are not used very much any more, although they were very popular with railroads at one time.[2]

---

[1] Although sinking funds are now almost universally incorporated into bond contracts, an extensive study made some years ago of their use in the railroad field is quite informative; *see:* W. H. S. Stevens, *Railroad Sinking Funds and Funded Debt* (Washington, D.C.: Government Printing Office, 1939).

[2] Charles A. D'Ambrosio, *Changes in Railroad Financial Structures, 1929–1958*. Unpublished Ph.D. dissertation, Department of Finance, University of Illinois, Urbana, 1962.

The third type of secured debt is the *equipment trust obligation*. As we mentioned earlier, this form of issue is supported by the lease of equipment to, say, a railroad by a trust, which is usually administered by a trust division of a large bank, the latter of which issues equipment obligations to the public. The railroad does not own the leased equipment, usually rolling stock; the title to it resides with the trust. The railroad's lease payments to the trustee provide for repayment of both the interest and principal. The railroad agrees to maintain and insure the rolling stock and make periodic reports concerning its condition. In the event the railroad fails to make its lease payments, the trustee can easily recover the rolling stock and sell or lease it to other railroads. Even in bankruptcy, equipment obligations are given preferential treatment over other forms of debt obligations.[3] Other industries have used equipment obligations, but not nearly as extensively as railroads.[4]

These equipment obligations are typically sold so that part of the issue comes due for retirement every six months or every year. These and other securities containing this provision are called *serial securities*.

Sometimes, interest on bonds is made contingent on income available from a firm's operations. Bonds possessing this covenant are called *income bonds*. They arise primarily out of reorganizations, and their most extensive use has been found in the railroad field. When they have been used there, most of them have had mortgage provisions also.[5]

Unsecured Bonds

Unsecured bonds are called *debenture bonds*. They are unsecured in the sense that no specific assets are pledged as security for them. In the event of default, their claim is equal to that of all other general creditors.

Many of the same covenants found in secured bonds are to be found in unsecured bonds, too. Typically, debentures are callable, have a sinking fund, stipulate a minimum working capital, can be open-end or closed-end, and might restrict dividends on stocks. Several provisions

---

[3] Although, strictly speaking, equipment obligations are not a debt of the firm, the nature of the fixed contractual payments—and the necessity of having the rolling stock in order to do business—has prompted the financial community and the Interstate Commerce Commission to view these leases as the equivalent to bonds. In effect, they may be viewed as capitalized leases.

[4] There are only a few comprehensive studies of railroad equipment financing. *See:* Kenneth Duncan, *Equipment Obligations* (New York: Appleton, 1924); Donald Macqueen Street, *Railroad Equipment Finance* (New York: Columbia U. P., 1959); and Donald M. Street, "The Role of Equipment Obligations in Postwar Railroad Financing," *The Journal of Finance,* 15 (September 1960), 333–40. For data pertaining to their use by twenty-seven leading Class I roads (90 per cent of all traffic), *see:* Charles A. D'Ambrosio, *Changes in Railroad Financial Structures, 1929–1958,* 72–88, 120–30, 167–76.

[5] Charles D. D'Ambrosio, *Changes in Railroad Financial Structures, 1929–1958,* 63–67, 69–74.

found in debentures, however, are not found in mortgage bonds. One of these stipulates that no bonds with a prior claim on assets may be issued unless the holders of debentures are treated equally and rateably with the new senior issue. This is called an *equal-and-rateable clause.* In effect, it bars the issuance of mortgage bonds unless a mortgage provision of status equal to that of the new bonds' provision is added to the debenture bondholders' contract.

A variant of this clause may even *restrict the issuance of new debentures.* Covenants containing this constraint, however, are usually so constructed as to permit the issuance of more debentures, provided (1) there is a stipulated amount of assets relative to the amount of debt outstanding, (2) there is a stipulated amount of earnings relative to the charges on debt securities, and/or (3) there is a minimum working capital position expressed in, say, a current ratio of 2.5:1.

In recent years debentures whose claim on assets in liquidation are subordinated to the claims of all the other long-term and some short-term creditors (usually banks) have come more and more into vogue. These *subordinated debentures,* as they are called, are designed to enhance the asset cushion of senior security holders.[6]

Sometimes, senior securities can be exchanged at the option of the bondholder for other securities, usually common stock. This privilege is known as the *conversion* feature and securities containing it are called *convertible securities.*

Preferred Stock

As the name implies, *preferred stock* is a security accorded certain preferential treatment over common stock. There are two ways in which one type of stock can be given preferential treatment over all other stocks taken as a class. The first is to extend to the one type of stock preference in the distribution of assets in the event of liquidation. A preferred stock possessing this preferred treatment is said to be *preferred as to assets.* The second is to extend one type of stock preference in the distribution of earnings. A preferred stock possessing this preferred treatment is said to be *preferred as to dividends.* If either of these two provisions is present, the stock is called a preferred stock. Customarily preferred stocks are preferred both as to assets and dividends. A variant of this preferential treatment is to be found in *classified common stock.* Sometimes, for control purposes, it is desirable to issue two types of "common stock"—one having voting privileges, the other lacking them. (Because one type of stock

[6] Robert W. Johnson, "Subordinated Debentures: Debt that Serves as Equity," *The Journal of Finance, 10* (March 1955), 1–16.

is receiving preferential treatment, in an extended sense of the term it too can be called *preferred stock,* although this is usually not what is meant by the term.)

Some preferred stocks possess many of the covenants found in bonds. For instance, it is not at all uncommon for preferreds to have sinking-fund requirements; usually they are callable; they may contain an equal and rateable clause; they may be convertible into common stocks; and they may restrict dividends on common stock.[7] A provision implied both in bond contracts and in preferred stock issues is the cumulation of dividends in the event that they are passed in any one or series of periods. The *cumulative* covenant, as it is called, requires the payment of these accumulated dividends before dividends can be paid on common stock. Unless the charter specifically states that the preferred stock is noncumulative in nature, dividends usually do accumulate when passed. Most preferreds are cumulative.

Also, preferred stock is usually entitled to some degree of *voting power.* Holders may be entitled to vote just as any other stockholders unless the charter specifically restricts it, a tendency which is becoming more and more prevalent. Most preferred stockholders, however, are allowed to vote for a stated percentage of the members of the board of directors upon the passage of a stipulated number of quarterly dividends, usually four to six. This is known as *contingent voting,* because the right to vote is contingent on the passage of several quarterly dividends.

OWNERSHIP SECURITIES

The only ownership type of security left to discuss is common stock. This stock is the residual claimant on the assets and earnings of the firm. It typically possesses all the voting power in the firm. Usually each share of stock is entitled to one vote per share and, when directors are elected, each position is voted on separately so that a holder of the majority of votes (stock or proxies[8]) can elect the directors he chooses. This is the regular voting method. Sometimes *cumulative voting* is allowed. This provision allows a shareholder to cast as many votes per share as there are directors to be selected. For example, in the absence of cumulative voting, a shareholder owning ten shares of stock can cast only ten votes for each of the seven directors to be elected. Under cumulative voting, he may cast seventy votes for any one director or spread them. The effect of cumula-

[7] *See:* Donald A. Fergusson, "Recent Developments in Preferred Stock Financing," *Journal of Finance,* 7 (September 1952), 447–62.

[8] Proxies are written authorizations by stockholders giving another party power to cast their votes.

tive voting is to allow a minority group of shareholders to elect a director or two of their choosing. A formula that can be used to determine the minimum number of shares needed to elect a given number of directors is

$$S_D = \frac{S \times D}{TD + 1} + 1$$

where

S_D = number of shares required to elect a given number of directors
S = total outstanding shares
D = the given number of directors to be elected
TD = total number of directors to be elected

If a firm has 150,000 shares outstanding, and we wish to elect four of the seven directors, the formula

$$S_D = \frac{150,000 \times 4}{7 + 1} + 1$$

$$= \frac{600,000}{8} + 1$$

$$= 75,001$$

shows we need 75,001 shares to elect four directors. If we wanted to elect only one director, we would need 18,751 shares.

APPENDIX C PRESENT VALUE TABLES AND TABLE OF NORMAL CURVE AREAS

Table C-1
Present Value of One Dollar Due at the End of *n* Years*

n	1%	2%	3%	4%	5%	6%	7%	8%	9%	10%	n
1	.99010	.98039	.97007	.96154	.95238	.94340	.93458	.92593	.91743	.90909	1
2	.98030	.96117	.94260	.92456	.90703	.89000	.87344	.85734	.84168	.82645	2
3	.97059	.94232	.91514	.88900	.86384	.83962	.81630	.79383	.77218	.75131	3
4	.96098	.92385	.88849	.85480	.82270	.79209	.76290	.73503	.70843	.68301	4
5	.95147	.90573	.86261	.82193	.78353	.74726	.71299	.68058	.64993	.62092	5
6	.94204	.88797	.83748	.79031	.74622	.70496	.66634	.63017	.59627	.56447	6
7	.93272	.87056	.81309	.75992	.71068	.66506	.62275	.58349	.54703	.51316	7
8	.92348	.85349	.78941	.73069	.67684	.62741	.58201	.54027	.50187	.46651	8
9	.91434	.83675	.76642	.70259	.64461	.59190	.54393	.50025	.46043	.42410	9
10	.90529	.82035	.74409	.67556	.61391	.55839	.50835	.46319	.42241	.38554	10
11	.89632	.80426	.72242	.64958	.58468	.52679	.47509	.42888	.38753	.35049	11
12	.88745	.78849	.70138	.62460	.55684	.49697	.44401	.39711	.35553	.31863	12
13	.87866	.77303	.68095	.60057	.53032	.46884	.41496	.36770	.32618	.28966	13
14	.86996	.75787	.66112	.57747	.50507	.44230	.38782	.34046	.29925	.26333	14
15	.86135	.74301	.64186	.55526	.48102	.41726	.36245	.31524	.27454	.23939	15
16	.85282	.72845	.62317	.53391	.45811	.39365	.33873	.29189	.25187	.21763	16
17	.84438	.71416	.60502	.51337	.43630	.37136	.31657	.27027	.23107	.19784	17
18	.83602	.70016	.58739	.49363	.41552	.35034	.29586	.25025	.21199	.17986	18
19	.82774	.68643	.57029	.47464	.39573	.33051	.27651	.23171	.19449	.16351	19
20	.81954	.67297	.55367	.45639	.37689	.31180	.25842	.21455	.17843	.14864	20
21	.81143	.65978	.53755	.43883	.35894	.29415	.24151	.19866	.16370	.13513	21
22	.80340	.64684	.52189	.42195	.34185	.27750	.22571	.18394	.15018	.12285	22
23	.79544	.63414	.50669	.40573	.32557	.26180	.21095	.17031	.13778	.11168	23
24	.78757	.62172	.49193	.39012	.31007	.24698	.19715	.15770	.12640	.10153	24
25	.77977	.60953	.47760	.37512	.29530	.23300	.18425	.14602	.11597	.09230	25

$$* \; PV = \frac{\$1}{(1+d)^n}$$

548

Table C-1 (Cont.)
Present Value of One Dollar Due at the End of *n* Years

n	11%	12%	13%	14%	15%	16%	17%	18%	19%	20%	n
1	.90090	.89286	.88496	.87719	.86957	.86207	.85470	.84746	.84034	.83333	1
2	.81162	.79719	.78315	.76947	.75614	.74316	.73051	.71818	.70616	.69444	2
3	.73119	.71178	.69305	.67497	.65752	.64066	.62437	.60863	.59342	.57870	3
4	.65873	.63552	.61332	.59208	.57175	.55229	.53365	.51579	.49867	.48225	4
5	.59345	.56743	.54276	.51937	.49718	.47611	.45611	.43711	.41905	.40188	5
6	.53464	.50663	.48032	.45559	.43233	.41044	.38984	.37043	.35214	.33490	6
7	.48166	.45235	.42506	.39964	.37594	.35383	.33320	.31392	.29592	.27908	7
8	.43393	.40388	.37616	.35056	.32690	.30503	.28478	.26604	.24867	.23257	8
9	.39092	.36061	.33288	.30751	.28426	.26295	.24340	.22546	.20897	.19381	9
10	.35218	.32197	.29459	.26974	.24718	.22668	.20804	.19106	.17560	.16151	10
11	.31728	.28748	.26070	.23662	.21494	.19542	.17781	.16192	.14756	.13459	11
12	.28584	.25667	.23071	.20756	.18691	.16846	.15197	.13722	.12400	.11216	12
13	.25751	.22917	.20416	.18207	.16253	.14523	.12989	.11629	.10420	.09346	13
14	.23199	.20462	.18068	.15971	.14133	.12520	.11102	.09855	.08757	.07789	14
15	.20900	.18270	.15989	.14010	.12289	.10793	.09489	.08352	.07359	.06491	15
16	.18829	.16312	.14150	.12289	.10686	.09304	.08110	.07078	.06184	.05409	16
17	.16963	.14564	.12522	.10780	.09293	.08021	.06932	.05998	.05196	.04507	17
18	.15282	.13004	.11081	.09456	.08080	.06914	.05925	.05083	.04367	.03756	18
19	.13768	.11611	.09806	.08295	.07026	.05961	.05064	.04308	.03669	.03130	19
20	.12403	.10367	.08678	.07276	.06110	.05139	.04328	.03651	.03084	.02608	20
21	.11174	.09256	.07680	.06383	.05313	.04430	.03699	.03094	.02591	.02174	21
22	.10067	.08264	.06796	.05599	.04620	.03819	.03162	.02622	.02178	.01811	22
23	.09069	.07379	.06014	.04911	.04017	.03292	.02702	.02222	.01830	.01509	23
24	.08170	.06588	.05322	.04308	.03493	.02838	.02310	.01883	.01538	.01258	24
25	.07361	.05882	.04710	.03779	.03038	.02447	.01974	.01596	.01292	.01048	25

6,000 received 5 years from now if the discount rate is 6%

Table C-1 (Cont.)
Present Value of One Dollar Due at the End of n Years

n	21%	22%	23%	24%	25%	26%	27%	28%	29%	30%	n
1	.82645	.81967	.81301	.80645	.80000	.79365	.78740	.78125	.77519	.76923	1
2	.68301	.67186	.66098	.65036	.64000	.62988	.62000	.61035	.60093	.59172	2
3	.56447	.55071	.53738	.52449	.51200	.49991	.48819	.47684	.46583	.45517	3
4	.46651	.45140	.43690	.42297	.40960	.39675	.38440	.37253	.36111	.35013	4
5	.38554	.37000	.35520	.34111	.32768	.31488	.30268	.29104	.27993	.26933	5
6	.31863	.30328	.28878	.27509	.26214	.24991	.23833	.22737	.21700	.20718	6
7	.26333	.24859	.23478	.22184	.20972	.19834	.18766	.17764	.16822	.15937	7
8	.21763	.20376	.19088	.17891	.16777	.15741	.14776	.13878	.13040	.12259	8
9	.17986	.16702	.15519	.14428	.13422	.12493	.11635	.10842	.10109	.09430	9
10	.14864	.13690	.12617	.11635	.10737	.09915	.09161	.08470	.07836	.07254	10
11	.12285	.11221	.10258	.09383	.08590	.07869	.07214	.06617	.06075	.05580	11
12	.10153	.09198	.08339	.07567	.06872	.06245	.05680	.05170	.04709	.04292	12
13	.08391	.07539	.06780	.06103	.05498	.04957	.04472	.04039	.03650	.03302	13
14	.06934	.06180	.05512	.04921	.04398	.03934	.03522	.03155	.02830	.02540	14
15	.05731	.05065	.04481	.03969	.03518	.03122	.02773	.02465	.02194	.01954	15
16	.04736	.04152	.03643	.03201	.02815	.02478	.02183	.01926	.01700	.01503	16
17	.03914	.03403	.02962	.02581	.02252	.01967	.01719	.01505	.01318	.01156	17
18	.03235	.02789	.02408	.02082	.01801	.01561	.01354	.01175	.01022	.00889	18
19	.02673	.02286	.01958	.01679	.01441	.01239	.01066	.00918	.00792	.00684	19
20	.02209	.01874	.01592	.01354	.01153	.00983	.00839	.00717	.00614	.00526	20
21	.01826	.01536	.01294	.01092	.00922	.00780	.00661	.00561	.00476	.00405	21
22	.01509	.01259	.01052	.00880	.00738	.00619	.00520	.00438	.00369	.00311	22
23	.01247	.01032	.00855	.00710	.00590	.00491	.00410	.00342	.00286	.00239	23
24	.01031	.00846	.00695	.00573	.00472	.00390	.00323	.00267	.00222	.00184	24
25	.00852	.00693	.00565	.00462	.00378	.00310	.00254	.00209	.00172	.00142	25

Table C-1 (Cont.)

Present Value of One Dollar Due at the End of n Years

n	31%	32%	33%	34%	35%	36%	37%	38%	39%	40%	n
1	.76336	.75758	.75188	.74627	.74074	.73529	.72993	.72464	.71942	.71429	1
2	.58272	.57392	.56532	.55692	.54870	.54066	.53279	.52510	.51757	.51020	2
3	.44482	.43479	.42505	.41561	.40644	.39754	.38890	.38051	.37235	.36443	3
4	.33956	.32939	.31959	.31016	.30107	.29231	.28387	.27573	.26788	.26031	4
5	.25920	.24953	.24029	.23146	.22301	.21493	.20720	.19980	.19272	.18593	5
6	.19787	.18904	.18067	.17273	.16520	.15804	.15124	.14479	.13865	.13281	6
7	.15104	.14321	.13584	.12890	.12237	.11621	.11040	.10492	.09975	.09486	7
8	.11530	.10849	.10214	.09620	.09064	.08545	.08058	.07603	.07176	.06776	8
9	.08802	.08219	.07680	.07179	.06714	.06283	.05882	.05509	.05163	.04840	9
10	.06719	.06227	.05774	.05357	.04973	.04620	.04293	.03992	.03714	.03457	10
11	.05129	.04717	.04341	.03998	.03684	.03397	.03134	.02893	.02672	.02469	11
12	.03915	.03574	.03264	.02984	.02729	.02498	.02287	.02096	.01922	.01764	12
13	.02989	.02707	.02454	.02227	.02021	.01837	.01670	.01519	.01383	.01260	13
14	.02281	.02051	.01845	.01662	.01497	.01350	.01219	.01101	.00995	.00900	14
15	.01742	.01554	.01387	.01240	.01109	.00993	.00890	.00798	.00716	.00643	15
16	.01329	.01177	.01043	.00925	.00822	.00730	.00649	.00578	.00515	.00459	16
17	.01015	.00892	.00784	.00691	.00609	.00537	.00474	.00419	.00370	.00328	17
18	.00775	.00676	.00590	.00515	.00451	.00395	.00346	.00304	.00267	.00234	18
19	.00591	.00512	.00443	.00385	.00334	.00290	.00253	.00220	.00192	.00167	19
20	.00451	.00388	.00333	.00287	.00247	.00213	.00184	.00159	.00138	.00120	20
21	.00345	.00294	.00251	.00214	.00183	.00157	.00135	.00115	.00099	.00085	21
22	.00263	.00223	.00188	.00160	.00136	.00115	.00098	.00084	.00071	.00061	22
23	.00201	.00169	.00142	.00119	.00101	.00085	.00072	.00061	.00051	.00044	23
24	.00153	.00128	.00107	.00089	.00074	.00062	.00052	.00044	.00037	.00031	24
25	.00117	.00097	.00080	.00066	.00055	.00046	.00038	.00032	.00027	.00022	25

1,000 received annually for 5 years if the discount rate is 6%

Table C-2
Present Value of an Annuity of One Dollar for n Year*

n	1%	2%	3%	4%	5%	6%	7%	8%	9%	10%	n
1	.9901	.9804	.9709	.9615	.9524	.9434	.9346	.9259	.9174	.9091	1
2	1.9704	1.9416	1.9135	1.8861	1.8594	1.8334	1.8080	1.7833	1.7591	1.7355	2
3	2.9410	2.8839	2.8286	2.7751	2.7232	2.6730	2.6243	2.5771	2.5313	2.4868	3
4	3.9020	3.8077	3.7171	3.6299	3.5459	3.4651	3.3872	3.3121	3.2397	3.1699	4
5	4.8535	4.7134	4.5797	4.4518	4.3295	4.2123	4.1002	3.9927	3.8896	3.7908	5
6	5.7955	5.6014	5.4172	5.2421	5.0757	4.9173	4.7665	4.6229	4.4859	4.3553	6
7	6.7282	6.4720	6.2302	6.0020	5.7863	5.5824	5.3893	5.2064	5.0329	4.8684	7
8	7.6517	7.3254	7.0196	6.7327	6.4632	6.2098	5.9713	5.7466	5.5348	5.3349	8
9	8.5661	8.1622	7.7861	7.4353	7.1078	6.8017	6.5152	6.2469	5.9852	5.7590	9
10	9.4714	8.9825	8.5302	8.1109	7.7217	7.3601	7.0236	6.7101	6.4176	6.1446	10
11	10.3677	9.7868	9.2526	8.7604	8.3064	7.8868	7.4987	7.1389	6.8052	6.4951	11
12	11.2552	10.5753	9.9539	9.3850	8.8632	8.3838	7.9427	7.5361	7.1607	6.8137	12
13	12.1338	11.3483	10.6349	9.9856	9.3935	8.8527	8.3576	7.9038	7.4869	7.1034	13
14	13.0038	12.1062	11.2960	10.5631	9.8986	9.2950	8.7454	8.2442	7.7861	7.3667	14
15	13.8651	12.8492	11.9379	11.1183	10.3796	9.7122	9.1079	8.5595	8.0607	7.6061	15
16	14.7180	13.5777	12.5610	11.6522	10.8377	10.1059	9.4466	8.8514	8.3125	7.8237	16
17	15.5624	14.2918	13.1660	12.1656	11.2740	10.4772	9.7632	9.1216	8.5436	8.0215	17
18	16.3984	14.9920	13.7534	12.6592	11.6895	10.8276	10.0591	9.3719	8.7556	8.2014	18
19	17.2261	15.6784	14.3237	13.1339	12.0853	11.1581	10.3356	9.6036	8.9501	8.3649	19
20	18.0457	16.3514	14.8774	13.5903	12.4622	11.4699	10.5940	9.8181	9.1285	8.5136	20
21	18.8571	17.0111	15.4149	14.0291	12.8211	11.7640	10.8355	10.0168	9.2922	8.6487	21
22	19.6605	17.6580	15.9368	14.4511	13.1630	12.0416	11.0612	10.2007	9.4424	8.7715	22
23	20.4559	18.2921	16.4435	14.8568	13.4885	12.3033	11.2722	10.3710	9.5802	8.8832	23
24	21.2435	18.9139	16.9355	15.2469	13.7986	12.5503	11.4693	10.5287	9.7066	8.9847	24
25	22.0233	19.5234	17.4131	15.6220	14.0939	12.7833	11.6536	10.6748	9.8226	9.0770	25

$$* PV = \frac{EO}{d}\left[1 - \frac{1}{(1+d)^n}\right]$$

Table C-2 (Cont.)
Present Value of an Annuity of One Dollar for n Years

n	11%	12%	13%	14%	15%	16%	17%	18%	19%	20%	n
1	.9009	.8929	.8850	.8772	.8696	.8621	.8547	.8475	.8403	.8333	1
2	1.7125	1.6901	1.6681	1.6467	1.6257	1.6052	1.5852	1.5656	1.5465	1.5278	2
3	2.4437	2.4018	2.3612	2.3216	2.2832	2.2459	2.2096	2.1743	2.1399	2.1065	3
4	3.1024	3.0373	2.9745	2.9137	2.8550	2.7982	2.7432	2.6901	2.6386	2.5887	4
5	3.6959	3.6048	3.5172	3.4331	3.3522	3.2743	3.1993	3.1272	3.0576	2.9906	5
6	4.2305	4.1114	3.9976	3.8887	3.7845	3.6847	3.5892	3.4976	3.4098	3.3255	6
7	4.7122	4.5638	4.4226	4.2883	4.1604	4.0386	3.9224	3.8115	3.7057	3.6046	7
8	5.1461	4.9676	4.7988	4.6389	4.4873	4.3436	4.2072	4.0776	3.9544	3.8372	8
9	5.5370	5.3282	5.1317	4.9464	4.7716	4.6065	4.4506	4.3030	4.1633	4.0310	9
10	5.8892	5.6502	5.4262	5.2161	5.0188	4.8332	4.6586	4.4941	4.3389	4.1925	10
11	6.2065	5.9377	5.6869	5.4527	5.2337	5.0286	4.8364	4.6560	4.4865	4.3271	11
12	6.4924	6.1944	5.9176	5.6603	5.4206	5.1971	4.9884	4.7932	4.6105	4.4392	12
13	6.7499	6.4235	6.1218	5.8424	5.5831	5.3423	5.1183	4.9095	4.7147	4.5327	13
14	6.9819	6.6282	6.3025	6.0021	5.7245	5.4675	5.2293	5.0081	4.8023	4.6106	14
15	7.1909	6.8109	6.4624	6.1422	5.8474	5.5755	5.3242	5.0916	4.8759	4.6755	15
16	7.3792	6.9740	6.6039	6.2651	5.9542	5.6685	5.4053	5.1624	4.9377	4.7296	16
17	7.5488	7.1196	6.7291	6.3729	6.0472	5.7487	5.4746	5.2223	4.9897	4.7746	17
18	7.7016	7.2497	6.8399	6.4674	6.1280	5.8178	5.5339	5.2732	5.0333	4.8122	18
19	7.8393	7.3658	6.9380	6.5504	6.1982	5.8775	5.5845	5.3162	5.0700	4.8435	19
20	7.9633	7.4694	7.0248	6.6231	6.2593	5.9288	5.6278	5.3527	5.1009	4.8696	20
21	8.0751	7.5620	7.1016	6.6870	6.3125	5.9731	5.6648	5.3837	5.1268	4.8913	21
22	8.1757	7.6446	7.1695	6.7429	6.3587	6.0113	5.6964	5.4099	5.1486	4.9094	22
23	8.2664	7.7184	7.2297	6.7921	6.3988	6.0442	5.7234	5.4321	5.1668	4.9245	23
24	8.3481	7.7843	7.2829	6.8351	6.4338	6.0726	5.7465	5.4509	5.1822	4.9371	24
25	8.4217	7.8431	7.3300	6.8729	6.4641	6.0971	5.7662	5.4669	5.1951	4.9476	25

Table C-2 (Cont.)

Present Value of an Annuity of One Dollar for n Years

n	21%	22%	23%	24%	25%	26%	27%	28%	29%	30%	n
1	.8264	.8197	.8130	.8065	.8000	.7937	.7874	.7813	.7752	.7692	1
2	1.5095	1.4915	1.4740	1.4568	1.4400	1.4235	1.4074	1.3916	1.3761	1.3609	2
3	2.0739	2.0422	2.0114	1.9813	1.9520	1.9234	1.8956	1.8684	1.8420	1.8161	3
4	2.5404	2.4936	2.4483	2.4043	2.3616	2.3202	2.2800	2.2410	2.2031	2.1662	4
5	2.9260	2.8636	2.8035	2.7454	2.6893	2.6351	2.5827	2.5320	2.4830	2.4356	5
6	3.2446	3.1669	3.0923	3.0205	2.9514	2.8850	2.8210	2.7594	2.7000	2.6427	6
7	3.5079	3.4155	3.3270	3.2423	3.1611	3.0833	3.0087	2.9370	2.8682	2.8021	7
8	3.7256	3.6193	3.5179	3.4212	3.3289	3.2407	3.1564	3.0758	2.9986	2.9247	8
9	3.9054	3.7863	3.6731	3.5655	3.4631	3.3657	3.2728	3.1842	3.0997	3.0190	9
10	4.0541	3.9232	3.7993	3.6819	3.5705	3.4648	3.3644	3.2689	3.1781	3.0915	10
11	4.1769	4.0354	3.9018	3.7757	3.6564	3.5435	3.4365	3.3351	3.2388	3.1473	11
12	4.2785	4.1274	3.9852	3.8514	3.7251	3.6060	3.4933	3.3868	3.2859	3.1903	12
13	4.3624	4.2028	4.0530	3.9124	3.7801	3.6555	3.5381	3.4272	3.3224	3.2233	13
14	4.4317	4.2646	4.1082	3.9616	3.8241	3.6949	3.5733	3.4587	3.3507	3.2487	14
15	4.4890	4.3152	4.1530	4.0013	3.8593	3.7261	3.6010	3.4834	3.3726	3.2682	15
16	4.5364	4.3567	4.1894	4.0333	3.8874	3.7509	3.6228	3.5026	3.3896	3.2832	16
17	4.5755	4.3908	4.2190	4.0591	3.9099	3.7705	3.6400	3.5177	3.4028	3.2948	17
18	4.6079	4.4187	4.2431	4.0799	3.9279	3.7861	3.6536	3.5294	3.4130	3.3037	18
19	4.6346	4.4415	4.2627	4.0967	3.9424	3.7985	3.6642	3.5386	3.4210	3.3105	19
20	4.6567	4.4603	4.2786	4.1103	3.9539	3.8083	3.6726	3.5458	3.4271	3.3158	20
21	4.6750	4.4756	4.2916	4.1212	3.9631	3.8161	3.6792	3.5514	3.4319	3.3198	21
22	4.6900	4.4882	4.3021	4.1300	3.9705	3.8223	3.6844	3.5558	3.4356	3.3230	22
23	4.7025	4.4985	4.3106	4.1371	3.9764	3.8273	3.6885	3.5592	3.4384	3.3254	23
24	4.7128	4.5070	4.3176	4.1428	3.9811	3.8312	3.6918	3.5619	3.4406	3.3272	24
25	4.7213	4.5139	4.3232	4.1474	3.9849	3.8342	3.6943	3.5640	3.4423	3.3286	25

Table C-2 (Cont.)
Present Value of an Annuity of One Dollar for n Years

n	40%	39%	38%	37%	36%	35%	34%	33%	32%	31%	n
1	.7143	.7194	.7246	.7299	.7353	.7407	.7463	.7519	.7576	.7634	1
2	1.2245	1.2370	1.2497	1.2627	1.2760	1.2894	1.3032	1.3172	1.3315	1.3461	2
3	1.5889	1.6093	1.6302	1.6516	1.6735	1.6959	1.7188	1.7423	1.7663	1.7909	3
4	1.8492	1.8772	1.9060	1.9355	1.9658	1.9969	2.0290	2.0618	2.0957	2.1305	4
5	1.9352	2.0699	2.1058	2.1427	2.1807	2.2200	2.2604	2.3021	2.3452	2.3897	5
6	2.1680	2.2086	2.2506	2.2939	2.3388	2.3852	2.4331	2.4828	2.5342	2.5875	6
7	2.2628	2.3083	2.3555	2.4043	2.4550	2.5075	2.5620	2.6187	2.6775	2.7386	7
8	2.3306	2.3801	2.4315	2.4849	2.5404	2.5982	2.6582	2.7208	2.7860	2.8539	8
9	2.3790	2.4317	2.4866	2.5437	2.6033	2.6653	2.7300	2.7976	2.8681	2.9419	9
10	2.4136	2.4689	2.5265	2.5867	2.6495	2.7150	2.7836	2.8553	2.9304	3.0091	10
11	2.4383	2.4956	2.5555	2.6180	2.6834	2.7519	2.8236	2.8987	2.9776	3.0604	11
12	2.4559	2.5148	2.5764	2.6409	2.7084	2.7792	2.8534	2.9314	3.0133	3.0995	12
13	2.4685	2.5286	2.5916	2.6576	2.7268	2.7994	2.8757	2.9559	3.0404	3.1294	13
14	2.4775	2.5386	2.6026	2.6698	2.7403	2.8144	2.8923	2.9744	3.0609	3.1522	14
15	2.4839	2.5457	2.6106	2.6787	2.7502	2.8255	2.9047	2.9883	3.0764	3.1696	15
16	2.4885	2.5509	2.6164	2.6852	2.7575	2.8337	2.9140	2.9987	3.0882	3.1829	16
17	2.4918	2.5546	2.6206	2.6899	2.7629	2.8398	2.9209	3.0065	3.0971	3.1931	17
18	2.4941	2.5573	2.6236	2.6934	2.7668	2.8443	2.9260	3.0124	3.1039	3.2008	18
19	2.4958	2.5592	2.6258	2.6959	2.7697	2.8476	2.9299	3.0169	3.1090	3.2067	19
20	2.4970	2.5606	2.6274	2.6977	2.7718	2.8501	2.9327	3.0202	3.1129	3.2112	20
21	2.4979	2.5616	2.6285	2.6991	2.7734	2.8519	2.9349	3.0227	3.1158	3.2147	21
22	2.4985	2.5623	2.6294	2.7000	2.7746	2.8533	2.9365	3.0246	3.1180	3.2173	22
23	2.4989	2.5628	2.6300	2.7008	2.7754	2.8543	2.9377	3.0260	3.1197	3.2193	23
24	2.4992	2.5632	2.6304	2.7013	2.7760	2.8550	2.9386	3.0271	3.1210	3.2209	24
25	2.4994	2.5634	2.6307	2.7017	2.7765	2.8556	2.9392	3.0279	3.1220	3.2220	25

Table C-3
Normal Curve Areas*

Z	Area	Z	Area
0.0	0.000	1.6	0.445
0.1	0.040	1.7	0.455
0.2	0.079	1.8	0.464
0.3	0.118	1.9	0.471
0.4	0.155	2.0	0.477
0.5	0.191	2.1	0.482
0.6	0.226	2.2	0.486
0.7	0.258	2.3	0.489
0.8	0.288	2.4	0.492
0.9	0.316	2.5	0.494
1.0	0.341	2.6	0.495
1.1	0.364	2.7	0.496
1.2	0.385	2.8	0.497
1.3	0.413	2.9	0.498
1.4	0.419	3.0	0.499
1.5	0.433		

* Z is the number of standard deviations away from the center of the normal distribution which is symmetrical such that this table also applies for negative Z.

INDEX

HIEBERT LIBRARY

3 6877 00122 6603

SOME FREQUENTLY USED SYMBOLS